Television Production

Thirteenth Edition

Television Production

Thirteenth Edition

Gerald Millerson

ELSEVIER

AMSTERDAM • BOSTON • HEIDELBERG • LONDON • NEW YORK • OXFORD
PARIS • SAN DIEGO • SAN FRANCISCO • SINGAPORE • SYDNEY • TOKYO
Focal Press is an imprint of Elsevier

Focal Press
An imprint of Elsevier
Linacre House, Jordan Hill, Oxford OX2 8DP
30 Corporate Drive, Burlington, MA 01803

First published 1961
Second edition 1963
Third edition 1964
Fourth edition 1966
Fifth edition 1967
Sixth edition 1968
Seventh edition 1969
Eighth edition 1970
Ninth edition 1972
Tenth edition 1979
Eleventh edition 1985
Twelfth edition 1990
Reprinted 1992, 1993 (twice), 1994, 1995, 1997
Thirteenth edition 1999
Reprinted 2001, 2003, 2004, 2005

British Library Cataloguing in Publication Data
Millerson, Gerald.
Television production. — 13th ed.
1. Television – Production and direction
I. Title. II. The techniques of TV production
791.4´5´0232

ISBN 0 240 51492 0

Library of Congress Cataloguing in Publication Data
Millerson, Gerald.
Television production/Gerald Millerson. – 13th ed.
p. cm.
Rev. ed. of: The technique of television production. 12th ed. 1990.
Includes bibliographical references and index.
ISBN 0 240 51492 0
1. Television – Production and direction. I. Millerson, Gerald.
Technique of television and production. II. Title.
PN1992.75.M5 98–49389
791.45´0232–dc21 CIP

For information on all Focal Press publications visit our website at www.focalpress.com

Composition by Genesis Typesetting, Rochester, Kent
Printed and bound in Great Britain by Biddles Ltd, King's Lynn, Norfolk

Contents

Preface to the thirteenth edition

Welcome to the *thirteenth edition* of this guide to the intriguing world of **Television/Video production** – to the world of ***ILLUSION***!

How can this book help you?

This book, which offers you a very **practical** guide to *professional TV/Video production techniques*, is a distillation of a lifetime's personal experience. Here you will find not only straightforward explanations of the equipment you will meet, but discover the best ways of using it. We shall discuss typical everyday problems and how you can overcome them quickly and easily. You will learn how to master a wide range of operational techniques. We shall be exploring all major *technical operations* including top-grade camera-work, persuasive lighting methods, successful sound treatment, the subtle processes of editing, etc. Similarly, you will discover the underlying principles of other associated production crafts, such as scenic design, make-up, graphics, etc.

In this comprehensive survey of TV program making we shall analyze the work of the TV Director and members of the team step by step, as we go through the various processes involved in organizing an effective TV show – whether working with a single mobile camera unit or with a multi-camera studio crew.

But in the end, successful program making is about **communication** and **persuasion**. So we shall not only be looking at *how to* but also *why* and *when* to use various productional styles. After all, ultimately program making is not a matter of knowing 'which buttons to press' but how to use your tools creatively. You will discover how the techniques you use can influence and persuade your audience, hold their attention, develop their interest, influence and arouse emotions in particular ways. When, for instance, your subject moves, should you . . . *move the camera to follow along with it; or widen the lens' coverage; or cut to another camera viewpoint . . .?* It certainly matters *which* methods you choose, for each will have a *different audience impact.*

Will this book suit a range of study courses?

Yes. First, the text does not assume you have previous knowledge or experience of the medium. Because *The Technique of Television Production* is used by many different kinds of courses, from media studies to television/video training, we have arranged the text to suit a wide range of readers at introductory, intermediate, and advanced levels of study. Although topics range from basics to the most innovative and progressive techniques, you will be able to read the text *selectively* to suit your particular needs.

This book has been designed to provide facts in an interesting, easily digested form. Here knowledge is encapsulated for you in many at-a-glance summaries in tables and lists that avoid your having to search through pages of text. Throughout, you will find extensive illustrations that concentrate on the essentials.

If you want technical information, it is there. If you would rather bypass the more technical aspects of the equipment, the text is arranged for you to do so. To avoid interrupting the flow of the general text, we have placed chapters covering technicalities of the TV system towards the end of the book. Specific technical details are included in digests within the extended encylopedic *Digests.*

What are the changes in this new edition?

Today the *Television/Video* medium draws on a wide range of techniques – from the long-established to the newest sophisticated technology – and this latest version of *The Technique of Television Production* has been updated and extended to reflect these current developments.

There have been important technical innovations since the last edition that directly affect production techniques in several ways. You will see, for example, how new *digital technology* has begun to revolutionize recording and program editing processes. *Desktop video* has evolved, and now enables quite modest computer-based devices to process picture and sound in ways that would previously have required major dedicated equipment. *Virtual sets* are increasingly used today and promise exciting opportunities for future scenic treatment. These and other developing fields are now included. But still the emphasis throughout is on *imaginative and creative interpretation*, and on *effective* program making.

Acknowledgements

As always, I would like to express my grateful thanks to the British Broadcasting Corporation, where over the years I have had widely based opportunities to develop experience and exchange ideas with many expert colleagues.

Finally, I would like to thank those who have so diligently translated my various titles into a diversity of languages (including Spanish, Italian, Japanese, Hebrew, French, German) yet managed so successfully to preserve the essence of the text.

I hope you will enjoy your journey into this very practical world of make-believe.

Gerry Millerson

To

my wife, Pamela

Typical development for a complex production

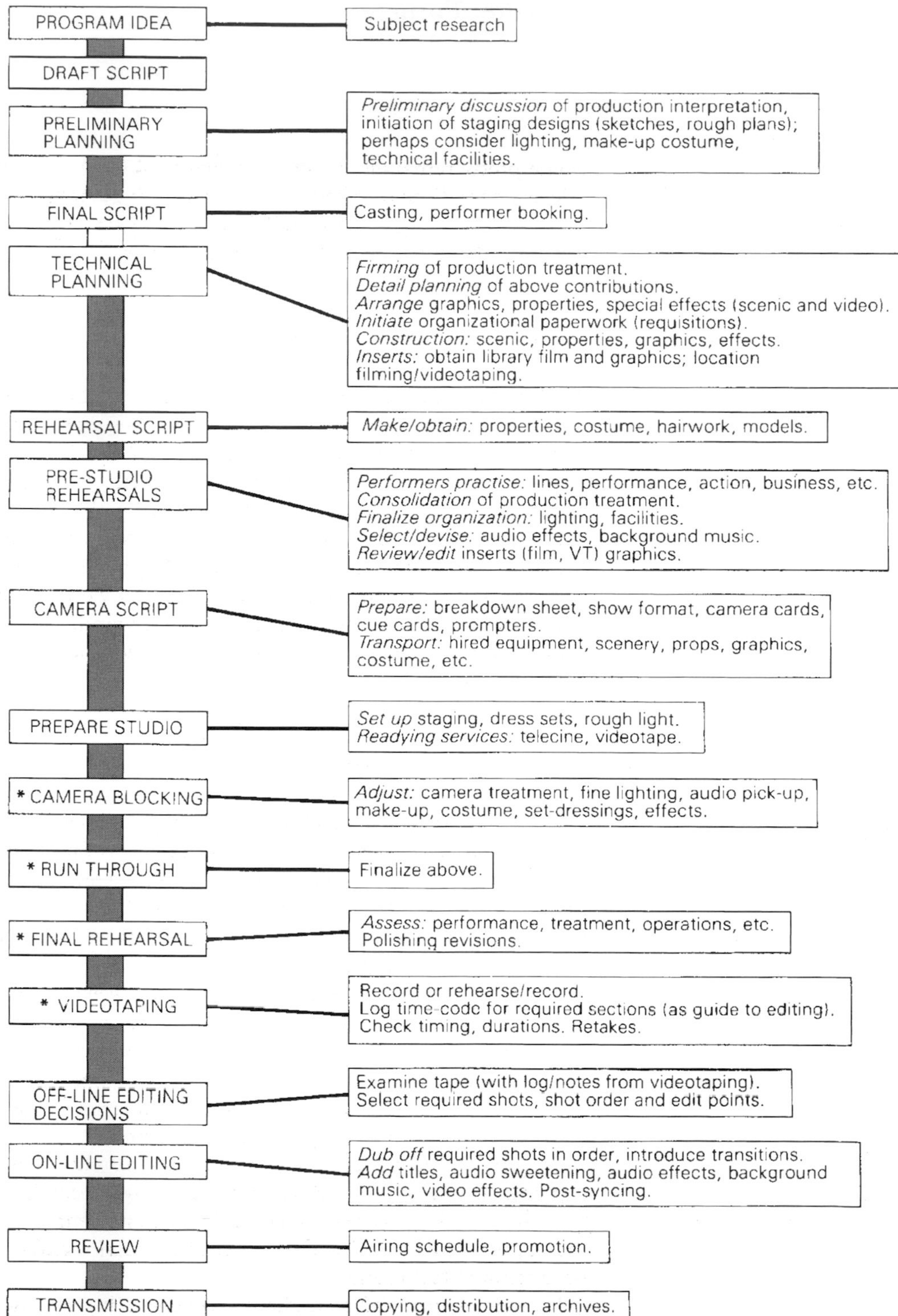

PROGRAM IDEA
Subject research
DRAFT SCRIPT
PRELIMINARY PLANNING
Preliminary discussion of production interpretation, initiation of staging designs (sketches, rough plans); perhaps consider lighting, make-up costume, technical facilities.
FINAL SCRIPT
Casting, performer booking.
TECHNICAL PLANNING
Firming of production treatment.
Detail planning of above contributions.
Arrange graphics, properties, special effects (scenic and video).
Initiate organizational paperwork (requisitions).
Construction: scenic, properties, graphics, effects.
Inserts: obtain library film and graphics; location filming/videotaping.
REHEARSAL SCRIPT
Make/obtain: properties, costume, hairwork, models.
PRE-STUDIO REHEARSALS
Performers practise: lines, performance, action, business, etc.
Consolidation of production treatment.
Finalize organization: lighting, facilities.
Select/devise: audio effects, background music.
Review/edit inserts (film, VT) graphics.
CAMERA SCRIPT
Prepare: breakdown sheet, show format, camera cards, cue cards, prompters.
Transport: hired equipment, scenery, props, graphics, costume, etc.
PREPARE STUDIO
Set up staging, dress sets, rough light.
Readying services: telecine, videotape.
* CAMERA BLOCKING
Adjust: camera treatment, fine lighting, audio pick-up, make-up, costume, set-dressings, effects.
* RUN THROUGH
Finalize above.
* FINAL REHEARSAL
Assess: performance, treatment, operations, etc.
Polishing revisions.
* VIDEOTAPING
Record or rehearse/record.
Log time-code for required sections (as guide to editing).
Check timing, durations. Retakes.
OFF-LINE EDITING DECISIONS
Examine tape (with log/notes from videotaping).
Select required shots, shot order and edit points.
ON-LINE EDITING
Dub off required shots in order, introduce transitions.
Add titles, audio sweetening, audio effects, background music, video effects. Post-syncing.
REVIEW
Airing schedule, promotion.
TRANSMISSION
Copying, distribution, archives.

* When 'Rehearse/Record' production techniques are used, these steps merge, as separate shots or sequences are individually blocked . . . rehearsed . . . taped.

1 An introduction

Some pretty remarkable technical changes have taken place in the television medium over recent years. As equipment has evolved and become increasingly adaptable, production techniques have developed to take advantage of new opportunities.

Equipment gets simpler to use

You've probably discovered already how even quite modest consumer camcorders can produce successful pictures under a wide range of conditions. Clever circuitry adjusts and compensates. Surely we need do little more than point the camera, follow the subject, and zoom in and out. To pick up the sound we can simply clip a small microphone onto a person's jacket, hand them a baton mic, or just use the microphone attached to the camera. As for the lighting, today's cameras work in daylight or whatever artificial light happens to be around. *So where's the mystery? Why do we need to **study** TV/Video techniques? Anyone can get results nowadays. It's all very obvious!*

The illusion of reality

One of the basic truths about photography, television and film media is that *the camera always lies*! On the face of it, it's reasonable to assume that if you simply point your camera and microphone at the scene you will convey an accurate record of the action to your audience. But as we shall see, in practice camera and microphone inherently *transform 'reality'*.

There can be considerable differences between what is *actually happening* . . . what your viewers are *seeing* . . . and what they *think* they are seeing. How they interpret *space, dimension, atmosphere, time, etc.* will depend on a number of factors, such as *the camera's position, the lens angle, lighting, editing, the accompanying sound* . . . and, of course, their own personal experience.

As you will see, we can turn this gap between the *actual* and the *apparent* to our advantage. It allows us to deliberately select and arrange each shot to create a particular audience impact. It gives us the opportunity to devise all manner of persuasive and economical productional techniques.

If a scene looks '*real*' an audience will invariably accept it as such. When watching an old film involving long-dead actors they still respond edge-on-seat to dramatic situations. Although they *know* that the character hanging by fingertips on a cliff is *really* safe and accompanied by a nearby production crew that does not override their *suspended disbelief*.

Even if you put together a disjointed series of totally unrelated shots your audience will still attempt to rationalize and interpret what they are seeing. (Some pop videos and experimental films rely heavily on this fact to sustain interest!) If you use a camera casually its pictures will still influence your audience – however unpredictably. Generally speaking, careless or inappropriate production techniques will usually be confusing, puzzling, and *a bore to watch*! The show will lack a logical and consistent form. Systematic techniques are a must if you want to catch and hold audience attention and interest.

It's not just academic

At first sight learning about *television production* would seem to be just a matter of mastering the basic mechanics. But let's think for a moment. How often have you heard two people play the same piece of music yet achieve entirely different results? The first instrumentalist certainly hits all the right notes but the performance sounds pedestrian, dull and uninteresting. The other person's more sensitive approach stirs our emotions with memorable sound.

Of course, we could simply assume that the second musician had greater talent. Bút this 'talent' generally comes from painstaking study and *effective techniques*. Experience alone is not enough – especially if it perpetuates wrong methods. Even quite subtle differences can influence the quality and impact of a performance. You'll find parallel situations in television production practices.

Techniques will tell

It's not unknown for three directors to shoot the same action, and yet produce quite diverse results:

- In a '*shooting by numbers*' approach the first director shows us everything that's going on, but follows a dull routine: the same old wide shot to begin with, followed by close shots of whoever is speaking, with intercut 'reaction' shots of the listener.
- The second director is so busy getting 'unusual' shots that these actually distract us from the subject itself.
- The third director's smooth sequence of shots somehow manages to create an interesting, attention-grabbing program. The audience feels involved in what is going on. Clearly it's not simply a matter of pointing the camera and keeping in focus!

Similarly, two different people can *light* the same setting. The first person illuminates the scene clearly enough, but the second somehow manages to build up a persuasive atmospheric effect that enhances the show's appeal. These are the kinds of subtleties we shall be looking into as we explore techniques.

Having the edge

Working conditions have changed considerably in recent years. Earlier equipment often needed technical understanding to operate it effectively, and keep it working. (Or as it was often put: '*You had to know where to kick it*!') Various operational jobs in a production unit – camerawork, audio, lighting, videotape operation, editing – were handled by specialist technicians or engineers.

In today's highly competitive industry where equipment is increasingly reliable and operation simplified, there is increasing use of multi-tasking. Individuals need to acquire a variety of skills, rather than specialize in a particular craft. Also, instead of permanent in-house production crews there is a growing trend to use freelance operators on short-term contracts for maximum economy and flexibility. Now it's even possible for a single person to go out on location with a lightweight camera . . . record picture and sound . . . use a laptop computer system to edit the results . . . and return to base with a complete program ready to put on air!

The person with greater know-how and adaptability has the edge! Job opportunities vary considerably. While a person who specializes in a single craft develops specific aptitudes in that field, someone who operates a camera today, lights a setting tomorrow, and subsequently handles sound has opportunities to appreciate a broader spectrum of skills. There is a marked difference, too, between working in a team where experience is shared and newcomers trained, and working as an individual within a group of freelance individualists hired for the occasion.

Ultimately, all television/video production is essentially a team effort. Results depend not only on each person knowing their own job but on their understanding what others are aiming to do. In many shows, where the action is live or cannot be repeated, there is only one opportunity, and if that is lost or the shot marred . . . If, for instance, a sound-boom operator does a poor job, not only will audio be sub-standard but the work of others is likely to be spoiled – as a distracting microphone comes into a carefully framed picture, microphone shadows fall across faces, and so on.

Studying this book will give you a number of major advantages:

- By taking the trouble to understand the fundamentals of the equipment you are using you'll be able to rapidly assimilate and

adapt when new gear comes along. It's then just a matter of discovering any operational differences, or different features, etc.
- It will help you to anticipate problems and avoid trouble before it happens! For example, because you realize how a bright window in an interior shot could upset the entire picture quality and balance you may avoid difficulties by framing the shot to avoid it altogether!
- When unexpected difficulties arise – as they inevitably will at some time – you will recognize them and quickly compensate. For example, because a speaker has a weak voice you might tighten the shot a little to allow the sound boom to work closer without coming into shot.

An overview

Before we begin our journey, let's take an overview of the terrain we shall be covering. This will help to familiarize you with typical features you are going to meet and give you a general idea of how they interrelate.

- **Organization** – Although organizational basics follow a recognizable pattern for all types of TV production, the actual format the director uses will always be influenced by such factors as:
  - Whether the production is taking place in a studio or out on location
  - Whether it is to be transmitted '*live*' (as it happens) or videotaped (*pre-recorded*) for transmission later
  - Whether the action can be repeated (to correct errors, adjust shots) or is a 'once-only' opportunity that has to be captured first time round
  - Any restrictions due to shortage of time, equipment limitations, space problems, etc.
  - How the director decides to shoot the action (camera viewpoints, shot changes, etc.)
  - Whether there is an audience . . . and so on.

  In some situations, a *multi-camera set-up* is the best solution to shooting the action effectively. (This is controlled by a production team in a distant control room.) At other times, the director may decide to stand beside a *single camera*, guiding each shot from a nearby picture monitor.
- **Planning and performance** – In order to create a smooth-flowing coordinated presentation the director needs to have clear ideas about the action: i.e. what is going to happen next, where people are going to stand, what they are going to do, their moves, what they are going to say, and so on. Although there will be situations where the director has no option but to extemporize, and select shots spontaneously, quality results are more

likely where action and camera treatment are planned to some extent.

In more complex productions it is usually necessary for performers and crew to work to an agreed scheme which is based on a prepared script. This serves as a regulatory framework throughout the show. Action and dialogue are rehearsed to allow the production team to check their various contributions (camera shots, lighting, sound, cues, etc.).

Even where dialogue and action appear to be quite spontaneous (as in an interview situation), there has generally been some preliminary preparation. Topic coverage may be agreed; shots and sound levels are checked before recording. In a drama production, actors have usually memorized all their dialogue ('learned their lines'), and every word and move is rehearsed beforehand.

However, in the majority of productions, performers do not have the time or opportunity to remember a detailed prepared script. Instead they read their lines from a prompter which displays an image of the script in front of the camera lens. In addition, they may also be guided by instructions or advice picked up on an inconspicuous earpiece fed by a personal radio receiver – typically in newscasts, magazine programs and similar productions.

- **Shooting the action** – You can shoot action in several ways:
  - As a continuous process (*'live on tape'*), recording everything that happens.
  - Divide the total action into a series of separately recorded sequences (*'scenes', 'acts'*).
  - Analyze each action sequence into a series of separately recorded 'shots' with variations in viewpoints and/or subject sizes. Action may be repeated to facilitate later editing.

  Later, we shall be looking at the advantages and limitations of these various methods.
- **Cameras** – Cameras in general use today range from the largest state-of-the-art versions on heavy mountings to shoulder-mounted lightweight designs which are adaptable to field and studio use. For documentaries and news gathering, even smaller hand-held units have a valuable role.
- **Videotaping** – For convenience and greater flexibility, most TV programs are videotaped. Their picture and sound are usually recorded on a long ribbon of magnetic tape in a videotape recorder (using analogue or digital methods). In some situations sound may be taped on a separate audio recorder too. The videotape recorder (*'VTR'*) unit may be:
  - Integrated into or attached to the actual camera unit
  - In a separate nearby portable unit, which is connected to the camera by cable or radio
  - Or housed in a central videotape recording area in a remotes van or nearby building.

In a *multi-camera* production, where the separate outputs of the cameras are to be interswitched or blended together, this is usually carried out on a *production switcher* (in a remotes van or a nearby building). The selection is taped on a central videotape recorder. Alternatively, each camera's output may be recorded separately and their shots edited together during a later session. A later method records picture and sound *digitally* on disks (magnetic or optical), or uses solid-state electronic stores to retain data.

- **Additional picture sources** – Further picture sources such as film (telecine), graphics, slides, contributions from *remotes* (outside broadcasts), titling, etc. may be inserted into the program during the main recording session, or added to the final videotape recording during the *postproduction ('post') editing session*.
- **Program sound** – Typically, a microphone is clipped to the speaker's clothing, or hand-held, or attached to a sound boom or other fitting. Any music, sound effects, commentary, etc. can either be played into the program's sound track during the main taping session, or added in a later *postproduction ('post') session.*
- **Lighting treatment** – Lighting treatment can make a major contribution to the success of a presentation; whether it is augmenting natural light or providing totally artificial illumination. Techniques involve carefully blending the intensities and 'texture' of the light (its 'hardness' or its diffusion), with selectively arranged light direction and coverage, to bring out certain features of the subject and the scene.
- **Scenic design** – Providing appropriate surroundings for the action, scenic design creates a particular ambience for the program. *Virtual settings* are increasingly used to simulate an environment.
- **Make-up and costume (wardrobe)** – In larger productions, these important contributions are overseen by specialists. But in smaller studios they are handled more incidentally.
- **Editing** – Fundamentally, there are two forms of editing:
  1. *Direct editing* 'on-the-hoof' during the actual performance; interswitching between sources using a *production switcher (vision mixer)* – typically in a 'live-on-air' transmission.
  2. *Postproduction editing.* Here, when all the program material has been compiled, the separate shots are selected and listed during a later editing session to form an *edit decision list*; *EDL.* The chosen shots or segments are then copied onto a new 'clean' videotape, arranged to form coherent sequences, and create a particular audience impact. This forms the '*transmission* or *master copy*'. The original tapes are retained for any later editing rearrangements or for archiving.

  Two basic systems are used in video/audio editing:
  - In *linear editing*, you 'shuttle' the original recorded program tapes to and fro to select the sections you want, copying these

individually in the EDL order onto the 'clean' tape of another videocassette recorder to form the master tape.

- In *non-linear editing*, you copy all your taped program material onto a *disk storage system* to provide a digital duplicate. Disk systems have the important advantage that they allow very rapid random selection – unlike tape systems, where it takes some time to find individual sections, especially where several tape reels are involved.

- **Audio (program sound)** – As well as direct sound pick-up from the action, most productions include other contributions such as music, sound effects, narration, fed in from various sources; e.g. audio tape or disc equipment, VTRs, film reproducing equipment (telecine, film island), remotes.

  As with picture editing, all this program sound may be selected and blended (*mixed*) during performance. Or alternatively, the final soundtrack may be built up during a *postproduction ('post') session*. Most shows combine both practices.

Audience impact

It's pretty obvious that to achieve professional-quality results we need to be able to use equipment smoothly and unobtrusively. But it's all too easy to develop slick techniques while overlooking the most important issue – the kind of impact that particular treatment is going to have *on your audience*.

Ideally, the techniques you choose should arise from the nature and purpose of the production. The camera treatment, lighting, sound treatment, the design of the setting, should all be selected to suit the occasion. Many an otherwise excellent documentary program, for instance, has been ruined by an obtrusive, repetitive, irrelevant musical background.

We shall be exploring various ways in which techniques can influence your audience's response to what they are seeing. There is nothing sinister about this idea, for program making is a *persuasive craft*; quite as much as marketing, advertising, and all other presentational fields. Learning how to control and adjust production mechanics to achieve the kind of impact you are aiming at is part of the director's skills.

Audiences don't usually give much thought to whether the program they are watching is actually *television, video, film, computer* magic, or a mixture of all these systems. In fact, in today's multimedia world it is becoming increasingly difficult to discern where one medium ends and another begins! The viewer is only concerned with the nature and effectiveness of the material; whether it holds the attention, is interesting, amusing, stimulating, gripping, intriguing, entertaining . . .

Demarcations between these various communications media have become blurred. Nowadays you can find the same program material appearing in a public *television* transmission, on a *video* cassette watched on a home TV, or as part of a *CD-ROM* viewed on a *computer* screen. To confuse matters further, *motion pictures* may be shot with *video* cameras; the videotape being edited and transposed onto film for theater projection. Little wonder that people talk about '*filming*' or '*photographing*' with the video camera!

'Television' or 'video'?

Whether you are involved with *television* or *video production*, you will find that the program-making *principles* and the equipment used can be virtually identical.

- '**Television**' is a *broadcast* medium in which programs are promulgated via land transmitters, cables, or satellites to a general audience, and seen '*off-air*' as part of a regular *public service*.
- '**Video**' program making, on the other hand, is usually concerned with productions which are intended for single-program selective viewing by *closed-circuit* audiences. In some cases, it is designed for repeat-viewing. But even these broad distinctions are really very arbitrary!

TV organizations

While some *television* organizations make most of the programs they transmit, others primarily replay bought-in program packages. Because production costs rise, strategic marketing and co-production (in which program budgeting is shared between two or more companies) become increasingly important. As with film making, audience ratings strongly influence both subject choice and production formats. There may be less opportunity for experiment and a greater tendency to follow proven 'formula' approaches.

Television organizations vary in size from small local stations to large multi-studio production centers. Most permanent TV studios are equipped with anything from two to six video cameras and a selection of sound and lighting equipment. *Network studio operations* will normally be supported by various in-house facilities (specialists, technical and supply services, etc.). Regular production teams or crews may be allocated on a scheduled basis to cover a variety of programs ranging from newscasts, talk shows, magazine programs, comedy, to soap operas . . . In larger organizations, a production crew may tend to work on a particular style of show such as *Comedy* or *Drama* – for as you will see, each type of production tends to require noticeably different skills and aptitudes.

In some TV systems, crews may work both in the studio and away from base (i.e. on *remotes/outside broadcasts*). But more usually, units will specialize; in *studio* production, *location* assignments (e.g. public events, sport, etc.), or in *news gathering*.

Cable TV systems take several forms, from small studios that cater for community groups to specialist providers (news organizations), and relay systems that supply multi-source programs but have no actual production facilities of their own.

Video production units

A variety of organizations meet the ever-expanding needs of the *video* market:

- There are the small *in-house units* that make video programs for their own organizations. *Corporate video* units attached to businesses and public services cover such topics as staff training, internal liaison, publicity, etc. *Campus* studio units produce educational or experimental material of various kinds.
- Freelance commercial organizations make contracted shows for broadcast and/or video distribution. Program topics range from advertising, promotional material and pop videos to instructional videos (e.g. courses on management techniques, equipment maintenance, safety).

  The production team is often assembled specifically for each project. Equipment is hired (or augmented) from facility houses, and where necessary, additional facilities (e.g. studio space) rented. A high proportion of the program material is shot on location. Lacking the back-up amenities of larger, more extensive set-ups (i.e. news archives, stock film libraries, sound effects, etc.), these are obtained from commercial libraries as they are needed.
- Finally there are the large-scale *video* production units with similar facilities to those found in regular television production organizations.

The technical world

Meeting new equipment

Most of us feel somewhat uneasy when meeting new equipment for the first time. Whether it's a new version of equipment we are used to, or an entirely unfamiliar gizmo, there's always that apprehension that we might break it, or make a fool of ourselves by using it incorrectly. But don't worry. This *technofear* soon passes, and the new technical terms soon trip off the tongue. As you will see, the technology we shall be meeting is straightforward enough. Mastering it will leave you free to concentrate on the *creative aspects* of the job.

However, a word of warning! As you become accustomed to your equipment, certain temptations can develop! *Directors*, for example, often get an urge to try out various of the 'bells and whistles' available simply to introduce variety: adding a wipe here, some astounding multi-image superimpositions there, putting in a dynamic 'page turn' or some other exciting video effect. *Camera operators*, too, may be tempted to use their equipment with a certain 'panache': an impressively rapid dolly move here, a fast zoom there . . . There's the temptation to dramatize the lighting treatment, or add a little extra to the sound . . . *Appropriateness* is the watchword!

Terminology

Because Television has developed in many centers throughout the world, you will find that terminology varies between organizations. Some terms are universal, while others are local. Stick to those that are used in your group! Fashions change too, so that, for example, what were once widely called *spot effects* in radio and early TV have now developed into the art of *Foleying*.

Regrettably, there has been insufficient space here to include the picturesque slang that pervades the industry; to explain, for instance, why '*a baby is hot, and needs to be boxed in with a jelly*' (i.e. an overbright small spotlight needs its barndoors closed and a plastic diffuser added). But that is a separate study in itself!

Technical developments

In recent years there have been many exciting developments in television/video technology. Some have given rise to passing novelty effects, such as squashed, stretched, or color-distorted multi-images, morphing, reverse action . . . Other devices such as the *Steadicam* have provided the director with even greater flexibility and additional techniques.

Viewers soon take for granted the most complex technical innovations: satellite communication that allows an on-the-spot camera report direct from a disaster area, or conversations between people thousands of miles apart, or continuous coverage of a road race, or views from outer space . . . Yet not so long ago these 'routine' transmissions would have been quite impracticable.

Less obvious are such behind-the-scenes developments as the freedom with which pictures can now be adjusted and digitally manipulated; the ways in which non-linear videotape editing has revolutionized news production; the effects of the introduction of desktop workstations and servers; the fascinating potentials of digital audio processing . . . and so on.

Today's equipment

Broadly speaking, the equipment used for television/video program making today tends to fall into three categories:

- *Consumer* equipment: Intended for hobbyists, family use, etc.
- *Portable professional*: Equipment used by in-house units, video teams, small studios.
- *Broadcast* equipment: In-built (rack-mounted) used by larger TV/video organizations.

Consequently the type of gear you may be handling can range from compact lightweight units to the robust heavy-duty facilities needed for the rough-and-tumble of continuous everyday use.

Broadcast equipment has to

- Function to the highest standards, providing high definition and color fidelity under a variety of conditions, low picture noise, no visible defects or distortions (artifacts).
- Be extremely stable and reliable.
- Be adjusted and maintained to stringent limits, and provide consistent results. (For instance, a tape recorded on one machine must reproduce identically on another machine to the same standards.)
- Be able to operate hour after hour, and still produce results to the laid-down standard. There should be no noticeable changes in performance; e.g. no drifting as the system warms up.
- Withstand quite rough handling (vibration, bumps and jolts, dust, heat, rain . . .) when used under very demanding conditions.

Any piece of equipment will have its shortcomings, which manufacturers gradually overcome through design and invention. But generally speaking, state-of-art quality performance only comes from equipment that is rigidly constructed, well ventilated, has robust controls, and incorporates sophisticated electronics which ensure precise stability.

Small low-cost cameras often incorporate lots of '*special features*' that are not found in professional units, and thanks to ingenious design can produce remarkably good picture and sound quality. But when results are compared directly with those from typical broadcast equipment, quality differences become noticeable that would be unacceptable under broadcast conditions where deterioration is cumulative – especially in multi-generation recordings.

The production team

The journey ahead

Most people in television operations find themselves specializing to some degree; in the kind of job they do, and in the sorts of production they meet. The particular skills you develop will largely depend therefore on the kinds of production you encounter, and the type of equipment available. Where, for example, a sound crew largely relies on clip-on personal microphones for sound pick-up, they are unlikely to discover the features and idiosyncrasies of working with a large sound boom. Problems on a live show are noticeably different from those on an identical production where the action is taped and edited during postproduction.

Teamwork

In a well-coordinated production group, members continually interrelate. A good director will allow for the practical problems that a set designer has to face. The designer arranges a setting to help the lighting director to achieve the most effective results. Similarly, the lighting director needs to rationalize treatment with the make-up artist. Of course, there are always individuals who concentrate on their own contribution to the exclusion of others. But when you work in a cooperative team where each member appreciates the other person's aims and problems, difficulties somehow seem to become minimal!

Practical production

The hidden factors

As you will discover, there are many hidden factors that directly affect how a TV director working on a studio production can approach a subject, such as:

- The program's budget
- The amount of time allocated for rehearsal and recording
- The free studio space
- The type of equipment obtainable, and its flexibility
- The size and the experience of the production team
- Support/back-up facilities. Etc., etc.

All aspects of the production have to be arranged and adjusted to suit these parameters.

The daily routine

In a surprisingly short time many of the procedures and operations that mystified you not so long ago will quickly become second nature. Therein lies a trap for the unwary! It's all too easy to learn techniques by rote, and go on to apply them as a comfortable routine. In a busy schedule it is a temptation, of course, to apply regular 'off-the-peg' solutions that have been successful before, rather than work out innovative 'tailor-made' approaches. During daily TV viewing, you can see many a show where only the talent and the scenery seem to change! In the end, repetitious routines become as wearisome to the audience as to the production team.

The pressures of production

Program making is an absorbing, extremely satisfying process, but one is always aware of underlying practical pressures. *Aspirations* are one thing – but the *achievable* can be quite another. In the real world one has to rationalize and cope with the various organizational mechanics that influence the form and development of program making: *How much will it cost? Is there time? What happens if it overruns scheduled time? Is there enough skilled labor available? Do we have the equipment/materials? Are there any regulations/restrictions preventing it?*

Very few productions evolve without a hitch of some kind. There will always be the planned action that does not work, the last-minute hang-up, the prop that breaks, the missed cue . . . Particularly when things go wrong, it's very easy to become more preoccupied with the mechanics of the situation – e.g. how much taping time remains, camera moves, boom shadows – than aesthetic niceties or potential audience responses. These can get pushed into the background.

It is not surprising that, especially during a *live* show on-air, program makers can lose sight of the value and purpose of the end product their audience will see. The more fully you understand production principles and problems, the freer you are to think about the *significance* of what you are doing.

The detached viewpoint

One of the greatest difficulties that everyone working on any production will have, is to assess how the *audience* will respond. The viewer is seeing it for the first, and usually the only time. The production team has become overfamiliar with all its aspects. Every person in the team is concentrating on their own particular contribution:

While the *director* is worried about the talent's performance . . .

The *set designer* has noticed where some scenic flats do not fit properly. . .
The *lighting director* is fretting about a boom shadow. . .
The *sound specialist* finds air conditioning noise obtrusive behind quiet speech . . .
The *make-up artist* is disturbed by a perspiring forehead . . .
The *costume designer* has noticed creases in a collar . . .
The *video operator* is preoccupied with picture matching . . .
The *producer* is concerned with costs of overrunning the scheduled time . . .

It is not easy to assess from a detached viewpoint. And when you have put all that effort into a project, it's hard to accept that your audience may be watching the show with less than 100 per cent attention, unaware of any of these problems!

2 Television in action

Nowadays someone with a hand-held camcorder and quite a modest computer system can produce results that not so long ago would have needed the combined services of a large production team and a deal of equipment!

Today, the television camera is free to shoot virtually everywhere. Our audience has come to accept the camera's flexibility. Whether the pictures they are watching are from a camera in the studio or from outer space, intimate shots from an endoscope or from a '*critter camera*' attached to a swimming seal, or thrilling shots from a sky diver's helmet camera . . . these diverse channels are all grist to the endless mill of television programming and accepted as 'normal'!

Production methods

The way you set about developing any production will depend on a number of factors:

- Whether the show is *live* (i.e. being seen by the viewers as it is happening), or whether you are recording the action for subsequent editing and postproduction treatment
- You can choose to record continuously or selectively: in the order in which the action will be seen, or in an order arranged to suit the production mechanics.
- Then again, much will depend on whether you are able to control and direct the action you are shooting, or whether you are obliged to snatch shots wherever you are able.

As new facilities have been developed, established methods of creating programs have extended. Wherever possible, productions are videotaped or filmed, and have come to rely more and more on postproduction editing techniques; using all kinds of digital video effects to enhance audience appeal.

- As you will see, although many situations involve little more than uncomplicated switching between shots, in others the *editing* process – which determines how shots are selected and arranged – becomes a subtle art.

  Although, as you would expect, all television productions have a number of common features, the particular skills required of the director and crew can vary considerably with the *type* of show you are working on. The program material itself can determine how you present it. Some kinds of production follow an exacting prepared plan, while others have to rely heavily on spontaneous decisions. Let's look at some examples:

- *Interviews and talks shows* – As you will see, approaches here are inevitably somewhat standardized, with shots concentrating on what people have to say and how they react.
- *Newscasts* – Most news programs follow a similar format. '*Live-on-air*' in the studio, a pair of newscasters present the news seated behind a central desk, reading from camera prompters, and introducing stories from various contributory sources – videotaped inserts, film, live on-site reporters, library photographs, graphics, etc. There may also be brief interviews; either in the studio or via a display screen. Continuously reviewed and revised, there is a behind-the-scenes urgency, particularly for late-breaking news stories. The closely coordinated team is continually assessing and editing incoming material, preparing commentary, assembling illustrations, library clips, graphics, titling, etc.
- *Sports programs* – Each type of sport or game poses its own particular problems for the director. Shooting conditions vary considerably. On the one hand, we have the relatively localized action of the boxing ring or the snooker table. On the other, there is the fast ebbing and flowing action of the football field. When presenting the wide-ranging action of a golf tournament, marathon runners, a horse race, or a bicycle race, will the cameras follow along with the action or shoot from selected vantage points? Sometimes, several different events are taking place simultaneously. Can they all be covered effectively on-air or will selective taped shots be shown later? In each case, the director's aim is to always be 'in the right place at the right time'. While conveying a sense of continuity, the camera must not only capture the highlights but be ready to record the unexpected. Slow motion replays help to analyze the action.
- *Comedy* – Most comedy shows follow the familiar 'realistic' *SitCom* (situation comedy) format. The studio production is staged to enable the studio audience (seen or only heard) to see and react to the action. They can watch any videotape or film inserts on hanging picture monitors. Additional 'appropriate' laughter/applause or even 'reaction shots' may be added during postproduction editing.
- *Music and dance* – Productions can range from straightforward performance to elaborate visual presentations in which pictures (and sound) involve considerable postproduction aftertreatment (e.g. creating multi-image montages, slow-motion sequences, color changes, animation effects, etc.). Particularly where the sound arrangements are complex, the on-camera performance may be *mimed* to a previously recorded soundtrack.

- *Drama* – Drama productions usually follow a very carefully planned process in which camerawork, sound and lighting treatment can be very exacting. The dialogue, action, camera and sound treatment are fully scripted. The show may be taped continuously or in segments. Most drama today relies heavily on postproduction editing and aftertreatment (e.g. adding sound effects, music, post-syncing).

The venue

Today TV productions are shot under a variety of conditions:

- In a regular fully fitted TV/video studio.
- In an extemporized studio, set up for the occasion.
- On location, in an existing interior (e.g. a public building).
- On location, in the open air (EFP – *Electronic field production*).

Each locale has its particular advantages and limitations. While, for example, a *studio* has all the facilities you need ready to hand, we have to face the fact that there is nothing to shoot there (except the walls) until we create settings of some sort, which then need to be decorated and lit appropriately. The running costs of providing these conditions can be considerable.

On location, you may have a ready-made environment in which to shoot, and perhaps daylight to provide the illumination. But here there are various new problems; from variable weather conditions and background noises to traffic and bystanders. You are normally away from your base, with its back-up services (spare equipment, maintenance, etc.).

The television studio

A high proportion of TV production is studio based. So what could be better than starting our journey with a visit in our imagination to a typical studio and its associated control center?

Although in practice, TV studios vary from the modest, to purpose-built giants, all seem somehow to share a certain indefinable atmosphere. At first, as we push through heavy soundproof entry doors, the studio has the impersonal silence of a deserted warehouse. Despite its emptiness, the acoustically padded walls reduce all echo. Looking across the stark expanse of smooth floor, we see the blank screen of a picture monitor over in one corner. Various cables and connectors hang from the walls. On the framework of bars or battens suspended from the ceiling, clusters of lamps await . . .

But bring in the scenery, switch on those lamps to bathe the settings in light and shade . . . and this atmosphere will become

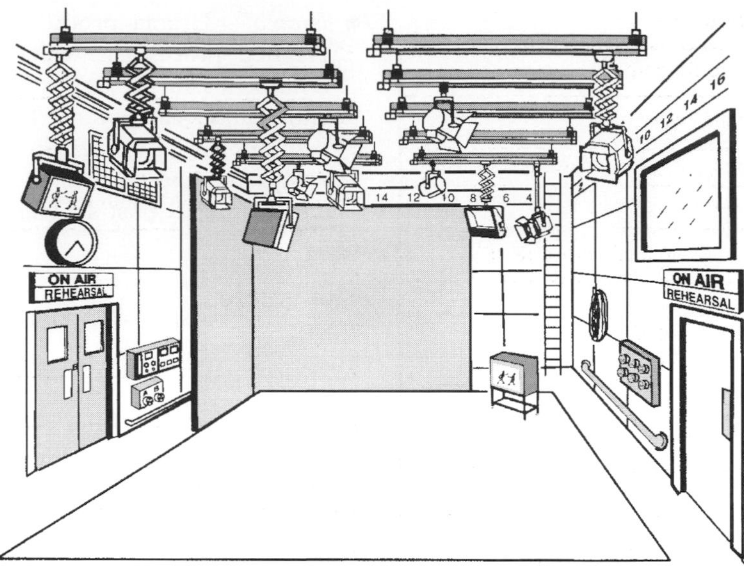

Fig. 2.1 The television studio
A typical view of the empty studio with uncluttered staging area, surround safety lane, overhead lighting battens and control-room observation window.

expectantly transformed. And with this magic comes a feeling of urgency; a purposeful tension conveyed to performers and crew alike.

Let's watch as preparations begin. A busy crew trucks in a mass of scenery – preformed units of all shapes and sizes. A variety of furnishings arrive, accompanied by containers of intriguing bric-à-brac. Working from detailed plans, the crew sets up the scenic flats, each piece in its prescribed place . . . a window here, a wall, and a doorway there. And before our eyes, a 'real' lived-in environment is beginning to form. Furniture is positioned, drapes are hung, as the sets are *dressed*. A lighting crew begins to position and adjust each lamp to a meticulously prepared *plot*. The newly arrived camera and sound crews move their equipment from store into the opening positions ready for rehearsals. Everywhere is urgent action; completing tasks, tidying away, making last-minute changes . . .

By a daily organizational miracle, the various pieces of the productional jigsaw are combining to provide the show we have been planning and preparing. The cameras set up their shots, seen there on the monitor screens. The illusion begins to live!

Yet, within a time span of hours the production will have completed rehearsals; the crew will have learned and practiced the director's treatment; performances hopefully reached their peak . . . and the program has been recorded or transmitted. And then the whole 'magic cave' will be dismantled. Unbelievably quickly, the settings will be 'struck' and tucked away for stock or junking; equipment stored; and floors cleaned off. The original emptiness will return.

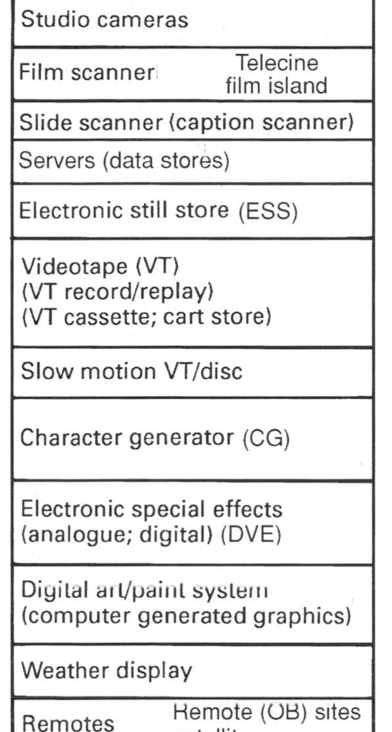

Sources
Studio cameras
Film scanner
Telecine film island
Slide scanner (caption scanner)
Servers (data stores)
Electronic still store (ESS)
Videotape (VT)
(VT record/replay)
(VT cassette; cart store)
Slow motion VT/disc
Character generator (CG)
Electronic special effects
(analogue; digital) (DVE)
Digital art/paint system
(computer generated graphics)
Weather display
Remotes
Remote (OB) sites
satellites

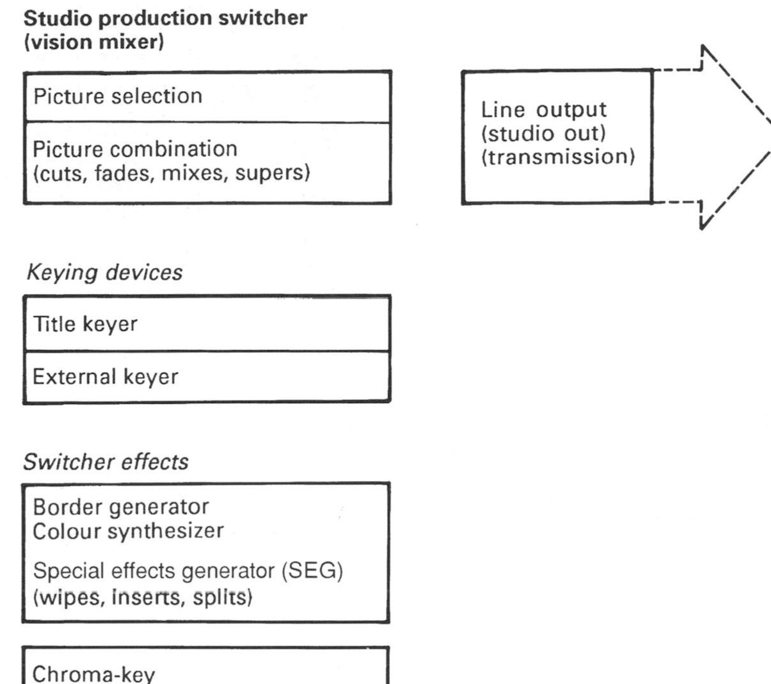

Studio production switcher (vision mixer)
Picture selection
Picture combination
(cuts, fades, mixes, supers)
Line output
(studio out)
(transmission)
Keying devices
Title keyer
External keyer
Switcher effects
Border generator
Colour synthesizer
Special effects generator (SEG)
(wipes, inserts, splits)
Chroma-key

Fig. 2.2 Contributory video sources

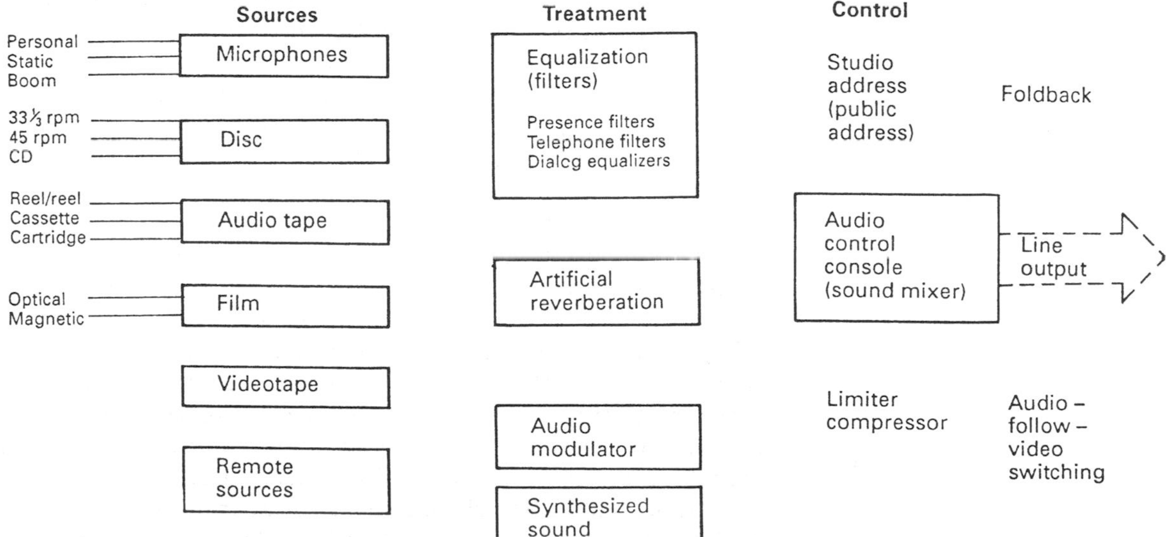

Sources
Personal
Static
Boom
Microphones
33⅓ rpm
45 rpm
CD
Disc
Reel/reel
Cassette
Cartridge
Audio tape
Optical
Magnetic
Film
Videotape
Remote sources
Treatment
Equalization (filters)
Presence filters
Telephone filters
Dialog equalizers
Artificial reverberation
Audio modulator
Synthesized sound
Control
Studio address (public address)
Foldback
Audio control console (sound mixer)
Line output
Limiter compressor
Audio – follow – video switching

Fig. 2.3 Contributory audio sources

These are the conditions in which our theories and hopes become reality. And it is only when we relate our aspirations to the relentless pressure of practical conditions that we see TV production in its true perspective.

The television studio in action

Turn back the clock now, to earlier in the day when camera rehearsal was in progress for a drama production. The illuminated wall signs show that the studio is in closed-circuit rehearsal. So, although all the equipment is *hot* (operating), its output is only being monitored locally. At the scheduled time the studio video (pictures) and audio (sound) signals will be fed via the coordinating *master control room* (the central switching/routing control point) to the videotape recorders or immediately to the transmitters for *live* telecasting.

While the occasional production may shoot action against the studio walls alone, or use electronically inserted backgrounds, most will make use of scenery to create an environmental effect. This may range from a simple arrangement of background drapes or a few free-standing scenic units to elaborate architectural or decorative structures of various kinds. Many studios have 'permanently' arranged scenery ready for their regular newscasts, cookery programs, interviews, etc. For our visit, let's imagine that today's show is a drama of some kind . . .

Around the studio you can see examples of the *set designer*'s art: the three-walled rooms, a section of a street scene, and a summer garden. After surprise at the colorful realism of these sets the first impression is one of endless lights! Suspended, clamped to sets, on floor stands . . . it is hard to appreciate that each has been placed and angled with precision, for a particular purpose.

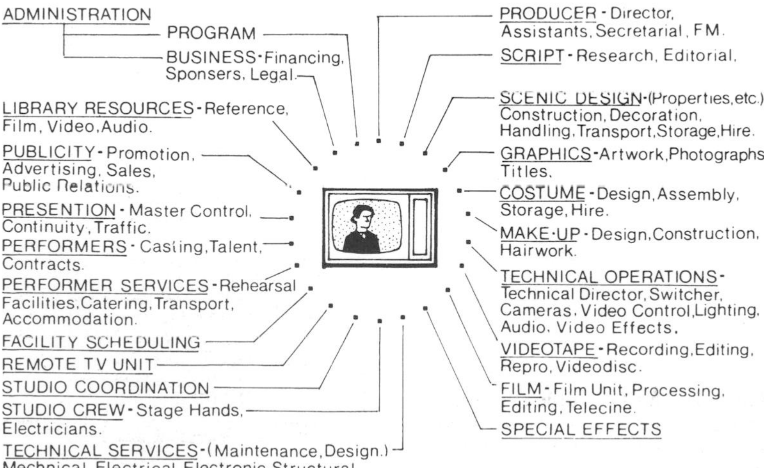

Fig. 2.4 Contributory services

At the moment, action is in a 'living room' (an *interior*). Despite the number of people working around, everywhere is surprisingly quiet. Only the dialogue between the actors is audible.

A camera dollies gently over the specially leveled floor – where the slightest bumps could judder the picture. Its long cable snakes away to a wall outlet. As we watch, people and equipment move around silently, almost as if choreographed, systematically and smoothly, to an unspoken scheme.

But plug your earphones into the studio intercom circuit and you enter a different world! Now you can hear the continuous instructions from the unseen director in the production control room: guiding, assessing, querying, explaining, cuing, warning, correcting . . . coordinating the studio crew through their headsets.

Outside the 'living room' you see the 'sunny garden' (an *exterior*). Close scrutiny reveals that the convincingly flowering trees are really plastic blossoms wired to lopped-off branches and the artificial turf is laid over sandbags. But on camera, the effect is idyllic. Quiet birdsong fills the air from a nearby playback speaker (foldback/program loudspeaker).

The *floor manager* (FM), the director's link with the studio floor, hand cues an actress to enter the garden. The sound boom's telescopic arm swings, its microphone following her as she speaks. The cameras within the room pull away quickly and move to the next set.

Behind the tinted glass window in one wall of the studio is the *production control room*. Here the director sits watching a large

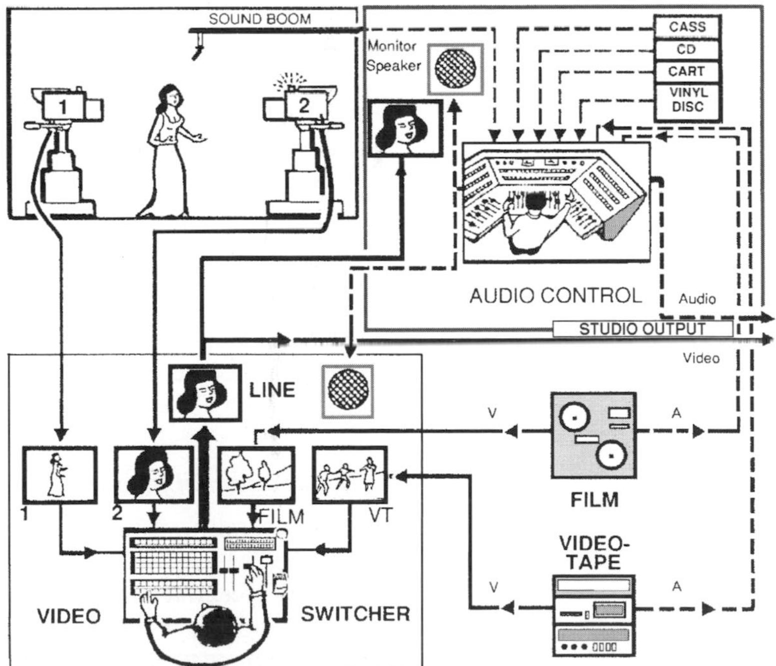

Fig. 2.5 The TV studio system
This simplified diagram shows how video and audio sources are routed to their respective selection points.

group of *picture monitors*. These continuously display each camera's shot and the outputs of the various other picture sources – videotape and film channels, graphics, etc. Program sound can be heard over the *monitor speakers*.

Through an *intercom (talkback)* microphone the director guides the rest of the production team. In the studio, the crews working on cameras, sound, lighting, scenery, etc. hear this intercom through their earphones, unheard by the performers/talent or the studio microphones. The FM diplomatically relays the director's instructions and observations to the performers, cues action with hand signals, guides and advises where necessary.

The director has just seen a bad shot, as someone in the foreground obscures (*masks*) another person, and asks the FM to stop the action. '*Hold it please*,' calls the FM. Action pauses while the problem is sorted out. A slight position change is the solution, and the floor is crayon-marked (*toe* or *location mark*). The talent goes through the revised moves and all is well. But the director now feels that the shot now looks too close. '*Can you pull back on Two?*' (dolly the camera back away from the action). Camera Two's operator shakes the camera's head to signal 'No'. '*Can you zoom out a little?*' And with a wider lens angle, picture composition improves. On the director's go-ahead, the FM calls for silence. '*Right. Back to Shot 54, as Joe enters*,' and checking the shot on a nearby wheeled floor monitor (which displays the studio's *line* picture), gives an arm signal to cue the action. The game of make-believe springs back to life . . . as if no mere technicalities had interrupted. The rehearsal continues.

The production control room

Here is the production nerve center, where the director accompanied by a support group controls the production. There are two basic approaches to control room design – a *communal* arrangement and a *sectionalized* layout. Each has its advantages and its limitations.

Most production control rooms have a large soundproof window with tinted glass which provides a good overview of the studio. This can help you to solve at a glance various routine rehearsal problems that may not be apparent on camera (e.g. crowded equipment, staging difficulties, lighting faults).

The communal layout (Figure 2.6 part 1)

This uses open-plan arrangements in either a single-level or split-level form. Here everyone concerned with production control sits at a long central desk: the *production director*, an *assistant* (who checks program timing, calls shot numbers and stand-by cues), the *switcher* (*vision mixer*), the *technical director* and *audio technician*, and

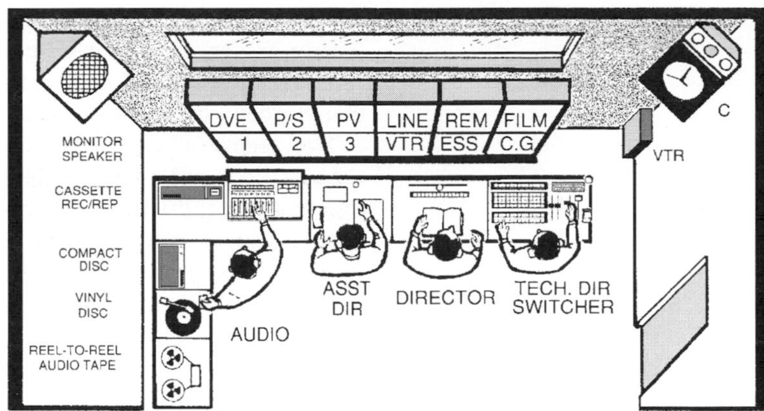

Fig. 2.6 part 1 The 'communal' production control room
All production operations are concentrated at a central desk. Video and lighting may be controlled locally or elsewhere.

For key to abbreviations, see page 25.

perhaps the *video control operator* (*shader*). (As you will see, the jobs, titles, and names vary considerably!) See Table 16.1.

The desk faces a row of picture monitor screens. The *preview (channel) monitors* show the outputs of the various video sources and continuously display each camera's output as well as film, videotape, slide scanners, and remote sources. Any source may be selected and switched (or faded) by the *production switcher* to the *studio output* (line output to master control). The *master monitor* (*line, main channel, transmission*) displays the result.

Many production control rooms use small black and white monitors for all previews, and rely on two or three large color monitors for assessing color quality. One serves as a general-purpose preview that can be switched to check upcoming shots, video effects, combined sources, etc. Another is the master monitor, showing, in color, the program output (*line, studio out*) from the switcher.

This arrangement is not only more economical than having a large bank of color monitors but overcomes the problem of making all their color pictures match. It can be confusing if monitors drift over a period. On the other hand, one has to switch any picture source onto the preview color monitor before being able to check its color quality, and this is not always convenient.

The director's attention is divided between the various preview monitors, the selected output on the master monitor, and the *program-audio* from a nearby loudspeaker. In a communal layout, the director instructs the production team and floor crew (cameras, sound booms) through a headset (earphone and microphone) plugged into the communal intercom circuit (PL – private line). Although this shared-line arrangement is simple, it has the disadvantage that everyone overhears other people's instructions and exchanges, and this can become wearying or confusing in a busy production.

The production director may operate the production switcher (video switching panel, vision mixer) – particularly on remotes

(OBs). But for more complex operations a specialist switcher (vision mixer) or the technical director usually does this job, enabling the production director to concentrate on controlling the many other aspects of the show.

The technical director's responsibility can vary between one organization and another. He/she may direct cameras, actively assisting in production treatment, and carrying out video switching. As a supervisory engineer, he/she may oversee the engineering aspects of the production such as aligning effects, checking shots, ensuring source availability, and monitoring quality.

At the far end of the desk the audio specialist (*audio technician, audio control*) sits at the audio console (board, panel) adjusting and blending the various sound sources; wearing earphones in order to check and cue-up audio inserts (from disc, tape, film).

Depending on the show and its organization, others directly involved in its presentation may include:

1 The *set designer* (*scenic designer*) responsible for the *scenic treatment* (*staging*).
2 The *lighting director* who designs and arranges the studio lighting.
3 The *producer, editors* (script, film, videotape), *sponsor*, special assistants, researchers . . . and so on *ad infinitum*.
4 Where a program uses elaborate *video effects* these can take some time to prepare. So an extra operator may be needed to devise and control them. Otherwise the person at the production switcher has to arrange these, in addition to the regular inter-source transitions(!).

In practice, where a production is being videotaped it may be more convenient to leave all video effects and image manipulation until a postproduction (*post*) session rather than attempt them during production.

Whether various pieces of ancillary equipment – such as videotape recorders – are included within the productional control room or housed elsewhere varies between organizations.

As far as cameras are concerned, each studio camera's cable is routed via a wall outlet to its separate *camera control unit (CCU)* or *base station*, where an engineer (*shader*) monitors the picture quality; checking and adjusting the video equipment as necessary. (See Chapter 23.) This control position may be located in a nearby *master control room (apparatus room)* or within the communal production control room itself.

The sectionalized layout (Figure 2.6 part 2)

In this arrangement the entire control area is subdivided into a series of separate rooms. Large glass wall panels and an intercom system enable the groups to intercommunicate:

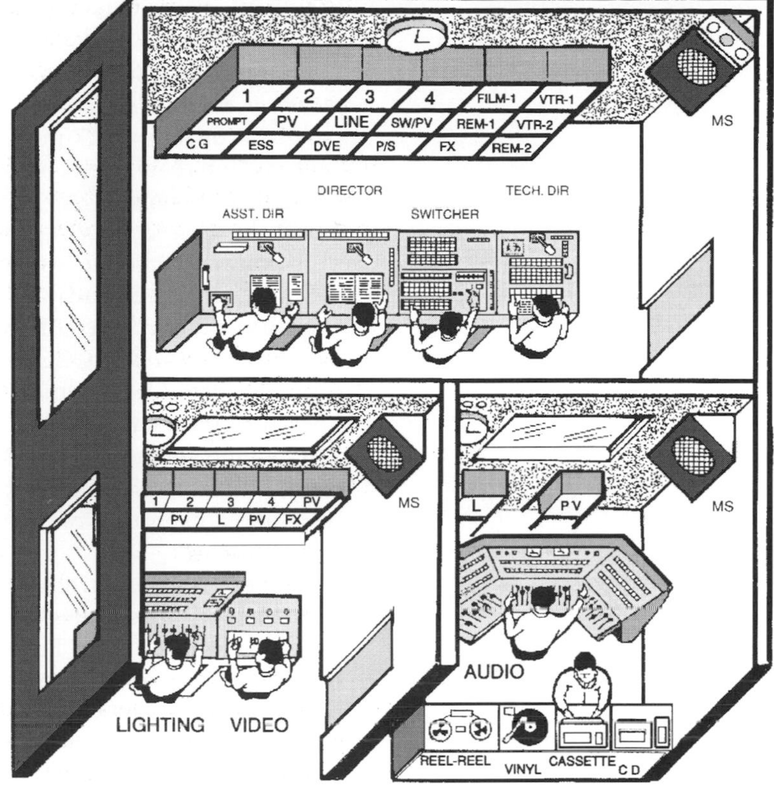

Fig. 2.6 part 2 The 'sectionalized' production control room
Production control, audio control and video/lighting control are located in separate rooms, to avoid interaction. They have private wire intercom, as well as communal production intercom (talkback).

CG	Character generator
DVE	Digital effects
ESS	Electronic still store (server)
FILM	Film island/telecine
FX	Effects (chroma-key)
LINE	Studio output (transmission)
PROMPT	Camera prompter
PS	Preset (combined sources)
PV	Preview
REM	Remote (OB)
SW/PV	Switchable preview
VTR	Videotape channel
MS	Monitor speaker

1 *Production control room* – Where the director, assistant(s), producer, switcher and technical director are located.
2 *Vision control room* – Video quality and lighting coordination.
3 *Sound control room* – Audio coordination and control.

This layout has the real advantage that it allows each group to concentrate on their own particular activities without distracting others. So, for example, the director will not be diverted as the sound and lighting specialists sort out the reason for a boom shadow. All intercommunication is through local microphones and loudspeakers. (Nobody wears headsets.)

The director's desk microphone relays the *general intercom* (communal *production talkback*) which is heard over other rooms' loudspeakers. Each room also has switched *private wire (party line)* circuits. So, for instance, someone at the audio console can talk to the sound-boom operator without intruding into the general intercom.

1 **Production control room** – As you would expect, the main features here are similar to those in the *communal layout*. A bank of monitors shows the outputs from all picture sources. Wall

loudspeakers provide the program sound. At the production desk, the *director* sits together with an *assistant*(s) in front of the main intercom microphone and a private wire switchpanel. The *technical director* (*crew chief*) at the end of the desk has switch panels to display check pictures on a local preview monitor, as well as intercom, telephone lines and private wires to all contribution points. A *switcher (vision mixer)* operating a *production switcher panel* works directly to the director's instructions. Various personnel who need close contact with the director will also be seated nearby (e.g. the producer).

2 **Vision control room** – All the operational video controls for the *camera control units* (*CCU*) or *base stations* are extended to a central control desk in the video control room, where a single operator continually monitors and adjusts the picture quality from studio cameras, slide/film scanner and other contributory sources. Here, if necessary, the color quality, contrast and brightness (exposure) of pictures can be adjusted and matched (*color balance*).

Because video control adjustments and lighting are interdependent, this control desk is usually located beside the *lighting console* at which studio lighting is controlled and cued. These operators – who share the same picture monitors – can therefore coordinate their work guided by the lighting director.

3 **Sound control room** – Sitting at the *audio console* (*sound desk, mixer, or board*) the person controlling the program sound (variously named *audio engineer, sound mixer, sound supervisor, audio control!*) is responsible for monitoring sound dynamics and quality, blending the sources to suit the production's artistic and technical requirements. In complex drama or musical productions this requires not a good ear but a great deal of dexterity and split-second operations. Incoming sources will include not only the studio microphones but discs (CD and vinyl), audio tapes, film and videotape soundtracks, announce booth, remotes . . .

At the same time, the audio control technician guides the sound crew on the studio floor by private wire intercom. Where sound booms are being used the boom operators will need guidance:

- To avoid the microphone or its shadow appearing in shot
- To give warnings of changes of shot (e.g. to keep the microphone out of long shots)
- To provide action reminders (e.g. when talent is going to move to a new position)
- To adjust the microphone distance, so that the resulting *sound perspective* suits the shot.

Whether a separate technician operates all the additional sound equipment (i.e. discs, CDs, carts, cassette players) largely depends on the complexity of the production and the control room layout.

Master control

The *Master Control Room* is the engineering coordination center for a TV station. It provides a master control point where a *routing switcher* interconnects the various production units – e.g. studios, film chains, VTRs, remotes, etc. Because of the technical complexities of source routing, switching is increasingly automated.

The Master Control Room houses such items as synchronizing generators, distribution amplifiers, camera control equipment (CCUs), and may include audio equipment, film chains, VTRs, slide scanners, etc., when these are not located in separate areas elsewhere.

Television programs from larger studio centers are often routed to a transmitter via a *Continuity/Presentation suite*. Arranged rather like a production control room, it may have a small studio (and/or announce booth) for station announcements, newscasts, weather, interviews.

Table 2.1 Typical approximate TV studio sizes

			Typical	*Ceiling*
Local TV/campus studios	Small	150 m^2 (1600 ft^2)	15 × 10 m (50 × 30 ft)	3.5 m (11 ft)
	Medium	216 m^2 (2400 ft^2)	18 × 12 m (60 × 40 ft)	7 m (23 ft)
Network studio center	Small general purpose	330 m^2 (3500 ft^2)	22 × 15 m (70 × 50 ft)	9 m (30 ft)
	Medium	672 m^2 (7200 ft^2)	28 × 24 m (90 × 80 ft)	10 m (33 ft)
	Large	1024 m^2 (10 000 ft^2)	32 × 32 m (100 × 100 ft)	13 m (43 ft)

Continuity control is mainly concerned with providing a smooth-flowing program output from the station: switching between program sources at the scheduled times, inserting commercials, trailers/promos (promotions) for upcoming shows, station idents (channel identification logos), covering breakdowns, etc. In addition, there will be liaison with program sources (studios, remotes, VT and film channels) relative to go-ahead cues, scheduled timing, introductory announcements, etc.

Services and support areas

Most studios have a variety of storage and service facilities nearby that help in the smooth running of day-to-day production. Their size and scale vary, but typically we find:

A *scene dock* – Here the scenery constructed in the *scenic workshop* is temporarily stored, ready for the current production. Either here, or in a nearby *properties (props) storeroom* various items such as furniture, drapes, ornaments, etc. are stored in readiness to dress the settings.

A *technical store* – All the mobile technical equipment is housed here ready for immediate use: camera mountings, lighting equipment, sound booms, picture monitors, cables, etc. This not only helps to protect the equipment but leaves the studio floor clear for scenery to be moved around during the setting period.

Leading off the studio may be:

- *Make-up rooms* (for individual make-up and in-program repairs)
- *Changing rooms* (where clothing/costumes can be changed or valeted)
- A circulation area with rest rooms (*Green Room*) where people can wait during production breaks
- *Dressing rooms* (where performers can dress, rest, await their calls).

Various technical areas for electronic, electrical, and mechanical maintenance are also located near the studios.

3 How television works

You don't need to study technology in depth in order to make good programs! But understanding the principles involved will certainly help you to anticipate and avoid various everyday problems. Although the actual electronics are extremely sophisticated, the basics we need are really surprisingly straightforward.

The video signal

Let's look first at a simple 'black-and-white' camera system. The picture from the lens is focused onto an *image sensor* within the video camera. This is usually a '*CCD*' – *a charge-coupled device.** (*See Digests – CCD, Camera tube.*)

A pattern of electrical charges forms on the light-sensitive area of this CCD, which corresponds in strength at each point to light and shade in the lens image. As special scanning circuits systematically read across this charge pattern in a series of parallel lines a varying signal voltage or **video** is produced relating to the original picture tones. After amplification and certain compensatory electronic corrections this *video signal* from the camera (with added *synchronizing pulses*) can be sent along a cable or transmitted by radio.

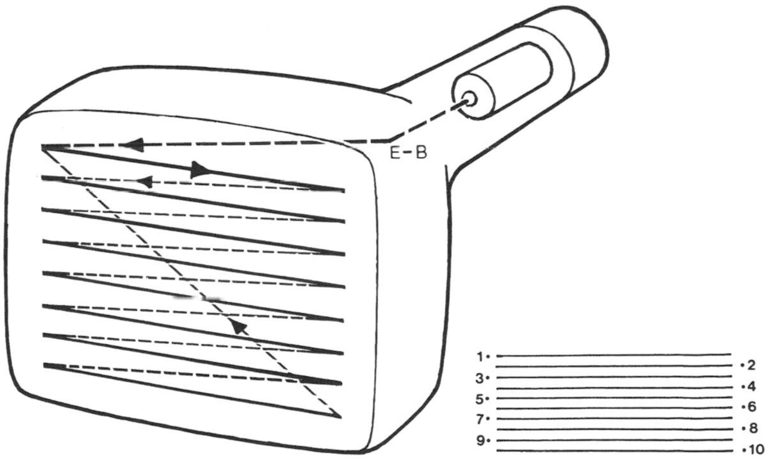

Fig. 3.1 The monochrome picture tube
A gun in the picture tube produces an electron beam (E-B), which fluctuates in intensity with the video signal. As the beam scans across the screen in a series of close parallel lines. It causes the fluorescent coating to glow correspondingly, building up the light and shade pattern of the original image. The picture (frame) is scanned in 525 lines (485 active) 30 times each second (Europe – 625 lines, 25 per second). To conserve bandwidth and decrease flicker effects, the odd lines (*odd field*) are scanned, and then the even lines (*even field*) fitted between them (*interlacing*). In simple TV systems, this interlacing varies (*random interlace*) and definition deteriorates.

* Earlier TV camera systems used various forms of vacuum tube pick-up device. Of these *camera tubes*, the later *plumbicon* designs were particularly effective. Now apart from certain special applications these are largely superseded by more robust, cheaper, solid-state *CCD* devices.

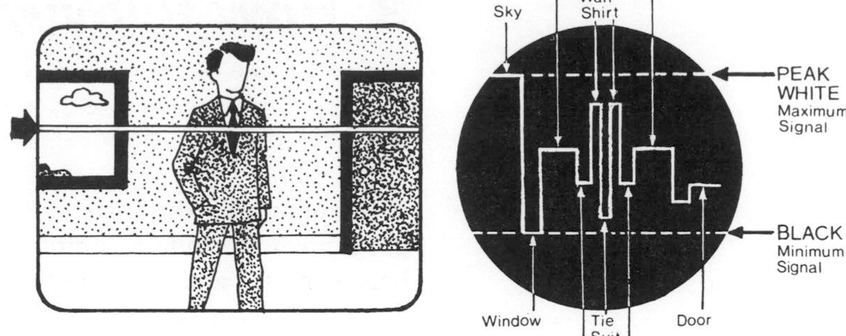

Fig. 3.2 The picture and its video
Showing a typical scanned line and its corresponding video signal.

At the *monochrome TV* receiver or monitor the *picture tube* has a phosphor coating inside its front face. As a fine beam of electrons from a '*gun*' at the rear of the tube scans across this display screen – exactly in step (*in sync*) with the camera system – it causes the phosphor at each point it passes to glow momentarily. How brightly depends on the strength of the beam.

Because the beam is controlled by the *video signal*, its video fluctuations are traced as a pattern of light and shade on the screen, to build up a complete multi-tone image. This is all happening so quickly that the eye sees only the overall result, which we interpret as a reproduction of the original scene.

Color analysis

Looking at the apparently endless range of colors and shades in the world around us, it seems incredible that they can be reproduced on a TV screen simply by mixing appropriate proportions of red, green, and blue light. Yet that is the underlying principle of color television.

- **The color camera** – Like all types of image sensor, the CCDs in the television camera can only respond to variations in *brightness*. They cannot directly detect differences in *color*. However, if we place a color filter in front of a CCD the video signal it produces will then correspond to the proportions of that color in the scene.

  While a *monochrome* ('black and white') camera requires only one CCD, a *color* camera may have from one to four CCDs analyzing hues and shades. The simplest systems use a multi-colored *striped filter* fitted over a single CCD. But for more accurate color and detail, three separate CCDs are used. Here the image from the lens passes through a special *prism* block with *dichroic filters*, which produces three color-filtered images corresponding to the red, green, and blue proportions in the scene (*see Digests – Dichroics*). The video signals from the respective CCDs will correspond to the three primaries needed to reproduce a picture in full color. In some camera designs, an additional fourth *unfiltered* CCD is also included, which provides a black-and-white image (*luminance component*) for optimum picture quality.

- **The color display** – In a color system the phosphor display screen inside the face of the picture tube is made up of three kinds of *phosphors*, arranged in a close pattern of tiny dots or stripes. When a stream of electrons from a *gun(s)* at the rear of the picture-tube scans over these different phosphors they glow red, green or blue respectively. How brightly depends on the strengths at each moment of the red, green and blue video signals controlling the gun(s). So precise is this synchronized scanning action that these tiny phosphor elements in the screen can be energized independently. If, for instance, there is only video information from the red channel, while the green and blue channels are at zero, just phosphors within the set of red will glow, tracing an image on the screen corresponding to proportions of red in the scene. Video signals from the green and blue camera channels will similarly produce images on their green and blue screen phosphors, corresponding to variations in the green and blue video signals.

Of course, this all sounds a lot simpler than it is in reality. In practice, the process is technically complex. For instance, one needs to ensure that the entire system from camera to display screen is scanning exactly in step; for any *synchronizing* errors would cause the picture to tear, break up, distort, or become displaced. Similarly, maintaining optimum and consistent color quality and picture detail (*definition*) poses all manner of problems to the circuit designer.

Color mixtures

Because these phosphor patterns are so tiny, our eyes do not see them as individual dots – although you can do so if you use a magnifying lens. Instead, colors of adjacent dots merge together, and produce a color mixture; an effect termed *additive color mixing*.

When you see a similar amount of light from the red, green, and blue dots in an area you experience the sensation of *white light*. Equal amounts of red and blue produce a purplish or *magenta* hue. Blue and green together appear as *cyan*. But, unexpectedly, equal amounts of red and green light produce *yellow* – a strange result until you get used to the idea!

Light and shade

So it's clear enough where the full range of colors comes from in the TV picture. But what about its light and shade, its brightness variations?

Well, as we saw, **R + G + B = white**. If they are all equal but very weak they will result in a very weak white – or what we would call a dark gray. If the signals are stronger, the area on the screen will be brighter. If most parts of the screen are energized by strong video signals, we interpret this as a bright picture; and vice versa.

So, to summarize: the effective *color (hue)* results from the actual proportions of red, green, and blue, and the *brightness* of each part of the screen depends on the overall strength of the mixture.

Transmitting color

You could have a color TV/video system that involved sending three separate video signals (R, G, B) from camera to receiver. The sound (audio) signal would be sent separately. This principle would work. But there would be various technical difficulties.

Instead, it is more practical to send a specially *encoded* signal that incorporates all color and brightness information. This encoded signal is *decoded* at the receiver, and reconstituted as separate color signals that drive the picture-tube.

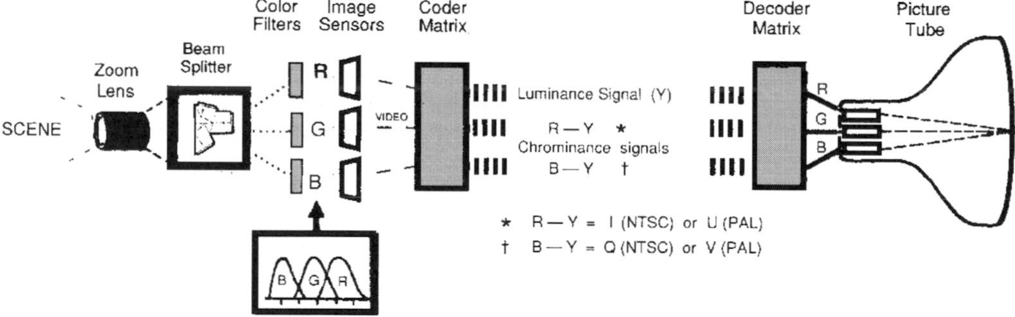

Fig. 3.3 Color TV principles
The focused image is split by a prismatic block (or dichroic filter-mirrors) into three light paths – covering the red, green, and blue regions of the spectrum. Camera sensors produce corresponding video signals. These signals could be transmitted in this form, and recombined to recreate the original color image (as in color printing processes). However, to provide a *compatible color* TV picture (that will reproduce on monochrome receivers) a complex intermediate system is necessary – NTSC, PAL or SECAM. This involves *coding* to derive special *luminance* (brightness) and *chrominance* (hue, color) video signals. (Monochrome receivers respond to the luminous component of the signal.)

In the color picture-monitor or receiver, the separate RGB components are recovered by a *decoding matrix* (decoder), each video signal being used to control their respective electron-beam strengths in the picture tube.

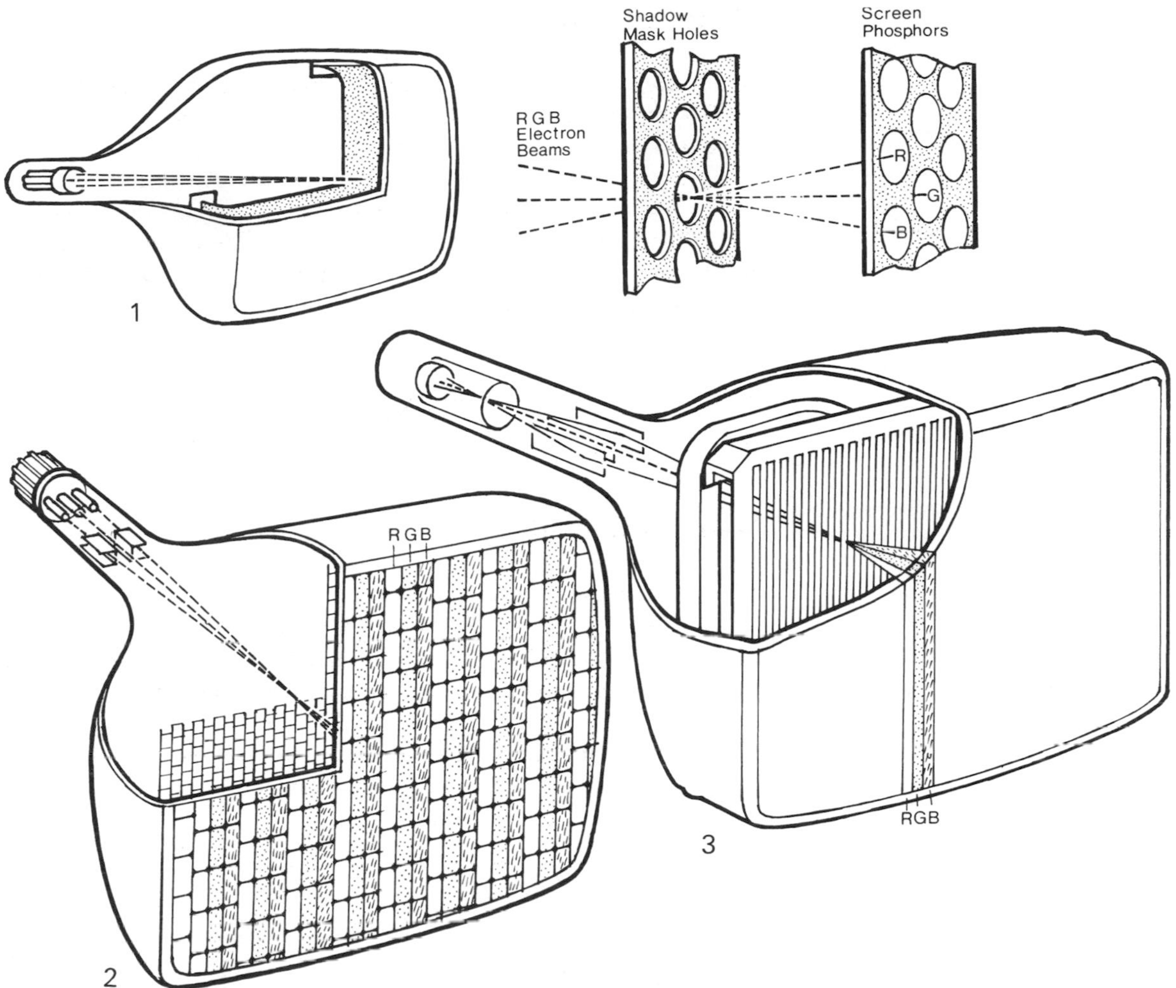

Fig. 3.4 Color TV picture-tubes
The tube screen comprises three patterns of phosphors (dots or stripes) that glow red, green, or blue when energized by their associated electron beam. The eye merges these tiny RGB patterns, seeing them as color mixtures; when proportionately activated they appear white to gray.

The color picture-tube may take three forms: (1) delta-gun dot mask (shadow mask): (2) self-converging precision in-line (PIL) slot-mask design, or (3) single-gun (three beams) aperture-grille type (Trinitron). The last two avoid the convergence color-fringing problems of 1.

When public color TV services began, it was important that anyone using a '*black-and-white*' *receiver* should be able to see good monochrome pictures from color transmissions. Color TV standards had, therefore, to relate to existing black-and-white systems. Technically, this proved to be very limiting. However, the ingenious American *NTSC* method of color encoding television pictures (while still scanning at a standard rate of 525 lines and 60 scans per second) managed to do just that! Admittedly there were shortcomings, but overall results were very satisfactory.

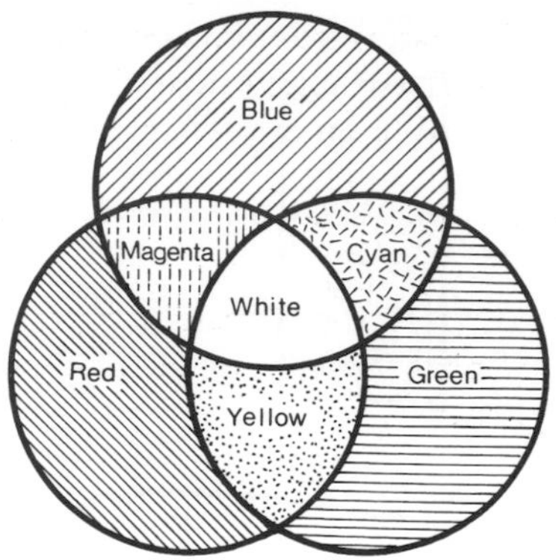

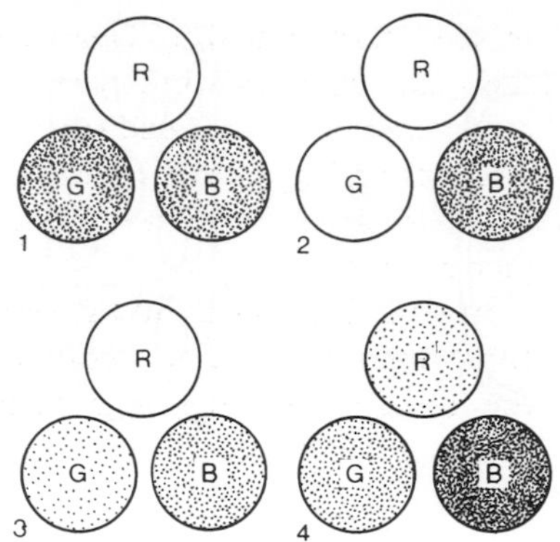

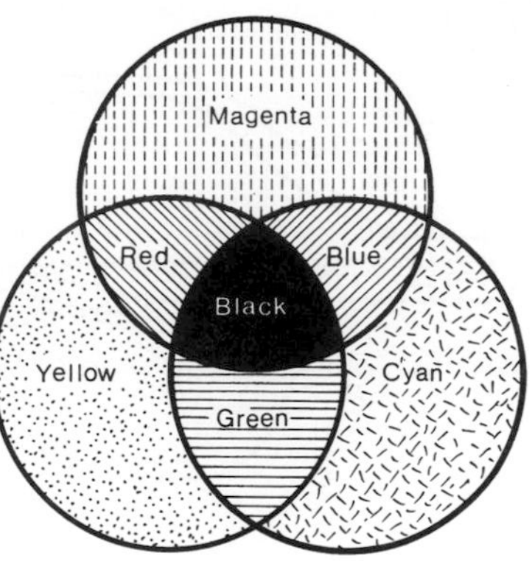

Fig. 3.5 Color mixing

Part 1 Light mixtures – additive primaries
If you project beams of red, blue and green light, these *additive primaries* will blend where they overlap, to produce new secondary colors (*subtractive primaries*). In equal proportions.

R + B = magenta (purple)
B + G = cyan (blue-green)
R + G = yellow
R + G + B = white

A secondary color is often termed a 'minus' of the third primary hue: hence yellow is *minus blue*, cyan is *minus red*, and magenta is *minus green*.

Part 2 Hue and luminance
Hue derives from the *proportions* of red, green, and blue present. *Luminance* (brightness) results from their *quantities*.

1 If only one phosphor is activated, the screen appears of primary hue.
2 Two or three phosphors produce additive color mixtures (e.g. R + G = Yellow).
3,4 If three phosphors are combined, various shades or degrees of color dilution (saturation) result (e.g. diluted red = pink; dim orange or yellow = brown).

Part 3 Pigment mixtures – subtractive primaries
If you print magenta, yellow, cyan pigments onto a white surface (using ink, paint, dyes), new hues appear where they overlap. The surface colors we see are just the remaining part of the visual spectrum, after all other colors have been absorbed by the pigments. So this is termed a *subtractive* process.

Other countries developing color television systems and faced with similar problems adopted this technology, while taking the opportunity to improve its color stability, and reduce its color/luminance interference. That resulted in the three different *incompatible* color television systems which are now used worldwide – NTSC, PAL and SECAM. Unfortunately, pictures transmitted or recorded on one system cannot reproduce directly on another. Subsequently *standards converters* were devised which enabled material originating in one system to be translated into another (e.g. from NTSC to PAL or *vice versa*). At best, these can be extremely effective, and allow the free interchange of programs between organizations using different systems.

The television picture

There are times when television engineers may seem to be obsessed with 'picture quality'; with color fidelity, definition, tonal gradation, gamma, and the like. But this preoccupation is not technical pedantry. The quality of the pictures we produce, like that of the accompanying sound, directly affects audience enjoyment. If a camera's picture is not sufficiently sharp the viewer will not be able to see detail or texture clearly. If color varies from one camera to the next, changes will distract when interswitching their shots. If tones are not reproduced successfully, subtle variations will be lost, surfaces will appear flat and unmodeled.

Clearly, picture quality matters, but how good can a TV/video picture be?

Initially it depends on the system used. At best, it can be superb. But there are inevitably various losses between the camera lens and the home screen that degrade the picture.

Picture detail

All electronic and photographic systems have a maximum limit to the amount of detail they can convey. In TV the *definition (resolution)* is initially influenced by the number of picture lines the system uses. But it is also affected by system design. As the image of the scene is scanned in the camera the video should ideally be able to change in strength to correspond with tonal differences. The faster it can change, the finer the detail it can resolve. This rate of change is measured as 'frequency' (4 MHz for a 525-line system; 5 MHz for 625 lines).

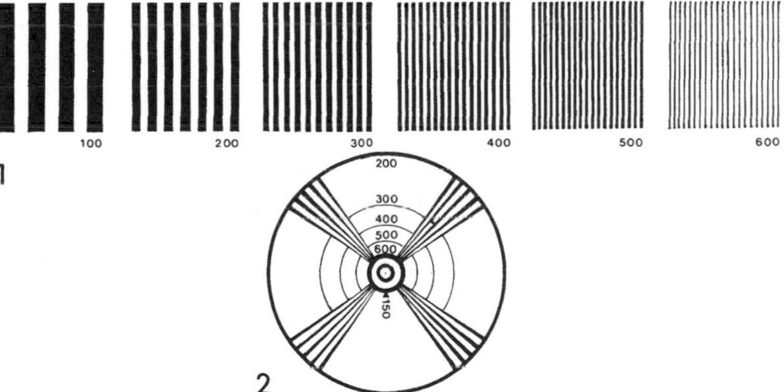

Fig. 3.6 Picture detail
The TV system's ability to resolve detail (its resolution) is checked with standard test charts. These contain *gratings* (1) or *resolution wedges* (2). The finest information that can be discerned reveals the system's maximum resolution. (The calibrations indicate the 'number of picture lines' that could be resolved in the picture width.) In a 525-line *NTSC* system, typically '320 lines' (4 Mhz)* represents maximum transmitted detail. Maximum closed-circuit resolution may be '640 lines' (8 MHz).

* PAL 5.25 MHz

Apart from these technical parameters, many other factors can affect picture clarity, including the lens's performance. It may be dirty or badly focused. Lighting may be producing lens flares. The glass of a prompter attached to the camera can degrade picture quality. Video equipment may have drifted. Or you may be watching a poor videorecording. There can be many reasons for unsharp pictures!

Picture tones

Although it is not immediately obvious in most pictures, the range of tones a TV or photographic system can normally reproduce is quite restricted compared with those in the original scene.

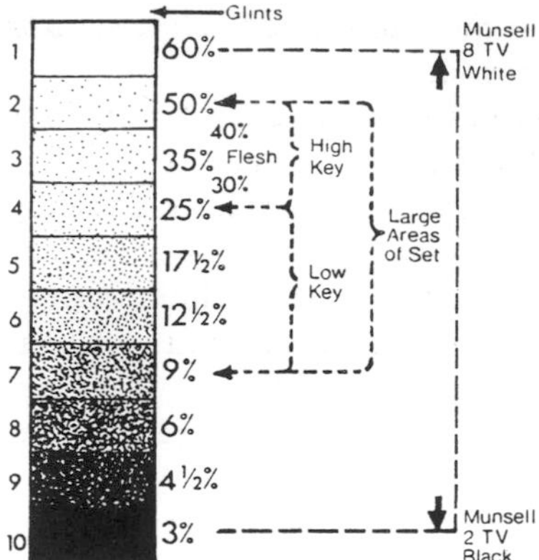

Fig. 3.7 The gray scale
The standard gray scale takes the maximum-to-minimum tonal range readily reproduced by the TV system (overall 20:1 contrast), and divides it into 10 steps. (Relative light reflectance 60–3%.) Each step is √2 times brightness of the next: the logarithmic scale looking linear to the eye. (What appears mid-gray, is only 17½% reflectance; not the 50% you might expect.)

Our *eyes* appear to detect subtle tonal differences over a remarkably wide range – even when the lightest areas are as much as thousand times brighter than the darkest (a 1000:1 contrast range). This impression, however, is largely thanks to the brain's *adaptation*; the ability to readjust instantaneously to the brightness of localized areas we are looking at. Picture reproduction systems have considerably less accommodation. Color negative film, for example, may only handle a contrast range of about 100:1 (10 stops) and still reproduce subtle half-tones in between. If the subject contrast is greater than this range, it will result in tonal gradation and details being lost in the highlights and/or shadows.

Most CCD cameras can easily handle a 40:1 contrast, but where you can control subject tones (as in the studio), it is preferable to restrict the overall contrast range to a maximum of about 30:1 if half-tones are to be reproduced accurately. Home TV receivers are more likely to be limited to a range of around 20:1. Any picture tones that exceed this range (e.g. bright highlights, deep shadows) will appear as detailless white or black areas on the screen. If the TV receiver itself has not been adjusted for optimum contrast/brightness, or light is falling on its screen and diluting darker tones, reproduced picture quality can be considerably impaired. Many display little more than a 10:1 or 15:1 range

Whether such limitations matter in practice will depend on how important tonal subtlety is in your shot. If a map you are showing reproduces as a blank sheet because lighter tones have *blocked off (crushed out)* it does become embarrassing! On the other hand, if dark clothing lacks subtle modeling, this may be quite unimportant. Cunning compensatory circuits (*gamma adjustments; exposure 'knee'*) can prevent this restricted range from being too obvious, but they do not enable you to extend the system's inherent tonal limits. Sometimes you may have to adjust the lighting contrast or the actual tones of the subjects (costumes, scenery) to keep within them, and improve the overall effect.

Digital magic

Exciting technical developments are taking place today which are revolutionizing many aspects of program making. And yet we can summarize their basics in a couple of paragraphs!

For many years, electronic techniques in the audio and video fields relied on '*analogue*' processes. The continuously varying *audio signal* in the sound channel, from microphone to loudspeaker, corresponded directly to the fluctuations of the original sound waves. Similarly, the *video signals* from camera to TV picture-tube changed with brightness variations as the scene's image was scanned. Unfortunately, these analogue signals can easily become impaired as they pass through their respective systems. We become aware of degraded quality, distortions, background noise, and various other unwanted effects. For decades, we were stuck with such problems.

Then gradually an alternative method evolved – *digital technology.* Now, instead of sending an amplified *analogue* signal through a system it can be converted into a *digital* form. This is done by sampling the intensity of the original analogue signal at regular intervals, and transmitting this data instead, in the form of corresponding packages of pulses. Now, even if this pulse pattern becomes weakened or distorted, or is accompanied by interference, it becomes possible to interpret it, and convert it back into an analogue signal that is virtually identical to the original.

At first sight, this seems like a roundabout process, but we have only to compare today's audio CDs with earlier vinyl discs to appreciate how audio techniques have advanced as a result of digitization. Later, we'll be looking at these developments more closely, and seeing ways in which they have extended production opportunities.

4 What your camera can do

Video/television cameras have become increasingly user-friendly over recent years. Various controls that previously needed watchful readjustments can now be left to clever auto-circuitry that tweaks them automatically! On the face of it then, there may seem little point in getting involved with the technicalities of its controls. It looks as if you only need to point the camera, zoom in and out to adjust the size of the shot, and can leave circuitry to take care of such 'esoteric' matters as *exposure, light quality*, etc. Why do we need to learn about '*lens apertures*' '*depth of field*', '*lens angles*' and the rest?

Frankly, it really depends on how critical you are of the results. Where you want successive pictures to match in brightness, contrast and color quality, with consistent perspective and controlled focusing, you will need to understand the effects of the various camera controls. Although automatic compensatory circuits can certainly ease pressures when working under difficult conditions, and are valuable fall-back devices that prevent your being caught out, they do have their limitations. *Good cameracraft* involves making subtle *artistic judgments*, and as we shall see, auto-circuits simply can't do that for you. But more of that later. Knowing about the various camera adjustments, and the effects these can have on your pictures, will not only enable you to make the best judgments but will prepare you for problems that arise under everyday conditions.

Types of television camera

A wide range of television/video cameras is available today; from modestly priced designs for home video to very sophisticated state-of-the-art cameras. The market spread of models suits a variety of applications; and as you would expect, both design and performance vary with cost. While cameras at the lower end of the range can provide very satisfactory picture quality under optimum conditions, the more advanced equipment designs produce consistently excellent pictures for long periods; even in difficult circumstances.

A number of factors can influence one's choice of camera, including

- *Cost:* initial and running costs.
- *Physical aspects:* e.g. weight, portability, method of mounting, reliability.

- *Operational features:* e.g. facilities, controls, handling, flexibility (e.g. zoom range).
- *Electronic/optical performance:* e.g. definition (resolution), color quality, picture noise, any picture impairment (artifacts), performance stability, sensitivity.

Which features are most important to you depends on how you are going to use the camera. Are you shooting 'live' (i.e. showing events as they are happening) or recording them? Are you working as a single-camera unit or one of a group? Are you using a videocassette recorder directly linked to the camera or are your video and sound being recorded elsewhere? Are you editing what you shoot 'as you go' or will the material be edited later? Some camera systems are more appropriate than others for particular situations.

One factor can strongly outweigh others. If, for instance, a news unit is working under hazardous conditions where the likelihood of equipment loss or damage is high, it may be wiser to use a small low-cost consumer/small-format camcorder rather than a larger expensive broadcast camera!

Studio cameras

Nowadays, studio productions make use of a wide range of camera designs, from hand-held to built-in units. But the term '*studio camera*' has long been established for the larger top-quality designs which are the workhorse of bigger studio centers. In practice, you will also meet this type of camera away from the studio, at major sports meetings and large-scale indoor events such as public meetings and concerts.

With advances in technology and design it has become possible to create remarkably small and compact high-grade TV cameras. But where state-of-the-art performance is essential, larger equipment is still unavoidable. So we find that unlike the portable lightweight types of camera which are self-contained, the *studio camera* remains bigger, heavier and more cumbersome. And

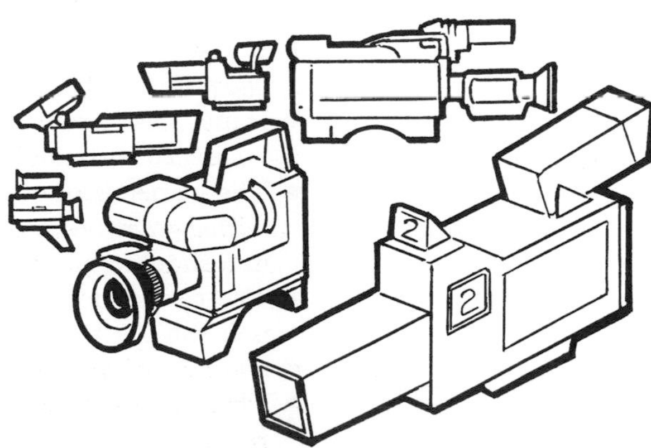

Fig. 4.1 Camera design
Television/video cameras today come in a wide variety of designs, from compact hand-held forms, to large studio camera systems.

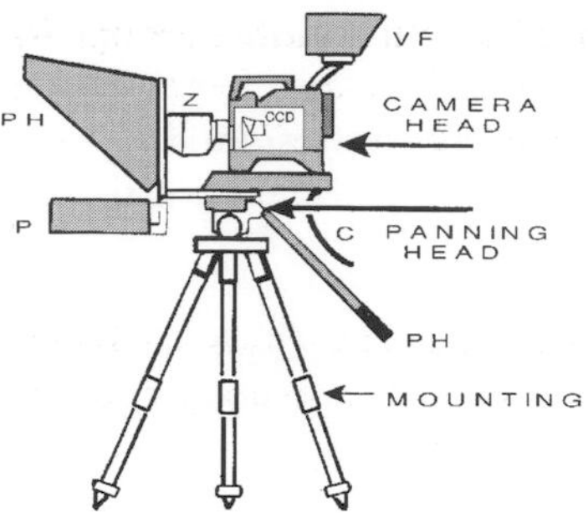

Fig. 4.2 The television camera
The *camera head* is fitted onto an adjustable *pan head (panning head)*, which is attached to a supporting *mounting*.

A *zoom lens* (*Z*) focuses the scene onto *CCDs* (*image sensors*) which create the electronic picture signal.

A two-way *camera cable* (*C*) carries the camera's video to the distant control unit (CCU), which provides various technical supplies.

The *viewfinder* (*VF*) monitors the camera's picture.

The program script on the *prompter screen* (*P*) is reflected in an angled glass sheet within the *prompter hood* (*PH*).

A quick-release *wedge-mount* under the camera head slides into a corresponding recessed plate on the *pan head* (*panning head*). This device enables the camera to tilt and turn (*pan*) smoothly. Variable friction controls (*drag*) steady these movements. The head can also be *locked off* in a fixed position. *Tilt balance* adjustments position the camera horizontally to avoid its being nose- or tail-heavy.

One or two *pan* (*panning*) *handles* (*PH*) attached to the pan head allow the operator to accurately direct and control the camera.

The *camera mounting* support can take various forms: e.g. a *tripod, pedestal, jib,*

much of its associated apparatus has to be housed separately outside the studio.

Studio cameras are mounted on heavy-duty wheeled *dollies – pedestals or rolling tripods* – on a *panning head* (*pan and tilt head*) which enables it to turn (*pan*) and tilt. Its *focus* and *zoom* controls are usually fixed to the *panning handles* (*pan handles*) which position the head.

To make it easier for the operator to accurately focus and compose pictures, a full-size 5- or 7-inch (12.5 or 17.5 cm) viewfinder is usually fitted to the studio camera. (Small viewfinders can impede panning when the camera is fixed to a mounting, and are fatiguing to use for long periods.)

By the time a large high-grade *zoom lens* has been attached, a large *viewfinder* mounted at its rear, and a video *prompter* fitted to the front of the camera, the combined assembly needs careful handling. As you will remember from our tour, each camera is connected to a long multipurpose *camera cable* which trails along the floor, and is plugged into a studio wall outlet. This outlet is permanently wired to the main equipment located in a nearby technical area (*apparatus room*). There at its *camera control unit/CCU* (in an *analogue* system), or the *central processing unit/CPU* (in *digital* systems), the picture quality is checked and adjusted. (In some organizations, instead of adjusting a series of separate units, all main controls are extended to a central *video control* (*vision control*) console.)

Portable cameras

Although the large '*studio cameras*' produce superior picture quality, they do have the drawbacks of being costly, bulky and heavy. So, as high-performance *portable cameras* became available, they were adopted by many organizations throughout the world, for both studio and location production. Portable camera designs (Figure 22.1) have proved to be not only more convenient, but more adaptable, with much lower operating costs.

The portable cameras can be used in several different formats:

- It may have its own *in-built* videocassette recorder – *integrated* or *one-piece camcorder.*
- It may have a *separate* compact video cassette recorder attached – *dockable* or *combined camcorder.*
- The camera's output may be routed via a cable or a portable *microwave radio link* to a nearby videotape recorder (e.g. carried in a shoulder pack or on a wheeled *trolley-pack*).
- The camera may be routed to a nearby *base station* or control point in the vicinity, where a central VTR records its pictures and sound.
- The camera may be connected to an *up-station* (*portable* or *van*), which transmits its output via a satellite to the control center.

- The portable camera may be part of a multi-camera group. Its pictures are routed to a distant CCU or CPU, and after selection at a production switcher, are taped at a central VTR.

Convertible cameras

Where a camera is *convertible*, you can use it in various *configurations* – i.e. fitting different kinds of lenses, viewfinders, videotape recorders, etc., to suit a particular production.

- For a studio show, the camera is mounted on a dolly, with the larger viewfinder that is essential for flexible dolly operation. While you can use its standard zoom lens, one with a wider coverage can prove more effective when space is very limited. Its controls are best extended to the panning handles. In the studio you would not normally use an attached VTR.
- When you want to shoulder-support your camera for maximum mobility, you can fit lightweight attachments instead: a smaller hand-operated zoom, and a compact eyepiece viewfinder because you are working up close to the camera. Where you need them, you can attach a small *camera light* and a *microphone*.

While the *studio* camera requires a centralized group of rack-mounted precision equipment, the *portable* camera is designed to be virtually self-contained, so includes miniaturized versions of all this circuitry. There are necessarily technical compromises, but the camera's performance can be excellent notwithstanding, and its greater mobility outweighs any shortcomings. Portable cameras generally rely on battery power supplies (attached or carried separately); but where household current is available, you can use a converter unit to transform the supplies (e.g. 120/240 volts AC to 12 volts DC).

To simplify operation, the portable camera is fitted with various automatic devices which control the video as shooting conditions change. We shall look at these in detail later. Its camcorder operates on the same principles as the small-format VTRs, and includes the usual VTR controls for record/replay/rewind, etc. You can replay the recorded tape to check/review/cue, using either the camera's eyepiece viewfinder or an attached monitor.

ENG/EFP cameras

Although systems are often designated as ENG (*Electronic news gathering*) or EFP (*Electronic field production*) cameras, these are, in fact, just variations on the portable cameras we have just met.

- *ENG* – The camcorders used for news gathering invariably work alone, are generally shoulder-mounted with a small camera-light and microphone attached, and powered by a *battery belt* power supply. Typically CCD versions weigh 2 to 6 kg (4–14 1b).

- *EFP* – Shooting away from the studio for program inserts, documentaries, magazine features, commercials, etc., higher-grade portable cameras may be used in various configurations. Most productions shoot with a single camcorder, but sometimes (e.g. drama or a sports event) a multi-camera shoot is controlled at a central point (CCU, CPU), and recorded on a separate VTR. The cameras may be set up on mountings ranging from a *tripod* to a portable *pedestal* or a *jib arm*.

Consumer or small-format cameras

Certain equipment formats found in the low-budget non-professional market are now increasingly used in a more refined form for local station and corporate TV/video program making. The *Hi8, S-VHS*, and *DVC* videotape recorder formats in hand-held camcorders, and the various *desktop video* facilities based on the personal computer (such as the *Video Toaster*), reflect the high technical standards that are now achievable in modestly priced compact equipment.

Camera basics

Let's now take a closer look at the various features you will meet on your camera, and how they can affect the way you use it.

- The camera's *viewfinder.*
- The camera's *main controls.*
- The camera *lens* and how it behaves.
- The techniques of adjusting exposure for the best picture quality.
- Methods of *supporting* the camera.

The viewfinder

An effective viewfinder is an essential for successful camerawork. It enables you to select, frame and adjust the shot, to compose the picture, and to assess focus adjustment. When you are working alone, with a *portable camera*, the viewfinder will usually be your principal guide to picture quality and exposure, as well as providing continual reminders about videotaping, the battery's condition, etc.

Most viewfinders are fitted with a black-and-white picture tube, displaying a high-grade *monochrome* picture of your shot. Although LCD screens do have the advantage that you can see the shot in color (although not necessarily identical to that on the picture monitor) one cannot see fine detail so easily, and manual focusing can be more difficult.

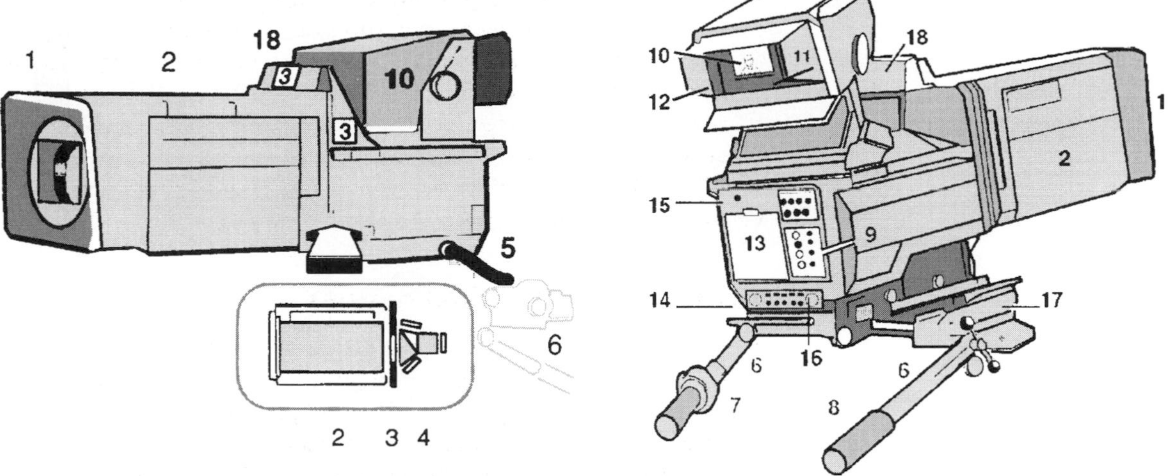

Fig. 4.3 part 1 The camera head

1 Lens hood (sun shade, ray shade).
2 Zoom lens.
3 Filter wheel.
4 Prism block (beam splitter).
5 Camera cable.
6 Adjustable panning handle (pan handle, pan bar).
7 Twist-grip zoom control.
8 Focus control (many cameras use a control mounted on a panning handle RHS).
9 Shot box (mounted on the camera head, or on a panning handle – RHS).
10 Monochrome viewfinder (perhaps with magnifying lens).
11 Viewfinder controls (including hi-peaker, crispening image detail).
12 Indicators: mimic tally light, lens-aperture indicator (*f*-stop), zoom lens setting (focal length/lens angle), etc.
13 Camera card clip.
14 Headset jack points (intercom and program) with volume controls. Mixed viewfinder feeds switch.
15 Zoom lens range-extender switch.
16 Call button (contacts shader/video control).
17 Camera mounting head (panning head/pan head), with drag adjustment for tilt and pan action, and tilt/pan locks. Also tilt fore-aft balance adjustment.
18 Tally light with camera number, illuminated when camera selected to line on switcher.

Some camera systems show just a little more than the actual shot being transmitted, so that you can see whether there is anything just outside the frame that might inadvertently come into the picture. Where the viewfinder shows exactly the same shot area as the transmitted picture, the camera operator has no warning if an unwanted subject (a microphone, a bystander) is just about to intrude into the shot.

Because the viewfinder is a *monitoring* device, any adjustments you make to its brightness, contrast, sharpness or switching will not affect the camera's output. Normally a viewfinder is fed with the camera's own video, but, whenever necessary, it can be switched to display another camera's picture as well (*mixed feeds*). That enables you to compare two or more cameras' shots, or to show them

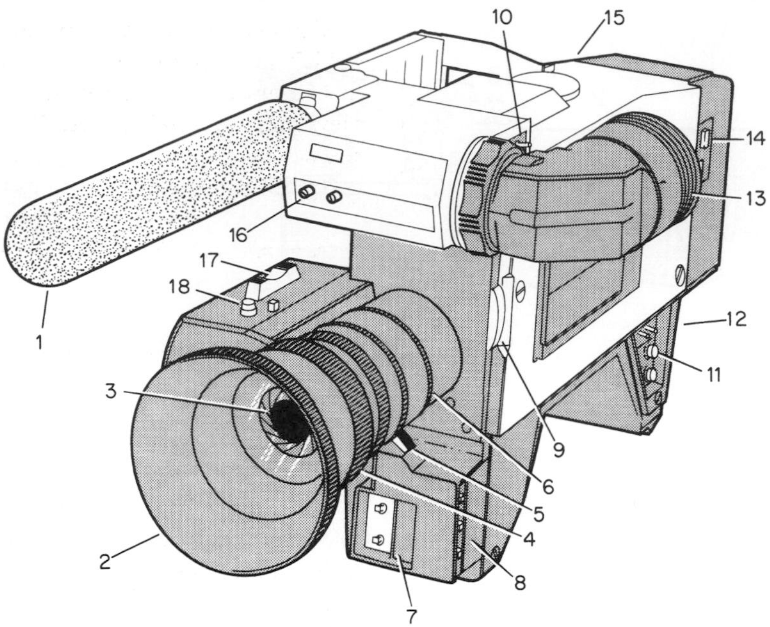

Fig. 4.3 part 2 Parts of the camera
Camera designs vary, but the following are typical facilities found in the video camera:

1 Microphone – electret, unidirectional.
2 Lens hood.
3 Lens aperture (iris) – *f*/1.6 max.
4 Focus control.
5 Manual zoom control.
6 Aperture control.
7 White balance adjust; black adjust.
8 Video gain (0 dB, 6 dB, 12 dB), color bars, camera standy-by/operate switch.
9 Color compensation filter – 3200 K, 5600 K, 5600 K + 12.5% ND, closed.
10 Viewfinder, adjustable – 1.5 in (37 mm) with LED indicators.
11 Power selection, intercom, audio monitoring jack.
12 Camera back: VTR connector, video output, camera cable, monitor video output, genlock connection for multi-camera set-ups.
13 Eyepiece.
14 Snap-on battery pack.
15 Side of camera: microphone input connector, external DC socket.
16 Viewfinder controls.
17 Power zoom switch.
18 Auto-iris on/off.

combined them in a composite effect. You can also use the viewfinder to display test patterns (e.g. color bars), which check the camera channel's performance.

■ **Indicators** – To aid framing the picture, the viewfinder screen may be marked with a *central cross* showing the exact middle of the shot. An engraved *safe area* line around its edges reminds you how important information and titles near picture edges can be lost inadvertently through edge cut-off on overscanned TV receiver screens (see Figure 15.1).

Various indicators keep you informed about the camera's and VTR's settings and status. They may take the form of inbuilt lights or meters around the viewfinder or small visual displays on the viewfinder screen itself. Additional indicators are often arranged on the sides and rear of the camera.

Typical arrangements include:

- A *mimic tally light* which shows when the camera is recording or 'on-air'.
- A *zoom lens setting* indicator, shows the len's focal length/lens angle, its aperture (*f*-stop), and whether a *lens extender* is being used to increase/decrease its coverage.
- *Exposure/video level* indicator designs vary from a simple *low light indicator* lamp to an on-screen *zebra* visual exposure indicator. (With the latter, any parts of the picture exceeding a preset brightness level will display *diagonal stripes* warning you to reduce exposure (e.g. stop down).)
- The camera's *video gain (boost) settings* are indicated to show the amount of video amplification you have selected.
- Indicators show whether *corrective filters* are in use – e.g. to compensate for the color temperature of the light.
- *A call light* indicates whenever someone on the *private wire intercom system* (e.g. the CCU operator) wants to contact the camera operator.

ENG/EFP cameras can include further indicators:

- *Videotape recorder*: Shows if VTR is set up on *standby, record, replay*, or is *rewinding*.
- Shows whether tape cassette is loaded, the amount of tape remaining, or if tape has run out.
- *Battery status*: Showing the *battery charge remaining* (or has been used).
- *Moisture or dew indicator*: Shows if *humidity* will impair the recording. (An *auto lock-out*.)
- *White balance/color temperature/color balance*: Shows whether the camera system is *color balanced* to match the prevailing light.

Consumer/small-format cameras can also include further features:

- *Indicators* showing *auto-focusing zone* selected, *back-light exposure correction, shutter speed, full auto-control* indicator, *manual focus correct*, standard or long-play *VTR setting*.
- *Viewfinder displays* such as *date/time stamp, titling*.

■ **The studio camera viewfinder** – The full-size 5- or 7-inch (12.5 or 17.8 cm) viewfinder fitted to most studio cameras has an adjustable hood, which shields its screen from random light that would dilute its picture. It is often possible to tilt (and sometimes turn) the viewfinder housing so that you can see its picture clearly, whatever the camera's height and your position.

When you are focusing manually, it is essential to have a viewfinder with the best possible resolution to enable you to focus accurately. Otherwise there is the danger that your audience who are watching a larger TV screen may be able to detect focus errors that you can't see in the camera viewfinder! Although it would seem more logical to fit all cameras with color viewfinder screens, so that the operator can identify colors and judge color relationships in the picture, this is not general practice. Pictures on monochrome screens have a fine, even unbroken surface finish. Color screens, on the other hand, have an inherent 'texture' (of stripes or dots) which make it more difficult to detect the finest details. The lightweight *LCD viewfinder* color screens fitted to some cameras have similar drawbacks, but for lower-definition video systems or where focusing is not critical (e.g. for shots with considerable depth of field) this may not prove too limiting.

When you are operating a camera fitted with a larger viewfinder the commonest operating position is to stand back, holding a panning handle in each hand (focus control on the left handle, the zoom on the right), looking ahead to the viewfinder. When working under very bright conditions, however, you may find it better to work closer, leaning in with your forehead touching the viewfinder hood to shield off all stray light.

■ **The portable camera viewfinder** – Whenever you are shooting with the camera supported on a shoulder, it is fitted with a compact *eyepiece viewfinder* (1.5 in./3.8 cm). This can usually be swivelled to either side of the camera (and perhaps tilted), to suit your operating position. With its flexible rubber eyepiece pressed against one eye, and its optics adjusted to suit your eyesight, the viewfinder's high-resolution monochrome image is shielded from stray light or reflections. Where the viewfinder is fitted with a magnifier to provide a larger screen image it is practicable to use it further from the eye; an advantage when shooting from awkward angles.

The viewfinder starts up an instant after the camera is switched on, but a word of warning! All the time you are using it – even just to check around for potential shots, to line up action, to rehearse, to tape, and finally to review the recording – the viewfinder system is drawing power from the supply batteries! The larger the viewfinder, the more power it is likely to use. It has been known for directors and operators to become so preoccupied with checking shots and rehearsing that they find that they need to change the battery for the actual take!

Although it is natural when working with an *eyepiece viewfinder* to close one eye and concentrate on the picture, get into the habit of keeping *both* eyes open! You will remain more aware of your surroundings (particularly when working with a wider or narrower lens angle), and will be less likely to bump into nearby obstructions as you move around.

Whenever you are shooting over long periods (e.g. at a sports event, or a conference) it is worth attaching even the smallest camera to a firm mounting, and fitting it with a larger viewfinder. Continual operation with an eyepiece viewfinder can become tiring. Then the *focus* and *zoom* controls can be extended to the pan bars.

An important advantage of a larger viewfinder is that you tend to be more aware of your surroundings. Your eyes can continually flick around to check nearby action, and so anticipate problems or shot opportunities. When concentrating on a small monocular screen, one can become surprisingly 'isolated'. The larger screen also makes it much easier to read and identify details, recognize faces, etc. that can be indecipherable on a small screen.

The camera's controls

On the television camera you will find three kinds of controls:

- Those you need to readjust *continually* during picture making – e.g. focus.
- Those you alter only *occasionally* – e.g. to compensate for changing light quality.
- And those involved in aligning the camera electronics to obtain optimum consistent performance – which once set up, should not be 'tweaked' casually!

There are really two quite distinct aspects to picture making – '*camerawork*' and '*picture quality control*'. These can be controlled manually, semi-automatically, or even completely automatically. Let's look at practical cases:

■ **Studio cameras** – Here the camera operator concentrates on the subtleties of *camerawork* – selecting and composing the shots, selectively focusing, zooming, controlling dolly movements, etc. The reproduced *quality* of the picture is controlled remotely by a separate operator at the *camera control unit (CCU)* or *remote control unit (RCU)*. Here two sorts of adjustment are carried out:

- **Pre-set adjustments**: During a *set-up (line-up) period* camera circuitry is adjusted to ensure optimum color and tonal fidelity, definition, picture geometry and shading for the system. This can be done manually using test signals displayed on oscilloscopes and vectorscopes. Or in digital systems, the process can be semi-automated by inserting *programmable 'memory cards'*.

- **Dynamic adjustments**: During production, the vision *control operator/shader* continually adjusts the cameras' pictures (exposure, black level, gamma, color balance) to optimize the subjective quality of shots and intermatch their pictures. This approach not only leaves the camera operator free to concentrate on effective camerawork, but results in the highest and most consistent picture quality.

■ **Portable cameras** – As we shall see, portable cameras offer us a great deal of productional flexibility.

- They can work as a *group*, as in regular studio systems; picture quality being adjusted remotely at a communal control desk.
- They can work *independently*, relying on their inbuilt automatic circuitry to readjust the camera's performance as local conditions change.

When used as a self-contained unit, you have several options:

- Adjust preset controls to arbitrary settings, hoping that these will provide satisfactory results when shooting.
- Readjust presets while shooting. (For example, changing color balance controls to try to compensate for variations in light quality when moving between daylight and artificial lighting conditions.)
- Preview the scene before shooting, and adjust various preset controls until pictures appear optimum in the viewfinder or a nearby monitor – and then shoot with these settings.
- Rely on *automatic (auto) circuits* to correct/improve performance as the shot changes. We shall discuss these in detail later.
- In certain situations, all camera operation (tilt/pan. zoom, focus) may be entirely remotely controlled – e.g. when used on a *jib/boom arm/camera crane.*

The camera lens

Meet your lens

Although we may begin by handling our new camera equipment with tender loving care, familiarity can result in casual habits. Experienced camera operators develop a considerable respect for their lens systems! They appreciate that a moment's distraction can cause a deal of expensive damage to these precision optical devices, especially when working under adverse conditions. Liquid, dust, or grit can in a moment wreck the lens or degrade its performance.

Lens systems

Most television/video cameras are fitted with the familiar *zoom lens* system, which provides the director with a remarkably flexible production tool. But occasionally, for special purposes, this may be replaced by a *prime* or *primary* lens system.

Prime or *prime lenses* have *fixed optics*; that is, their focal length or scene coverage cannot be varied. However, this design is particularly useful where

- The highest optical quality is necessary
- To create a special optical effect (e.g. an extremely wide-angle *fisheye* lens)
- When shooting in low-light situations (they have lower light losses, so transmit a stronger image)
- And when using special *light-intensifier* systems.

Because its focal length is fixed, the prime lens will only cover a particular angle of view – according to whether it is designed as a *narrow-angle* (or '*long lens*'), a *wide-angle* (or '*short lens*'), or as a *normal* lens system. You can only change a *prime lens's* coverage by adding a *supplementary lens*. Prime lenses are available with fixed focal lengths of just a few millimeters (for wide-angle work), to long-distance lenses with focal lengths of over 1000 mm.

A *zoom lens* system, on the other hand, has the great advantage that its *focal length* is adjustable. You can alter its coverage of the scene simply by turning a lever. This gives the subjective impression that the camera is nearer or further from the subject – at the same time, modifying the apparent perspective. At any given setting within its range the zoom lens behaves like a prime lens of that focal length.

Lens controls

Your lens system normally has three separate adjustments, which can be made manually or semi-automatically:

- *Focus* – adjusting the distance at which the image is sharpest.
- *f*-stop – adjusting a variable iris diaphragm inside the lens system.
- *Zoom* – altering the lens's 'focal length' to adjust how much of the scene the shot covers.

Broadly speaking, how you adjust the *lens controls* will affect:

1. How clear-cut detail is ('focusing')
2. Exactly what appears sharply defined in the shot ('depth of field')

3 How much of the scene appears in the shot ('angle of view')
4 The impression of distance, space and size that the picture conveys
5 The overall brightness of the picture, the clarity of lighter tones and shadows ('exposure').

Identifying your lens

On the front rim of your lens system you will find two pieces of information:

1 The *maximum available lens aperture* or '*f-stop*'. This indicates how 'fast' the lens is; i.e. how much light it lets through. A 'fast' lens (e.g. *f*/1.8) will still provide good pictures under lower light levels. A 'slow' lens (e.g. *f*/3.5 maximum) would need considerably more light, even at maximum aperture.
2 The *focal length* (Figure 4.4). On a zoom lens, the range of focal lengths is marked either directly (e.g. 9–126 mm) or as a *zoom ratio* (e.g. 9 mm × 14).

Focal length

If you move a lens to and from a surface until far-off objects are sharply focused the distance from the optical center of the lens to this surface (e.g. the CCD or film) is called its *focal length.* That is an inbuilt optical property. In a *prime lens* the focal length is fixed. In a *zoom lens* it can be adjusted within limits.

How much of the scene your lens shows, and the size your subject's image appears on the screen, will depend on several things:

- The size of the subject itself.
- How far you are from it.
- The *focal length* of the lens you are using.
- The size of your camera's *CCD light sensor* (i.e 2/3 in., 1/2 in., 1/3 in.).

The coverage of a *prime lens* is fixed according to its particular focal length. So to alter the shot you have to move your camera, attach a supplementary lens, or change to a lens with a different focal length.

Because the *angle of view (field of view) of a zoom lens* varies as its focal length is altered, you have the choice of moving your camera either nearer or further away from the subject, or controlling the lens's focal length when you want to alter the shot size.

■ **Why bother**? – Does it *really* matter what focal length setting you use on your zoom lens? *Apparently* all one has to do is to stand wherever it happens to be convenient, zoom in and out on the subject until you get the size of shot you want – and there we are!

But if you really care about picture making the focal length of your lens is not a 'mere technicality'. As you will see, the setting you choose is going to simultaneously affect.

- How much of the scene your shot shows.
- The apparent proportions, sizes, and distances of everything in the shot (*perspective*).
- How much of the scene is in focus, and how hard it is to focus accurately.
- Camera handling; i.e. how difficult it is to hold the shot steady, and to pan around smoothly.

So it's certainly worth taking a closer look at this major control in some detail!

Fig. 4.4 part 1 Fixed optics lens (prime lens)
Adjustable focus (distance) and lens stop. Fixed lens angle (focal length).

Focal length and image size

Let's suppose that you set your lens's focal length to 20 mm (0.8 in.) and then change the focal length to 40 mm. As you alter the focal length, the subject appears to get closer (*zoom in*). Its image will now be *twice* as large on the screen. But now the shot shows less of the scene – only *half* the previous overall height and width is taken in.

What if instead you had changed from the 20 mm focal length to a 10 mm setting? Then the subject would appear further away – only *half* as big – but the shot would now cover *twice* the previous height and width.

- A *long* focal length lens setting (*long-focus lens*) covers only a narrow segment of the scene – (a telescopic effect. But it shows a correspondingly larger image of the subject.
- A *short* focal length lens setting (*short-focus lens*; *wide-angle lens*) gives you a wide view, but subjects usually appear quite small and far away.

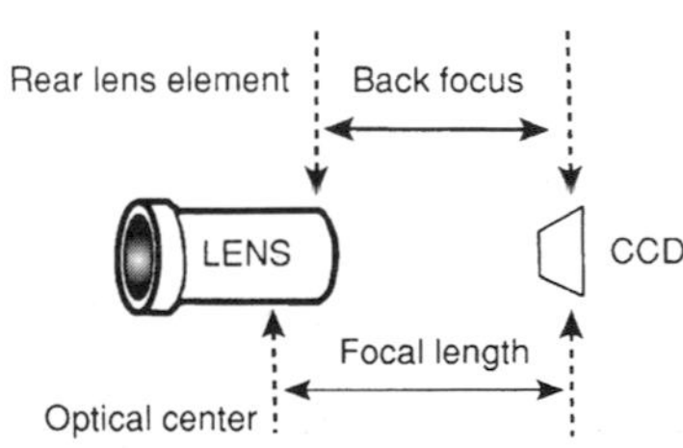

Fig. 4.4 part 2 Basic lens characteristics
Focal length – the distance from the lens' optical center (rear nodal point) to the CCD when focused at infinity.
Back focus – the distance from the back lens surface to the CCD, when focused at infinity.

Relative focal lengths

If the focal length of	the equivalent focal length for	the equivalent focal length for
2/3 in. CCD is 1	1/2 in. CCD is × 0.75	1/3 in. CCD is × 0.6
1/2 in. CCD is 1	2/3 in. CCD is × 1.3	1/3 in. CCD is × 0.75
1/3 in. CCD is 1	2/3 in. CCD is × 1.7	1/2 in. CCD is × 1.3

Working practices

There are several ways of working out the sort of shot you will get at various distances:

On-the-spot assessment

- *Trial and error* – A 'try it and see' approach, in which you move the camera around to potential positions, changing the lens's focal length setting until you get the result you want. This is not only a very laborious process, but leads to perspective and scale errors.
- *Portable viewfinder* – Here the director stands in the planned camera position and checks out the scene through a hand-held *calibrated portable viewfinder*. Adjusting its zoom lens to give the required shot size, the corresponding focal length is then read off the viewfinder's scale and the camera's lens set to this figure.
- *Experience* – When you are working regularly in certain surroundings (e.g. a news studio) you soon come to associate various shot sizes with particular camera positions and focal length settings. However, these proportions will alter if you happen to change to a camera with different CCD sizes.

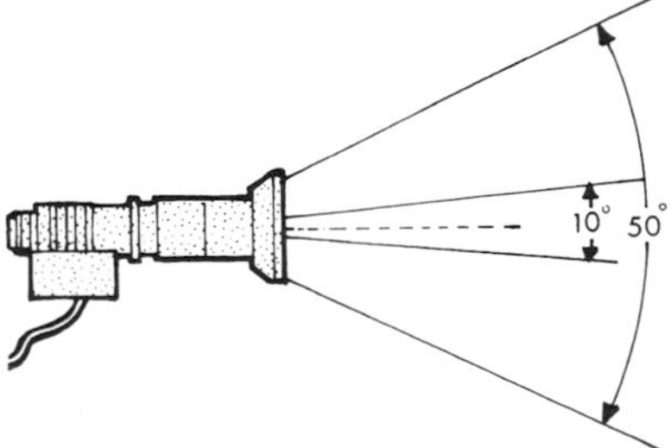

Fig. 4.5 Zoom lens
Adjustable focus, stop, and focal length (lens angle). Altering focal length varies the field of view. Usually set at a pre-selected angle. Changing the angle in shot produces 'zooming in' (as angle narrows, F increases), or 'zooming out' (angle widens, F decreases). Typically 12–120 mm focal length adjustments.

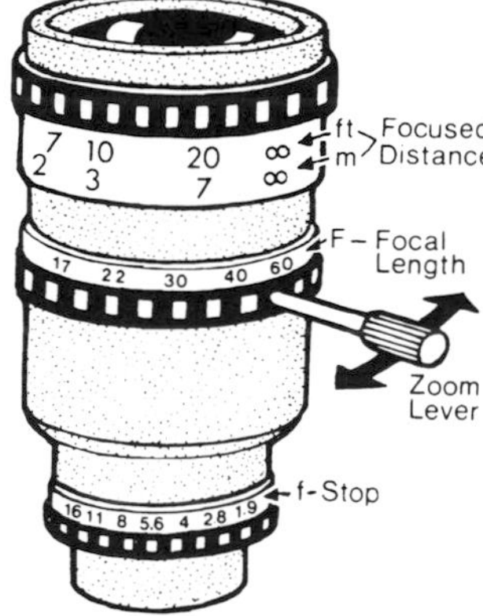

Lightweight zoom lens showing focus (distance) control, zoom lever (focal length/lens angle). *f*-stop (lens aperture).

Preliminary planning

The great weakness of these 'try-it-and-see' methods is that you have to be *on the spot facing the action*. But suppose you are *planning* a production. How do you assess beforehand whether you will be able to get the shots you are hoping for? The answer is to work on a *scale plan*.

Table 4.1 Typical lens angles

Lens angle	*5°*	*10°*	*15°*	*20°*	*25°*	*30°*	*35°*	*40°*	*45°*	*50°*	*55°*	*60°*	
2/3 in. CCD	101	50	33.5	25	20	16.5	14	12	11	9.5	8.5	8	Focal length (mm)
1/2 in. CCD	73	37	24	18	14.5	12	10	9	8	7	6	5.5	Focal length (mm)

See Figure 18.7 for the lens coverage at various distances

- *Focal length* – Here you can check tables (as in Table 4.1) to see the horizontal coverage of any focal length setting at various distances.
- *Lens angle* – Where the camera is fitted with a lens *shot box* having an indicator showing lens coverage in degrees you can relate shots directly to angles shown by a protractor laid on a scaled plan.

What is a lens angle?

The regular TV screen is a rectangle. Its sides are in 4 by 3 proportions; i.e. if the screen is 40 cm (16 in.) across, it will be 30 cm (12 in.) high. The TV camera's lens covers a similarly shaped field, stretching away to infinity.

If we draw an imaginary line from the left and right edges of the picture to the camera lens the angle they make at the lens is called the *horizontal lens angle* or, more usually, 'the lens angle'.

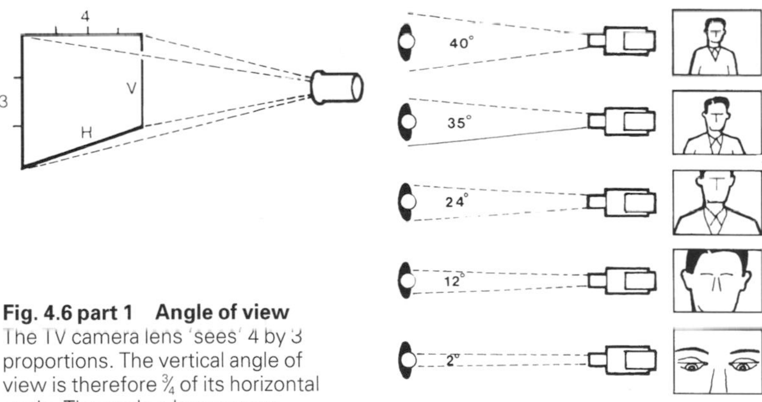

Fig. 4.6 part 1 Angle of view
The TV camera lens 'sees' 4 by 3 proportions. The vertical angle of view is therefore ¾ of its horizontal angle. The angle a lens covers depends on its *focal length* relative to the size of CCD used.

For a given camera position, the longer the lens focal length (narrower lens angle) the closer the subject appears; but less of the scene is visible. The shorter the focal length (wider lens angle), the more distant the subject appears.

Fig. 4.6 part 2 Lens angles
Changes are proportional as the lens angle alters. Using a lens of three times the present angle (i.e. ⅓F), the subject now appears ⅓ of former size and × 3 of scene width is now visible. The effect is that of increasing the camera distance by 3 times. Changing to a narrower angle has the opposite effect.

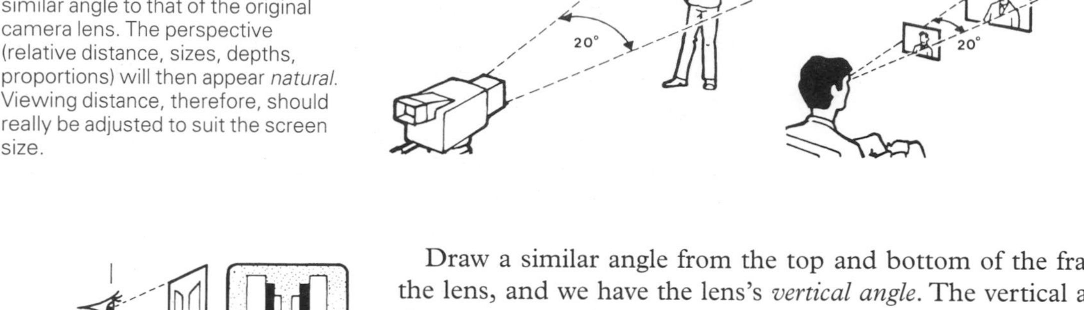

Fig. 4.7 Viewing distance
Ideally, a photograph should be viewed so that the image subtends a similar angle to that of the original camera lens. The perspective (relative distance, sizes, depths, proportions) will then appear *natural*. Viewing distance, therefore, should really be adjusted to suit the screen size.

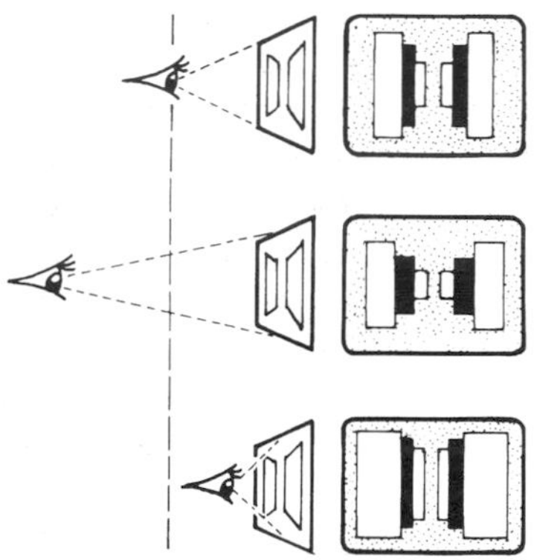

Fig. 4.8 Natural perspectives
When the viewing angle equals the camera's lens angle our impression of the picture's perspective will be similar to that of the original scene. Viewing the picture from too far away or using a camera lens of too wide angle for normal viewing conditions gives a false impression of perspective. Depth and distance are exaggerated; distant subjects unduly small. Viewing the picture too closely or using a too narrow angle lens for normal viewing conditions again gives a false impression. Depth and distance are compressed; distant subjects unduly large.

Draw a similar angle from the top and bottom of the frame, to the lens, and we have the lens's *vertical angle*. The vertical angle is three-quarters of that value.

Although you can calculate the lens angle from its focal length (*see Digests: Lens angle*) it is easier to check the manufacturer's figures for the lens, and go from there.

For example, a studio zoom lens may have a focal length varying from 8 to 120 mm, covering an angle from around 57° to 4°. Multiply one focal length limit (e.g. 8) by the angle it provides (57 in this case), and you obtain a factor 8 × 57 = 456.

When you want to know the lens angle for any intermediate focal length, divide this factor 456 by that focal length. In this case, a 100 mm setting gives an angle of 456 ÷ 100 = 45.6°. Use the factor you have found for your particular lens system.

Figure 18.7 shows a useful chart for planning or checking your lens angles.

For *HDTV (high definition television)* systems a different picture aspect ratio is used. Instead of a 4 by 3 (1.33:1) screen shape, the picture shape is now 16 units wide, and 9 units high (1.77:1). So the vertical angle of view is now 9/16ths (or around 0.56) of its horizontal angle, compared with the former 3/4 proportions. This shape which appears to give a wider horizontal view compared with the 4:3 aspect ratio brings its problems, particularly when using material (films, graphics, titles) that has been shot in the earlier proportions. But more of that later. To avoid confusion, let's concentrate here on the established 4:3 screen shape.

Table 4.2 CCD image sizes compared

The format or aspect ratio for charge-coupled devices here is 4:3; but the size of the sensor is not the equivalent of the sensor's active area

2/3 in. (17 mm)	8.8 mm horizontal × 6.6 mm vertical	11 mm diagonal
1/2 in. (12.7 mm)	6.4 mm horizontal × 4.8 mm vertical	8 mm diagonal
1/3 in. (8.5 mm)	4.8 mm horizontal × 3.6 mm vertical	6 mm diagonal
1/4 in. (6.4 mm)	3.2 mm horizontal × 2.4 mm vertical	4 mm diagonal

The pixel area on 2/3 in. CCD is double that of 1/2 in. and four times that of 1/3 in. CCDs.

HDTV CCD image area 14 mm horizontal × 7.9 mm vertical 16 mm diagonal

Perspective distortion

Perspective distortion is not a lens fault. It is essentially an *effect*. If the angle from our eyes to the left and right edges of the TV screen is, for example, around 20°, and the camera is using a 20° lens angle, the picture will appear to have *natural* ('*correct*') *perspective*. The apparent sizes, proportions, and distances of everything within the shot look as they would if you were actually standing there in the scene.

But where the lens and viewing angles differ appreciably strange effects can arise. (Theoretically, by moving closer or further from the screen, or altering the picture size so as to match the angles, one could compensate, and perspective would then appear correct.)

This is all a very arbitrary, subjective effect. Many directors and camera operators just ignore such finesse. But when the *perspective distortion* in a picture is extreme, even the least observant will react to the impressions of squashed or exaggerated space! Vertical columns can look bowed and bent. Close shots appear grotesquely deformed (close wide lens angle); or flattened as if cut out of board (narrow lens angle). There are odd occasions when you want exactly that kind of distortion to give the picture a dramatic impact. But take care that it doesn't arise through your accidentally using an inappropriate lens angle!

Some scenes contain very few clues to perspective – e.g. deserts, seascapes, countryside, arctic wastes – so that the lens angle you use may not be at all critical in general shots. But where there are innumerable visual clues – as in shots of city streets or inside buildings – exaggeration or compression of perspective, and unlikely proportions, can be all too obvious.

When you are shooting with a '*normal*' lens angle of say 20° to 27° – e.g. 17 mm for a 2/3 in. CCD – your audience will get a reasonably accurate idea of space and proportions. With many zoom lenses this will be when you are using a focal length around the middle of its range.

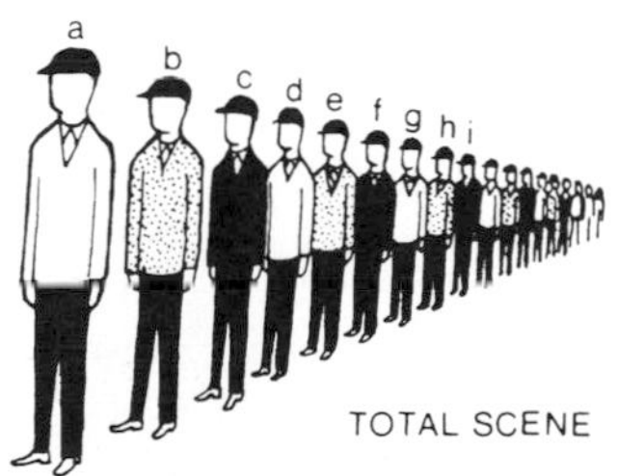

Fig. 4.9 Perspective distortion
(see *Digests*)
Reducing the lens angle (increasing F) provides a magnified image of part of the scene. This emphasizes perspective effects normally associated with distant subjects, and produces an illusion of space compression.

The narrow-angle lens (long-focus lens)

As you move the zoom lens setting towards the '*T*' or '*telephoto*' end of its range, its focal length increases and the lens angle becomes narrower. The effect becomes progressively 'telescopic' as the lens's 'angle of view' is reduced. You get closer and closer shots of the subject.

Using a narrow lens angle has major advantages:

- When you cannot get the camera nearer the subject because of *obstructions*.
- When the subject is *out of reach*.
- When there is *insufficient time* to move the camera nearer.
- When the camera is *fixed* in position.
- When the camera operator is unable to move smoothly and unobtrusively.

There are often occasions both in the studio and in the field when the only way you can hope to get an effective shot of the subject is by using a narrow lens angle.

Distortion effects

However, the narrow-angle lens does have its drawbacks!

- *Depth can appear unnaturally compressed* – Foreground-to-background distance seems much shorter than it really is. Solid objects look shallower and 'depth-squashed'.
- *Distant subjects look much closer and larger than normal.* Things do not seem to diminish with distance as we would expect.
- Anyone moving towards or away from us seems to *take an interminable time* to cover the ground, even when running fast. At the racetrack, horses gallop towards us, but appear to cover little ground despite their efforts.
- Where the camera using a narrow lens angle shoots end-on to a long subject *it will look strangely foreshortened*:
  - A large oil tanker may look only a few meters long.
  - Shooting along a piano keyboard we see considerable compression.
  - In a rowing eight, flat cramped figures squat in a foreshortened boat.

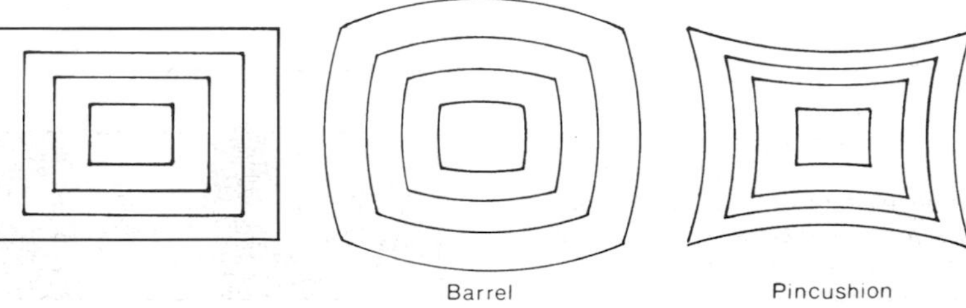

Fig. 4.10 Geometrical (curvilinear) distortion
Optical distortion in which lines parallel to the frame edges appear progressively bent outwards (barrel distortion) or inwards (pincushion distortion).

If you try to get close-ups of people some distance away by using a lens angle of around 5° to 10° you will notice that their features are unpleasantly flattened and facial modeling is generally reduced. Shot from the front (i.e. in full face), or when slightly angled (three-quarters face), this effect can be very obvious.

Camera handling

There are moments when the unexpected happens, and we want to grab a close shot of a fleeting moment – to emphasize someone's reaction perhaps, or show detail in a passing parade. Only a narrow-angle lens can change in an instant, from the wide view it

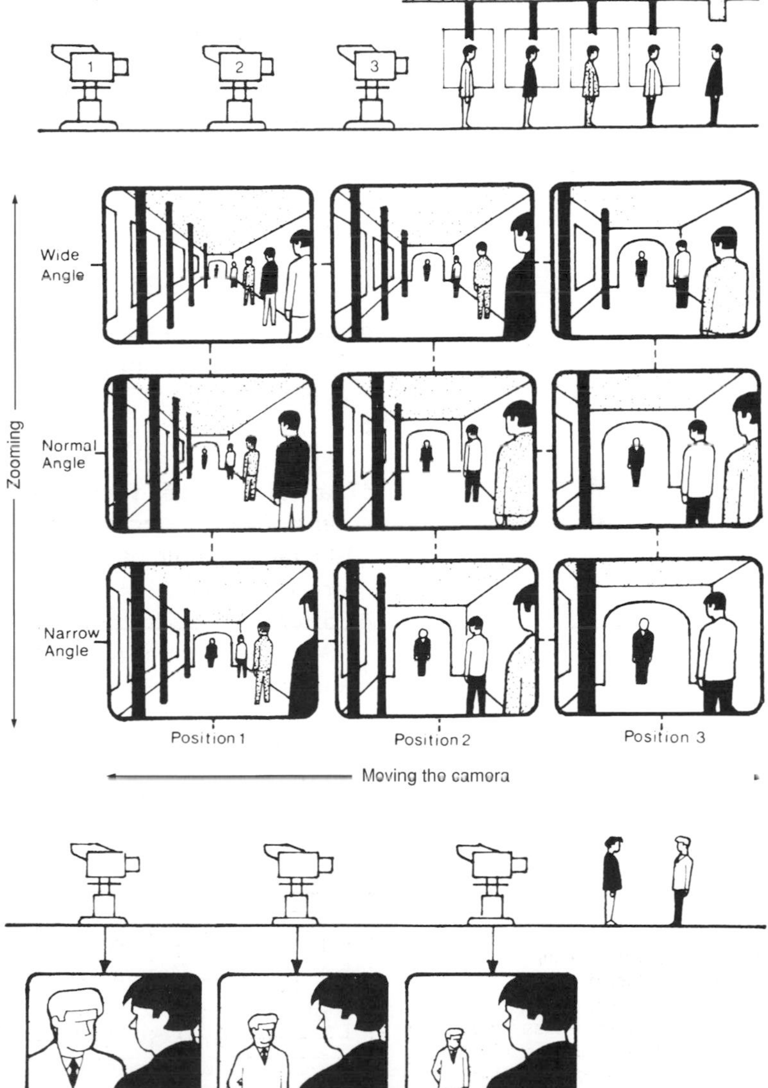

Fig. 4.11 part 1 Lens angles and camera movement
Here we see the effect of moving the camera (positions 1, 2, 3) with wide-angle, normal, narrow-angle lenses.

Fig. 4.11 part 2 Maintaining foreground subject size
If lens is changed, and camera distance altered to maintain the same foreground subject size, proportions change too. (1) Narrow; (2) normal; (3) wide-angle lens.

was taking, to get that unplanned shot. The audience will be too interested to notice such niceties as spatial distortion. (It may not be very bad anyway!)

But for the camera operator, narrow-angle lenses spell trouble! Camera handling becomes increasingly harder as the lens's focal length is increased. Even slight camera movement, caused by a wavering hand-grip or dollying over an uneven floor, causes disturbing picture judder. It is no mean feat to follow a fast-moving subject, such as a flying bird, in a close shot with a narrow-angle lens and keep it accurately framed throughout its maneuvers! Apart from handling difficulties, there is the additional focusing hazard of working with a shallow depth of field!

When using a narrow-angle lens it is difficult to hold the camera still for any length of time without a shudder or shake from one's breathing, heartbeart, or tiring muscles. A gust of wind can be a disaster! But it is virtually impossible to hand-hold it when set to a *very narrow* lens angle.

For cameras in the field, lens angles as small as ½° to 5° may be necessary to bring the action close enough. Then the problem is acute. You may even have to *lock-off* the panning head, to keep the picture steady.

In hot weather, close shots of distance subjects taken with a narrow-angle lens can be marred by heat haze rising from the ground. Light diffraction produces an overall shimmering that distorts the picture, and destroys detail. Then there is no remedy except to move nearer to the subject with a wider lens angle.

The wide-angle lens (short-focus lens)

For all practical purposes, we can say that any lens with a horizontal angle of 30° or more has wide-angle characteristics. The shorter the focal length, the wider the lens angle will be.

As you might expect, wide-angle ('short-focus') lenses have exactly opposite characteristics from narrow-angle lenses.

Distortion effects

The wide-angle lens appears to *exaggerate perspective*. Depth and space are overemphasized. Things seem further away than they really are.

If you move the camera while on a wide-angle lens it appears to be traveling faster than it really is. Anyone approaching or walking away from the camera seems to be moving much more quickly than normal.

You can use these various effects to advantage. A short-focus lens can give quite a wide overall view of the scene, even when it is relatively close.

Table 4.3 Lens angles *(see Table 6.2)*

	Advantages	*Disadvantages*
'Normal' lens (20°–27°)	Perspective appears natural. Space/distance appears consistent when intercutting 'normal' lenses. Camera handling feels natural and is relatively stable. Focused depth is generally satisfactory, even though fairly shallow for closer shots.	Inadequate width-coverage in confined spaces. Camera must move close to subject for detail; so may be seen by other cameras taking longer shots of the same subject.
Narrow-angle long-focus lens (less than 20°)	Brings distant subjects closer. Permits 'closer' shots of inaccessible subjects. Can flatten or reduce emphasis on surface contours. Enable objects spaced-out away from the camera to be compressed into a more cohesive group (e.g. a string of automobiles). Can suggest aborted effort in subjects moving quickly to/from the camera (e.g. running). Defocuses distracting background.	Depth appears compressed. Heat haze may shimmer the picture. Flattening of subject modeling can appear unnatural. Camera handling is considerably more difficult (pan, tilt, smooth dollying). Restricted depth of field makes focusing critical.
Wide-angle short-focus lens (greater than 30°)	Can obtain wide views at closer distances, especially in confined space. Camera handling causes negligible judder. Because of extended depth of field, focusing is less critical. Enables modeling and space to be exaggerated. Impressive spatial effects possible. Useful for grotesque or dramatic shots. Provides considerable depth of field.	Depth appears exaggerated. (Confined spaces cannot be shown in correct proportions.) Pronounced geometric distortion, at widest angles. Susceptible to lens flares. On close-ups, problems with camera shadows falling on subject.

This can be a great help when you are shooting in restricted spaces and shots taken with a normal lens angle look far too close.

Occasionally, when you set up a shot you may find that something nearby is visible as a defocused blur in the foreground. If you move closer until the obstruction is out of shot your subject may appear too large or too close. Moving closer with a wider lens angle can be the answer.

Even a small room can look quite spacious when shot on a wide-angle lens – a very useful deception when you want to emphasize space, or make small settings in the studio appear more impressive.

But there are times when this effect can be an embarrassment. If, for instance, you are shooting within a very confined area such as a cell, only a wide-angle lens will give you a general view of the location. (Any other lens angle would only provide close shots.) But at the same time, the wide-angle lens exaggerates perspective, and makes the surroundings seem very spacious . . . In these circumstances the only alternative is to use a normal lens angle, and move outside the room, shooting in through a window or door.

If you take close shots of people on wide-angle lenses you will get extremely unreal, bizarre distortions: puffed-up bulbous heads, large protruding noses, stumpy legs, and enlarged chests. Fine for grotesques, but totally unacceptable for flattering portraiture!

Never use wide-angle lenses for close shots of geometrical subjects such as pages of print, graph paper, or sheet music. The geometrical distortion can be very pronounced! Better still, try it and see what happens! Panning on a shot containing straight vertical or horizontal lines, you will see them bend as they near the picture edges.

The wider the lens angle (shorter focal length), the more obvious will these effects be. The *fisheye lens*, which has a coverage of from 140° to 360°, can only be used for those odd situations where their gross distortion can be accepted.

Camera handling

On the plus side, camerawork is much easier when using a wide-angle lens. Camera movements appear smoother, and any slight bumps as the camera moves are less likely to cause picture judder. As an extra bonus, focusing is less critical as the available depth of field is much greater.

Summarizing

To summarize these points:

Narrow-angle lenses

- The field of view is restricted. Only a small segment of the scene appears in the shot.
- At the narrowest angles you can get a blow-up 'telescopic' image of the subject.
- Space, distance, depth are compressed.
- Camera handling and focusing become difficult.

Wide-angle lenses

- The wide field of view takes in a large segment of the scene.
- The widest lens angles can give a 'wrong end of the telescope' impression.
- Space, distance, depth are exaggerated.
- Camera handling and focusing are easy.

In Table 6.2 you will see the practical features of various lens angles. A typical *zoom lens*, with its adjustable focal length, behaves

- As a narrow-angle or long-focus lens when zoomed fully in,
- As a wide-angle or short-focus lens when zoomed fully out,
- Somewhere about mid-range it has 'normal' lens-angle characteristics.

Supplementary lenses (also see Extender lens)

By adding an extra 'supplementary' lens in front of your lens you can alter its focal length, and hence the lens angle. The power of this 'add-on' lens is quoted in *diopters*. You can use such supplementary lenses with a prime lens or a zoom lens system.

A *positive supplementary lens* reduces the effective focal length, and therefore widens the lens angle. It also allows the lens system to focus on subjects closer than normal. You can identify a positive supplementary lens by holding it at arm's length, when you will see a small *inverted image*.

When you hold a *negative supplementary lens* the tiny image is *upright*. When placed over the lens the negative lens narrows the lens angle. However, if you position it beyond the main lens's focal length the overall lens angle will *increase*.

The zoom lens

Let's take a closer look at the *operating features* of the zoom lens. Its main productional advantage is that you can select or change between any focal lengths within its range without interrupting the shot. You can *zoom out* to get an overall view of the action and *zoom in* to examine details. The fact that in the process you are playing around with the spatial impressions your picture conveys, is usually incidental to the convenience of getting shot variations from a camera viewpoint. Many directors would argue that the artificial effects of perspective distortion, and the action of zooming, have been accepted by audiences as *conventions* in the media, like cuts, dissolves, wipes, etc.

In order to alter the effective focal length of a lens system it is necessary to move certain of its lens elements to adjust its overall magnification while still maintaining sharp focus, and avoiding optical distortions. This involves very precise mechanical readjustments.

If the focal length of our lens system when zoomed fully in (to *narrow angle*; *telephoto*) is, for example, fourteen times that when

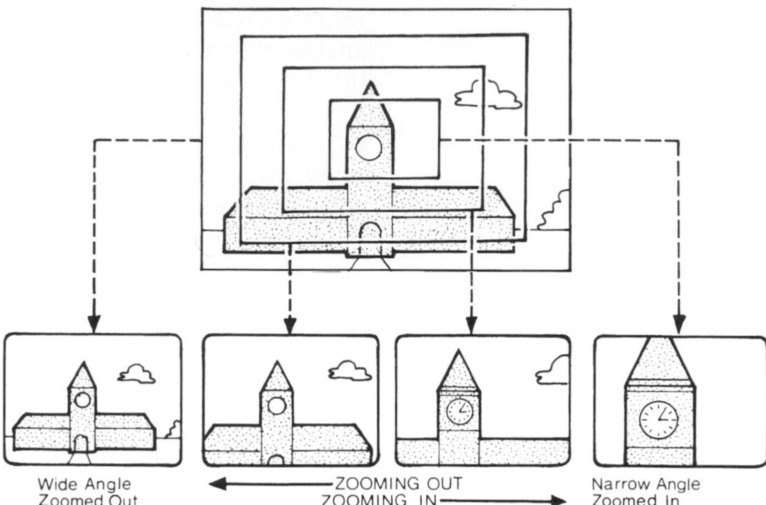

Fig. 4.12 Zooming
Zooming in progressively fills the screen with a smaller section of the scene. (Narrowing lens angle, increasing focal length.)

fully zoomed out (*wide angle*), we say that it has a *zoom ratio* of 'fourteen to one'. This can be written in several ways as *×14, 14× or 14:1.* With this lens you can change the size of a subject's image size in the picture by a magnification factor of fourteen. You might, for instance, zoom from a full-length of a person to a close shot of their face. The greater the zoom ratio, the bigger the angular change available. A really high ratio – e.g. 44:1 – could fill the screen with a person's eye . . . then zoom back until they became a speck in the landscape!

Another way of indicating a zoom lens specification is e.g. *14 × 8.5 (a 'fourteen by eight point five' lens)*. That simply means that the lens has a zoom ratio of *14:1*, with a minimum focal length of *8.5 mm* (i.e. when zoomed right out to its widest angle). Its longest focal length when fully zoomed in is therefore *14 × 8.5 = 119 mm.* Used with a 2/3 in. CCD, this lens will cover angles from 4.2° to 54.7°.

Types of zoom lenses

You can get zoom lens systems in a range of designs to fit all types of cameras, and to match specific CCD formats. The largest high-quality systems may weigh as much as 25 kg (55 lb), while more compact lightweight systems could weigh around 1.3 kg (3 lb). The large precision zoom lenses are fully corrected for various optical distortions (aberrations), and retain accurate focus throughout their range.

■ **In the studio** – The actual zoom range you need will really depend on the size of the studio and the type of production you are involved in. You can assess the most likely range by checking out typical camera distances (e.g. roughly around 3–9 m/10–30 ft) and the angles that will give you shots from about 0.5–3.5 m/2–12 ft wide (i.e. *close-up to long shot*). In practice, a 10:1 zoom covering about 5° to 50° has proved very successful, but 15:1 systems are also used.

The narrowest angle is useful for general close-up work, and the widest angle for overall shots of the action. However, where wider angles are used on distant cameras there may be problems in continually *over-shooting* (*shooting off*) the setting, and seeing lamps or getting *lens flares*

■ **In the field** – Working away from the studio, in open spaces or public places, you are more likely to need really narrow lens angles in order to get close enough shots from considerable distances.

Many cameras in the field work from fixed viewpoints, isolated way up on a balcony or a scaffold tower perhaps, and the only way they can give a variety of shots is by changing their lens angle. The wide-angle end of the zoom's range is limited but sufficient for most purposes.

For ENG/EFP work with a 2/3 in./18 mm format a zoom lens that can be adjusted over a range from 10.5 mm (at 45.5°) to 378 mm (0.67°) offers wide scope – a magnification of ×36. Adding a ×2 *extender lens* will convert the lens's range to become 21 mm (11.8°) to 756 mm (0.34°). However, lens systems of this kind can be quite heavy – e.g. 4.4 kg/10 lb. Certainly, a larger lens system can add considerably to the weight of the camera.

When subjects are a considerable distance away, an even larger lens system with a range of up to ×70 (9.5 to 665 mm on a standard 2/3 in. mount) may be the best solution. However, this must not only be firmly supported and well balanced (it is likely to weigh some 20 kg/44 lb), but firmly locked off when using its narrower angles in order to hold the shot steady.

The zoom lens range that is most appropriate for a production really depends on whether your camera is to be highly mobile, getting in among the action to take shots, or is to be set up in a fixed or semi-fixed position.

Where a camera is to be *hand-held* or *shoulder-mounted* there is a tendency for the operator to use wider lens angles. This makes it easier to hold shots steady. The disadvantage here is that the camera has to work closer to the action otherwise subjects will look too distant. And perspective can appear exaggerated.

As the lens angle is reduced, it becomes increasingly difficult to hold the camera steady and avoid shots wavering; especially as you become tired. An image stabilizer or a special harness mounting can be invaluable here.

Zoom lens controls

There are three methods of adjusting the focal length of a zoom lens:

- *Direct control* – By turning a ring or a lever on the lens barrel. Although subtle zooming action is not easy with these types of direct control, they are simple to use, and allow you to make very rapid zoom changes.

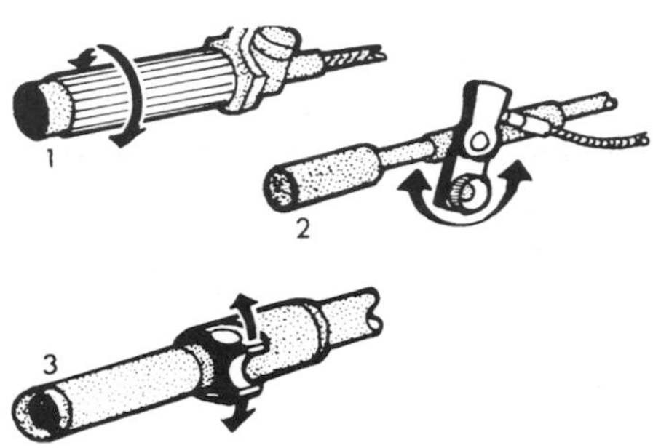

Fig. 4.13 Zoom lens controls

Forms of zoom control

On studio cameras:

1 Twist-grip.
2 Hand-crank.
3 Thumb-lever.

On lightweight cameras, thumb-operated switches by the handgrip operate the zoom motor.

Panning handle controls. When a camera is fitted to a mounting, the lens is usually adjusted with extension controls: *zoom control* (1 – twist grip) fixed to the left panning handle; *focus control* (2 – hand crank) to the right.

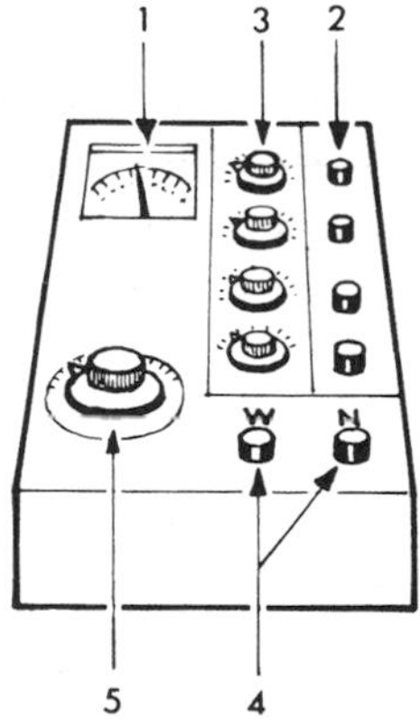

Shot box (integrated into camera head, or clamped to a pan handle). This provides pre-selected zoom settings; overriden by pan-bar thumb control.

1 Zoom meter shows focal length/lens angle.
2 Buttons select pre-set angles adjusted by knobs at 3.
4 Auto-zoom switch, zooms the lens in/out towards narrowest/widest angles when pressed.
5 Adjusts auto-zoom speed.

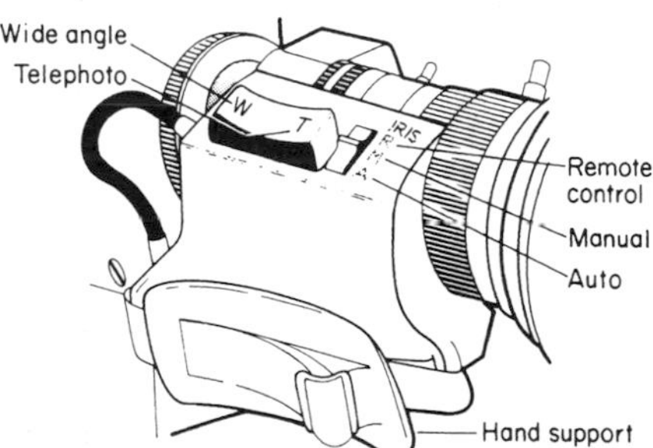

Focal length (lens angle) may be adjusted manually (zoom lever on lens barrel), or with a motor system (*power zoom*) operated by a rocker-switch, from Wide-angle to Telephoto (narrow angle). Nearby switches also control the lens *aperture (iris)*: auto, manual, remote control.

The major advantage of this form of control is that it does not use valuable *battery power* or make any noise; unlike motorized systems. On most ENG/EFP cameras you can override the motorized *lens servo-switch control* and operate the zoom action manually. So to conserve power some operators set up *all* shots using the manual control, only switching to the servo system when they intend to zoom.

- *Cable control* – In this mechanical system there is a a flexible cable from the zoom lens to a hand-operated *hand crank* control on the right-hand panning handle. Turning this crank alters the lens's focal length – forward to *zoom in*; towards you to *zoom out*. The faster you turn, the faster the zoom.

  Many *hand cranks* have a small speed lever which adjusts the control's coarseness; i.e. the number of turns needed to cover the zoom range. Its 'slow' ratio, which is more subtly controlled, is used for most purposes and its 'fast' for rapid zoom changes. (When a cable-controlled zoom is fitted, *focusing* is usually controlled by a twist-grip control attached to the left panning handle.)
- *Servo control* – In this design the lens's zoom action is controlled by a small two-way, vari-speed electric motor.

  – *On lightweight cameras a* rocker-switch forms part of the lens housing, or is set in a pistol grip attached below the lens. When the camera is hand-held or shoulder-mounted, and your right hand secure within the lens strap, your fingers can easily operate the two-way rocker switch to adjust the zoom. Pressing **W** causes the lens to *zoom out* towards its widest angle, while pressing **T** makes it *zoom in*, towards its narrowest angle (longest focal length). On releasing the switch you can stop travel at any mid-point. Some lens systems also allow you to adjust the zoom speed.

  – *On studio cameras:* On larger studio and field cameras the zoom servo motor is controlled remotely by a control on the left panning handle. This can provide a very smooth, even change, particularly during a very slow 'creep-in'. Servo systems can be designed to give the same 'feel' to the zoom (and focus) controls, whatever the focal length being used. (Others feel coarser towards the narrower end of the zoom range.) This type of control has the advantage that you cannot inadvertently 'overzoom' (or 'overfocus') and ram the lens against its end stop as it reaches its limits – jerking the picture and even damaging the lens system.

  The spring-loaded *thumb-lever* control is turned to the *left* to zoom *out*, and to the *right* to zoom *in*. Light thumb pressure results in slow zooming, while heavier pressure gives a fast zoom. You soon learn to adjust thumb pressure to control the zoom rate.

  Another form of zoom control is the *twist grip*; a rotating sleeve which turns right to zoom in and left to zoom out.

The shot box

Studio cameras are often fitted with a *shot box* at the rear of the camera head; or fastened to the right-hand panning handle. This automated zooming facility shot box has a number of useful features:

- At the touch of a button, the lens will change to any of 4–6 prearranged lens angles, adjusted to suit your production's needs.
- A 'field of view' meter shows the current horizontal lens angle or focal length.
- A pair of selector buttons will automatically zoom the lens in (narrow) or out (wide).
- A knob adjusts the speed of this auto-zoom action.
- Operating the thumb-lever control on the panning handle overrides the selection of the shot box controls.

  Apart from the convenience of being able to select specific camera angles rapidly the shot box ensures that you use identical lens angles in both rehearsal and taping sessions.

Zoom performance

Now that we have looked at the fundamentals, let's think about the practicalities. Zoom lenses have unquestionably added an important dimension to camerawork. However, zoom lens design involves many technical compromises, especially in less expensive versions. To achieve smooth progressive zooming throughout the range, without the focus drifting, varying image brightness, geometrical distortions, and other aberrations is a considerable technical challenge. Even the best systems can have their inherent limitations (e.g. varying light transmission throughout the zoom range). That we usually overlook such vagaries is a tribute to their designers' skills.

Zoom advantages

We can summarize the zoom lens's chief *advantages* as:

- It provides a wide selection of lens angles.
- You can rapidly select any angle within its range.
- Zooming can be controlled *manually* or by a motor-driven *auto-zoom* at various preset speeds.
- It allows you to slightly adjust the size of the shot to improve composition/framing, without having to move the camera nearer or further away from the subject. This is quicker, and much less tiring.

- Zooming is easier than dollying. (Sometimes *too* easy!) It needs experience and skill to move a dolly smoothly at an even rate – particularly if you have to reposition it fast or over some distance.

Zoom disadvantages

But we must not forget that the zoom lens does have its *disadvantages*:

- The zoom lens behaves differently at various zoom settings. (Depth of field, perspective, and handling vary).
- It is easy to select an *inappropriate* lens angle so that perspective varies between shots, distorting people and space.
- If you are continually varying the zoom settings during a rehearsal it is important to repeat these angles and camera positions exactly when taping. Suppose, for instance, that you are now further away than previously and zoom in to compensate. This 'corrected' shot will not have the same relative subject proportions. You might now be in the way of another camera or a sound boom! (To avoid such discrepancies, note details of the lens angle on your *camera card*, *shot sheet*, or *script*, and mark or tape the camera's floor positions during rehearsal.) If your camera does not have a reliable indicator or shot box you may have to rely on the marked floor and your shot memory.
- Zooming can be misused, as a lazy substitute for more effective *camera movement*.

Zoom handling

Focusing and camera handling are very easy when you have the lens set to a *wide angle*. But things become increasingly difficult as you zoom in to *narrower* lens angles. Fast-moving subjects are harder to follow and frame accurately. (If you pan your camera just 1° while using a 60° lens, subjects will move sideways only 1/60th of the picture width. On a 1° lens, they would move from one side of the picture to the other! It's not surprising that the slightest camera shake is so obvious with narrow lens angles!)

If you happen to be working on a wide-angle lens setting and the subject moves away you may find it necessary to both move and zoom in to follow it. Then some disconcerting things can happen. While you are concentrating on maintaining focus and framing you may fail to notice that you are now moving around with a narrowing lens angle, and barely able to hold the shot steady!

Parallactic movement

Why bother to move the camera, when you can simply zoom in and out to change the shot? After all, when you zoom, it looks as if the camera is moving nearer and further away. Or does it?

If you are shooting a *flat surface* such as a photograph or a painting, the effect of zooming is identical with that of dollying – an overall magnification or reduction of the image.

There are important differences though, when shooting *three-dimensional* situations. Suppose the scene contains a person standing behind a tree. From where we stand, they are hidden. If we zoom in on the scene, simply magnifying the image, they remain hidden.

But if instead of zooming we dolly the camera forward we see quite a different effect. Our viewpoint continually changes. As in everyday life, the picture shows us going *past* different objects in the scene. Their relative positions in the shot alter.

In this example, as we move forward past the tree part of the person comes into sight. Continuing forward, they become increasingly visible . . . until eventually we see them quite clearly, separate from the tree.

This effect, as relative positions change, is known as *parallactic movement*. When the picture zooms, we miss this displacement, and the result looks false, even if one does not recognize why. So zooming is seldom a completely convincing substitute for moving the camera.

Extender lens

Some zoom lens systems include an in-built supplementary lens – a flip-in *extender lens* (range extender). Typically this changes the available zoom range by ×1.5 or ×2.

With a ×2 *fixed extender* in position the basic range of an 8–101 mm zoom lens (60°–5°) would effectively be increased to become a 16–202 mm (30°–2½°) system. With the extender lens in, the widest shots available will be limited; but you are able to get closer shots than normal.

Variable extenders (sometimes called 'double zooms') allow the amount of magnification of the basic zoom range to be adjusted (e.g. up to ×2 maximum). To a limited extent, this arrangement minimizes the usual disadvantages of extenders.

There are drawbacks to using any extender lens:

- There is inevitably an overlap between the two ranges.
- The image quality when using the extender is not as high as the normal range; although the softer focus may not be obvious.
- You should not switch the extender lens in/out while on shot, for it will disrupt the picture. So you may need to choose the moment for changeover carefully.
- There can be practical difficulties due to the overlap between the two ranges. Suppose you are on the lower range, and zoomed in to its narrowest angle. Switching to the higher range, you will find that the lens is now *at its narrowest angle* on the high range;

a considerable jump in image size! You cannot zoom smoothly from the widest angle (low range) to the narrowest angle (high range).

- There can be a considerable light loss when switching to the extender. A ×2 extender, for example, may require a fourfold light increase for the same exposure! It may not be practicable to open up to a larger lens aperture to compensate.
- The minimum focusing distance can change between the ranges. You may not be able to focus on closer subjects on one range.

Nevertheless, the extender does provide an opportunity to increase the effective range of a zoom lens, and this can be very useful at times.

Focusing

When you focus the camera, you adjust its lens to produce the sharpest possible image of your subject. With a prime lens, this involves altering the distance between the lens and the camera's CCD (or film, in the case of a photographic camera). With the zoom lens, focus adjustment is by readjusting the positions of internal lens elements.

Why focus?

Simple photographic cameras have no focusing control, yet everything in the shot looks reasonably sharp. Why does the TV camera need to be focused continually? There are several reasons:

- A fixed-focus system does not provide maximum sharpness in your subject. The lens is set at the *hyperfocal distance* (*see Digests*) so is in 'acceptable focus' from the far distance up to about 2.4 m (8 ft) away. Anything closer is defocused.
- The lens aperture is reduced (small stop), so high light levels are needed for good results.
- Everything in the shot is equally sharp. There is no *differential focusing* in which subjects can be made to stand out against a defocused background.
- The camera cannot focus on close subjects (although a supplementary lens may help).

  If, for some reason, you wanted to use your TV camera as a fixed-focus system, so that you were free to move around and concentrate on other things, you could set the lens to the hyperfocal distance. But this is a very limiting technique.

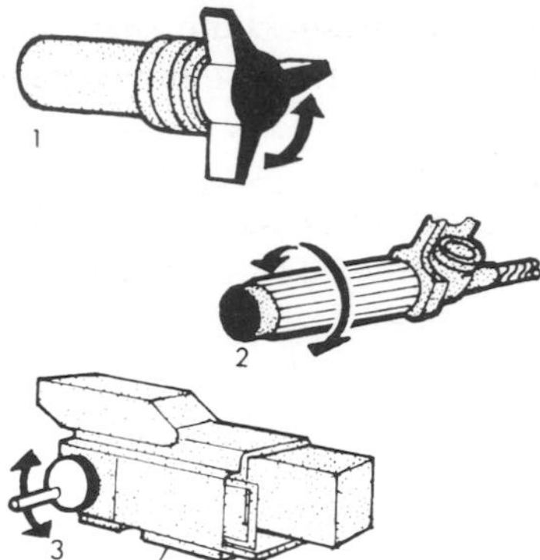

Fig. 4.14 Forms of focus control
Typical systems of focus control include:

1 Spoked capstan control
2 Twist-grip
3 Camera-head focus control.

Focusing methods (Figure 4.14)

Several different methods are used to focus the camera's lens system:

1 A *focus ring* on the lens barrel.
2 A *twist grip* attached to a panning handle.
3 A focus knob on the side of the camera, or on a panning handle attachment.
4 Some form of *auto-focus* – an automatic focusing system.

1 *Focus ring* – Lens systems on hand-held and lightweight cameras can be focused by turning a ring on the *lens barrel*, until subject details are as sharp as possible. To make it easier to focus more accurately, a *crispening* control may be fitted, which exaggerates detail in the viewfinder display. (A local effect which does not affect the transmitted TV picture itself.)
2 *Twist grip* – When a camera is fixed onto a mounting, *panning handles* are usually attached to its *panning head* to direct and steady it. A rotating sleeve *twist grip* control clamped onto the left panning handle turns to adjust the lens focus.

   Designs vary. Some allow you to re-adjust the focused distance rapidly. A single turn of the grip moves focus from the closest (*MFD*) to the furthest point (*infinity*), to *throw focus/pull focus* instantly between a subject in the foreground and another in the distance. However, focus adjustments feel quite coarse in close-up shots where the depth of field is shallow. In other twist grip designs, it takes two or three complete turns to cover the range. Now focus changes can be quite subtle, but rapid focus changes are impracticable.

   In the simplest remote-control systems, the twist grip is linked to the lens focusing mechanism through a *flexible cable*. Although quite trouble-free, focusing can be quite coarse at *narrow* lens angles, while at *wide-angle* setting you need turn the grip over an appreciable range before you can detect changes.
3 *Servo motor system* – Here a small servo motor adjusts the lens focus mechanism. This has considerable advantages, for its focus control can be located on the side of the camera, attached to a panning handle, or even remotely at a separate control point. Moreover, this system can be designed to have the same operational 'feel', whatever the lens angle (focal length).
4 *Auto-focus* – An increasing number of cameras include *automatic* focusing facilities. Ideally, you just point the camera, and it focuses on the subject. Auto-focus is particularly useful when you are moving around with a hand-held or shoulder-mounted camera, for it maintains focus wherever you move, allowing you to concentrate on framing the shot and checking out your route.

   However, it is best to think of the auto-focus facility as an aid, rather than assuming that it will relieve you of all focusing worries. There can be all kinds of nasty surprises, depending on which system you are using! Normally, auto-focus systems sharpen focus on the nearest object in the center of the shot, but there are several different techniques: *infrared light*, *piezo control*, *digital AI*, *auto-tracking*, *fuzzy logic*, and '*eyeball focus*' *systems*. You will find details of these processes in the *Digests – Auto-focus*.

Auto-focus problems

- If your subject is not *central*, auto-focus may sharpen up on whatever happens to be there, leaving your subject defocused.
- Although you may want two subjects at different distances from the camera to appear equally sharp, the auto-focus may indiscriminately sharpen on one or neither.
- If you are shooting through a foreground framework of e.g. branches, a grille, netting, railings, the system will focus on this, rather than your subject beyond.
- If your subject is behind glass (show case, shop window), or beneath the surface of a pool, the auto-focus system can be fooled.
- If someone or something moves in front of the camera, the system may refocus on it, defocusing your subject. If, for instance, you pan over a landscape, and a foreground bush comes into shot, the lens may defocus the distant scene and show a well-focused bush. Similarly, when following a moving subject (e.g. someone in a crowd) the system may continually readjust itself, focusing randomly on passing subjects.
- When you zoom to alter the shot size, the system may refocus as you recompose the picture.
- If the subject is dark-toned, or covered with a black material, focusing may be inaccurate, as such surfaces do not reflect infrared well.
- When shooting in rain, snow, mist or fog, auto-focusing may not be accurate.
- Sometimes detailed backgrounds close behind a subject can cause ambiguous focusing.
- Highly reflective surfaces, and areas that are shiny or reflect a lot of light can be a problem.
- Horizontal subjects with strong tonal stripes can cause ambiguous auto-focus settings.
- Subjects that are moving rapidly or continuously can beat the system.
- Subjects that are angled away from the camera may produce false results.
- Subjects that have little contrast may not provide accurate focusing.
- When shooting at night, results can be uncertain.
- When using a lens filter for effects, it may interfere with the auto-focus system.

These problems may not arise or course, but it is as well to be warned. If in doubt, switch to *manual* focusing instead.

Depth of field

When you focus a lens you are adjusting the *distance* at which it gives maximum sharpness. Anything that is nearer or farther away than this focused distance appears progressively defocused.

The range of distances over which subjects are apparently sharp is called the *depth of field* – not *depth of focus*, which refers to an entirely different thing (focal plane tolerances). The focused area in front of the subject is much shallower than that behind it.

How far sharpness can deteriorate before you notice it depends on the detail in your subject, and how good the system is. If the subject lacks detail, or the system has poor definition, you may have difficulty in seeing exactly what *is* in focus!

Provided a subject remains within this depth of field, you do not need to readjust the focus control. At times, the focused depth may be considerable, especially when the lens is focused at the hyperfocal distance (*see Digests*). But it can also become embarrassingly shallow, particularly in close shots. Then when the distance of the subject or the camera changes even slightly you may need to readjust the focus control to maintain sharpness (Figure 4.15).

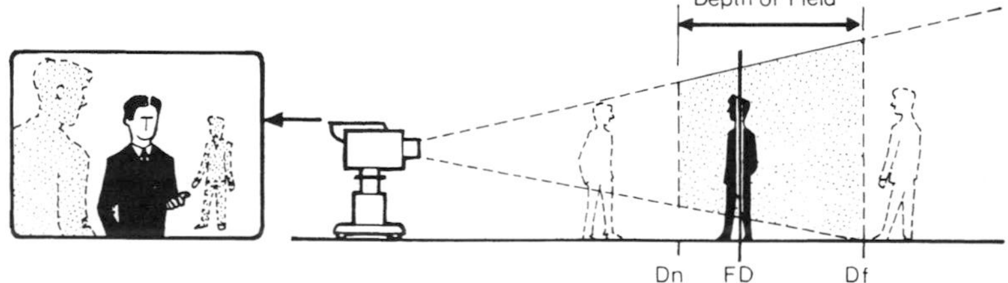

Fig. 4.15 Depth of field
Within the depth of field, subjects appear sharp: although definition is optimum at the *focused distance* (FD). Beyond the furthest acceptable distance (Df) and closer than the nearest limits (Dn), subjects are defocused.

As you can see in Figure 4.16, the depth of field in a shot alters noticeably when you vary

- The distance at which the lens is focused
- Or the lens angle (the focal length)
- Or the lens *f-stop*.

Rather than continually following focus as subjects or cameras move around it would seem preferable to stop the lens right down (e.g. *f*/22) to obtain the maximum depth of field. The hard fact of life is that this could necessitate light levels that are anything from eight to 30 times the normal light intensity! (Hardly practicable in a studio.) And as we shall see, all-over focus (*deep focus*) is not always desirable artistically.

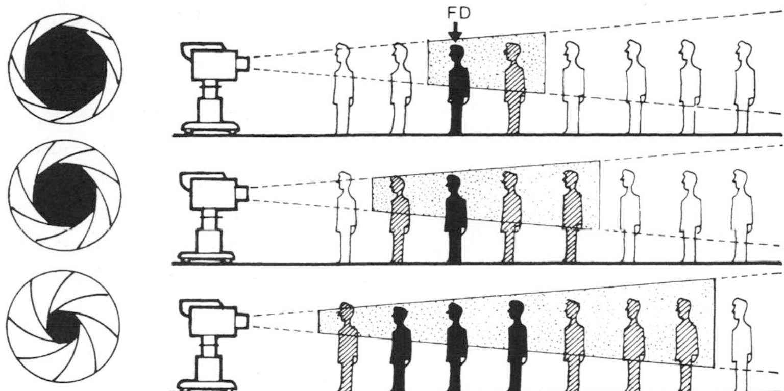

Fig. 4.16 part 1 The effect of aperture on depth of field
Keeping the focal length and focusing distance (FD) constant, the depth of field increases as lens aperture is reduced (stopped-down).

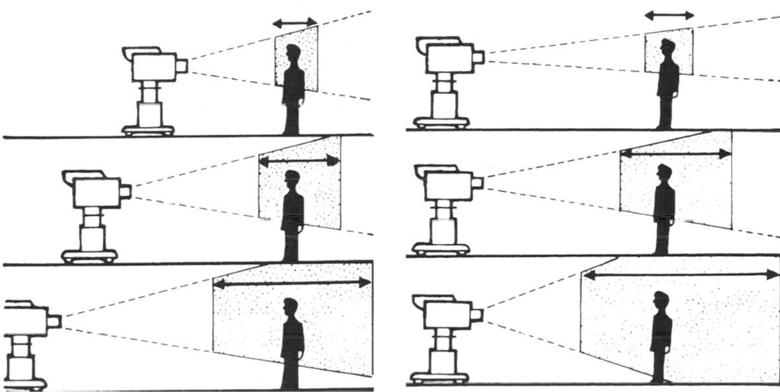

Fig. 4.16 part 2 The effect of subject distance on depth of field
Keeping the focal length and aperture constant, the depth of field increases as the camera gets further from the subject; but image size decreases.

Fig. 4.16 part 3 The effect of focal length on depth of field
Keeping the aperture and subject distances constant, the depth of field increases as focal length decreases (lens angle is widened), but image size decreases.

Focusing problems

If a shot is correctly focused, zooming in or out should have no effect. If focus does vary (tracking error), this may be because the lens needs setting up, or may be due to shortcomings in lens design.

However, even a correctly aligned high-performance zoom lens has a regular operational hazard you should know about (Figure 4.18).

Imagine your lens is fully zoomed out, and the picture sharply focused. You zoom right in to a close shot . . . and find that the picture is now *completely out of focus*. Why?

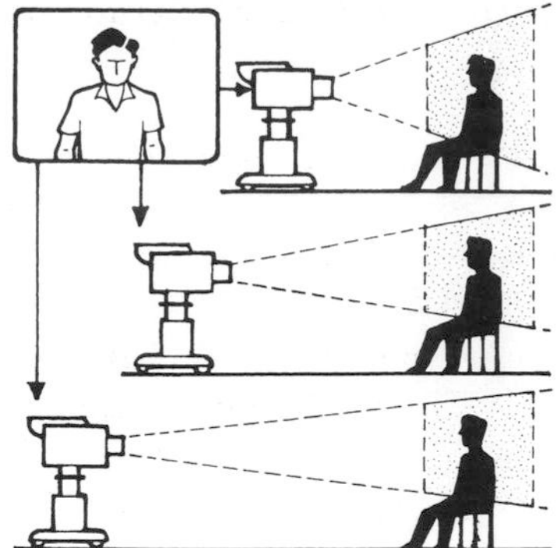

Fig. 4.17 Constant depth of field
If the camera distance is adjusted for each lens angle to keep the same subject size, the depth of field will remain the same (for a given *f*-stop).

Focusing with a wide-angle lens setting (short focal length) is so uncritical that whether your lens is actually focused at e.g. 8 m or 10 m (26–32 ft) the shot appears equally sharp. That is because there is a considerable depth of field. The exact focused distance is not easy to see.

However, when you zoom *in*, the focused depth becomes progressively shallower as the lens angle narrows. If you were originally focused at 10 m but your subject is at 8 m, the error will now be very obvious; it will be out of focus!

The only solution is to wait until you are off shot, and *pre-focus* the picture. You zoom in, sharp focus, and then zoom out to the wide-angle shot, ready to start shooting, and zoom in on cue. If you are taken by surprise, or do not have the opportunity to prepare the zoom-in, you have no option but to correct any defocusing during the take. It looks sloppy, but sometimes the lapse can be edited out afterwards.

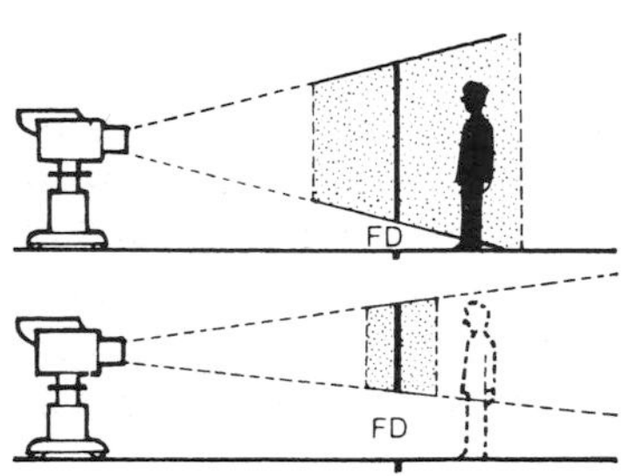

Fig. 4.18 Zoom lens focusing problems
Unless the camera has been pre-focused, the close-up after zooming it may be unsharp.

Zoomed out – although the focused distance is incorrect, the subject appears focused due to the considerable depth of field available (wide lens angle).

Zoomed in – without re-adjusting focusing, we zoom in. Now the depth of field has become shallower (narrower lens angle) and it no longer includes subject, which appears defocused.

Minimum focusing distance

Any lens can be focused over a range from *infinity* to a plane a short distance from the lens. Nearer than this *minimum focusing distance (MFD)* the shot remains defocused, the control having reached its limit. This MFD varies with the type and design of the lens. A wide-angle (short-focus) lens can focus down to a few centimeters away. But the MFD for a very narrow-angle (long-focus) lens may be several meters from the camera. For a zoom lens, the minimum focusing distance varies with the angle selected.

Many zoom lenses have a *macro* setting, which provides a sharp image almost up to the actual lens surface. You can fill the screen with a postage stamp. Whether you can get light on the subject at that distance and avoid camera shadowing is another matter! When you use the macro setting, the lens's zoom action is inoperative.

Setting up the zoom lens

It's easier to understand how the zoom works if you think of it as a fixed-focus lens with a telescope of variable magnification in front of it. While its field of view changes as you alter the focal length (i.e. zoom), the distance between the rear lens element and the CCD remains constant. To ensure that the zoom lens maintains focus as you zoom (i.e. correct *focus tracking*), the lens system has to be carefully adjusted.

If you change the lens system for any reason, not only must you check that the image size produced by the new lens is appropriate for the CCD format but you will need to adjust the *back- focus (flange-back)* distance to suit the camera (e.g. 48 mm). Setting up the lens involves:

- With the lens at maximum aperture (manual), zoom right in to distant detail and adjust the normal *zoom focus control* (i.e. *focus ring* on the lens barrel, or main focus control) for maximum sharpness.
- Zoom right out to the widest angle, and adjust the internal preset *back-focus (flange-back) control* for the sharpest image
- Now you should be able to zoom in/out without focus drift. If necessary, repeat this setting-up procedure for optimum results. Once set up, the lens tracking should remain satisfactory for some time.
- Finally switch in any *range extender*, and check that the lens tracking remains satisfactory.

Lens aperture (*f*-stop)

Looking into a lens system, you will see an adjustable circular *diaphragm* or *iris*, made up of a number of thin overlapping metal blades. The size of the hole formed by these plates is carefully calibrated in graduated stops. These *f-numbers/f-stops* (or *transmission – T* numbers) are marked around a ring on the lens barrel. Turning the ring alters the effective diameter of the lens opening over a wide range.

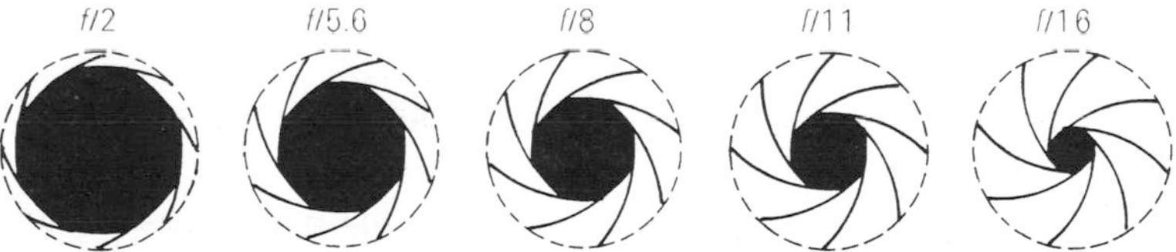

Fig. 4.19 Lens aperture
Lens aperture is adjustable from a maximum (e.g. *f*/2 for a fast lens *f*/5.6 for a slow lens) to a minimum (e.g. *f*/22). *Large aperture* – small *f*-number, shallow depth of field, but less light needed. *Small aperture* – large *f*-number, increased depth of field, but more light needed.

Adjusting the lens aperture, two quite separate things happen simultaneously:

1 It changes the brightness of the lens image falling on the camera-tube or image sensor – i.e. the picture's *exposure*.
2 It alters *depth of field* in the shot – which, we know, is also affected by the lens's focused distance and focal length.

f-numbers (f-stops)

The larger its maximum opening, the more light the lens will let through. Typical maximum stops for a 'fast lens', suitable under lower levels, would be *f*/1.4 to 1.7 'wide open'. A 'slower lens' with a maximum opening of e.g. *f*/3.5 would not produce optimum pictures under these conditions.

A typical maximum aperture for a 2/3 in. CCD camera is *f*/1.7; and for a 1/2 in. CCD system, *f*/1.4 maximum.

As you reduce the lens aperture (stop down) the *f*-stop number increases. The lens's minimum aperture may be around *f*/22. For each complete stop you open the lens its image brightness light will double (halved when stopping down). But a whole stop number is an inconveniently large calibration, so subdivisions are normally used. The standard series of lens markings is:

f/1.4 2 2.8 4 5.6 8 11 16 22 32

In practice, intermediate points such as 3.5, 4.5, 6.3 are also used.

You can calculate the difference in the light passed at two apertures with the formula:

$$\frac{(\text{First } f\text{-no.})^2}{(\text{Second } f\text{-no.})^2} = \text{light change}$$

So opening up the lens from *f*/8 to *f*/4, the image brightness increases by four times. Stopping down from *f*/4 to *f*/8, the image brightness changes to one-quarter. If, for instance, you wanted to increase the depth of field in a shot, and stopped down to improve focused depth, light levels (intensity) would need to be increased fourfold to compensate.

Working apertures

The highest grade lenses provide sharp pictures, even at their maximum aperture (e.g. *f*/1.7). You may be working fully open because lighting is insufficiently bright to stop down further, or because you want to isolate a subject, using a shallow depth of field. But clarity (*definition, resolution*) falls off discernibly towards the edges of the picture at large apertures.

Some lenses only produce optimum picture quality at around *f*/5.6. But with improved lens design, many are now very efficient at larger apertures. Although stopping down to small apertures (e.g. *f*/16) may make the subject look sharper (as the depth of field increases), it does not provide maximum lens definition.

Exposure

There is a lot of misunderstanding about 'correct exposure'. We might say that a picture is correctly exposed when the subject tones you are interested in are reproduced most convincingly.

As we saw in Chapter 3, the camera's CCD can only respond accurately over a relatively restricted range of tones. Brighter areas will crush out above its upper limits; darker tones are lost below its lower limits. The trick is to adjust the lens aperture to suit the prevailing conditions, so that the tones you particularly want to see lie within these limits.

If you want more detail in the shadows you will need to open the lens aperture a little to increase exposure. But, of course, this will cause *all* the other tones in the picture to appear brighter, and the lightest might now pale-out badly, or even crush-out to a blank white.

Occasionally, you may deliberately *over*-expose a shot to create a high-key '*notan*' effect of lightness, bleaching-out lighter tones.

Conversely, if you want to see better tonal gradation in a white dress you may need to reduce exposure by closing down to a slightly smaller stop. This will, however, cause *all* the other tones in the picture to appear darker, and the darkest might now merge, or even crush-out to black.

So exposure is an artistic compromise. But it is also a way in which you can manipulate the image. You might deliberately over- or underexpose the picture to achieve certain effects (e.g. stormy skies, mystery, night effects). It is quite possible to set the exposure to suit the prevailing light levels, and shoot everything in the scene with that stop. But for more sensitive adjustment of picture tones one really needs to be alert, and continually readjust the exposure (e.g. ± half a stop as camera angles change).

Over- or underexposure can cause visible defects in the picture (Figures 4.20 and 4.21). We'll discuss the subtleties of exposure adjustment in more detail in Chapter 23.

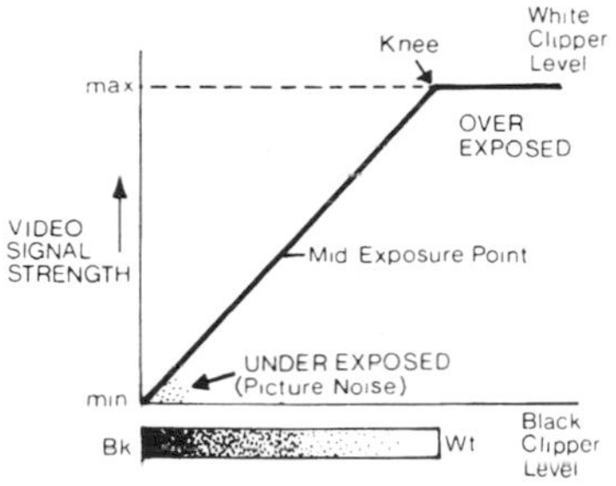

Fig. 4.20 Exposure curve
Ideally, as the camera scans various tones in the lens image, its video signal should vary correspondingly. Relative tonal values will then be reproduced accurately in the picture.

Darker tones will only produce a weak video signal; comparable with inherent background noise in the system. We see this noise reproduced as 'snow' or grain in dark areas of the picture.

If tones in the scene reflect more light than the camera sensor can handle, the video strength will reach the system's upper limits, and block off to produce a blank white area in the picture.

To avoid the brightest tones clipping-off abruptly, circuitry can make the upper limit more gradual (soft), by introducing a *knee* in the exposure curve; as with photographic film. Highlights are then reproduced more realistically.

Automatic iris

Lightweight and portable cameras are usually fitted with an *auto-iris*. Switched in, this automatically adjusts the lens aperture to suit the prevailing light levels. At first sight, the auto-iris frees the camera operator from the chore of adjusting exposure for each shot. It is a particularly useful facility when you are very mobile; moving around quickly, concentrating on framing the shot, and not tripping down stairs or bumping into things. Shooting in a sunny exterior, the lens may need to be stopped down to e.g. *f*/16 for correct exposure. But go into a building where light levels are much lower, and the lens now needs to be opened up to perhaps *f*/2 for the camera's CCD to receive sufficient light. The auto-iris will make this compensation automatically. Without it, you would have to continually check tonal gradation in the viewfinder picture, and open the iris until the new scene was correctly exposed.

Unfortunately, like any automatic set-up, the auto-iris system cannot make *artistic* judgements, and is easily fooled. Ideally, you

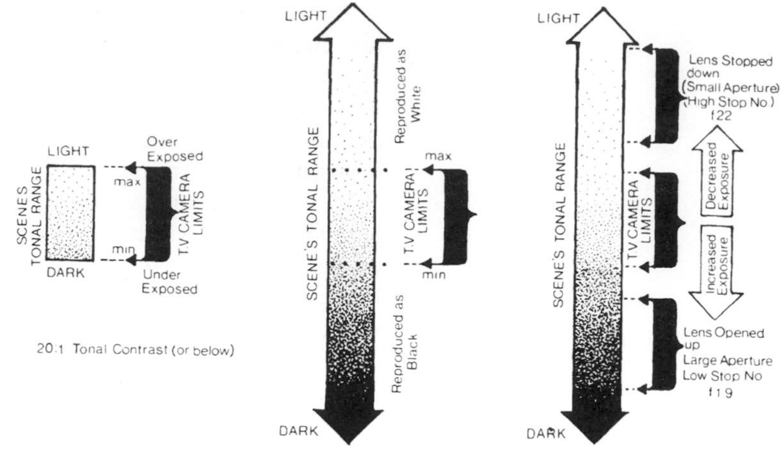

Fig. 4.21 Exposure
The camera can only reproduce a relatively limited range of tones accurately. This *contrast range* may be as little as 20:1. If scenic tones fall within this range, the *f*-stop can be adjusted to accommodate them. If subject tones or lighting contrast exceed the system's range, detail and tonal gradiation in the lightest and/or darkest areas will appear as solid white or black.

Opening the lens aperture, progressively (e.g. to *f*/2) improves shadow detail, but increasingly *overexposes* the lightest tones, which block off to white.

Reducing the lens aperture progressively (e.g. to *f*/16) improves detail in lightest tones, but increasingly *underexposes* darker tones, which merge to black.

want the exposure of your main subject to remain *constant*. But an auto-iris is activated by all other tones in the picture.

- Move in front of a light background, or bring a newspaper into shot, or take off a jacket to reveal a white shirt, and the iris closes and reduces exposure. *All* picture tones now appear darker.
- If a large dark area comes into shot, the iris may open up 'to compensate', and all picture tones appear lighter.
- Walk through trees, where areas of sky and foliage come and go, and exposure can yo-yo up and down quite inappropriately.

Under certain conditions the auto-iris can cause bad under-exposure – against a window; very light backgrounds; a shiny background with strong light reflections. Some cameras have a *backlight* control that opens up the lens an arbitrary stop or so above the auto setting, to improve subject exposure.

In some camera designs the auto-iris system sets both the *lens aperture* ***and*** *the shutter speed* to 'correctly' expose the picture. But this can cause problems, particularly when the system chooses *high shutter speeds*. There can be difficulties too, where a subject approaches the camera and moves into shade. The auto-iris opens up, reducing the depth of field, and leaving the subject defocused! To avoid such dilemmas, the camera may be fitted with an *exposure lock*, which allows you to choose the lens aperture you want for optimum exposure.

Auto-iris systems work by measuring the brightness of the lens image falling on the CCD. Most concentrate on the central area of the frame. Some are designed to avoid being over-influenced by the top of the frame, where bright skies, for example, could falsely reduce the exposure. The best systems judge exposure by sampling all parts of the image.

■ *Manual iris adjustment* – Turning the iris/diaphragm ring on the lens barrel allows you to decide for yourself exactly how you want the picture to be exposed. You can adjust the overall picture brightness, compensate for features in the scene that would fool an auto-iris system, and even produce fades to or from a black screen. But some cameras do not give us *complete manual control* of the iris when set to this position. Instead, although the lens aperture is set manually, the auto-iris still opens and closes to compensate relative to that setting. Normally, an auto-iris system will function independently, over the complete aperture range.

Summarizing, we can say that at best the auto-iris, like the auto-focus, can be a 'lifesaver'; but at worst the cure is worse than the disease, and results are very uneven. Exposure inaccuracies may be too small to notice; or in news gathering may be unimportant compared with getting clear shots.

Remote iris control

When a camera is connected to a *camera control unit* (*CCU*) or *remote control unit* (*RCU*) its lens aperture is usually set up during *camera line-up* to suit prevailing light conditions.

In the studio one aims at reasonably constant light levels (e.g. 1600 lux (150 fc)). During production, the lens aperture of each camera can be remotely controlled, either with coarse adjustment (several stops) or more usually with a fine control (e.g. ± half a stop) to vary exposure subtly for the best picture quality.

Neutral density filters

When the scene is too bright for the aperture you want to work at, a *neutral density filter* is used to cut down the overall intensity. These transparent gray-tinted (neutral) discs are usually fitted in a filter wheel behind the lens (*see Digests*). Otherwise they must be clipped over the front of the lens, in a *filter holder*. Typical values range from 1/10 (10 per cent) to 1/100 (1 per cent) transmission. A 10 per cent filter will, for example, cut light down by nearly three stops (e.g. *f*/5.6 to *f*/16).

Neutral density (ND) filters may be used when shooting in very strong sunlight, to prevent overexposure or the need for unduly small apertures. Again, should you want to open up the lens of a particular camera to restrict focused depth for artistic reasons, while perhaps other cameras use smaller stops, a ND filter can be used to compensate exposure.

Camera sensitivity

All TV cameras require a certain minimum general light level to produce clear, crisp pictures with good tonal gradation. The actual intensities needed depend on the camera's inherent sensitivity, scenic tones, the atmospheric effect required, and suitable depth of field (hence the *f*-stop).

Camera sensitivity varies with design and line-up. High sensitivity allows you to get satisfactory pictures under lower light conditions, when otherwise you would have to increase video gain (amplification) despite greater picture noise, to try to strengthen the dim underexposed shot.

In the studio, however, very dim lighting provides depressing and uncomfortable working conditions. Artistic lighting balance becomes difficult, as the eye cannot evaluate light values accurately, or detect extraneous shadows or spill light that are very evident on camera. Instead, when using high-sensitivity systems we normally find ourselves lighting to comfortable intensities and stopping down or filtering to prevent overexposure.

Cameras are quoted as needing a particular incident-light level at a certain lens aperture or *stop*. In practice, you will find quite wide divergences in the quoted '*sensitivity*' of various camera systems. A lot depends on how it is measured, and on various technical parameters. (*See Digests – Sensitivity.*) It can be influenced by scenic tones (light-toned surroundings require less light). Is the light even or patchy? Is it from the camera direction? How has the camera channel been adjusted (e.g. gamma, color temperature, video gain)? To achieve high picture quality, tests have shown that consumer cameras and low-end industrial cameras with a single CCD may require ten times or more the quoted minimum illumination specified!

Light intensities (*light levels*) are measured in *lux* (*lumens per square meter*) or in *foot-candles* (*lumens per square foot*); 1 fc = 10.7639 lux. 1 lux = 0.0929 fc. The light levels a camera requires to work efficiently are only a guide to its sensitivity when they are related to the lens's working aperture or *f*-stop.

Typical light levels required for modern cameras are often quoted as 200 lux (18.5 fc) at *f*/2 for 2/3 in. CCD format, rather than the 1500–2000 lux that earlier color cameras needed. But in practice, allowing for light losses in prompter mirrors, 500–600 lux (46.5–55.7 fc) at *f*/2.8 may be more typical in a news studio.

By adjusting the camera channel's amplification (*video gain*) its effective sensitivity can be considerably increased – but at the cost of higher picture noise. Much depends on the lens aperture that you wish to work at. For instance, a camera requiring 2000 lux (186 fc) at *f*/8, will only need 13 lux (1.2 fc) when opened up to *f*/1.8 with 18 dB gain. Open up further to *f*/1.4, and even 7.5 lux (0.7 fc) will provide satisfactory pictures!

There are camera systems that will work effectively under really low-light conditions, producing acceptable pictures with excellent color balance down to around 1 lux. But for near-darkness or moonlight level conditions, a special *image intensifier* is needed, which will still produce useful pictures with as little as 0.02 lux illumination!

The relative amount of light needed on the scene at various lens apertures (taking *f*/4 as unity) varies:

f/1.4	*f*/2	*f*/2.8	*f*/3.5	*f*/4	*f*/4.5	*f*/5	*f*/5.6	*f*/6.3	*f*/8
1/8	1/4	1/2	3/4	1	1/4	1 1/2	2	2 1/2	4
← Less light					→ More light				

Video gain adjustment

Although superficially the effect may be similar, there are important differences between increasing the *camera channel's gain* to boost picture strength and opening up the *lens aperture*. Extra video amplification boosts the inadequate video signal, and so increases picture noise. Increasing the *lens aperture* provides the CCD with improved exposure, so results in a stronger, less noisy video signal – although depth of field will be reduced in the process. Here is a comparison between the two methods:

Increased gain	+3	+6	+9	+12	+18	+24 dB
Equivalent increase in lens aperture (stop)	1/2 stop	1 stop	1 1/2 stops	2 stops	3 stops	4 stops

Shutter speeds

Because the TV system provides images at 1/60th second (NTSC) or 1/50th second (PAL, SECAM) intervals, anything that is moving at a faster rate is normally reproduced as a blur. We are not usually aware if this. It can even add to the impression of speed; as when watching a pirouetting skater. But if you freeze a frame while watching a videotape replay it becomes very obvious. Detail is blurred. By shortening the duration of the electronic pulse that reads out the image charge on the camera's CCD it is possible to shorten the *effective exposure time*. This may be switchable (e.g. 1/60th (in PAL)–1/125th–1/500th–1/1000th–1/2000th of a second), or continuously variable, depending on camera design. The briefer the setting of this *electronic shutter*, the more clearly will moving subjects be reproduced in a slow-motion replay or a still. Now instead of a bicycle wheel appearing as a blurred disc in a single video frame, all its details will be clearly visible. This technique also reduces the problems of traveling bars or flicker when shooting computer screens or TV receivers.

However, there is a price to pay. Now we may see an unnatural flicker or break-up when a recording of moving subjects is replayed at normal speed. In some cases – e.g. flames, waving flag, wind-blown foliage – this can be quite distracting.

Because the briefer shutter time reduces the amount of light available for the CCD, it's necessary to open up the lens aperture proportionally to compensate:

Shutter speed	1/50	1/125	1/250	1/500	1/1000	1/2000	second
Open lens aperture (approximate)	0	1	2	3	4	5	stops

Supporting the camera

If you are shooting while traveling over uneven ground, climbing stairs, in amongst a crowd . . . your audience expects pictures to bounce around. At times this can even add to the excitement! But pictures that weave about, bounce up and down, lean on one side soon become tiring to watch. Smooth subtle movement and rock-steady shots are essential for effective camerawork, and there are various forms of support to help you achieve this.

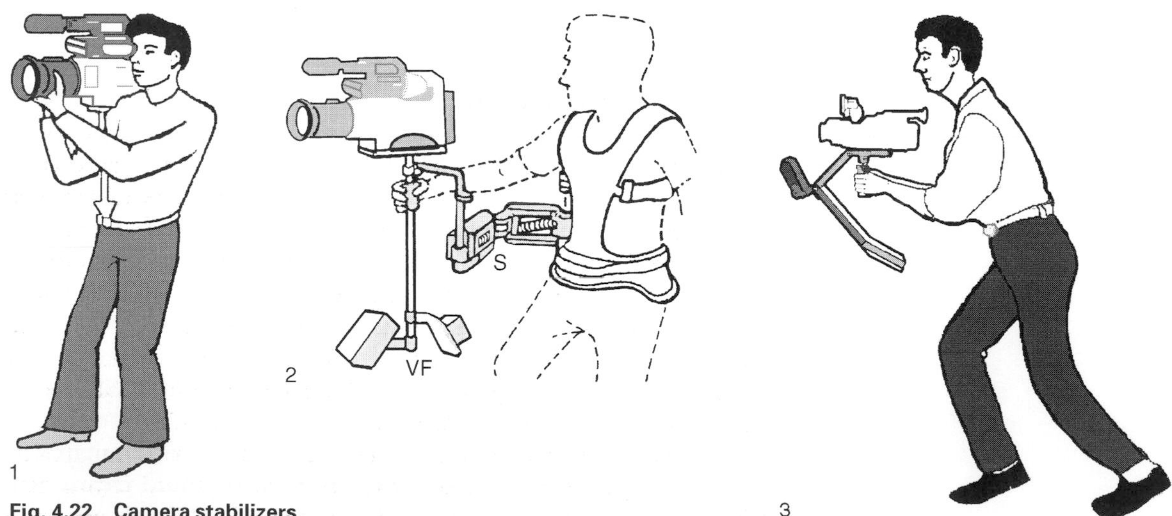

Fig. 4.22 Camera stabilizers
To increase the stability of hand-held cameras:

1 Some form of shoulder-support/ shoulder-pod, brace or body harness may be worn.
2 In the *Steadicam* system, an elaborate spring-stabilized harness (S) is used to hold the camera steady, even during violent movement. A 4-inch electronic viewfinder (adjustable position) is fitted to the support arm (VF).
3 A smaller form of hand-held spring-balanced camera stabilizer is available for lightweight cameras.

What type of support?

Before tackling any project, consider whether you have an appropriate camera mounting (or a suitable substitute). Otherwise you may not be able to get the kind of shot that the director is aiming at! The kind of camera support you need will depend on a number of very practical factors.

- The size and weight of your camera. Do you intend *hand-holding* or *shoulder-mounting* the camera? Will the shots be brief or are you shooting sustained action?
- Are you shooting from a *fixed position*, moving only while '*off-shot*', or moving while shooting ('*on-shot*'). Will there be any *quick moves* to other camera positions?
- Do you expect to be *moving around at a preset height* or expect to vary the camera height? Will you be changing height while shooting, or off-shot?
- Will you want *high/very high or low/very low* shots? Will you be raising/lowering the camera to these positions or even swooping or gliding within the action?
- Your surroundings can influence the type of mounting you use – the floor surface, the operational space, height. Does the mounting have room to move around within the scene, round furniture, through doorways, between trees . . .?
- Is the camera likely to be unsteady? Are you shooting while walking/running or from a moving vehicle?
- Finally, there are those situations where the solution is a remotely controlled camera mounted on an overhead rail system, a robotic pedestal, or even a self-propelled camera car.

The hand-held camera

If you are holding a *compact lightweight camera* the trick is to support it firmly; but not so tightly that your own slightest movements are transmitted to the shot. Your right hand is through an adjustable support strap near the zoom controls or holding a molded grip beneath the camera. Your left hand holds the lens barrel. Holding the eyepiece viewfinder against an eye helps to steady the camera. (Whether you make hand adjustments or rely on auto-controls (*auto-focus, motorized zoom, auto-iris*) will largely depend on camera design and shooting conditions.)

The lighter the camera, the more difficult it is to hold it steady. Make use of a nearby stable structure such as a wall if you can. (You'll see various regular ways of steadying a hand-held camera in Figure 4.23.) Where you need to rest your camera on a rough or uneven surface a small bag containing sand ('*sandbag*') or filled with plastic or ceramic granules ('*bean bag*') will help to support it firmly.

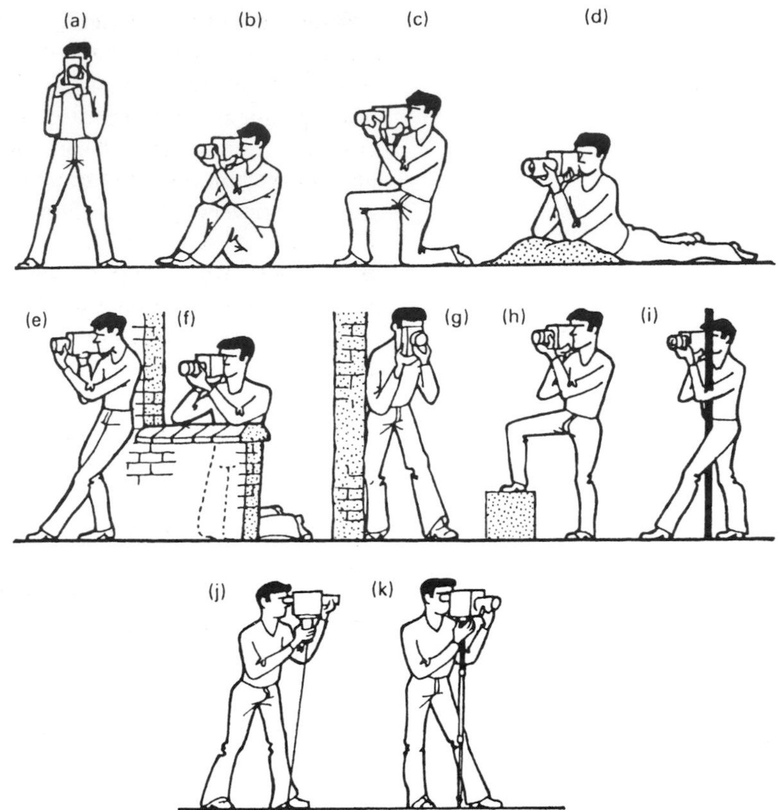

Fig. 4.23 Hand-held supports
Any camera shake causes the picture to weave and hop about, so it is essential to hold it as rigidly as possible. Grip your camera firmly (but not too tightly) with your eye against the eyepiece and both arms tucked well in. Various techniques help to steady the camera:

1 Stable body positions: (a) legs braced apart; (b) seated, elbow on knees; (c) kneeling; (d) ground support.
2 Nearby supports: (e) back to wall; (f) resting on low wall, fence, railings, car etc: (g) leaning side against wall; (h) foot on step or box; (i) resting against post.
3 String or chain support (j) attached beneath camera, trapped under one foot and pulled upwards.
4 Monopod; (k) single-leg telescopic tube, or pole.

Some camera lens systems include an *image stabilizer* that is inbuilt or attached to the lens system to steady slight picture movements (*see Digests – Image stabilizer*).

Camera stabilizers

The widespread technique of supporting the camera on one shoulder has its limitations. Its success largely depends on your stamina! Some people can continue shooting over long periods, without their pictures leaning over to one side, wavering or drooping. But arms tire and back muscles ache after a while, and it is not easy to sustain high-grade camerawork, particularly when shooting with narrower lens angles.

A U-shaped molded saddle or *shoulder mount* attached beneath the camera makes it more comfortable to support, and prevents it from slipping. Your left hand adjusts the *focusing ring* and the *lens aperture ring (f/stop)* on the lens barrel and the *manual zoom control lever*. The right hand fitted through the support strap on the zoom lens operates the *power-zoom switch* (to auto-zoom in/out), and the *iris selection switch* (**M** – manual: **A** – auto-iris; **R** – remote iris control). Your right thumb may press the VTR pause switch.

When shooting for long periods with a shoulder-mounted camera you may find that wearing a *body brace* or *shoulder harness* helps to keep pictures steady. A metal prop fastened beneath the camera rests in a chest pad or a belt-support. However, such body mounts can be restrictive, and 'breathing bounce' may cause vertical picture movement and be difficult to avoid.

The *monopod* is a very useful 'just-in-case' device to carry around. It simply consists of a collapsible metal tube of adjustable length, which screws into a socket beneath the camera. By bracing it against your foot, knee, or leg, a monopod can provide a surprisingly firm camera support. No panning head is needed, and you can carry the camera around with it fitted ready to shoot. Although not self-supporting, this mounting works equally well on flat or uneven ground. You simply swivel round or tilt the camera to follow moving subjects – taking care to avoid sloping horizons.

The most advanced form of camera stabilizer such as the *Steadicam* system uses a body harness with ingenious counterbalance springs. Stabilizers of this kind will not only absorb any camera shake but actually allow you to run, climb stairs, jump, shoot from moving vehicles . . . while still providing smooth controlled shots! The operator uses a small electronic viewfinder attached to the stabilizer. Near-magical results are possible that are unattainable with other camera mountings. But underneath it all there is still a vulnerable human operator, and extended work under these conditions can be very tiring.

For *small-format/consumer cameras* a simpler, more compact balanced support is available (e.g. *Steadicam Jr*) that offers similar stabilization while moving around.

Fixed cameras

There are occasions when you want a camera to work from a fixed or static position.

- *Isolated camera* – Here the camera is set up to cover a particular area, and *locked off*. This situation could arise on a *remote*, where there is no room for an operator. Similarly, you can attach an isolated camera to the outside of a *moving vehicle* using *limpet mounts* (powerful suction cups), or fitted to clamped-on *support beams*.
- *Remote control* – Here a distant operator controls the movements (zoom/focus/pan/tilt) of one or more cameras, following a picture monitor(s) display.
- *Auto-control* – This isolated camera uses *lock-follower* electronics to pan/tilt/focus on a chosen subject.
- *Isolated operator* – The camera operator works on a camera tower, balcony, or similarly isolated spot.

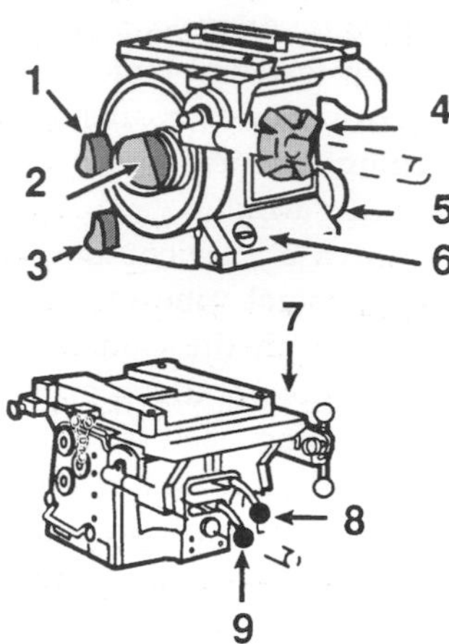

Fig. 4.24 Camera mounting head (panning head, pan head)
This takes several different forms (*see Digests*). Attached to the top of a camera mounting (e.g. a tripod), it allows the camera head to be tilted up and down on a central pivot, and turned on a central turntable. Controlled by an attached *panning handle* (*pan bar*), friction (*drag*) can be introduced to improve handling. Further controls lock off the head, and adjust balance.

A wedge plate beneath the camera head fits into the quick-release housing on the mounting head.

1 Tilt lock
2 Tilt drag
3 Pan lock
4 Camera head horizontal balance
5 Pan drag
6 Level bubble
7 Tilt drag
8 Tilt lock
9 Pan lock

The panning head (pan-and-tilt head; camera mounting head)

As you might expect, there are several types of head designed to suit different types and weights of camera. (You will find details in the *Digests – Panning head (camera mounting head)*.)

If you simply bolted your camera onto a mounting it would be held firmly enough but quite unable to move around to follow the action. Instead you need a *panning head/camera mounting head*, which goes between the camera head and the top of the camera mounting. It firmly anchors the camera, yet allows it to be turned (*panned*) and tilted, or fixed at any required angle.

The regular method of fastening uses a wedge-shaped plate (*wedge mount/camera wedge*) attached to the underside of the camera head. This slides into a corresponding recessed plate on top of the *panning head*. (Lightweight cameras often use quick-release *wedge mounts*.)

Panning handles are attached to either side of the panning head for the camera operator to support and guide the camera. They may have a center-joint that allows them to be hinged to a convenient angle. (Zoom and focus controls are clipped to the panning handles.)

If the camera head moves around too easily it can be difficult to make smooth, even panning and tilting movements. So *drag* controls allow you to introduce a controlled amount of friction, to steady movements. They should never be overtightened to 'lock-off' the camera. If you want to prevent panning or tilting (e.g. when holding a superimposed graphic, or when leaving or storing the camera) use the separate *head locks*.

Balance adjustments ensure that the camera remains level when it is not being supported by the camera operator. Careful balancing is absolutely essential when you have large zoom lenses, prompting devices, camera lamps attached to the camera, or it will be front-heavy and difficult to operate. In some situations it might even overbalance the mounting!

A point to bear in mind when assessing mountings is that when the camera head is fitted on the pan and tilt head its actual lens height can be some 30–45 cm (12–18 in.) higher than their quoted heights.

Choosing the camera mounting

Camera tripods

Collapsible tripod

Although the tripod cannot be repositioned quickly it does have advantages. It is simple, robust, and can be folded up into an easily

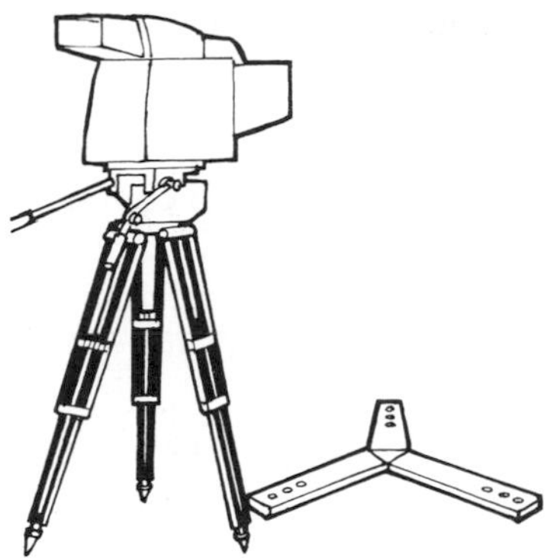

Fig. 4.25 The tripod
A simple 3-legged stand with independently extensible legs. Height is preset. Unlike other mountings it can be set up on sloping or uneven ground.

A *spider* (spreader) may be used to prevent tripod feet slipping.

transported pack. It can be used in situations where no other could go: on rough, uneven, overgrown surfaces, on staircases, in vehicles . . .

Basically, the tripod has three legs of independently adjustable length. They may be wooden or metal (steel or aluminum) or carbon fiber. These are spread apart to form a stable base for the camera. You can screw the camera onto the tripod's panning head and simply close the tripod legs together, when moving to a new position. Better still, use a quick-release *mounting plate (wedge)* which allows the camera to be detached in a moment.

Tripods can be preadjusted to various heights (e.g. 600 mm (20 in.)) to 1600 mm (63 in.) by altering the leg lengths. Some units have a central camera-support column, which can be hand-cranked to adjust height while off shot.

Tripods are a great help if they are used properly, but they are not foolproof. Here are some useful warnings:

- Don't use a flimsy lightweight tripod. It will be flexible and insecure for a video camera.
- Don't be tempted to use the tripod partly open, for it will overbalance! Always adjust camera height by altering leg-length, not by changing the spread.
- At maximum height the tripod tends to be unstable. Bottom weighting (e.g. a bag of sand or stones slung under the center of the tripod) or ground-lashings (rope-fastening to a ground-spike) may be a wise precaution – particularly if the ground is sloping, or slippery.
- Don't leave your camera standing unattended on its tripod. People (or animals) may knock it over; a pulled cable may overbalance it.
- Tripods usually have two types of feet: retractable spikes for rough surfaces and rubber pads for smooth ground. (Take care not to use spikes on carpets, wooden floors, etc.!)
- On uneven ground (rocks, stairs) you can fix tripod legs at different lengths, so that the camera remains level as you pan. A level indicator (spirit-level) helps here. Some panning heads incorporate an adjustable *leveling bowl* which can be quickly released and repositioned to compensate for uneven terrain.
- The feet of a tripod can be fitted onto a Y-shaped *spreader* or *spider* to prevent its feet from slipping. On soft ground, sand, or mud it is best to use a flat triangular wooden base.
- At maximum tripod heights you may have difficulty seeing into the viewfinder (have a step or box handy). Low-angle shots, too, can pose difficulties when following moving subjects.
- If you have a wide panning movement, stand with your body at a midway point, ready to twist from side to side. It may be easier to follow action in a nearby picture monitor than in the viewfinder.

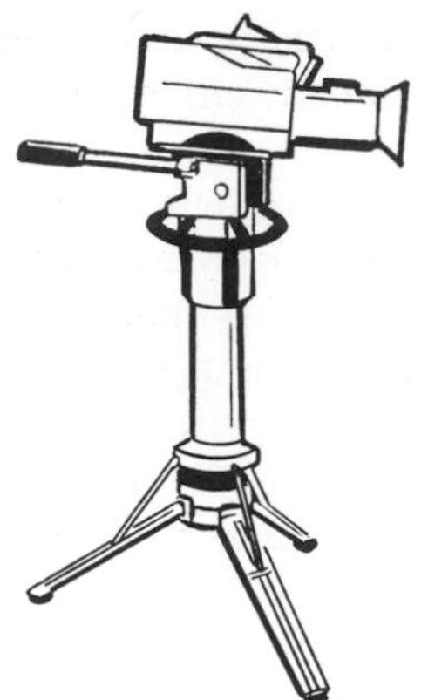

Fig. 4.26 Lightweight pneumatic tripod (Hydro-Ped, PortaPed)
A robust tripod mounting, widely used in ENG/EFP production.

Pneumatic tripod (Hydro-Ped; PortaPed)

Although quite portable (e.g. 13 kg (30 lb) in weight) the *pneumatic tripod* provides a very adaptable rigid support for cameras weighing up to e.g. 45 kg (100 lb), even when panning or tilting. It comprises two concentric columns, which can be locked at any point over their 48 cm (18 in.) travel. It uses a pneumatic counterbalance system, in which the center column is pumped up and down, before locking off a valve.

The hinged legs at the lower end occupy little spread (40 cm (16 in.)), so can be used in very confined spaces. The mounting remains balanced, even when one of the independently adjusted legs is up on a step or curb. It can be used with its legs turned out at right angles to the column (0.69–1.14 m (27–45 in.) height), or in a tripod mode (0.94–1.4 m (37–55 in.) height).

Although normally a fixed mounting, it can be fitted onto a *crabbing dolly* to provide a very flexible mobile mounting.

Rolling tripod/tripod dolly

This is basically a tripod on wheels. It can be very suitable for simpler studio operations, and its portability makes it extremely useful for remotes.

The tripod fits onto a detachable three-castered base (*skid; skate*), which can be folded for transportation. Although the dolly moves around quite easily on a flat level floor, uneven surfaces will judder the picture, especially when you use narrow lens angles. In practice, it is not always easy to control the dolly's direction

Fig. 4.27 The rolling tripod/tripod dolly
The tripod can be mounted onto a castered base (skid/skate/rolling spider). Height is preset (pneumatic or hand-crank). Easily wheeled on a flat smooth floor (although steering may be imprecise). Caster foot-brakes, and cable guards may be fitted.

accurately. It often helps to give the dolly a slight push beforehand, to align the casters in the appropriate direction. Otherwise the picture may jerk as you start to move.

The casters can be left to move in any direction (freewheel), or locked to dolly in a straight line. Cable guards prevent the wheels overrunning floor cables. To hold the mounting immobile, you can either lock off each angled caster or wind down *screw-jacks* (taking care not to damage the floor surface).

In some designs it is necessary to reset the tripod leg lengths to change camera height, and this takes some time and effort.

Camera pedestals

The *pedestal (ped)* is the most widely used studio TV camera mounting. Fundamentally, it consists of a central column of adjustable height, fixed to a three-wheeled base which is guided by a steering wheel and/or a handle (tiller arm).

The rubber-tired wheels can be switched into either

- a *'crab'* mode in which all three wheels are interlinked to move together,
- or a *'steer'*/*'dolly'* mode where a single wheel steers while the other two remain passive.

Pedestal designs range from preset lightweight hydraulic columns on casters to heavyweight monstrosities that can need two people to move them. The ideal pedestal is stable, easy to move, and quickly controlled by one person.

Lightweight/field pedestal

Pedestals for use away from the studio need to be robust but compact, and preferably demountable. Simpler forms have hand-cranked column-height adjustment. (Height-changes are jerky, so have to be made off-shot.) The camera is steered around by its panning handles.

More sophisticated pedestal designs have pneumatically controlled height adjustment. Their height can be changed smoothly while on shot, and the mounting steered accurately by a central surround-ring.

Column and base may be separated for easier transportation. The camera height range is typically around 0.6 m (2 ft) to 1.5 m (6 ft). Where lightweight cameras are used in a studio they have proved very adaptable.

Studio pedestal

Pushing a pedestal around for long periods, with a full-size studio camera, large heavy-duty zoom lens, attached video prompter and a trailing camera cable, can take stamina and dexterity. In a complex show, you may find yourself needing to zoom, refocus, pan, tilt, change height, push, and guide the dolly simultaneously – yet control all these movements smoothly and accurately! When shooting at eye level this can be a difficult feat. At maximum or minimum column heights it becomes impracticable. Then you may well need someone to help by pushing the pedestal while you handle the camera head.

When using a pedestal the camera height can be adjusted smoothly and precisely, even while on shot, and held firmly in position at heights from about 1–2 m (3–6 ft). A large ring steering wheel around the central telescopic column is used to raise/lower the camera, as well as guide dolly moves. There may be a subsidiary ring to lock off the column height.

The method of adjusting the column height of the pedestal varies. It may be hand-cranked, motor-driven, counterbalanced, hydraulic, or pneumatic. In practice, some types are slow to operate, erratic, heavy; others are smooth and easy, but require expert attention.

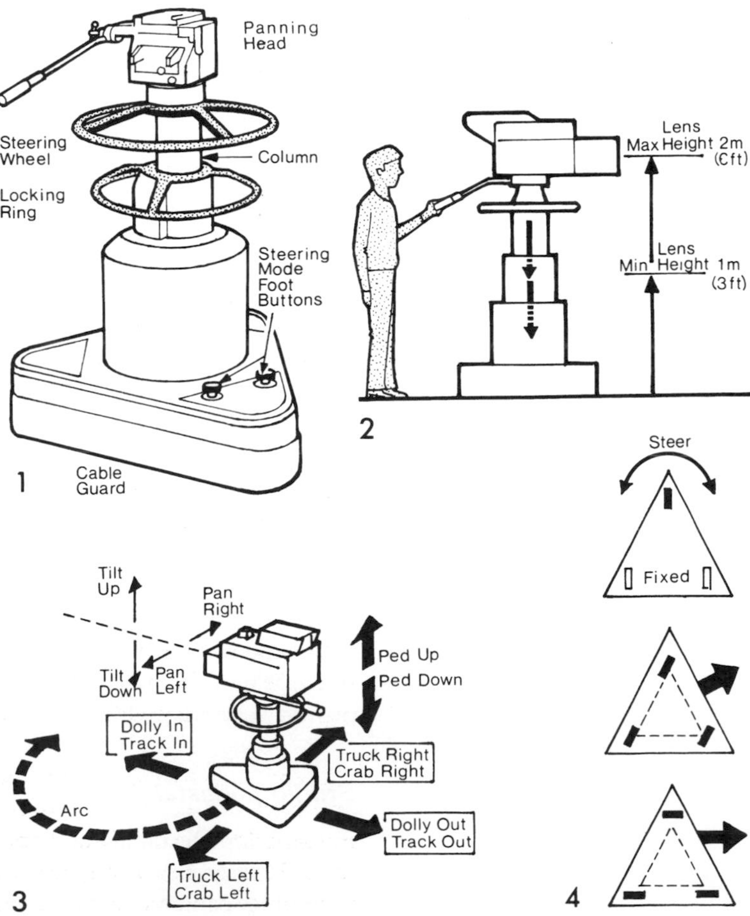

Fig. 4.28 The studio pedestal

1 A surround wheel or ring at the top of the column is used to adjust column height (hence the lens height) and to steer the pedestal. A second ring may be fitted to lock-off the column.
2 The lens-height range is typically 1–2 m (3–6 ft).
3 The camera can be moved around and repositioned in various ways.
4 The rubber-tired tricycle wheels can be steered in either of two ways (foot-pedal selection).
Dolly (*tricycle, tracking*) *mode*: single wheel steered, other two fixed. Used for general dolly moves and curved tracks (arcs).
Crab (*parallel*) *mode*: all three wheels interlinked, steered simultaneously. Used for trucking – crabbing, sideways movements, moving into confined spaces.

■ *Counterweight type* In this widely used type of pedestal a series of traveling weights and springs counter the weight of the central column. These can be adjusted to compensate for the weight of different types of camera. The system is reliable and works smoothly – but the overall weight of the mounting is formidable, particularly when a large zoom lens and a prompter are fitted to the camera head. Fast dolly moves are impracticable. Because its height range is limited to about 1.2–2 m (4–6.5 ft) its productional use is restricted.

■ *Pneumatic type* The *lightweight ped* is considerably lighter than the counterweighted form. It can be moved around quickly and smoothly, so it allows much more mobile camerawork. It uses compressed air (or an inert gas) from a small tank to control the height of the multiple central column. The mounting has a useful lens-height range – e.g. 1 to 2 m (3 to + 6 ft)

One disadvantage of the pneumatic pedestal is that changes in camera weight (e.g. adding or removing a heavy prompter) can require the air-pressure to be readjusted ('re-gassing') by releasing or adding compressed air to the system.

Camera cranes

Jib arms

As film makers have demonstrated so successfully over the years, a large *camera crane* offers the director an impressive range of shot opportunities. It can hover . . . then swoop in to join the action. Or it can draw back . . . rising dramatically, to reveal the broader scene. It allows the camera to travel rapidly above the heads of a crowd, or to sweep around near floor level as it follows dancers' movements. But such visual magic is only achieved at a price! Larger camera cranes are cumbersome, need a lot of room to maneuver, and require skilled and closely coordinated crews. Today, relatively few TV studios make use of such camera cranes. Instead the modern *jib arm* in its various forms or a small *studio crane* satisfy most directors' aims.

The main feature of the *jib arm* is its long extendable *jib* (*boom, beam*). This is counterbalanced on a central column, which may be supported on a tripod, a camera pedestal, or a four-wheeled platform. The camera itself is usually suspended in a cradle at the upper end of the jib and remotely controlled (tilt, pan, focus, exposure) by an operator who is standing beside the counterweight at the lower end, watching a picture monitor.

Smaller lightweight jibs are easily disassembled and transported, and have proved to be extremely adaptable both in the studio and in the field. The crank-up tripod on which the jib is mounted takes up a floor space of only around 2 × 2 m (6 × 6 ft). Typically the preadjusted telescopic jib elevates to a height of around 3 m (10 ft).

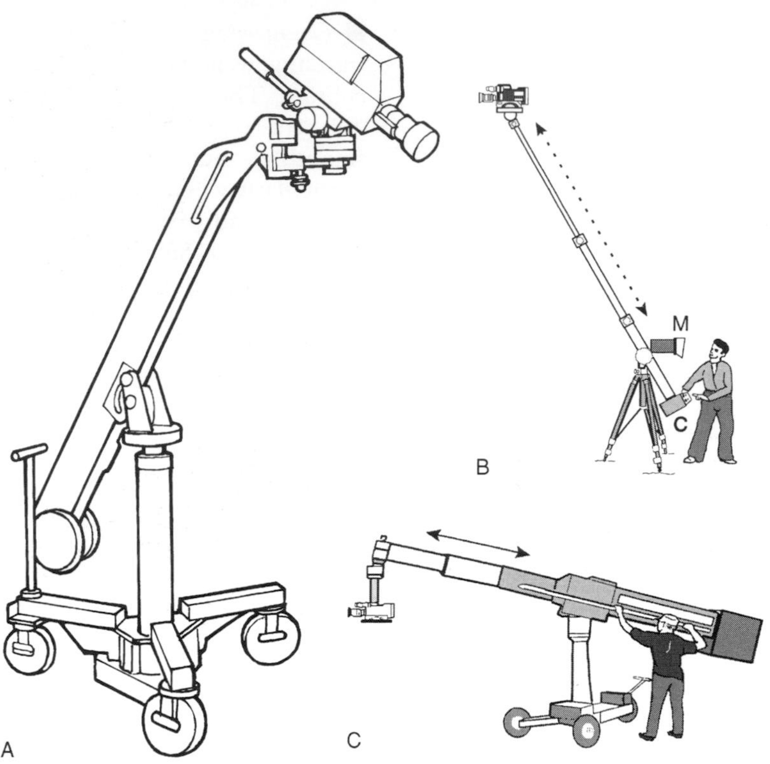

Fig. 4.29 Jib mountings
Part 1. A The jib is a counter-balanced beam attached to a pedestal, tripod, or wheeled base. It enables the camera at its end, to move in an arc over a range of heights from ground level to an overhead position. The camera may be pre-adjusted, or controlled remotely.
Part 1.B The jib arm of this lightweight design, can be extended to pre-set lengths. The camera is remotely controlled from a control box (C) at its lower end, by the operator who follows an attached picture monitor (M).
Part 1.C For larger cameras, or when working at much greater heights (e.g. 40 ft (12 m)) the heavy duty jib provides increased opportunities.

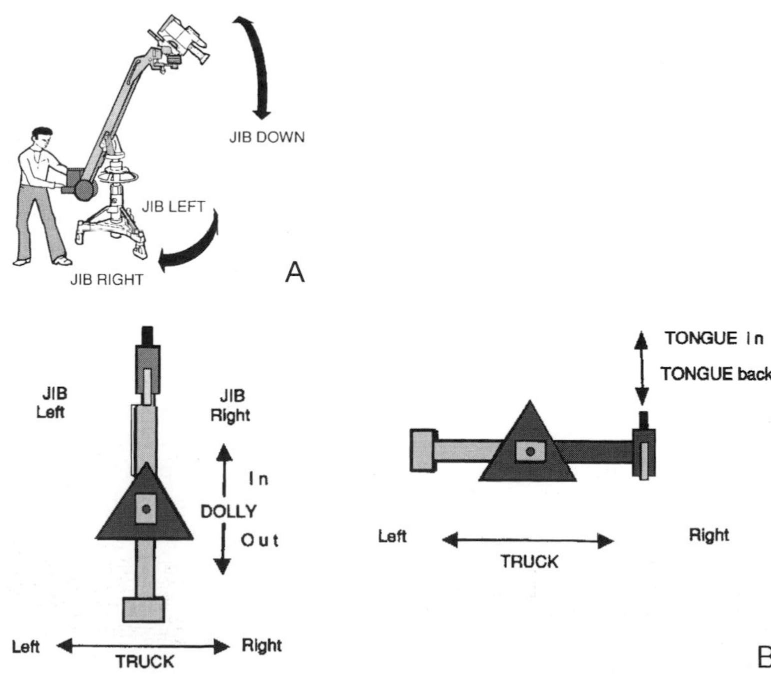

Jib movements
Part 2. A The main beam of the jib may be swung up/down (*jib up, jib down*), or turned left/right (*jib left, jib right*). Where the camera is remotely controlled the usual *pan* and *tilt* instructions apply. Movements of the jib or crane arm are also referred to as *craning, booming, jibbing.*
Part 2. B Swinging the jib or crane arm sideways is *tonguing* (or *craning*) *left/right.* Swinging it to or from the action is tonguing *in/back.* The more robust mountings may be moved and steered; using a tracking line to/from the action (*dollying/tracking*), or move across the action area (*tracking, crabbing*).

Fig. 4.30 The small crane
Lightweight versions of the small crane are sometimes used.

Particularly for remotes, the height range (0.6–2 m, 2–7 ft) with 360° seat and camera-mounting rotation offer improved shot flexibility (Vinten–Kestrel)

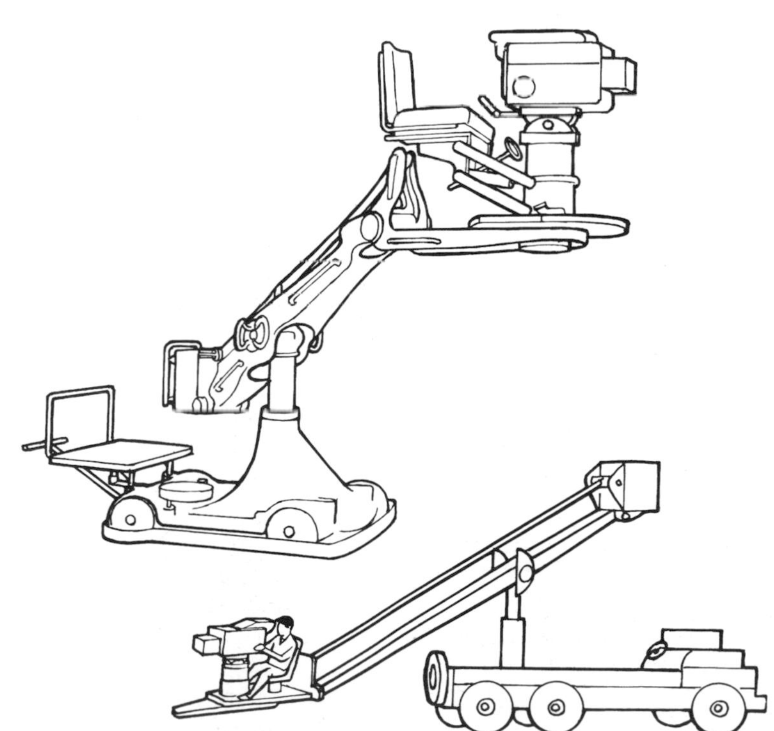

Fig. 4.31 Larger cranes
Heavy-duty cranes are normally used where extensive camera viewpoint changes, high-angle or swooping shots are required for large-scale action. Thanks to precision counter-balancing, the boom can be swung manually by a single operator (guided by a picture monitor and camera operator's finger-signals).

SPECIAL MOUNTINGS

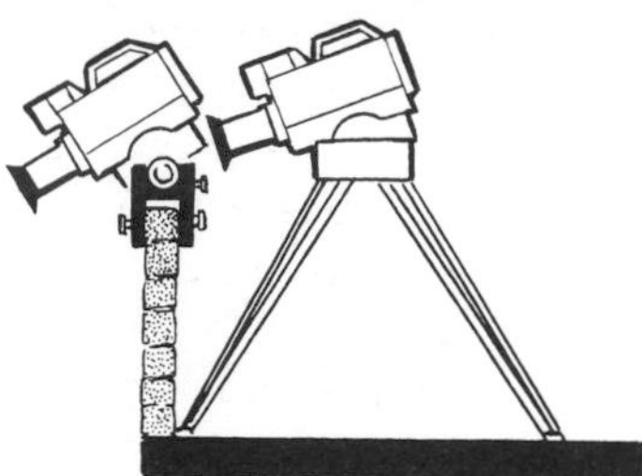

Fig. 4.32 part 1 Tripod limitations
When a tripod is positioned on a platform or balcony, it has to be set back some distance from the edge. As a result, its downward view is limited, particularly where there is a protective wall. If instead the camera head is fastened to a wall clamp fitting, it will have greater coverage.

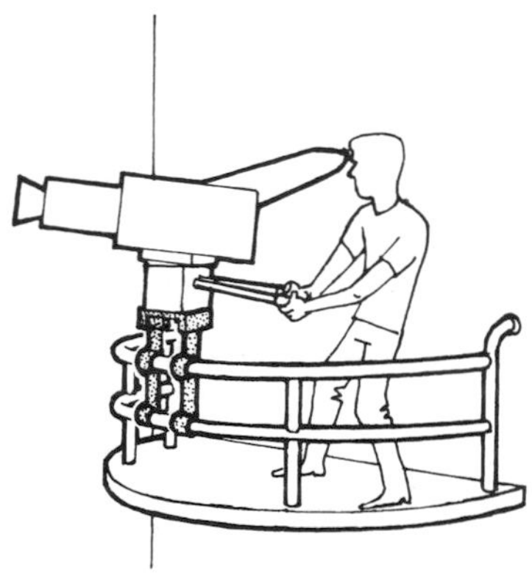

Fig. 4.32 part 2 Camera clamps
The panning head may be clamped to a firm tubular-rail structure at a vantage point.

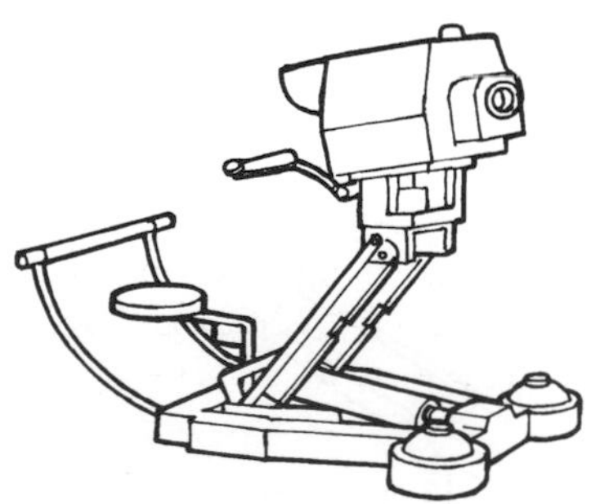

Fig. 4.32 part 3 Low angle dolly ('sled')
Gives height-mobility for low-angle shots, together with considerable maneuverability

(Some systems can be extended to 7 m (21 ft) in just 30 seconds.) All the camera controls including focus, iris, zoom, tilt and pan are precision adjusted remotely, using hand or foot operation.

Large mobile jib-cranes which have controllable jib length are used on location and are capable of attaining impressive heights at open air events, e.g. for elevated vista shots surveying a golf course or a race track.

- *Advantages* – A *jib arm* is more compact than the traditional camera crane, much more portable, and a lot less costly to buy or hire. The camera on a jib arm may be handled by a single operator. It can stretch out over the action (like a crane), overreaching any foreground objects. (A pedestal or tripod dolly reaching an obstruction can go no further.) It can support the camera at any height within its range, moving smoothly and rapidly from just above floor level up to its maximum, and swing round over a 360° arc. Its camera can also pan freely over a 360° arc.
- *Handling limitations*
  Smaller jib systems. Although some operators assert that they can dolly and swing smaller jib systems *while on shot*, results can be very uncertain. Like the *small sound boom*, this type of mounting can be rather unwieldy; and when fully extended there is a certain amount of instability. The camera on its end always swings in an *arc*; whether you are raising, lowering or turning the jib. So it cannot travel along *parallel* with action.
  Large jib arms require two or three operators. One controls the camera, another the jib, and a further operator pushes/guides the mounting. The jib can be successfully raised/lowered/tongued, while panning and tilting and dollying – although to do this reliably every time, with well-framed shots throughout, requires subtle coordination, and a deal of practice!

Small cranes

On the *small crane* (*studio crane*) the camera with its operator seated behind it is mounted at one end of a short *jib* (*jib-arm*, *boom*, *tongue*, *crane-arm*). The lower end is hinged to a steerable four-wheeled platform or dolly. The crane's jib may be raised/lowered manually (hand-crank), hydraulically, or by an electric motor. On some cranes the entire jib can be slewed sideways on a turntable for *tonguing* movements.

In some cranes the camera together with its operator can rotate over a wide arc at any height to follow the action. Where only the camera turns, it becomes increasingly difficult for the stationary operator to follow its viewfinder as the camera is panned.

The camera operator is assisted by a crew, who adjust camera height, push and steer the dolly, and feed the camera cable –

variously called *camera assistants, dolly operators, grips, trackers.* They are guided by intercom instructions, an attached picture monitor, and by finger signals from the camera operator.

Cranes which are steered by only one set of wheels can need a fair amount of floor space to reposition. Where *all* the mounting's wheels can be turned (*crabbing*), it can be moved in any direction within a much smaller area.

When a camera mounting is fitted with *solid-tired* wheels a level even floor surface is essential to ensure smooth dollying. Where the ground is uneven, special *camera rails* or *tracks*, or *floor boarding* may be necessary. On location, pneumatic tires are fitted to larger cranes to absorb ground irregularities.

Typical camera heights for smaller cranes range from around 0.6 to 2 m (2 to 7 ft). All crane and jib operation needs a watchful eye. It is all to easy to depress the jib onto something or someone beneath its overhang, or to raise the camera and hit suspended lamps, ceilings, etc.

Film dollies

Camera mountings that are widely used in film making have been equally successful in TV production. *Crab dollies*, which are similar to small cranes (i.e. camera supported on a column or a jib), have the advantage that they can be steered by the rear wheels or crabbed sideways to move around in any direction. The *spyder dolly* which resembles a camera pedestal is very adaptable on location. At its base, the four outstretched legs can be spread or confined as needed (e.g. to pass through doorways), with its wheels selected to run on the floor or on tubular track. For full camera movements, the spyder dolly can be fitted with a centrally pivoted counter-weighted *crane-arm (jib, boom)*

Special mountings

There are situations where more traditional forms of camera mounting cannot get the shot you want. Then various other approaches may solve the problem.

Low shots

■ *Low tripod* Short fixed tripods, which are considerably more stable than full-size versions, can be effective for many low shots.

■ *High hat* Surprisingly versatile, the *high hat*, and its smaller *lo-boy* version, can be useful if you need a very low viewpoint. The camera fits onto a short cylindrical base, which is bolted or screwed onto any firm foundation – a platform, a rolling tripod base, or a heavy-duty lighting stand.

■ *Low-angle dolly (sled; creeper)* Here the camera operator sits on a very low wheeled base, which is pushed by an assistant. The camera may be fitted to a high hat (fixed height) or a short crane-arm (rising from e.g. 0.5 to 1.1 m (1½ to 3½ ft).

■ *Alternative methods* You can also get low-angle shots by shooting into a low mirror, or using a mirror periscope attached to a pedestal mounting.

High shots

In the studio you might be able to get suitable high-angled shots by shooting up into an overhead mirror, or using a crane at full elevation. But on location the scale of operations changes.

■ *Camera clamp* If your camera is to be located on a balcony, a camera frame/camera tower or some similar structure, the obvious mounting to use is a firmly based tripod. However, there is a major drawback. The camera's vertical field is very limited. It cannot tilt down past the edge of the structure (Figure 4.25 part 2).

Instead, it may be better to fasten its panning head to a tubular steel scaffold framework, with a *camera clamp* (*scaffold clamp*). Wire safety bonds ensure that nothing is going to fall down onto unsuspecting passers-by.

■ *Large camera cranes* A truck-mounted giant camera crane or boom which has a typical range of e.g. 1–8.2 m (3½–27 ft) may be hired, together with its own crew. The camera operator with safety helmet and harness, sitting at the end of the long counterweighted boom, needs total confidence in the crew . . . and a good head for heights!

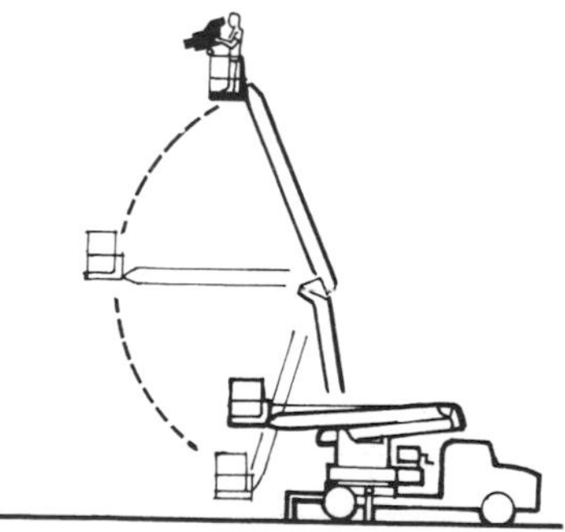

Fig. 4.33 Hydraulic platform Considerable platform-height variation is possible (even while on shot), giving a high stable viewpoint.

■ *Hydraulic platform (cherry-picker; Simon crane)* If you need really high shots on location this hired facility can provide staggering viewpoints. It comprises a truck-mounted hydraulic lifting platform, which can raise the camera from 1.8 to 26 m (6 to 85 ft) above the ground. It can also be used to position microwave dishes (radio links) for remote telecasts or ENG work.

If you want to go higher than 26 m you need the services of a helicopter (or a blimp) – with a special camera-stabilizing device to avoid rhythmic vibration. Extremely effective aerial shots have been obtained from video cameras attached to radio-controlled small-scale helicopters.

■ *Flying camera, cable cam, sky cam* This specialized facility has been used successfully over sports fields to provide a 'flying camera'. The remotely controlled camera (which is gyro-balanced) is suspended in the center of an X-pattern of overhead cables. Independent computer-controlled winches simultaneously adjust cable lengths, to rapidly reposition the camera at rates up to 43 kph (27 mph) anywhere over the action area. The camera's wide-ranging aerial views can go from zoomed-out vista shots to zoomed-in detail.

Remotely controlled cameras

In some types of production, where people always sit in pre-arranged fixed positions (e.g. newscasts), camera and sound operations are really minimal. So it becomes both practicable and more economical to reduce the normal studio crewing arrangements.

Some small off-base news studios are completely automated. A visiting reporter simply switches the equipment on entering, and picture and sound are routed to a distant news center. The system may be auto-controlled, or adjusted remotely.

Remotely controlled cameras are increasingly used for studio shows that follow a regular production pattern. Operated from a central desk in a nearby control room, typical shots are set up during rehearsal using joystick/trackball controls, and the system stores all information about the camera adjustments involved. Then at the touch of a key each camera self-adjusts to provide these prearranged shots.

Two kinds of camera arrangements are used in such systems:

- *Suspended pan-and-tilt systems* – In low-cost studios permanently fixed suspended cameras simplify operations and reduce

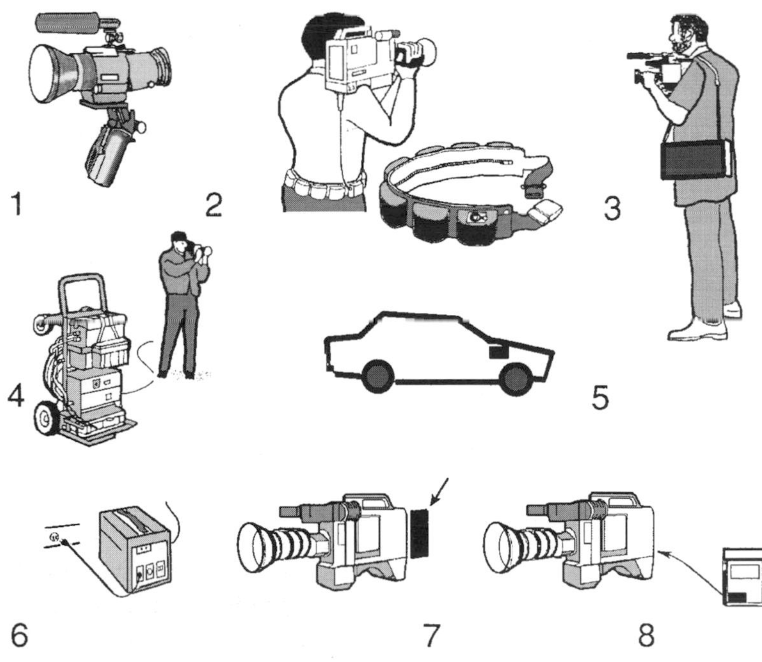

Fig. 4.34 Camera power
The camera can be powered in a number of different ways

1 Internal battery.
2 Battery belt.
3 Battery in shoulder pack.
4 Battery on camera trolley.
5 Car battery (using cigar-lighter socket).
6 A.C. adapter from public supply.
7 'On-board' attached battery.
8 Power from portable VCR.

staffing. But even for more complex situations, where a large assembly is covered from many angles by a series of camera positions (e.g. a parliament), this approach provides a very effective way of selecting and coordinating shots. Cameras can be arranged in optimum positions, as no space is required for operators. (Lens apertures are selected to give a generous depth of field, so focusing readjustments are unnecessary.)

- *Fully robotic systems* – In this arrangement, as well as controlling pan, tilt, and zoom, the *cameras' heights* and *positions* can be selected at the remote control desk. Shots are recalled by pointing to miniature stills of the preset shots on a *touch-screen display.* To guide camera moves, metal-foil tracking lines may be stuck to the floor.

In a further development, the program's computerized *prompter script* can include operational cues, which automatically carry out the selected changes. Needless to say, the system can be overridden and operated manually in an emergency!

Currently, robotic cameras are primarily used in news studios, where you have the choice of covering localized areas with their own separate cameras (i.e. anchor, newscaster, guests, weather-caster), or moving fewer cameras between areas. Typically, two cameras cover the newsdesk, then one moves over to the weather map for the forecast that follows.

Similarly, in general-purpose studios where the same working area is used for several different production set-ups (interviews, cooking), robotic cameras can be individually programed to suit each of the shows.

5 Handling your camera

Now that we have examined the camera's various features, let's turn to the *operational techniques* that are the foundation of good camerawork.

Standard shots

As film making developed, a universal system for classifying shots evolved. These provide convenient quick reference points for all members of the production team – especially for the director and the camera operator.

A series of 'standard' terms have evolved for the most effective shots of a single *person*. You'll find them in Figure 5.1. Terminology can vary from place to place, but the most widely recognized ones are included here. Use those that are current in your group! If in doubt, remember how these shots are framed; e.g. 'cutting *just below* the waist', '*just below* the knees'. Avoid framing that cuts through the body at natural joints.

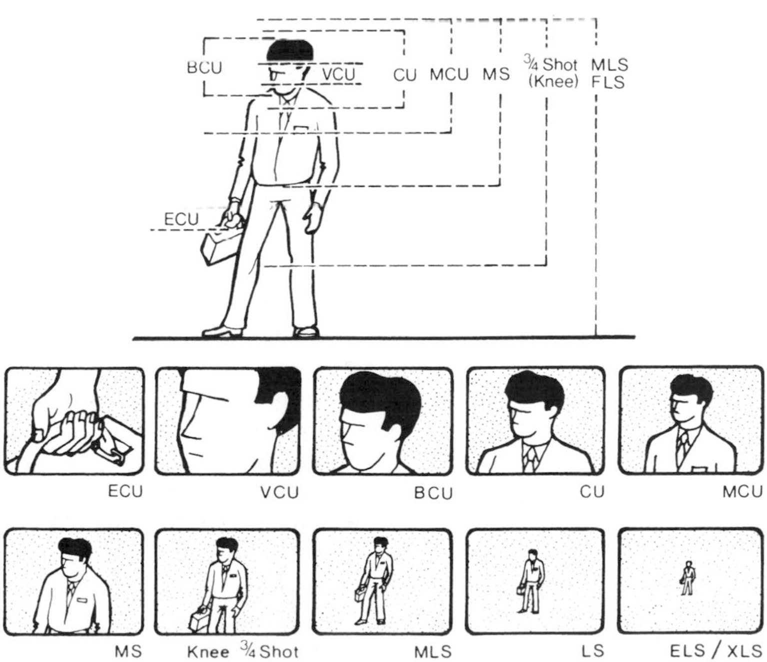

Fig. 5.1 Shots of people
Shots are classified by the amount of a person taken in:

ECU	Extreme close-up (detail shot) – isolated detail.
VCU	Very close-up (face shot) – from mid-forehead to above chin.
BCU	Big close-up (tight CU, full head) – full head height nearly fills screen.
CU	Close-up – just above head to upper chest (cuts below neck tie knot).
MCU	Medium close–up (bust shot, chest shot) – cuts body at lower chest (breast-pocket, armpit).
MS	Medium shot (mid-shot, close medium shot. CMS, waist shot) – cuts body just below waist.
KNEE	Knee shot, three-quarter length shot – cuts just below knees.
MLS	Medium long-shot (full-length shot. FLS) – entire body plus short distance above/below.
LS	Long shot – person occupies ¾ to ⅓ screen height.
ELS	Extra long shot (XLS). extreme LS.

Exactly *how* you get a particular shot does not affect the term used. For instance, you can take a *close shot* on a nearby camera with a wide-angle lens or with a distant camera on a narrow-angle lens. There will be differences, of course, in perspective distortion, camera handling, depending on which method you use. (Remember, the depth of field will remain the same for a given type of shot.)

Although you can be very specific when composing shots of *people*, pictures of other subjects have to be described more loosely. Sometimes it is more convenient to use broader terms:

- Indicating the lens's *coverage*:
  A '*long shot*' or '*full shot*' – A distant view.
  A '*wide shot*' or '*cover shot*' – A view taking in all the action.
  A '*close shot*' or a '*tight shot*' – A detailed shot, excluding other subjects nearby.
- Giving a general indication of the camera's *viewpoint*:
  A *frontal shot*, a *side view, three-quarters frontal, a back* or *rear view.*
- Referring to the camera's height (actual or apparent):
  A *low shot, level shot, high shot*, an *overhead* or *top shot.*
- Defining the camera's position relative to the performers:
  An '*over-shoulder shot*' or '*point-of-view shot*'.
- Describing the number of people to be included in the shot:
  A '*single shot*', a '*two shot*', a '*three shot*', or more generally, a '*group shot*'.

Remembering the shot

Most shots or sequences are rehearsed before being recorded. Ideally, during taping you want your shots to be an identical polished version of the rehearsal. There are three ways of ensuring this:

- Look around the shot carefully, and see what is just visible at the edges of the frame.
- Make a note, on a shot sheet/camera card attached to the camera, of shot details (e.g. '25°; *avoid doorway as she enters*'). If you are not given shot sheets, keep your own notes during rehearsal, on a card clipped to the camera. Don't rely on your memory alone.
- For the main camera viewpoints, make a clear but unobtrusive floor mark showing the exact position of one corner of the ped or dolly. Chalk or crayon may be suitable; but no form of permanent marker. (Masking tape or plastic tape is only acceptable *if* it is peeled off afterwards.)

Checking the shot

- Once a shot is established, a quick glance away to the overall scene can warn you of potential problems; e.g. that you are nearly shooting off the setting; that a lamp or another camera will come into shot if you pan right. It will let you know that someone is about to move into the shot, and that you may need to recompose the picture to include them.
- Only lock off the head during breaks, or when pushing the pedestal to a new position, or when shooting titles and graphics on *floor stands*.
- Check your viewfinder picture to see if something is about to move out of shot, or is going to be partly cut off by the edge of the picture.
- Check the composition of your shot (framing, headroom, offset-framing, etc.), subtly correcting for changes that develop (e.g. people moving to different positions in the shot). We shall discuss *composition* in detail in Chapter 7.
- Keep a look-out for the unexpected, such as scenic lines 'growing out' of subjects (Figure 17.23). Are microphones, cameras, lamps, or their shadows just appearing in shot? You can often re-frame the shot slightly to avoid them.

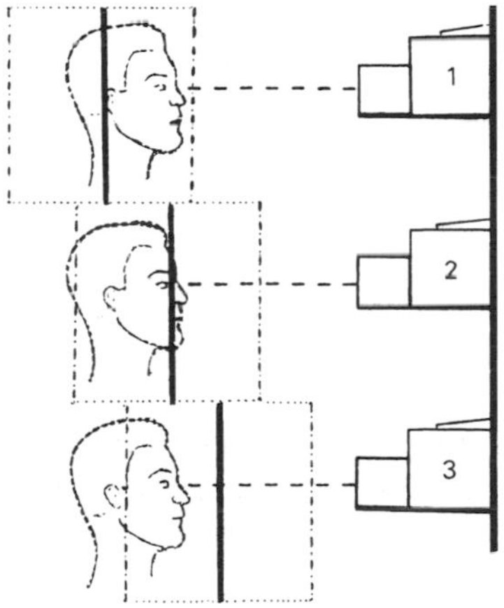

Fig. 5.2 Incorrect focusing
When *accurately focused* (2), the most important part of the subject is sharpest. Even in closer shots the subject can move to some extent, and remain clearly focused (i.e. within the available depth of field).

If you focus beyond the correct distance (i.e. *focused back* (1) close subjects moving towards the camera are liable to go out of focus.

If you focus nearer then the correct distance (i.e. *focused forward* (3)), close subjects moving away from the camera are liable to go out of focus.

Camera operation

Focusing

Focusing is not always as straightforward as it looks. When the subject has well-defined patterns you can easily detect maximum sharpness – *hard focus*. But with less-defined subjects you may *rock focus* either side of the optimum, and somehow, they still look *soft-focus*.

- The *exact point* at which you focus can matter. As you'll remember, there is more focused depth beyond the actual focused plane than there is in front of it. So in closer shots there can be advantages in focusing a little forward of the true focusing point (nearer the camera), to allow for subject movement (Figure 5.2). If you are focused too far back (away from the camera), the problem worsens. When shooting people, the eyes or the necktie are favorite focusing points. Hair-lines can be misleading – especially on thinning hair.
- Many focus controls are quite 'coarse', and the slightest readjustment produces obvious changes. This is great when you need to change focus rapidly (*throw focus/pull focus*); but subtle focus-following can be difficult, and is liable to appear jerky. A control which has 'fine' adjustment needs to turn quite a lot

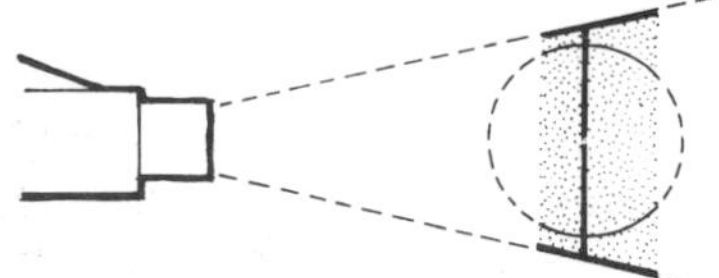

Fig. 5.3 Restricted focus
In close shots, the depth of field may be so restricted, that only parts of the subject are sharply focused.

before focus changes are obvious in the picture; so you may have problems keeping up with fast moves to and from the camera. If it takes two to three turns of the control to change focus from *MFD* (minimum focusing distance) to infinity, you may find that you need to readjust your grip midway! Some systems provide coarse/fine selection on the focus control.

- Depth of field is continually changing, as you focus at different distances, select different lens angles, or zoom in or out. This is something you quickly become accustomed to, but it can't be ignored. Focusing is simple in longer shots, but the closer the subject, the greater the focusing problems. You shoot two people speaking, yet can only get a sharp image of one of them at a time. In very large close-ups, focusing can be so critical that only *part of a subject* is sharp, while the rest is completely defocused. In Figure 5.5 are regular solutions to this dilemma.

Moving people

- Watching people in your shot closely, you can anticipate whether they are just about to adjust their position, get up (rise), or move . . . and this alerts you to pan and tilt to follow the action.
- Whenever anyone starts to move, the director has to make a decision that will affect what you do. If people are 'breaking' (moving apart) you need to know how to treat the action.
  - ○ Are they going to remain within the frame? If you are in a long shot there may be room for them. Otherwise you may need to zoom out. If so, how far? Probably just enough to include them.
  - ○ If someone is going to move out of the frame (i.e. you will 'lose them'), you may need to gently recompose the shot to balance the picture. Perhaps the director is cutting to another camera at that point, and you simply get to your next shot.
  - ○ Are you going to follow the person? By panning to watch them leaving? Panning and zooming in? Dollying after them? Dollying along with them? Each method has its own audience impact.
- If you are on shot, and then someone moves into frame, is there room for them, or do you need to widen the shot a little (pull back or zoom out)? Avoid overwidening then having to correct.

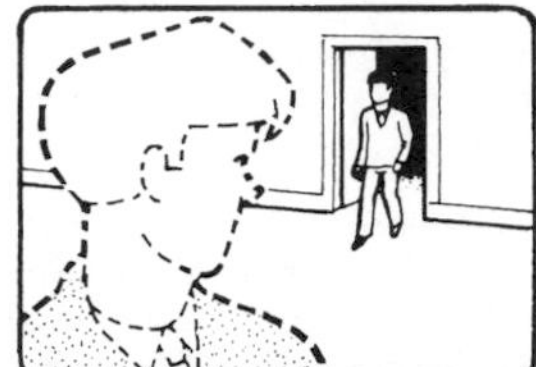

Fig. 5.4 Throwing and pulling focus
As a dramatic effect, you can deliberately refocus while on shot; from a nearby subject to a more distant one (*throw focus*), or from a distant subject to a nearby one (*pull focus*).

Fig. 5.5 The problem of limited depth of field
Where depth of field proves too *limited* (1), the solutions are:

2 *Stop down* – depth of field increases, but higher light intensity necessary.
3 *Focus on one subject* – permitting other(s) to soften.
4 *Split focus* – spread available depth between both subjects (both are now softer than optimum).
5 *Move subjects closer together* – making subjects more equidistant from camera.
6 *Use wider lens angle* – depth of field increases but subjects now appear smaller. (Moving closer for larger image, reintroduces limited depth.)
7 *Pull camera back* – depth increases but shot is smaller.

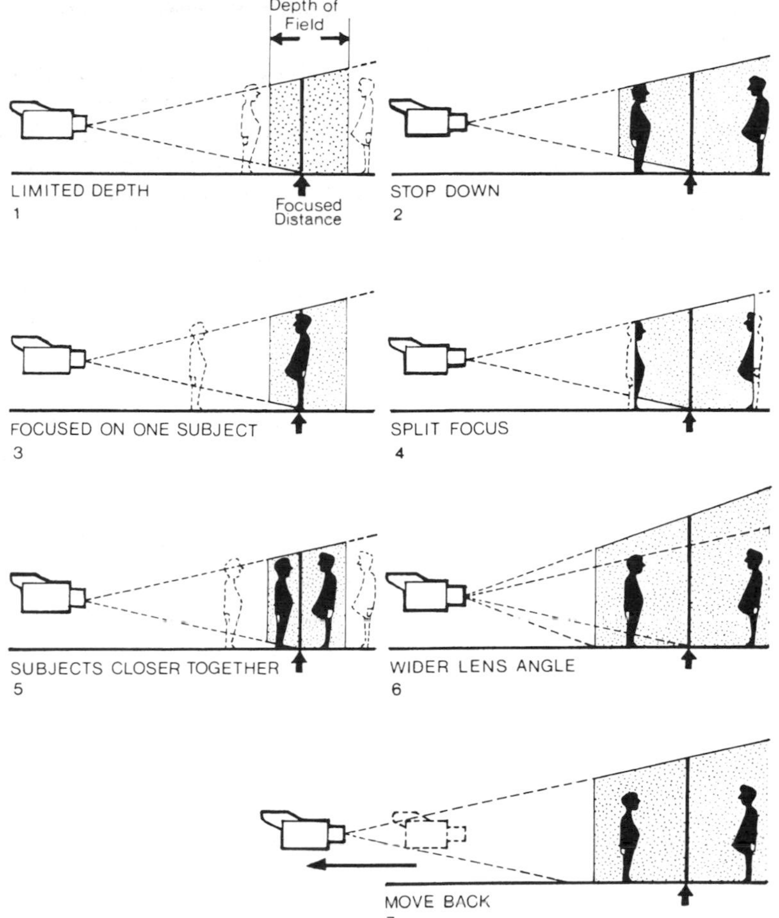

- When people move towards the camera be prepared to follow focus. The closer they are, the quicker you need to refocus. If they are moving diagonally towards you, you'll need to adjust focus and pan simultaneously.
- If you are panning with a moving subject do not keep it in the center of the frame. Instead, offset it so that it lags behind center-frame. This offset should be greater, the faster the subject. (The offset distance is often called 'looking-room', 'nose-room', or 'lead-room'.)
- Although you can rely on most actors to repeat the moves they made during rehearsal, and to 'hit their marks' every time, never assume this – especially with inexperienced talent. You may need to slightly readjust your previous position or lens angle to get the same shot.

Camera moves

- Whenever you are going to move your camera there are a number of preliminaries. First of all, check your route for obstructions and people. In most studios there are floor cables, scenery, floor lamps, sound booms, picture monitors, loud-speakers, and other cameras to be avoided! Your camera mounting can only run smoothly over the studio floor, so avoid dollying over floor cloths or rugs. During the move, take care not to displace furniture, parts of the set, floor lamps. All very obvious, but in a quick move backwards during a fast-moving show you can overlook the obvious.
- If you are simply moving the mounting *to get to another position* lock off the camera head – preferably pointing slightly downwards, so as not to point it into lights. Then dolly as quietly as possible, causing minimum cable drag noise across the floor. Silence may be more important than speed! Rather than try to pull the stretched cable after you, ensure that you have sufficient slack beforehand (or get help in handling it while you dolly). Never pull a cable which has a tight loop in it. You'll damage it.

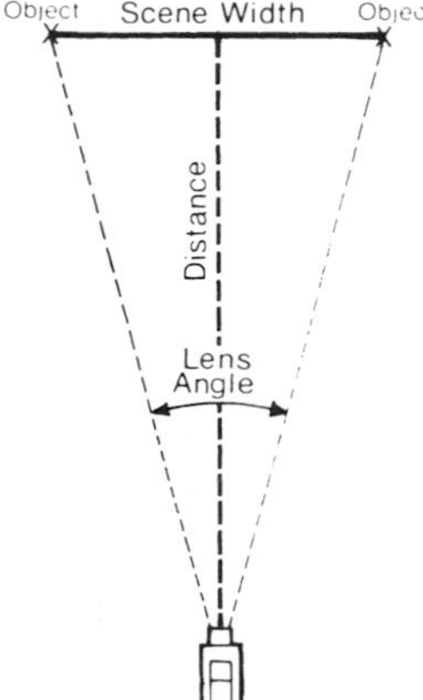

Lens Angle	Width at 3m Distance	Width at 10ft Distance
5° —	0.26 m	10 in
10° —	0.53 m	1 ft 9 in
15° —	0.79 m	2 ft 7 in
20° —	1.06 m	3 ft 6 in
25° —	1.33 m	4 ft 5 in
30° —	1.61 m	5 ft 5 in
35° —	1.89 m	6 ft 4 in
40° —	2.18 m	7 ft 4 in
45° —	2.49 m	8 ft 4 in
50° —	2.80 m	9 ft 4 in
55° —	3.12 m	10 ft 5 in
60° —	3.46 m	11 ft 7 in

Fig. 5.6 Checking your camera's angle

1 *To find the angle of your lens.* Place two small objects on a crossline 3 m (10 ft) away, moving them so that they just appear within the left-right frame edges. Measure how far apart they are and check in the table the angle that covers this width.

2 *To set the shot-box to a particular lens-angle.* Look up the required angle in the table and find the screen-width it takes in at 3 m (10 ft) away, place them this distance apart (e.g. for 30° they must be 1.61 m (5 ft 5 in) apart). Adjust your lens to just take in the objects at the frame edges, and it is now at the required angle. Adjust shot-box preset, or note zoom setting. You could make up a regular zoom-lens line-up graphic for adjusting all lens angles at this distance.

- If you are going to change position *to follow a moving subject*, check out the route and cable as before. But now you leave the camera head free. With one hand on the steering ring, and the other on the focus control, push firmly in the appropriate direction. You can push two-handled lightweight tripods by the panning handles for simple moves over short distances.
- If you are using a *rolling tripod*, remember the preliminary push that aligns the wheels. On a *pedestal* you will have selected the dolly (steer/track) mode for the wheels, or the truck (crab) mode. The dolly mode offers precise steering for straight-line moves. The truck mode is best for moving in confined spaces,

changing directions, traveling sideways. Camera operators develop their own preferences.

- Start dollying with gentle pressure, and have your foot ready to push the pedestal base.
- At the end of a move, slow the dolly to avoid overrunning the floor marks at your destination, or bringing it to an abrupt halt.

Raising and lowering the camera

- In action, it is best to leave the pedestal column unlocked, ready to 'ped' up or down at any time.
- Particularly from low camera positions, look out for lens flares from light shining towards the camera, degrading picture quality. You can often clear lens flares by raising your viewpoint slightly, or by stretching a piece of masking tape across the top edge of the lens shade (lens hood).
- Whenever you raise or lower the camera-head, take care not to momentarily tilt the lens up or down as you do so. And when changing height quickly, remember it's easy to hit the column's maximum or minimum height limit, and judder the picture. And, of course, there are situations where you can inadvertently crush the camera down onto something just in front of it, or raise the camera and strike something overhead!

Camera shadows

Always be on the look-out for shadows of your camera appearing in shot. This is most likely to occur when you are close in to a subject, and when you are high, looking downwards. You may be able to clear it by moving sideways a little, or pulling out and zooming in (i.e. using a narrower lens angle). Or it may be necessary to relight the subject. Let the lighting director know if the shadow is unavoidable.

Production format

Film making customarily uses a single camera, shooting action in a series of brief sections ('takes') which are edited together afterwards into a coherent program. The television director can emulate this approach; using a single video camera to videotape brief sequences which are later edited, and enhanced in a post-production process.

However, although you can shoot studio shows with a single-camera, there are distinct advantages in using two or more simultaneously in a *multi-camera* setup. Not only does this provide greater flexibility, but the entire production process is much faster.

When shooting on location though, this multi-camera approach can become far too complex and unwieldy for many projects. Instead, a single camera's no-fuss mobility is far more practicable.

The single-camera shoot

If you are on a shoot for a documentary or a news item, there will always be a fair amount of improvization. You need to make the most of any opportunity that offers itself. Clearly, a lot depends on whether you are working indoors or in the open; whether you are on your own, or backed by a team. The weather and light conditions may affect shooting.

Especially when travelling to remote spots therefore, it's particularly important to ensure that your camera is fault-free. So we have included a helpful table here, of typical points to look out for (Table. 5.1 – page 107).

Some people on a single-camera shoot prefer to 'travel light', setting off with just a camcorder, a spare battery, a videotape or two . . . and a song in the heart. But for peace of mind, there's a lot to be said for using a systematic *check list* routine. This list can be as brief or comprehensive as you like; including whatever stuff you personally find invaluable on that kind of project. (The item you'll need in an emergency, is sure to be the one you've left behind!) Lists also help to avoid losses when hurriedly repacking equipment after a shoot. (Table 5.3 – page 113.)

The multi-camera shoot

Whether you are working out on location or in a regular studio, you will find that all multi-camera setups have a common theme. Unlike a single camera unit, which often relies on a spontaneous and improvized approach, a multi-camera team is essentially a closely coordinated group, working to a planned pattern. We shall be looking in some detail here at the ways such a team is organized and managed.

Working in the studio

Productions vary considerably in their complexity. Some follow a familiar routine, with cameras taking standard shots from limited viewpoints. In other shows, cameras are very mobile, and follow

Table 5.1 Single camera checkout

The exact procedures will depend on the design of your particular camera.

Camera support	If you are using a *shoulder support pad* check that it is firmly attached, and the camera is balanced (fore/aft). With a tripod, check the *camera base-plate* and *quick-release* housing on panning head.
Lens	Preferably keep the lens in a protective case with silica gel desiccant. Examine the lens surface for any splash-marks, dust, finger marks, scratches. If you have a permanently fitted protective *UV filter*, check this. First clean *dust* off surfaces with a *lens brush* (preferably incorporating a bellows), or a *clean-air aerosol blower*. Then breathe gently on surfaces and clean them with fresh *lens tissue*. Remove lens, inspect rear element.
Filter wheel	Check that filters are in place, clean and unscratched. Leave in appropriate position for light source color temperature.
Power	Check power sources (clip-on battery, battery belt, adapter) – no damage; connections OK; fully charged (as indicated on *charger*, and on *camera indicator*). Attach e.g. battery to camera. **Switch on**.
Viewfinder	Check viewfinder position adjustments. Adjust eyepiece optic to suit your eyesight. Check viewfinder performance, with *color bars* or *test pattern*: Adjust *focus* (sharpest detail); *brightness* (scanning lines just disappear in black area); *contrast* (all tonal range clearly visible). Compare results with *picture monitor* showing camera's output.
Indicators	Check all *indicators* in viewfinder and on camera body, showing present state of camera: e.g. *humidity OK*. Check *TIME INDICATORS* and *TIME CODE* display.
Preset controls	(Preferably compare viewfinder and monitor versions.) Check *FOCUS* operation in *manual* and *auto* modes (near and distant). Check pre-focus tracking. Check *macro* position. Check *ZOOM* operation in *manual* and *auto (rocker-switch)* modes; at various speeds. Check again with *RANGE EXTENDER* in operation, if fitted. Check *IRIS (LENS APERTURE)* operation in *manual* and *auto* modes in light and shadowy areas. Watch *exposure indicator (zebra operation)* for *overexposure* or *underexposure*. Manually underexpose picture, and check if *auto-iris* mode compensates. Check *GAIN* (leave at 0 or OFF). Shooting shadow or low-light areas, increase gain, and check changes in iris settings. Check *SHUTTER SPEED* (leave at 1/60th). Changing speed causes auto-iris to operate. Set *WHITE BALANCE* (with appropriate *filter* setting for the light source) using white reference card (or translucent lens cap). Set *BLACK BALANCE* (*iris* completely closes; or use opaque lens cap). Open iris after check. Check *BACK FOCUS (FLANGE BACK)* IF NECESSARY.
Warning indicators	Where possible, present 'incorrect' conditions, such as wrong *white balance* and *black balance, exposure*, and check that indicator reveals the error. Correct the condition and recheck indicator.
Audio checks	Check that the *CAMERA MIC* plug fits firmly, and that the audio channel(s) is switched on. With someone speaking normally about a couple of meters away (6.5 ft), using AGC setting, check that the audio indicator is peaking appropriately. Switch to *manual* position, and recheck. Adjust audio gain if necessary. Attach an *EXTERNAL MIC* and check audio indicator similarly.
Recording check	Check general state of **VTR** (cleanliness, heads and guides clean?), and its operation (i.e. record, replay, rewind, fast fwd). Check tape at start of cassette with protective tag or plug in position to record. Record *color* bars and zero-level *tone* (e.g. 30 seconds). With appropriate color balance (white balance) shoot typical scenic tones, panning to lighter/darker areas, zooming, refocusing, etc. Check picture replay on a color monitor if possible. (Perhaps check vectorscope.)

complicated action. They can require the skilled, highly controlled camerawork that only comes with experience.

Each camera operator is on their own, having to find a way round particular problems; yet at the same time, you are part of a crew, working together to achieve a coordinated result. In some shows you can help the director by 'offering up shots'; while in others this would be a distraction from a planned treatment. You cannot know what shots other cameras have.

If the production has been planned in meticulous detail the camera operator's role may be to reproduce exactly what the director drew in *storyboard* sketches weeks before. On the other hand, the entire show may be 'off-the-cuff' with the director relying on the camera crew to find the best shots of the action.

Although a senior member of the camera crew may be briefed about the project beforehand, camera operators usually only discover their role on the day, during the actual studio rehearsal. Each camera is issued with a *shot sheet/camera card* showing its main positions and shots throughout the show. From then on, the camera crew relies on intercom instructions during camera

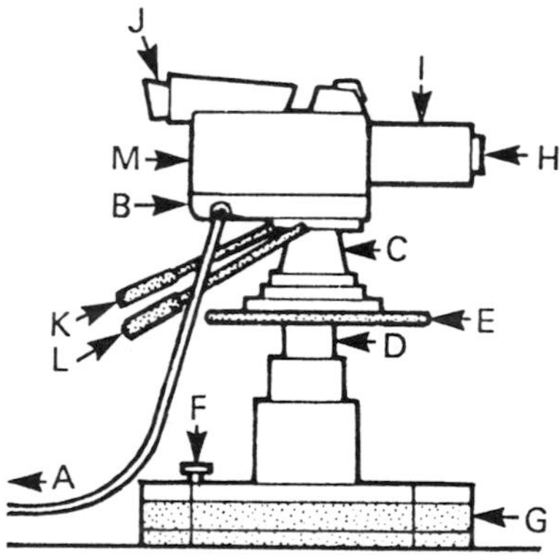

Fig. 5.7 Preliminary camera check
Make it a regular routine to check out your camera before rehearsal.

A Is it switched on, warmed up, and set-up (lined-up)?
B Cable connections OK at the camera and wall outlets?
C Camera head security and balance OK?
Check the panning head (adjust drag).
D On a *pedestal mounting* check the vertical column movement.
On a *tripod/rolling tripod*, check leg securing screws. Check height/level.
E Steering OK?
F Try out both the dolly and truck steering modes.
G Check that cable guards are not set *too high* (or camera will overrun small cables), or *too low* (scraping the floor).
On *rolling tripods*, check caster brakes, caster movement.
H Remove lens cap. Is the lens clean?
I What is the working lens aperture? Are any filters in position?
J Is the viewfinder correctly adjusted and working efficiently? Check all indicators.
K *Focus.* Check overall focus, and that focus does not vary while zooming.
L *Zoom.* Check the zoom action throughout its range, and any extender lens. Set up the shot box.
M Intercom, program feeds etc. OK?

Table 5.2 Multi-camera pre-rehearsal checkout

1 Preliminaries
Camera switched on, warmed up, and set up (lined up)?

2 Camera cable
Are the cable plugs at the camera and wall (or equipment) sockets tight?
Is the cable firmly secured to the *camera mounting*?
(Don't leave the cable just hanging free from the outlet on the camera head, or when you dolly, it will pull on the head outlet.)
Is there sufficient cable for the camera moves?
Is it suitably routed, and free to move around (e.g. not trapped under scenery)?

3 Camera-head
Is the camera-head firmly attached to the panning head?
Are the *panning handles/pan-bars* firmly attached, and at a comfortable angle?
Unlock the *tilt-lock* and check the camera-head *balance*. Is it nose or back heavy, and needing adjustment?
Check and adjust *vertical drag/tilt friction*.
Unlock the *pan-lock* and check if panning is smooth, with just sufficient resistance. Adjust *horizontal drag/pan friction* if necessary.

4 Mounting
Rolling tripod
Check the tripod's height, fixing, base fittings (brakes, caster movement).
Pedestal
Unlock the column, raise/lower it slowly. Is its movement smooth and easy?
Check that the column does not drift up or down. If it does, it requires re-balancing. (Likely if prompter has been added or taken off since last used.)

5 Steering
Check freedom of movement in all directions.
Check dolly (track) and truck (crab) modes.

6 Cable guards
Adjust cable guards to prevent the dolly from overrunning floor cables (lighting, sound, camera), but avoid guards scraping the floor.

7 Lens cap
Remove the cap from the front of the lens (*lens cap*).
Switch electrical capping out (this may be on the CCU).
Is the lens clean? If not use a compressed-air can, lens brush, or lens-cleaning tissue.

8 Viewfinder
Check focus, brightness, contrast, *picture shape* (aspect ratio), edge cut-off (you must be able to see right to the edge of the picture frame).
Adjust image sharpening (crispening) for maximum definition.
Are the indicators around the viewfinder working?
Are tally light and indicator cue-lamps OK?
Check mixed viewfinder feeds.

9 Focus
Check the smoothness of focusing action from close-up to the far distance (infinity).
In a servo system, does the focus control tend to overrun or hunt (rhythmical changes)?
Check focus when fully zoomed in, and when zoomed out.
Pre-focus on a distant subject; slowly zoom out checking that focus does not wander (i.e. tracking is correct).

10 The *f*-stop/lens aperture
Check the *f*-stop you will be working at. This lens aperture has been set during camera set-up/line-up to suit standard lighting levels, e.g. 1600 lux (150 fc).

11 Zoom
Is the zoom action smooth throughout the range?
Check any zoom extender lens.
Check any zoom meter or indicator.
Check the *shot box*, and adjust it to the preset angles you will be using.

12 Intercom/talkback
Check all intercom circuits (general/production intercom and private-wire circuits) and associated indicators.
Is your headset *one earpiece* (intercom only) or *two earphones* (separate intercom and program sound) OK?
Is the switched intercom to the video engineers/shader/vision control working?

13 Filters
Check the filter wheel, making sure that an incorrect filter is not accidentally left in position.

14 Lock off and cap up
Lock off panning-head and cap up.

15 Prompter
If a prompter is fitted, check that it is secure, connections and cables OK.

16 Shot sheet/camera card
Read through, check camera positions in the studio sets, and clip the card to the camera.

rehearsal, to guide their camerawork. During breaks, the director may discuss particular shot problems.

Preparing for rehearsals

You could simply move your camera into the opening position, focus up, and wait for intercom instructions. But don't be caught out! Check over your camera and its mounting beforehand – especially if someone else was using it earlier. In the checkout list (Table 5.2) you will find the main points you should look at. It takes very little time, and soon becomes a rapid routine.

During rehearsal

Relaxed yet alert

Of course, there are no 'rules' for effective camera operation. But there are approaches that make life a lot easier, and produce more consistent results. Other people have found out the hard way, so why not benefit from it?

You can tell inexperienced camera operators at a glance; standing poised rigid and tense, eyes glued to the viewfinder, gripping controls tightly . . . Relax! The best posture is an alert, watchful readiness; very aware of what is going on around. Not so relaxed as to be casual, but continually waiting to react.

- In a multi-camera show you need to keep a watchful eye on the *tally light* on top of your camera (repeated as a viewfinder indicator). It shows that *your* camera has been selected on the production switcher. You are 'on-air'. When the light is out, you can move to new positions, adjust zooming or focus, check composition, and so on. But do not get caught out. Do not move off shot (*clear*) until your tally light goes off. It is useful to check other cameras' lights, when moving around, to ensure that you are not going to get into their shots.
- Is your viewfinder at a comfortable angle, easy to see, and not diluted with spill light? Its tonal adjustment can be critical, to give optimum detail in both the shadows and lightest tones.
- Make it a habit to note the *lens angle* (*focal length*) at which your lens is set at any time. This helps you to anticipate handling and depth of field problems.
- Another good habit is to *pre-focus* your lens whenever you move to a new position (i.e. zoom right in, focus sharply, zoom out to your present shot). You will then be ready to zoom in from a wide shot to closer detail.
- For most shots, the lens should be around the talent's eye-level – unless the director wants higher or lower angles for some reason. If the camera is slightly lower, at chest height, this tends

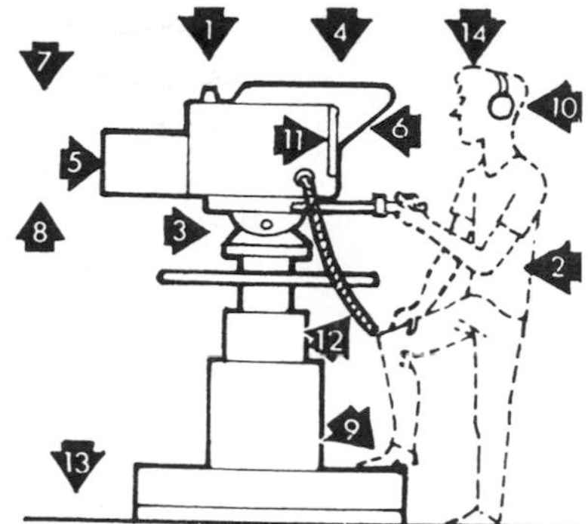

Fig. 5.8 During rehearsal
During rehearsal, make regular checks on:

1 The tally light. It shows whether your camera is on-air.
2 Aim to be relaxed, comfortable yet alert.
3 Be ready for your next shot. When off shot, don't let the camera tilt up onto lights or the sun, and avoid strong specular reflections.
4 Check the viewfinder performance, indicator lights, call-lights, etc.
5 Check your present working lens angle. (It directly affects camera operations.)
6 Check your shot (focus accuracy, depth of field, composition, etc.). *Pre-focus* the zoom.
7 Check for unwanted effects in the shot (e.g. shooting off, lens flares, camera or boom shadows, etc.)
8 Action. Watch the action, to anticipate the need to reframe the shot refocus, follow action, etc.
9 Be ready to help dolly movements.
10 Continually check intercom (and program sound).
11 Check your shot sheet for moves and camera positions.
12 Is the camera cable free and sufficient for all camera moves?
13 Are there any obstacles that will impede camera moves, or get in the way of the next shot?
14 If any problems develop while the show is on-air, seek help (e.g. tell the FM, call the shader/vision operator), but try not to miss shots.

to give the talent a more imposing look (but they may look down slightly, and develop shadowed eye sockets). A higher camera improves lighting, as the person looks upwards, but they are more likely to be dazzled by lights if they are using a prompter attached to the camera. Items on tables or the floor are usually shot from a height of about 1.2–1.8 m (4–5 ft).

- Continually check your shot sheet/camera card, and be ready to move to your next position once each shot is completed; then prepare for the next shot.
- When you want to match with another camera's picture you will usually switch to *mixed viewfinder feeds*, which shows both shots superimposed. But there are occasions when a *color* floor monitor in the studio can be used instead to check and match the headroom and height of other camera's shots, and to line up elaborate combined shots (e.g. when using *chroma key*).
- Listen to all intercom/production-talkback instructions, including those for other cameras. Where there is no intercom circuit, or you cannot speak to the director (e.g. when on-air), you may

use visual signals such as: '*Yes*' (tilt up and down); '*No*' (pan left and right); '*I've a problem*' (pan/tilt round in circles); '*I've focus problems*' (rapidly rock focus); '*I need to speak on the private wire*' (quick in/out zooms).

- You will meet problems during rehearsal that only the director can solve, by making changes or reorganizing camera treatment. These include such situations as: one subject masking (obscuring) another, insufficient time for dolly moves, compositional problems, focusing difficulties, etc. Let him know, for it may mean stopping rehearsal to work things out. Don't assume that it will be alright next time. It may be worse!
- Be on the lookout for strong specular reflections that may damage the cameras' CCD, can cause picture defects, and will certainly distract.
- *Occasionally*, an experienced camera operator can help the director by suggesting slight changes in the camera treatment that would improve a sequence, or simplify a complicated situation. What is obvious on the floor may not be evident on monitors in the production control room. But avoid appearing to 'subdirect' the show!
- Sometimes, when there is a difficulty during rehearsal, it can help the director if a neighboring camera turns to give a wide shot of the situation. For example, it might reveal that the on-air dolly is backed against a wall, with no further room to move.
- Avoid the temptation to find odd shots for your own amusement, or 'hint shots' of the studio clock when a break is due.
- Be calm. If you are late on shot, try not to lose it altogether. Do not lose the next! If you misjudge, then try to correct the fault as unobtrusively as possible.
- Things go wrong during a busy production. What you have to decide quickly is whether:
  You can ignore the problem – because you are on-shot, or have a shot coming up, or others know about it and will deal with it.
  It would be helpful to inform others (e.g. about a lamp knocked out of position by moving scenery).
  You should use your intiative, take immediate action to help.

In most cases the floor manager is your on-the-spot contact. Teamwork is the essence of good production.

Production techniques

A director can tackle a production in several different ways. These may vary with personal temperament, experience, and with the type of show (see Chapter 19):

- An improvised, spontaneous, 'let's see what happens!' approach(!).

- An outline shooting plan; that cannot be rehearsed before taping or transmission (e.g. a dance group who are arriving later, during air-time).
- A rehearsal with stand-ins in place of the actual performers (e.g. checking shots beforehand, for an interview).
- A closely planned show, in which the director walks round the sets beforehand, explaining action/shots to camera and sound crew, before beginning rehearsals (*dry run*).
- A '*stop–start*' arrangement in which action is rehearsed on camera while the director guides shots; stopping and correcting errors/problems as they arise. After a complete *run through* rehearsal (occasionally followed by a final *dress run*) the show is taped or transmitted from beginning to end.
- A '*rehearse–record*' approach, in which each shot, segment, or scene is rehearsed **and recorded** before going on to the next. Shots will not necessarily be in the final program order. (They will be edited later.)

Table 5.3 Have you forgotten anything?

Camera (*Camcorder or stand-alone + videotape recorder*) Standard zoom lens Any additional lens (prime) Supplementary lens Filters (UV, sky, ND, fluorescent, etc). Matte/filter box Lens hood extension Lens cleaning kit Large (5 in.) viewfinder Light meter (light levels, color temp) White/black 'standard' cards **Camera protection** Carrying/transit case Weather and/or water protection (rain, sand, dust, etc.) Underwater camera housing **Batteries** (Fully charged) Fitted and standby Battery storage container Battery belt (if used) Camera battery (on-board) Battery charger AC power (mains) adapter **Videotape** (*Ready to use*)	**Communications/ monitoring** Earpiece/earphones/headset On-camera antenna (IR/ Radio) **Camera mounting** Shoulder support Pistol grip support Body brace Monopod Tripod Lightweight pedestal Spreader (spider) Base triangle (for sand, mud) Wheeled base Limpet mount, bean bag, clamp. Pan and tilt head + quick release Panning handle(s) Remote zoom/focus controls **Sound equipment** Camera microphone Hand-held (interview) mic. Radio microphones + receiver(s) Special purpose microphone (shotgun/rifle, parabolic reflector) Portable audio mixer Lightweight microphone stand Audio cables/extensions*	**Lighting equipment** Camera light (working OK?) Lamp power supply (e.g. battery belt)Hand-held lamp Portable light fittings: ***Additional lighting equipment*** Reflector boards/panels (white, silver, gold) Redheads with barndoors Broad with doors Lightweight stands Gaffer grip. Profiled wall plate Sandbags Lighting cables with extensions, adapters* Spare lamps (*check power supply/ voltage re lamps used*) Diffusers (spun glass, scrim) Color filters (daylight, tungsten) ND filters	**Supplementary equipment** Trolley-pack (for heavy duty battery, monitor, vectorscope or other test equipment) Portable videotape recorder Portable picture monitor with light hood Portable videocassette recorder (replay to check/ monitor tape) Prompter? Nylon rope (secure equipment, barriers, haul equipment, etc.) Cord, Gaffer tape Flashlamp Watch (stopwatch) Note–pads, pens, adhesive tape Mobile phone(s) Keys to all equipment locks Small tool kit *Check all cables' connectors (video, audio, lighting, power) to ensure that they are appropriate and in good condition!

As you will see, the problems and opportunities for the production crew can be very different with each method; ranging from a '*one-chance-only*' situation to '*retake-until-we-get-it-right*' approach.

After the show

At the end of a production, when any videotaping retakes have been completed and checks made, the director and the technical director will announce on intercom that the studio is cleared. The floor manager will repeat this for everyone in the studio, including performers.

You should then lock off the camera head (tilt and pan), ped down to the lowest column position, and lock it off. If prompters or camera lights have been used, their cables may need to be removed at this stage. Cap up the lens to protect it, and move the dolly to its arranged parking area or a technical store. When the video engineer confirms that the camera has been switched off, remove the cable, and store it either in a neat figure-of-eight pile or on a cable reel. Cable care now avoids a tangle next time! Don't forget to remove your shot sheet (or script), and to clear any masking tape from the studio floor! If the headset is your personal issue, remember to recover it from the camera.

6 The persuasive camera

This chapter discusses how you can use the camera to present your subject effectively.

Why do we need techniques?

Shooting style

The simplest way to use a camera is to set it up at a suitable viewpoint, then zoom between overall *cover* (*covering*) shots showing general action, and closer shots showing detail. But this mechanical, unstimulating routine soon becomes very boring to watch. Good techniques add to the subject's appeal; they arouse our interest. Bald statements are not enough. Rather like listening to a hack pianist who plays the right notes without any sort of expression, our attention falls.

When you point a camera at a scene you are doing much more than simply showing your audience what is going on there. You are selecting particular features in the scene. You are drawing their attention to certain aspects of the action. The way you use your camera will influence the audience impact of the subject.

In an interview, for example, you can shoot the guests from a low viewpoint and give them an air of importance or self-confidence. From a higher viewpoint they might look diminished. Concentrating on detail shots of their nervous finger movements, they may appear insecure or ill at ease.

The camera *interprets* the scene. How you use it will affect your audience's responses. If you use the camera casually you will get haphazard results.

Whenever you point a camera at action you have to make a series of fundamental decisions, such as:

- Which is the best viewpoint? Can the action be seen clearly from there?
- Which features do you want to emphasize at this moment?
- Do you want the audience to concentrate on a particular aspect of the action?
- Do you want to convey a certain impression?

Of course, we seldom analyze in this fashion before deciding on a shot. Instead, we develop an instinctive feeling that a particular type of shot is most suitable for the situation.

Screen size

The size of the screen on which the audience watches the production can influence how they respond to what they see there. It is difficult to distinguish detail on a *small* screen (or a larger screen at a distance). The picture is confined and restricted, and we tend to feel detached as we closely inspect the overall effect. On the other hand, when watching a *large* screen we become more aware of detail. Our eyes have greater freedom to roam around the shot. We feel more closely involved with the action. We are onlookers at the scene.

At typical viewing distances most TV receivers allow us to effectively present a wide range of shot sizes, from vistas to microscopic close-ups. Although wide shots of large-scale events, panoramic views, or spectacular situations are not particularly impressive, this limitation is not too restrictive in practice.

Selecting the shot

Each type of shot has its particular advantages and disadvantages. You can use *longer shots*

- To show where the action is taking place
- To allow the audience to follow broad movements
- To show the relative positions of subjects
- To establish mood.

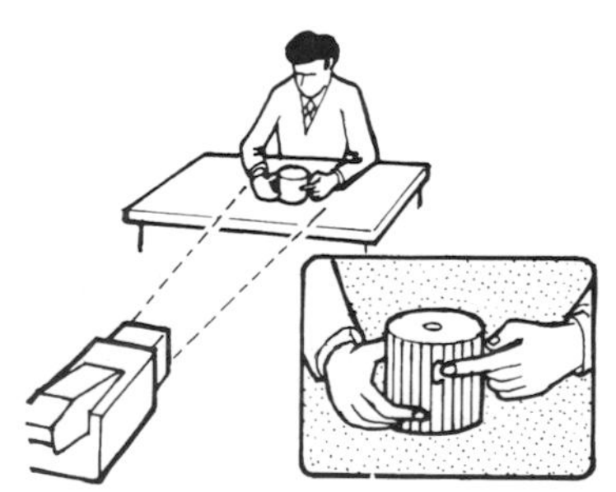

Fig. 6.1 Restricted framing
In close shots, action must be kept within the frame area. Avoid moving items in/out of frame (it draws attention to limited viewpoint).

But long shots do not allow your audience to see details, and you can leave them overaware of what they are missing. For example, in a wide shot of an art gallery they may feel that they are being prevented from seeing individual paintings clearly.

Closer shots are used

- To show detail
- To emphasize
- To reveal reactions
- To dramatize.

Use too many close shots, and the effect can be very restrictive. You can leave your audience feeling that they are being prevented from looking around the scene; from seeing the responses of other performers, from looking at other aspects of the subject, from following the general action.

Occasionally you may arrange a shot to show both a wide view of the scene and close detail, at the same time, in a combination shot (Figure 6.2).

Of course, any situation can be shot in many different ways. But there are always wrong or inappropriate shots for any given situation.

Fig. 6.2 Combined close-up and wide shot
Combined shots can show detail and wider view simultaneously. This can be achieved by *detail insert* (left) or showing foreground detail (right). The latter method requires considerable focused depth.

If action is *incidental* to the purpose of a sequence (e.g. someone speaking about their forthcoming vacation happens to be making an omelette) then shots should concentrate on the people involved, watching their interreactions. But if the purpose of the sequence is to show us how to cook, then we need detail shots of the action, with little or no interruption from reaction shots. Obvious enough, but directors do make the wrong choice, and annoy or puzzle the audience.

A shot that is appropriate at one moment could be very unsuitable the next. In fact, there are times when an inappropriate or a badly timed shot can totally destroy an entire sequence.

The very long shot (vista shot)

This is a very distant view of the scene. The environment predominates, and people appear as tiny figures in the landscape. Normally, one can only arrange such shots on location; although it can be achieved in a large studio, using very wide lens angles and electronic insertion.

The *very long shot* enables you to establish broad locale, and to create an overall atmospheric impression. You can use it to cover very wide-spread action, or to show various activities going on at the same time. It usually takes the form of a high shot from a hilltop, or an aerial view (e.g. a distant view of a battle).

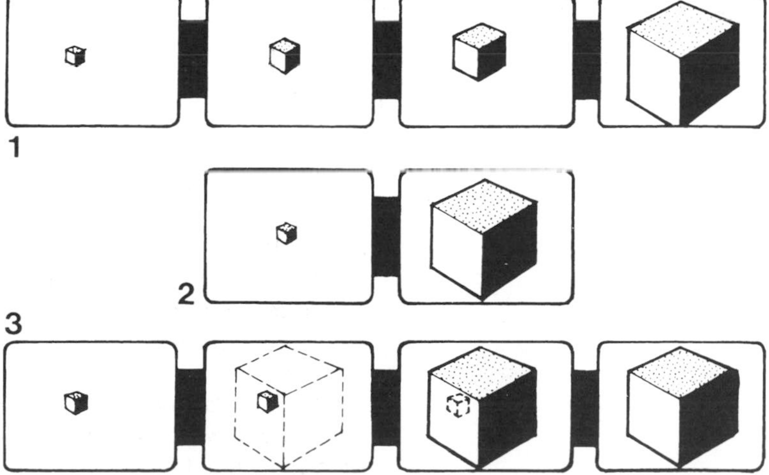

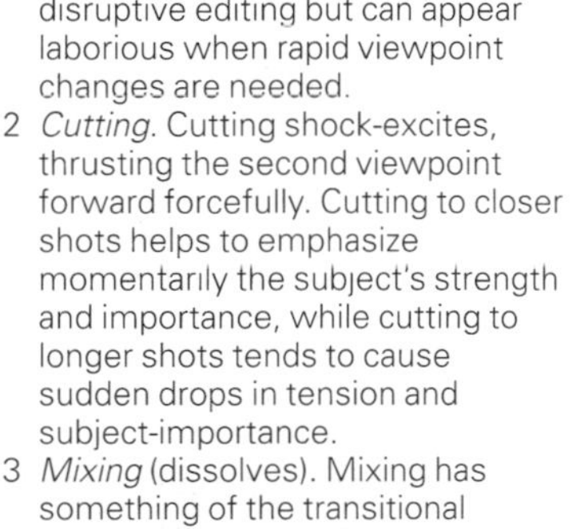

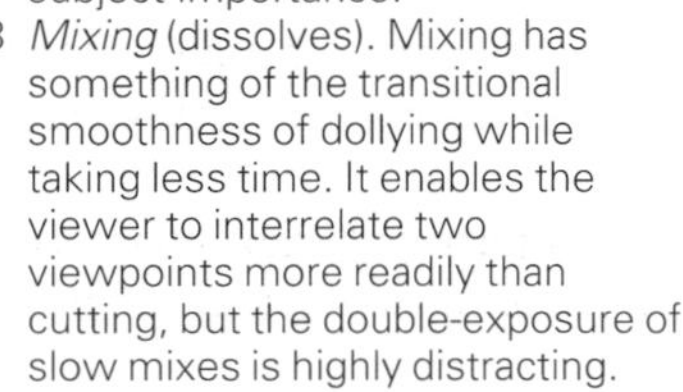

Fig. 6.3 Varying the length of shot

1 *Dollying*. Forward dollying can offer a gradual build-up of interest or tension, the importance of the subject growing progressively. Dollying back allows interest, tension or importance to be released gradually. The change can be made imperceptibly or fairly rapidly, the size and rate being controlled throughout. (Zooming has a similar effect for many purposes.) Dollying avoids disruptive editing but can appear laborious when rapid viewpoint changes are needed.
2 *Cutting*. Cutting shock-excites, thrusting the second viewpoint forward forcefully. Cutting to closer shots helps to emphasize momentarily the subject's strength and importance, while cutting to longer shots tends to cause sudden drops in tension and subject-importance.
3 *Mixing* (dissolves). Mixing has something of the transitional smoothness of dollying while taking less time. It enables the viewer to interrelate two viewpoints more readily than cutting, but the double-exposure of slow mixes is highly distracting.

The audience takes a rather detached, impersonal attitude; surveying the scene without any sense of involvement.

The long shot

Often used at the start of a scene, the long shot immediately shows where it's all happening. This *establishing shot* sets the location and broad atmospheric effect. It allows the audience to follow the purpose or pattern of action.

As you tighten the shot, and show less of the scene, the audience is influenced less by the setting and the lighting. The people within the scene have a greater audience impact, their gestures and facial expressions becoming stronger and more important.

Medium shots

These range from full-length to mid-shots; their value lying somewhere between the environmental strength of the long shot and the scrutiny of closer shots. From *full-length* to *three-quarter shots*, large bodily gestures (outflung arms) can be contained. But they are likely to pass out of shot if the shot becomes tighter. Then you have the option of restricting performer movement, taking a longer shot, or tightening to exclude arm movements entirely.

The close-up

An extremely powerful shot, the close-up concentrates interest. With people, it draws attention to their reactions, response, and emotions. Close-ups can reveal or point out information that might otherwise be overlooked, or only discerned with difficulty. They focus attention, or provide emphasis.

When introducing close-ups, you have to ensure that the audience wants to look that close, and do not feel that:

1 They have been cheated of the wider view, where something more interesting may be happening.
2 They have been thrust disconcertingly close to the subject – the audience may become overaware of facial blemishes in over-enlarged faces.
3 Detail that is already familiar is being overemphasized.
4 Picture clarity is actually being *reduced*: because there is no fine detail, or irrelevant details have become prominent, or restricted focus has blurred details.
5 Through continually watching close-up fragments, they have forgotten how these relate to the main subject, or have become disorientated.

Where shots do not contain enough detail to sustain continued interest, take care not to hold them so long that they entirely satisfy the curiosity, or encourage attention to wander.

Instead of beginning a sequence with a long *establishing shot*, you can build up impressions gradually, shot by shot; satisfying curiosity a little at a time. This encourages a sense of expectation, speculation.

But take care that delayed piecemeal introductions do not confuse; especially where the locale is unfamiliar. There must be sufficient pointers for our audience to be able to interpret the time, place, and action correctly. Where action has been seen from closer viewpoints for some time, longer shots may be desirable to remind, or re-establish the locale in the viewer's mind.

The prudent director remembers, and allows for, the camera operator's various operational problems when shooting close-ups:

1 Restricted depth of field, which therefore requires critical focusing.
2 Handling difficulties with narrow-angle lenses:
3 Depth compression.
4 The distortions and camera shadowing hazards when using close wide-angle lenses.
5 The difficulties in framing and following close movements.

Sometimes you will need to pan over close-up detail on a large flat surface (map or photograph). Then you must avoid the geometric distortions (keystoning) of a close short-focus (wide-angle) lens, or the restricted focused depth of a long-focus (narrow-angle) lens. It is best to move the lens parallel to the surface by trucking (crabbing) past it; with a long mural this is the only successful solution.

Deep-focus techniques

As you saw earlier, the *depth of field* in a scene varies with the lens *f*-stop, lens angle, and focused distance. You can change it by altering any of these parameters.

Stopping the lens down (e.g. *f*/11), everything from foreground to far distance appears sharply focused. The camera has no problems in following focus and there is little danger of subjects becoming soft focused. There is an illusion of spaciousness and depth; enabling shots to be composed with subjects at various distances from the camera. (But higher light levels are necessary.)

One weakness of this technique is that where there is little camera movement or few progressively distant planes in the picture it can appear unattractively flat. Surfaces or subjects at very different distances can merge or become confused. *Too much* may be sharply and distractingly visible.

Fig. 6.4 Focus techniques
Deep focus (top illustrations) provides overall clarity. This technique allows the camera operator to compose in depth and also accommodate close shots of three-dimensional subjects. *Shallow focus* (bottom illustrations) isolates subjects from distracting or confusing backgrounds, softens off unwanted detail.

Shallow-focus techniques

Using a wider lens aperture (e.g. *f*/2) restricts focused depth. It enables you to *isolate* a subject spatially, keeping it sharp within blurred surroundings; and avoids the distraction of irrelevant subjects. You can display a single sharply focused flower against a detailless background; concentrating attention on the bloom and suppressing the confusion of foliage. Sharply defined detail attracts the eye more readily than defocused areas.

By deliberately restricting depth of field you can 'soften' obtrusive backgrounds, even if these are strongly patterned, so that people stand out from their surroundings.

On the other hand, restricted depth can prove embarrassing when essential details of a close object are badly defocused. The camera continually refocuses to keep a close moving subject in focus. For instance, close shots along a piano keyboard can demand considerable dexterity, when following focus on quickly moving fingers. Where there are two or more subjects in shot, you may not be able to maintain sharp overall focus but have to split focus between them, or select one to focus on.

Occasionally, by changing focus between subjects at different distances (*pulling focus*, *throwing focus*) you can move the viewer's attention from one to another; however, this trick easily becomes disturbing unless coordinated with action. Blurred color pictures can be frustrating. Whereas in monochrome defocused planes merge, in color the viewer may be unable to decipher unsharp detail and the effect can be less acceptable.

Moving the camera head

In everyday life we respond to situations by making particular gestures or movements. These reactions and actions often become very closely associated. We look around with curiosity; move in to inspect an object; withdraw or avert our eyes from a situation that we find embarrassing, distasteful, or boring.

It is not surprising to find, therefore, that certain *camera movements* can evoke associated responses in your audience; causing them to have particular feelings towards what they see on the screen. And these effects underly the impact of persuasive camera techniques.

Table 6.1 Why change the lens angle?

To adjust framing	**A slight change in lens angle**: Where you want to exclude (or include) certain foreground objects, and repositioning camera or subject would spoil proportions; Where a normal lens would not provide the required size or framing, without repositioning the camera or subject.
For otherwise unobtainable shots	**Using a narrow-angle (long-focus) lens:** To shoot remotely situated subjects – where they are separated from the camera by uneven ground or inaccessible: Where the camera is isolated – on a camera platform (tower), shooting through scenic openings: Where the camera cannot be moved – static tripod, obstructions. **Using a wider-angle (shorter-focus) lens:** Where the normal lens does not provide a wide enough shot – space restrictions: To maintain a reasonably close camera position (e.g. so talent can read *prompter*) yet still provide wider shots.
To adjust effective perspective	Altering lens angle and changing camera distance to maintain same subject size, alters relative subject/background proportions and effective distances (Table 6.3). **Using a wider lens angle (short-focus lens)** – enhances spatial impression, increases depth of field. **Using a narrower lens angle (long-focus lens)** – educes spatial impression, compresses depth, e.g. bunching together a straggling procession.
Insufficient time to change camera distance	**Altering apparent camera distance (shot size) by changing lens angle**: During fast intercutting sequence: When camera repositioning would involve complicated moves.
To provide simpler or more reliable operations	**Zooming in/out instead of dollying** may produce smoother, easier changes in shot size (but perspective and handling affects change). Zooming provides **rapid changes in image size** more safely than fast dollying (for dramatic effect or to suddenly reveal detail). **Zooming in/out on a flat subject** is indistinguishable from dollying, but avoids focus-following problems Lens angle changes can avoid close-up cameras coming into picture.
To increase production flexibility	Where dollying would distract talent or obscure the camera action from audience. When using only one camera.
To produce distortion	For grotesque close-ups, or to flatten modeling.

Panning the camera

Panning shows us the spatial relationship between two subjects or areas. Cutting between two viewpoints does not provide the same sense of continuity or extent. When panning over a wide arc the intermediate parts of the scene connect together in our minds, helping us to orientate ourselves. We develop an impression of space. But avoid panning across irrelevant areas – such as the 'dead' space between two widely separated people.

Panning should be smooth; neither jerking into action nor juddering to a halt. Erratic or hesitant panning irritates. With a correctly adjusted panning head (suitable drag/friction) and a proper stance, such unevenness usually occurs only when using very narrow lens angles or where a subject makes an unpredicted move.

■ *The following pan* This is the commonest camera movement. The camera pans as it follows a moving subject. In longer shots the viewer becomes aware of the interrelationship between the subject and its surroundings. Visual interaction can develop between the subject and its apparently moving background pattern, creating a dynamic mutual impact (*dynamic composition*). In closer shots the background becomes incidental; often indecipherably blurred.

■ *The surveying pan* Here the camera slowly searches the scene (a crowd, a landscape), allowing the audience to look around at choice. It can be a restful anticipatory action; providing there is something worth seeing. It is not enough to pan hopefully.

The move can be dramatic, with high expectancy – the shipwrecked survivor scans the horizon, sees a ship . . . but will it notice him? But the surveying pan can build to an anticlimax, too; the fugitive searches to see if he is being followed . . . and finds that his 'pursuer' is a friendly hound.

■ *The interrupted pan* This pan is a long smooth movement that is suddenly stopped (sometimes reversed) to provide visual contrast. It is normally used to link a series of isolated subjects. In a dance spectacle, the camera might follow a solo dancer from one group to the next, pausing awhile at each as it becomes the new center of interest.

The technique has comic applications: the camera follows a bunch of sailors. They pass a pretty girl. The camera stops in mid-pan to watch her. One sailor comes running back and grimaces to the camera, beckoning it to hurry and catch them up.

In a dramatic application: escaping prisoners slowly stagger over treacherous marshland. One man falls exhausted, but the camera stays with the rest. A moment later it stops and pans back – to see only the last traces of the straggler remain.

Fig. 6.5 Slow panning
To provide a dramatic development
Panning slowly from the sleeping victim . . . along the intruder's shadow . . . then a rapid upward-tilt, revealing the intruder's identity.

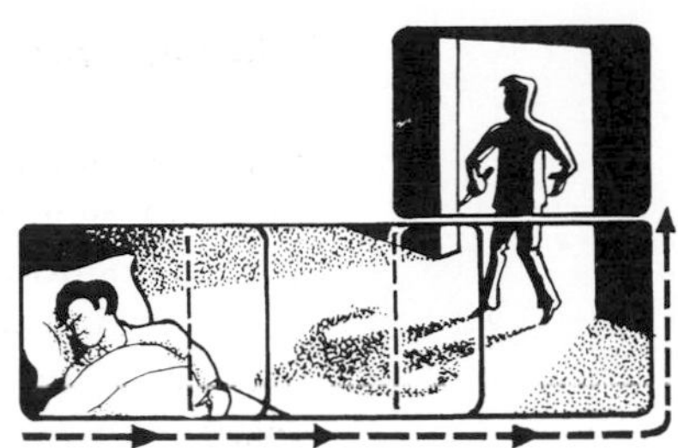

■ *Panning speed* A slow, prolonged pan can create opportunities or disappointments, according to how it is used. If the camera pans slowly over a series of objects that are increasingly interesting or significant the movement will continually hold our attention; even build up to a climax. But a slow pan around without any real points of interest will quickly pall, as the viewer's initial expectancy falls.

■ *The whip pan* A *fast* pan may produce nothing but a series of broken-up, half-seen images due to stroboscopic effects. But a *whip pan (swish, zip, blur pan)* turns so rapidly from one subject to the next that the intermediate scene becomes a brief, streaking blur.

Whether the effect arouses excitement or annoyance largely rests on how the preceding and following shots are developed. As our attention is dragged rapidly to the next shot it gives it transitory importance.

The *whip pan* usually produces a dynamic relational or comparative change:

1 *Joining different viewpoints of the same scene* – the pan *direction* should be compatible with the location of these viewpoints, i.e. panning right to a viewpoint located to camera right.
2 *Providing continuity of interest* – connecting a series of similar subjects or themes.
3 *Changing centers of attention* – from one area of concentration to another, e.g. a golfer drives . . . we whip pan to the awaiting hole.
4 *Showing cause and effect* – a whip pan from a cannon . . . to the demolished castle wall.
5 *Comparing or contrasting* – relating situations, e.g. wealth with poverty, old and new.
6 *Transferring in filmic time and space* – an aircraft takes off . . . whip pan to it landing at the destination.
7 *Dramatic change of direction* – changing the viewpoint with a sudden climax, e.g. the camera subjectively scans the distance, we hear a noise, and it whip pans to see an intruder behind, about to attack.

A whip pan continues the pace between two rapidly moving scenes. It can provide a tempo-bridge between a slow scene and a fast one. But at all times it remains something of a stunt.

A whip pan has to be *accurate* as well as appropriate, to be successful; no fumbling, reframing, refocusing at the end of the pan! To avoid such problems, the effect may be cheated by intercutting a brief separately recorded shot of 'blur' between two static cameras' shots.

Tilting the camera head

Although, strictly speaking, pointing the camera upwards and downwards is *tilting*, most of us talk about '*panning up and down*'. But we'll stick to the correct term here, for the sake of clarity.

Tilting, like panning, allows you to visually connect subjects or areas that are spaced apart. Otherwise, you would need to intercut different shots, or use a longer shot to include both subjects.

Tilting can be used:

1. To emphasize *height* or *depth* – tilting up from a mountaineer . . . to show the steep cliff face to be climbed.
2. To show *relationships* – as the camera tilts from the rooftop watcher . . . down to his victim in the street below; or from the victim . . . up to the rooftop, revealing that he is not alone.

Fundamentally, *tilting upward* creates feelings of rising interest and emotion, expectancy, hope, anticipation. Conversely, *tilting downward* is allied to lowering interest and emotion, disappointment, sadness, critical inspection.

Where the viewer is conditioned beforehand by dialogue or action, responses become more complex. The *downward* tilt can become an act of enquiry; the *upward* tilt, a gesture of despair. Again, where a subject no longer holds our interest, the relief of a downward tilt can produce an anticipatory feeling – although the movement is not itself anticipatory.

In practice, of course, you will not stop to hypothesize about each camera movement. You come to recognize the 'feel' of such treatment in a dramatic situation. For example, a woman hears of her son's death, and the camera *tilts down* with her, as she sits. This treatment conveys her grief more convincingly than either a static shot or a depressed viewpoint.

Camera height

The angle from which you shoot a subject can have a considerable influence on the audience's attitude towards it. Intercut high – and low-angle shots of a person demonstrate this immediately. In a drama you may deliberately choose the camera's height to emphasize or diminish a person's dramatic strength, or to control the impact of dialogue. Similarly, if you shoot a piece of sculpture from a low viewpoint it will appear imposing, forceful, and impressive; while shot from above it loses vitality and significance.

How you get that viewpoint is immaterial. Shooting an architect's miniature/model of land development, for example, you could equally well obtain an overhead view from a crane shot, a suspended camera, a mirror shot, or by attaching the subject vertically to the studio wall and shooting straight on to it. The effect is the same, although in some cases camera movement will be very restricted.

Extreme camera angles

Extreme angles have an unhappy knack of drawing attention to the abnormality or ingenuity of the camera's position. If your audience is left wondering how we got that shot, mechanics have intruded over artistic purpose. Similarly, during the now-familiar swooping and climbing of helicopter shots, the viewer can become overaware of wind-beaten grass or telltale shadows of the aircraft on the ground below.

Where extreme angles arise *naturally*, viewers accept them readily: looking down from an upper-storey window; looking up from a seated position; even an eavesdropper peering through

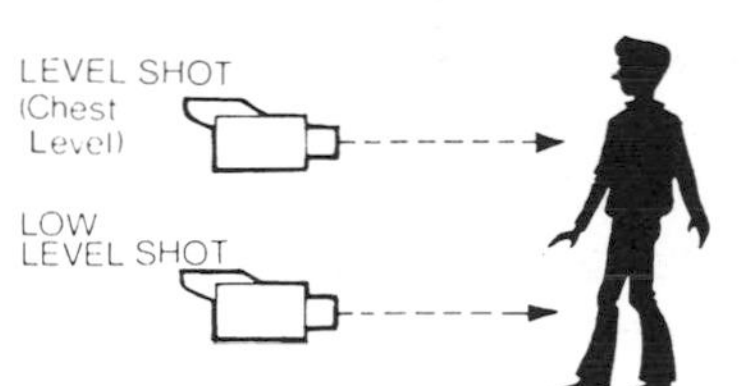

Fig. 6.6 part 1 Level shots
A normal viewpoint, usually around chest height; carries no special significance. Camera height: 1.2–1.8 m (4–5 ft) for a standing person. 1.1 m (3½ ft) for a sitting person.

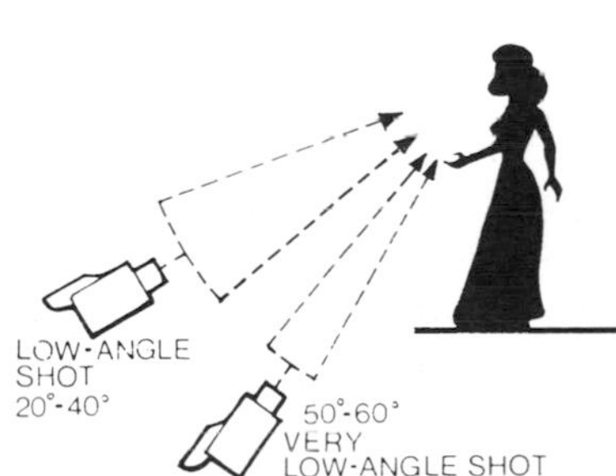

Fig. 6.6 part 2 Low shots
Low angle shots make most subjects appear stronger, more imposing, overpowering, strange, ominous. A person can seem threatening, pompous, authoritative, determined, dignified, benevolent, according to their attitude and environment. Dialogue and movement become significant and dramatic. The closer we are, the stronger these impressions. In a very-low-angle shot, the subject takes on a strangely distorted, even mystical, appearance. At greater distances, it appears remote and unknown.

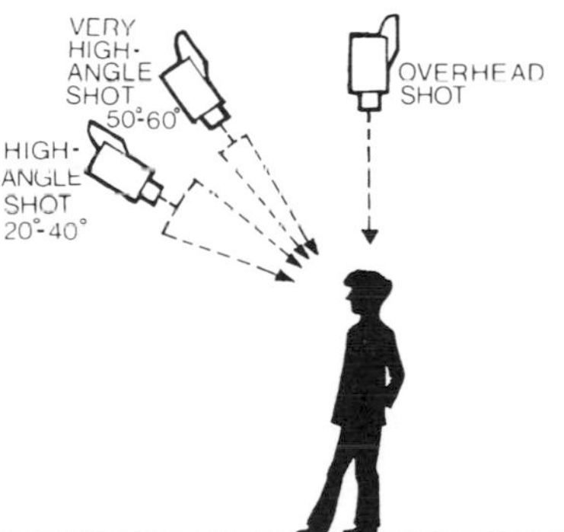

Fig. 6.6 part 3 High shots
High angle shots give the audience a sense of strength or superiority, an air of tolerance, even condescension, towards the subject; this feeling increases with distance. Therefore high shots can be used to imply unimportance, inferiority, impotence, etc. Very high angle shots give an attitude of peering down, scrutinizing. From a height of 3–6 m (10–20 ft) surveillance gives way to complete detachment. Overhead shots emphasize pattern and movement in formation (as in ballet and dance spectacle). They reveal isolation or congestion.

plank flooring to the room below. But an unexplained extreme usually becomes a visual stunt; for example, a bird's-eye view of a prisoner pacing a ceilingless cell, or shooting up through glass floors.

Emotional impact of extreme viewpoints

As you have seen, while *high shots* generally create an audience-strength/subject-weakness relationship, low shots reverse this influence. But the associations are often much more subtle than that. Imagine a high-angle shot of an old man trudging through rainswept streets. The audience does not feel 'strength' or 'superiority', but pities him, or feels sorry for his loneliness. But these are, of course, psychological variations on the fundamental theme of 'viewer-strength/subject-weakness' that the high shot provides.

In a very high angle shot, the viewer has an overall view; in fact, more than people on the spot. This underlying response colors our attitude to what we are seeing.

In an *aerial view* we survey the extent of the landscape; we follow the course of a river, seeing houses clustered along its banks, and its toy-like boats. We feel remote, seeing it all at a glance. We see the searchers moving towards the hiding fugitive. We see the magnitude of the invading army. But there is emotional detachment in this inspectional viewpoint; none of the involvement of more

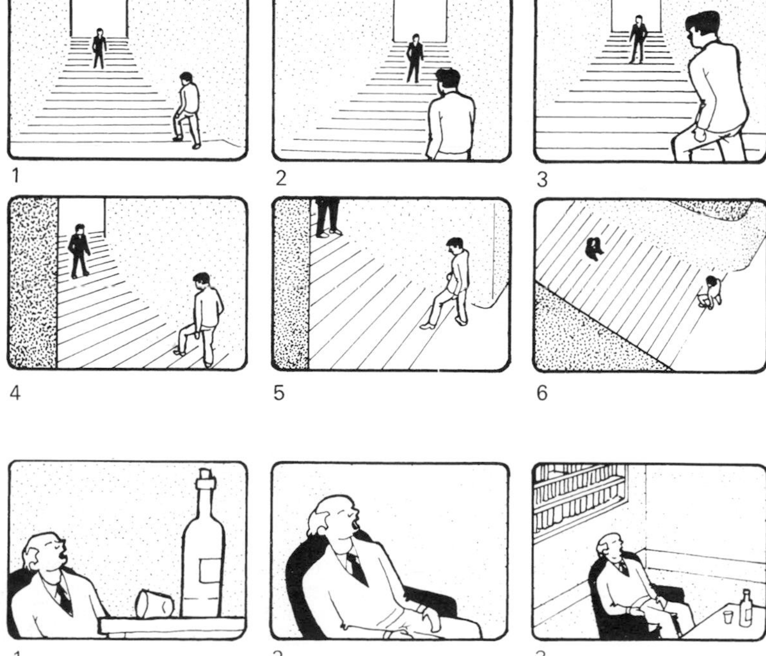

Fig. 6.7 The influence of viewpoint
The viewpoint you choose can influence how your audience responds to the action and to the location.

Part 1 Are we just seeing two people meeting (1), or a confrontation (2), or a challenge (3)? Is the person in white dominant (3), or the person in black (4) (5)? Are we detached observers (6)?

Part 2 Viewpoint can affect how the audience interprets the action, the mood, the dramatic impact. Here an old man sits sleeping. But our first impressions are that (1) he is drunk . . . or (2) just sleeping quietly . . . or (3) lonely, deserted.

Fig. 6.8 Verticals in overhead shots
In overhead shots, the position of the camera relative to strong verticals in the scene can considerably affect shot impact.

1 Verticals at the bottom of the frame cause tension and instability.
2 This impression is absent where foreground verticals are at the top of the frame.

normal camera positions. Dynamics are reduced. Some subjects, such as high-wire acts, juggling, balancing feats, can lose their appeal entirely if shot from above, whereas a very low angle position emphasizes their difficulty and suspense.

Portraiture

The camera's height modifies what people look like, too. *Elevated shots* (especially on wide-angle lenses) emphasize baldness and plumpness in women; also through foreshortening and distortion, they can produce a dumpy sawn-off effect.

Low-angle shots can emphasize dilated nostrils, upturned or large noses, heavy jawlines, and scrawny necks. Men with high foreheads or receding hair may look entirely bald. Protruding ears may appear very prominent.

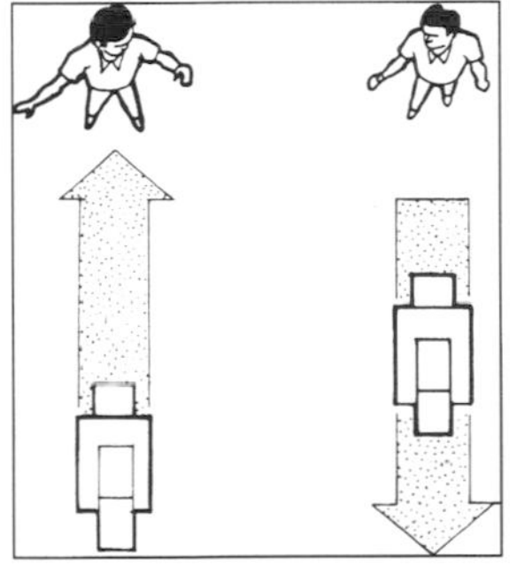

Fig. 6.9 Dollying (tracking)
Moving to or from the subject. *Dollying in* causes increased interest, build-up of tension, but the closer view may result in disappointment, disillusionment and, consequently, diminished interest. Dollying back results in lowered interest, relaxed tension; unless unseen subjects are revealed, or when curiosity, expectation, or hope have been aroused. Attention tends to be directed towards the edges of the picture. Rapid dollying is visually exciting, but space and safe speed restrict fast moves. (Controlled zooming may produce allied effects.) Dollying (like subject movement to and from camera) appears faster than it really is, on a wide-angle lens, and slower on a narrower lens angle.

Moving the camera

How freely you can move the camera around is determined by the type of mounting used. Whereas a crane boom shot offers considerable flexibility, it may not be able to relocate the viewpoint as rapidly as a highly mobile pedestal. Well-chosen camera moves add visual interest and vitality, as well as engendering certain audience reactions. The inter-movement of planes (parallactic changes) that takes place as the camera moves provides an illusion of solidity and depth; a realness that no static zooming camera can achieve.

But camera movement needs to be motivated, appropriate, smoothly controlled, and at a suitable speed, or it can become restless and disturbing.

Prominence of camera movement

The effects of camera movement are most obvious when shooting a static subject. Movement impact is correspondingly lessened where the camera moves with the subject; e.g. following it in a *tail-away shot* as the subject moves away; or dollying out as the subject approaches the camera in a *head-on shot*. And if respective direction and speeds match in a *traveling shot*, the dynamic effect of movement will come largely from the passing background. Whenever camera and subject are heading toward or away from each other, the overall impression is considerably heightened.

Move the camera – or the subject?

There are intrinsic differences between the effects of moving the *camera* or moving the *subject*. You can see this by watching a mute TV screen in a darkened room. You will feel your peephole vision moved around, almost physically, as the moving camera *subjectively* examines the scene. Where the camera is static, the performers will seem to move to and from you; an *objective* effect.

Camera movement (or zooming) becomes 'our behavior' by proxy, towards the subject. *We* the audience are moving; going up to look at or meet the subject . . . to satisfy our curiosity or to see detail more clearly. Forward camera movement is strong and exploratory; while dollying back is usually a weak move.

When a performer moves towards or away from the camera, we the audience become recipients of 'his attitude towards us'. Our

1 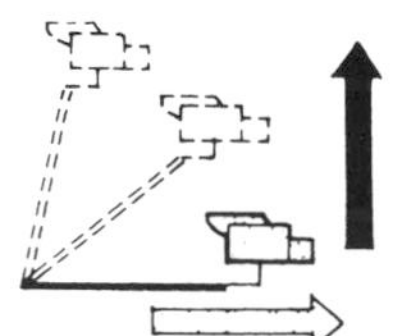
2 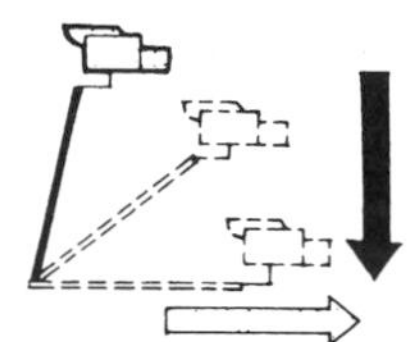
3 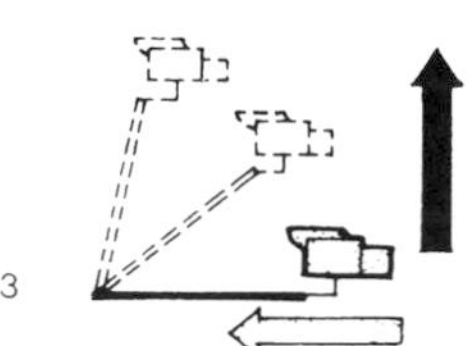
4 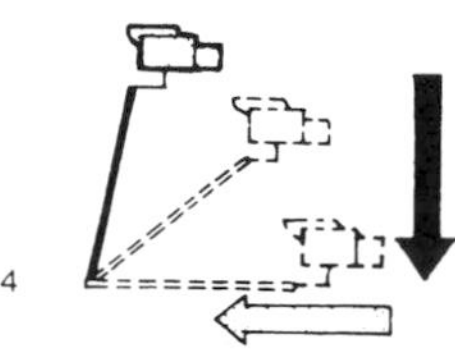

Fig. 6.10 part 1 Height changes on a static dolly (craning or booming)
1 When craning up from level, audience response is elation, superiority, eventual detachment as height increases; while the subject becomes less significant, even unimportant.
2 When craning down from level, the response is depression, inferiority, even a feeling of being dominated; and the subject becomes more important, impressive, significant.
3 Craning down from an elevated height with superior viewpoint will produce an effect of return to normality, with some sense of depression.
4 Craning up from low-level to level produces the same effect, but with a slight feeling of elation.

1 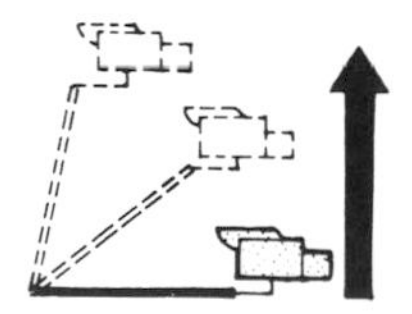
2 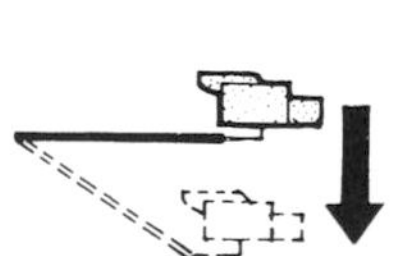
3 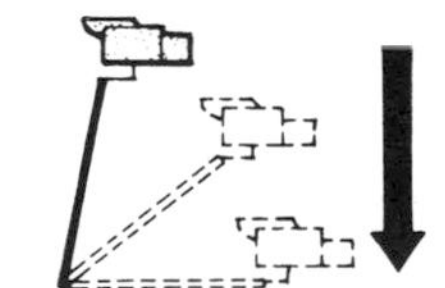
4 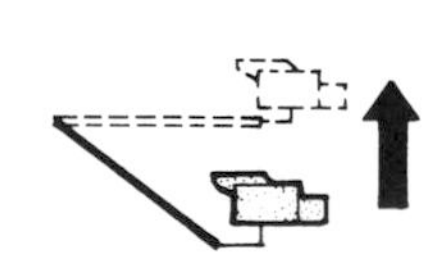

Fig. 6.10 part 2 Height changes on a moving dolly (craning or booming)
1 Forwards and craning upwards creates an air of freedom, flight, lack of restriction, elevation, joy.
2 Dollying forwards and craning down, implies swooping, power, strength, importance relative to subject when fast; but when done slowly suggests depression, return to normality.
3 Dollying back and craning upwards gives a feeling of complete release: detachment from the subject or action.
4 Dollying back and craning down is a recessive move, often saddening or disillusioning; a return to earth: no longer detached from subject or action.

Fig. 6.11 Arcing

1 Circling round a subject to see it from a different viewpoint, tends to be a self-conscious move, drawing attention to the action. Spurious side-slip effects can arise.
2 Slight position changes can help when one performer masks (obscures) another.

reactions to his move largely depend upon his demeanour; whether his action is forceful or casual. Circumstances may alter situations – we may experience an 'audience superiority' effect as someone walks the length of a corridor to meet us, but 'inferiority' if they sit while we (the camera) have to move up to meet them. And remember, the impact of all movements to and from the camera will be influenced by the lens angle you are using.

Subjective treatment

When you use the camera *subjectively*, it is as if the viewer is actually walking about within the scene, following the action. The camera pushes through a crowd, moves up to inspect something, glances up at nearby detail. We encounter this approach regularly, of course, when shoulder-mounted cameras are used, instead of shooting from the static viewpoint of a fixed tripod.

Subjective camera movement creates a participatory effect for the audience. But if a director moves us when we do not want to do so, or fails to show us something we wish to see, we feel resentful

Fig. 6.12 Camera and subject movement

Someone enters a room (in long shot) and crosses to a table (arriving in close-up). There are two methods of single-camera treatment, each providing a different audience impact.

1 The entrance and walk are taken in long shot. When the subject has stopped, the camera dollies in to close-up.
2 The camera pans and trucks throughout the walk, with subject and camera arriving simultaneously in a close-up.

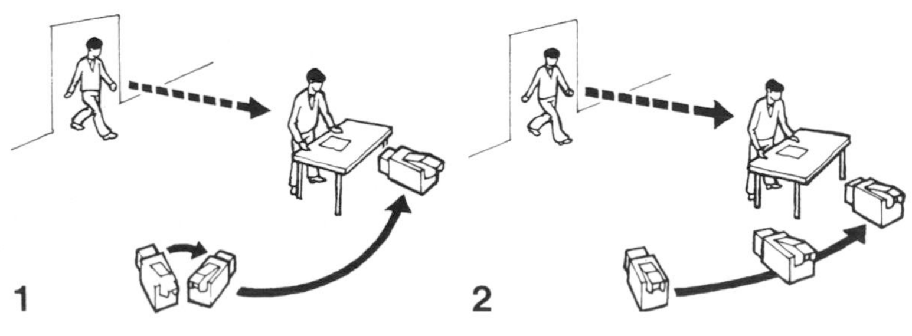

Fig. 6.13 part 1 Following the subject – long shot throughout
Audience impact comes chiefly from the moving environment, subject importance being limited. The pace of action is relatively slow. Varying composition or tone during the pan, can produce emotional changes – e.g. the 'uplift' on panning from low to high key. Sudden mood changes are achieved by, for example, having the actor raise window blind to let in daylight, or switching room lights.

Fig. 6.13 part 2 Following the subject – close shot throughout
The subject dominates, its strength depending on camera height. The influence of the environment is limited, and pace varies with dynamic composition. Slightly off-centering the subject in the direction of movement creates a feeling of anticipation, expectancy.

1 Profile – weak against a plain background, but an impression of speed and urgency against a detailed background.
2 Three-quarter frontal – can be dramatically strong. By preventing us from seeing the subject's route or destination, marked curiosity can be encouraged.
3 Elevated frontal – although weakened, the subject dominates the environment.
4 Depressed frontal – the subject is especially forceful, dominating the environment. *Rear shots introduce a subjective effect.*
5 Three-quarter rear – partially subjective; the viewer moves with the subject, expectancy developing during movement.
6 High rear shot – almost entirely subjective; produces increased anticipation; searching.
7,8 In level and low shots there is a striking sense of depth. The subject is strongly linked to the setting and other people, yet remains separate from them.

Fig. 6.13 part 3 Following the subject – long shot to close-up
The subject walks up to the camera. Environment predominates at first, but the subject grows increasingly stronger as it approaches. The impact can be modified by dollying or zooming as the subject approaches.

Fig. 6.13 part 4 Following the subject – close-up to long shot
A weak, recessive movement, generally accompanied by lowering tension as the subject's strength falls and that of the environment increases. Used to depict pathos, anticlimax.

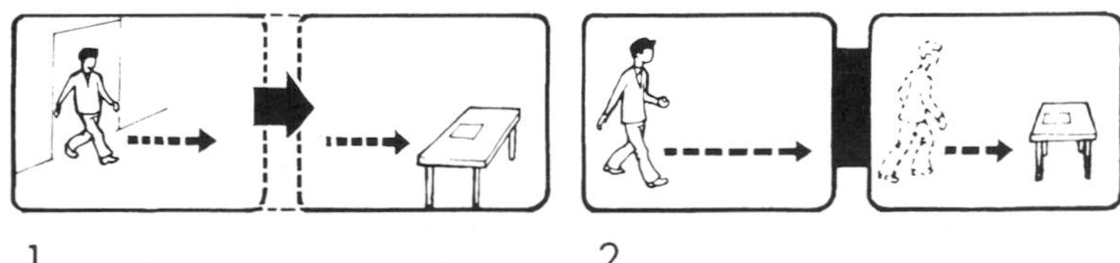

Fig. 6.13 part 5 Following the subject – then arriving at the destination beforehand

1 The camera moves more quickly than the subject, to the destination – the quickening pace providing an exciting introduction to the new position; but it must be sustained to be effective. The shot shows spatial relationships and gives the viewer time to assimilate the destination before the subject arrives.
2 Here the person begins to move, you cut to the destination, and he/she then arrives. Often mechanically convenient, the cut gives the destination shot impact. Audience-superiority can arise through foreknowledge of the subject's destination, and provide pathos, bathos, stage irony, climactic effects. It avoids lengthy dollying shots, and can imply non-existent spatial relationships. Irrelevant intermediate movement is eliminated and pseudo-filmic-time effect achieved, but interest and tension can flag while awaiting the subject.

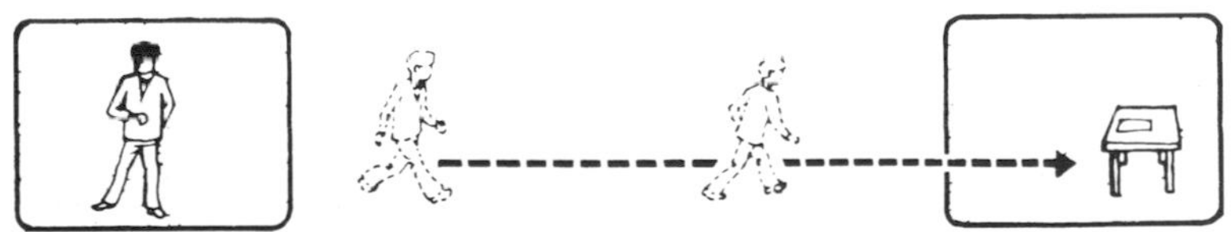

Fig. 6.13 part 6 Following the subject – cutting from the static subject to the destination
A simple but weak treatment, unless dialogue or gesture has indicated that the person is going to move. Spatial relationship or significance may not be clear to the viewer. Static action cuts of this kind can make the viewer over-conscious of the time taken for the subject's move. On commenced-action cuts, as in part 5 above, this is less pronounced.

or frustrated. The skilled director persuades his audience to want a change in viewpoint, or a move. The unskilled director thrusts it upon them.

Imitative camera movement

Apart from the familiar ploy of moving cameras to suggest jogging vehicles or rolling ships, camera movements can provide subjective comments on the action itself. Staggering as it dollies after a drunk;

Fig. 6.14 The canted shot

1 Canting is most pronounced with subjects inherently associated with horizontal or vertical stability. Left: slight slanting (about 10°) is ineffectual. Centre: typical tilt around 20–30° is used to convey instability, abnormality, dynamism. Right: excessively canted (50–60°) the effect is excessive overbalancing.

2 From low-angle (or high-angle) positions, canting causes subjects to lean into, or out of frame.

copying the bounce of a dandy's gait; swaying in waltztime as we follow a girl home from her first dance.

Drawing attention to itself quite openly, the camera movement becomes a tongue-in-cheek observation between the director and his audience. When it comes off, this device has persuasive appeal.

Using the zoom lens

As you saw in Chapter 4, the zoom lens brings both advantages and pitfalls for the unwary. It is too easy to use lens angles indiscriminately, just to change subject image size.

There is a great temptation to stand and zoom, rather than move around with a normal lens angle. It is an easy operation, demands little of the camera operator or director, and avoids problems such as keeping close cameras out of long shots. There is just the need for a pre-zoom focus check, before zooming in.

Zooming is extremely convenient. But it only simulates camera movement. There are no natural parallactic changes; and scale, distance, and shape become distorted through zooming. A slow zoom made during panning, tilting, or subject movement may disguise these discrepancies. A rapid zoom during an exciting fast-moving ball game would scarcely disturb even the pedant. Much depends on the occasion.

Zooming can provide a visual bridge from the wide view to the close-up, without the time and effort involved in dollying or the

Table 6.2 The effects of lens angles

About 50°	The widest lens angle generally used in the studio. Used for wide shots at close camera distances. Used to exaggerate setting size, space, distance, scale. Exaggerates dolly movements and speed. Exaggerates performer movements to and from the camera. Used to frame fast on erratically moving subjects. Allows very smooth camera handling. Provides considerable depth of field. (It may be excessive.) Used to create deliberate grotesque geometric (barrel) distortion – e.g. of CU faces, forward arm movements. But camera is liable to *overshoot* (*shoot*-off), and get lens flares.
*About 35°**	Frequently used for close shots of small objects, but camera shadows may arise. Enhances the impression of space and distance, but without the extreme exaggeration of wider lens angles. Generally emphasizes dolly movements and speed. Provides easy camera handling. Greater depth of field makes focusing much easier. Appreciable camera movement may be necessary to correct framing.
About 25°	The 'normal' lens angle, used for most purposes and providing natural perspective in the picture. A generally effective lens angle for good camera handling. Allows convenient working distances when shooting close-ups, title cards, etc. The associated depth of field suits most shots. It is sufficient for longer shots (deep focus), yet allows closer subjects to be isolated from their defocused background.
About 15°	Useful narrow angle for 'close shots' from a distance – whether due to subject inaccessibility, or to avoid other cameras coming in shot. Isolates individuals from a group. Noticeable compression of depth and perspective distortion. Camera handling is not easy. The lens angle is only really suitable for slight dolly movements. Depth of field is somewhat restricted.
About 10°	Achieves close-ups from around 3.5 m (11½ ft) but depth compression is considerable. Very 'compressed' perspective. Depth of field is very limited for close shots. Camera handling becomes coarse; needs skilled operation, even for limited movements. Movement of close subjects is often hard to follow accurately.
About 5°	Used for static close shots on a distant camera. Considerable depth compression. Mainly suitable for flat subjects, where perspective distortion is absent. Most unsuitable for close-ups of people, because of extreme perspective distortion. Camera handling is extremely coarse. Subject movement is very difficult to follow. Depth of field is extremely limited.

Typical lens angles

Approx. angle	*CCD size* 1.2 in. (12.5 mm)	⅔ in. (18 mm)
50°	7 mm	9.5 mm
35°	10 mm	14.0 mm
25°	14.5 mm	20.0 mm
15°	24 mm	33.5 mm
10°	37 mm	50.0 mm
5°	73 mm	101.0 mm
	Focal length setting	

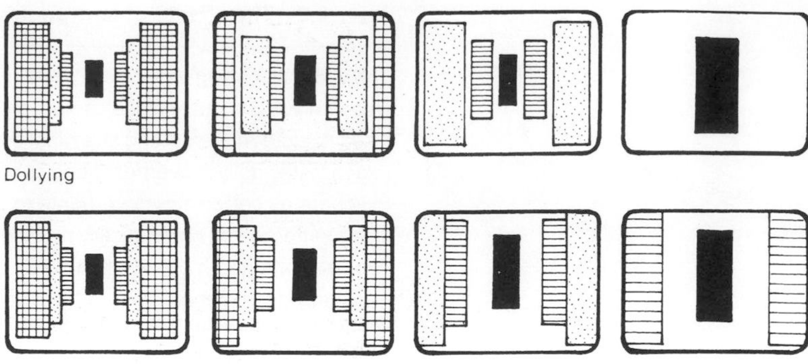

Fig. 6.15 Comparing dollying and zooming

1 *Dollying:* when a camera moves through a scene, relative sizes and spacing of subjects change proportionately. This continual parallactic movement causes planes to become visible and disappear with position changes. Perspective remains constant.

2 *Zooming:* as the field of view alters with lens angle, the shot is simply enlarged or diminished. There is no parallactic movement, no planes appear/disappear, or change relative proportions. So effective perspective appears to change (unless the viewer adjusts his viewing distance to compensate) and visible 'depth-stretching' or compression results.

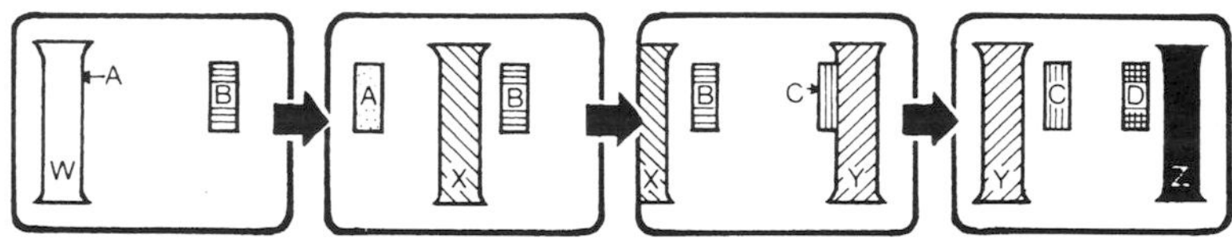

Fig. 6.16 Trucking (crabbing)

Moving across the scene, parallel with it. Trucking becomes associated with an attitude of inspection, critical observation, expectancy, intolerant appraisal. The lateral displacement of planes (*parallactic movement*) introduces a strong illusion of depth and solidity, but the restriction of the picture's frame becomes over-apparent if trucking stops abruptly.

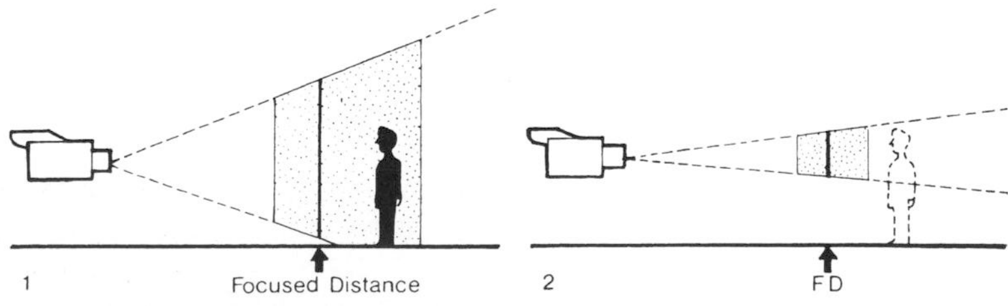

Fig. 6.17 The need to pre-focus

1 The considerable depth of field available with a wide lens angle broadens focusing, so that subjects may appear sharp although not at the focused plane.

2 However, on zooming in to a narrow lens angle (without re-focusing) depth of field becomes restricted, and the subject now falls outside the available depth of field.

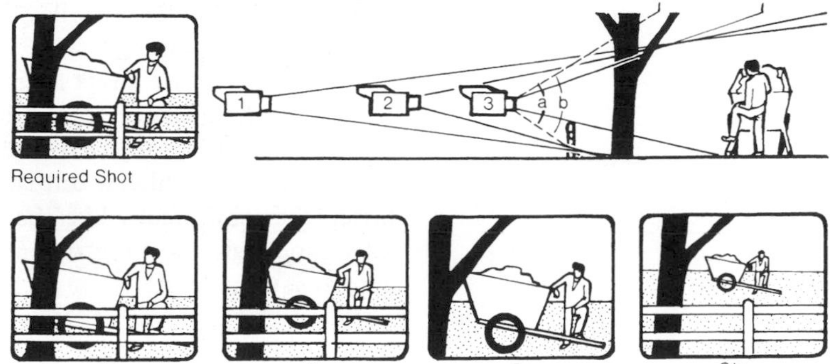

Fig. 6.18 Adjusting proportions
Altering relative subject proportions in the picture can be achieved by changing to a different lens-angle and readjusting camera distance (see Fig. 4.11 part 2).

1 A distant narrow-angle lens provides the required subject/foreground proportions.
2 A closer position using a normal lens angle, shows required foreground proportions, but the subject appears too small.
3a Dollying-in will correct the subject size but loses the foreground fence.
3b Widening the lens angle now will bring the fence into shot again, but the subject image appears small and the subject-foreground distance increased.

Table 6.3 Adjusting picture proportions

Subject size	*Background appears*	*Lens angle correction*	*Camera position*
Too large	Too large*	Use wider lens angle (zoom out)	Keep camera still
Too small	Too small*	Use narrower lens angle (zoom in)	Keep camera still
Satisfactory	Too distant	Use narrower lens angle	Increase camera distance
Satisfactory	Too near	Use wider lens angle	Move camera closer
Too large	Satisfactory	Use narrower lens angle	Increase camera distance
Too small	Satisfactory	Use wider lens angle	Move camera closer

** But relative subject/background proportions satisfactory.*

interruption (and possible disorientation) of *cutting*. A *rapid zoom-in* produces a highly dramatic swoop onto the subject. An instant *crash (snap) zoom-in* flings subject detail at the audience. Such effects can be fantastically forceful – or plain annoying!

All zooming should be decisive. Avoid the nauseous results of rhythmical or jerky in-out zooms, or quick *slight* angular changes that look like an operational error.

Zooming on *flat surfaces* (maps, illustrations) avoids the need to follow focus that dollying would entail. On title cards you can produce carefully controlled size changes (titling growth or shrinkage) by zooming.

Use zoom-ins to direct attention, to increase tension, to give powerful emphasis, or to restrict the coverage. But the zooming action itself should be used discriminately for particular occasions – like wipes, star filters, diffusion discs, and similar productional tinsel. Certain effects, like that of zooming in and dollying back simultaneously (keeping the subject-size constant), are bewildering, to say the least!

7 Effective picture making

Why do some pictures look very attractive, while the eye passes over others disinterestedly? Why do some draw the eye to a particular subject, while in others we look around? Why are some pictures so atmospheric, while others appear so 'ordinary'? The answers lie in effective picture making.

Behind the picture

One tends to think of picture making as the prerogative of the camera operator. For the camera on location that is largely true. But in the studio, where the entire environment is *contrived*, it is the culmination of many combined talents.

The design of the setting, the way it has been lit, the viewpoint selected by the director, can all be controlled to provide appropriate conditions for the occasion. The tonal quality of the picture, too, can be adjusted electronically over a wide range.

The camera operator's opportunities to create a meaningful composition depend directly on the way the scene has been developed, how action has been arranged. Stand someone in front of a flatly lit plain background, and the prospects for interesting shots are very limited. Sit the same person in a well-designed, attractively lit setting, and the camera can explore the situation, producing arresting shots.

Persuasive picture making is the result of successful teamwork. If the lighting is inappropriate, or the director selects an ineffective camera position, the result will be inferior pictures – and lost opportunities.

Composing the picture

What is *composition*? Some people think that it is the idea of arranging pictures to provide an attractive harmonious effect. It is much more than that. It is a way of arranging pictures so that the

Fig. 7.1 Why compose the picture?
The unguided eye wanders around the scene, finding its own centers of interest.

viewer is directly attracted to certain features. You can influence how viewers respond to what they are seeing. You can compose a picture to create anticipation, unease, apprehension, excitement, restful calm. The mood can be depressed, or expansive.

The principles we shall explore here are guides, rather than 'rules' to be slavishly copied, but they are essentially *practical.*

Practical composition

Under everyday working conditions you will meet three basic approaches to composition:

1 Composition by **design**.
2 Composition by **arrangement**.
3 Composition by **selection**.

Composition by design

This occurs where you have an *entirely free hand* in composing your picture. The artist approaching a blank canvas can arrange line, tone, and color in any way he or she chooses, without concern for accuracy or feasibility. The physical limitations are minimal and are inherent in this medium. Canaletto 'improved' his paintings of Venice by actually repositioning entire buildings for effect, whatever the resulting topographical errors. Only occasionally does this freedom exist for the camera (e.g. in process work).

Composition by arrangement

Here you *deliberately position subjects* before the camera to produce an appealing, meaningful result. A set designer dressing a setting does this by placing furniture, flowers, and ornaments to form appropriate arrangements. Sometimes even a single carefully introduced foreground object (a leafy branch, perhaps), will help the camera operator to devise appropriate composition.

More usually, a designer creates *potential* rather than specific composition opportunities; an environmental package suiting the mood and mechanics of the occasion, rather than calculated composition arrangements.

There is always the danger when arranging natural situations that the resultant effect will look deliberately contrived. You can become over-aware of how 'cleverly' the picture has been manipulated.

Composition by selection

This is the situation most camera operators encounter. The camera is positioned at a certain viewpoint chosen by the director (or the camera operator) and the director composes the shot *using what is there*, to show the subject most effectively. In this situation you can adjust the picture's composition in several ways:

- *Adjust framing.* Positioning the shot to deliberately include/exclude parts of the scene, or to alter subjects' positions in the frame (balance).
- *Increasing/decreasing the lens angle.* The lens angle of view will determine how much of the scene appears in the picture from that viewpoint.
- *Adjusting the camera position.* As the camera moves up/down or sideways, foreground objects change position in the frame more noticeably than distant ones. So even slight readjustments can considerably alter the compositional relationships.
- *Proportions.* By altering the lens angle, and changing the camera distance to compensate, you can keep the same sized shot but adjust proportions within it.

The director and composition

The director's attitude to pictorial composition varies between individuals, and with the type of production. For many shows, the director is so preoccupied with what is being said, with performance, continuity, and mechanics, that he or she does not arrange the composition of shots specifically. Instead, indicating the shot size required (CU, singles, two-shots, group shots) and leaving details of lens angle, framing, etc. to the camera operator.

In other types of production (primarily drama), the director deliberately groups actors to provide particular compositional arrangements – for dramatic effect, or to direct audience attention. In some cases, the director (or the set designer) may have prepared a *storyboard sketch*, showing the detailed composition of certain *key-shots.*

Composition principles

Composition principles are not laws. They are indications of how people respond to distribution of line and tone. Whether you put that tone into the scene, or are selecting from whatever is already

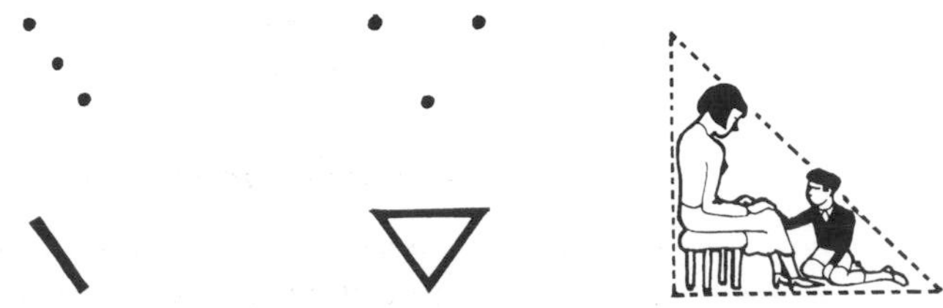

Fig. 7.2 Subjective lines
The mind tends to seek pattern and to see relationships, even where none really exist. Individual subjects seem to combine or interact to form patterns.

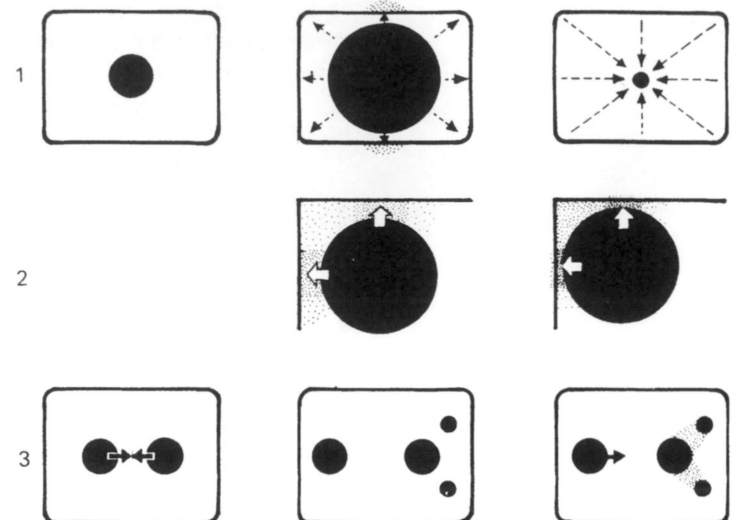

Fig. 7.3 Illusory attraction
1 A disk in the center of the frame appears at rest, surrounded by empty areas of equal tension. A change in subject size alters this reaction between the subject and its frame. An over-large subject bulges the frame, squeezing-out the surrounding space, while a too-small subject becomes compressed by the large area of empty space surrounding it.
2 This compression effect gives way to a forceful thrusting as the intermediate space lessens.
3 Tension is built up between subjects in a picture. The two close subjects convey a feeling of mutual interlinking – illusory attraction. In a more complex example, the isolated subject appears to be attracted towards the more stable supported group.

there, is not important. What *is* important is that if you do not organize pictures appropriately, your audience may well react by looking at the wrong things, interpret the picture inappropriately, or become bored by unattractive shots. *Composing shots* is not just a matter of 'pictorial packaging' but a method of controlling continuity of thought.

The effect of the picture frame

The camera does much more than 'put a frame' round a segment of the scene. *It inherently modifies whatever it shows*. Because the screen *totally isolates* its subjects (the viewer cannot see whatever else is happening), and because the resultant picture is flat (and cannot reproduce stereoscopic depth) unique relationships develop within it that are not present in the actual scene.

No shot directly portrays *reality*. In many cases our own experience enables us to rationalize and interpret, so that we make a pretty accurate assessment of what we are seeing, e.g. a tourist photograph composed to make the Statue of Liberty rest on someone's outstretched hand . . . or is it a model after all? But this does not always happen; particularly where the viewer is not familiar with the situation.

The subjective effects that arise in the flat framed picture take several forms:

1 Although one plane may be some distance behind another, they can appear conjoined or even merge in the shot.
2 Spatially unrelated areas of tone and color are often juxtaposed in the picture; interacting and influencing pictorial balance. Simultaneous contrast effects result.

3 Seen in perspective on the flat screen, the shapes of objects and composition lines can change with camera angle.
4 A series of quite unrelated subjects at varying distances can combine pictorially to form a composition group.
5 Within the picture, *imaginary* composition relationships can seem to develop between subjects, and visual tensions form between them.
6 As subjects approach the edge of the screen, impressions of tension or compression can develop; particularly in screen-filling shots.
7 The lateral position of subjects influences their composition impact.
8 Various dynamic effects arise (dynamic composition).

Proportions

There are no formulae for beauty. But centuries ago, artists discovered a widely accepted principle guiding harmonic proportions – the Golden Section or Golden Mean. Great painters, sculptors, architects have used these ratios in many ways (often unwittingly, perhaps) when expressing their concepts of beauty.

If you cut a straight line into sections that provide the most pleasing relationship, you will find with incredible regularity that the line lengths are divided according to the Golden Section, in a constant ratio, so that the small part is to the larger, as the larger is to the whole. These proportions work out in practice to about 8:13 (often quoted as 3:5).

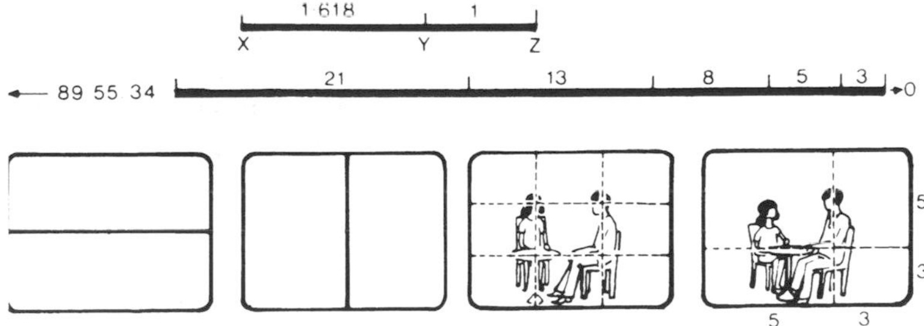

Fig. 7.4 Proportions
The Golden Section. Dividing for ideal proportions tends to produce YZ:XY in the same proportions as XY:XZ. Making several such divisions, a series appears, and this ratio of division, the Golden Section, is about 3:5.

Dividing the frame. An equally divided frame allows only formal balance – usually dull and monotonous. Thirds can lead to quickly recognized mechanical proportions. Dividing the screen in a 2:3, or a 3:5 ratio achieves a far more pleasing balance.

Such proportioning has quite far-reaching applications, for it gives us a guide to ratios that most readily please the eye. Be suspicious of such formulae; but see how often they seem to validate themselves.

Rule of thirds

When composing a shot, you should avoid mechanically dividing the screen into regular sections. A screen cut into halves or quarters can produce a dull, monotonous balance.

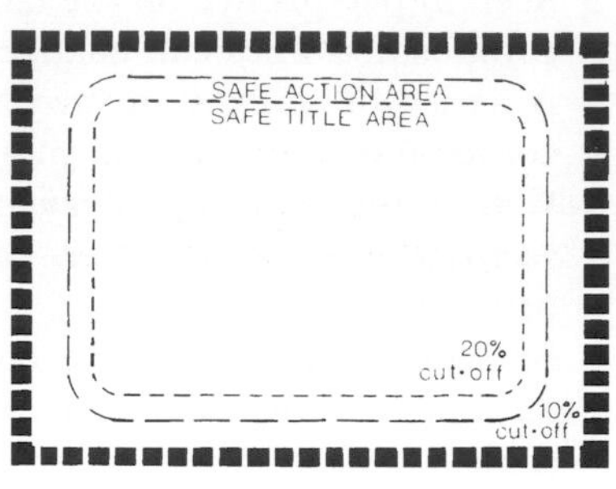

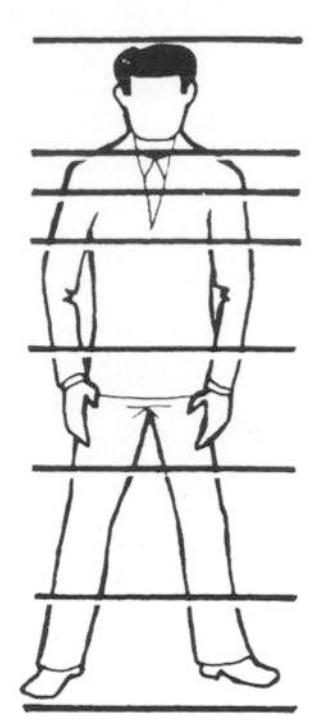

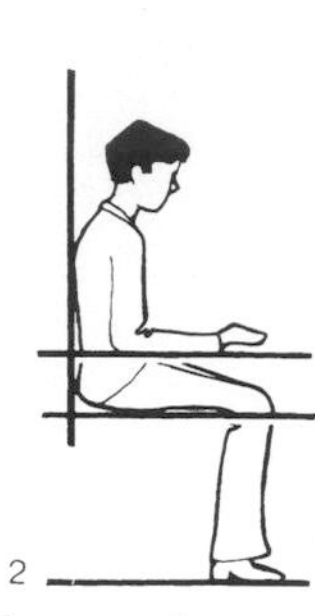

Fig. 7.5 part 1 Safety margins
As TV screen edges are usually masked off, avoid placing important action or titling near the frame edges. Some monitors and camera viewfinders indicate the safe area (engraved, or from a special generator).

Fig. 7.5 part 2 Framing people
1 Avoid frame-cutting people at natural joints: as shown intermediate cutting-points appear more attractive. Similarly avoid framing so that they touch the screen edge as in 2.

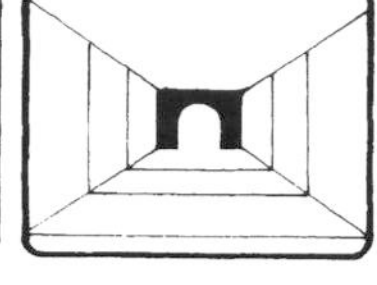

Fig. 7.5 part 3 Framing – frame positions
1 Center screen is generally the weakest area for holding the viewer's attention. Continual or sustained use of picture-center becomes monotonous.

2 Positions near frame edges seldom give good balance (particularly scenic lines running parallel with them). Frame corners exert an outward pull on subjects placed there. Subject strength and importance tends to increase higher in the frame and towards the right.

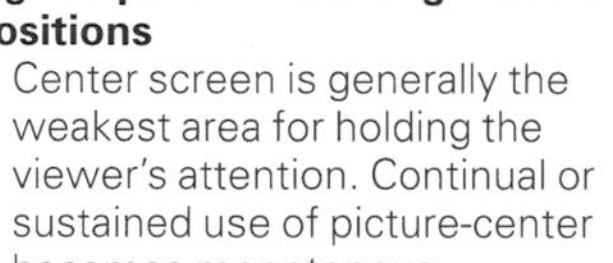

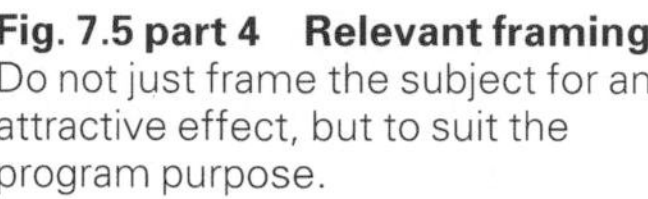

Fig. 7.5 part 4 Relevant framing
Do not just frame the subject for an attractive effect, but to suit the program purpose.

Fig. 7.5 part 5 Tight framing
Close shots of people bring problems such as arm gestures, or explanatory items remaining unseen out of shot. Tight framing emphasizes the screen's confines. Head movements can pass out of frame, leaving it empty; thus requiring catch-up panning, which is a fidgety and obtrusive operation.

You will find the 'rule of thirds' often advocated when selecting proportions. Main subjects are placed at the intersections of lines dividing the screen vertically and horizontally into three equal parts. A useful enough mechanical concept to guide in composing pictures, it should not be followed overslavishly for it can develop a recognizable sameness.

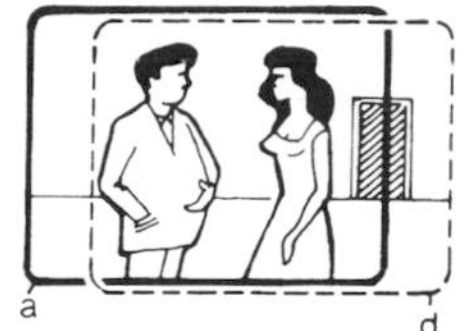

Fig. 7.5 part 6 Offset framing – still subjects
For side or 3/4 views, center-frame positions (*a*) provide an unattractive balance. Slight offsetting (*b*), sometimes referred to as 'looking room', is usually preferable; although this must not be overdone (*c*) unless you want to draw attention to that side of the frame, or imply isolation.

Horizontal framing can affect significance too. Notice when the door is included in the shot, someone's entry is expected (*d*).

Framing

As you frame or line up a shot, you are doing several important things:

1 First of all, you are choosing *exactly* what the viewer is going to see; what is to be included within the picture (*on-frame, in-frame*); and what is to be excluded from it (*off-frame, out-of-frame, out-of-shot*). You may be selecting to concentrate attention and avoid distractions, or to show more subject detail. You might omit information deliberately – or reveal it in another shot.

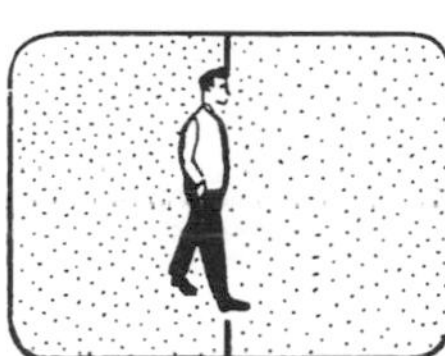

Fig. 7.5 part 7 Offset framing – moving subjects
When a subject moves, keep it slightly lagging behind the center of the frame. The amount of offset needed increases slightly with the speed of movement.

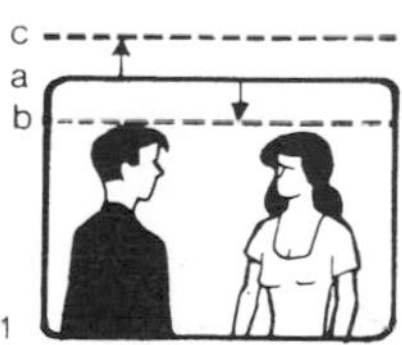

Fig. 7.5 part 8 Headroom
1 For good vertical balance, people should be framed with appropriate headroom (*a*). Avoid the cramping effect of insufficient headroom (*b*), or the bottom-heavy effect of excess (*c*).
2 Whether compositional elements become an incidental border, or oppressively overhang the action, largely depends on how they are framed.

Fig. 7.5 part 9 Reframing
As subjects leave or enter frame, the cameraman normally readjusts framing unobtrusively for the next situation. For dramatic purposes you may deliberately NOT reframe: the tension from the unbalanced composition emphasizing the second subject's departure or absence.

2 As you alter a shot's framing, you are repositioning line and tone within the picture, and modifying its audience impact.

All parts of the frame do not have equal pictorial value. The effect changes, depending on where you place the main subject.

How you frame a shot will not only alter compositional balance but can influence the viewer's interpretation of events. Framed in a certain way, a two-shot might lead him to expect someone is about to enter the room, or that an eavesdropper is outside a door.

Headroom changes proportionally with the length of shot; lessening as the shot tightens. In a multi-camera production the

Fig. 7.6 part 1 Adjusting balance

1 Balance pivots about the picture center.
2 Unbalanced shots are visually unstable and unattractive.
3 But formal *symmetrical* arrangements usually prove monotonous and uninteresting.
4 Certain compositional grouping has considerable stability, but must be correctly framed to appear balanced.
5 To reduce symmetry, you may angle subjects (avoiding head-on positions); for balance can change with shape.
6 Or you can adjust relative sizes of subjects.
7 Altering the subject's relative distances from center-frame changes pictorial balance. (Try adjusting positions of cut-out card shapes.)
8 Isolation gives a subject weight.
9 By *grouping* individual subjects, they have greater collective 'weight'. (See Fig. 7.7.)
10 *Size and tone* combine to affect overall balance. Larger areas and darker tones should be framed carefully. Dark tones towards the top of the frame produce a strong downward thrust – top-heaviness, a depressed closed-in feeling. At the bottom of the frame, they provide a firm base for composition, lending it solidity (See Fig. 7.12.)

headroom can vary considerably between different cameras. So it is as well for the director to check that comparable shots match.

Pictorial balance

For most purposes you will want *balanced* composition. Not the equal balance of formal symmetry, for that is uninteresting, but a picture with *equilibrium*.

Balance in a picture is affected by:

1 The *size* of a subject within the frame.
2 Its *tone*.
3 Its *position within the frame*.
4 The *interrelationship of* subjects in the shot.

A balanced picture has a coordinated, structured look. Balance unifies the subjects within a shot. Occasionally, you may deliberately arrange the picture so that it is *unbalanced*, to create a dynamic restlessness or tension. But use this effect sparingly. A balanced arrangement does not have to be static. You can continually readjust the balance of a shot – by moving a person, altering the framing, etc. – so as to redirect attention to a different subject, or to alter the picture's impact. *Balance* is a very subjective effect. You cannot measure it. But there are number of useful guiding principles:

1 A center-frame position is satisfactory; safe but dull to watch.
2 As a subject moves from picture center, the shot feels progressively unbalanced.

Fig. 7.6 part 2 Changing balance
Balance and emphasis can be altered in several ways.
1 By changing the lens-angle (zooming) – size change.
2 By altering the camera-distance – proportions change.
3 Readjusting subject height.
4 Altering subject grouping.
5 Changing camera height.
6 Changing viewpoint – different tones, masses come into shot.
7 Lighting changes – altering tones or colors of areas.

3 This effect arises more strongly with bigger and/or darker objects; especially if high in the frame.
4 A subject or tonal mass to one side of the frame usually requires compensatory counterbalancing in the remainder of the shot. This could be an equal opposite mass (symmetrical balance), or a series of smaller areas that together counterbalance the main offset region.
5 Tone influences visual *weight*: darker tone subjects look heavier and smaller than light-toned ones.
6 A small darker area, slightly offset, can balance a larger light-toned one further from picture center.
7 Darker tones towards the top of the frame produce a strong downward thrust – top-heaviness, a depressed closed-in effect. At bottom frame they introduce stability and solidity.
8 Balance is more influenced by vertical elements than horizontals; although the overall horizontal effect determines the final balance.
9 Regularly shaped subjects have greater visual weight than irregular ones.
10 Warmer colors (red, orange) appear heavier than cooler ones (blue, green), bright (saturated) hues looking heavier than desaturated or darker ones.

Unity (order)

When the composition of a shot is *unified* all its component parts appear to hang together, and form part of a complete pattern. Without unity, one has the impression of randomness; of items being scattered around the frame.

Wherever possible, try to group subjects (either across the screen or in depth) so that they appear interrelated – by real or imaginary compositional lines (Figures 7.19 and 7.20).

If you intercut between shots of a scene that give a very different impression from various viewpoints this can destroy *inter-shot unity*. So aim for visual continuity in style and tonal balance between successive shots.

Visual rhythm

In music and poetry the ear prefers a recognizable, but not too elementary, rhythmical beat; the eye also is attracted by a variety of

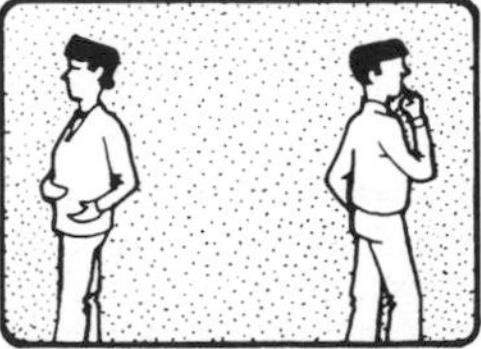
1

2

3

Fig. 7.7 Unity (order)
Unity is cohesion, interrelationship of masses. A picture can be balanced, yet not be unified (1), or a group unified without overall balance (2). Real or imaginary compositional lines create visual unification. Lines or tones that divide the screen (3) disrupt unity.

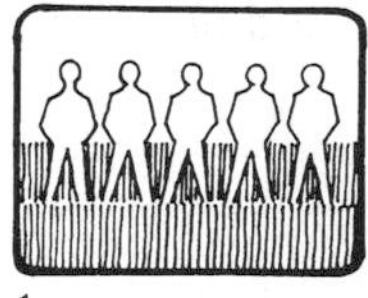

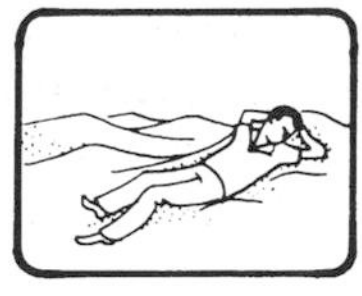

Fig. 7.8 Visual rhythm
1 Pictorial arrangements can produce a monotonous repetitive effect, or interesting variety of emphasis in shape or tone; a visual rhythm.
2 While verticals and diagonals give an emphatic rhythm, horizontals and slow curves convey a restful rhythm.
3 Although identical repetition is dull, used as a progressive visual development, repetition can build and strengthen a theme.

pattern. *Visual rhythm* is a pattern term; a variation of visual emphasis, of outline. While a solemn, quiet mood is suited by slow, smooth-flowing lines; a rapid, spiky staccato would match an exciting, dramatic situation.

The emotional influence of tone

The set designer and the lighting director use light and shade to create the picture's emotional key.

Large areas of contrasting tone can give a picture strength, vigor, significance. And in practice, most attractive shots usually include a wide variety of tones.

Where tones in a picture are predominantly light, the effect is open, simple, perhaps weak. Add small distinct areas of dark tone, and the picture develops a liveliness, cheerfulness, delicacy. Darker tones give a shot strength and significance. They can add force and dignity.

But pictures with large areas of unrelieved dark tone can look somber, heavy, or sordid. The overall impression can be disappointingly dull and uninteresting. Little detail or tonal gradation is generally visible, and video noise is often prominent. When there are smaller distinct light areas within the dark tones the overall effect tends to be mysterious, dramatic, or solemn.

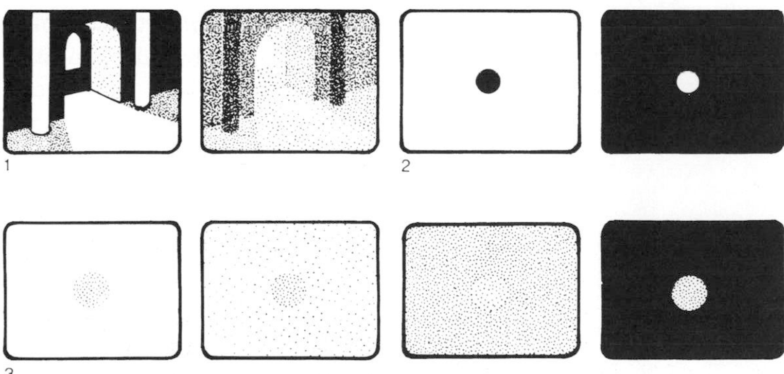

Fig. 7.9 part 1 Tonal impressions
Sharply defined tonal contrast (left) is used to isolate and define areas, suggest crispness, hardness, vitality, dynamism.

Graded tone (right) blends areas together, guiding the eye from darker to lighter regions. It suggests softness, beauty, restfulness, vagueness, lack of vigor, mystery.

Fig. 7.9 part 2 Tonal emphasis
Tonal contrast emphasizes shape and mass. A small dark area becomes subjugated within a large white background, whereas a small light area stands prominently from a dark tone.

Fig. 7.9 part 3 Simultaneous contrast (spatial induction)
Adjacent tones interact. A light tone can make a nearby one look darker; while a dark area apparently lightens a light tone further. The same central tone here appears different as its background changes. The sharper the contrast and borders, the stronger this effect.

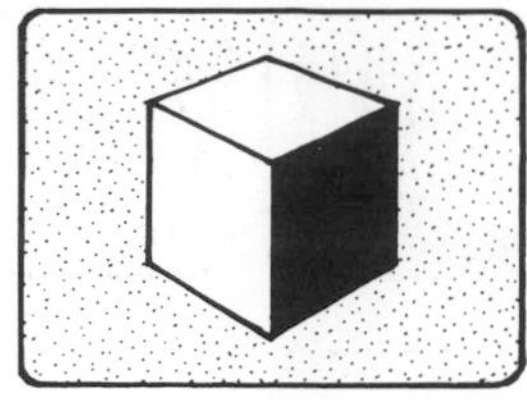

Fig. 7.10 Scale
The viewer judges scale subjectively, by how fully the subject fills the screen and by the presence of other objects of known size.
If size-references are omitted (absent or obscured by viewpoint) accurate interpretation of scale may be impossible.

Scale

We judge how large or small a thing is by comparing its size and proportions with familiar items we recognize in the picture. Without a comparative scale, we can only guess. A finger moves into shot, and we realize that a chair we are looking at is a skillfully made miniature. The eye is easily fooled, as you can see in Figures 7.10, 10.26 and 10.27.

Perspective lines can influence our impression of scale and relative size.

Again, although there is no relationship between shot size and the size of the subject, we often assume when an unfamiliar subject fills most of the frame that it is larger than it really is.

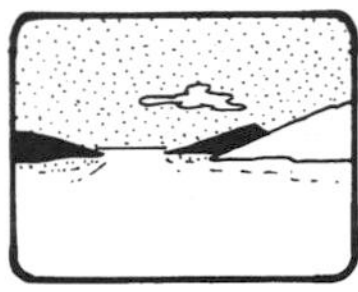

Fig. 7.11 Foreground and scale
Foregrounds influence our impression of scale and distance; particularly for isolated and remote subjects. Try to include foreground and perspective clues to define and unify depth; but avoid over-emphasized, stylized, and artificial relationships.

Subject prominence

A subject's *surroundings* have a considerable influence on our attitude towards it. Consider the difference between a coin imposingly displayed on a velvet cushion . . . or heaped with others in a rusty junk box. Depending on how you present a subject, it can appear important or trivial. It can look powerful or weak; interesting or incidental. It may even be overlooked altogether!

Isolation gives a subject emphasis. You can create this emphasis in many ways:

- By the subject's attitude
- By contrasting tones
- By the camera height
- By the composition of the picture
- By the subject's position and size relative to its surroundings
- By using background pattern or form to make the subject look more prominent.

You will find typical methods summarized in Figure 7.12.

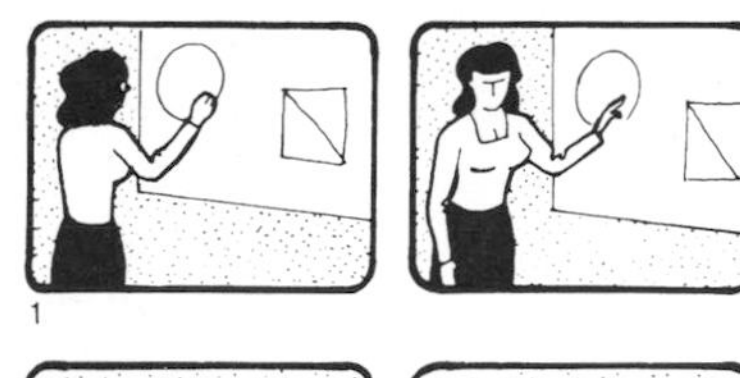

Fig. 7.12 part 1 How subject strength is influenced by viewpoint
1 Unsuitably arranged, a subject's strength is diminished.
2 Low-angle shots emphasize subject strength and importance; while high-angle shots suggest weakness, unimportance.
3 Subject-strength grows as the shot gets closer.

Fig. 7.12 part 2 Subject strength – frame position
Set higher in the frame, the subject gains strength.

Fig. 7.12 part 3 Subject strength – size proportions
Relative proportions of subject size and surroundings will affect the subject's 'power'.

Fig. 7.12 part 4 Surroundings influence subject strength
1 A supported subject appears weaker than an unsupported one.
2 A subject can be dominated by dynamic scenic lines, or by other stronger subjects.
3 Background line and tone can strengthen or weaken the subject.

Subject attitude

A performer's associative attitudes can modify his effective strength, whether he looks forceful, cowed, submissive.

His general *posture* is significant too. *Weak attitudes* include side or rear views, lying down, looking down, bowed, stooping, clasped hands, and slow movements. *Strong attitudes* include frontal view, uptilted head, hands clenched, stamping feet, and fast movement.

Camera treatment can have a considerable influence on our reactions to a subject. Shooting a ranting dictator in a high-angle long shot would make his gestures appear futile, weak, and ineffective. However, a low-angle mid-shot would give them a powerfully dramatic force.

Where you use a strong camera treatment for weak performance attitudes you strengthen them; so that an old woman making weak submissive gestures could seem to have a dignity and an inner strength against adversity when shot from a depressed viewpoint.

Picture shape

A picture's shape can affect the viewer's feelings towards the scene. A *horizontal* format can give it stability, restfulness, extent . . . A *vertical* format can imply height, balance, hope . . .

The original motion picture screen shape (aspect ratio) had 4:3 (1.33:1) proportions. But subsequently, to enhance big-screen presentation, several others were developed (1.65 to 2.55:1). Television adopted the original 4:3 format; and while this cannot be intrinsically altered, you can change its *effective shape* by introducing mattes (wipes), masks, scenic restriction or by lighting restriction.

Currently, television standards are changing. The demand for larger, sharper TV pictures has resulted in a new HDTV (High Definition TV) format with a picture in 16:9 proportions (1.77:1).

There is no *ideal* picture shape. The wider format that most effectively shows the entire sweep of a landscape in one shot will pose problems when you come to shoot a tall subject such as a skycraper or a tree. If you zoom back to take in the entire subject, the shot will now reveal a great deal of the scene on either side of it. This may be advantageous – e.g. demonstrating how tall the skyscraper is relative to its neighbors. But the picture may now include unwanted subjects (e.g. advertisements) that draw our audience's attention away from the subject itself.

Wide-format screens can make it more difficult to concentrate the audience's interest on central subjects. There can be a greater tendency to overshoot the side edges of a setting, and to get lens flares from back light in long shots, than when using a 4 by 3 picture shape.

In practice, you have to adapt to the format you are working with. If, for instance, when shooting a drama on an HDTV system, distracting subjects appear at the sides of the shot, you have the

1

2

3

Fig. 7.13 Picture shape
The effective picture shape can be modified by (1) electronic wipes, camera mattes (vignettes); or (2) by using a scenic opening as a border; or (3) by restricted lighting.

options of removing them, taking a closer shot, or introducing some foreground masking (e.g. a bystander, a piece of furniture, a bush) to hide the unwanted items.

For the director, there is a temptation to distribute subjects across the screen, and even to have dramatic interaction between people on the extreme left and right of the frame. Supposing, for example, the wide-format screen shows the villain entering frame on screen left, while the victim is seated on screen right. This could be a moment of high tension as the audience's concentration hops between them, watching their interreactions. But what if some of your audience are watching on 4 by 3 screens?

Unifying interest

You should normally arrange a picture so that the eye can find satisfaction within the frame; concentrating on certain features, while the rest become a subordinate background. Avoid three-ring circus techniques, with several things happening simultaneously. They divide attention, creating ambiguity and confusion. One picture – one focal point.

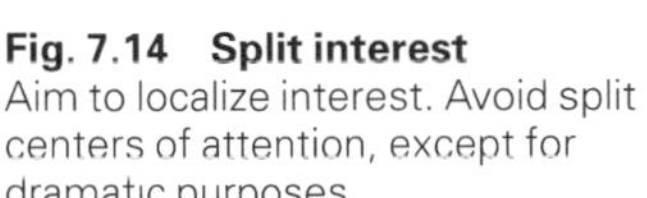

Fig. 7.14 Split interest
Aim to localize interest. Avoid split centers of attention, except for dramatic purposes.

Unifying the center of interest does not prevent you moving it around freely. This continual flow, linking together parts of the picture, is often termed *transition* or *continuity*. The eye moves naturally from one area to the next.

Speed of compositional lines

The eye scans some shapes at a leisurely rate (gently curved lines), while others are appreciated quickly (straight lines, zig-zags). Through suitable selection, you can adjust the picture's vitality and the speed with which the eye examines it. Faster lines move attention quickly and would allow fast intercutting.

Simple lines and shapes direct attention more readily than complex or disjointed ones. Interest is strongly attracted by clear-cut geometrical shapes, particularly when they seem to arise accidentally. An excess of simple line soon palls though, and leads to a stark unsympathetic atmosphere.

Fig. 7.15 Speed of composition lines

1 A pattern or direction-of-line over which the eye lingers is termed 'slow'. Predominating curved lines suggest leisure, beauty, deliberation.
2 'Fast' lines are usually straight or angular, creating an impression of speed and vitality.
3 Unbroken lines are faster than broken ones.
4 Direction of movement will affect 'speed'; the first three directions being generally faster than the remaining four directions.

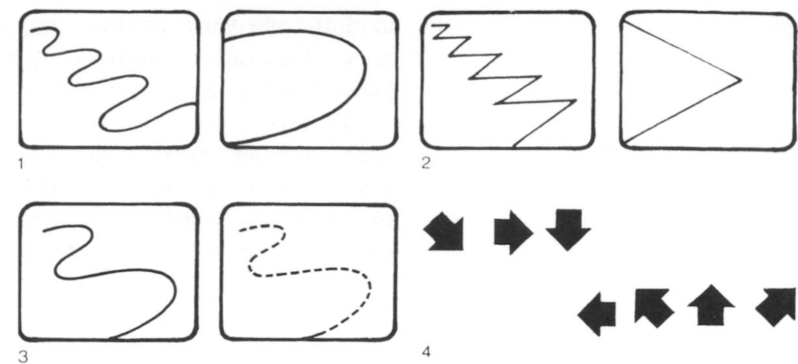

Continuity of centers of interest

Although our eyes continually move around the picture, we usually find that interest is localized at any given moment to about one-twelfth of the screen area. You can divide the 4 by 3 frame into twelve equal segments.

Where successive centers of interest are widely spaced, the viewer's concentration must be disrupted to some extent while he seeks each new spot. Fast interlinking composition lines help here. This situation particularly arises, of course, whenever you cut to another shot. If the new picture presents an entirely different interest location, the audience becomes overaware of the transition; so the points should be reasonably matched.

Poorly matched transitions, especially between numerous brief-duration shots, can accelerate mild audience resentment into marked hostility. This situation arises all too regularly where editors

Fig. 7.16 Related shots
The compositional arrangements and action can move the eye about the picture. On cutting to another shot, a new center of interest presents itself. If the centers are too dissimilar, as in the first pair of illustrations, the viewer becomes overaware of the change. But where reasonably matched, the transition may be almost unnoticed.

Fig. 7.17 Movement of interest
Good visual continuity between shots does not necessitate static arrangements. Composition and action can introduce unlimited interest-movement, providing successive shots match at the transition.

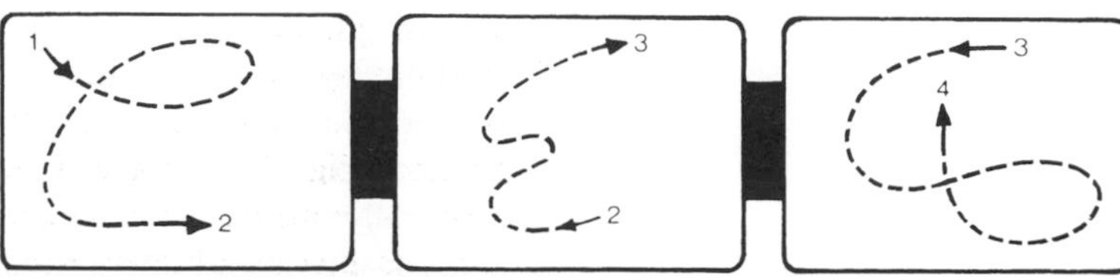

demonstrate their prowess by rapid cutting to the beat of fast music. Even if synchronism is perfect, inept matching of centers of interest (often with too little time to examine each shot) becomes totally frustrating.

In certain types of program (e.g. pop videos, program trailers) a vogue has developed for fast cutting between a series of completely unrelated shots. The result can be an exciting montage, as one unexpected image after another hits the screen, and the eye searches for points of interest. Or it can be a haphazard, meaningless confusion. Clearly, a technique to be handled carefully!

Composition continuity in multi-camera production

A regular problem in multi-camera production is that a composition set-up that looks great from one viewpoint may be quite disappointing from another. On cutting, you find that the new shot is unbalanced, or lacks unity. It may draw attention to the wrong subject. The more complex the set-up, the greater is the chance of this happening.

Fig. 7.18 Cross-cut shots
1 If successive pictures are matched accurately, some visual confusion can arise when inter-switching between cameras.
2 Where alternative foci are continually being intercut, it may be less disturbing to space (offset) centers of interest.

There are several ways of overcoming this problem and controlling compositional continuity:

1 You might rely on the well-composed main shot, and just accept the shortcomings of the other brief shots.
2 You can arrange subjects so that they suit all shooting angles – as in most interviews.
3 If shooting is *discontinuous*, you might slightly rearrange the composition of each shot in turn (cheat) – people's positions, set dressing, lighting. This is a regular practice during filming, for it produces optimum results. But it can be very time consuming, and cause continuity errors.

Fig. 7.19 Care in grouping
Cameras shooting actuality, have to select from available grouping. But by attention to people's positions a wider range of shots becomes possible.

1 People must normally work closer together than in everyday life, to avoid widely spaced shots.
2 Where close spacing is inappropriate, cross-shooting groups them.
3 Although parallel face-to-face conversation may seem more natural, slight angling improves shot-opportunity.
4 Similarly, closed groups are better opened up.

Fig. 7.20 part 1 Continuity of composition – two shot
The subject can be arranged to provide appropriate composition from several viewpoints.

Fig. 7.20 part 2 Continuity of composition – three shot
Although composition continuity becomes more difficult with larger groups, a variety of shots is available with careful grouping.

4 You can recompose the first shot so that it is still satisfactory . . . but more suitable for the next shot's composition.
5 You can reposition performers just at the moment of the transition. So having delivered a line, the actor turns away . . . on the cut . . . to a new position.

Color impact

Most of us take color for granted. We accept that a surface is a particular shade of green, for example. But in fact, what we are interpreting as 'green' can vary considerably: with the color of the light falling on the surface, its angle, any other nearby color, and various other factors.

Surface effect

The color of a smooth surface generally looks 'purer' (more saturated) than a rough-textured one of identical color; its brightness, too, will change more noticeably with the light direction. The color of a surface can seem to vary with the quality of the incident light, appearing brighter and more saturated under hard light than under diffused lighting. A color surface may reflect light onto a nearby subject – so the face of a person wearing a yellow sweater may be tinged yellow by its reflected light.

Fine color detail

Our eyes cannot readily detect fine detail in color. Where a scene contains tiny areas of color (whether small patterns or distant subjects) these will seem to get paler as they grow smaller. The actual color of fine detail can become difficult to identify. Yellow, for instance, tends to become indistinguishable from light gray, and blue detail can become confused with dark gray. Similarly, bright areas of green, blue-green, and blue appear identical when very small. Eventually, as detail size diminishes, even strong reds and blue-greens become indistinguishable, so that you can only detect differences in brightness between them.

Warm and cold colors

Colors are often associated unconsciously with warmth and distance. Red, yellow, and brown seem 'warm', and areas of these colors tend to look bigger and nearer than the 'cool' hues such as blue and green. You will find, too, that darker and more saturated colors seem nearer than lighter or desaturated ones.

Subjectively, the pictorial 'weight' of a color is often affected by its 'warmth': warmer tones seem heavier than cooler ones, saturated colors look heavier than duller desaturated ones. For these reasons, it is desirable when composing masses in a picture to keep areas of saturated color small, for they can easily balance much larger ones of desaturated color.

Simultaneous color contrast (lateral color adaptation)

The appearance of any color can be considerably affected by the background against which it appears; an effect known as *simultaneous contrast*. A green dress against gray drapes will not only look greener than normal, but the gray background itself may tend to take on the complementary hue (magenta) and appear 'warmer'. If you place a white object in white surroundings, and illuminate it with both white and magenta light, its shadow appears to be green! Clearly, the eye and the brain can play strange tricks!

The same turquoise object may look lighter, darker, bluer, greener, according to its background colors. When a strong color appears against a pale version of the same hue the background seems grayer. A strong color will appear more vibrant when backed by white, than against black. Conversely, a darker color is more pronounced against a black background. Any color will look brightest and strongest against its complementary color.

Even *neutral tonal values* (white, grays, black) are modified by their background. The darker the background, the lighter will the subject tones appear to be (and vice versa). Light tonal areas look larger. Darker tones look heavier. All these factors can strongly influence our impressions of size, distance, and pictorial balance.

Separation of color

Although color surfaces may in reality be some distance away from each other, they can appear adjacent when seen together within the shot. So there is a mutual interaction between them.

Bright colors

Bright colors hold the attention – particularly scarlets, bright yellows, and orange. But their prominence can become embarrassing when they are defocused, for the eye turns to them yet cannot see detail there. Pastel (desaturated) hues do not pose this problem – but they, on the other hand, can lack vigor and visual appeal if widely used.

Where there are reasonably equal areas of strong color a disharmonious tension can develop between them, particularly where they are not complementary. So it is preferable to have one or more of them desaturated (i.e. grayed-off, less vivid).

Approximate color constancy

This illusory effect continually influences our evaluation of color. We experience it when looking at a picture containing a familiar subject of known color – a mailbox, perhaps. Having fixed on this item, we go on to judge other colors in the picture accordingly. Even where the reproduced color of this subject is considerably different from that of the real thing, the brain adjusts its interpretation, so that we are predisposed to see it as 'correct'; perhaps regarding others nearby as inaccurate, although they are actually satisfactory.

All interpretation is subjective. We regularly misinterpret as 'white' areas that in reality are quite blue or yellow. Blue puddles on the sidewalk may look unnatural, although they truly reflect a blue sky. A 'black' object in bright sunlight may actually be reflecting more light than a dimly illuminated 'white' – although our brain, making a comparative judgement, refuses to believe this.

After-images

After looking at a color for some time you will often experience a brief color 'hang-over' on switching to the next shot. Following exposure to red, you will see a blue-green (cyan) ghostly after-image on a black screen. After orange, a peacock-blue after-image follows. Yellow gives blue; green gives purple (magenta); while after blue an orange-yellow image is seen.

Bearing this in mind, you would expect some interaction between a succession of colors. Such *successive contrast* causes white to appear bluish-green after looking at a red screen. Similarly, yellow appears bright green; blue appears more intense and greenish; while repeated red has a grayed appearance.

Admittedly, these are extreme situations, but color distortion on quick cuts and the visual fatigue that follows overexposure to a strong color are not to be disregarded.

Color associations

Color and emotion are inextricably interlinked. Color associations are legion. For example:

Red – with warmth, anger, crudity, excitement, power, strength.
Green – with spring, macabre, freshness.
Yellow – with sunlight, the Orient, treachery, brilliance.
White – with snow, delicacy, purity, cold.

Dynamic composition

So far, we have been discussing the composition of *still* pictures, or pictures with little movement – principles that have long been widely accepted. But what happens when the subject and/or the camera *moves*? Then a series of interesting dynamic effects develop that offer us exciting opportunities. We have termed this previously unexplored field *dynamic composition*.

The still picture

Still photographs have become such a regular part of our daily life – in newspapers, magazines, books, our own snapshots – that we accept them as perfectly natural. Yet these 'frozen moments' really have interestingly different characteristics from the real world we experience. They encapsulate what something looked like at a particular *instant.* It may not even be typical. The picture shows a segment of the world, and puts a frame around it. This frame affects our impression of the subjects within it.

Look at a video of any interview and examine a person's expressions *frame by frame!* An animated face will appear to switch instantly, appearing coy, surprised, bored, threatening, asleep, wistful . . . The brief glimpses produce totally uncharacteristic effects that are not there when seen at normal speed.

In everyday life we see a solid three-dimensional world. We do not think about the 'composition' of the scene we are looking at. Arrangements change continually as we move around.

In a still picture, whether it is a photograph or a painting, subjects within the frame become part of an enclosed pattern. We become aware of the *tonal masses*, *directional lines*, *perspective.* In the real world, we do not respond to this degree.

Part of the attraction of a still picture lies in the fact that we can study its details at leisure. We can concentrate on any aspects that interest us. Action that is intriguing when we catch only a fragmentary glimpse may prove uninteresting when we watch it in its entirety. A situation that is effectively composed in a still may become less attractive when movement rearranges its component parts. The underlying appeal of many great paintings and sculptures lies in this indefinable feeling of 'suspended animation about to commence'.

Compositional balance that appears so forceful in a still often goes unnoticed during motion. Take a photograph of a horse leaping a fence, and the shot can look dynamic, strong, graceful. Show a moving picture of the same action, and the result may seem quite commonplace and unexciting.

Certain production techniques spring from this idea of *uncompleted action* in order to savor and emphasize thc dynamics:

- During a fight scene the director cuts to a *freeze frame*, or a sequence of stills showing people flying through the air, or crashing to the ground.
- Intercutting between brief shots of action without showing us the results of the action. The executioner's hand moves forward . . . a bystander starts to speak . . . a head turns . . .
- Showing an action sequence, then fading out before it ends. The hero walks into the distance . . . the picture fades.

Such methods create a *climax* – which, if left to follow through, would often lead to an anticlimax.

Potentials of the moving picture

A still picture seldom holds the attention for long. The moving picture offers *continued interest.* Movement attracts. Through change, the director can introduce variety in the picture, and hold the audience's attention concentrated on the particular subject he chooses. Changes enable him, for example, to:

- Alter a subject's prominence
- Redirect the viewer's attention
- Add or remove information as the audience watches
- Transform the mood of the scene
- Show movement, growth, development.

Even this brief list reminds us of the potential persuasive power of the moving picture.

The *still picture* allows viewers freedom to scrutinize and assess. The *moving picture* often gives them time to grasp only the essentials, before it is replaced by the next; particularly if action is fast or brief.

If the information in a succession of pictures is obvious, simple, or familiar to the audience, changes can be rapid. (A sophisticated or informed audience may actually find the fast pace stimulating, as they rapidly assess each new shot.) But if the pace is too great for your audience, they are likely to build up resentment as you snatch away each shot before they have finished looking at it. In the end their attention and interest can lapse.

Movement can be dynamic and stimulating – or confusing and tiring. It depends on the subject, and your audience.

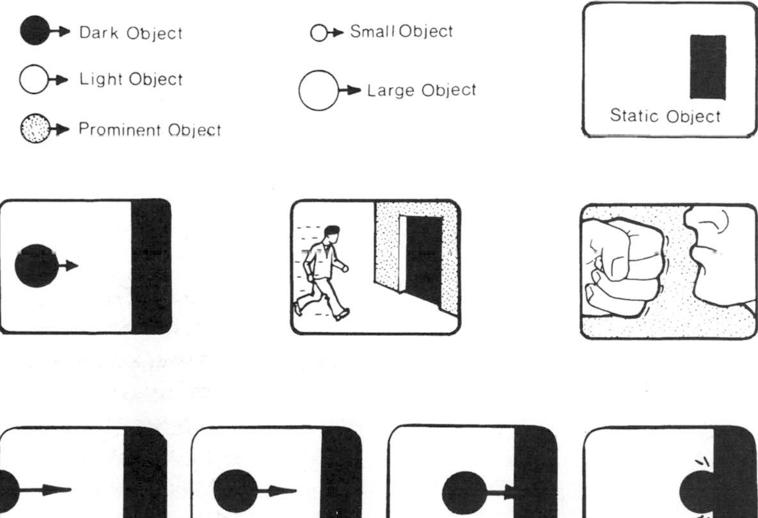

Fig. 7.21 part 1 Representing movement
Symbols can represent many different dynamic situations – the subjects, their direction, and their path within the TV frame.

Fig. 7.21 part 2 Dynamic effects
As the symbol moves within the frame and approaches other symbols, we sense dynamic changes in relationships. Similar effects occur as subjects move around within a real picture.

Fig. 7.22 Gravity
There is a tendency to interpret movement within the picture as if gravity were always involved. So in these illustrations movement is seen as:

1 Normal progress.
2 Moving uphill; climbing.
3 Moving downhill; descending.
4 Rising.
5 Falling.

Such movement is regarded as difficult easy, forceful, weak, etc.

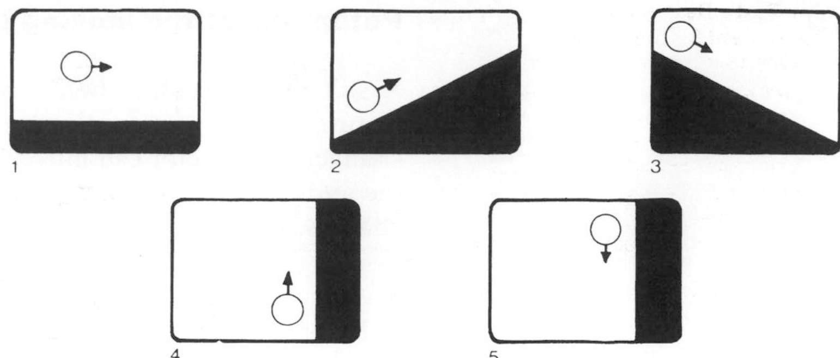

A theory of dynamic composition

In daily life we continually make very subjective judgements as we assess the movements and speed of things around us. As we drive through flat, featureless country we feel that the car is traveling at a much slower speed than the speedometer shows. Driving along a tree-lined road, the reverse happens, and we tend to overestimate speed.

Fig. 7.23 The impression of movement
1 Our impressions of movement in a picture often depend on the way the subject is framed, on the apparent speed of other subjects, and on the passing background. Firmly framed against a plain background, there is no sense of movement. If the subjects's position wavers and it is known to be moving, the movement is assumed to be so fast as to be difficult to follow. Add signs of a background racing past (e.g. aircraft in clouds) and the sense of movement and speed grows considerably.
2 To this there can be added four general axioms. Movement across the screen tends to appear exaggeratedly fast. Movement to or from the lens seems slower for narrow-angle, faster for wide-angle lenses. Camera movement in the direction of subject movement reduces its speed. Camera and subject moving in opposite directions increase their mutual speed and impact.
3 The flat screen can cause the viewer to misinterpret spatial movements. On camera the people seem to be running to meet – but the plan view shows otherwise!

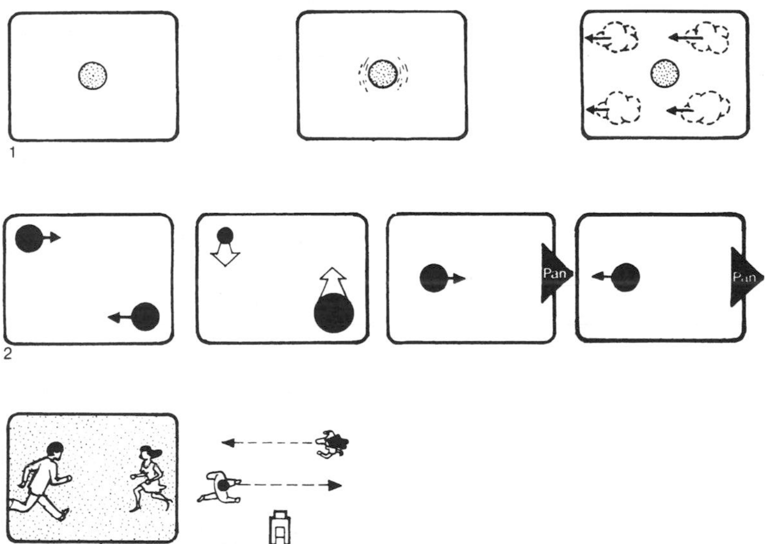

Watching moving pictures, we carry over these arbitrary interpretations. Because the image is within a frame, and two-dimensional, there are further influences.

We cannot *see* speed and movement in the picture, we can only interpret from clues that are there. Against a plain white sky, a fast-moving aircraft appears stationary. When we see the landscape beneath streaking past, we have an impression of speed.

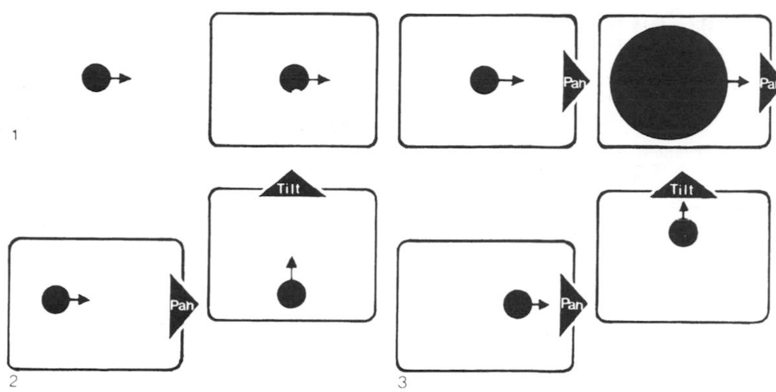

Fig. 7.24 Restriction of movement by the frame

1 When we see movement in *free space* (e.g. a flying bird), it appears to have total freedom. But when we see the same action within the frame of a picture, an illusion of *restriction* develops. The frame subjectively 'inhibits movement'. If we hold the subject center-frame as it moves, this sense of restriction is limited. But in closer shots, the frame appears to impede movement.
2 When we frame the picture to keep the moving subject near the *lagging edge* of the picture, restriction is much less.
3 But when we frame the subject near the leading edge, its restriction becomes emphasized.

Here are a few typical ways in which we react to movement in a picture:

1 *Effort.* Slower speeds can suggest effort; that a movement is difficult; especially if it is accompanied by sounds that are similarly associated (e.g. low pitched, forceful, percussive). If we replay a normal action in slow motion, this can increase the impression of effort involved. We also interpret the amount of effort, from signs of strain, tension, slipping, etc., even when these have been faked.
2 *Relative speeds.* We assess the speed at which someone is running towards us by the rate at which their image size grows. (Shot on a narrow-angle lens, this increase is slow, so we lose a sense of speed.)

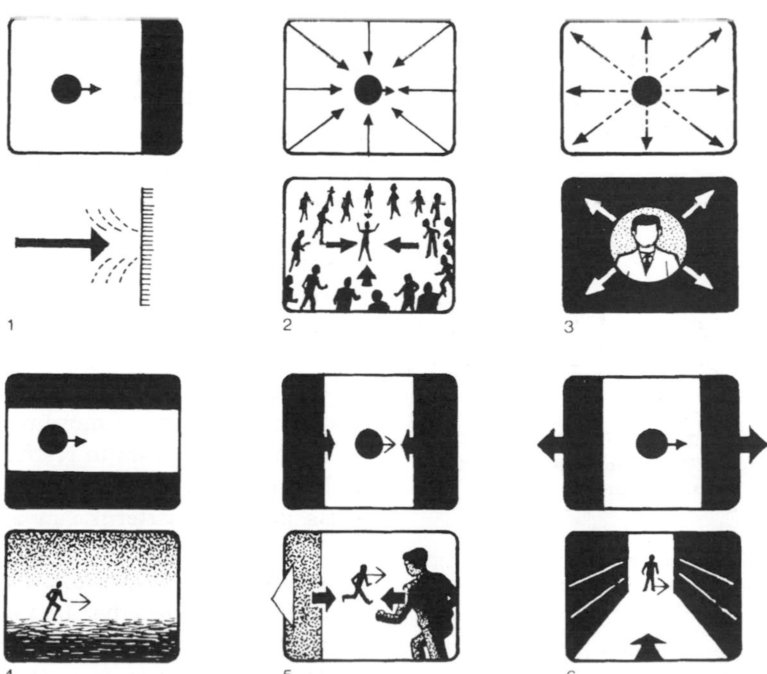

Fig. 7.25 Restriction of movement by masses

The shape and position of masses (moving or still) in the picture can alter the interpretation of events.

1 The mass in the path of the moving subject suggests imminent impact or arrest.
2 Converging, encircling, crushing, as when a crowd presses in on a central figure.
3 Expansion, new freedom, isolation, as when using an iris-out wipe.

Even complicated situations can be arranged to emerge quite naturally.

4 The restricted feeling aroused by the traveler moving at dusk between darkened sky and ground.
5 The compression effect as the camera pans left (following the pursuer), and the wall moving frame-right create a pincers compression movement towards the distant victim.
6 As the camera dollies down the alley, the distant light area grows – creating an expansive effect.

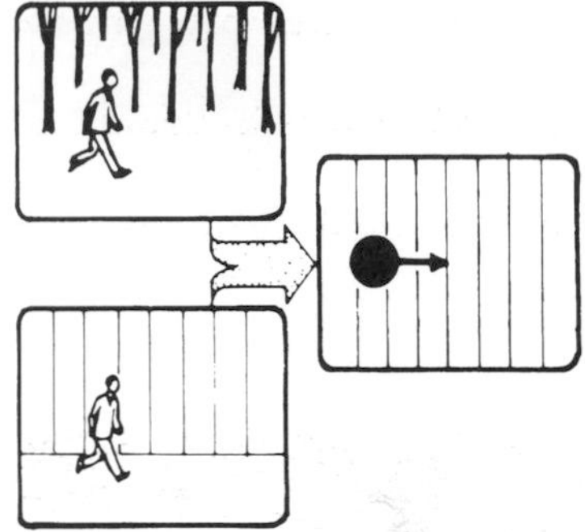

Fig. 7.26 Background patterns
As subjects move past them, background patterns can exert strong effects upon picture impact.

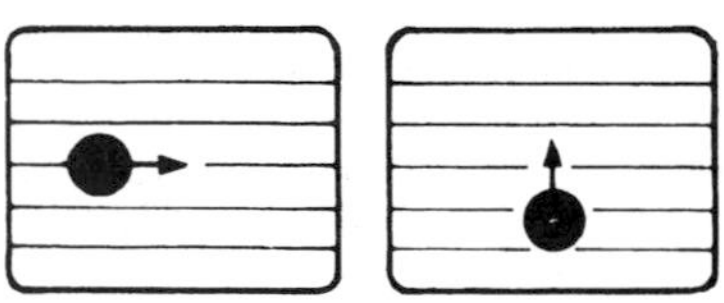

Fig. 7.27 Background and subject movement
Where movement is in the direction of background pattern, the movement will appear unimpeded if slightly restricted. The line emphasizes direction. Where the subject moves across (against) the pattern, effort is emphasized; movement appears stronger. Subject shape may modify these effects.

Fig. 7.28 Moving background and subject 'strength'
Against a plain background, the effect of this low-angle shot remains constant as the subject walks and the camera dollies back. But if a series of horizontals move downwards (crossboards in a ceiling) during the move, it is considerably strengthened.

3 *Space.* When there is a lot of space (border) around a subject in the picture it can modify our impression of speed, compared with a closer shot.
4 *Relative movement.* Where more than one plane is moving within the frame we sense an underlying pattern of *compression* (impact, collision), or *expansion* (parting, stretching, strain).
5 *Gravity.* Although gravity is irrelevant, we subconsciously associate movement and position within the frame with gravitational forces. Something moving from top to bottom appears to be moving downwards, sinking, falling, collapsing. Moving from bottom to top of the shot, it is rising against gravity, floating, climbing.
6 *Fixation point.* The visual impact of movement can depend on where we happen to fix our attention. Looking skyward, we see moving clouds and static buildings . . . or static clouds and toppling buildings.
7 *Power.* Slower movements tend to suggest greater power and force. If a car hits a wall in fast-motion, the wall simply falls down. We judge that the wall was weak. In a slow-motion replay the car seems to crash into the wall, which breaks apart under great force. The dynamics are changed.
8 *Strength* Something that is large in the frame, and is moving towards the camera, appears to grow stronger and more threatening. Seen from a side viewpoint, the same action (e.g. a truck backing) can seem quite incidental.

Using dynamic composition

As you can see in Figure 7.21, we can represent subjects and their movement within the picture by symbols. These provide a convenient 'shorthand' method of showing complicated effects. You could test these effects for yourself by drawing a succession of frames at the edge of these pages, and flicking through them to animate an example.

Whether we are looking at symbols or real subjects, the effects of movement can considerably affect the way we interpret what we are seeing:

- The apparent effects of gravity (Figure 7.22).
- Our impressions of movement (Figure 7.23).
- The frame appears to restrict movement (Figure 7.24).
- Tonal masses appear to restrict movement (Figure 7.25).
- Background patterns can affect our impression of movement (Figure 7.26).
- Background patterns can affect the effort of movement (Figure 7.27).
- Background patterns can affect apparent subject strength (Figure 7.28).

- Changes in the background can appear to interrelate with the moving subject (Figure 7.29).
- The apparent speed of a subject can be affected by its shape, and by the background pattern (Figure 7.30).
- The passing background can build up a visual rhythm (Figure 7.31).

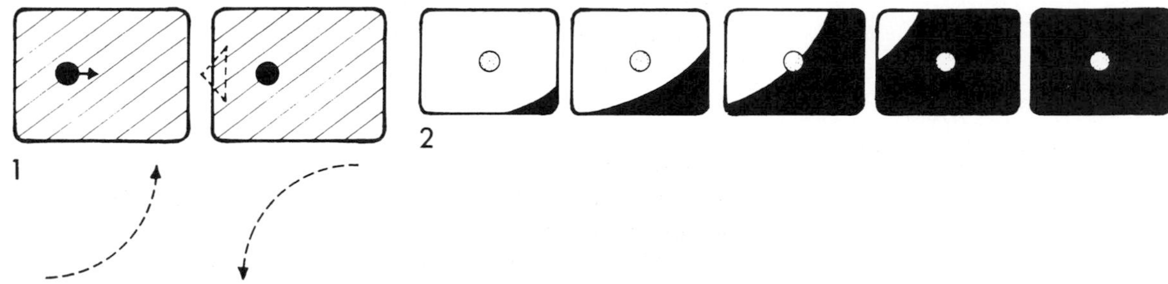

Fig. 7.29 Background and directions

1 When the subject moves across a static patterned background the viewer feels an undertow of movement. Where the subject is held in frame and the background passes the direction of this undertow changes.

2 As the subject moves over the upward-sweeping background, an upward force seems to be exerted on the subject. In addition, background tones modify its apparent size and importance.

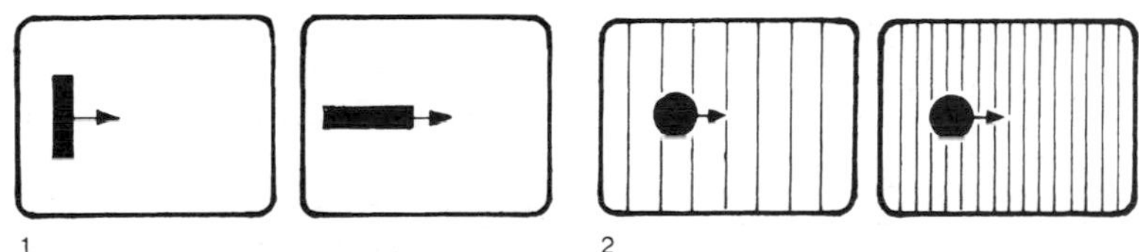

Fig. 7.30 Speed

The subject's shape can affect its apparent speed.

1 Although moving at the same speed the 'tall' object appears to be moving faster than the 'flat' object.

2 The apparent speed is also increased as the background becomes more detailed. Shot-size will modify how much of the background is visible and hence effective speed-impact.

Fig. 7.31 Rhythm

Visual rhythm from the passing background will seldom be as regular as these examples, although quite strong rhythmical patterns can be built up naturally from passing flags, trees, palings, etc.

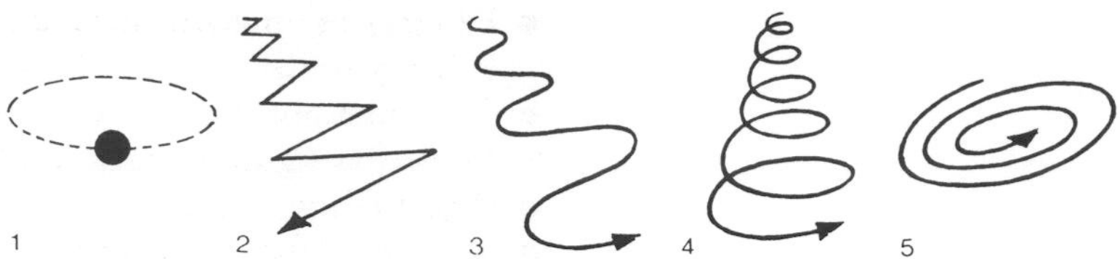

Fig. 7.32 part 1 Patterns of movement
Some movement patterns have widely accepted associative feelings.

1 Continuity. 2 Vigor; excitement, indecision. 3 Beauty, charm.
4 Expansion. 5 Contraction, collapse.

Smooth action suggests control, evenness, simplicity; while *jerky* irregular motion suggests the clumsy, erratic, uncontrollable.

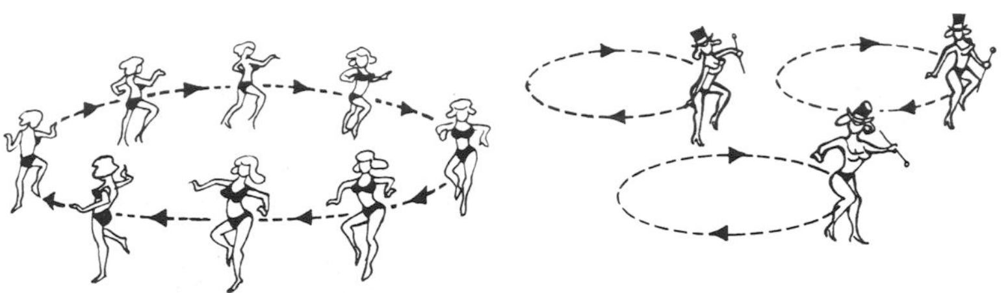

Fig. 7.32 part 2 Patterns of movement
In massed dance and marching, the viewer sees simple pattern formations from group movement, and individual movements.

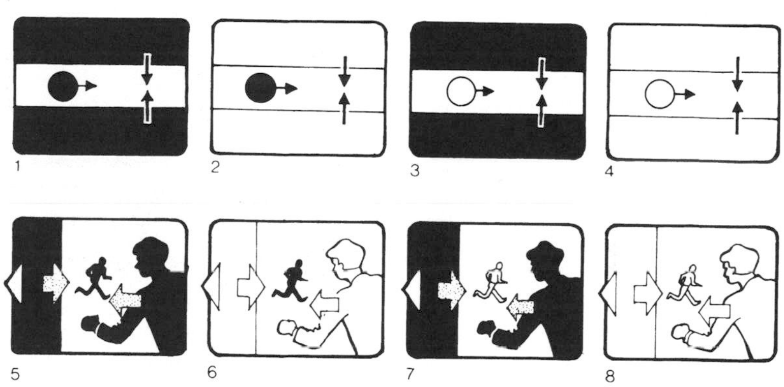

Fig. 7.33 The dynamic effect of tone
The effective strength of static and moving masses varies with tone.

1 When a dark subject moves through converging dark areas, the mutual impact is powerful.
2 For lighter tones the 'crushing' effect is lightweight against a heavy substantial subject.
3 The *apparently* larger but lightweight subject suggests less resistance to approaching forces. There is a hint of destruction.
4 Both subject and approaching forces are lightweight, so the effect is less dynamic than in the first example.
5 Dynamic pursuit.
6 Ineffectual pursuit of strong subject.
7 Annihilation of vulnerable subject.
8 Undramatic. Following rather than pursuing.

- Patterns of movement can create an emotional response (Figure 7.32).
- The tones involved can affect a picture's dynamics (Figure 7.33).
- Movement can change the visual significance of a picture (Figure 7.34).
- Dynamic effects can result from a succession of shots (Figure 7.35).

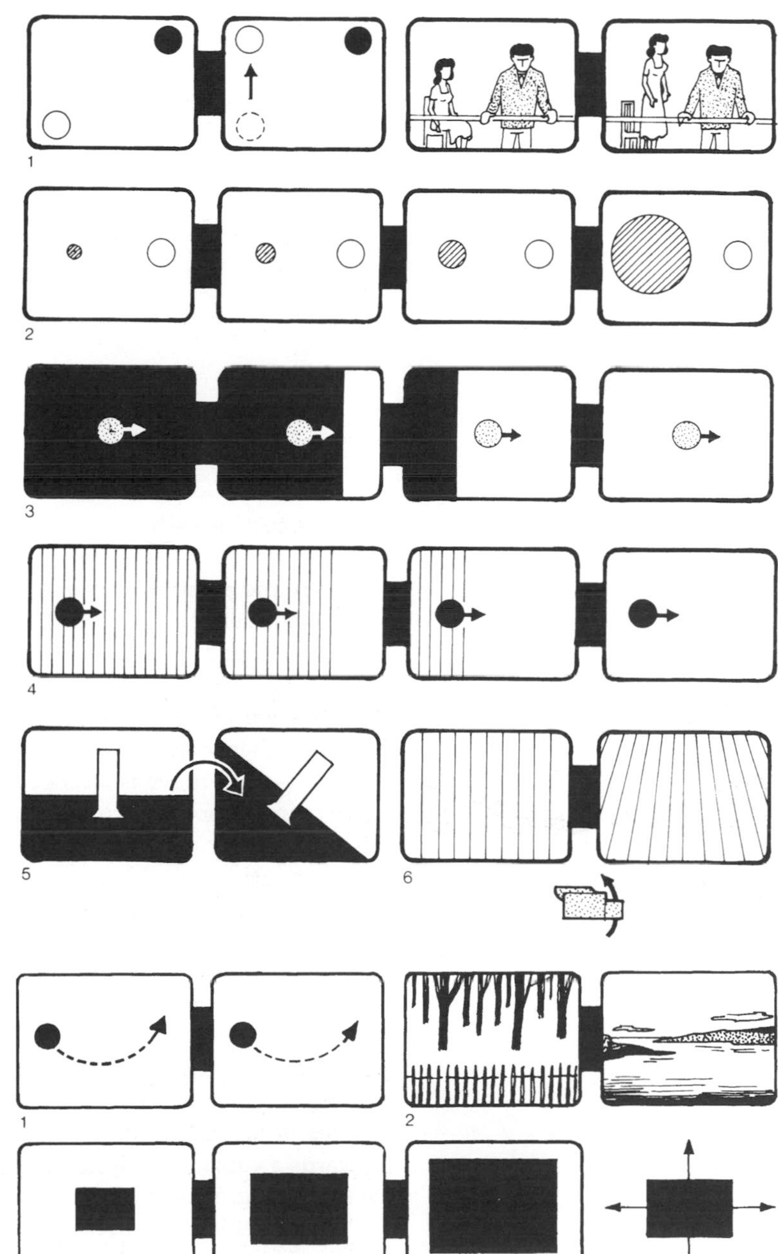

Fig. 7.34 Changing visual significance
You can alter the strength of a subject by changing its *position*, its *size*, or its *background*.

1 The upward movement and higher position strengthens the left-hand person.
2 Striped object is approaching. At first it is insignificant, but with increasing size, its importance and interest exceed that of the static subject.
3 As the subject passes from the dark background to the light one, there is an emotional uplift.
4 Passing from a region of restrictive verticals to a plain background produces a sense of freedom, and an effective speed change (fast to slow).
5 As the shot cants off the horizontal, pictorial balance becomes unstable.
6 The camera tilts upwards, and the verticals in this background converge into diagonals.

Fig. 7.35 Dynamic effects between pictures
Seeing a rapid succession of shots (still or moving), the viewer subconsciously compares or contrasts them.

1 Cutting between scenes with similar movement-form or shape, emphasizes this effect.
2 The vigorous verticals of one scene contrasts effectively with the restful horizontals of the next.
3 The successive size differences here produce expansive jumps.

Fig. 7.36 Area of interest
1 With a slope to the right, the eye tends to favor the distance and so run out of frame.
2 With the reverse slope, the eye tends to favor the foreground.

Fig. 7.37 Concentration of interest
1 Placed on the left, the window is just part of the scene; the foreground person dominates. When it is on the right, the viewer anticipates important action through the window; the person becomes less important.
2 The viewer is very conscious of the watcher on the right, but only half-aware of his victims. Placed on the left, the watcher is nearly overlooked, attention focusing on his victims.

Accepted maxims

You see the principles of dynamic composition applied daily; and from experience, some excellent widely accepted working axioms have emerged.

Fig. 7.38 Direction of slope
Direction of the slope can alter a picture's attractiveness, there being a tendency for version 1 to seem more dynamic than 2.

■ *Direction of movement* Like vertical lines, vertical movement is stronger than horizontal, which is the least arresting.

A left–right move is stronger than a right–left action.

A rising action is stronger than a downward one. Hence a rise from a seated position has greater attraction than a downward sitting movement.

An upward move generally looks faster than a horizontal one.

■ *Diagonal movement* Like diagonal lines, this is the most dynamic movement direction.

■ *Movement towards the camera* All forward gestures or movements are more powerful than recessive action away from the camera: a glance, a turned head, a pointing hand. Similarly, a shot moving towards a subject (dolly/zoom in) arouses greater interest than one withdrawing from it (dolly back/zoom out).

Where someone moves in front of another person (or scenery) they attract more attention than when moving behind them. Avoid such cross-moves in shots closer than mid-shot.

■ *Continuity of movement* While a moving subject attracts attention more readily than a static one, continuous movement at constant speed does not maintain maximum interest. Where action is momentarily interrupted or changes direction, the impact is greater than one carried straight through. Converging movements are usually more forceful than expanding ones.

Mirror images

If you look at any collection of photographs direct and then in a mirror you invariably find a difference in the appeal of the two versions. Differences may be great or slight; but they do modify the picture's impact.

Table 7.1 Mirroring the picture

Pictorial balance	Subjects tend to look heavier (affecting balance more markedly) on frame *right*. So frame left can support more weight (i.e. greater density or mass) than right. A predominant mass on frame right can make the picture unbalanced or lopsided. The space between subject and left frame may appear excessive where masses predominate on frame right.
Pictorial stability	The picture may look more stable one way round than another; dormant in one version – but dynamic when reversed.
Apparent proportions	Large dark foreground areas on frame right may produce a crowded, shut-in, or heavy feeling; while the reverse gives a more open impression.
Subject strength	A composition element that seems unimportant when located on the left can become obtrusive on frame right (although the reverse seldom holds). A subject overlooked on left frame may become compositionally or dramatically significant on the right.
Area of interest	Our reaction to diagonal lines can vary with their slope direction. So our attention center can be directed in depth within the scene.
Concentration of interest	The eye tends to wander towards frame right (even with a predominant frame left subject). Where strong subjects are positioned frame right, left-hand subject may go almost unregarded.
Picture significance	Part of the scene may take on an implied significance in a mirrored version.
Visual interpretation	Our interpretation of what is happening or what the picture depicts may be modified by left–right disposition.
Direction of slope	A down-slope to the right tends to be interpreted as downhill, and an up-slope as uphill. This influences how difficult or forceful lateral movements along such slopes appear to be as they move in an 'uphill' or 'downhill' version. Similarly, a vertical object learning or falling to the right tends to 'fall forward', rather than backward.

Fig. 7.39 Mirror images
Check these examples, and see what differences you notice in the feel of the left- and right-handed versions. (See Table 7.1.)

The various effects that arise regularly through 'right-handedness' in composition treatment can influence which way round you arrange your picture to suit any particular purpose.

8 Video editing

As film editors have demonstrated for decades, skilful editing can make a vital contribution to a production's impact. The way you interrelate shots will not only affect their visual flow but will directly influence how your audience reacts to what they are seeing: their interpretation; their emotional responses. Poor editing can leave them confused. Proficient editing can create interest, tension or build up excitement that has them on the edges of their seats! At worst, editing can degenerate into casual switching between shots. At best, it is a sophisticated persuasive artform.

An introduction to editing

To appreciate the skills of editing techniques, we need to study two diverse aspects of the craft:

- The *mechanics* – the ways in which editing is carried out.
- The *aesthetics* – the artistic impact that these techniques have on our audience.

In *film making*, a specialist film editor aided by assistants is entirely responsible for the mechanics and techniques of the editing process. The material goes through a series of stages (from the initial *rough-cut* to the final *fine-cut* version of the film), which are reviewed and appraised by the director.

In *television production* we shall meet a number of quite different editing situations. Depending on the nature of the show, and how it is organized, editing can range from impulsive switching (e.g. during a live sports event) to the painstaking empiricism possible when editing a taped drama. Technicalities can vary considerably with the equipment available, and how it is used. Let's look at these variants more closely.

Editing techniques in television

1 Editing during a live show

How the director shoots live action, will ultimately depend on

- Whether the event is taking place in front of an audience
- Whether it is a public event on which the television camera is 'eavesdropping'

- Whether the action is being staged specifically for the camera before an invited audience who participate or provide background reactions.

There are two broad approaches:

- *Spontaneous selection* – In the first, the director sits in the production control room, watching an array of picture monitors, spontaneously choosing and switching between sources. Action is continuous, and recorded just as it happens (*'live-on-tape'*). All the editing needed is carried out at the time on the production switcher. At most, a few corrective shots or inserts may be added later, or supplementary sound treatment introduced (e.g. music or applause) during brief postproduction editing.
- *Preplanned selection* – In the second, the director adjusts each shot to comply with a carefully planned and prepared script, in which all the cutting points and transitions have been considered and marked beforehand.

In each situation the director (or an assistant) calls shots to cameras over the intercom system, and the *technical director* or a specialist *switcher/vision mixer* (occasionally the director) will operate the *production switcher.*

2 Editing during a videotaped show

Where the show is essentially staged for taping, the director is free to record the action in its entirety, or in long or brief sequences. All the editing, titling, effects, etc. may be carried out on the production switcher during performance, or left until a *postproduction ('post')* editing session. Consequently, the videotape editor may be faced with quite different tasks, depending on how the director has decided to shoot and interpret the material. Editing opportunities become much more flexible.

- *Small format dupe* – A typical method of working is to make a duplicate recording of all the production tapes on a small-format VTR such as a VHS system. (A *numeric time code* 'burned-into' the pictures, identifies each moment throughout.) The director scrutinizes these *working copy* tapes and makes an *edit decision list*. This indicates which shots are to be used from the total material. The *videotape editor* then edits the show to this basic preference list to prepare a *rough-cut copy.*
- *Cutting to script* – In another method the *videotape editor* examines all the taped material (original or copy), and using the production script as a guide, edits this to produce a *rough cut*, which is then evaluated by the director.
- *Submitted copy* – Where the videotape editor has been involved with the show from its planning stages, and knows the director's

general aims, he or she may examine the whole of the recorded material, selecting, arranging and editing shots to produce a *show copy* which the director assesses. (This approach may be used, for example, on a documentary program where narration is to be written after a disparate collection of shots have been fused into a coherent sequence.)

When the editor has created a master tape, further important contributory elements can then be added: sound treatment (dialogue, narration, sound effects, music, etc.), titling/subtitling, video effects, etc. Of course, these are only the bare bones of typical editing procedures. In reality, there is usually a very close working relationship between the director, the switcher, and the videotape editor. Each may contribute observations, suggestions, criticisms that could enhance the end product, as might other members of the production team.

Editing basics

Editing decisions

During the editing process, we need to make a series of decisions:

- *Which shots do you want to use from the total available?* When editing a *live* show, choices are irrevocable. You can only select from the shots being presented at each moment by cameras, videotape, film channels etc. When you are editing a *videotaped* show there is time to ponder, to select, to reconsider. After editing, unused material is usually retained for a while to allow for any subsequent revisions or archiving (total or sectional).
- *What is the final order of shots to be (sequence)?* The relative durations of shots can affect their visual impact (*cutting rate; cutting rhythm*).
- *At exactly which moment in the action* do you want to change from one shot to the next (the cutting point)?
- *How is each shot to be joined to the next*: i.e. the *transition* (e.g. a cut or mix/dissolve)?
- *How fast or slow will this transition be*, if it is a mix/dissolve, wipe, etc.? (*Transition rate.*)
- *Is there good continuity between pictures (and sound)* that supposedly show continuous action (but were actually shot discontinuously or at different times/places)?
- *Are there to be any special effects involved in the editing* (e.g. superimpositions, montages)?

Each of these decisions involves your making both a *mechanical* operation and an *artistic* choice. Even the simplest treatment (a cut from one picture to the next) can create a very different effect, according to the point at which you decide to edit the action. Let's look at an example:

- You can show the entire action, from start to end:

  The intruder reaches into a pocket, pulls out a pistol and fires it. The victim falls. (The action is 'obvious'.)

- Identical action and treatment; *but deliberately misleading. The shot was from someone else, out of frame*
- You can interrupt an action, so that we do not at that stage, know what is going to happen:

  The hand reaches into the pocket/CUT/to the second person's face. (What is the intruder reaching for?) **Or** *The hand reaches into a pocket, and pulls out a pistol/CUT/to the second person's face. (Is the intruder threatening, or actually going to fire it?)*

- You can show the entire action, but hold the audience in suspense about its consequences:

  We see the pistol drawn and fired/CUT/but did the shot miss?

Editing opportunities

As we examine editing techniques, you will begin to see how subtly they contribute to the success of the production:

- You can join together a series of separately recorded takes or sequences to create a continuous smooth-flowing picture development – even where none originally existed.
- Through editing, you can omit action that would be irrelevant or distracting.
- You can seamlessly cut in *retakes* to replace unsatisfactory material – to correct or improve performance; to overcome camera, lighting or sound faults; to improve ineffective production treatment.
- You can increase or reduce the overall duration of the program – by adjusting the duration of sequences, introducing cutaway shots, altering playing speed, or repeating strategic parts of an action sequence,
- *Library* material (*stock shots*) can be introduced and blended with the program material – to establish location; for effects; or to introduce illustrations.
- When a subject is just about to move out of shot . . . you can cut to a new viewpoint and show the action continuing, apparently uninterrupted. (Even where it is possible to shoot action in one continuous take, the director may want to change the camera viewpoint or interrupt the flow of the action for dramatic impact.)

- By intercutting shots recorded at quite different times or places, you can imply relationships that did not exist (*filmic space*, *filmic time*).
- Editing allows you to instantly shift the audience's center of interest, redirecting their attention to another aspect of the subject or the scene.
- You can use editing to *emphasize* or to *conceal* information.
- You can adjust the duration of shots in a sequence to influence its overall pace.
- Editing can change the entire significance of an action in an instant . . . to create tension, humor, horror.
- By altering the order in which the audience sees events you can change how they interpret and react to them.
- You can integrate selections from different productions, to create a *compilation program*.

The mechanics of editing

The actual process you use can have an important influence on the ease and accuracy with which you can edit and on the finesse that is possible. There are several systems:

1. *Editing in-camera* – Editing '*on the fly*' while shooting; by strategically starting/stopping the recording process.
2. *Production switcher (vision mixer)* – The regular hands-on method of interswitching or combining video sources, using the switcher located in the production control room.
3. *Linear editing* – The process of editing videotapes by replaying sections, in the order you require while making a copy on a master tape.
4. *Non-linear editing* – The latest and most flexible editing process, in which the original pictures and sound from the camera or videotape are copied in digital form onto a *hard disk* (or a recordable videodisc) ready for editing. Any point in any shot on this disk can be selected immediately.
5. *Film editing* – The editing process used for *filmed* material. (See Figure 13.1.)

Editing in-camera

With care, it is possible to stop and start the *videotape recorder* itself while shooting the action so that when this tape is replayed one sees a continuous coherent program. So, for example, you might shoot a person getting out of a car . . . *stop (or pause) recording* . . . then begin recording again as they enter a building. When the tape is played through, unnecessary intermediate action is removed and the edited sequence appears quite normal.

However, assembling a program in this way has its drawbacks:

- You have to shoot the action *in the final running order*. That may not be practicable or convenient.
- If you rewind the camera's videotape a little, to record new material over a faulty part (*insert recording*), it is hard to do this accurately. There is always the chance that you will accidentally wipe wanted parts of the original takes. It is all too easy to clip the end of the previous action or the start of the new shot. And unfortunately, you usually cannot correct such errors.
- Videocassette recorders usually *back-space edit* as they start to record; automatically rewinding a few frames in order to stabilize sound and picture at start-up. So precise editing in-camera is impracticable. Although you may overcome this particular problem by keeping the recorder running in a *record pause* mode in between takes, that results in bad local tape wear (and possibly *head-clogging* from tape debris) as the heads continually re-scan the same spot on the tape, over and over.
- When using in-camera editing you really need to reply (review) the tape to check each edit, and ensure that it is successful. There is always the possibility that the shots may be spoiled at the join, and an immediate retake may be necessary – where this is practicable.

The main advantage of this method of *in-camera editing* while shooting is that you finish up with a *first-generation* recording. All other editing methods involve *making copies* of the original, and unless you are using a digital system, these must be of lower quality than the original; even although that may not be obvious.

Where a television camera records digitally on an integrated *videodisc recorder* instead of a videotape cassette there are certain advantages, particularly for newsgathering. In-camera editing becomes rather more practical, particularly when the camera is used in conjunction with a *laptop editor/editing deck*. (*See Glossary – DVC system*.)

Editing with the production switcher (vision mixer)

As you saw earlier when touring the production control room (Chapter 2), the *production switcher* or *vision mixer* enables us to intercut or combine various picture sources, and to introduce certain basic video effects.

During a production, conditions in most production control rooms are generally a world apart from the relative calm of an editing suite. In front of the director, an extensive bank of small monochrome monitors presents a continually changing display of pictures. These are the many *channel monitors* showing the individual outputs of the various video sources: Cam. 1, Cam. 2, Cam. 3, etc., VTRS, telecines, slide scanner, character generators, video effects, electronic still stores, videodiscs, prompter display, etc.

In addition there are two larger *color* monitors:

- *The MASTER MONITOR (line monitor, main channel, program, transmission monitor* – This shows the main output of the production switcher, i.e. the source(s) you have selected to be recorded (or transmitted).
- The *switchable (selectable) PREVIEW MONITOR* – You can switch any picture source to this check monitor; usually whatever you have selected on the *PREVIEW BUS* on the switcher unit.

This arrangement is not only less costly than having a complete bank of color monitors, but it overcomes difficulties in accurately color-matching (*color balancing*) all their screens.

At first sight, a multi-display of this kind can be quite daunting. Not only can we see the 'real' shots that are ready to be switched to *line (transmission)* but there are also the 'accidental' outputs of cameras moving into position and setting up their shots . . . film and videotape channels shuttling between sequences, running up to their next cue point . . . graphics being set up . . . lighting adjustments being made . . .

While all this is going on, the director's attention is divided between the current shot on the *line (transmission)* picture and upcoming shots – guiding the production team, instructing, correcting, selecting, coordinating their work . . . All of this in addition to checking performance, keeping on schedule, and coping with those various contingencies that always arise. It is little wonder that under such conditions, '*editing*' with the production switcher can degenerate into a mechanical process!

■ **From the simple to the complex** Some switchers are very easy to use, but are limited in the number of things they can do. Others have extensive facilities; but need a quick mind to work out how to set them up quickly. How difficult a particular switcher system is to operate largely depends on the circumstances in which you are using it. Straight cuts are simple, but intercutting on-air between complex combined shots can be intimidating. Do you have time to anticipate and prearrange each set-up?

It's a far cry between operating a switcher during a studio situation where any errors can be retaken and working on a live sports meeting with off-the-cuff shooting, concurrent events, inserts of results boards, slow-motion replays, inlays of commentators . . . and so on! Different pressures; different needs!

Fig. 8.1 Sequential inter-cutting
Each subject accuses the other of treachery, tension is rising. The camera dollies closer and closer, shots become larger and larger and of increasingly shorter duration.

What the production switcher can do

The production switcher is an ingenious piece of equipment, that enables you to do a number of quite different things:

1 *Select and interlink shots.* You can select one or more of the various picture sources and send your choice to line to be recorded or transmitted (*studio output, main channel, program, transmission).* You can *cut* between channels (i.e. by switching), *mix (dissolve)*, *fade*, or *superimpose* pictures

   When you select any channel, that switcher button lights up, indicators are illuminated beside the corresponding picture monitor, and at the camera (a main tally light and an on-air warning light in the viewfinder).

2 *Wipes.* Another group of controls on the switcher enables you to wipe from one picture to another, in a wide range of patterns. This facility can also be used to segment the screen (e.g. split screen), or to combine parts of different shots.

3 *Titles.* Titles from any type of source (title card, slide, character generator, computer graphics, can be adjusted in outline, tone, and color, and inserted into a picture.

4 *Picture manipulation.* Some switchers include controls that can change the appearance of the picture in several ways – e.g. make it negative, ripple, invert, mirror.

5 *Special video effects.* There are usually controls enabling you to insert a selected subject or section from one picture into another (e.g. chroma key). More elaborate digital video effects are usually controlled by a separate *effects unit*: operated, perhaps, by a second person.

6 *Preview facilities.* Larger switchers include a row (*bus; bank*) of *PREVIEW* buttons. When you select any of the incoming picture sources here, it appears on the *SWITCHABLE PREVIEW MONITOR.* (This is a picture-checking facility; it does not affect the studio output at all.)

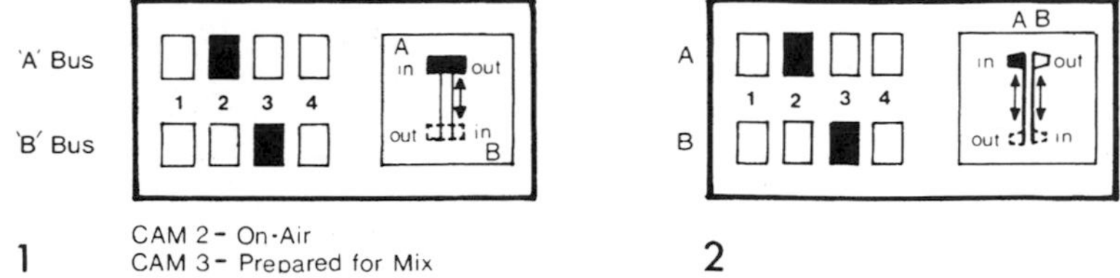

Fig. 8.2 part 1 The production switcher – principles of the A-B switcher
There are two identical rows of push buttons called buses or banks, labelled A and B (or BUS-1, BUS-2). Each pair of A and B buttons selects a particular video source (typically 6 to 20 sources per bus: cameras, film VTR, slide scanner, etc.). The *BUS fader lever(s)* position determines which bus is in use.

1 A single fader may be fitted (mixing or superimposing between A and B buses).
2 If twin faders are included, they may be operated together. or 'split' to fade A and B buses separately.

With the fader moved to the top. A-bus is active.
Switching buttons on A-BUS cuts the chosen source (e.g. Cam 1) to the studio's line output (main channel: on-air). (B-bus switching produces no visible result unless connected to a preview monitor: when it becomes a preparatory bus.)

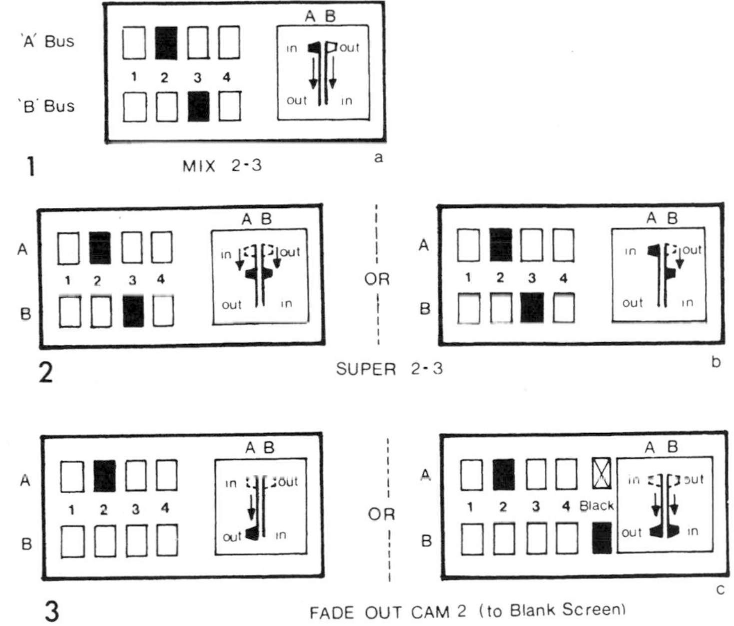

Fig. 8.2 part 2 The production switcher – basic operations
1 MIX (DISSOLVE) between Cams 2 and 3.
Select 2 on A-bus. It is now on line (on-air) as the bus fader is at A. Prepare for a Mix, by pressing 3 on B-bus.
Push down bus fader(s) from A to B, and output mixes from Cam 2 to 3. Move fader to A-bus: output mixes back from Cam 3 to 2.

2 SUPER CAMERAS 2 and 3.
Either as for a Mix: stopping when superimpostion strength is as required. Or split faders, moving appropriate lever towards the bus to be added.

3 FADE OUT CAM 2 (to blank screen).
Either split faders, pushing A-bus lever to OUT (B-bus is already faded out): or where the system would lose chroma using this method, select special *black level* button in the other bus and mix to black.

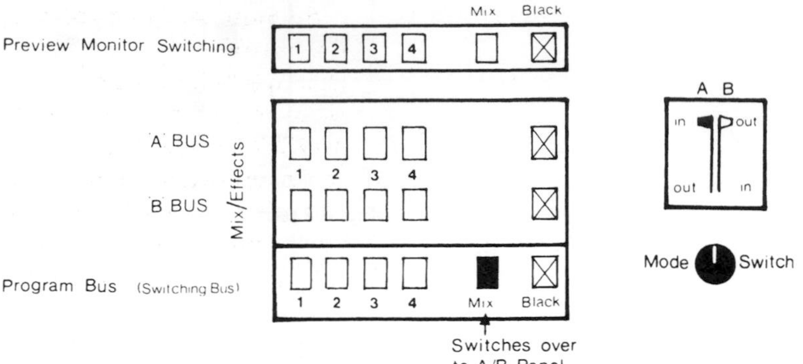

Fig. 8.2 part 3 The 'A-B-C' switcher
A separate program bus is used only for cutting (switching to line). The A/B buses are used for setting up *mixes and effects* (supers, split-screen, wipes, chroma-key, inserts).

The A/B fader lever can be used in either of two ways: (a) *Mix mode*, to provide mixes/dissolves/superimpositions between buses. (b) *Mask key mode*, in which it fades in a keying signal, or makes a pattern *transition*, or operates a wipe-pattern *movement*.

A *take* button or bar may interswitch between A and B buses. Preview buttons switch chosen channels onto preview monitor for checking before use. (Do not affect output to line.)

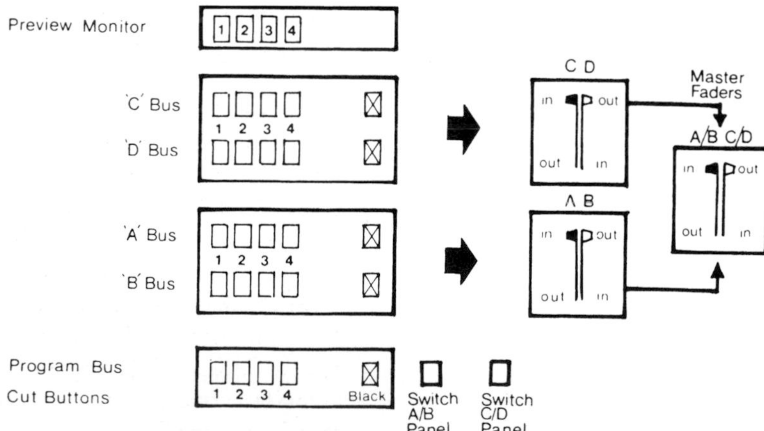

Fig. 8.2 part 4 The 'A-B-C-D' switcher
An elaboration, providing two duplicate pairs of buses – A/B and C/D. Now a prearranged combination of cameras can be set up on one pair of buses (e.g. for titling or effects), while the other pair is used for cuts and/or mixes.

Master fader levers to select the entire A/B and/or C/D combinations are required. A pair of buses (A/B or C/D) is called a MIX/EFFECTS (M/E) BANK.

Suppose you have only four preview monitors available but five or more sources. How can you check the extra incoming channels before switching them 'on-air'? You use the *PREVIEW BUS* to switch them onto the *SWITCHABLE PREVIEW MONITOR* beforehand. Similarly, if you have any shots that combine several sources (supers, inserts), or any video effects, you select the MIX button on the preview bus to check them on this monitor. If you use a *flip-flop* facility to intercut between two cameras, whichever is off-air will be displayed on the *SWITCHABLE PREVIEW MONITOR*.

7 *Remote controls*. Extra switches may be located at the switcher to remotely operate a slide scanner, film scanner, VTR channel, etc. (e.g. remote start, stop, change).

Switching conditions

People using production switchers for the first time are often puzzled to find that

- Some controls have an obvious effect, while others apparently do nothing!
- At one moment a control appears to be working, while shortly afterwards it seem inoperative!

This situation is easier to understand if you think of most controls as having three different conditions, which we might call:

'*ON-AIR*', '*PREPARATION*', '*AVAILABLE*'.

The condition of any given control will depend on how you have set up the switcher board.

- *ON-AIR*. If you operate any control that is selected for on-air use, you will see the result immediately on the *MASTER MONITOR* (line monitor).
- *PREPARATION*. Before putting any pictures on-air you want to be able to preview and adjust them. Any straightforward shot will appear on the channel preview monitors. But suppose you have a *combination shot* involving two or more sources. It might be a superimposition, a split screen with an inserted title, or a special effect. This will need to be prepared beforehand. The switcher enables you to adjust the associated controls while checking the effect on preview, then switch this prepared picture to line at the right moment. Instead of using the *SWITCHABLE PREVIEW MONITOR* for this purpose (it can be distracting for the director, and prevent his using it for program previews), some organizations have a separate additional monitor for shot preparation.

- *AVAILABLE*. Finally, there will be a number of controls that have not yet been selected for any purpose. They are available but inactive. They do nothing until you actually *route* them to preview or line.

Operating the switcher

At first sight, the switcher seems to be a mass of switches and levers. But things are not as complicated as they look. The answer to mastering any switcher is to take each function a step at a time.

The switcher is laid out systematically. At the top is the row of **PREVIEW** buttons for the *SWITCHABLE PREVIEW MONITOR*. Its buttons can be routed as you wish, but typically, they will be arranged in order (left-right): CAM 1, CAM 2, VTR, FILM, SLIDES, C-G (character generator), etc. The more sources/ channels you have, the more switches you need. All the buses below it follow a similar order.

To help the operator to see which parts of the switcher are in use at a glance, push-buttons often light up *dimly* when selected and *brightly* when the function controlled by that button is on-air.

Cutting (switching)

Let's begin with straightforward cutting (switching) between sources. This is normally done on a row of push-button switches marked **PROGRAM**. As with the **PREVIEW** buttons, each key on this *PROGRAM BUS (BANK)* is connected to a corresponding picture source.

Press **CAM-1** button on the program bus. The key lights, Camera 1's shot is switched 'on-air' to be videotaped or transmitted, and it appears on the *LINE MONITOR (TRANSMISSION)*. Press **CAM-2** switch, and the switcher output cuts to Camera 2's picture.

Faders

The video fader is similar in principle to the gain control (volume pot) on an audio amplifier or a radio. It would seem logical to have a switcher with a fader and switch for each picture channel, but this arrangement can become very unwieldy when combining and manipulating several sources. Instead, switchers use a very ingenious system, that allows considerable flexibility.

As well as the **PROGRAM BUS** which cuts between channels, you will see two more identical horizontal rows of switch-buttons, marked **MIX A** and **MIX B**. (Again, each button corresponds with the picture source in that vertical line.) At the end of these twin rows is a communal T-shaped control lever – the **fader bar**

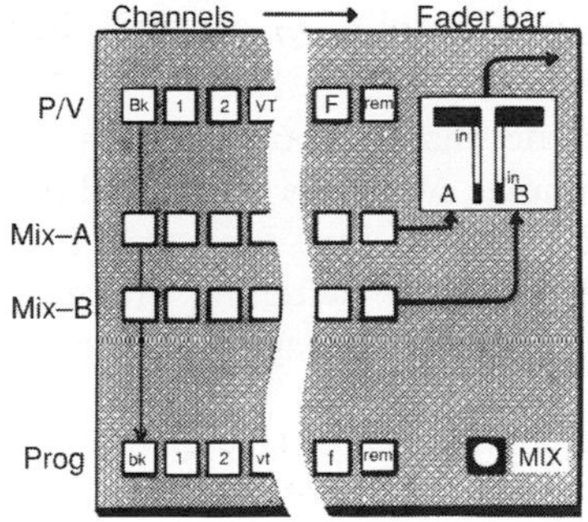

(T-bar). You move this up and down to select which of the rows of switches is active.

A nearby push-button switch marked **MIX** selects whether the **PROGRAM** bus or the **FADER BAR** selection affects what is happening on-air. This fader bar actually consists of two separate faders that are normally used locked (ganged) together. The left-hand **A-FADER** operates on whichever channel is selected on the bus **MIX-A**; and the right-hand **B-FADER** controls the channel on **MIX-B** bus.

If you separate ('split') the fader levers, and push the **A** lever up, it fades up the channel switched on in **MIX-A**. Push downwards, and the **A** channel fades out. Fader lever **B** does the *opposite* for the **MIX-A** bus. (Down for max. **B**; up for min. **B**.) So when you move the *combined* levers upwards you will fade up the channel selected on **A**, and fade out the different channel on **B** at the same time. The result is a **MIX**.

At the end of each row of source buttons is one marked **VIDEO BLACK**. If you select this button on one of the banks and fade over to it . . . the result is a *fade* to *black*.

When you have the fader bar right up to the **MIX-A** bus, then any switching on the **MIX-B** bus will not have any visible effect on-air (although you can check what is happening by watching on **PREVIEW**). You can switch **MIX-B** bus to another channel, ready for the next mix.

Suppose, for example, you are taking *CAM-1* on **A** bus, then mix to *CAM-2* on **B** bus. The studio output mixes from *CAM-1* to *CAM-2*. You are now free to switch **A** bus to a different source (e.g. **FILM**) ready for the next transition. Later, when you mix back from **B** to **A** you will see Camera 2's picture mix to the film channel. (A lot more straightforward in practice than it sounds.)

Superimpositions

To superimpose two shots you simply set up one source on the **A** bus and the other on **B** bus, then move the combined fader bar part way. In the middle, both pictures will be of equal strength. Move the control lever a little nearer **A** bus, and that picture becomes stronger while **B** weakens.

Any *switching* on either bus during the superimposition will show on-air. So whenever you use combined pictures, avoid switching on those buses, unless that is exactly the effect you want (e.g. to switch a superimposed title).

Alternative methods

There are often alternative ways of doing the same thing. For example, you would normally switch between channels on the **PROGRAM** bus. But suppose that you have been using the **MIX (MIX/EFF)** buses, and have just mixed to a camera on the **MIX-A** bus. You now want to *switch* to another camera. Do you have to move over to the **PROGRAM** bus to do so?

No. You can interswitch between the channel buttons on your present **MIX-A** bus. People using simpler switchers do that all the time, for they have no separate **PROGRAM** bus. However, it is better practice to use the **PROGRAM** bus for switching wherever possible, so that the **MIX-A/MIX-B** buses are always available for mixes, fades, and supers.

One quickly learns various tricks. Suppose you have been interswitching on the **PROGRAM** bus. You are on *CAM-1*, but want to *mix* to *CAM-2*. A typical solution is to set up **MIX-A** with *CAM-1* (fader bar to **A**) and transfer to it (**MIX** button). There will be no effect on the transmitted picture, for you've changed to the same channel. But now you are on the **MIX** buses, you can *mix* to *CAM-2* whenever you're ready.

To get back from the **MIX** buses to the **PROGRAM** bus, do the reverse. With *CAM-2* on a **MIX** bus, punch up the same channel on the **PROGRAM** bank, and go to it with the **MIX** button.

So here you have the basics. You now know how to *CUT, MIX, FADE*, and *SUPER*. And how to move between the **PROGRAM** and **MIX** buses. From now on, much depends on the design of your particular switcher.

Additional switcher features

Today's switchers contain an ever-increasing range of facilities, to make operation easier and to allow more elaborate treatment. They also incorporate various *video effects* that we shall discuss in detail later, in Chapter 21 (Table 21.3).

Most of the regular features found in production switchers are summarized in Table 8.1. But let us look in more detail at some particularly useful facilities.

- Wipes
- Re-entry
- Downstream keyer
- Take bar (cut bar)

Wipes

Most switchers have a facility for *wiping* between pictures, creating split screens and inserts. In some you press an appropriate **EFFECTS** switch and are routed into a side-chain, consisting of two more **EFFECTS** buses. A separate control bar (looking like another fader-bar) selects between them. If you put *CAM-1* on **EFFECTS-A** bus and *CAM-2* on **EFFECTS-B** bus, adjusting the control lever will cause one camera's shot to wipe out the other.

The *direction* of the wipe will depend on which way you move the lever. You can move it at any speed, stopping mid-way if you wish to produce a split or divided screen. The actual form of the wipe depends on which pattern you have selected from the menu.

Smaller switchers do not have these extra **EFFECTS** buses. For economy and compactness, they have just the one pair of **MIX** buses. When you press the **EFFECTS** button your regular **MIX** bank is transformed into an **EFFECTS** bank. Now, when you move the 'fader bar' it no longer mixes but *wipes* instead – between the channels selected on the two sides **A** and **B**.

In this switcher design the system is termed a **MIX/EFFECTS** bus or bank.

Some switchers extend this idea of multi-use, and, for example, the **PREVIEW** bus can double as an **EFFECTS KEYING** bus and the **PROGRAM** bus as a **MIX** bus.

Similarly, it may be possible to have a mix-effects set-up on the **PROGRAM** output and a different set-up on the **PREVIEW** output. Pushing a **TAKE PREVIEW** button switches the **PREVIEW** arrangement over to the **PROGRAM** output. Whether such ingenuity proves to be helpful or limiting mainly depends on what you want to do.

Re-entry

The *re-entry* or *cascading* facility allows you to combine two or more sources in one part of the switcher (e.g. a person with a chroma-key insert), and then take this prepared 'package' as if it were a single source and route it to a different **MIX** or **EFFECTS** bank, where it can be combined with a *further* source.

This *double re-entry* technique is regularly used in newscasts, sports programs, demonstrations, where you have a simulated display screen behind the speaker (Figure 21.20), and want to *fade* a series of titles or insets in/out without affecting the composite. (Using other methods, they would have to be abruptly *switched* in/out.)

Some switcher designs allow you to *take* that 'composite plus re-entry package' and enter it into yet another section of the switcher for further treatment – a process termed *cascading*. ('Cascade' simply means connected in a series; one after another.) This circuitry enables you to create and intercut multi-source images.

Downstream keyer

When you have set up various effects, wipes, supers, chroma-key combinations, it may not be particularly convenient or easy to key in subtitles or graphics in addition. That is where the downstream keyer is particularly useful. This feeds into a point at the *output* of the main switcher unit (*line-out*), so is quite independent and does

Table 8.1 Production switcher terms
For terms associated with *electronic insertion*, see Table 19.4.

Audio-follow-video	Facility providing mike-channel switching to correspond with video switching (e.g. intercutting between both ends of a phone conversation).
Auto-switching	Provides automatic interchannel switching at an adjustable rate.
Black input/black buttons	On some switchers, one simply fades out the channel or line fader to obtain a black screen. On others, this would result in a loss of color (chroma) during the fade-out. so a 'black-level' channel button is selected to fade to. (Fade-out is caused by loss of 'color-burst' when fading out a composite video signal.)
Border generator	A narrow line (tone or color) of adjustable width and sharpness, around a picture segment or lettering.
Bus/bank	A series of selector cut buttons (one for each source) associated with a particular function.
Cascading re-entry	An arrangement in which a composite picture (e.g. a quad-split screen derived from several sources) can be further treated (e.g. title insert), by re-entering it at a later point in the switcher routing/chain.
Composite/coded signal	The combined NTSC (PAL or SECAM) signal including picture and sync pulses.
Cut buttons	Push-buttons used to intercut sources (*Program bus*).
Decoded signal	The individual red, green, blue video signals of the total TV picture.
Double-take/double-cut	Switching the foreground subject shot, and the background scene shot simultaneously, in a combined picture.
Downstream keyer	Switching arrangement that enables graphics/titling to be inserted over the main program output from the main switcher unit, without involving a mix/effects system (so leaving that section available for wipes or chroma-key use).
Effects bus/mix-effects bus	A bus used for intersource mixes (dissolves), or for combined-source effects.
Flip-flop controls	A circuit that interswitches the line output between a channel selected on the program bus, and a channel selected on the *preview (pre-set)* bus. On operating the take switch, the previewed channel is transferred to program bus and put on-air. Simultaneously, the channel that was on-air switches away to the preview bus and its monitor. This arrangement provides an automatic preview display of each upcoming shot (on a single-*line preview monitor*) before transferring it to line.
Flip-flop mix	The system mixes from program to a preset selection, for either direction of the fader lever.
Channel fader	Individual video fader for each picture source.
Group fader	Fader controlling a group of sources (e.g. a bus/bank).
Inputs	Switches routing selected video sources to each channel on the switcher.

Table 8.1 (cont.)

Joystick	A vertical stick (or roll-ball) controlling the movement, position, direction of wipes, mattes, etc. around the screen.
Knob-a-channel mixer	A vision mixer favored in some European studios, in which each video channel has its own independent fader. A switch bus facilitates cutting. Its simplicity eases operation for many types of program; particularly when mixing/dissolving fully modulated pictures.
Linear key	A system used for keying in titles without extraneous edge effects. (When used to key in video, can provide color to monochrome dissolves, negative monochrome pictures, and tinting effects – e.g. 'sepia toning'.)
Lock-out	With some switchers, a 'lock-out' situation can develop when you arrange a succession of picture treatments (series insertion: cascade). No intermediate stage can be altered without disrupting the entire composite. (For instance, having combined mattes, titles, chorma key, colorized background, you cannot then decide to put borders around titling.)
Mix-effects (M/E)	A switcher arrangement in which a subfader enables sources on two separate buses to be combined (super, inset, wipe), then selected simultaneously in this form by the master fader.
Non-composite signal	A composite video signal with sync pulses removed (station sync being re-added after processing).
Preview bus/preset bus	Switch buttons enabling any picture source(s) to be selected on a single preview monitor (to check effects, supers, split screen, insertions etc.).
Program bus	Cut buttons interswitching program sources. The result is seen on the line output (studio output, transmission).
Re-entry	A facility allowing a picture treated in one part of a switcher to be fed into another section: e.g. the output from one **M/E bank** can be switched into another **M/E bank** for further treatment.
Sync/non-sync mode	Adjusts switcher to accept video-sources that are *in-sync or out-of-sync* with local synchronizing pulses.
Take-bar/cut-bar	A facility in some switchers that enables you to record a program's transitions (cut/mix/wipe, etc.) and composite effects in a memory/file/store and play them out to line as required, simply by pressing a *take-bar.* (Similarly *AUTO-TAKE. AUTO-DISSOLVE, AUTO-WIPE.*)
Wipe	A picture transition in which one shot progressively displaces another, usually in a decorative pattern, automatically, or by moving a control lever. A wide range of different patterns can be selected by thumbwheel switches or push-buttons (tablet switches).

not involve any controls set up on the main board, leaving them free for other functions.

The downstream keyer unit normally includes a **MASTER FADER BAR**, which controls the entire switcher output, allowing the transmission picture to be faded to black.

Take button (cut bar)

The **TAKE BUTTON/CUT BAR** enables you to switch from one set-up to another simply by pressing a single button. You can use this facility to continually interswitch between two cameras. After pressing a **FLIP-FLOP** key, you punch them up on the **PROGRAM** and the **PREVIEW/PRESET** buses, respectively. One will appear on the *MASTER MONITOR* (*LINE/TRANSMISSION*) and go to line, while the other appears on the *SWITCHABLE PREVIEW* monitor. (Their corresponding indicator lights are illuminated on the switcher and beside the monitors.) Press the **TAKE** button, and they change over; the on-air camera switches to preview, and the camera that was previewed is now on-air. (The indicators, too, will change.) Press **TAKE**, and they switch back. Although the result is the same as when using the **PROGRAM** bus alone for switching, it reduces the danger of hitting the wrong button during repeated interswitching, and one's reaction time is faster.

The **TAKE BUTTON** is most valuable, however, when you want to interswitch between a series of complex combined pictures.

In the most advanced switchers the operator can organize and set up elaborate transitions or multi-source effects at any time, and store all details (including the direction, speed, and position of wipes) in a *file/memory* ready for the moment they are required. These preset effects can then be selected in any chosen order, and introduced simply by pressing a *TAKE BUTTON/CUT BAR*.

Linear editing

Linear-editing requires a *master monitor* to show the selected material being recorded onto the master videotape and a *preview monitor(s)* to display the sections being replayed from the original tapes. The process simply involves your playing the original tape(s) on one VTR, and copying (*dubbing off*) selected parts onto a clean tape (i.e. blank, unmodulated) on another machine. As you add each shot or sequence to the end of the previous one, you *assemble* a new composite master tape. This type of *manual linear editing* can be quite laborious and time consuming, as you shuttle to and fro on the original tapes to find the chosen sections.

If you have a 'bad take' on the original tape, and want to replace just this piece with a corrected version, you have the choice of either copying in an *assemble* (*assembly*) mode as before, or using a different editing method called *insert editing*. When switched to the *insert editing* mode, you can record replacement material 'over' (in place of) the faulty section. Ideally, that has the advantage that you are left with the optimum quality original recording, into which the corrected shot has been imperceptibly dovetailed. In practice though, unless your new insert is precisely timed to match the original section, frames at the head or tail of the insert will be lost or duplicated. A hazardous process!

In a more refined form of *linear editing*, you note which shots you want to use, and where they are to go during an *off-line editing session*. This information is then fed into a computerized *edit controller* system which shuttles the tapes to find the items, and then assembles the master tape automatically.

Non-linear editing

Although videotape is a remarkably cheap method of recording program material, it has one major drawback. When editing, you find yourself spending a lot of time running to and fro searching for each section you want to use. You can't go directly to a particular point in the tape. Even with the aid of *fast forward/rewind, shuttling* at variable speeds, and electronic *markers* on the tape, time is wasted arriving at each selected edit point. (The situation is akin to that between audio tapes and CD discs.)

In the world of *computer technology*, high-capacity *hard disks* are used to magnetically store a considerable amount of *digital* data, which can be retrieved instantaneously at the press of a button. Information can be recorded on the disk and wiped, over and over again. Not surprisingly then, this technology has been applied to the process of editing TV picture and sound – in a process called *non-linear editing.*

The non-linear editing set-up

Originally all television picture and sound took the form of *analogue* signals – i.e. continuously fluctuating voltages corresponding to the brightness or loudness of the original sources.

In *non-linear editing systems* these analog video and audio signals are converted into coded digital form (*digitized*) similar to that in regular computer technology. This transformation has many advantages. Picture and sound are of much higher quality, and unlike analogue signals, can be copied over and over without deterioration. Information can be more compactly stored, and can be manipulated in various ways. When this information is stored on a magnetic disc as *digital data* (like the hard disk in a computer system) you can search out and replay any part of the recording in an instant; unlike the play-through delays of tape recordings. (*See Digests – Desktop video.*)

The main control on the desktop *editing console* is typically a *shuttle wheel*, which allows you to replay program picture and sound forward and backwards, in sync at adjustable speeds. You can jog frame-by-frame, or jump directly to its head, tail or to any cue-marks. Alternatively, the system may be controlled from a computer *keyboard, mouse*, a *track-ball (tracker ball)*, a *light-pen, a digital tablet*, or by pointing to *a touch-screen* over the monitor picture.

Some non-linear editing systems use a single color monitor picture, which is switched between the preparatory *menu mode* and the *editing mode*; displaying small frames of the various shots and the sound tracks. Other systems use two separate monitors. A further monitor might display the *edit decision list (EDL)*, providing a database which shows shot identification, the start/end timecodes of a sequence, shot durations, audio track data, director's comments, etc.

The system may also include various additional facilities, including automatic sorting of clips, storyboard displays, trimming facilities (i.e. adding or removing individual frames to clips), motion effects (freeze, slow or reverse motion), audio mixing, etc.

Non-linear editing processes

You begin editing by making a complete copy of the original videotape recording, on the hard disk of the non-linear editing system. In the process, the equipment automatically creates a visual log on the editing monitor screen. This shows the *in* and *out* frames (*tops* and *tails*) of all the shots recorded as a series of small still pictures, together with their *time code addresses*. Now you have a total record of all the material available, and can rapidly locate any frame simply by calling up its code reference.

Next, using this visual log as a guide, you play through the original videotape again, selecting the particular shots you want to use. This builds up a new *edit decision list* display on the screen – a sequence of stills in the new order you have now chosen, with details of the transitions you require between them, and any special transition effects (e.g. wipes). Remember, these shots may have been located *anywhere* in the original videotapes. The corresponding sound appears as graphical audio strips below the picture displays.

It is important to appreciate that what you are creating is a '*dummy*' arrangement, giving an overall view of your *anticipated* editing treatment for that sequence. This is a 'probability list'. You have not actually edited anything yet. Next you instruct the computer to play through the sequence to see how effective this picture and sound arrangement is going to be. (The replay speed is adjustable.) During this rehearsal, you can make any changes you wish; altering the shots' order, durations, transitions, etc., without having to revise earlier or later sequences. (That is a particular problem in *linear editing* processes.) Once you are satisfied with this *edit-master*, you store it on hard disk, videotape, or recordable videodisc.

If your *edit-master disk* has been recorded in *compressed* form (*see Digests – Compression*), you now use it to instruct a computer-assisted system which auto-assembles a new master videotape from the original videotape recording using a *linear* editing process. (In *auto-assembly* the computer runs the VTRs to locate the required shots and copy them in the chosen order.)

If you have a *full-resolution (high-end)* system with high-quality images that have not been compressed, the edit-master disk can be copied directly onto the transmission videotape (*'printing to tape'*) via a digital/analogue convertor unit.

As with most of the technical processes we are meeting, this all sounds a lot more complicated than it really is. The real complexities are within the electronics. Once you operate the equipment for yourself, everything soon becomes an instinctive routine.

■ *Digital store* – One of the drawbacks of the non-linear recording process is that the original videotapes from the camera copy usually have to be copied onto the editing system's hard disk(s) *in real time*. So if you have shot a couple of hours' worth of tape, it can take that long to copy it all onto disk. To avoid this delay before editing can begin, some people make a separate *digital recording* while shooting in analogue. That can speed the preparation of the edit-master disk considerably, as the *digital* version is copied into the editing system in minutes.

The features of non-linear editing

Currently there are several types of non-linear editing systems. These have operational differences, but produce virtually similar results.

- Because there is immediate access to any part of the program, non-linear methods are undoubtably quicker for routine editing. But most editors find that in practice, instead of appreciably shortening the overall editing time, the increased flexibility encourages them (and others!) to refine and rework edits, trying out alternative treatments than would previously have been impossible in the time available.

  During any creative process, there is a lot to be said for 'sleeping on it' wherever possible; coming back to critique results after a break. While working, you become overfamiliar with each feature, so even a brief time gap helps to develop a 'fresh eye', improving one's critical judgment. Every time you review a sequence, you tend to see aspects you've overlooked before. That kind of rethinking was less practicable when using lengthy *linear editing* processes.

There are many other advantages to *non-linear editing:*

- The order and duration of shots, or any part of a shot can be changed rapidly – unlike linear editing processes, where alterations can involve re-making entire sequences. In tape systems, you have to rebuild, or rerecord (i.e. *go down another generation*).

- After any change, the overall duration of the program can be checked in a few seconds; and if necessary, material can be reinstated immediately. Every new change you make need not spoil the work you have already completed.
- A number of different formats can be accommodated, so that a single program might include such diverse sources as Hi8, Betamax, D-5, S-VHS, as well as Super 8, Super 16 film formats, which are all converted to common digital form.
- Non-linear editing can be used for both *off-line editing* (i.e. making pre-editing decisions) and *on-line editing* (during the actual editing process). However, it is generally agreed that where compression is involved, non-linear editing is more suitable for an *off-line* approach, because of the extra time involved in copying.
- When working with *digital data*, there is no quality loss during copying. When duplicating *analogue* tape, or converting up and down between digital and analogue, there is an opportunity for deterioration.

The art and techniques of editing

From the mechanics of television editing, let us turn to the artistry of editing – to the subtle ways in which you can influence your audience through your editing treatment.

Three types of editing are widely used: *continuity cutting*, *relational cutting*, and *dynamic cutting.*

Continuity cutting

In *film editing* the editor may spend considerable time and thought in deciding on the final shot order, the exact cutting points, cutting rhythm, etc. Although this is possible with more sophisticated VT editing systems, time usually precludes this precision.

In most TV productions editing is simplistic, serving the practical purpose of interrelating viewpoints, creating a feeling of consecutiveness and order, interlinking dialogue and action. At best, the technique provides a clear straightforward narrative, a smooth pictorial flow, and unobtrusive transitions. At worst, such *continuity cutting* becomes a purely functional routine.

Example
Mr Brown speaks – cut to CU of Brown.
Mr Smith speaks – cut to CU of Smith.
Anchorman speaks – cut to three-shot of group.

Relational cutting

Here, through intercutting, shots that have no direct connection in reality are deliberately given an implied relationship.

Examples

Woman seen walking up to house, *cut* to woman in a room. We assume she entered house, and is now in a room there. (Actually shot with different women in similar costume, at different locations).

Shot of aircraft in flight, *cut* to pilot at controls. (A library model shot has been intercut with a studio mock-up. Neither is real.)

Man approaches foot of stairs, *cut* to him coming upstairs. (Action may have been shot on different occasions.)

In *parallel cutting* (*parallel action*), shots from two different locations or action groups are repeatedly intercut; usually as a dramatic development to heighten tension, e.g. fast intercutting between fugitive and pursuers. *Cross-cutting*, on the other hand, intercuts between different viewpoints of the same subject, usually for visual variety.

Whenever you join two shots together by a *cut* you immediately establish a relationship between them. This juxtaposition is both *physical* and *intellectual*.

Physically, the viewer's eyes become aware of the change, and begin tracing a fresh interest pattern in the new picture.

Intellectually, the viewer has to interpret the new picture. (Where are we now? What is this? What is happening?).

These responses are, of course interrelated. Where the shots are compositionally matched (matched cuts) and the significance of the second shot obvious, it will be a *smooth cut*.

Where shots are pictorially unmatched (jump cut, mismatched cut) the effect can be very disturbing, as the audience has to search around for the subject in the new shot. Similarly, their attention is disrupted if they do not instantly realize how the second shot relates to the first, or what it is all about.

Dynamic cutting

Sophisticated intercutting can create dramatic emphasis, convey moods or abstract ideas that are not readily expressed in more direct terms. The ideas themselves may not be implicit in the component shots. Cause–effect relationships are often interpreted.

Examples

Shot of broken window, *cut* to small boy crying. (A lost ball? Punished after breaking the window?)

Intercut shots symbolically suggesting 'Spring', 'Progress', 'Terror', etc.

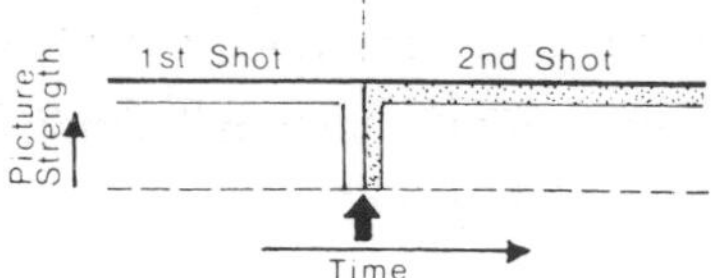

Fig. 8.3 The cut
The mechanics of picture transitions can be shown graphically. Here the *cut* (straight cut, flat cut) is shown – from one shot or scene to another.

The cut

The cut is the simplest transition. It is dynamic, instantly associated two situations. Sudden change has a more powerful audience impact than a gradual one, and here lies the cut's strength.

Cutting, like all production treatment, should be purposeful. An unmotivated cut interrupts continuity and can create false relationships between shots. Cutting is not akin to repositioning the eyes as we glance around a scene, for we move our eyes with a full knowledge of our surroundings and always remain correctly orientated. On the screen, we know only what the camera show us; although guesses or previous knowledge may fill out the environment in our minds.

Fig. 8.4 Intercut shots of the same subject
1 Avoid cutting between similar or near-similar shots.
2 Extreme changes in shot size (e.g. over 5:1) are distracting, unless explained by dialogue or story-line (see Fig. 17.1).
3 Viewpoint angle cuts of less than 20° or over 60° can be visually disturbing.

Fig. 8.5 Visual continuity
1 The viewer can lose sense of direction where there are dissimilar backgrounds.
2 This is unlikely to happen where there is background continuity, or (3) compositional links between pictures.

Cutting jumps attention between new viewpoints or locations, so the viewer has continually to relocate and interpret each new shot. This is a problem during fast intercutting between different locations.

Where quite dissimilar shots are intercut, your audience may have some difficulty in appreciating continuity or relationships. But you can establish an immediate connection through:

1 *Dialogue* – introducing or implying the next shot's substance.
2 *Action* – establishing a cause–effect relationship.
3 *Common reference points* (a person) in both shots.
4 *Audio continuity.*

Occasionally, and *only* occasionally, you may want to mislead the viewer's continuity deliberately for a comic or dramatic purpose.

Where a quick viewpoint change seems obtrusive it has usually not been clearly *related*, and has not fulfilled the *purposes* outlined earlier. It is a change that the viewer has no reason to want or expect. Unmotivated changes rarely satisfy.

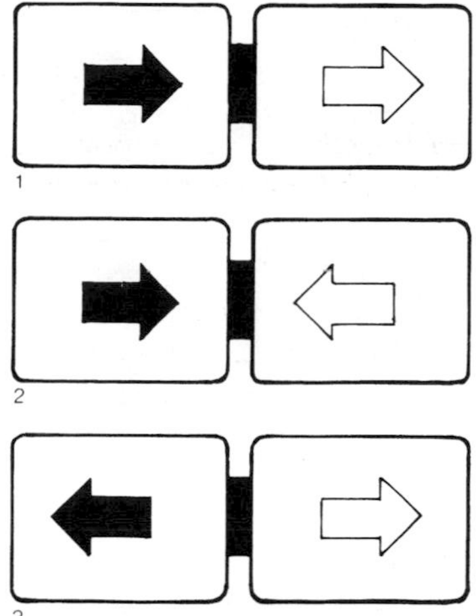

Fig. 8.6 Cutting between moving pictures
Cuts during movement create strong subjective effects.

1 *Directional* cuts between subjects moving in the same direction suggests continuity of action or direction, pursuit, similar purpose.
2 *Reverse* cuts between opposite directions can suggest converging forces, impending meeting or collision, or (3) diverging forces, parting, expansion.

It is generally inadvisable to intercut between shots of widely differing size (LS to BCU), or over a wide angle unless the attention is tightly localized.

■ *The moment for the cut* Cut should preferably be made on an *action* or *reaction* – turning head, gasp of astonishment, a rise. However, there are two philosophies about the moment to make the cut. Some editors contend that the cutting moment should be *just before* or *after* an action. A transition during a movement can disrupt it and create a spurious cutting rhythm. Others maintain that by cutting *during* a movement you avoid the illusion of its being jerked into action or suddenly halted (from an in-motion shot to a static one). Where the aim is to transfer attention rather than create a visual shock, the cut can be hidden within action, as the audience is preoccupied with the movement itself.

■ *The delayed cut* A *late* cut is frustrating. Badly timed, it has missed the optimum moment for change. But the *delayed cut* has exciting possibilities. It deliberately withholds the new shot until after the expected moment – in order to create audience suspense, interest, and anticipation. For example:

1 *Cutting on a reaction:*
Knock at door. Writer looks up –
Cut – Door opens. Woman enters. 'May I come in?'

2 *Delaying the cut:*
Knock at door. Writer looks up. Door heard opening.
Woman's voice, 'May I come in?'
Cut – To woman at door, who enters.

■ *Cutting between moving pictures* When moving shots are intercut, you invariably create spatial interactions between them, even when none exists. Intercutting such shots suggests:

1 Moving together (meeting, collision).
2 Moving apart (parting, expansion).
3 Moving in the same direction (following, chasing, similar destination).

To avoid these effects, cutaway shots or intermediate movement directions (to or from camera) can be introduced. Where the viewer

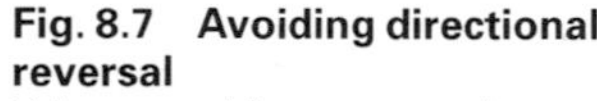

Fig. 8.7 Avoiding directional reversal
Where a subject appears in successive shots showing movement in opposite directions, you can avoid accidental subjective effects by introducing an intermediate buffer shot showing a head-on view (perhaps including the actual change in direction).

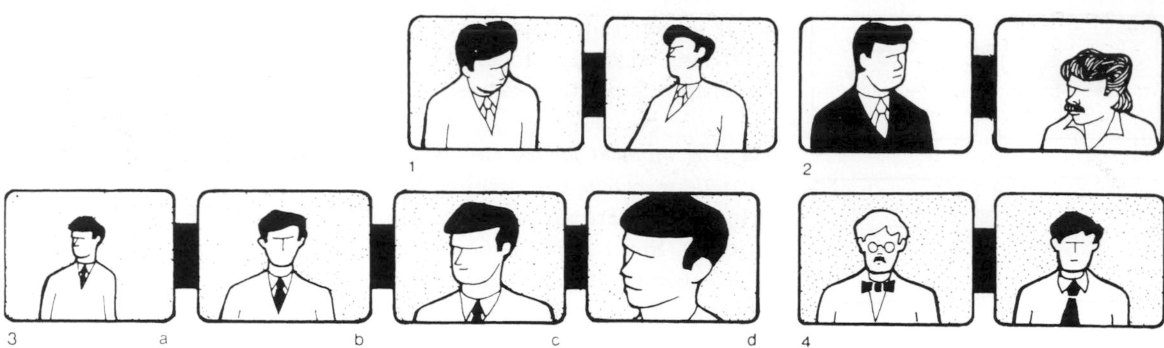

Fig. 8.8 part 1 Matched and mismatched cutting
Mismatching on cutting can take several forms, but in each case results in visual disruption.

1 *Height change* – mismatched lens-heights (for no dramatic purpose).
2 *Headroom changes* – mismatched headroom.
3 *Size jumps* – instantaneous growth or shrinkage occurs if subject size changes only slightly on the cut (e.g. a-b, or b-c). A difference of at least a-c (4:3 previous size) is desirable.
4 *Transformations* – if too closely matched, the viewer may see 'magical transformations' on the cut!

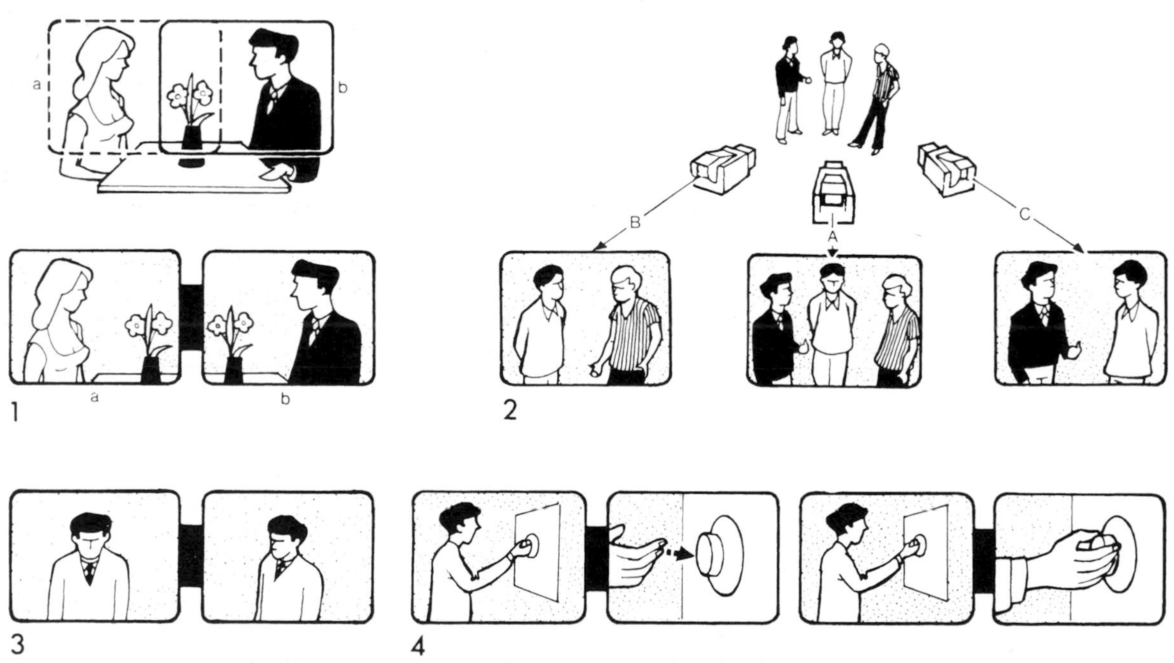

Fig. 8.8 part 2 Matched and mismatched cutting
1 *Jump cuts* – if the same subject is included iin successive shots, it may jump frame-position on the cut – a common dilemma in table shots.
2 It can arise also in group shots. Cameras A-B or A-C intercut, but not B-C.
3 *Twists* – a slight difference in the viewpoint can produce a turn or twist on cutting. Hopefully, the disruption may be disguised by 'motivating' the change (e.g. a singer turns to face the new camera), or by a slow dissolve.
4 *Continuity matching* – when shooting *discontinuously*, you must match shot detail and action for each cut, during editing: e.g. the moment of turning a knob, opening a door, lifting a glass. Otherwise continuity is disrupted.

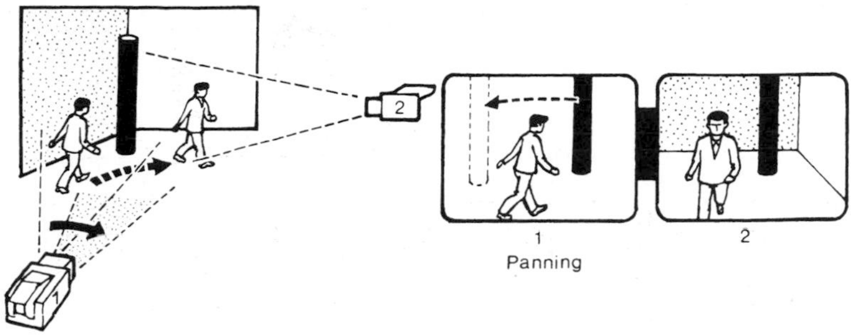

Fig. 8.9 Rediscovery on a cut Camera 1 pans, following the action. The black pillar passes out of shot (frame left). *Cut* to Camera 2 (to prevent shooting off) and the pillar is rediscovered on frame right again! A similar situation arises when someone who has just entered a shot is seen, after a cut, to re-enter the next.

is watching a single moving subject any direction changes should be obvious or deducible. Otherwise he will see distracting direction-jumps or may lose orientation.

■ *Cutting between static and moving pictures* Cutting from a static scene to a moving one suddenly accelerates audience interest. The new shot springs into action; its speed, energy, or violence being accentuated by its sudden appearance.

Cutting from a moving scene to a static shot causes a sudden collapse in tension; which, if unsatisfied, can lead to a rapid fall-off in interest. Or it can produce a highly dramatic interruption. For example, panning with a searcher around an empty room . . . and then *cut* – to a static shot of someone watching his actions.

■ *Cut to begin or end action* These devices must be used with caution. They can too easily look like operational errors!

The cut-in: a shock introduction to vigorous action, catastrophe, chaos.
The cut-out: a severe, definite conclusive action as you cut to a blank screen at the end of a shot. An emphatic gesture or comment of finality.

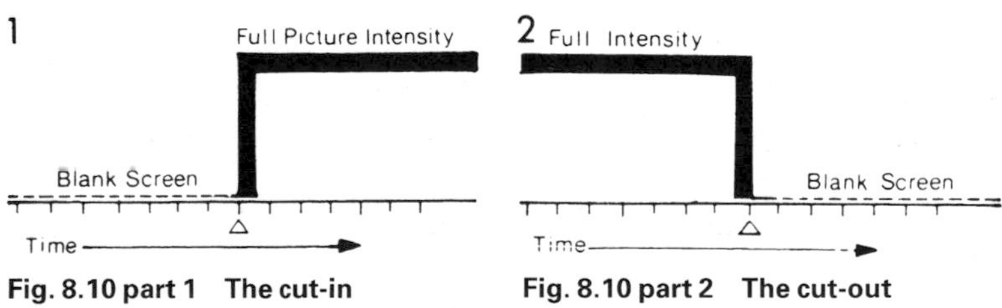

Fig. 8.10 part 1 The cut-in **Fig. 8.10 part 2 The cut-out**

The fade

■ *The fade-in* This provides a quiet introduction to action. A slow fade-in suggests the forming of an idea. A fast fade-in has rather less vitality and shock value than the cut.

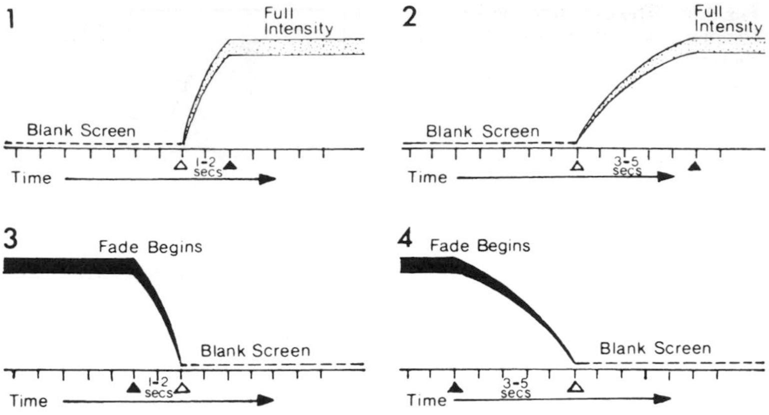

Fig. 8.11 The fade-in and fade-out
1 Fast fade-in.
2 Slow fade-in.
3 Fast fade-out.
4 Slow fade-out.

The fade-out and fade-in may be combined in permutation (slow-out, fast-in etc.) to link two shots producing a fade out-in.

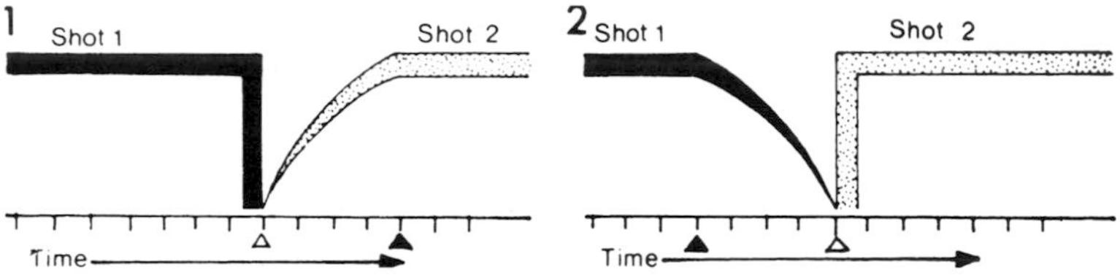

Fig. 8.12 Combinations of fade and cut
1 The cut/fade-in results in a surge, a visual crescendo, strongly introducing the new shot.
2 The fade-out/cut-in produces a visual punch; used between a succession of static shots (e.g. of captions, paintings), provides a dynamic introduction to each.

■ *The fade-out* A quick fade-out has rather less finality and suspense than the cut-out. A slow fade-out is a peaceful cessation of action.

■ *The fade-out/in* Linking two sequences, the fade-out/in introduces a pause in the flow of action. Mood and pace vary with their relative speeds and the pause time between them. You can use this transition to connect slow-tempo sequences, where a change in time or place is involved. Between two fasting-moving scenes it may act as a momentary pause, emphasizing the activity of the second shot.

A cut-out/in with a pause between shots is valueless. It always looks like a lost shot – or a mistake.

The mix (dissolve, lap dissolve)

The *mix* is produced by fading out one picture while fading in the next. The two images are momentarily superimposed; the first gradually disappears being replaced by the second.

Mixing between shots provides a smooth restful transition, with minimum interruption of the visual flow (except when a confusing intermixture is used).

A *quick-mix* usually implies that their action is concurrent (parallel action).

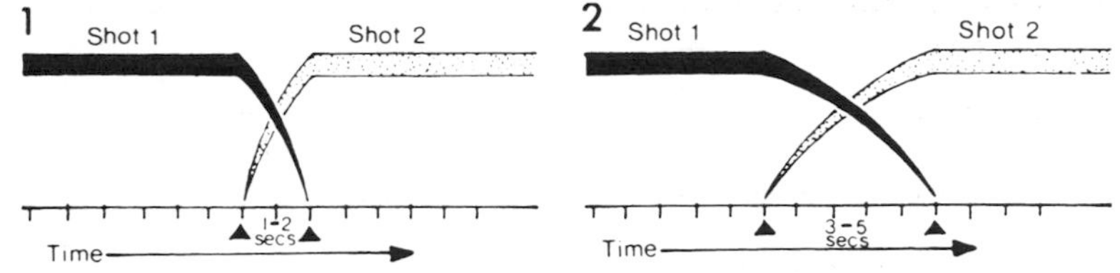

Fig. 8.13 The mix (dissolve) The mix usually compares successive shots.

1 Fast mix.
2 Slow mix.

A *slow-mix* suggests differences in time or place.
Mixes are generally comparative:

1 Pointing similarities or differences.
2 Comparing time (especially time passing).
3 Comparing space or position (mixing a series of shots showing progress).
4 Helping to relate areas visually (when transferring attention from the whole subject to a localized part).

Mixes are widely used as 'softened-off' cuts, to provide an unobtrusive transition for slow-tempo occasions where the violence of a cut would be disruptive. Unfortunately, they are used also to hide an absence of motivation when changing to a new shot!

A very slow mix produces sustained intermingled images that can be tediously confusing. Between different viewpoints of the same subject, they result in twin images.

■ *Matched dissolves* By mixing between carefully matched shots with similarly framed subjects you can obtain a transformation effect. Its main applications are to suggest time changes (boy to man, seasonal change), or *flashbacks* (reversed time), or magical changes (pumpkin to Cinderella's coach).

■ *Mixes on movement* Mixes during movement are usually only completely satisfactory when their relative directions are similar. Mixing opposite directions can arouse feelings of confusion, impact, or expansion, without necessarily indicating that these subjects are involved. But it is a transition to be used cautiously.

■ *Defocus dissolve* The first camera gradually defocuses, while you mix to a second completely defocused shot which then sharpens. Normally used for *flashbacks*, but sometimes introduced for transformation effects, or decorative interscene transitions.

■ *Ripple dissolve* Here the first shot becomes increasingly broken up by horizontal rippling (weave), during which you mix to a second rippling shot . . . which steadies to a normal image. Generally introduced for flashback effects.

Fig. 8.14 part 1 Uncover wipe
Second image is progressively uncovered.

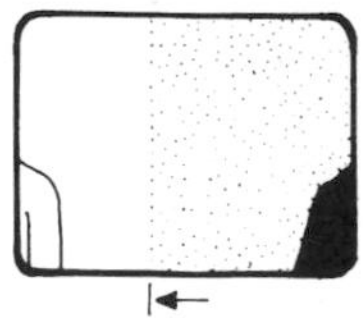

Fig. 8.14 part 2 Pushover wipe
Second image pushes over, displacing original one. (Push-off/pull-off/push-on wipe).

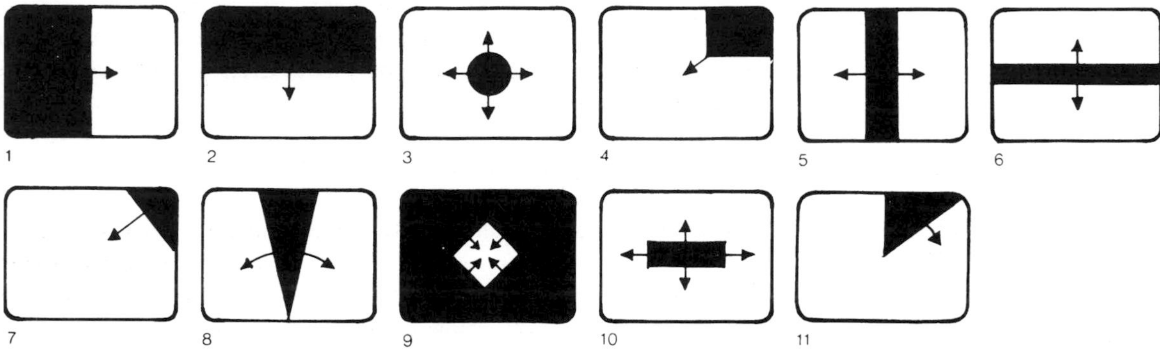

Fig. 8.14 part 3 Common wipe patterns

1 Horizontal wipe/line-split. (When static, this provides a split-screen).
2 Downwards vertical wipe.
3 Iris/circle wipe (out or in, expanding or contracting).
4 Corner wipe – top right. (When static, this provides a *corner inset*).
5 Barndoors/line bar/horizontal split wipe (expanding or converging).
6 Vertical split wipe/field bar (wipes out or in).
7 Diagonal (top right).
8 Fan wipe (in or out).
9 Diamond wipe-in.
10 Box wipe-out.
11 Rotary/clock wipe.

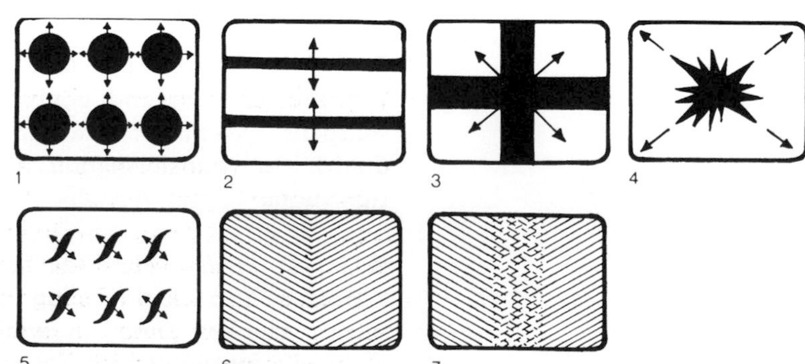

Fig. 8.14 part 4 Multiple and complex wipes

1 Multiple iris (out).
2 Blind wipe (out).
3 Cross wipe.
4 Explosion.
5 Multiple wipe with ripple (only the wipe-pattern ripples, not the pictures involved).
6 Hard-edge wipe.
7 Soft-edge wipe.

The wipe

The wipe is a visual effect, mainly used for decorative transitions. It can be produced by several methods, but most production switchers include electronic wipe facilities. It had a particular vogue in early movies, and is now mainly used in trailers and commercials. There the visual impact of the wipes tends to disguise the raw edges of compositionally unrelated fragments.

The effect of the wipe is to uncover, reveal, conceal, fragment; according to how it is applied. In all forms it draws attention to the flat nature of the screen, destroying any three-dimensional illusion.

The wipe direction can aid or oppose the subject's movement, modifying its vigor accordingly. The edge may be sharp (hard-edged/hard wipe) or diffused (soft-edged/soft wipe), the latter being much less distracting. Broad soft-edged versions can have the unobtrusiveness of a mix.

Wipes take many geometric forms with a variety of applications. A circular (*iris*) wipe, for example, may be used as a transition between close-up detail (a soloist musician) and a wider viewpoint (the full orchestra).

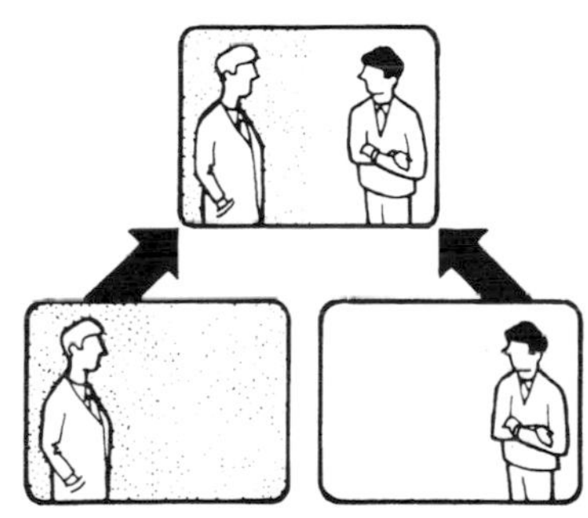

Fig. 8.15 Split screen
The screen is split into two or more segments, showing a series of pictures or respective portions of these components.

The split screen

If a *wipe* is stopped during its travel, the screen remains divided; showing part of both shots. In this way you can produce a localized *inset*, revealing a small part of a second shot, or where the proportions are more comparable, a *split screen.*

The split screen can show us simultaneously:

1 Events taking place at the same time
2 The interaction of events in separate locations (phone conversations)
3 A comparison of appearance, behavior, etc. of two or more subjects
4 A comparison of before and after (developments, growth, etc.)
5 A comparison of different versions (comparing a relief map with its aerial photograph).

Superimpositions (half-lap dissolves, supers)

In film, superimposition necessitates exposing each frame twice or more (double exposure) in the camera, or more usually in the laboratory's optical printer. In television, you simply fade up two or more picture channels simultaneously.

Because the tones of superimposed pictures are additive, the light areas of any picture generally break through the darker tones of other shots with which it is superimposed.

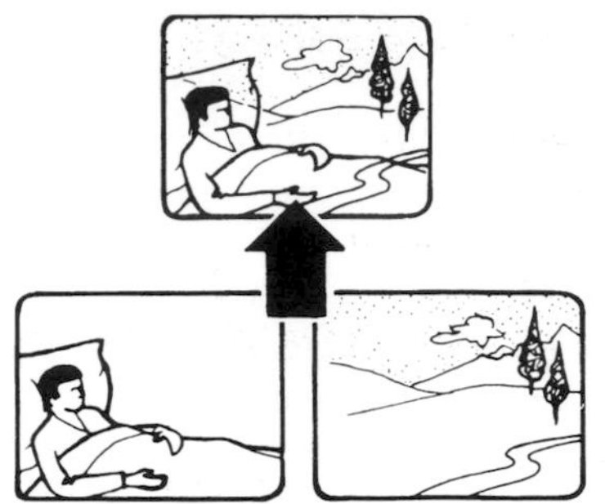

Fig. 8.16 Superimposition
Two or more pictures faded up at the same time: their relative strengths being controlled by video faders.

Whether superimposed subjects appear solid or transparent will, therefore, depend on relative picture tones. Where a lighter-toned subject is superimposed on a *black background*, it will appear solid. On lighter-toned backgrounds, it will be proportionately diluted. Superimposed over multi-tones, the result appears 'transparent'.

But you must always guard against messy confused images, particularly where multi-colored or multi-tone shots are combined (color mixtures and lightness variations result). You should also avoid any movements (or zooms) of superimposed cameras where supers are being used to provide subject inserts, unless you want growth, shrinkage, or side-slip effects.

Superimposition can be used productionally to convey several ideas:

1 *Spatial montage*: suggesting that two or more events are occurring concurrently in different places.
2 *Comparison*: showing the similarity or difference between the subjects juxtaposed. (Bringing together action, events, locale, having parallel significance.)
3 *Development*: displaying stages in a process. (A half-built house with architectural sketches superimposed.)
4 *Relationship*: showing subjects' interrelationships, how components are positioned. (A mechanism superimposed on a faint image of the entire machine.)
5 *Thoughts*: a close shot of a person, with images of his thoughts superimposed.

Superimposition has a number of practical mechanical applications:

1 To obtain transparent-looking images (ghosts).
2 To achieve larger or smaller proportions (giants, dwarfs), by 'solid' superimposition.
3 To permit appearances and disappearances.
4 To combine titling with another picture.
5 To insert subjects (solid or transparent) into a separate background shot.
6 To add 'surface texture' (e.g. canvas), or a decorative border.
7 To emphasize or identify detail (map route, selected area pointer).

Order of shots

It is a characteristic of the human mind that we continually seek meaningful relationships in what we see and hear – even where none exists. In any rapid succession of shots we subconsciously try to establish a connection between them (slow mixes between them reduce this effect).

We can interpret a succession of shots in several ways:

1 Shot A may cause (or lead to) Shot B's situation.
2 Shot A may be explained by Shot B.
3 Shots A and B together may give rise to Shot C.
4 Shots A and B together may be explained by Shot C.
5 Shot A juxtaposed with Shot B may imply an idea 'X' that is not implicit in either A or B alone.

In various circumstances you may find that the order in which you present a series of shots will influence your audience's interpretation of them.

Even a simple example shows the nuances that easily arise. *A burning building – a violent explosion – men running towards an automobile.*

Altering the order of these shots can modify what seems to be happening:

1 Fire – automobile – explosion:
Men killed while trying to escape from fire.
2 Fire – explosion – automobile:
Running from fire, men escaped despite explosion.
3 Automobile – explosion – fire:
Running men caused explosion, firing the building.

Not only is the imagination stimulated more effectively by *implication* rather than direct statements but indirect techniques overcome many practical difficulties.

Suppose you join two shots: *A boy looking upward . . . tree falling towards camera*. One's impression is that a boy is watching a tree being felled. Reverse the shots and the viewer could assume that the tree is falling towards the boy who, sensing danger, looks up. The actual pictures might be totally unrelated; a couple of library shots.

Cause–effect relationships

Sometimes pictures convey practically the same idea, whichever way they are combined: *woman screaming* and *lion leaping*. But there is usually some distinction, especially where any cause–effect relationship is suggestible.

Cause–effect or effect–cause relationships are a common link between successive shots. Someone turns his head – the director cuts to show the reason. The viewer has become accustomed to this concept. Occasionally, you may deliberately show an unexpected outcome:

1 A bore and his victim are walking along a street.
2 Close-up of bore . . . who eventually turns to his companion.
3 *Cut* to shot of companion far behind, window gazing.

The result here is an amusingly sardonic comment.

But sometimes the viewer expects an outcome that does not develop and he feels frustrated or mystified, having jumped to wrong conclusions:

1 A lecturer in long-shot beside a wall-map.
2 *Cut* to a close-up of map.
3 Lecturer now in an entirely different setting.

The director used the map-shot to relocate the speaker for the next sequence, but the viewer expected to find the lecturer beside the map, and became disorientated.

Even more disturbing are situations where there is no visual continuity, although action has implied one:

1 Hearing a knock at the door, the girl turns . . .
2 *Cut* to a shot of a train speeding through the night.

The director thought that he would create tension by withholding who was outside the door, but he inadvertently created a false relationship instead. Even where dialogue or action explains the second shot, this is an unsuitable transition. A mix or fade-out/in would have prevented misunderstandings.

Quite often, in an attempt to shorten scene duration and to create filmic time, directors cut from one shot to another in which the same person appears in different costume at a different time and place. Whether the technique is acceptable or confusing is challengeable.

Montage

In a montage we present a series of images which combine to produce an associative effect. These pictures can be displayed sequentially, as a multi-image screen, or superimposed.

1 *Sequential montage*. One brief shot follows another in rapid succession, usually to convey an abstract concept, such as 'Development, Prosperity, Civilization, Industry'.
2 *Multi-image montage*. We can show several images at the same time by dividing the screen into two, four, eight or 16 segments. Any smaller, and each section loses its impact and becomes part of an overall pattern. These images may be of the same subject, or of several different subjects. They can be *stills* (e.g. showing various stages as an athlete clears a pole vault) or *moving pictures* (e.g. showing different people using the same product).

   You can use a multi-image montage series for many purposes – to show steps in a process, to compare, to combine different viewpoints, to show action taking place at different places, to

Fig. 8.17 Montage
1 A rapid succession of related images, or
2 juxtaposed images (quad split/segmented shot), or
3 superimposed images developing a common theme.

demonstrate different applications of a tool, to show variety, and so on.

3 *Superimposed images*. This form of montage is less used nowadays, for as images overlap each other the color picture quickly becomes confused; particularly where there is a lot of detail (see *Superimpositions*).

Duration of shots

If a shot is too brief the viewer will have insufficient time to appreciate its intended information. Held too long, and attention wanders. Thoughts dwell on the sound, eventually giving way to rumination – or channel switching! The limit for most subjects is probably around 15–30 seconds; and for a static shot, much less. For a mute shot, it could be as little as 5–10 seconds. The belief that a close shot can sustain interest longer is arguable.

The 'correct' duration for a shot depends on its purpose. We may show a hand holding a coin for half a minute as its features are described by a lecturer; whereas in a drama, a one-second shot would tell us that the thief has successfully stolen it from the owner's pocket. Given the right occasion, even a single subliminal frame (1/30 or 1/25 second) can be seen and responded to!

Many factors influence how long you can usefully hold a shot:

1 The amount of information you want the viewer to assimilate (general impression, minute detail).
2 How obvious and easily discerned the information is.
3 Subject familiarity (its appearance, viewpoint, associations, etc.).
4 How much action, change, or movement the shot contains.
5 Picture quality (marked contrast, detail, strong composition, all hold most interest).

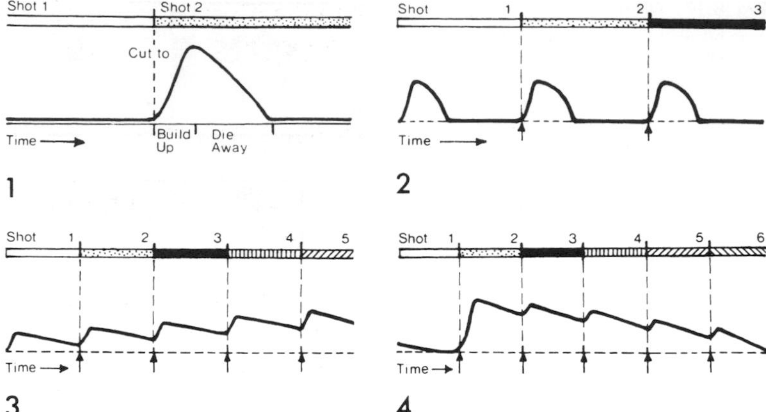

Fig. 8.18 Response to cuts

1 The viewer's response to a cut is not instantaneous. When the cut is made, the audience impact is slightly delayed; building to a peak and dying away gradually.
2 A series of cuts may achieve individual impacts: there being sufficient time for each reaction to subside.
3 Faster cutting may produce a cumulative build-up.
4 Through repetition, surprise may diminish with each cut, resulting in declining tension.

Audience attention is normally keyed to production pace. A short flash of information during a slow-tempo sequence may pass unnoticed, while in a fast-moving sequence it would have been fully comprehended.

Cutting rate

The frequency with which you can cut within a series of shots depends initially on successful shot matching, continuity, whether the transitions are motivated, and their purpose. Cuts may be used relatively unobtrusively; or as deliberate interruptions to shock, surprise, emphasize, accentuate. With the latter, you have to judge carefully the borderline between pleasurable shock and distracting annoyance.

Where the picture contains fast action, the cutting rate can be high: whereas in a slow-moving scene, fast cutting would usually be intrusive – unless perhaps the accompanying sound has a rapid tempo.

Although fast cutting is simple enough on the switcher, it may not be so easy for the cameras to get onto new shots between each cut. Unless you are repeat-intercutting the same set of pictures you may quickly run out of shots!

In a live program a fast average cutting rate during continuous action imposes considerable strain on the entire crew, as cameras rapidly readjust positions and compose their next shots. Unless the production treatment is straightforward, camera moves limited, and action reliable, operation standards are liable to deteriorate. A half-hour live telecast may contain some 200 shot changes; but figures tell us little, unless we know details of the camerawork involved.

Videotape recording, like filming, permits any cutting rate we choose. But clearly the briefer the shots to be selected and inserted into the program, the more exacting and time consuming the VT editing will be.

Cutting rhythm

Within a picture sequence we can become aware of certain intrinsic rhythms:

1 Subject movement – rhythm of moving machinery.
2 Composition changes – the dynamic effects of passing backgrounds (a line of trees).
3 Superimposed movement – regularly flashing street sign.

If you take two pictures (each with its own internal rhythms) and intercut them, a comparative effect results.

A *cutting rhythm* can be set up according to the durations of successive shots. Shot duration might, for example, be progressively shortened as tension rises – an increasing cutting rate. Long and short durations might be contrasted to compare leisurely and urgent paces. Similarly, you can use cutting rhythm to emphasize audio rhythm, or vice versa.

9 Lighting

Effective lighting makes a vital contribution to a television production. We quickly recognize bad lighting when we see it, but good lighting is so unobtrusive and 'natural' that we take it for granted. In this chapter, we shall discuss the secrets of successful lighting techniques.

The aims of lighting

Lighting in television and film is about much more than just making things *visible*. It has to satisfy a number of often conflicting objectives:

- *The lighting must enable all the TV cameras to produce pictures of the highest quality.* This means that the light levels (light intensity) must be appropriate for the camera lens aperture (*f*-stop) being used so that the picture can be exposed correctly.
- *The lighting must be consistent.* It must suit all camera positions.
- *The lighting treatment must take into account the mechanics of the production.* It must fit in with the scenery, the camera treatment, the sound boom's positions, etc. Badly positioned lamps can prevent talent from reading the prompter, cause flares in a camera lens, result in boom shadows, spoil a skilfully designed setting, degrade make-up. . .
- *Good lighting creates a three-dimensional illusion in the flat picture.* It imparts an impression of solidity and depth in subjects and surroundings.
- *Lighting should usually produce an attractive visual impact.* It should enhance the appearance of people.
- *Lighting must be appropriate.* It should create the right sort of atmosphere for the occasion. The lighting in realistic settings should look natural, not seem contrived. It can suggest the time of day, or weather conditions.
- *Successful lighting guides the audience's interest.* It directs their attention towards important features.
- *Lighting can create compositional opportunities for the camera.*
- *Lighting should not make us aware of staging defects.* For example, the viewer's attention should not be drawn to wrinkles in a cyclorama, joins in sets, strong reflections, cables, shadows . . . through unsuitable lighting.

Why is lighting necessary?

The technical reasons.

As you know (Chapter 4), the TV/video camera needs a certain amount of light reflected from the scene to be able to produce a good tonal range in the picture, without various distracting defects (such as noise and picture lag).

If there is too little light, the lens aperture has to be opened up to compensate, and the available depth of field is considerably reduced. Too much light, and pictures become overexposed, unless you stop down the lens (depth may now be too great), or use neutral density filters. In the studio, excess light wastes power, causes ventilation problems, and is unpleasant to work in. Light levels need to be related, wherever possible, to the preferred working *f*-stop.

The TV camera can only handle and reproduce relatively limited tonal contrasts. If the lighting is contrasty, details in the lightest and darkest tones will be lost.

On location, the existing lighting may not be suitable. From the camera position, it may prove to be

- Too bright – e.g. strong sunlight causing performers to squint their eyes.
- Too dim – e.g. insufficient for well-exposed shots.
- Too flat – e.g. diffuse light, in which subjects lack form or definition.
- Too contrasty – e.g. lighter tones burned out, and shadows clogged.

Under these conditions we need to augment or replace the natural lighting . . . or tolerate the results. Sometimes the only solution is to alter the camera position.

The artistic reasons

Our impressions of space and form when looking at a picture depend on a number of factors, such as perspective, scale, the way planes overlap, comparative details, relative sizes, and so on. But lighting, too, plays a major part in how we interpret what we see. Even when structure and outline give us leading clues, the play of light and shade strongly influences our judgements of size, shape, distance, surface texture, contours.

Lighting is strongly associated with mood. Through carefully chosen light direction and contrast you can change a scene's entire atmospheric impact. It can impart fun or fantasy, mystery or dramatic tension. Lighting can enhance a setting, and create pictorial beauty, or it can deliberately create a harsh, unattractive, sordid effect. Lighting can transform a rich imposing environment into a garish tasteless display, or reduce it to a boringly dull characterless emptiness.

You can use light selectively, to emphasize certain aspects of the scene while subduing others; avoiding or reducing distracting features. You can exaggerate form; draw attention to texture, or suppress it. You can merge planes, or cause one to stand out prominently from another. Through shadow formations, lighting can suggest structures that do not exist, or hide what is there.

You *can* illuminate the action and the setting simply by spreading enough light around to ensure that the cameras get good pictures. Some people do that! But if you want pictures in which subjects stand out solidly from their backgrounds, which have an attractive appropriate atmosphere, and which are free from distracting shadows and hot spots, it is necessary to apply systematic lighting techniques.

The nature of light

When you use light you can apply it with large 'brush strokes', or with fine delicate attention to detail. You can wash it across the scene, or pick out and emphasize certain features. But to exercise this control you need to appreciate the subtleties of light itself. So we begin by looking at the practical basics of illumination.

1 *Light intensity.* The strength of light we require on the subject and the surroundings will determine how powerful the lamps need to be, relative to the area they have to cover. (In practical terms this will affect the sizes of fittings, the power required, ventilation, etc.)
2 *The color quality* of the light (its *color temperature*). Light and camera performance need to be matched to avoid inaccurate color quality.
3 *The light dispersion.* Some light sources produce *hard light* which casts strong shadows, while others create *soft light* which is diffused and shadowless. This range of fittings offers us the choice of bold brush strokes or subtly graded half-tones.
4 *Light direction.* The direction of light affects the way light and shade falls on a subject. It determines which features are highlighted, and which fall into shadow.

Light intensity

The amount of light needed to illuminate a setting and the action within it is partly a technical decision, and partly an artistic one. You might, for example, use one strong keylight to cover both the action and the background, or a series of restricted lamps, each lighting a carefully chosen area.

Camera systems are usually quoted as having a particular sensitivity – requiring a certain light level (intensity) for a given

Table 9.1 Methods of light measurement

Incident light method	*Reflected light method*	*Surface brightness method*
Meter positioned beside the subject, pointing at light sources.	*Meter* positioned beside the camera, pointing at the subject.	*Meter* positioned beside the camera, pointing at the subject.
Measures light intensity falling upon subject from each lamp direction in turn.	*Measures* average amount of light reflected from scene and received at camera lens.	*Measures* brightness of surface at which the instrument is directed.
Checks: Whether the *relative incident light intensities and balance* are suitable for the camera's sensitivity and lens aperture. Measure the base light, key light, fill light and back light in turn, and compare relative intensities.	*Checks*: Standing at different camera positions, measuring whether the *average intensity of light reflected from the scene* is suitable for the camera's sensitivity and lens aperture. *Also*: Standing closer within the scene, measuring lightest and darkest tonal areas, and using a midway reading to guide exposure/contrast.	*Checks*: Whether the *brightnesses of typical surfaces* (skin tones, 'standard white' and black) are satisfactory – i.e. have suitable amount of light falling on them. *Also*: You can measure the *tonal contrasts* within the scene, to avoid over-contrasty lighting, over-lit areas, highlights, underlit shadows.
Ease of operation: method is simple and consistent. Does not require experienced interpolation. Widely used in motion-picture lighting.	*Ease of operation*: readings vary with meter angling and experience is needed to make allowance for subject tones and contrast. Large dark areas cause readings to be falsely low, encouraging overexposure of highlights. Large light areas give high readings, which may cause underexposed shadows.	*Ease of operation*: method requires some experience in judging the importance of individual surfaces' brightness relative to overall exposure.
Advantages: when a show is to be repeated original levels can be duplicated readily. Balance between various light directions readily checked.	*Advantages*: method provides a quick rough check of average light levels. Can facilitate evenness of lighting.	*Advantages:* method is capable of assessing surface brightness and contrast very accurately.
Disadvantages: arbitrary allowance has to be made for subject tones. The amount of light required depends upon the subject – which this method cannot assess. Method only directly useful for 'average' subject tones. Does not take into account tonal values, proportion of tones, and tonal contrast.	*Disadvantages*: meter readings are only of an 'average' nature: which varies considerably with tonal values and proportions. Method does not indicate contrast range of subject or lighting. Meter's 'angle-of-view' is seldom identical with the camera-lens's. Where a single surface (e.g. a face), is to be equally exposed in a variety of settings, measured exposure *should be* constant; but will vary as adjacent tones change.	*Disadvantages*: several separate readings are necessary to check evenness of lighting and contrast. Method measures scenic tones, but does not distinguish their relative importance: and hence the desired exposure. Tonal contrast measurements may not signify: if the tones measured do not appear together in picture; if their proportions are small and unimportant; if they *may* be acceptably 'crushed out' without injuring pictorial quality.

Note: Where the meter is held close to subject, measuring individual surface brightness, method becomes as for surface brightness method.

f-stop. But this is only a general guide. Much depends on the nature of the surroundings. To reveal detail in the walls of a dark-paneled room will require much more light than would be needed with light-toned walls.

Lighting intensities can be influenced by the surface finish; whether walls are smooth or rough textured; whether they are plain or strongly contoured. The contrast range of the set dressings used can also affect the amount of light needed to illuminate a situation effectively.

Paradoxically, a spacious light-toned setting may require less intense lighting than much more confined dark-toned surroundings. Lighting quality cannot be judged in kilowatts!

Of course, ultimately light intensity from various directions must be adjusted to suit the atmospheric effect and mood you are aiming for (*lighting balance*).

We have one great advantage when using the TV/video camera. Unlike the *film maker*, who has to await processing, we can immediately see the result of our lighting treatment. We can assess its artistic effect, and judge its technical suitability.

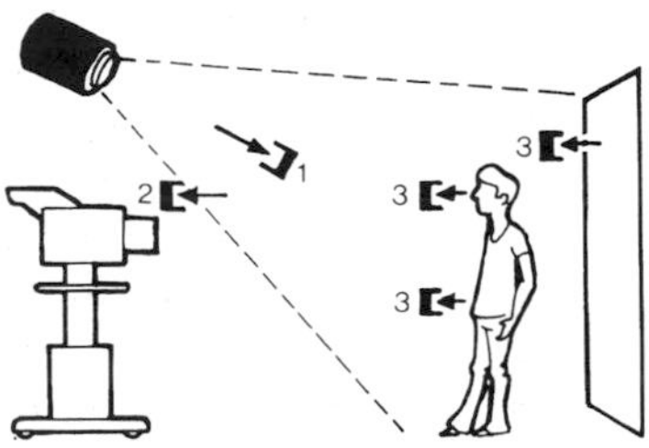

When first lighting, or when lighting under unfamiliar conditions (e.g. on location), it is advisable to make careful measurements of light levels. With experience, one becomes accustomed to lamp performance at various distances, and only occasionally needs to make light checks. Any slight variations are readily compensated by dimmer or lens aperture adjustments.

Fig. 9.1 Light measurement
Light measurements avoid gross over- or underexposure. Basic methods:

1 Incident light falling on subject.
2 Average light reflected from scene at camera.
3 Measuring surface brightnesses (tonal values and contrast).

- *Incident light* measurement helps to assess the relative intensities of lighting from various directions.
- *Reflected light* measurements provide a general indication of the amount of reflected light reaching the camera.
- *Surface brightness* checks help to assess the contrast range within the scene (Table 9.1).

Color quality of light

Eye and brain are astonishingly adaptable. We appear to see effects that are not really there (as in optical illusions), and we overlook effects that can clearly be measured by suitable instruments. An everyday example of the latter is the way we accept a very wide range of quite different light qualities as representing 'white' light.

If we analyze 'white' light we find that it is really a mixture of a range of colors. The spectrum is red, orange, yellow, green, blue, indigo, violet light in similar proportions. In many forms of illumination some parts of the spectrum are much more prominent than others, and the result is far from true white. For example, light from candles or dimmed tungsten lamps actually has a warm yellowish-red color quality; or, as we say, a *low color temperature*. Daylight can vary considerably, from cold bluish north sky light (a *high color temperature*) to the low color quality of light around sunset. Yet our brains compensate, and accept all these luminants as 'white light'. (*See Digests–Color temperature.*)

Television and film cameras are not fooled in this way. They do not self-compensate. If the illumination has bluish or yellowish characteristics the pictures would show this as a pronounced color cast. To avoid such coloration, we have two solutions:

- *Adjust the* **camera** to *compensate for variations in the color temperature of the prevailing light.* Either by using a suitable color-correction filter (in the filter wheel) and/or altering the relative gains of the camera's RGB channels – the *color balance.* On many cameras we electronically readjust the system's color balance by pressing the camera's WHITE BALANCE button while shooting a white surface.
- *Adjust the color temperature of the* **light** to *suit the camera's color balance.* If you are using tungsten lamps when shooting in daylight (e.g. to illuminate shadows) you can place compensatory blue filter material or special dichroic filters over them, to raise their effective color temperature (e.g. from 3200 K to 4500–7500 K).

Conversely, if daylight is illuminating a room in which you are using quartz or tungsten lamps a large sheet of filter medium (amber-orange) can be stretched over the window to reduce the effective color temperature of the daylight to match the interior lighting.

Cameras are usually set up to suit the prevailing light quality; e.g. 2950 K. But this varies between different types of luminant. Tungsten-halogen lamps ('quartz lights') burn at 3200 K, while tungsten lamps can have a noticeably lower color temperature of e.g. 3000 K. High-powered HMI lamps produce light of 5600 K, which blends well with daylight but does not mix with tungsten sources.

As tungsten and quartz lamps are dimmed their color temperature falls – the light lacks blue, and develops a 'warmer' yellowish-red quality.

Light dispersion

Soft light

Soft light is the scattered diffused shadowless illumination that in nature comes from a cloudy overcast sky, and is reflected from rough surfaces of all kinds (walls, sand, snow). You can create soft light artificially, by using:

- Large-area light fittings (e.g. multi-lamp banks)
- Heavy diffusion in front of light sources
- Internal reflection within large light fittings
- Or by bouncing light from large white surfaces (e.g. matte reflector boards, or a white ceiling).

Only large areas produce really diffuse light quality. Many so-called soft light sources cast discernible shadows. We use *soft* light when we want:

- To illuminate shadows without creating additional shadows.
- To avoid emphasizing modeling and texture (e.g. for flattering portraiture).
- To provide delicate tonal gradations. (They may be too subtle to register on many TV screens.)

However, *soft light* does have practical disadvantages:

- Really diffused light can be difficult to control, for it spreads around and is not easy to restrict.
- Badly used, soft light can produce flat unmodeled illumination. Texture and form can be difficult to see in the picture. If used as an overall *baselight* it can reduce the impression of depth, overlight the walls of settings, destroy atmosphere, and produce flat, uninteresting pictures.
- The intensity of soft light falls off rapidly with distance, and very approximately follows an 'inverse square law'.*

Hard light

Hard light is the directional illumination that produces sharp shadows, and in nature comes from direct, unobscured sunlight. This light comes from any concentrated small-area source. (Although the sun is large, it behaves as a 'point source', because it is so far away.) Compact light sources such as candles, small spotlights, open-bulb fittings, gas-discharge lamps (e.g. HMI), and arc lamps all produce well-defined shadows. We use *hard light* when we want:

- To create bold well-defined modeling; a sharp clear-cut vigorous effect.
- To cast pronounced shadows (e.g. tree-branch shadows).
- To localize light to specific areas.
- To produce coarse shading; an abrupt brightness fall-off.
- To project light over some distance, at a reasonably constant intensity. (The light rays from focused spotlights are roughly parallel and do not 'fall off' quickly with distance.)

However, *hard light* does have practical disadvantages:

- The shadows from hard light may prove to be unattractive, inappropriate, distracting.
- Hard light can overemphasize texture and surface modeling.
- High contrast can produce crude, harsh, unsubtle tones.
- Multiple shadows arise when the subject is lit by more than one hard light source.

* The *inverse square law* strictly applies only to point sources. The light intensity at 1 m falls to 0.25 (1/4) at 2 m, 0.06 (1/16) at 4 m, 0.016 (1/64) at 8 m.

Clearly, for effective lighting treatment you need a suitable blend of *hard* directional light and *soft* diffused light. Usually the hard light reveals the subject's contours and textures, while the soft light reduces undue contrast or harshness, and makes shadow detail visible. You may deliberately emphasize contour and texture; or minimize them, depending on the blend and direction of the illumination.

The direction of the light (Figure 9.2)

The effects of lighting will vary as you alter the angle at which it strikes the subject. Raising or lowering a lamp, or moving it round

Table 9.2 Light direction

Direct-frontal (from camera position)	Direct frontal lighting along the *lens axis* reduces texture and modeling to minimum. Valuable for disguising wrinkles or avoiding confusing shadows.
Edge lighting (side lighting)	Light skimming along a surface (from above, side, or beneath) emphasizes texture and surface contours. Ideal for revealing shallow relief such as in coins, embossing, wood grain, fabric, and stonework. Produces poor portraiture on full-face shots (ugly facial contouring).
Back lighting	Light directly behind the subject and along the camera lens axis is largely ineffectual unless the subject is translucent or has edge-detail (fur, hair, feathers). Slightly offset back light illuminates the subject's outline, modeling its borders and helping to distinguish it tonally from its background.

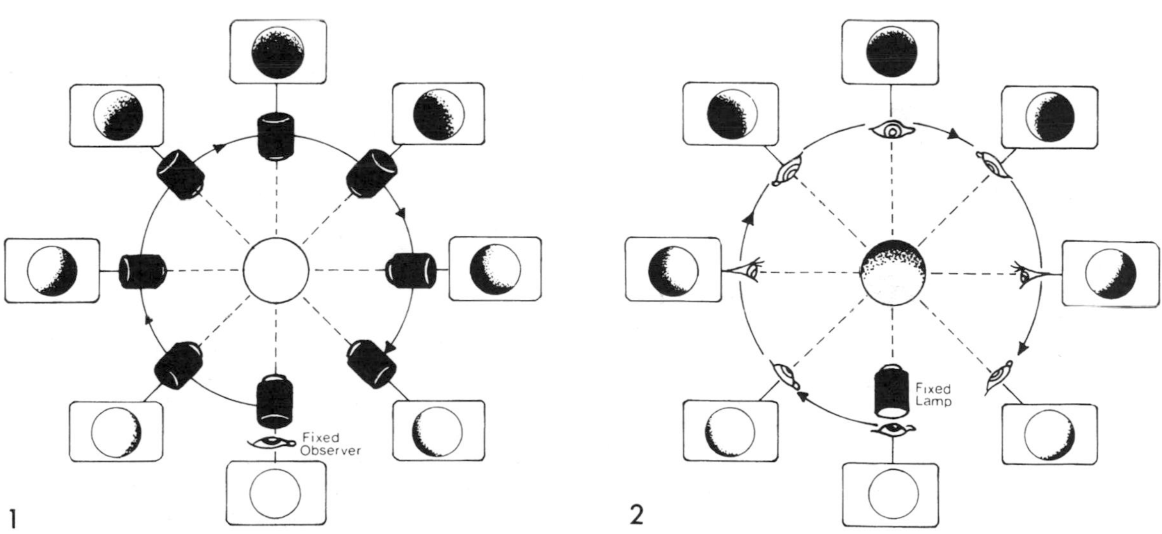

Fig. 9.2 Light direction
1 From a fixed viewpoint, the effect of the lighting changes as *the source* moves round the subject (shading develops on the side opposite the illumination).
2 Using a fixed lamp, appearance alters as *our viewpoint* changes.

the subject, will change which parts are lit, which are thrown into shadow. It will affect how contours and texture are reproduced. Surface markings and decoration become more or less obvious. If you reposition the light, or alter the camera's viewpoint, the appearance of various features of the subject can change.

The technique of lighting

Let us turn now from the way light behaves, and the general effects it can have, to basic lighting techniques. At this stage, the actual *types* of equipment you use to provide the 'hard' light and the 'soft' light are unimportant. Each will have its particular advantages and disadvantages.

Lighting a flat surface

You might think that you couldn't go wrong when simply lighting a flat surface. But there can be problems.

There are situations when you want patchy, uneven lighting to create a more interesting, dramatic effect. But at others, the surface must be lit evenly overall. Any shading or patchiness would be quite unacceptable – e.g. on a title card, graphic, photo blow-up, or skycloth.

The *edge lighting* that is great when we want to emphasize texture in a brick wall would show up wrinkles, bumps, and creases in the backdrop or cyc! The frontal lighting that can produce a flatly lit

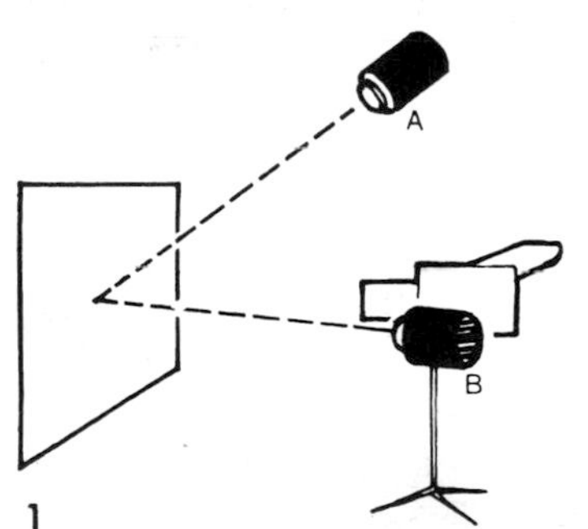

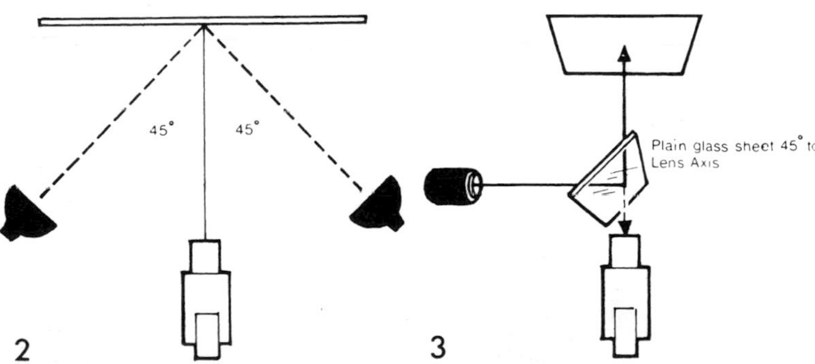

Fig. 9.3 Lighting a flat surface

1 Light from a frontal position near the camera (B), may reflect to produce hotspots, flares. Offset at (A) will overcome reflections, but may cause uneven illumination.

2 For critical work, dual lighting from either side (30–45° offset) is preferable. Soft light sources reduce spurious surface texture or irregularities (blisters, wrinkles).

3 Shadowless lighting (along the lens axis) is necessary for multi-layer graphics (Pepper's ghost).

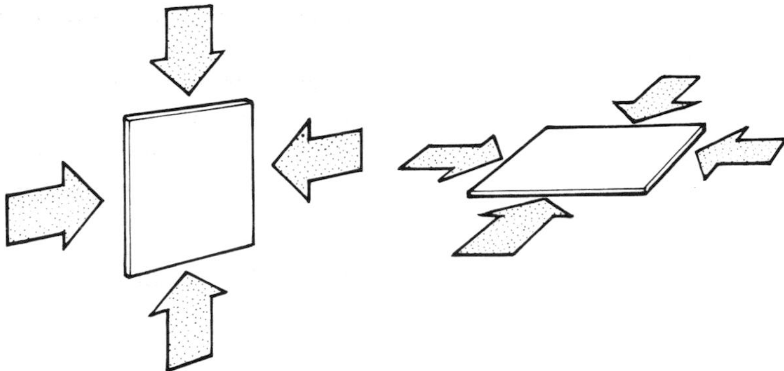

Fig. 9.4 Edge-lighting
Whatever the position of a surface, if light skims along it at an acute angle, any texture or unevenness will be emphasized.

cyclorama can cause hot spots of reflected light on an oil painting, making it difficult to see properly.

Hard light can exaggerate texture and surface undulations. And it can be difficult to blend adjacent spotlight beams together, without light fall-off or patchiness. Soft light provides more even lighting, but it shades off with distance, and can spill around uncontrollably. The greater the angle at which the light falls on the flat surface, the more uneven its illumination.

Lighting an object

Most solid subjects require three basic light-source directions – referred to as *three-point lighting*. The exact angles depend on the subject and the aspects you want to emphasize.

■ *Key light* This is a predominant hard light, normally in a cross-frontal position – for example, up to around 45° vertical, 45°

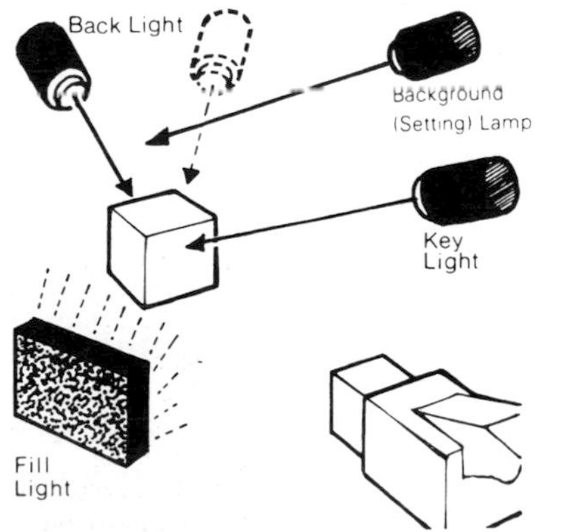

Fig. 9.5 Lighting an object
Effective lighting treatment usually involves four basic lighting functions:

Key light. Usually one lamp (spotlight) in a cross-frontal position.
Fill light. Usually a soft light source illuminating shadows and reducing lighting contrast. But may not be required, or alternatively a reflected hard light is used (rarely a direct spotlight).
Back light. Usually a spotlight (for two) behind the subject pointing towards the camera. (Occasionally soft light is used.)
Background (setting) light. Backgrounds are preferably lit by specific lighting, but they may be illuminated by the key or fill-light spill.

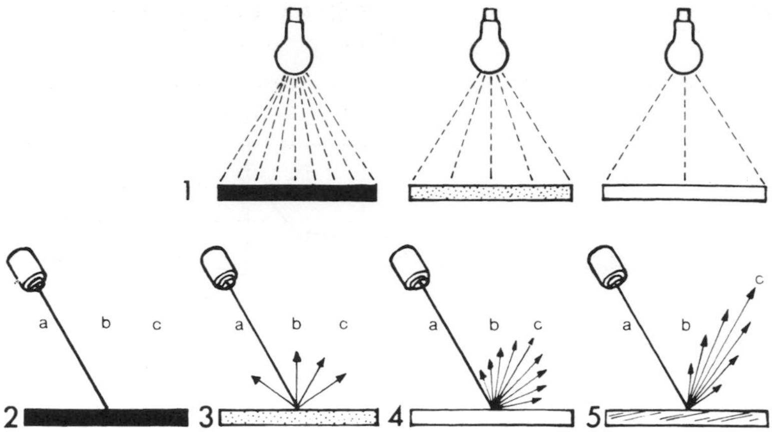

Fig. 9.6 Surface brightness
1 Apparent surface brightness depends on both surface tone and incident light intensity. Each of these examples would appear equally bright. The surface texture and finish affect how brightness changes with light direction and the viewing angle.
2 Complete absorption (e.g. black velvet). Little or no reflection. Surface appears dark from all viewpoints.
3 Diffuse reflection (rough irregular surface). Light scatters in all directions, fairly bright from all viewpoints.
4 Spread reflection (glossy surface). Fairly dark at a; fairly bright at b; bright at c.
5 Specular reflection (shiny surface). Fairly dark at a, b. Very bright at c.

horizontal from the lens axis. This lamp creates the principal shadows; reveals form, surface formation, and texture; and largely determines the exposure. Only one key light should normally be used for a subject.

■ *Fill light (fill-in, filler)* This soft shadowless illumination reduces tonal contrast between highlights and shadows, revealing shadow detail. It should not modify the exposure nor create additional shadows or modeling. The fill light is usually located 0–30° from the lens axis and on the opposite side from the key light.

■ *Back light* This is a hard rimming light behind the subject, separating it from the background. It helps reveal edge contours, transparency, and tracery. A single lamp or two spaced back lights may be used.

There is nothing mandatory about these arrangements. The key light is positioned to suit the object's particular features. If a single *side key* is sufficient, neither back light nor fill light may be needed. If the object is transparent or translucent you may only back light it, or even rest it on an illuminated panel for the best effect (e.g. engraved glass).

Lighting people

Although facial details vary between individuals, the basic head formation remains similar enough, so that the unattractive effects produced by poor lighting are much the same for most people.

Table 9.3 Lighting terms

Base light or foundation light	Diffuse light flooding the entire setting uniformly – used to prevent underexposure of shadows or excessive contrast.
Rim light or rimming	Illumination of subject edges by back light.
Modeling light or accent light	Loose term for any hard light revealing texture and form.
Cross light, counter key or balance light	An occasional second frontal key – positioned 30–60° horizontally from lens axis. Not used for portraiture.
Kicker, cross-back, or 3/4 back light	Back light some 30° off lens axis.
Effects light	Light producing specific highlight areas on backgrounds – e.g. around a light fitting.
Bounce light	Diffuse illumination obtained by reflection from a strongly lit surface such as a ceiling or a *reflector* board.
Set light or background light	Light illuminating the background alone.
Eye light or catch light	Eye reflection (preferably one only) of a light source, giving lively expression. Sometimes from a low-powered camera light.
Camera light, basher, headlamp. Camera fill light, or spot bar	Small light source mounted on camera to reduce contrast for closer shots, improve/correct modeling, and for localized illumination (e.g. title card).
Hair light	Lamp localized to reveal hair detail.
Clothes light	Hard light revealing texture and form in clothing.
Top light	Vertical overhead lighting (edge lighting from above). Undesirable for portraiture.
Underlighting	Lamp below lens axis used to illuminate, relieve, or disguise downward shadows. Also used to create uncanny effects.
Side light	Light located at right-angles to the lens axis. Reveals subject's contours. Creates ugly portraiture for full-face shots, but effective for profiles.
Contrast control light	Soft fill light from camera position illuminating shadows and reducing lighting contrast.
Edge light	Light skimming along a surface, revealing its texture and contours.

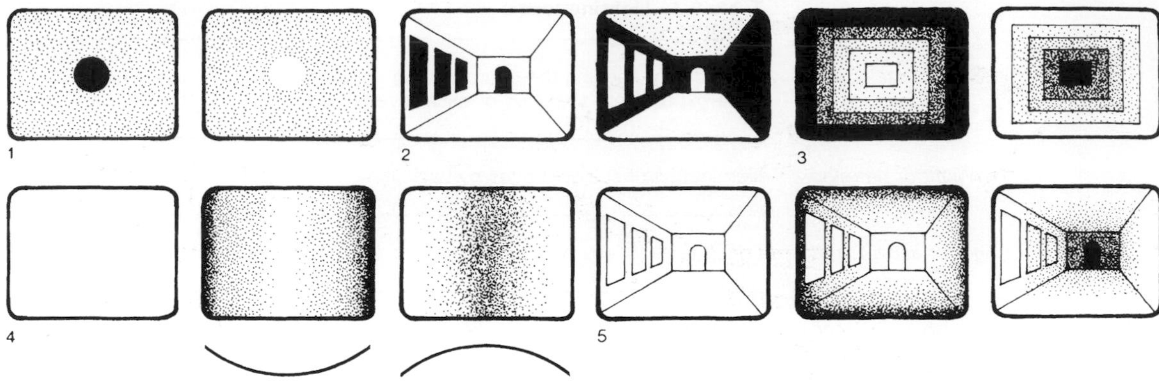

Fig. 9.7 The effects of surface tones

1 A subject's tones affect its prominence (relative to background and other adjacent tones), its apparent size, and its apparent distance. Lighter tones generally appear more prominent, larger, and more distant than darker ones.
2 While our eye stops at the black openings, the white ones suggest space beyond.
3 Progressively lighter planes recede. Progressively darker ones advance.
4 Tonal gradation (shading) affects our impression of form. If a flat plain area is shaded, it appears to have shape.
5 Pictorial perspective conveys an impression of space, which is enhanced by appropriate tonal change – and largely destroyed by unsuitable treatment.

General maxims

There are a number of generally accepted principles when lighting people:

1 Place the key light within about 10–30° of a person's nose direction.
2 Have them look *toward* rather than away from the key light, if re-angling their position.

Fig. 9.8 Pitfalls in portrait lighting
Various unattractive effects can arise from unsuitable portrait lighting.

1 *Steep frontal key light.* Black eyes, harsh modeling, long nose shadow.
2 *Two frontal keys.* Twin nose-shadows and shoulder shadows (latter can also arise from two backlights).
3 *Steep backlight.* Hot head-top: bright nose-tip, and eartips: long bib-shadow on chest.
4 *Oblique frontal key.* Talking profile seen on shoulder. Bisected face.
5 *Side key.* In full face bisects the face. Half of it crudely edge-lit, half unlit.
6 *Dual side-keys.* Create central badger shadow effect, and coarse modeling.

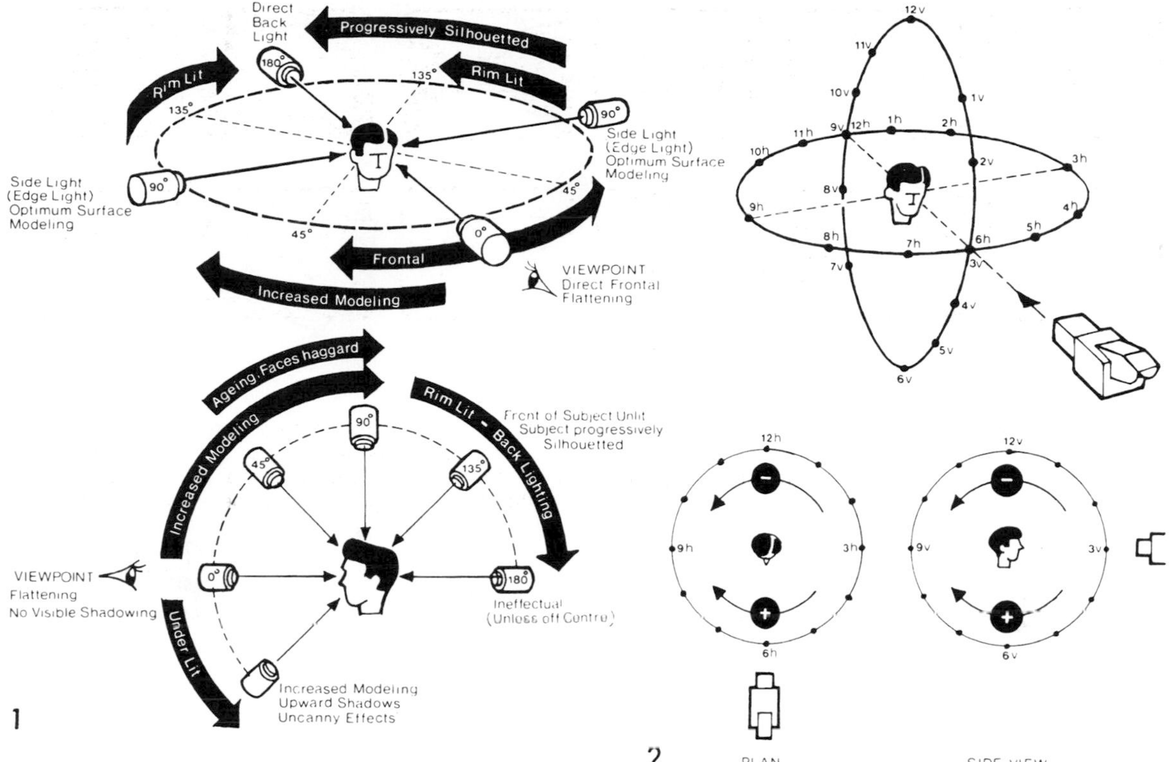

Fig. 9.9 Lighting angles
1 The lighting angle chosen depends on the particular features you want to emphasize or suppress.
2 Using two imaginary clock faces, lamps' positions are easily designated. The camera is always shown as at 3 o'clock V (3V), 6 o'clock H (6H). (Hours are 30° steps, minutes are 6° each.) Intermediate positions between hours are shown by + (clockwise) or – (anticlockwise) signs.

3 Avoid *steep* lighting (above 40–45°) or oblique angles.
4 Avoid a very wide horizontal or vertical angle between the fill light and the key light.
5 Do not have more than one key light for each viewpoint.
6 Use properly placed soft light to fill shadows.
7 Avoid sidelight on full-face shots.
8 For profiles it is generally best to place the key light on the far side of the face (upstage). This gives improved solidity and avoids casting shadows of the sound boom.

Lighting groups of people

Check the direction in which each person is looking, and arrange their key/back/fill lights to fit (Figure 9.10). One appropriate lamp may suit a whole group, but problems can arise if there are big differences in the relative tones of their costumes, skin, and hair. Light intensity may be too strong for one; too weak for another.

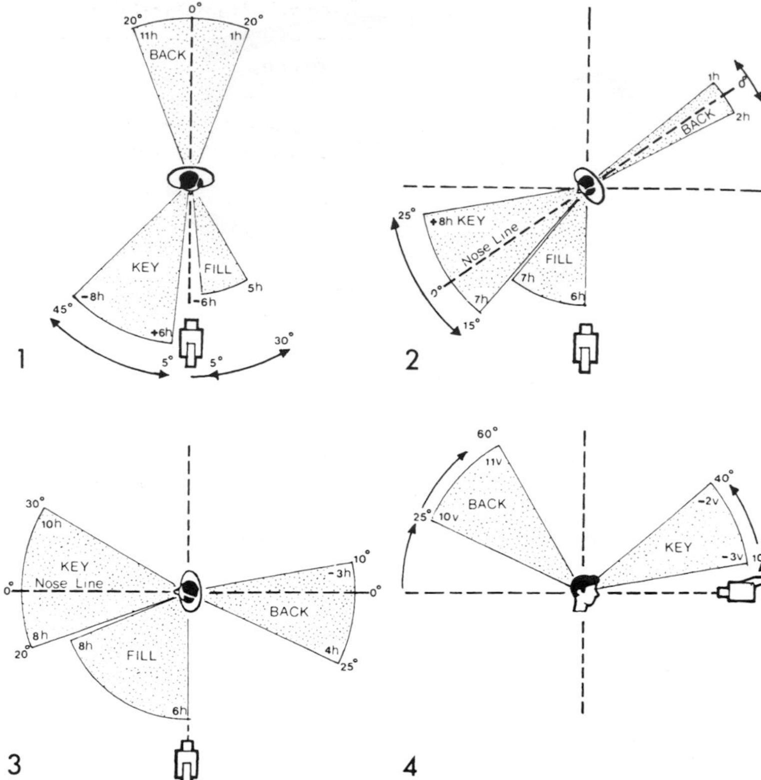

Fig. 9.10 Lighting a single person The plans and elevations show typical range of lighting angles within which good portraiture is achieved.

1 Full face.
2 Offset head (3/4 front, 45° turn).
3 Profile.
4 Vertical angles for each are shown.

Then localized reduction with diffusers or shading off light with a barndoor or flag may be the solution.

Where subjects are close, or you have few lamps, one light may have to serve two different purposes – e.g. as a key for one and a back light for someone else (Figure 9.11).

Where there are groups of people (audience, orchestra) you can either light them as a whole or in subdivided sections, still using three-point lighting principles and keeping overlaps to a minimum.

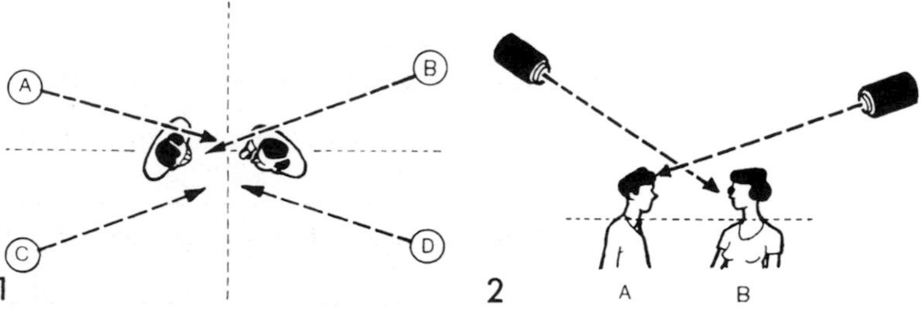

Fig. 9.11 Lighting two people
1 Several arrangements are effective (each has particular advantages) with keys at A and B, C and D, A and D, or C and B.
2 The lamps here may be shared, as Key A/back B, and Key B/back A. Or used specifically as keys, with extra backlights.

Table 9.4 Lighting people

	Front light	*Back light*
Lamp's vertical angle too steep	Harsh modeling which gives a haggard and ageing appearance. Gives black eyes, black neck, and long vertical nose shadow. *Emphasizes*: forehead size, baldness, and deep eyes. Figure appears busty. Casts hair shadows onto forehead. Hat brims and spectacles produce large shadows.	Nose becomes lit while face in shadow ('white nose'). Effect most marked when head tilted back. 'Hot top' to forehead and shoulders.
Lamp's vertical angle too shallow	Picture flat and subject lacks modeling. Produces shadows on background.	Lens flares or lamp actually in shot.
Underlighting	Inverted facial modeling. Shadows of movement beneath head level (e.g. of hands) appear on faces. Shadows may be cast up over background. 'Mysterious' atmosphere when underlighting used alone. Useful to soften harsh modeling from steep lighting. Reduces age lines in face and neck.	Largely ineffectual but can be used for back lighting women's hair. Shadows from ears and shoulders cast on face.
Light too far off camera axis	In full face, long nose shadow across opposite cheek. An asymmetric face can be further unbalanced if lit on wider side. One ear lighter than the other.	Ear and hair shadows are cast on cheek. One side of nose is 'hot'. Eye on same side as back light appears black – being left in shadow while temple is lit.

Note: All lamp positions are relative to camera viewpoint.

Table 9.5 Lighting balance

	Too bright	*Too dim*
Frontal light	Back light less effective. Skin tones are high and facial modeling lost. Lightest tones tend to be overexposed. Gives a harsh pictorial effect.	Back light predominates and often becomes excessive. Darker tones are underexposed. Can lead to muddy, lifeless pictorial effect.
Back light	Excessive rim light. Hot shoulder and top of heads. Exposing for areas lit by excess back light causes frontal light to appear inadequate.	Two-dimensional picture which lacks solidity. Subject and background tend to merge. Picture appears undynamic.
Filler	Modeling from key light reduced and flattened.	Produces excessive contrast and subject too harshly modeled.

Lighting areas

It is best to avoid flooding areas with light; e.g. spreading high-intensity soft *base* or *foundation light* and superimposing spotlights for modeling and intensity variations; unless you are seeking a really high-key effect.

Except for high-key pictures, the visual appeal of intense soft light is limited – although it does make key light positioning less critical, as ugly modeling is strongly diluted (*lit out*). Such treatments flatten modeling and produce overlit backgrounds.

Dynamic lighting requires appropriately positioned spotlights, relieved by suitably placed and carefully controlled fill light. (The amount of fill light due to random reflections from floor and scenery is usually minimal.)

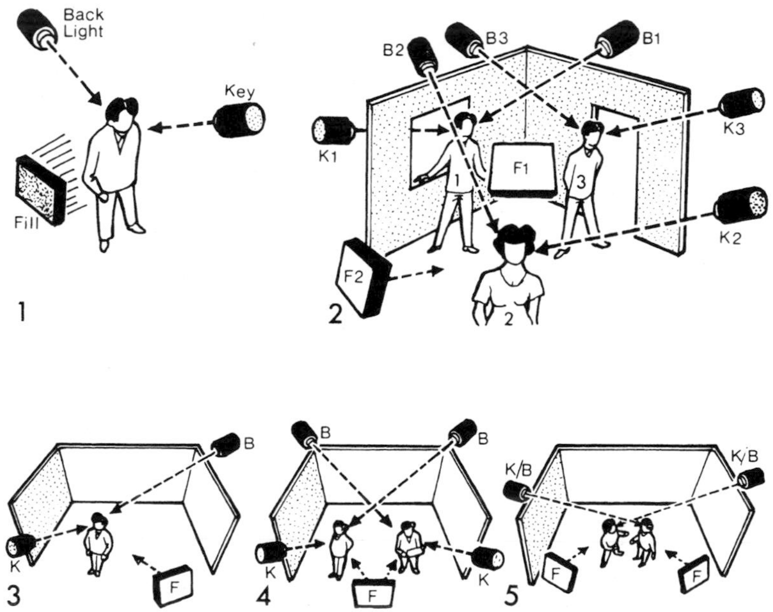

Fig. 9.12 Lighting areas
Where action is localized, the three-point lighting technique (1) can be applied at specific positions throughout the setting (2).
One lamp may be used for several positions. Overall three-point treatment can be used for general action (3) or the area can be sectionalized (4).

5 For cross-shooting cameras, lamps over the set's side-walls can be used as key/backlights, with suitable positioned soft-light.

The most attractive picture quality usually comes from analyzing the performance area into a series of *locating points* (by the table, at the door, looking out the window) and tailoring the three-point lighting at each to suit the action. One lighting arrangement will often suit other shots or action in that area (perhaps with slight lighting rebalance).

Given sufficient lighting facilities (enough lamps, dimmers, etc.) and adequate time to readjust lamps, you could light to suit each individual shot. But such elaboration is not normally feasible.

Where action is more general or widespread you must cover the area in a systematic pattern of lamps.

Light fittings

Light sources (luminants)

Several kinds of luminant are used in TV and film lighting: regular tungsten lighting, quartz lights (tungsten-halogen), gas-discharge lamps (with metal halide sources), regular and high-frequency fluorescent tubes. (*Carbon arcs* were used in film and television lighting, but had various limitations. So they have now been superseded by gas-discharge lamps.)

■ *Regular tungsten lamps* Confusingly also called 'incandescent' (which *all* TV luminants inherently are!) or 'tungsten' (used in quartz lamps too!). Still extensively used, the regular tungsten filament lamp is relatively cheap, has a reasonably long life, exists in a wide range of intensities (power ratings), is generally reliable, and can be mounted in many types of fittings.

Against this, tungsten lamps waste much electrical energy as heat. Their relatively large filaments prevent them being true point sources and providing crisp, clear-cut shadows. Their color temperature is normally relatively low and decreases as they get older. The light output also decreases due to the bulb (globe) envelope blackening.
Typical color temperatures 3000–3200 K.

■ *Overrun lamps* These tungsten lamps are deliberately designed for a supply voltage that slightly exceeds the filament's normal rating. By this means, you achieve a much greater light output and a higher color temperature – but at the expense of a considerably shortened life (e.g. *Photoflood*).

Such lamps can be used in *practical fittings* (wall brackets, table lamps) on sets, or location interiors.

Portable lightweight systems make use of overrun lamps in traditional tungsten or quartz form. For example, a *Colortran* unit using only 3 kW of power can provide the light output of a regular 10 kW tungsten rig. So, too, *Sun-guns* run from belt-batteries can offer intense hand-held illumination on location.
Typical color temperatures 3400–3500 K.

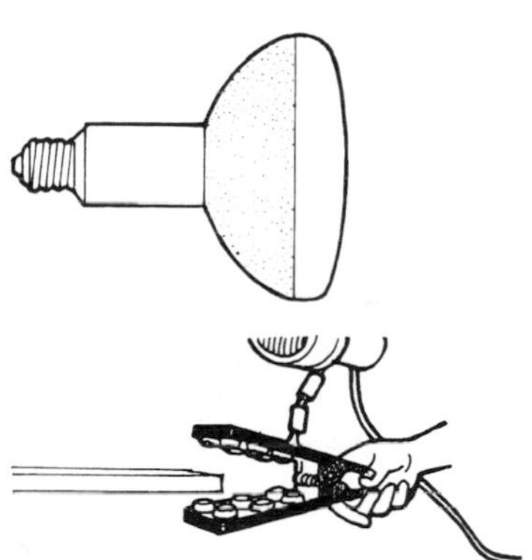

Fig. 9.13 Internal reflector lamp (sealed beam)
Available in regular tungsten and quartz (tungsten-halogen) forms. Used individually in clamps or grouped (Fig. 9.14 part 1, section 3). The glass front may be clear, ribbed or frosted, to give a wide, medium or spot beam, *hard* or 'softened' quality. A color compensating filter (integrated, or attached) matches the luminant to daylight. Widely used *PAR lights* incorporate a parabolic aluminized reflector (650–1000 W, 3200 K).

■ *Tungsten-halogen* (*quartz lamps*, *halogen lamps*, *quartz iodine*) Here the tungsten filament is enclosed within a quartz or silica envelope filled with a halogen gas. This restricts the normal filament evaporation and bulb blackening, so providing a longer lamp life and/or a higher, more constant light output of increased color temperature (e.g. 3200 K) that is ideal for color television.

The bulb must not be handled since body acid attacks the surface, and the lamp becomes brittle and extremely hot in use. Tubular strip and compact designs are available, making lighter and much smaller fittings possible. Twin-filament lamps are

produced which provide three intensities of similar color temperature by switching.
Typical color temperatures 3200 K.

■ *Gas discharge lamps* These lamps are compact, extremely efficient sources, using a mercury arc ignited within argon gas. Special 'rare-earth additives' result in near-daylight illumination (5600–6000 K). Luminants of this type (e.g. HMI lamps) are increasingly used for effects/pattern projectors, follow spotlights, high-intensity interior and exterior lighting.

Discharge lamps necessarily require auxiliary circuitry (ignitors and ballast units), and there is usually a 1.5–3-minute build-up time from switch-on (striking) to full light. Dimming methods are restricted and a lamp cannot usually be restruck quickly after switch-off; a disadvantage for 'shoot-and-run' types of production (documentaries, ENG).

Film shot with an HMI light source may exhibit flicker problems (visible beat, dark-frame) unless special equipment is used.

The highly efficient HMI lamp is particularly convenient for use on location to fill shadows in exteriors and to light within large daylit interiors, for its color temperature blends well with daylight. It provides some three to five times as much light as a quartz light of equivalent power, while producing less heat. A single 2.5 kW HMI lamp can give as much light as *two* color-corrected 10 kW tungsten lamps; while a 6 kW HMI unit has a similar output to a 225 A carbon arc but uses only half the power. Typical power ratings range from 200 W (with a light output similar to a 1 kW quartz light) through to 1200 W (equivalent to 6 kW quartz light), and can be run from normal 120-V 60-cycle household supplies (mains). The power ratings of gas discharge lamps range from as low as 200 W up to some 6 kW. For large-scale exteriors, lamps up to 18 kW are available, with 90 kW multi-unit giants for more extreme situations! Most HMI sources are fitted with a Fresnel lens, which in some cases may be changed to alter the beam pattern. Although the lighting fitting itself is remarkably compact, an associated ballast unit or ignitor (starter) is also necessary.

■ *Fluorescent sources* *The traditional tubular fluorescent lamp* – This consists of a sealed gas-filled glass tube with a phosphor-coated inner surface. When switched on, the mercury vapor within the tube ionizes, causing the phosphor coating to glow brightly (fluoresce); the color depending on the particular materials used.

The fluorescent lamp has many practical advantages. Its initial cost is low. It is 3–4 times more efficient than a tungsten source (more light per watt), so power consumption is correspondingly lower for the same light intensity. There is little radiant heat in the light beam. (Half of the power used by tungsten light sources may be wasted as heat!) Because fluorescent lamps provide a broad light source, the illumination is relatively soft and easier on the eyes than intense spotlights. Fluorescent tubes have a relatively long life.

So why aren't they widely used in the television studio? Although units have been used to some extent for base light or cyclorama lighting, and in locations illuminated solely by fluorescent sources (e.g. supermarkets), they have major limitations. The light fittings are bulky and rather fragile. Where television cameras require quite high light intensities (levels), the output from fluorescent tubes is inadequate. The light spreads around, and is difficult to localize. Its color quality is very variable (e.g. Ra 60), and does not match other luminants. (A *color rendering index* of around CRI 82 is probably optimum.) The traditional fluorescent lamp has other practical disadvantages, including an inherent flicker, and a fall-off in light output after 150–200 hours' use,

Fluorescent lamp developments – Later changes in design have transformed the fluorescent lamp while retaining its high efficiency and long life. Tri-phosphor tubes in conjunction with high-frequency ballasts produce light sources with a more suitable color quality, and free from flicker (they now operate at e.g. 28–39 kHz).

Available in various forms and sizes with very good color quality, (around Ra 90–95), this type of lighting unit has proved a useful addition in many studios and on location, with more sensitive color cameras (e.g. *f*/2.8 at 500–600 lux). The main shortcoming of this type of source lies in the light spread, for even with shutters and grilles (*egg-crates, louvers*) it is not easy to direct or confine light and avoid spill or overlit backgrounds.

Types of light fitting (luminaires)

Four basic forms of light fitting are used in TV:

1 Soft lights/floodlights.
2 Spotlights/Fresnel spots.
3 Effects projectors/pattern projectors.
4 Follow spots.

■ *Soft light fittings* These include *scoops, broads, floodlight, banks, internally reflected units, striplights, cyclorama lights.* They are used mainly for fill light and for broad lighting of backgrounds. They can be hung, supported on floor stands, or rested on the ground, according to the design.

Adjustment of soft light sources is limited. Many can be turned or titled, and any louvers, flaps, egg-crate shields, barndoors can be used to restrict the coverage to some extent. Multi-lamp fittings can be switched to adjust the light output. Otherwise diffusers or dimmers are used to control their light intensity.

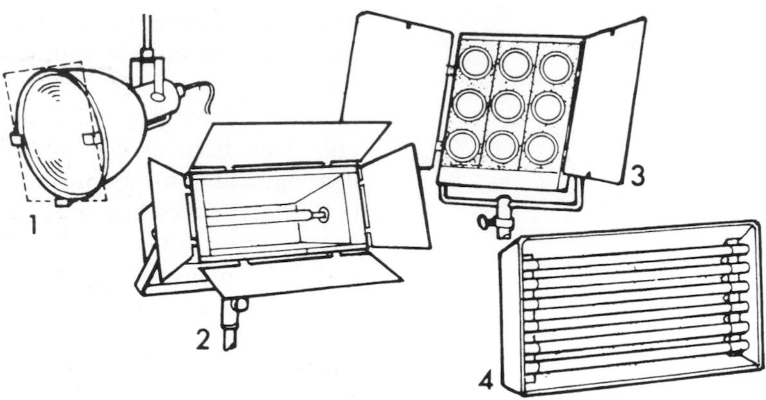

Fig. 9.14 part 1 Soft-light sources – open-lamp types

1 *Scoop* (1–1½ kW) has spun aluminium bowl of diameter 0.3–0.46 m (1–1½ ft). Emergent light is not particularly soft (or controllable) where an open lamp is used (tungsten or quartz). Spun-glass scrim fits into supports. aiding diffusion. The lamp is obtainable in fixed-focus and adjustable (ring-focus) forms: the latter has adjustable light spread. (Versions with lamp-shields are available to prevent direct light emergence.)

2 *Small broad* (½–1 kW) is a tubular quartz light. Flaps or barndoors restrict the light spread. The emergent light from an open bulb is fairly hard. That from versions using a light shield is softer. Broads of 1 kW, 2 kW, 5 kW are widely used.

3 *Floodlight bank* (*nine-light, cluster*) consists of groups of internal reflector lamps (650–1000 W each). They create soft-light through multi-source light overlap. Its sections may be switchable and adjustable. Widely used for location lighting.

4 *Fluorescent bank* is a group of fluorescent tubes, regular or high frequency, providing diffuse illumination.

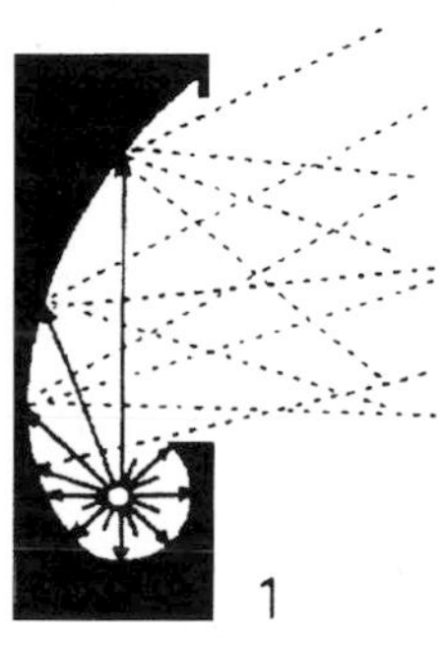

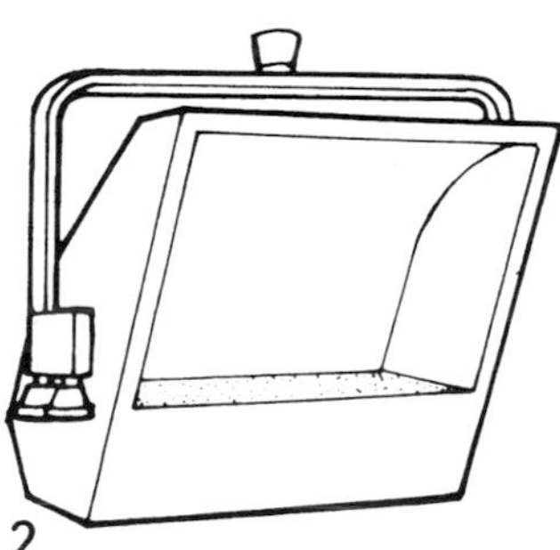

Fig. 9.14 part 2 Soft-light sources – internal reflection types

1 Internal reflection from shielded tubular quartz-light(s), produces diffused high-intensity illumination.

2 *Large broad* 'Softlight' (1–6 kW typical) has reflected internal lamps (tubular quartz or fluorescent). A diffuser may also be attached.

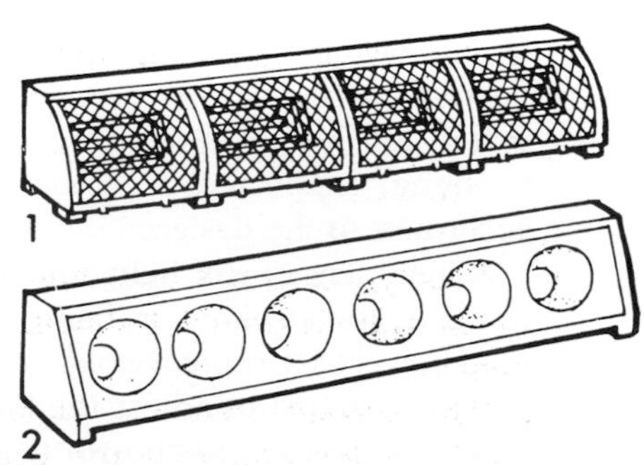

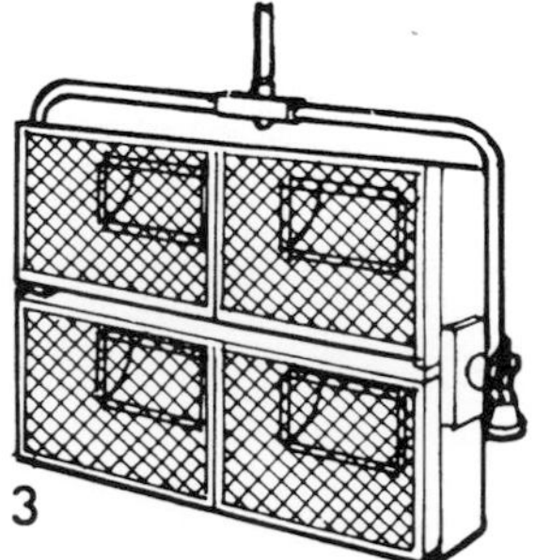

Fig. 9.14 part 3 Soft-light sources – cyclorama lighting

Special fittings used to provide an even spread of light over a vertical surface (cyc, backdrop). Fitted with color medium where colored illumination is required.

1 *Ground-row* (*trough*) containing tubular quartz units (625 W–1500 W).

2 *Strip-light* (*border light*) consists of a row of internal-reflector lamps.

3 *Suspended cyc* light is a single or multi-unit fitting (for color mixing) with strip quartz-lights.

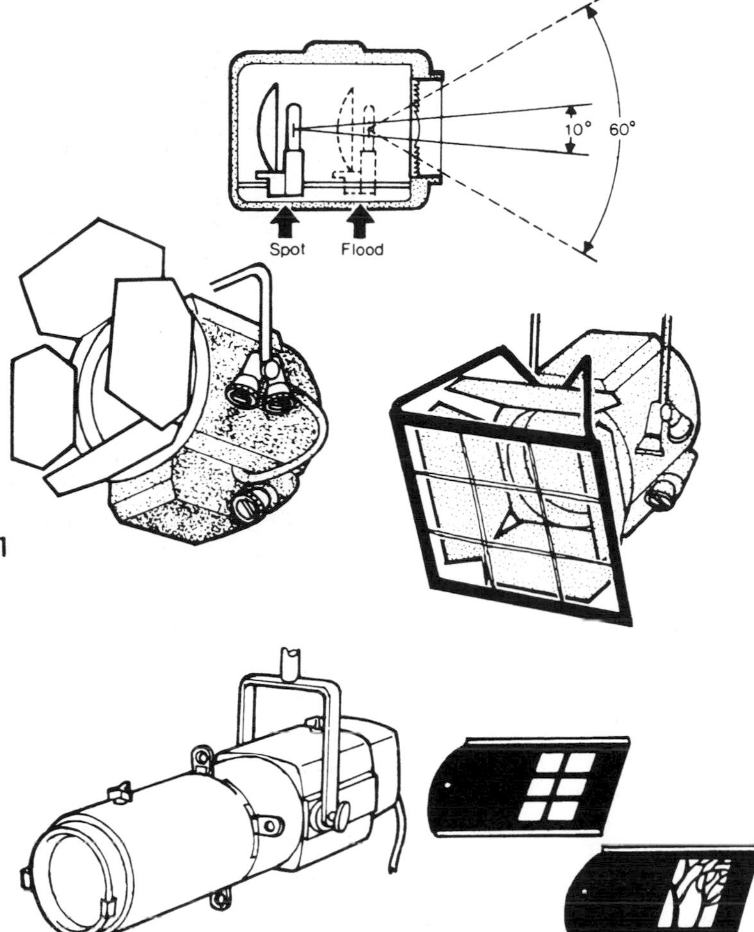

Fig. 9.15 Hard-light sources

1 *Fresnel spotlight* (100 W–10 kW. 8–38 cm (3–15 in) lens diameter). Sliding the lamp assembly to/from Fresnel lens adjusts light-spread – spot to flood. Adjusted by hand crank (crank or sweep lever), by pole (loop, ring, or T-fitting), or remote electronics. *Controls*: Focus, tilt, pan, filament-switch (where dual-filament lamps used). Barndoor may be permanently attached. Color-frame, French flags, etc., can be attached.

2 *Ellipsoidal spotlight* (profile spot) provides precisely-shaped hard-edged beams which are controlled by shutters, iris diaphragm, or metal plates (profiling blades). Shadow patterns can be projected, using an etched stencil plate of stainless steel (gobo, mask). Typical ratings 500 W, 750 W, 2 kW.

■ *Spotlights/Fresnel spots* Focused spotlights with Fresnel lens and internal reflector are used as key lights, back lights, background/set lighting, and for effects (sunlight, broad decorative patterns, dapples). The light spread of the spotlight's beam is adjustable (*focusing*):

- By moving the lens and mirror assembly (in the Fresnel spotlight)
- By moving the position of the mirror (in lensless spots)
- Or, in some designs, by moving the lens alone (in 'ring-focus' spots).

Ideally, the beam intensity should remain even overall as the beam width is altered; but many designs develop hot spots or 'dark centres'.

The *external reflector/lensless spotlight/'Redhead'/'Blonde'* is widely used on location and for confined places in studio settings.

Basically a bare tungsten-halogen bulb within a reflector, its design is compact, lightweight, and highly efficient. Its wide light spread (+80°, compared with a typical 60° Fresnel spot) makes it a valuable light fitting in confined spaces, although its beam is somewhat uneven. Power ratings range from 250 W to 2 kW.

■ *Effects/pattern projectors* These include effects spots, projection spotlights, profile spots, ellipsoidal spotlights, and pattern projectors. They are used to project precisely shaped areas of light (soft or sharp-edged cut-off) for localized effects lighting, or to project patterns of stencils or slides (windows, tracery, leafy branches, decorative motifs).

■ *Follow spots* Used for isolating static subjects or following moving performers (singers, skaters, dancers) in a confined pool of light. These large spotlights (e.g. 5 kW) are carefully balanced for continuous accurate handling and are usually stand or scaffolding mounted. The beam intensity is often shutter-controlled, and its circular spot area (hard- or soft-edged) is adjustable to suit the subject.

Lamp supports

Several methods have become standardized for supporting lamps.

■ *Ground lamps* Lamp fittings may rest on the ground for certain purposes. *Ground rows*, *cyc lights*, *strip lights*, *troughs* are used to light backgrounds; *spotlights* can provide underlighting effects or be used to reach otherwise inaccessible areas.

■ *Floor stands* Floor lights are mounted on telescopic three-castered stands. They have the disadvantages of occupying valuable floor space (perhaps impeding camera or sound-boom movement), casting shadows onto backgrounds, having trailing cables, and being vulnerable. But they do permit easily adjusted precision lighting.

In fact, most TV lighting is suspended, to leave floor space uncluttered by lamps or cables.

■ *Pipe grids* Smaller studios frequently use a pipework lattice or ladder beams fixed below the ceiling. This piping (37–50 mm (1.5–2 in.) diameter, at 1.2–1.8 m (4–6 ft) apart) enables lamps to be clamped or suspended as required. Catwalks may allow overgrid access.

■ *Battens/barrels/bars* These are arranged in a regular parallel pattern over the staging area and individual battens may be height-adjusted (counterbalanced by wall weights or motor-winched) to allow lamps to be rigged, or related to staging requirements.

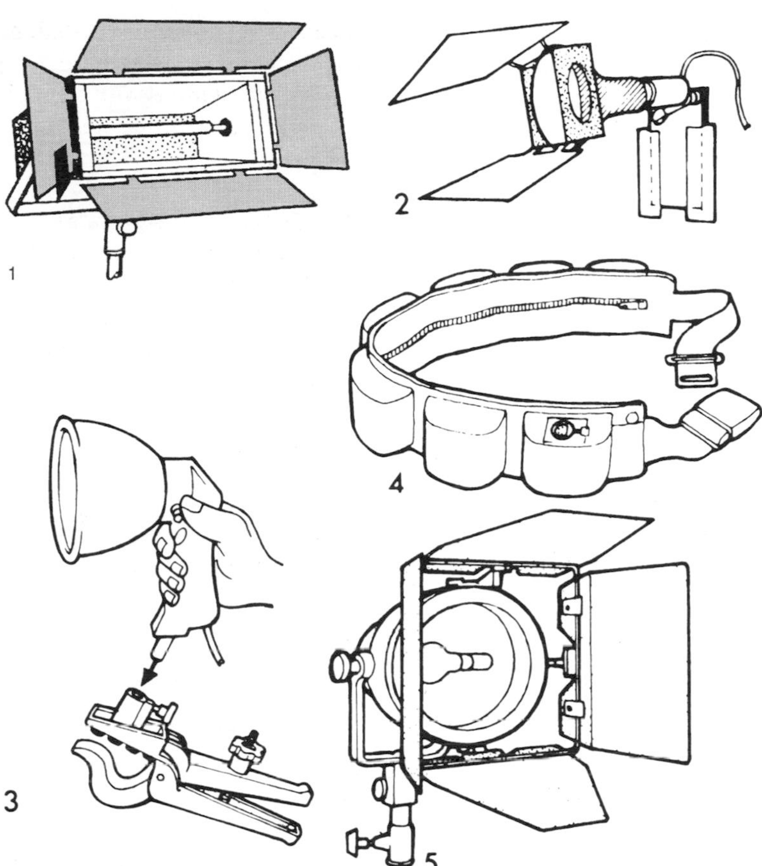

Fig. 9.16 Portable lighting
Typical portable lighting units include:

1 Small broad (600–1000 W).
2 Internal reflector lamp on plate (gaffer taped to wall, hung, hooked on bar) or fitted into clip-light.
3 Sungun (250 W) hand-held or clamped (gaffer-grip, or alligator clip). Powered from utility supply, or 30-volt battery belt (4).
5 External reflector spotlight, lensless spot, in lightweight stand.

■ *Ceiling tracks* Crossbars that can be slid along parallel ceiling tracks offer flexibility in lamp-rigging density. Power rails in single- or dual-track forms may support telescopic hangers or pantographs for individual or twin lamp arrangements.

■ *Lamp adjustment* When working from treads (stepladder) lamp adjustments are precise but time consuming. So many lamps are now designed with loop or 'T' controls to be operated from below by a long, extendable pole. Lamp adjustments by remote electronic control are effective (focus, pan, tilt, barndoors) and invaluable for isolated lamp positions, but add to expense and maintenance complications.

Improvised lighting

Small mobile lamps are widely used when shooting under difficult conditions for news stories, documentaries, etc. where regular light fittings are impracticable.

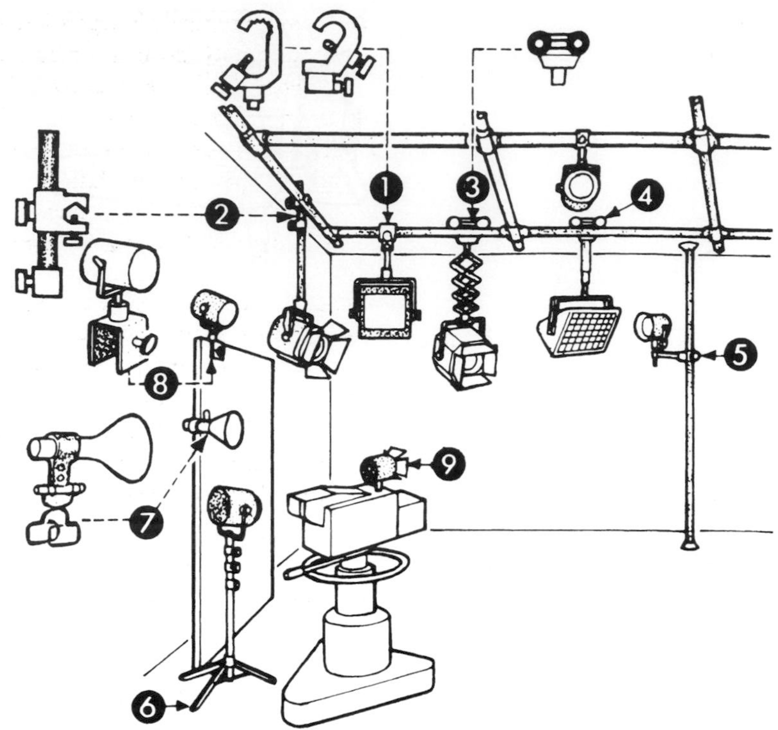

Fig. 9.17 Lamp supports
Studio lighting is mainly suspended (from a pipe-grid in this example).

1 Clamped directly to the grid (with a C-clamp fitting).
2 Lowered from an extendable hanger (sliding rod, drop-arm).
3 A movable trolley holding a vertically adjustable spring counter-balanced pantograph (extension 0.05–3.6 m/2–12 ft).
4 Telescopic hanger (skyhook, telescope, monopole).
5 In confined space, a spring-loaded support bar (barricuda, polecat) wedged between walls or floor/ceiling.
6 Telescopic floor stand (0.45–2.7 m/1½–9 ft).
7 Clip-lamp (spring clamp) attached to scenic flat.
8 Scenic bracket screws to top of flat.
9 Camera light (headlamp, basher). Low-power lamp for eye-light or local illumination. Safety bonds (wire or chain) are fitted to all hung fittings and accessories.

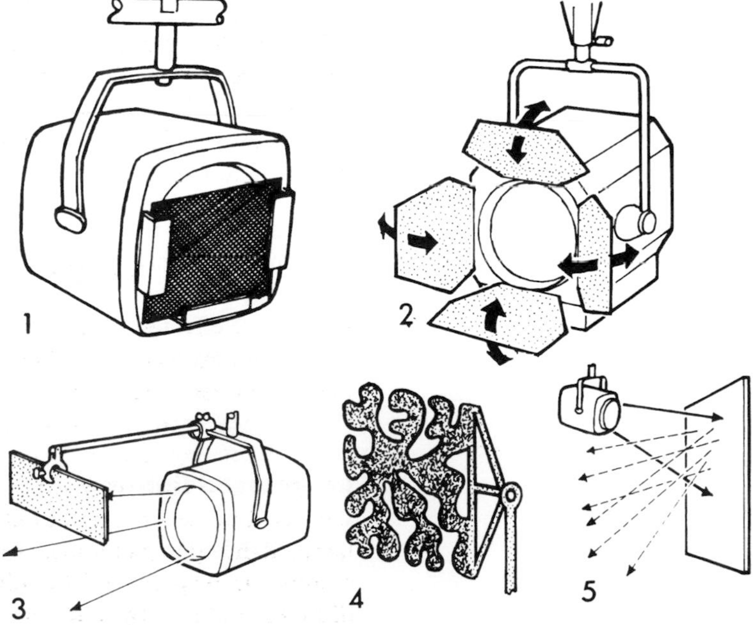

Fig. 9.18 Lamp accessories
Various attachments control the light.

1 *Diffuser* consists of a translucent material (wire mesh, frosted plastic or spun-glass sheet). Diffuses light (overall or locally) and reduces intensity.
2 *Barndoor* has independently adjustable flaps (2 or 4) on rotatable frame; cuts off light beam selectively. Used to restrict light, shade walls, prevent backlight from shining into camera lens (causing lens flares).
3 *Flag* is a small metal sheet (gobo) preventing light spill or cutting off light beam.
4 *Cookie* (*cucaloris, cuke*) is a perforated opaque or translucent sheet that creates dappling. shadows, light break-up, patterns.
5 *Reflector* is a flat sheet (white or silver surface) reflecting light to re-direct or diffuse it.

- Compact quartz lamps such as small *lensless spots/external reflector spots* (e.g. Sun-guns, omni-lights) are often attached to cameras (*camera lights*). *Hand-held*, they provide a mobile light source.
- *Internal reflector lamps*, or *PAR* fittings, may be clipped temporarily onto nearby structures or furniture (using gaffer grips, gator clips, sprung clip-lights). Lightweight telescopic standards (0.6–2.4 m (2–8 ft)), spring-loaded support bars are also used to temporarily position lamps.

Size and power are necessarily limited (e.g. 150–350 W) when using mobile supplies (e.g. a 30 V DC battery-belt); but when household current is available (110/230 V AC) increased ratings may be used. Lamps are often overrun, so are relatively short-lived (perhaps 10–20 hours). It is important, therefore, not to leave them on unnecessarily, and to be aware of how long you have used the present bulb. Always carry spares!

Lighting control

Earlier methods of light control used several types of electrical dimming, including resistances, transformers, reactance dimmers, and magnetic amplifiers. But these have mostly been replaced by solid-state *SCR* (*silicon-controlled rectifier*) *dimmer/thyristor* devices. This system is extremely adaptable, and equally suitable for portable and complex computerized equipment. Control levers (faders) and channel switchers are grouped on a *lighting board* (*console*), remotely controlling the actual dimmer units. Intensity adjustment is smooth, and proportional over their range, even for varying loads (consumption).

The SCR dimmer is a semiconductor device which controls lamp current according to the timing of a series of electrical 'gating pulses' applied to it. Earlier problems causing 'lamp sing' (filament vibrating at audible rates) or audio injection (mike cables picking up interference) can now be overcome by suitable suppression.

Dimmer board design

Every *lighting bar* (batten, barrel) in a studio has a number of permanent outlets fitted. These are numbered, e.g. Bar 22A, 22B, 22C, 22D. Each lamp on a bar is plugged into a separate outlet. This outlet is not itself a power supply. It is simply a tie-line, permanently routed to a corresponding patch cord (marked e.g. 22A) on the central *patch bay*. Any patch cord can usually be plugged into any power outlet receptacle or channel. Thus all the lamps lighting a cyclorama, for instance, wherever they are in the studio, can be patched into adjoining power channels; so that their dimmers are side by side for convenient operation.

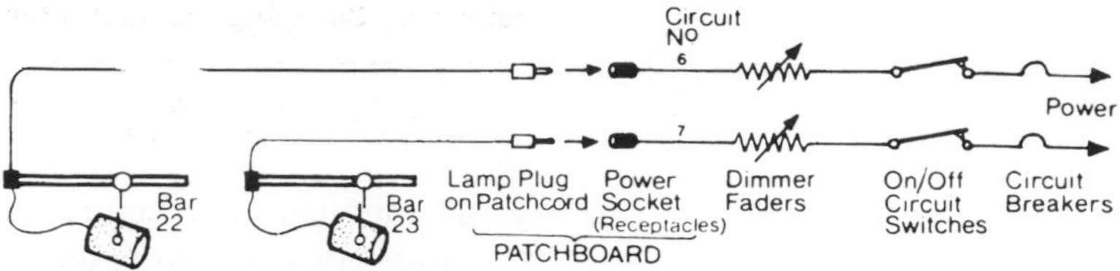

Fig. 9.19 part 1 Patching and control – basic patching
The *lamp* on the hanging bar/batten 'Bar 22' is plugged into a numbered *outlet* fixed to the end of the batten. All batten outlets are permanently routed to a central *patchboard*, where they appear as a series of numbered cables (*patch cords*), each marked with its bar/batten outlet number.

A patch cord is plugged (*patched*) into any one of a series of numbered power-circuit outlets (*channels*) – circuit No. 6 in this example. Each power supply incorporates its own *control dimmer or fader* and *channel switch*. Similarly, the lamp on bar 23 is being fed from power circuit outlet No. 7.

Each channel can be switched and dimmed independently. Avoid exceeding the power loading limit of a channel (e.g. 2 kW). Also switch off channels before patching lamps, to prevent burning contacts due to arcing.

Some installations use patch cords; others have permanent connections, switched patching, or minature peg-board patching.

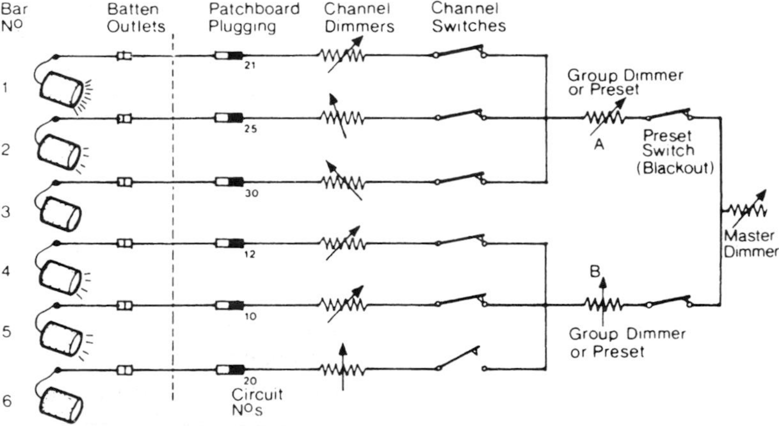

Fig. 9.19 part 2 Patching and control – group presets
A series of individually adjusted circuits can be grouped, to be dimmed/switched communally, e.g. fading cyclorama lighting up/down. Typical situation is shown here:

Preset A (fully faded up). Lamp 1 – Switched on, fully faded up (bright). Lamp 2– On, faded down (dim). Lamp 3 – On, but faded out (out).

Preset B Faded down, reducing supply to all groups. Lamps 4 and 5 – On, individually faded up (but dim due to preset dimmer.) Lamp 6 – Channel switched off.

Basically, you want to switch lamps (on/off) singly or in groups, and to adjust lamp intensities individually and/or in groups (to a chosen or variable level). Dimmers (faders) are usually scaled (10 = full, 0 = out) and normally worked around '7', to extend lamp life and permit 'above-normal' intensities when needed.

The simplest dimmer board comprises a row of channels, each with its separate switch and dimmer (fader). A *MASTER DIMMER*

Table 9.6 Changing the light intensity

When ***light levels*** are too low or too high they can be changed in several ways (INC = increase light intensity: DEC = decrease light intensity.)

- *Dimmers.* Alter dimmer settings to INC/DEC but check the picture for changes in color quality. Simple and immediate control, but can involve extensive equipment.
- *Diffuser.* Diffusers have the advantage that you can treat just part of a light beam if necessary. DEC: place a diffuser over lamp; add further diffuser material. INC: reduce/remove diffuser.
- *Spotlights.* INC: spot up the lamp slightly. DEC: flood the lamp slightly. Simple, but must be done manually, and affects the light spread.
- *Softlight sources.* Switch on/off sections of a multi-lamp softlight source. This does not affect color temperature. But the change in light level may be too great.
- *Lamp distance.* INC: move the lamp closer to the subject (now brighter, but its coverage will be reduced). DEC: move the lamp further from subject (light intensity falls, but its coverage will increase). Simple, but may not be practicable.
- *Lamp power.* Replace the lamp with another of higher or lower power. Except when lamp filaments can be switched (dual filament lamps), this involves rigging a new lamp.
- *Extra lamps.* INC: add more lamps. (Beware more shadows, or overlighting other areas.) DEC: remove lamps (e.g. switch off some of the soft light)

at the end of the row allows all the lamps to be *faded up/down together.* A *BLACK-OUT* switches them all on/off.

Many manual boards consist of two (or three) of these systems. Each group is then known as a *PRESET GROUP, PRESET,* or *BANK.* These presets may be lettered (Preset *A*, Preset *B*), or be given colors (*Red* preset, *Yellow* preset, *Blue* preset).

Each preset has its own *group dimmer* (*SUB–MASTER, GROUP FADER, PRESET DIMMER, BANK DIMMER*) and its *PRESET BLACK-OUT* switch. A *MASTER DIMMER* controls the overall output from several preset banks.

You can switch any lamp channel to any of the presets. Suppose you have a series of lamps lighting a cyclorama. If you route those particular channels to e.g. *PRESET A*, you will be able to fade the entire cyc lighting up/down, just by operating that preset's group dimmer.

Like production switchers, there are many available designs. Smaller dimmer boards are usually transportable – often as wheeled installations on the studio floor. Very sophisticated computerized facilities are used in larger studios. These can store considerable detail, including information on lamp intensities and switching, gradual or instantaneous lighting changes, cues, effects lighting, etc. These data can be recalled at the press of a button (or automatically) from computer memory (solid state, floppy disks, or cassette storage).

Basic lighting approach

Before lighting any production there are a number of preliminary questions you will need answered. Whether you get these answers at a full pre-production meeting with the director, set designer, audio engineer, etc. or from a chat in the studio while looking around the set will depend on the size and nature of the production.

What is going to happen?

- *The subject.* The main subjects in most programs are people. Even for a single person speaking to camera, or a seated interview, you must know where people are going to be positioned, and the directions they are facing. You will need details of the action. The answers will decide where you place *key lights.* If keys are badly angled, it can considerably affect portraiture. All subjects tend to have optimum directions for the main light direction.
- *The cameras.* Where are the cameras to be? Lighting must suit the camera's viewpoint. If the subject is to be shot from several positions the lighting has to take this into account – but that does *not* mean pouring light on from all directions!
- *The surroundings.* You will need to know about the general tones of the surroundings. Are they light-toned (then they could easily become overbright), or dark-toned (more light might be needed to prevent lower tones from becoming detailless shadows)? Will the subjects stand out from their background, or tend to merge with it?
- *Atmosphere.* Are you aiming at a particular atmospheric effect (happy upbeat spectacle, cosy evening interior, intriguing mystery)? This will influence how you distribute light and shade in the scene.
- *Production mechanics* These include such things as:
  Sound-boom positions (to avoid casting shadows that will be seen in shot).
  Lighting cues (e.g. someone apparently switching room lights on).
  Lighting effects such as fire flicker, lightning, moonlight.

There will be times no doubt, when you have to light a setting without knowing any of these details. In those circumstances you can only provide a more general pattern of lighting, as in Figure 9.12, and check pictures during rehearsal, to see where 'first-aid treatment' can improve matters. Results under these conditions can be unpredictable.

Check out the facilities

You now know various production details; about the series of lighting changes needed at the start of the show, the spotlight that

Table 9.7 Preliminary facility checks

Now you know details of the production, you need to check the studio facilities before drawing a lighting plot.

- What is the light level required at a typical working *f*-stop? (For example, 500–600 lux at *f*/2.8, 3200 K
- *Check out the lighting equipment.*
  What types of light fittings/luminaires are available?
  How many spotlights? (Sizes?)
  How many softlight sources?
  How many special-purpose lamps (effects projectors, follow spots)?
  What power is available?
  Is there likely to be sufficient spare cabling (e.g. to run to floor lamps)?
- *Check auxiliary fittings available*
  Do you have sufficient diffusers, barndoors, color medium, etc.?
- *Check the various methods of lamp suspension available.*
  What are the safety arrangements for lamps?
  Are there safety wires or chains on hung lamps?
  Sandbags/stage weights to steady floor stands?
- *Check the lamp patching and lighting control facilities available.*

Even if you work regularly in the studio, a particular facility may not be available on the day of your show (broken, being serviced, being used on another production).

is to follow the singer, the effects the set designer would like to see on the cyc . . . But do you have the resources to do these things?

It is wise to check at this stage. If you find that you have not, inform the director immediately! Some relatively simple lighting treatments (e.g. multi-color changes on a cyclorama) can require a large number of lamps. Where equipment is limited, you may have to make do with another different lighting treatment instead (e.g. a single-lamp shadow effect).

The lighting plot

Most people find the basics of lighting easy enough to understand, but are very apprehensive when it comes to the actual lighting process. How do you begin? Certainly, do not try to *imitate* 'standard plots'. They are, at best, only a general guide. Work out your lighting from first principles, to suit your own facilities. This is how to do so.

To start with, you need a scale plan of the studio, showing details of *scenery* and *main furniture*. If you just work from the back of an envelope, you'll get proportions and scale wrong. This *STAGING PLAN* (*FLOOR PLAN, GROUND PLAN, SETTING PLAN*) is usually provided by the set designer. It includes indications of the overhead lighting facilities, i.e. positions of lighting battens/barrels, power outlets, etc. If the main camera positions are also drawn, this becomes the *CAMERA PLAN.*

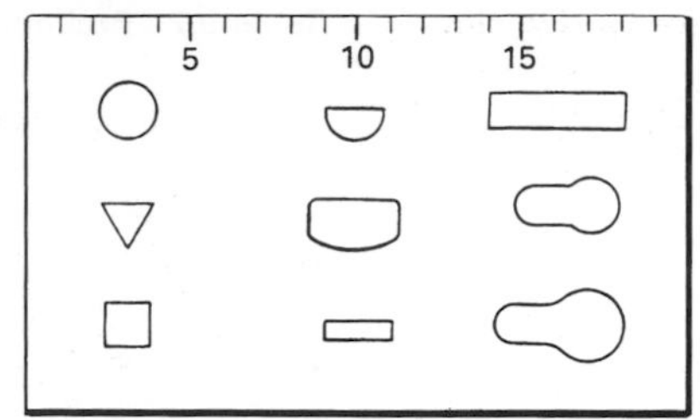

Fig. 9.20 part 1 Lamp stencil
A stencil with patterns for the main types of lamps used, to aid neat lighting plots.

Left column: Fresnel spotlight, lensless reflector spot. HMI arc.
Center column: Scoop, Softlight (internally reflected), small broad,
Right column: Cyc light/ground row, effects spot/profile spot, follow spot.

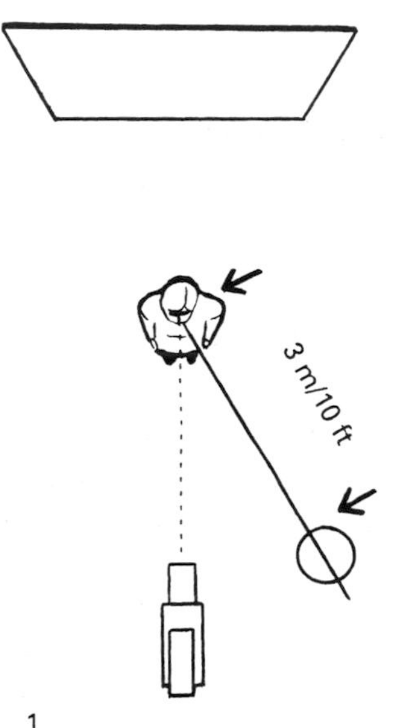

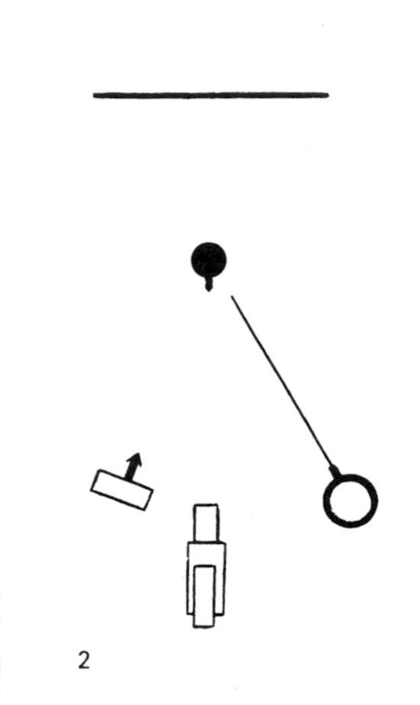

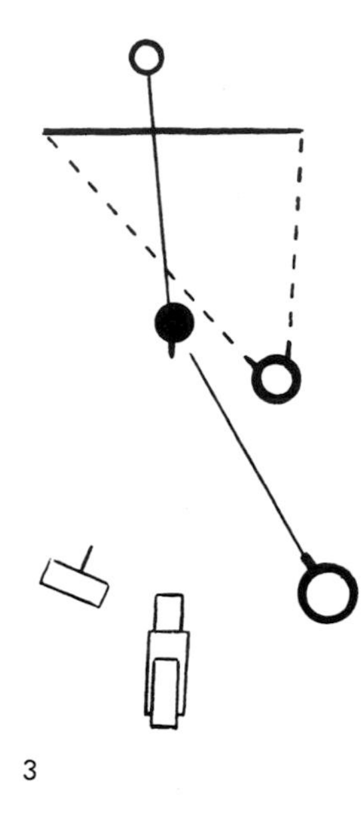

Fig. 9.20 part 2 Drawing the plot

1. The keylight direction is offset from the nose line, about 3 m (10 ft) away minimum.
2. Draw a symbol to represent the person (with nose direction), draw in the keylight. Fill light illuminates the shaded area of the subject.
3. A slightly offset backlight, and background lighting, complete the basic lighting.

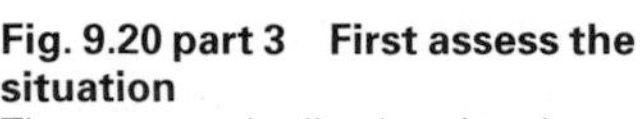

Fig. 9.20 part 3 First assess the situation
The scene to be lit, showing the main light directions (compatible with daylight).

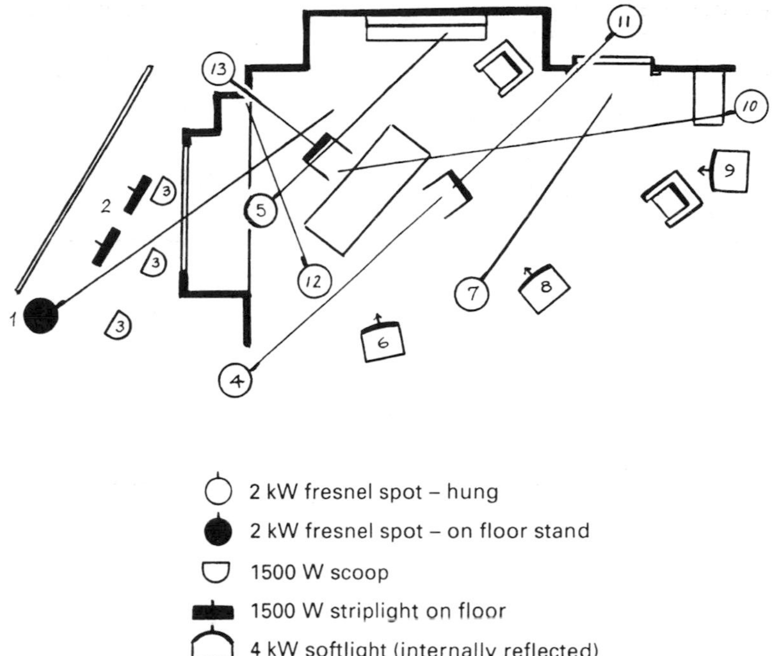

Fig. 9.20 part 4 The lighting plot After lighting the action areas (chairs), the set is systematically lit to simulate a sunny day. Lamps are patched into supply channels (here 1–13) and each lamp's channel number written within or beside it.

Keys 4, 10. Backlights 11, 13. Fill light 6, 8, 9. Sunlight through window 1. Background lighting 12,5,7. Backdrop lighting 3, 2.

It is helpful to have a lamp stencil, which includes scale symbols representing each type of lamp you are using: e.g. spotlight, scoop, floodlight, projection spot, cyc light, etc. An accurate lighting plot will enable you to immediately identify every lamp during rehearsal. Without a plot, you will be left wondering which lamp is causing the boom shadow, or why there is hot spot on the cyc.

Work systematically, taking the project step by step. The art and craft of lighting cannot be reduced to a 'painting by numbers' routine! But it is possible to develop a regular procedure.

Let's assume that the lamps are positioned at around 3–3.6 m (10–12 ft) above the ground, and that people are standing or are on chairs at floor level (i.e. not on raised areas). A typical vertical lighting angle is around 30–40° (max) viewed from the subject's position.

When you are in the studio you can stand in the subject's position and angle your stretched arm upwards to point at e.g. 35°. Generally, avoid much steeper or shallower angles. You can judge a lamp's height by comparing it with that of nearby standard flats.

In practice, to attain this angle, lamps hanging at 3.6 m (12 ft) should be above a floor mark about 3–3.6 m (10–12 ft) away from the subject. Lamps hanging at 3 m (10 ft) should be about 2.7–3 m (9–10 ft) away. If lamps must be higher, they will need to be further away.

Now to the lamp plotting!

1 Draw a circle to represent the person, with a *nose line* showing the way they are going to face.

2 Draw a *key light axis* (i.e. the light beam) about 30° to this nose line. Do this on the side of the nose furthest from the boom, or on the upstage side of the camera (see Figure 9.20).
3 About 3–3.6 m (10–12 ft) away on the plan, draw the spotlight symbol.
4 Draw the spotlight axis *through* the head and beyond. At about two-thirds of the key light distance (say 3 m (10 ft) away), draw the small spotlight symbol for the *back light.*
5 Assuming that fill light is necessary (as it usually is), place a soft light source at about 3 m high, 3–4 m (10–12 ft) away on the opposite side of the nose from the key light. (A soft light source on a floor stand will probably get in the way of the cameras, and be seen in long shots.)
6 The relative intensities of the lights will need balancing while watching the picture. Typical ratios are; key light and back light of similar levels; fill light half that of the key.
7 What power ratings should the lamps have? That depends on the light levels your cameras need, how close the lamps are to the subject, and on the efficiency of the lamps. On location, a lensless spot (e.g. 1 kW) may provide a suitable key light. But in the studio, where lamps are further away, higher powers will be needed. Typically, a key light may be 2 kW, a back light anything from 1 kW to 500 W, and softlight filler around 1.5 to 2 kW. But it really depends on the area involved and the lamp distances.

   In larger studios, with lamps further away, or cameras working at smaller lens apertures, 5 kW keys will probably be necessary.

   This completes the lighting plot for that person. The result may not be art, but it will be along the right lines. With experience, you will get the feel of your particular light fittings and how they behave at various distances.

   If you have an interview to light, follow a similar process, with a separate plot for each person. Prevent one person's light falling on the other, unless they are deliberately sharing lamps (e.g. a shared key, or one person's key is also another's back light).
8 Check out each person's head-with-nose symbol, and consider possible key/back/fill positions. Some will result in shared keys, others may have to be compromises. But try to localize treatment as far as possible. If you do have to provide '*area lighting*' instead, pay particular attention to rehearsal pictures, and see whether results can be improved by extra treatment.
9 When all action has been lit, start to light the setting itself. Unless you are lighting a sky cloth or backdrop, do not light the walls of settings with soft light (e.g. scoops). The flatly lit or overbright tops to walls are unattractive. In some cases a single spotlight can cover a wall (barndooring off the top), in others a series of spots can light the wall in sections.

These, remember, are only the basic mechanics of arranging the lighting plot; but they will certainly help you to light many regular types of production confidently and effectively. The techniques for coping with complex action, for creating and developing a particular atmosphere are another matter, and you will find these covered in *The Technique of Lighting for Television and Films* (3rd edn.) and *Lighting for Video* (3rd edn), by Gerald Millerson, published by Focal Press.

10 The final stage of the lighting plot involves patching the lamps. Each lamp is to be plugged into an outlet on the lighting batten/bar and fed from a selected power channel. Write each *channel number* by the associated lamp. Only use the same channel for two lamps, if there is sufficient power (e.g. a 2 kW supply point for two 1-kW fittings); and remember, *they cannot be dimmed independently.*

A *patching sheet* is necessary, so that someone can plug up lamps to correspond to the plot. You simply list the channel numbers and the batten outlets they feed. You do *not* need lamp descriptions on this list. A well-drawn plot is self-explanatory.

If there are *lighting cues* during the show (i.e. lights to be switched on or off at certain moments) you may write these on the production *script* and/or in a separate *cue sheet*, with details of when various channel numbers or groups are to be altered.

Lighting rigging

Armed with the plot, you can begin to arrange lighting treatment in the studio. The process of selecting, positioning, plugging, and patching lamps is called *rigging*. You can approach the job in several ways:

1. *Select and redirect appropriate lamps* from those already hanging in the studio. A workable system with experience, but it depends for its success on there being sufficient suitable lamps from which to choose.
2. *Position lamps one by one*, lighting and setting each in turn as it is rigged. This can be a time-consuming piecemeal approach.
3. *Hang all the lamps required*, then when the rigging is complete, light and set each lamp.
4. *Have all lamps rigged and tested before the lighting session.* Here the lighting crew is given a detailed lighting plot, showing the position and type of each lamp required, and all accessories (diffusers, color medium), together with patching channel numbers.

This is a systematic approach, allowing lamp rigging to be carried out whenever convenient, and providing a valuable reference and record of events. The lights are set at a later session.

Setting lamps

The mechanics of setting lamps

Now we are about to adjust the lamps so that they cover the planned areas. Sometimes the most convenient method is to switch on one lamp at a time, set it, then switch it off and go on to the next. Its disadvantage is that you will not be able to see if any lamps are doubling, or areas have been missed. And you will need to have a clear mental image of the exact purpose of each lamp.

The best approach is a progressive one. Having set a lamp, you then *add* the next, and gradually build up the overall effect. Sometimes you will have to work with all the lamps switched on at the same time, and set each in turn; probably waving a hand over it to check its coverage. If all lit lamps are initially pointing in random directions, the result can be confusing and dazzling; but unavoidable, perhaps, where switching facilities are limited.

When setting lamps look out for *overlapping key lights* which can cause hot spots, and unattractive *multi-shadows*.

Finally, always be cautious about judging the picture quality from a monitor in the studio. Apart from any spill light diluting its screen, the monitor may not be set up correctly.

Setting spotlights

Here are some hints on setting spotlights:

- Remember, when *flooded*, the spotlight's beam covers a greater area, but at lower intensity. The light coverage may not be *even*. *Spotting* the lamp reduces coverage, and increases light intensity considerably.
- Set a spotlight by *fully spotting* to position the center of the beam, then fully flood it to cover the required area. Or *wave over the light beam* (arm or lighting pole), watching the moving shadow to check its coverage.
- Avoid looking into lamps. After-images spoil your tonal judgement. Look at the scene through nearly closed eyes. It will help you to see tonal balance more accurately. (A 'monochrome' filter viewing glass can help, too.)

Lamp care and safety

- Avoid moving lamps when they are lit. *Filaments are fragile when hot.*
- Use gloves when handling hot lamps. (Preferably don't!) Never touch the new quartz lamp or HMI bulb (body acids destroy the envelope).

Table 9.8 The techniques of setting lamps

The subject	• Scrutinize the subject, and consider the particular features you want to emphasize or suppress. • Will there be any obvious problems with that subject (e.g. a person with deep-set eyes or a peaked cap, who needs a lower key light)? • Anticipate troublesome light reflections (e.g. on an oil painting). Will a carefully positioned key avoid bad speculars, or is dulling spray needed? • How critical will the shots be? If revealingly close, will there be sufficient depth of field? Possible camera shadow problems? • Is the subject stationary, or is it moving around? • Is it being shot from several angles? If so, from which directions? • Are shadows likely to fall on the subject from people nearby, or parts of the scenery (hanging chandeliers, arches, tree branches)? Lighting angles may need to be adjusted to suit the situation.
The key light	Arrange an offset key light, suitable for the camera position(s), subject direction(s), and action. • Does the key light cover the subject? If the subject moves, will it still be unsuitable? • Does the key need to cover more than one subject; an area perhaps? • Does the light coverage need restricting? Is there any unwanted spill light onto nearby areas (people, setting)? Use barndoors, flags. • Does that key suit the various camera angles? Will it be necessary to cross-fade to a second key for a different camera viewpoint? • Check and adjust the key light intensity. (Adjust light level by slightly spotting/flooding: switching lamps; adding diffuser.) • Is the key light likely to cause boom shadows? • Is the key light position – *Too steep* (i.e. too high)? Look for dark eye sockets; long nose and neck shadows. • *Too shallow* (i.e. too low)? It can dazzle talent; reflect in glasses; cause background hot spots; throw subject shadows onto the background; cast camera shadows onto people. • *Too offset* (i.e. too far round to one side)? Causes a head profile on the person's shoulder; produces a half-lit face. • Try to avoid placing people closer to the background than e.g. 1.8–2.7 m (6–9 ft) so that they can be lit properly, separately from the background.
The fill light	• Except for high-key or 'open-air' scenes, avoid high-intensity overall fill light (*base light*). It flattens modeling, reduces contrast unduly, and overlights backgrounds. • Do not use high-intensity fill light to disguise the effects of badly positioned keys. • Position the fill to illuminate the shadows; not to add illumination to the key light level. • Avoid steep or widely angled fill light. • Fill light must be diffused. If necessary, place diffuser over soft-light sources. • Check that the fill light does not overilluminate items nearer the camera than the main subject. Are the back and side walls of the setting too bright, due to excess fill light?

Table 9.8 (cont.)

	• Typical fill light intensity is around half key-light level. • The more frontal the key light (i.e. the nearer to the camera lens axis), the less the need for filler. • *Exceptionally*, in dark surroundings (e.g. a singer on a darkened stage) localized fill light can be provided by a dim, very diffused spotlight (despite the extra shadow it casts). • Do not rely on light bounced from the floor to provide fill light. It is uncontrollable, and of low intensity. • A lamp fixed to a camera can provide fill light, but its effectiveness varies considerably with camera distance. It is liable to be reflected in shiny background surfaces, glasses, etc.
The back light	• *Is the back light necessary*? It may not be needed for some subjects, or where edge lighting is used. • Avoid *steep back light*. It becomes ugly 'top light' – flattening the head, and hitting the nose tip. If someone is close to a background and cannot be backlit properly, omit it. Do *not* use top light or side light instead. • Avoid *very shallow back light*. Lamps come into shot. Lens flares may develop. • Check that back light for one camera position is not creating *ugly side light* for another viewpoint. • *Avoid excess back light*. Intensity is typically 1–1½ the key light level. (Excess creates unnatural hot borders to subjects, and overlights hair.)
Background lighting	• Is the background associated with a particular *style, atmosphere, mood*, that needs to be carried through in the lighting treatment? • Will the background *predominate*, or is it an *incidental* behind mainly close shots of the subject? This may decide how much detail is put into background lighting. • Is there any danger that the subject might *blend* into the background tones? • Do any areas of background tone need *compensatory* lighting (i.e. too dark-toned, too light-toned, excessive contrast)? • Does the background require *specific* lighting (e.g. a series of spotlit sections) or *broad* lighting (e.g. a flatly lit cyc)? • Are there any practical lamps (e.g. wall lamps) that will influence the lighting treatment? • Aim to *light the subject before lighting the background*. Any subject lighting falling on the background may make extra background lighting there unnecessary. Where possible, however, keep the subject and background lighting separate, for they usually require quite different treatment. • Wherever possible, relate the light direction to the environment; i.e. visible windows, light fittings. • Generally *shade off walls* above shoulder height to improve the subject's prominence. • Check background lighting for distracting shadows, hot spots, patches, specular reflections. • Avoid *bright* areas near the top of the picture. • Take care not to exaggerate *tonal contrasts*. • Avoid light *scraping along surfaces*, revealing and emphasizing surface blemishes, bumps, joins, etc. Look for spurious shadows from wall fittings.

- Allow plenty of ventilation around lamps, to avoid overheating. (Drapes, cloths, cyc and other scenery can *burn* if too close to lamps.) If you place diffuser material or color medium too close to a Fresnel lens you may crack the lens; so always use proper holders.
- Beware of overbalancing floor stands! Weigh the bottoms (weights, sandbags). Tidy away and secure cables, to prevent accidents.
- Have safety bonds (wire or chain loops) to secure all hanging lamps and accessories, in case they fall.
- Switch off lamps whenever possible, to reduce local heat, lengthen lamp life, and save power costs.
- Take great care when using ladders/steps. The main dangers are overbalancing (never lean over to one side to lift lamps), hitting suspended lamps and scenery, and dropping equipment from a height.

Lighting and camera rehearsal

Camera rehearsal is the moment of truth! Now you will see the results of your labors. Keep an eye on all preview monitors (even when cameras are off shot), and look out for lighting defects – e.g. distracting shadows, hot spots, unsatisfactory contrast, wrong light direction, unattractive portraiture, boom shadows, etc. If possible, readjust dimmers to improve the *lighting balance* (relative intensities) directly you see inaccuracies, for rebalancing could affect all subsequent shots.

The director will be arranging and readjusting shots. Many will be as expected; some may be quite different, and could require total relighting. Whether you correct lighting problems as they arise (and miss continuing rehearsal pictures while doing so) or list them to be corrected during a break depends on the circumstances. You may have an assistant who can help. It is reasonable enough to adjust the odd barndoor quietly with a lighting pole during rehearsal, but diffusers and color media, or hung lamps, cannot be changed unobtrusively.

After production

When the production has been taped, and it is time to clear away equipment, remember that the next person to use it will welcome neatly stored lamps, tidied and looped cables, a de-patched board. To have to sort out a confusion of lamps and rigging left by others before beginning to light can be a very time-wasting and frustrating business!

TV lighting problems

Lighting treatment affects and is affected by the work of most other studio activities. Consequently the lighting director needs to cooperate closely with others to achieve maximum pictorial standards and minimum mutual frustration. So let us now take a look in some detail at the main problem areas.

Electronic problems

The technical needs of the camera system can frustrate your artistic aims. If a situation requires us to switch all lights off, or to provide very dim illumination, or to shoot against a very bright background, or have a scene lit by a single (usually unsuitable) source such as a candle, the camera would normally respond by producing inferior picture quality. So instead, the lighting treatment must necessarily be a compromise; a 'cheated treatment' aided by sympathetic video-control adjustments (Chapter 21). (In film making a similar subterfuge is used when labs adjust processing and the printer light for exposure and color balance control.)

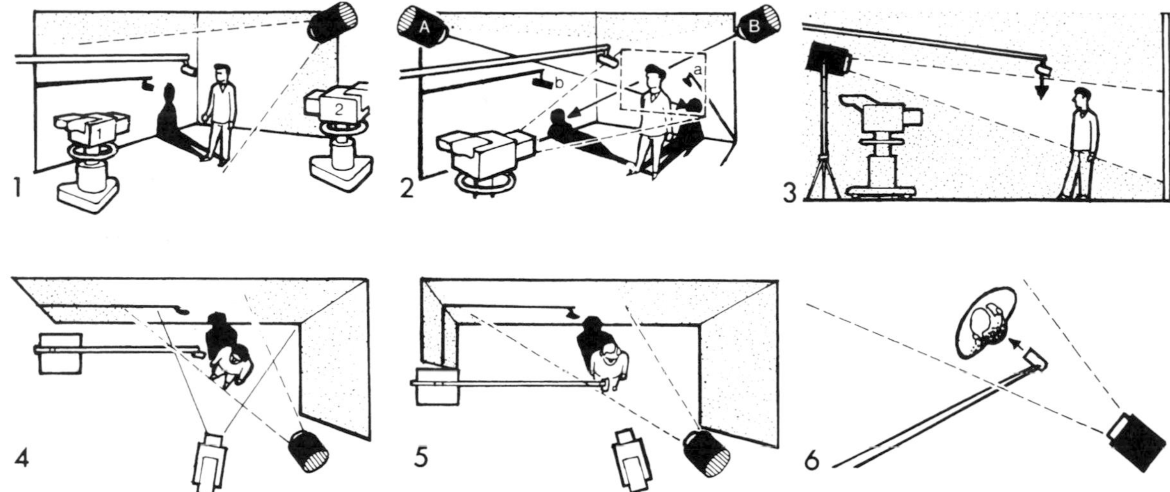

Fig. 9.21 Sound boom shadows

1 From Camera 1. microphone shadow is out of shot and lamp provides backlight, but from Camera 2 lamp is now frontal throwing shadow on background behind performer.

2 Microphone shadow (a) is caused by frontal key light being in line with boom-arm at A. while by placing frontal key at B, at a wide horizontal angle to the boom-arm, shadow (b) is thrown out of shot.

3 Floor lighting avoids microphone shadows unless the boom-arm dips into the lamp's beam.

4 Boom shadows can arise when the boom-arm is parallel with a wall, (5) when the boom operator cannot see boom shadows, and (6) when the performer is playing away from the boom. Where two booms pick up near and far action, the latter can shadow the closer source.

Sound-boom shadows

Shot anticipation and coordination are necessary to prevent boom shadows falling across people and backgrounds. The normal trick is to throw the inevitable shadow out of shot by careful key-light positioning. Obviously, difficulties arise when this lamp position is artistically incompatible.

Table 9.9 Methods of eliminating boom shadows

	Method	*Result*
By removing the shadow altogether	Switching off the offending light.	This interferes with lighting treatment.
	Shading off that area with a barndoor or gobo.	Normally satisfactory, providing the subject remains lit.
		Shading walls above shoulder height is customary, to make the subject more prominent.
By throwing the shadow out of shot	By placing the key light at a large horizontal angle relative to the boom arm.	A good working principle in all set lighting.
	By throwing the shadow onto a surface not seen on camera when the microphone is in position.	The normal lighting procedure.
By hiding the shadow	Arranging for it to coincide with a dark, broken up, or unseen angle of background.	Effective where possible, to augment other methods.
	By keeping the shadow still, and hoping that it will be overlooked.	Only suitable when inconspicuous, and when sound source is static.
By diluting the shadow with more light		Liable to overlight the surface, reduce surface modeling, or create multi-shadows. Inadvisable.
By using soft light instead of hard in that area of setting		Occasionally successful, but liable to lead to flat, characterless lighting.
By using floor stand lamps instead of suspended lamps		Light creeps under the boom arm, avoiding shadows.
		But floor lamps occupy floor space: can impede camera and boom movements; can cast shadows of performers flat-on to walls.
By altering the position of the sound boom relative to the lighting treatment		May interfere with continuous sound pick-up or impede camera moves.
By changing method of sound pick-up	By using a low fishpole, hand-held shotgun (rifle) mike, slung, concealed, personal mikes, prerecording, etc.	These solutions may result in less flexible sound pick-up.

How settings affect lighting treatment

The layout, shape, and finish of settings necessarily affect how you can light them.

■ *Size* Usually, the larger the setting, the broader will be the production treatment. Size alone is not significant since a series of small sets often require more lamps than one large set. Also, there are difficulties in providing precision lighting (e.g. for close-ups) over a wide area, without overlaps.

■ *Height of settings* Low-angle shooting usually necessitates higher sets (studio height permitting). This involves higher, steeper back and side lighting to ensure that lamps do not come into shot.

■ *Overhangs* Appropriate lighting can be difficult for people or scenery underneath any overhanging feature such as ceilings, canopies, beams, branches, and chandeliers. This is particularly true when using hung lamps.

■ *Shapes of settings* Deep narrow sets (e.g. corridors) and wide shallow sets restrict lighting angles, and can therefore frustrate good overall coverage.

■ *Surface tones* Very dark backgrounds and furniture easily lose modeling on camera, causing foreground faces to appear unduly light. Extra lighting may improve reproduced tones, but can spill onto performers. Overlight surfaces appear glaringly hot on camera, often making faces look unduly dark. You can try to keep light off them, but even the illumination from distant soft light sources may leave them overbright. Darkening by spraying down

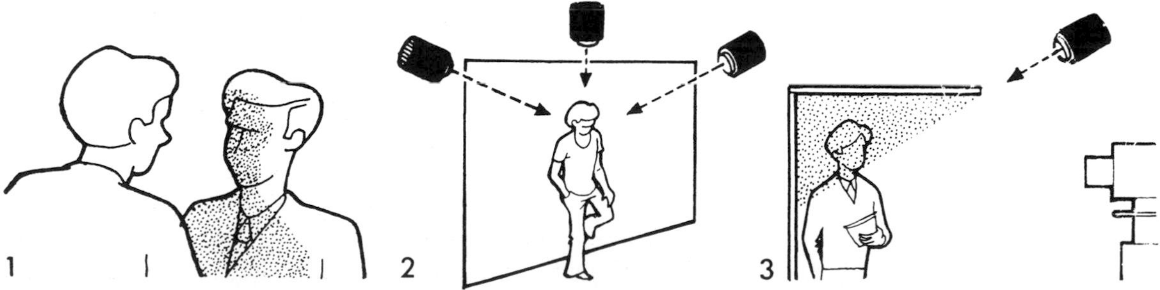

Fig. 9.22 Performer's positions

1 Mutual shadowing is often more easily remedied by repositioning people than by relighting.

2 Where people work too close to backgrounds, good backlight is impracticable. Side lighting or top-lighting (as shown) should be avoided.

3 Where action is in restricted or overhung positions, lighting can be a compromise – or even impracticable.

with a lower tone (impractical over large areas) can inadvertently cause patchiness, aging, or dirtying.

The illusion of depth requires good subject/background tonal separation. Contrast ratios of 1½:1 to 2:1 are typical. Backgrounds should rarely exceed 1½ times face brightness.

Shiny surfaces facing the camera can be particularly embarrassing, as lamps reflect in window glass, pictures, glossy walls, etc.

Overbright surfaces are a regular problem. Newspapers, scripts, table tops, light costume always require care; often having to be sprayed down (water-soluble color), dipped, or dulled down (wax dulling spray; antiflare) to prevent excessive light bounce. A 'hot' back light can aggravate the situation. Shiny glossy surfaces inevitably produce bright specular reflections or glare, and each problem has to be treated as it arises (dull down, re-angle, cover up, relight).

Practical lamps

Under typical studio conditions the low-power table lamps, wall-lamp fittings, stand lamps, etc., used within settings, will seldom provide enough illumination to serve as light sources for action. Sometimes their bulbs can be uprated (e.g. using overrun lamps) to make them appear more realistic. But normally it is necessary to cheat their effect by adding supplementary lighting – e.g. a localized spotlight forming a light patch on the nearby wall.

Other factors affecting lighting

■ *Studio facilities* How elaborate lighting treatment can be is often influenced by facilities available. It can depend on the number and type of lamps, how they are suspended, the type of dimmer board and power-patching arrangements, time, and labor. Where many lamps are prerigged (*blanket rig*) for immediate selection this saves time; particularly with fast turnrounds between productions.

Clearly, problems become more acute if there are a lot of settings, with numerous camera angles and many lighting changes or cues.

■ *Space limitations* Most staging representing interiors has to be built in reasonably naturalistic proportions. So the working space available *within* the set for cameras, sound booms, and lamps remains pretty restricted. When action or treatment is complicated or continuous, lighting treatment becomes that much more of a compromise. Further lighting difficulties develop when, to conserve space, staging is located near a cycloramas (spurious shadows on cyclorama), or backings are positioned too close to windows for appropriate lighting.

■ *Multi-camera production* Multi-camera shooting does not necessarily frustrate good lighting. Much depends on shot duration, shot variations, and duration of takes. Often one set-up can light several viewpoints successfully. Otherwise you will have to introduce lighting changes (unobtrusive or direct) to solve the difficulties.

Lighting for color

Color adds another artistic dimension to the TV picture, enabling you to distinguish between planes more easily (for now there is *hue* in addition to *tone*), and to perceive visual effects that are totally lost in monochrome.

■ *Lighting methods and color reproduction* Many people associate color systems with 'flat lighting' and the extensive use of colored light. Neither is true. Flat overall lighting is as undesirable in color as it is with black and white systems. But reasonably *even* lighting is important for controlled results – with neither *hot spots* (paling out and desaturating colors) nor *underlit* (insufficiently illuminated) areas darkening and emphasizing hues. Remember, too, that under soft light, colors tend to appear paler; while under hard light, they can look brighter and purer (more saturated).

■ *Exposure and color* Exposure and lighting balance are more critical in color. If you stop the lens down to correct the exposure of a brightly lit subject its surroundings will reproduce darker as a result. Conversely, if you open up to expose an insufficiently lit subject correctly, other parts of the picture will look much brighter. So exposure compensations for unbalanced lighting can lead to brightness and saturation changes when pictures are intercut.

Face tones and color can become considerably modified by changes in exposure or color-temperature variations of the light. So a high lighting contrast (key-to-fill ratio) can create color-bisection effects. This situation is further exaggerated when lamps are being run at high and low color temperatures. In color, too, you become more aware of the blocked-off white highlights from skin shine, or perspiration.

Colored light

In fantasy or highly decorative situations anything goes. Faces may be lit with outrageous color mixtures in the most startling combinations. But for most productions, colored lighting (if any) must be confined to the backgrounds.

Sometimes even the subtlest changes of color temperature will be sufficient to tint light; for instance, when one uses low color-temperature lighting to simulate an oil lamp or candle-lit atmosphere. Occasionally you may deliberately alter the camera channel's color balance, or use an incorrect 'white balance'.

Usually, we clip a sheet of color medium in a *color frame* in front of selected lamps. This material, bought in rolls or cut sheets, is of acetate, polyester, mylar, acrylic. Colored gelatin is cheap, but brittle, shortlived, and quickly changes color over hot lamps. Color medium is available in a wide range of hues and densities. But remember, deeper greens, blues, and purples can reduce the effective light output of a lamp to as little as one-tenth or less!

It is all too easy to misuse colored light. Certain treatments have been stylized to the point of cliche – blue to suggest moonlight; red-orange for fire; green for the uncanny. But when carefully introduced, colored light offers great visual opportunities. It enables you to ring changes on neutrally toned scenery and cycloramas. When combined with projected patterns, you can achieve impressive effects quite economically. However, take care that white lighting from other sources does not spill onto these surfaces and dilute the treatment.

Pictorial treatment

There are three broad styles of pictorial lighting through which we can depict the three-dimensional world on a flat screen: *notan, silhouette*, and *chiaroscuro*.

■ *Notan* Emphasis is on surface detail, outline, and surface tones. Pattern rather than form predominates. The impression is flat (two-dimensional). Notan effects come from high-key, low-contrast treatments, an absence of modeling light, reduced back light, and widespread diffused light.

■ *Silhouette* Here we concentrate on subject outline, suppressing all surface details. Apart from true silhouettes (black against a light background) used for dramatic, mysterious, and decorative effects; *semi-silhouettes* arise in contre-jour (against the sun) shots where back light predominates and frontal light levels are low.

■ *Chiaroscuro* In this approach, light and shade conjure a remarkable illusion of solidity, depth, and space. The style is so familiar that we are liable to overlook that it is actually contrived. When well handled, this treatment possesses arresting, vital qualities, as the Dutch master painters found and depicted so convincingly.

Where subjects are set up before a totally black background (cameo), or a white background (limbo), the pictorial effect is more strictly a scenic design treatment than a lighting style, although commonly referred to as such. In *cameo* situations side

Table 9.10 Approaches to pictorial treatment

Illumination – overall (flat)	Main consideration is visibility. Lighting is almost entirely frontal and flat. Tends to *notan*. At its best, subjects distinguishable from each other, and from their background. At worst: flat, characterless pictures: ambiguously merging planes; low pictorial appeal.
Illumination – solid	By a careful balance of frontal and back light, subjects are made to appear solid. This and clarity are the principal considerations of this chiaroscuro approach. The lighting suggests no particular atmosphere.
Realism – direct imitation	*Direct* imitation of effects seen in real life, e.g. sunlight through a window imitated by a lamp shining through it at a similar angle.
Realism – indirect imitation	Imitation of a natural effect, but achieved by a contrived method, e.g. simulating sunlight by lighting a backing beyond a window and projecting a window shadow onto an adjacent wall, from a more convenient position.
Realism – simulated realism	An imitation of a natural effect, where there is no direct justification for it from within the visible scene, e.g. a window shadow on a far wall, that comes from an unseen (probably non-existent) window. (This may be a projected slide, cast from a cut-out stencil, or a real off-stage window.)
Atmospheric – 'natural'	A lighting treatment in which natural effects are not accurately reproduced, but suggested by discreet lighting. A pattern of light that highlights and suppresses pictorial detail selectively, to create an appealing effect. Suggesting realism in most instances, but seldom strictly accurate for that particular environment. A typical motion-picture approach.
Atmospheric – decorative	Associative light patterns, e.g. of leafy branches on a plain background.
Atmospheric – abstract	Light patterns that have no direct imitative associations, but create a visual appeal: e.g. a silhouetted unknown person, lit only by a rectangular slit of light across his eyes. A flickerwheel pattern cast over an exciting dance sequence.

light usually predominates (for maximum modeling); while *limbo* situations are often a notan treatment, avoiding shadows on a white background.

Unfortunately, terminology has too often become confused, so that *limbo* becomes used to indicate 'neutral backgrounds' of any tone. Similarly, for some people 'Rembrandt lighting' defines selectively localized lighting treatment, while for others it implies strongly modeled portraiture.

Atmospheric lighting

Persuasive lighting treatment can considerably change the appearance and mood of a scene:

1 Concentrating attention – emphasizing particular features.
2 Revealing facts – showing form, texture, surface design, etc.
3 Concealing facts – preventing our discerning an object or plane; or seeing form, texture, detail, design, etc.

4 Associations of light – by light direction, intensity, distribution, recalling a particular atmosphere (firelight, sunset).
5 Associations of shade – shadow formations recalling certain subjects, environment, or mood (tree branches, prison-cell bars).

Mood lighting comes from selectively emphasizing and subduing. It is not enough to just imitate natural lighting, for under the camera's scrutiny true environmental illumination often produces ineffectual or ugly results; primarily hot tops, black eyes, half-lit faces, and steep harsh modeling. Instead, we must stimulate the imagination with light and shade – intriguing, hinting, evocative effects.

Animated lighting

You can introduce life and action into a scene by lighting. The movement of light may be used as a dominating effect, or as part of

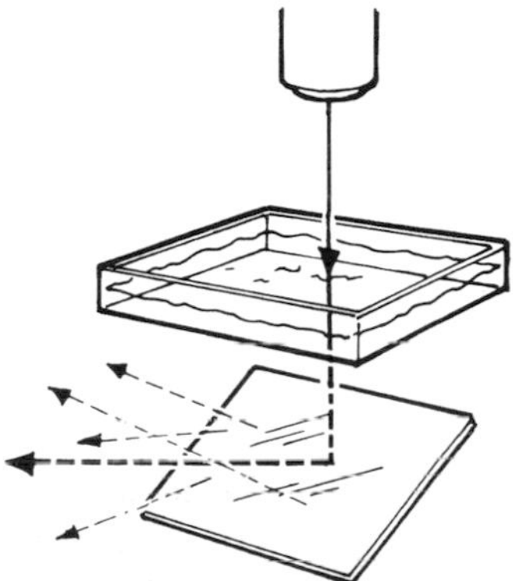

Fig. 9.23 part 1 Water ripple-tray
A spotlight shines through a water-filled glass tray, the rippling light being reflected on to the scene.

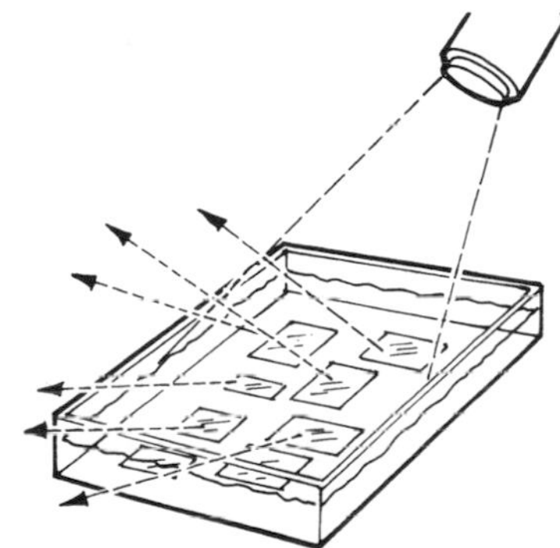

Fig. 9.23 part 2 Water ripple-trough
Light reflects from mirror fragments in water-filled trough.

Fig. 9.24 part 1 Shadow size, sharpness and intensity
Shadow size is always larger than the subject, increasing as lamp distance lessens. Close lamps give greater size changes, and exaggerated proportions. Shadow size increases with subject/background distance.

Shadow sharpness decreases with increased light source area, the lamp's closeness to subject, the subject's distance from background.

Shadow intensity depends on background tones and finish, and spill-light diluting shadow.

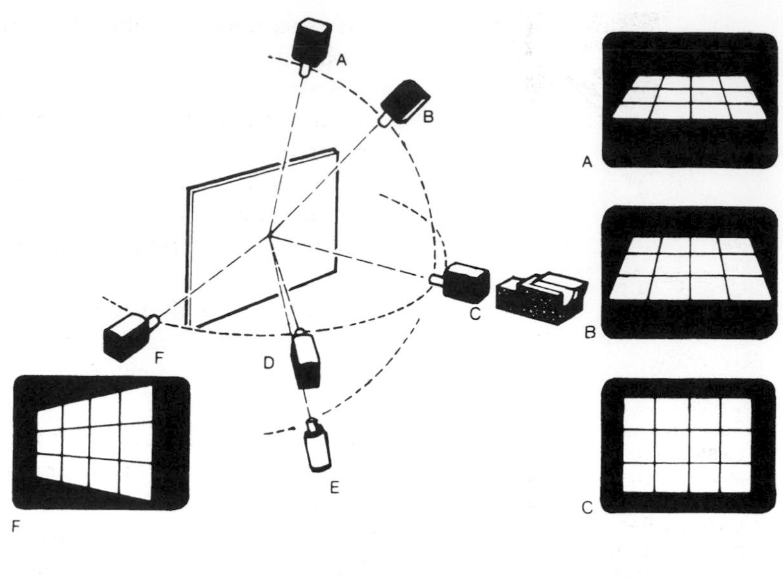

Fig. 9.24 part 2 Shadow distortion
Distortion arises when camera and lamp are not aligned, and not at right angles to background. Tilting the background or angling the lamp also creates distortion.

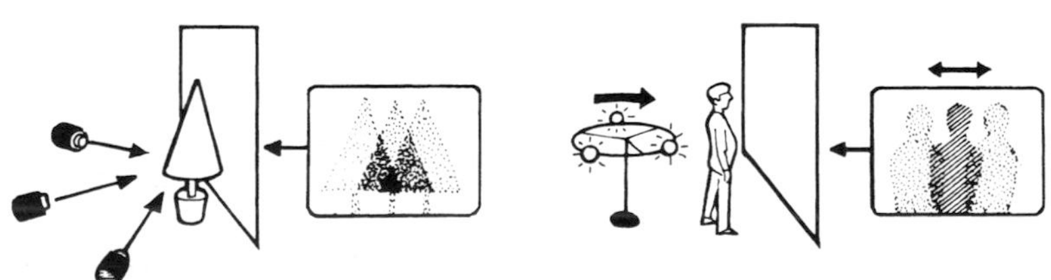

Fig. 9.24 part 3 Multiple shadow effects
These are produced when several lamps combine to light the same subject (particularly successful in color). If they rotate, the multi-shadows weave from side to side.

Fig. 9.24 part 4 Passing shadows
A rotating framework fitted over a lamp, and hung with a stencil cut-out, branches, etc., to create passing shadows. Patterns must not be obviously repetitive.

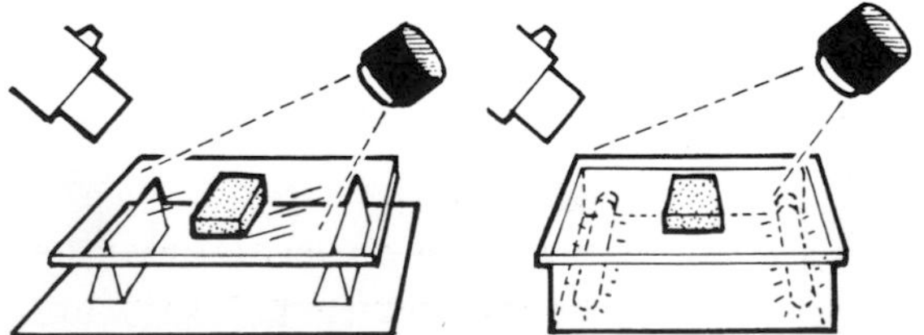

Fig. 9.24 part 5 To lose background shadows
This is achieved by displacing the subject from its background (e.g. on a glass panel), or by using a translucent illuminated panel.

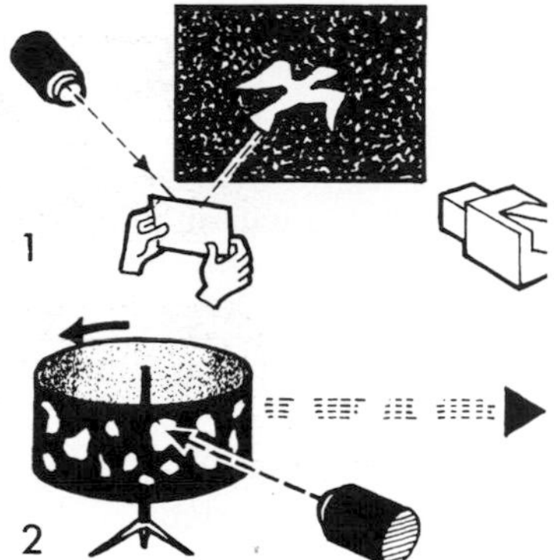

Fig. 9.25 Reflected shapes
1 Reflective material (metal foil, plastic mirror-sheet) held in a sharply-focused light-beam, projects its image on to nearby surfaces. Bending the reflector distorts the reflected shape.
2 Spotlight focused onto *mirror-drum* faced with plastic mirror, produces 'passing-lights' effect for vehicle interior shots.

an environmental illusion. You will often meet examples of this technique:

Rain running down a skylight throws streaking shadows into the room below.
Fluctuating light and shade patterning the interior of a moving automobile.
A room lit by a rhythmically flashing street sign.

Lighting has the particular merit of *flexibility*, for you can change mood or significance in an instant, or imperceptibly alter contrast and balance. For example:

A prowler is suddenly illuminated by a passing automobile . . . and we see that it is not the person we expected.
During a brawl, the room light is broken . . . tension rises, as we no longer know who is winning.
Opening a window blind, the room's appearance is transformed by sunshine.
A happy atmosphere . . . becomes sinister . . . and finally horrific.
The high key lighting gradually becomes contrasty . . . until finally underlighting predominates.

Lighting effects

■ *Reflected shapes* Light can be reflected from metal foil sheeting or silvered plastic to throw decorative patterns. As the surface is moved or flexed, the pattern shapes and position change. Even stenciled symbols or lettering can be reflected to animate or distort titles.

Countless visual effects can be produced in this way (including nebulae, abstract and magical illusions), reflected directly onto backgrounds, front-or rear-projection screens, or superimposed.

■ *Firelight* To simulate firelight, move a stick with close linen strips gently before a floor lamp. Smoke or gas jets are generally less convenient and most automatic devices provide mechanical-looking results.

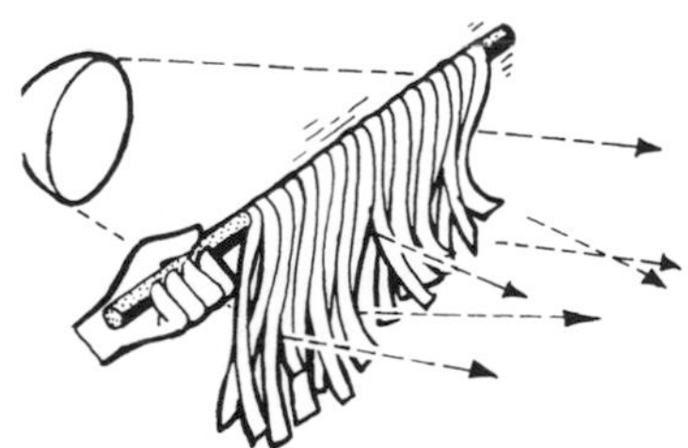

Fig. 9.26 Fire flicker
Narrow strips of rag attached to a stick are gently waved in front of a lamp to simulate firelight flicker.

■ *Lightning* You can achieve sheet-lightning effects simply by switching or uncovering a lamp for an instant. A group of lower power lamps (e.g. PAR lamps) may be more effective than a high-power tungsten source (e.g. over 2 kW), where the filament heating time slows the effect. Overrun lamps (e.g. photofloods) are liable to fail if switched on/off several times. Take care to avoid spurious shadows or unconvincing light patches on backgrounds, or gross overexposure during the flash.

Lighting on location

Varying conditions

When you are shooting away from the studio you will encounter a wide range of lighting conditions:

- *Day exteriors.* Varying from overcast skies to strong blinding sunlight with deep shadows.
- *Night exteriors.* Anything from pitch-black night to strong moonlight; from the odd street lamp to 'bright-as-day' surroundings.
- *Day interiors.* These can range from locations where sunlight through windows embarrassingly overwhelms any interior lighting to those where you need to provide a high-power lamp to simulate sunlight on a dull day!
- *Night interiors.* Conditions here can vary considerably; from total darkness to an extensively lit environment. Sometimes the interior lighting is quite unsuitable for the camera, and has to be switched off.

Lighting techniques on location

All the principles and practices of lighting we have discussed apply equally well on location. Faces still need key lights to be appropriately angled for the most attractive results, whether you are using the sun or a camera light to illuminate them.

Lighting on location is a matter of scale. Any given lamp fitting has its own 'dimension'. The intensity and spread of that light makes it suitable for a certain distance and coverage. Use a 10 kW lamp in a room, and it will be overwhelming; but used as fill light in a sunny exterior it might not be evident in the picture that it is there at all! Smaller lamps are useful for e.g. up to 6 m (20 ft) for fairly localized action. To light the inside of a large hall properly, bigger lamps at greater distances could be essential. Lots of small lamps would be difficult to position, and would probably come into shot.

A small production unit often has to light a location with a handful of lamps – because that's all they have! With modest facilities one's main concern is to make the subject *clearly visible* and as attractive as possible in the circumstances.

Given the option, one might well use a greater number of much larger fittings in order to achieve high-grade pictures from a number of camera positions, and create a more effective ambience.

Many factors can influence one's techniques. If, for instance, you were shooting during daylight in a hall with large ground-level windows, you might need few lamps, if any. But if instead, sunlight was shining in through windows located high up in the walls, you might need to introduce extra lighting to override its unattractive effects.

Much can depend not only on your resources but on how far you are able – even allowed – to modify conditions. Sometimes even a single lamp may considerably enhance the quality of the pictures. At other times only full-scale lighting treatment would really improve matters.

In Table 9.11 you will find a useful summary of typical equipment and techniques you can use when lighting on location.

Table 9.11 Lighting on location

Typical equipment

Lamps

- Camera light.
- Hand-held lamp.
- Lenseless spot (e.g. 250, 650, 800, 1000, 2000 W) with barndoor.
- Small broad (e.g. 600–1000 W).
- Floodlight bank/Minibrute (e.g. with four to nine 650 W PAR lamps).
- HMI arc (e.g. 200.575 W: 1.2, 2.5, to 6 kW).

Accessories

- Lightweight lamp stands.
- Medium/heavy-duty lamp stands.
- Spring-loaded support poles ('barricuda', 'polecat').
- Gaffer grips/alligator grips.
- Wall plates (for PAR lamps).
- Gaffer tape.
- Sandbags.
- Diffuser/scrim/wires.
- 'Daylight' color medium (gels).
- Dichroic filters.
- Window filter material (rolls and sheets) – Wratten 85/light orange gel.
- Neutral density filter material (rolls or sheets). May be combined with color correction.
- Reflector boards or sheets.
- Mobile power supplies (e.g. battery-belt, 30 V DC battery pack).
- AC power adapter (DC from household mains).
- Power cables, multi-outlet cables/spider boxes.

Typical household supplies

110–120 V, 15 A wall outlets (1650–1800 W max.).
220–240 V, 13 A wall outlets (2860–3120 W max.).

Treatment

Exterior shots – DAY

Sunlight

- Avoid shooting into the sun, or having talent looking into the sun.
- Reflect sunlight with a hard reflector (metallic faced) as key, or soft reflector (white coated) for fill light.
- In closer shots color-corrected lamp can fill shadows.
- Bright backgrounds are best avoided, especially when using auto-iris.

Dull day; failing light

- Color-corrected light can provide key light or fill shadows.

Table 9.11 (cont.)

Exterior shots – NIGHT	• Quartz lighting can provide key, fill, and back lighting for most situations. For larger areas, higher-powered sources are necessary (e.g. HMI arcs). • Where necessary, either rebalance the camera to suit any local light sources (and filter your own lamps to match) or overpower them locally with your quartz light, and ignore background color inaccuracies. Extensive background lighting for night shots can require high-power lamps. • Avoid moving the camera around where possible (lag effects visible; comet tails from highlights). Large lens apertures are often unavoidable (producing shallow depth of field). Extra video gain may emphasize picture noise.
Interior shots – DAY	• The camera has to be balanced to the color temperature of *either* the daylight *or* the interior lighting. • Where strong sunlight enters windows: pull shades or blinds, put filter material over windows, perhaps plus neutral density media to reduce sunlight strength. Or avoid shooting windows. Alternatively, filter your lamps to match daylight. • Camera or hand lights (e.g. held 30–40° off lens axis) can serve as keys or fill light for nearby subjects, but The light is very localized. (Very apparent in longer shots.) The very frontal lighting can easily dazzle people. The lamp casts adjacent shadows on a close background. A camera light flattens modeling. The light reflects in shiny backgrounds (e.g. glass, polished paneling). The light may be unsteady. The lamp may overlight close subjects, while leaving more distant ones underlit.
Interior shot – NIGHT	• Either supplement any existing lighting or replace it with more suitably angled and balanced lighting. • Where backgrounds are overlight, restrict main lighting to the subject. Overdark backgrounds may need extra lighting. Lighting arrangements may range from camera or hand lamps to three-point lighting. The most suitable form of lamp support depends on local conditions (on stands, clipped to structures or furniture, on telescopic poles from floor to ceiling, wall plates taped to structures, etc.).
	Safety
	On location it is important to take extra safety precautions in all aspects of lighting. For example:
Equipment condition	No frayed wires, loose parts.
Secure lamp fittings	Lamps should be firmly fixed and supported, and safety bonds fitted. All lamp stands should be secured or bottom-weighted to prevent overbalancing.
Power overloads	Keep within the power ratings of available sources. Remember, other nearby equipment may be sharing available power with your lamps.
Grounding/earthing	Have all lamp fittings individually fused and switched, and properly grounded/earthed.
Hot lamp fittings	Lamps can all too easily scorch or burn up nearby cables, drapes, paper. plastic, etc. In confined spaces, ventilation may be insufficient. Color medium can fume and smell. Overrun lamps can overheat fittings and nearby surfaces.
Floor cables	People can trip over cables, or inadvertently tug them and upset lamps. Tuck cables away, under rugs, near walls, hang them (gaffer tape or wire loops).
Water	Take great care when water is about! It can cause short circuits, or electrocute without warning. Water spray or rain on lamps will cause them to explode unless they are suitably designed for these conditions.

10 Scenery

Unless you are going to shoot on location or use studio walls as a background, you are going to need some sort of scenic treatment to create an environment for the action. Scenery can range in practice from a simple backdrop to extensive construction, but effective design is of paramount importance to the success of any show. Particularly when working with a very limited budget, it is essential to get maximum value for each buck. And as we shall see, with a little imagination and ingenuity, it is possible to create minor miracles to do just that.

Considerations in design

Television settings have to satisfy several requirements:

1 *Artistically*, settings must be appropriate to the occasion – the subject and the production's purpose.
2 *Staging mechanics* must be practical for the studio – its dimensions, facilities, and the production budget.
3 *Design* should provide suitable shot opportunities – operational freedom for sound, cameras, lighting, etc.
4 *The TV camera's characteristics* will influence the tones, colors, contrasts, and finish of settings.

Basic organization

Staging begins with the demands of the script and the aspirations of the director. Much depends on how effectively these can be related to the facilities, time, and budget available. As with all craftsmanship in television, optimum results come from a blend of imaginative perception and down-to-earth practical planning. TV set designers achieve minor miracles in making ingenious use and re-use of materials.

Planning begins with discussions between the director and the set designer. Using sketches, scale plans, and elevations, production concepts are transformed into the practicalities of man hours, costing, materials . . . For larger productions, there is close collaboration with various specialists, who consider:

Shot opportunities for cameras, performer action, and moves; the various lighting, audio pick-up, camera treatment, costumes, make-up and technical requirements.

In such an interdependent venture, teamwork is essential.

■ *The studio plan* The basis for much of the organization is the standard printed *studio plan*, showing the studio's permanent staging area with such features and facilities as exits, technical supplies, cycloramas, service and storage areas, etc. A typical metric scale of 1:50, i.e. 2 cm = 1 m, is replacing the widely used ¼ in = 1 ft scale.

■ *The staging plan (floor plan, ground plan, setting plan)* A rough plan of the staging layout usually begins with drawing potential scale outlines of settings, including their main features – windows, doors, stairways. By moving small tracing overlays around the

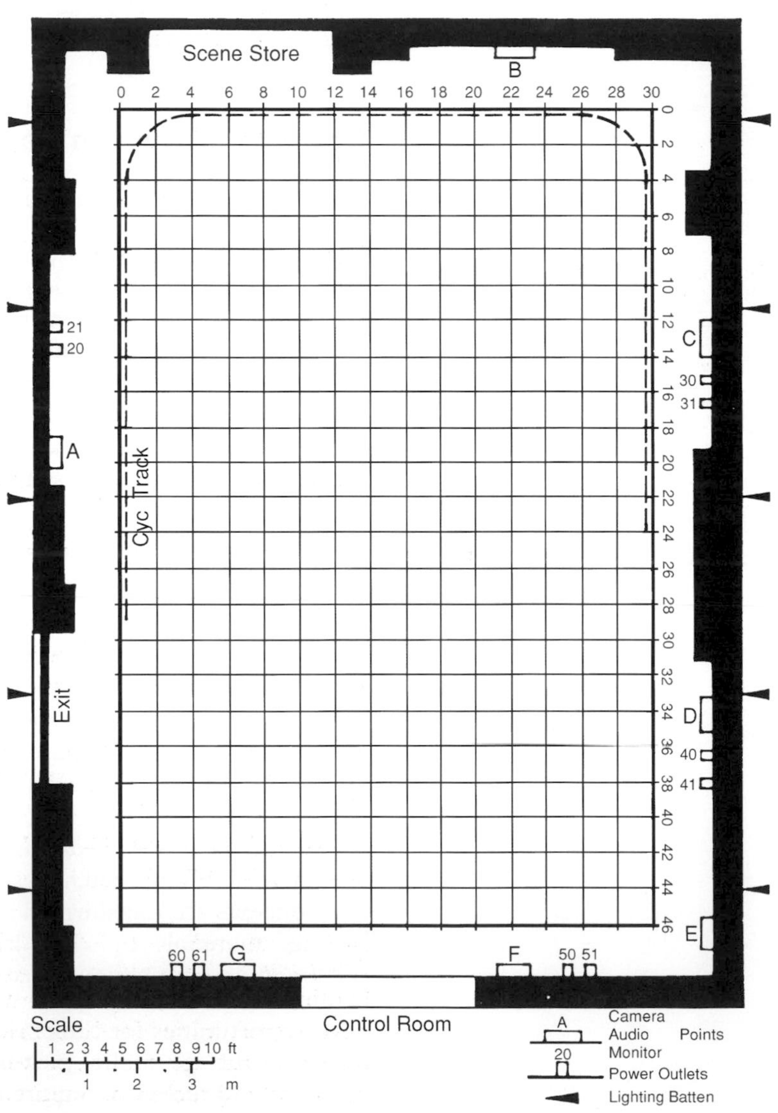

Fig. 10.1 part 1 Staging – studio plan

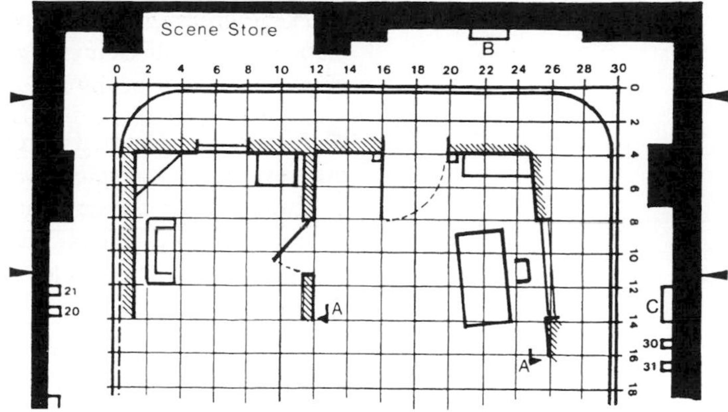

Fig. 10.1 part 2 Staging – staging plan

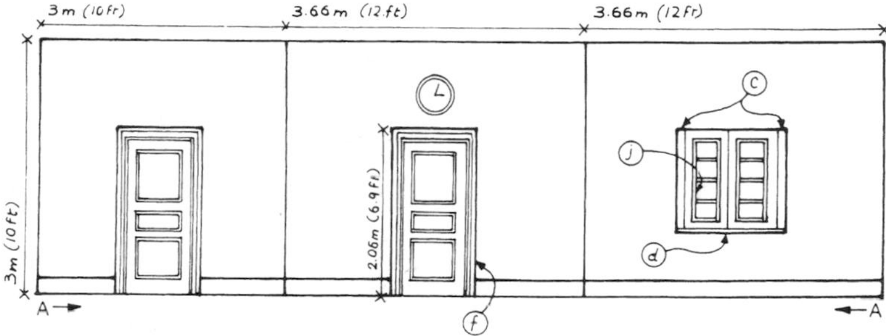

Fig. 10.1 part 3 Staging – elevations

studio plan you can make best use of available space, while ensuring maximum opportunities for cameras, sound booms, and lighting.

Standardized symbols representing scenic units, furniture, etc. are added until you have a mutually accepted 'bird's-eye view' of the entire staging area. Copies of a final plot are distributed to the production director, technical and lighting directors, scenic construction workshops, and anyone else who needs one.

■ *Camera plan (production plan)* The importance of the staging plan becomes clearer when you bear in mind that in a closely planned complex production it is used by the director to evaluate or calculate the shots and devise a *camera plan* showing principal camera positions (Chapter 18).

■ *Lighting plot* The lighting director overlays *the studio lighting transparency* (showing battens/barrels, lighting suspension points, lighting grid, rails, supply points, etc.), onto the staging plan. The next step, as we saw in the previous chapter, is to assess the lighting treatment and the types of equipment that will be needed, bearing in mind the production mechanics involved.

■ *Furniture/props plot* A series of larger-scale plans may show the disposition of all *set dressing* (furniture, drapes, etc.) and the main *props* listed on a props list.

■ *Elevations* Devised concurrently with the staging plan and to the same scale, *elevations* provide a scale side-view of surface detail, treatment, and dimensions of all vertical scenic planes (walls, doors, windows, pillars, etc.). These not only guide construction and decoration but help us to imagine the three-dimensional staging in the studio.

If cut out from thin card, these elevations can be attached to a staging plan to create a simple *scale model.* This is particularly useful in complicated situations, to aid visualization of the final scene (for director, performers, specialists, staging crew). A miniature viewfinder will even show shots obtainable from particular camera positions.

Basic scenic forms

Staging is styled to suit each production's particular needs.

- *Neutral settings* offer the simplest and most economical backgrounds. Non-associative, they concentrate the audience's attention on the subjects and the action. An open cyclorama or an arrangement of flats is generally used; simply decorated perhaps with surface designs, graphics, or lighting treatment.
- *Realistic settings* may represent a certain type of location (atmospheric realism), an actual place (replica), or through selected details conjure up a naturalistic impression (symbolic realism).
- *Decorative staging* takes several stylized forms, including abstraction, silhouette, limbo, cameo, in which design is predominantly arranged to delight the eye and stimulate the imagination.

Most studio settings are built from an assembly of prefabricated scenic units. Carefully positioned to the staging plan (using wall/ceiling/floor 'footage' marks), they are fastened together and supported where necessary and subsequently dressed or decorated to create the total scenic effect.

Sectionalized units make transport, *setting up* (erection), *striking* (dismantling), and storage much easier. Moreover, most of the component parts have been designed to be redecorated and reused over again, in different combinations, for many productions – as *stock units.*

The flat

Most scenic flats are made from fireproof burlap (hessian), plywood, or prepared boarding (fiberboard, hardboard) on wooden

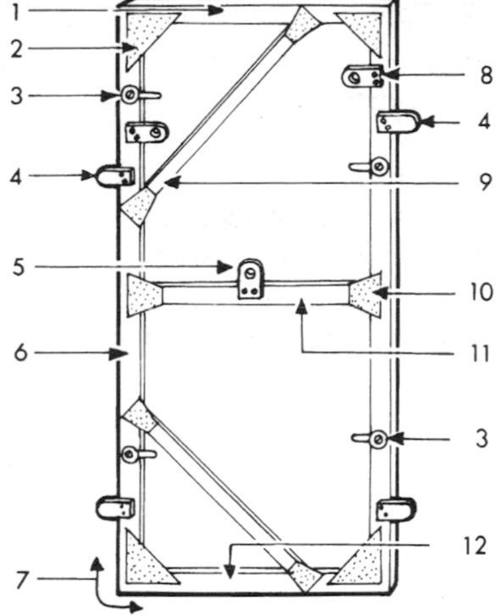

Fig. 10.2 part 1 Flat construction

1 Top rail.
2 Corner block.
3 Lash cleat.
4 Stop cleat (to align flats).
5 Brace cleat (brace eye).
6 Stile.
7 Frame (1 × 3 in pine)
8 Lash eye.
9 Diagonal brace (corner brace).
10 Keystone.
11 Toggle (stretcher).
12 Bottom rail.

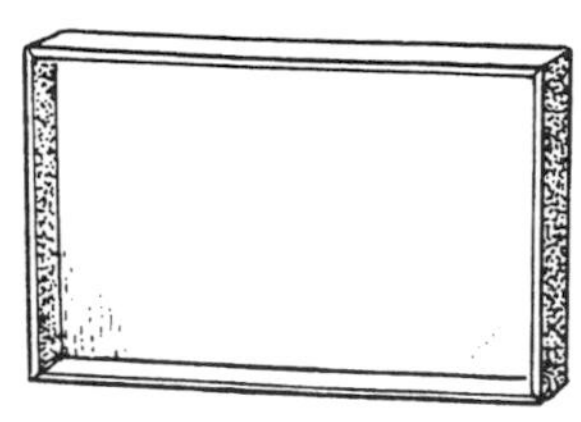

Fig. 10.2 part 2 The box flat
A simple board frame structure that may be bottom weighted or braced. Bulkier and heavier than standard flats, but provides a large flat surface (e.g. for window backings).

frames. Although canvas flats are lightweight, they are flimsy and lack rigidity. While 3.0–3.6 m (10–12 ft) high units are universal in larger studios, 2.5–3.0 m (8–10 ft) are more convenient in smaller studios where the camera is less likely to *overshoot (shoot off)* in longer shots. Widths from 0.15–3.6 m (6 in–12 ft) are used, the commonest being 1.2–1.8 m (4–6 ft).

Flattage can rise above 3.6 m (12 ft) but handling and safety problems increase. Tall flats are avoided where possible, for as lamps are forced upward to keep them out of shot their steeper angles cause coarser portraiture.

Surface treatments are legion. Cheapest are distemper or casein-prepared paints. Wall coverings (paper, vinyl) provide an extensive selection of patterns, tones, and textures. Finally, you can attach such materials as fabric or carpeting; or build up surfaces in relief with stuck-on forms or thin plastic-sheet mouldings.

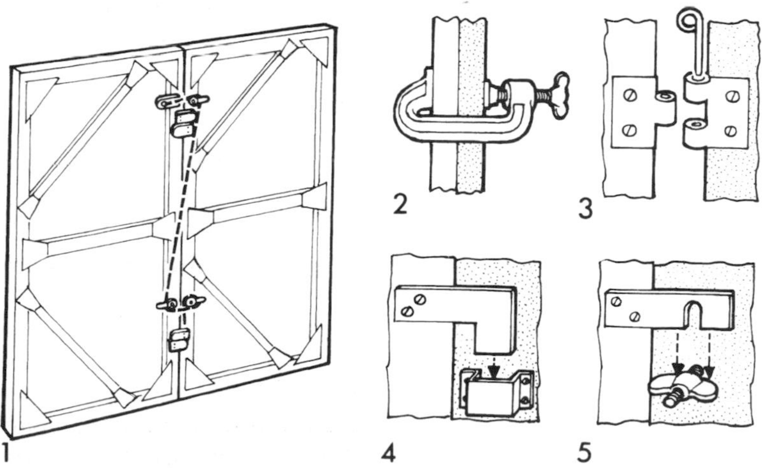

Fig. 10.3 part 1 Setting flats – method of joining

1 Scenic flats lashed together by line (sash cord).
2 Adjustable cramp/clamp butts firmly together.
3 Pin hinge.
4 L-plate clip.
5 Securing nut (wing-nut).

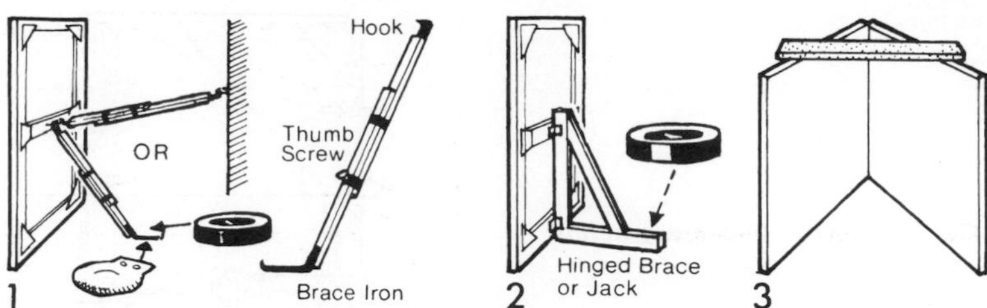

Fig. 10.3 part 2 Setting flats – supports
1 The flat can be supported by extendible stage-brace (held firm with a stage-weight or sandbag), or braced to studio wall plate.
2 A triangular wooden jack (French brace) can be hinged or hooked onto flat rail (preferably bottom weighted).
3 Top bracing struts may secure unsupported settings. Suspension lines or bottom weighting are alternative arrangements.

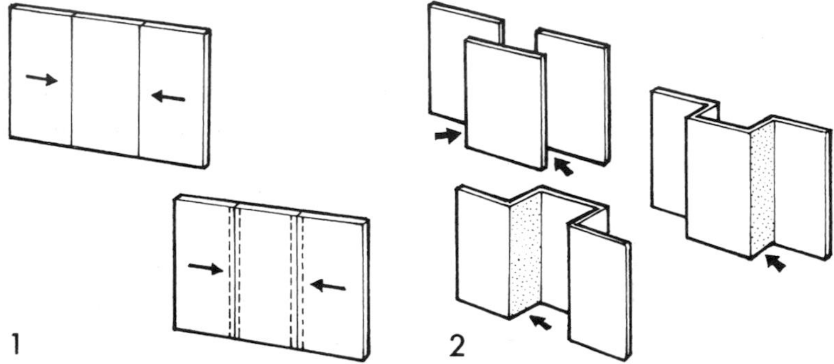

Fig. 10.3 part 3 Setting flats – disguising joins
1 When flats are set edge-to-edge, their joins show. But joins may be covered with pasted-on paper or fabric (stripping), although this prevents later re-angling. Joins still remain visible in plain light surfaces.
2 Where possible breaks or returns are introduced, disguising joins, providing a more interesting effect, and improving acoustics.

Most flats are single-sided (*single-clad*), but are made *double-clad* when you need to shoot them from either side. Curved flats are used for some applications (*sweeps*).

■ *Box flat* The *box flat* takes a different form. Its simple board frame is faced with canvas, plywood, or 3 mm (⅛ in.) masonite, and used mainly for large window backings.

Set pieces (built pieces, solid pieces, rigid units)

■ *Architectural units* Although one can construct scenery complete with features such as doors, fireplaces, niches, the resulting units tend to be heavy, bulky, and less adaptable. So instead, it is often more practicable to use profile flats (frames), into which these details, made in the form of plugs (shells), can be bolted

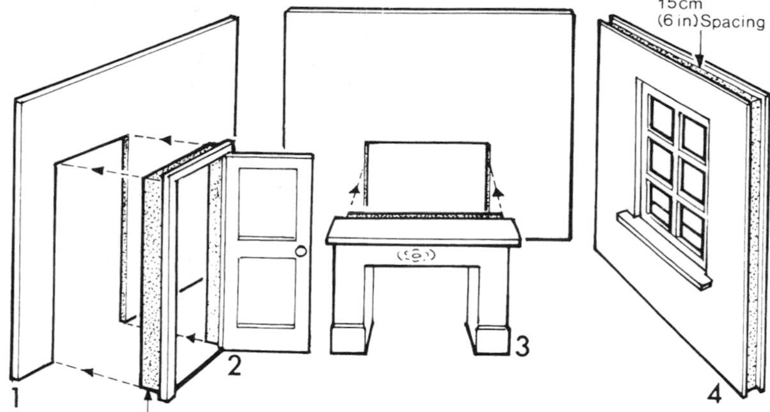

Fig. 10.4 Architectural units
Stock architectural features can be combined.

1 Contoured flat or frame (an example of a single-sided unit – viewable on one face only).
2 Door plug.
3 Fire-place plug.
4 Window unit (an example of a double-clad unit – viewable on both faces).

(Figure 10.4). Where features such as room doors, closet/cupboard doors are non-practical (i.e. unused), they can even be made in dummy form, and simply attached to the surface of a standard flat.

■ *Free-standing units* A second, more extensive group of solid pieces provides not only such architectural features as stairways and arches but structures for general production applications such as *parallels (rostra, risers)* to create platforms or raised areas.

Profile pieces (cut-outs)

These vertical profiles of plywood, prepared board, etc. may be arranged either free-standing or attached to stock flats to modify their outline. Typical applications include:

1 Isolated decorative pieces – flat cut-out representations.
2 Wings – masking off the edges of an acting area.
3 Ground rows – concealing background-to-floor joins.
4 Scenic planes – representing a skyline, and the intermediate terrain.

Profile pieces can provide cheap, very effective substitutes for elaborate scenic arrangements; for as the camera moves, parallactic movement between these planes can create a surprisingly convincing three-dimensional effect.

Although they may not deceive the camera in closer shots, profile units can appear very realistic at a distance – especially if cut from photo blow-ups. When shot from an angle, though, their flatness may become obvious – although this seldom matters with decorative units.

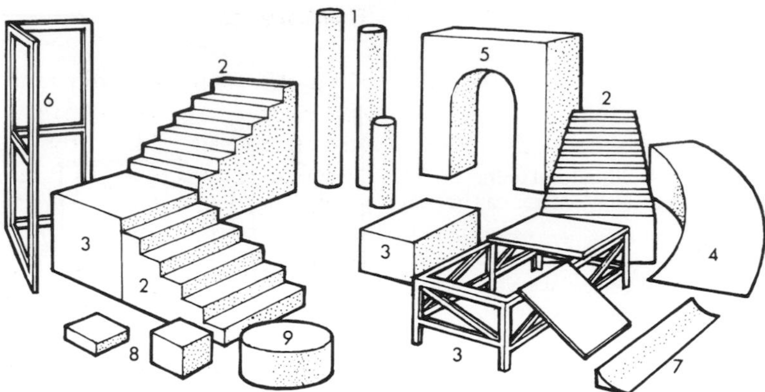

Fig. 10.5 Solid pieces/built pieces

1 *Pillars:* cylinders or half-shells of 0.15–0.6 m (0.5–2 ft) diameter and up to 4.5 m (15 ft) high.
2 *Staircases (stair units)*: groups of two or more treads, usually 0.15 m (6 in) risers, matching heights of stock parallels (rostra).
3 *Parallels (platforms, rostra, risers)* which are variously shaped level platforms on folding/dismantling frames with boarded-in sides.
4 *Ramp*: sloping plane surfaces.
5 *Arch.*
6 *Drape frame*: light framework in single or hinged units carrying draperies (otherwise suspended from batten or bar).
7 *Cove*: shallow sloping surface used to merge horizontal/vertical planes and hide cyc units.
8 *Step-box (riser block):* wooden shells from e.g. 0.15 m (6 in) to 0.6 m (2 ft) square. All-purpose unit that provides half-steps, display tables, for raising furniture, etc.
9 *Podium (drum).*

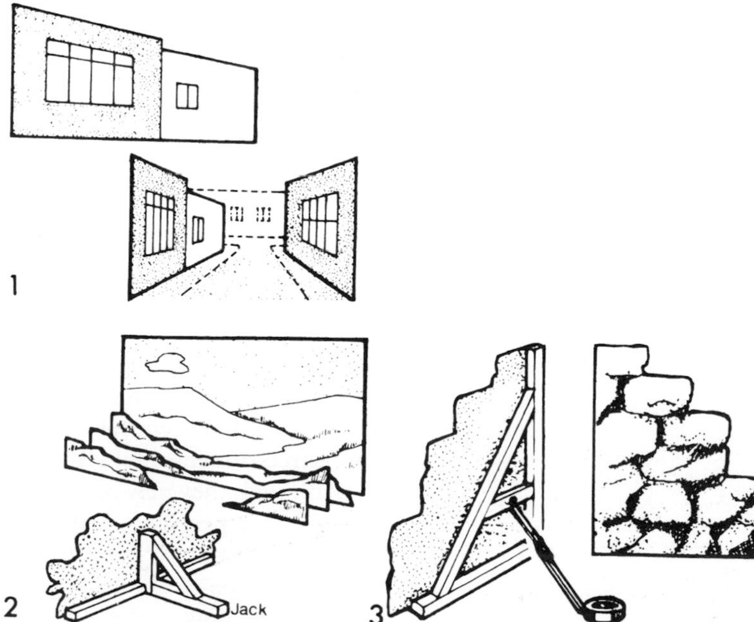

Fig. 10.6 Profiled pieces/cut-outs

1 Profiled flats painted in perspective, create a spatial illusion.
2 Profiled ground-rows suggest progressive planes.
3 Profiled flat supporting plastic-shell rock-face.

Cyclorama

Even the smallest studio makes full use of the cyclorama as a general-purpose background. The *cyc* (pronounced 'sike') is a suspended plain cloth; usually stretched taut by weights, battens, or tubular piping along its bottom edge where a totally wrinkle-free surface is required.

■ *Cyc track* The cyc is sometimes hung on straight or curved battens or scaffold tubing. But the most adaptable method is by gliders (runners) affixed to a permanent *cyc-track (cyc-rail)* round the staging area. Using this, the cyc can be repositioned, changed, and drawn back when not required. Sometimes a range of cyc tones is available for selection on parallel tracks.

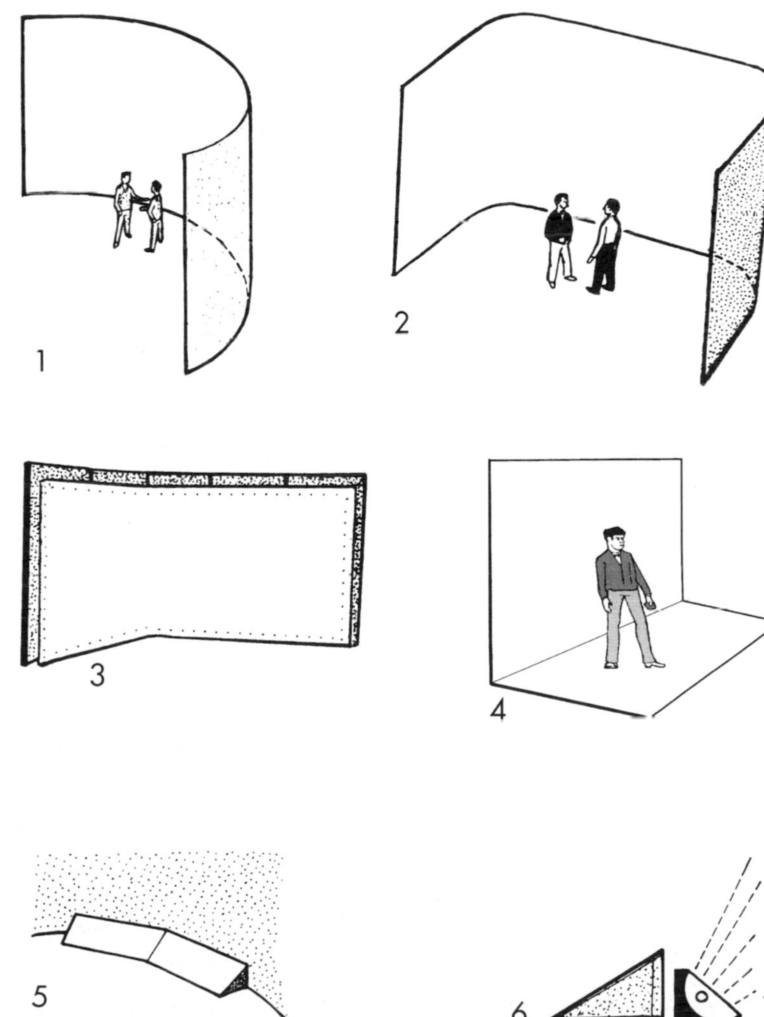

Fig. 10.7 The cyclorama

1 *Curved cyclorama.* A shallow C-shaped hung cloth background.
2 *Wraparound cyclorama.* A widely used form of cyc. Corners are gently curved, e.g. 2.7 m (9 ft) radius.
3 *Paper cyclorama.* A roll of background paper may be stapled to a run of flats, to form a continuous background.
4 *Backdrop of background paper,* used where space is insufficient for a full cyc.
5 *Merging coves/ground coves* can hide the join where the cyc meets the floor, and create a continuous plane.
6 *Cyc lighting* can be hidden behind a ground row.

■ *Materials* Various materials are used – including duck, canvas, filled gauze, shark's-tooth scrim, and occasionally velours. Usual colors and tones include 'white' (60 per cent reflectance), black, light gray, midgray, light blue, dark blue, and chroma-key blue. Although permanent (*board*) cycloramas are now seldom used, as they restrict staging areas and cause sound coloration, small shallow C-curved flats sometimes provide backings for windows.

■ *Adaptability* The plain light-tone cyc is extremely adaptable, for its smooth unbroken appearance can be considerably modified by lighting treatment. Its brightness and color can be changed; it can be shaded, or patterned, with projected shadows. With care, you can even attach very lightweight motifs to the cyc (double-sided adhesive tape, or pinned).

Backgrounds

Strictly speaking, any surface seen behind a subject is its *background*. Some people use the term *backing* synonymously, but that really refers to the planes beyond windows and other voids in the setting. These backings imply space and distance and prevent cameras from shooting off the set.

Neutral backgrounds

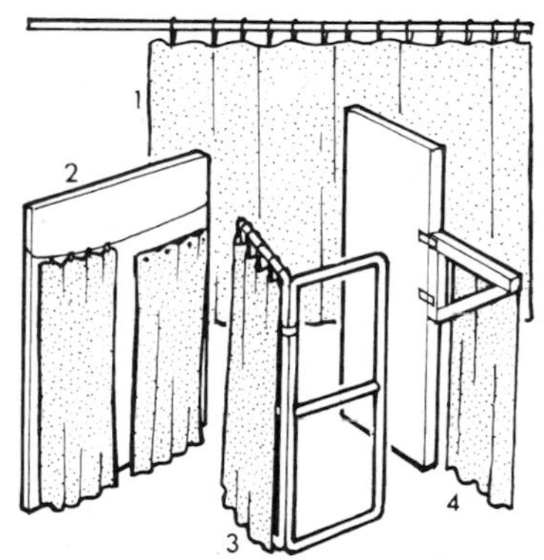

Fig. 10.8 Drapes
You can use drapes in many ways: to decorate a setting, to form parts of its structure, to provide the entire background. Drapes can be arranged:

1. Suspended from bars (battens).
2. Attached to a flat, or to a line hung across a flat.
3. Hung on a tubular *drape frame*.
4. Hung from a timber arm, hinged to the edge of a flat (*gallows arm*).

Neutral backgrounds are used wherever you want non-specific environments, e.g. for talks, *public (current) affairs* programs.

Because a setting is neutral it does not have to look plain and uninteresting; although to avoid distractions, any decorating is usually restrained. Surface texturing, uneven lighting (shading, dappling), decorative screens all have applications. Any drapes should avoid distinct patterning, for it easily becomes obtrusive and too recognizable for re-use.

Limbo (white) or *cameo* (black) backgrounds provide neutrality. Sustained viewing of either can be tiring, and similar subject or costume tones can inadvertently merge with them. The resultant effect easily vacillates between naturalism, fantasy, and abstraction. Essential furnishings, props, and set pieces (doorways, windows) can be set up in front of the background – either symbolically or to form 'open settings'.

The somber gloom of black backgrounds can be inappropriate for certain subjects, and on many TV receivers may reproduce as gray. Foreground subjects may look overlight against these tones. On the other hand, white backgrounds can appear ethereal and infinite, although subject tones may appear darkened.

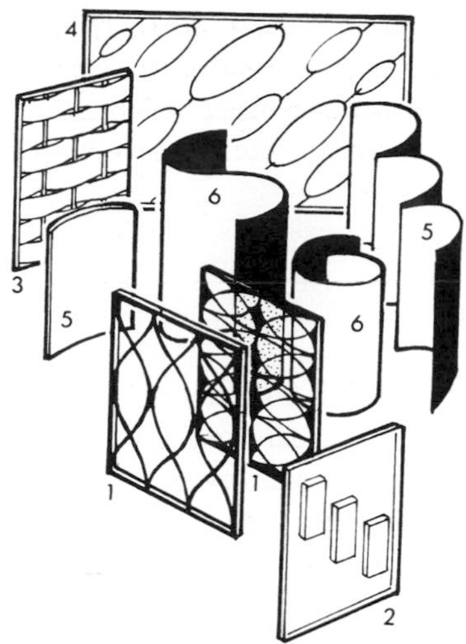

Fig. 10.9 Decorative screens
These take many forms. Stood or hung in front of a cyclorama, they provide a simple yet attractive background. Typical designs include:

1 Decorated screens of expanded metal, wire mesh, perforated board.
2 Flats with contoured forms attached (e.g. of plastic shell).
3 Woven screens.
4 Open screens of stretched wire or cord, poles, slats, etc. They may be used to support motifs or profiled areas.
5 Curved flats (*sweeps*).
6 Flexible screens.

Pictorial backgrounds

Because it is difficult to distinguish in the two-dimensional TV picture between distant objects that are flat and those that are solid, you can simulate three-dimensional effects convincingly using a flat pictorial background. Ideally, it would need to be free from blemishes, evenly lit, and show no spurious shadows; its perspective, proportions, tones, etc. should match the foreground scene; and it should be shot straight-on. In practice, you will find that even quite blatant discrepancies can still be very convincing on camera.

■ *Painted cloths (backdrops, backcloths, scenic cloths, canvas drops)* Ranging from pure vaudeville to near-photographic masterpieces of scenic art, these large painted sheets are used primarily as window backings. Of canvas or twill, painted cloths are normally hung on battens or pipes, or on wooden frames. In storage, a cloth may be rolled around the pole that weights its lower edge, or *flown* (hung high above the ground).

When used as backings, you may reduce a 'painted look' and suggest distance (the detail loss of *aerial perspective*) by introducing a light overall spatter or spray. Alternatively, you can stretch a black or white scrim over windows to soften the effect.

■ *Photographic enlargements (photomurals, photo blow-ups)* Although expensive, enlarged photographs represent the ultimate realism obtainable from studio pictorial backgrounds. Enlargements are made on sections of photosensitized paper stuck onto a flat, or a canvas support.

Color is normally underplayed. Monochrome versions carefully colored with aniline dyes are much cheaper, and can look much more realistic on camera than high-quality color photographs.

A *photographic backdrop* of a location can prove to be a very worthwhile stock item. It can be adapted and re-used by retouching or applying stick-on overlays. It can be hung so that different sections of it are visible on each occasion. Prominent parts may often be obscured by strategically positioning a bush, a wall, or similar object.

You can also use photo-enlargements to provide decorative features within a setting; as panels that are stood or hung within it.

■ *Projected backgrounds* Two systems are used: *rear projection (back projection. BP)* in which a still or moving background picture is projected onto the rear of a translucent screen situated behind the action; *reflex* or *front projection* in which the image is *projected along the lens* axis, onto a special beaded screen (see Chapter 21).

■ *Electronically inserted backgrounds (chroma-key, CSO)* By special electronic switching circuits, foreground subjects can be inserted into the background picture from any other video source (photograph, drawing, miniature, TV camera, etc.) (see Chapter 21).

Surface detail and contouring

■ *Painted detail* Because you can suggest solidity by suitable drawing and shading it is possible to create an illusion of brickwork, paneling, molding, etc. by brush alone. Realism depends on the scenic artist's skill, how closely the camera sees the effect, and whether oblique viewpoints or cast shadows reveal the true contours.

■ *Wallpapers* Various photographic wallpapers of brickwork, stonework, wood graining, are easily struck to flattage – retouched or sprayed over where necessary.

■ *Molded pieces* Ingenious lightweight imitations now exist for a diversity of subjects. Statuary, architectural features (beams, moldings), tree trunks, brickwork, roofing tiles, cobbled paving . . . are recreated with such conviction that they bear scrutiny – even up to fingernail scratching distance.

Earlier techniques with papier mâché and plaster or canvas on wire mesh have been largely superseded by fiber glass, molded rubber, and plastic forms. Solid items such as statues and rocks may be hand-carved by hot-wire cutters from lightweight styrofoam (expanded polystyrene foam blocks).

Most outstanding of all are the molded surfaces of thin plastic sheets (PVC). These are vacuum formed, up to about 2.5 × 1.25 m (8 × 4 ft) to produce realistic contouring shells depicting carved panels, rock face, stonework, brickwork, tiling, mullioned windows, as well as various wall furnishings (escutcheons, pistols, fish). These versatile panels are simply cut out, stapled onto stock scenic units, and painted. They have the merits of being low-cost, featherweight, adaptable. But they must be handled with care, to avoid compression damage.

Floor treatment

The studio floor's matte mid-tone surface serves as a neutral ground for most productions. But it can also provide some interesting staging opportunities.

■ *Painting* Temporary floor treatment can be applied, using special water-soluble paints, either to change the overall tone or

Table 10.1 Surface finish

	Method	*Purpose*
Flat lay-in	Even-toned surface painting.	Textureless finish.
Dry-brush work	Overpainting a flat tone with a nearly dry brush. Sparse brush marks across the ground color.	Suggests metal, wood, stone, fabric.
Stippling	Series of small close dots of color on a different ground tone: using coarse brush, sponge cloth, wrinkled paper.	Suggests stone, cement, earth.
Puddling	Wet colors flowed together, intermixed for random variations.	Suggests aging plaster, earth.
Daubing	Dabs of color with rolled rag, patted irregularly over a surface.	Varying density of tone.
Scumbling	Translucent coating, usually of darker tone over a lighter one.	Suggests surface undulations.
Glaze	Transparent dry-brush application of lighter tone.	Suggests highlight sheen.
Scuffing (dragging)	Skimming surface with brush, leaving textural depressions untouched.	Texturing a plain surface.
Wash	Thin coating of lighter or darker tone over background body color.	Suggests highlights or shadows.
Roughcast	Sprinkling material (sawdust, sand) irregularly onto freshly painted surface.	Random changes in tone or texture.
Spattering (dottling)	Mottling with random brush-thrown splashes.	Textural effect.
Stenciling	Applications of decorative motifs by stencils or rollers.	Decoration.

decorate the floor with realistic effects (floorboards, paving) or ornamental designs. Whether stenciled, hand-painted, or roller-printed, the treatment can be washed off after use. This means strictly avoiding spilled liquids for they destroy the treatment and make it treacherously slippery and sticky. Temporary adhesive floor tapes can simplify or augment painted designs.

Painted floors do not frustrate dolly movements as carpets and floor cloths can; but they are liable to become dirtied. Black floors all too readily show wheel and foot marks.

Where facilities allow, lighting may provide projected floor patterns; but these are very easily diluted by other lighting treatment.

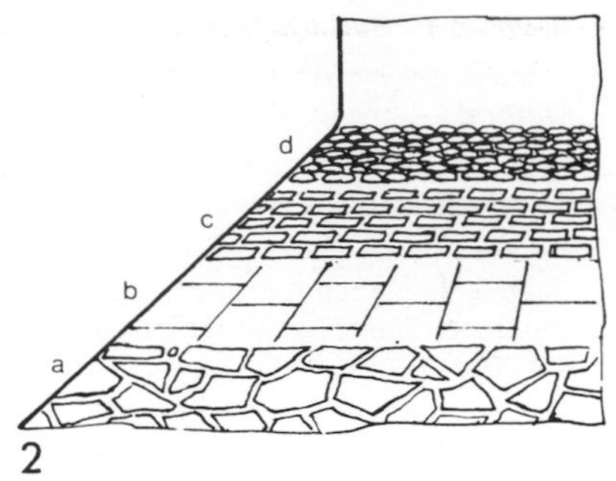

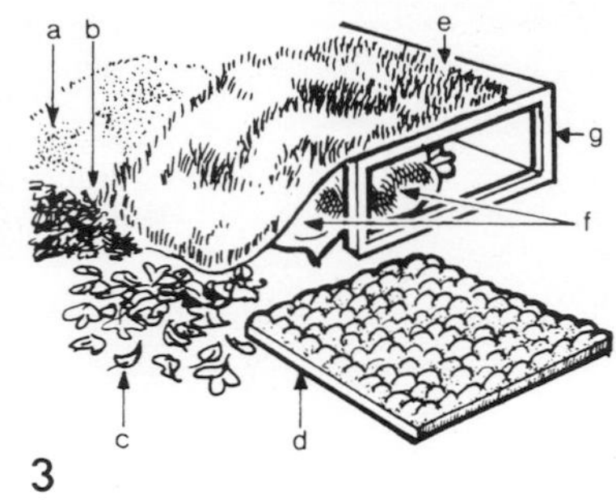

Fig. 10.10 Floor treatment

1 The studio floor may be treated decoratively (painted, stenciled, stuck-on designs).

2 Painting simulates surfaces economically, leaving them flat for camera moves: (a) crazy paving; (b) paving slabs; (c) pavé bricks; (d) cobbles.

3 The floor surface can be covered by; (a) sawdust; (b) scattered peat; (c) dead leaves; (d) sheets of rubber/plastic cobbles, brickwork, etc.; (e) grass matting (surface contours changed by (f) sawdust sacks, or (g) sack-filled platforms).

■ *Scattering* Scattering innocuous materials much as peat, sawdust, leaves, cork chips, bark transforms a surface rapidly for naturalistic effects. However, material tends to stray around the studio (particularly when using wind machines) and must be confined. Avoid salt or sand – they foul up equipment!

■ *Floor coverings* The floor can be decorated by covering it with a *floor cloth* made of heavy duck, canvas, or tarpaulin (plain or prepainted); photographic or patterned papers; or panels of prepared board. Thin materials may tear or ruck up under action or camera movements. Bulky materials such as turf or carpets can impede cameras.

■ *Adhesive patterns* Adhesive colored tapes and designs in plastic sheeting can be stuck to the studio floor in decorative patterns. They wear reasonably well, and are easily removed after the production.

Basic forms of staging

Most TV staging follows a number of regular forms.

1 Scenic background

Here the action takes place in front of a flat background. This may be anything from a single decorated scenic flat or a painted cloth to a chroma-key inserted background. It may be augmented by a few foreground items or scenic pieces.

Fig. 10.11 Basic forms of staging
Scenic background. A single plain or decorated flat, a photo blow-up, or a painted scene provides sufficient background for limited action (particularly when chroma key inserted).

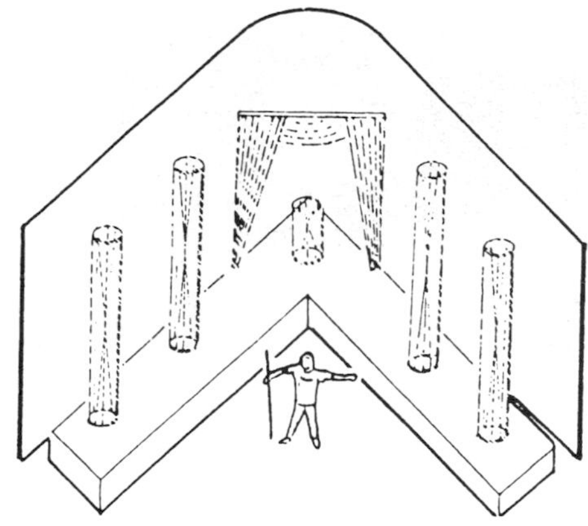

Area staging. Area staging is essential for broad action and widespread movement. Emphasis is on pattern and decorative effect.

Open sets. Economical and flexible, open settings are adaptable for stylistic and realistic situations.

Desk set-ups. Modular units or custom-built desks are adaptable to many regular show formats.

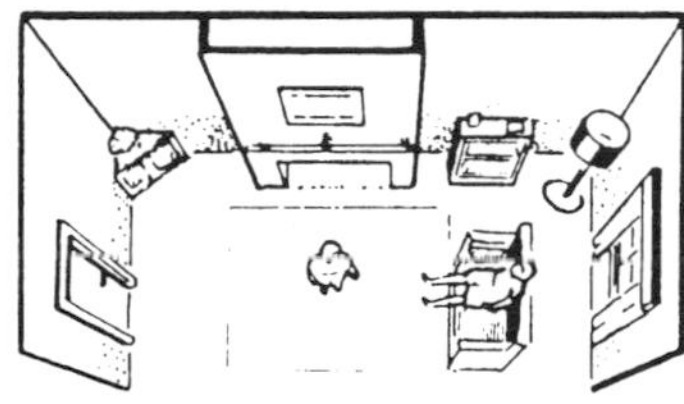

Box sets. The traditional three-sided set convincingly simulates rooms while providing maximum operational flexibility.

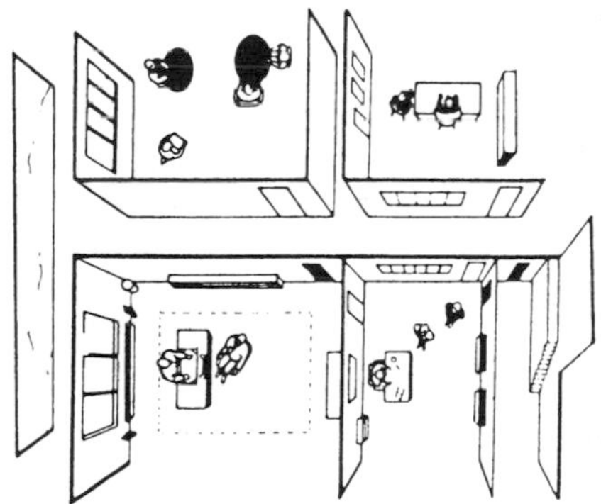

Composite settings. A series of interconnected or conjoining sets makes maximum use of the staging area.

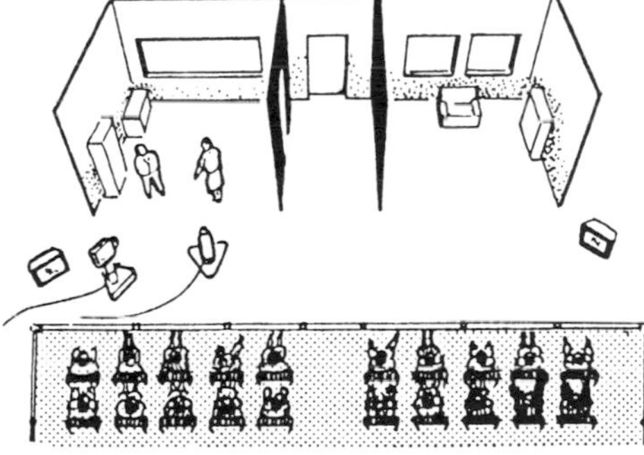

Audience shows. Sets are arranged to give the audience an optimum view of the action. The audience may be seen on camera or heard only as reactive background responses.

Two-tier staging. Very occasionally used where floor-level staging or subterfuges cannot be used. Requires well-designed scaffold framework for upper storey. Necessarily inhibits lighting, sound, and camerawork within the ground-floor setting.

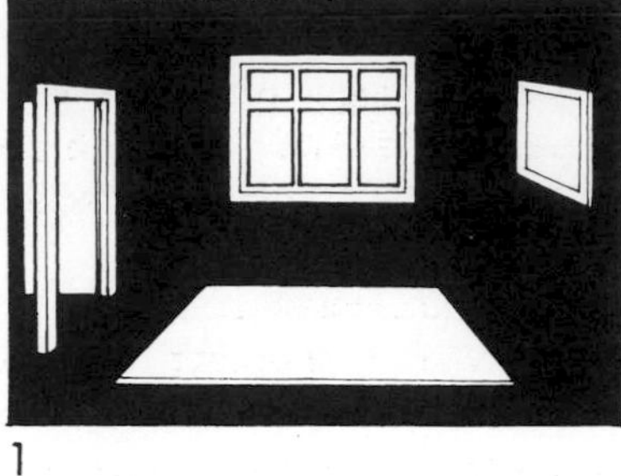

1

2 3

Fig. 10.12 Skeletal settings
This form of scenic treatment is essentially decorative (unlike *open sets* that usually simulate a real environment). Isolated scenic elements are set up in front of an open cyc:

1 To create a symbolically realistic effect.
2 Decorative symbolism.
3 Abstract patterns.

Extremely economical, the flat scenic background can be quite sufficient for fairly limited action. It is particularly useful in a small studio, where with a little ingenuity it can even be used to suggest extensive locations.

For example, suppose a person leaves their house and walks along a street. In a brief sequence, this could be shot as follows:

Person facing a street door flat, turns and walks towards the camera . . . (*STOP RECORDING*)
CUT to new shot Large brick flat with poster. They walk through the shot right to left . . . (*STOP RECORDING*)
CUT to new shot Same large brick flat (remove poster, insert lamp pole, leaf shadow on wall). They walk through the shot right to left . . . (*STOP RECORDING*)

Edited together, the few seconds of action are sufficient to create the 'environment' with just a couple of flats.

2 Area staging

This is the approach needed when presenting widespread action such as ballet, choirs, orchestras, bands, etc. To provide maximum space, area staging is usually based on the open cyclorama. In front of it are positioned a series of scenic units (e.g. pillars, arches, raised areas), hung screens, etc. to suit the occasion, without impeding the action.

Emphasis is usually on overall decorative effect, and, as we shall see, the cyclorama gives considerable scope for all manner of lighting treatment using light and shade, color, and projected patterns that can be changed at the flick of a switch.

3 Open sets

Basically, the open set simply consists of pieces of furniture or scenic units, set up in front of an open cyc. Yet on the screen the effect is remarkably convincing, and suggests a complete unified setting.

The result can be stylized or realistic, and against the dark cyc it can be hard to tell that cameras are not shooting a more conventional set. This low-cost arrangement is simple, extremely flexible, easy to stage, and allows cameras considerable freedom.

4 Desk set-ups

A wide range of productions use desk set-ups in one form or another as the central point for the action. As well as the newscaster's regular desk, we have desks used in discussion panels, quiz games, debates, demonstrations, displays, etc. The background to the action may be a regular three-walled box set; but a cyclorama is often used, augmented perhaps with a series of free-standing decorated flats.

The desks or benches used in these productions are usually demountable *modular* units. These consist of a metal or wooden framework to which decorative panels of plywood, prepared board, or plastic sheeting are attached.

5 Box sets (closed sets)

These are the traditional three-walled open-fronted arrangements used for many realistic room settings. It is not necessary to actually have *four* walls to an 'interior' setting to convey a convincing impression of completeness. You can even build various parts of a typical room around the studio, and, by careful intercutting, imply that they are part of the same room!

6 Composites

Here, instead of breaking an environment down into a series of separate settings the *composite* stages them interconnected as they would be in reality; part of a schoolhouse perhaps, with schoolroom and adjoining corridors, office, schoolyard. Where the camera *moves around* within this composite, passing from one section to another, the subjective effect can be completely realistic.

Most separate settings have a certain amount of wasted space around them, taken up with scenic supports (braces, jacks), through-ways, lamps, etc. By joining adjacent settings together as a composite, one can save the studio floor space that would normally be lost between them.

7 Audience shows

In this familiar situation a studio audience, on tiered seating faces a line of settings, a composite, an open set, or area staging. They have hung picture monitors and loudspeakers enabling them to follow the production while watching the floor mechanics.

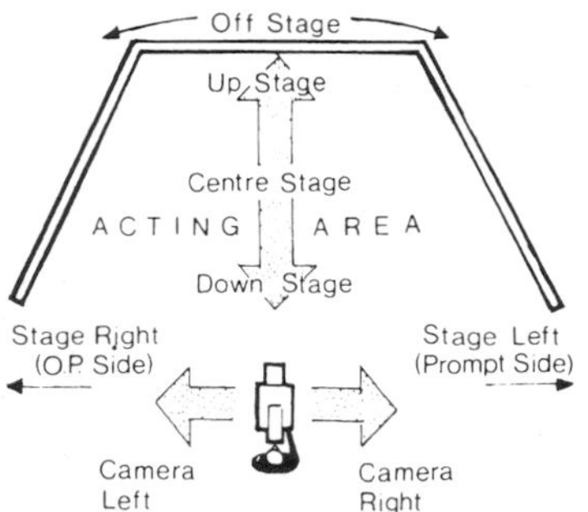

Fig. 10.13 The staging area
Locations are normally described in relation to a given camera's viewpoint.

8 Two-tier staging

Sometimes the story line calls for action to move upstairs or downstairs. Instead of actually building one set above another, it is far more convenient, and a lot cheaper, to 'cheat' the situation. You create the impression by intercutting between two sets at floor level.

Where the ceiling height of the studio permits, and two-tier staging is unavoidable, scenic construction can become a major project, for substantial scaffolding is usually necessary to support the upper floor with its scenery, furniture, performers, and cameras.

9 Enclosed sets

Another studio staging treatment that is avoided where possible. Here the action takes place within a complete four-sided room.

An actual four-walled room can be very restrictive to shoot, for the camera has difficulty in getting far enough away from subjects to provide wider (longer) shots. This occurs even when using wide-angle lenses or shooting in through doors or windows. Also, where several cameras are being used, they are liable to get in each other's shots if space is very restricted. On location, you just have to make the best of circumstances.

Where four walls are essential in a studio setting you may use intermittent videotaping to move in, or strike walls to shoot each viewpoint. Or you can actually build a complete four-walled set; arranging to raise, hinge, slide *wild walls* out when needed to give access to cameras and booms. In these situations lighting may become a compromise.

It may be simpler to provide peepholes for cameras – through doors, windows, fireplaces; *camera traps* as hinged wall flaps, e.g. behind pictures or camera-concealing drapes. When shooting a four-walled set you must particularly guard against *frame jumps* or disorientation by inadvertently cutting over the *imaginary* (*action*) *line*.

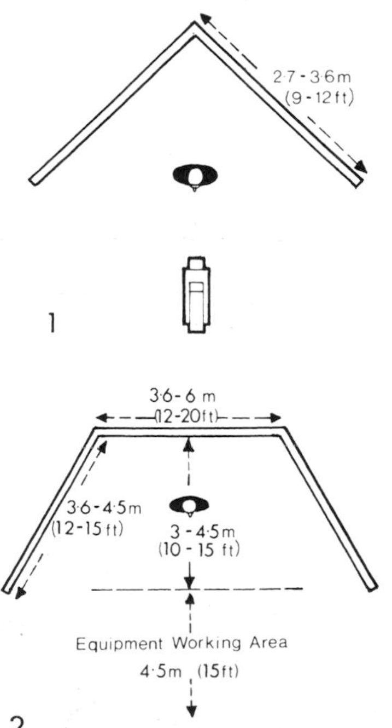

Fig. 10.14 Typical sizes of settings
1 *Two-fold set* – 'bookwing, book flat'.
2 *Three-fold set* – 'box set'.

Size and shape of sets

Space and budget restrictions usually prevent you from building sets much larger than they need be. Instead, you can *suggest* space by scenic treatment. Where spacious effects are required, wide-

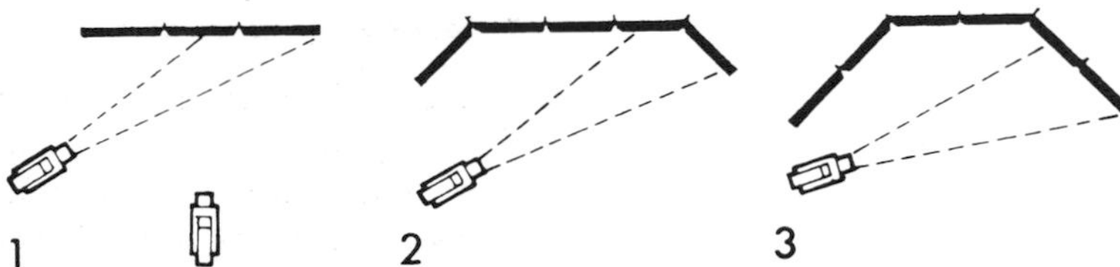

Fig. 10.15 part 1 Proportions of settings – flat backgrounds
On flat backgrounds cross shots shoot-off easily.

1 The set lacks depth and solidity, but occupies little room (can be piled or nested).
2 Slightly improved, but setting looks disproportionately wide in cross-shots.
3 Very satisfactory proportions for general use.

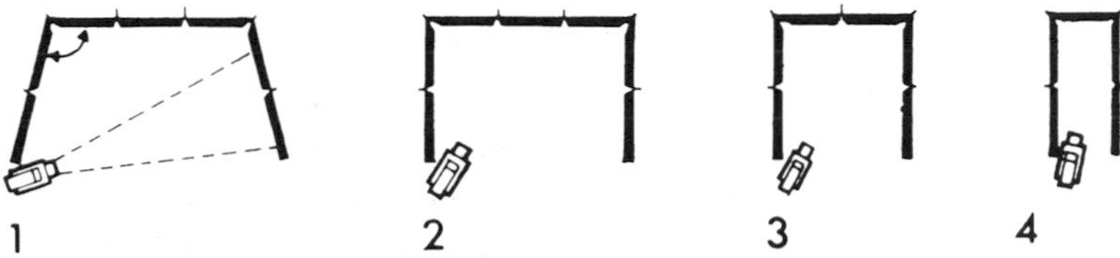

Fig. 10.15 part 2 Proportions of settings – walls
1 Walls may be splayed slightly to improve camera access.
2 Right angled walls may restrict camera movement, but prevent exaggerated room-size in cross-shots.
3,4 As sets narrow, little deviation from straight-on shooting is possible. Sound pickup may be 'boxy' and lighting tends to be steep.

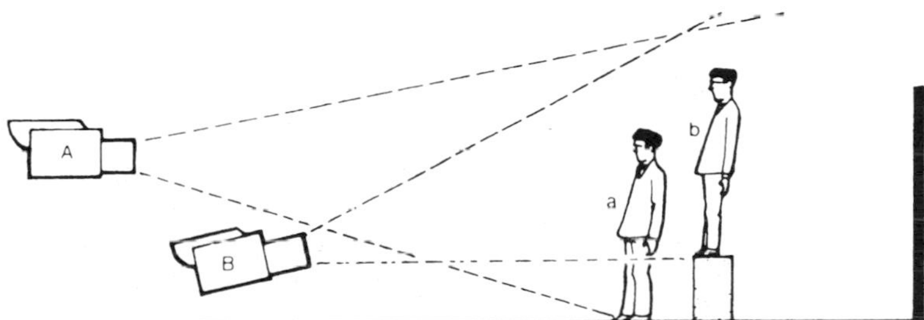

Fig. 10.15 part 3 Proportions of settings – staging height
The height necessary for staging depends on the longest shot to be taken (A), the lowest camera height (B), and the height of the subject (e.g. action on a staircase). A 3 m (10 ft) high flat is adequate for general use, a 3.6 m (12 ft) one being needed for larger settings. High backgrounds should be avoided to prevent steep lighting.

Fig. 10.16 Overshoot (Shooting off)
(1) Cameras can easily shoot past the edges of a set, and see the studio beyond. Solutions include (2) modifying the shot; (3) extending the set; (4) introducing appropriate masking pieces to prevent shoot-off (e.g. screen, wall, drapes).

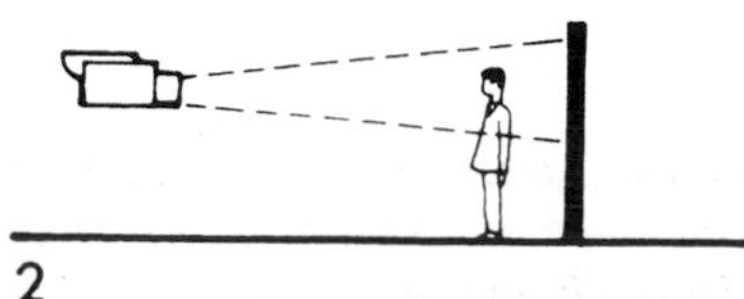

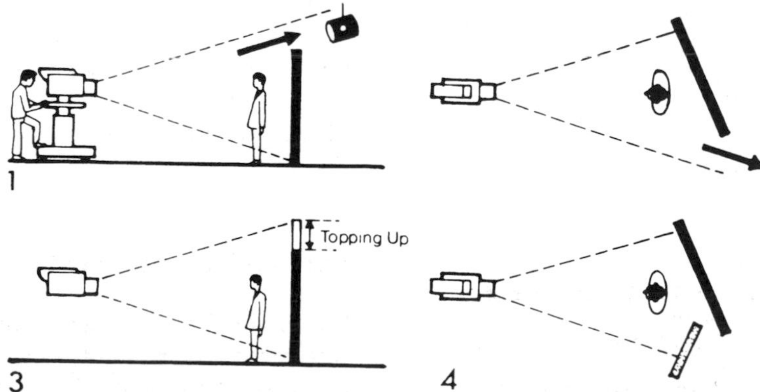

angle lenses can exaggerate distance, so that even quite sawn-off versions appear impressive on camera. The kind and extent of action anticipated will influence set sizes. The smaller the setting, the more restricted will the camera and lighting treatments normally be.

Overshoot (shooting off)

Wherever you inadvertently shoot past the confines of the setting the solution is self-evident: readjust the shot, or add *masking* (intermediate planes, a screen, border, wall extension, drapes, etc.). Anticipation during planning can prevent needless last-minute rearrangements.

Overshoot (shooting off) mostly arises when:

1 Cross-shooting on a shallow set.
2 Shooting downstage from an upstage viewpoint.
3 Windows or doors are inadequately backed.
4 Reverse-shooting into a set through a window or door.
5 Using low-angle shots.
6 Offstage areas seen in mirror/reflective surfaces.
7 Seeing through communicating openings (windows, arches) into adjacent sets.

Ceilings

Ceilings are introduced both to prevent cameras from shooting over sets into the studio beyond and to create environmental effects. However, unless carefully confined, a ceiling can frustrate the lighting treatment and produce boxy sound quality. Usually,

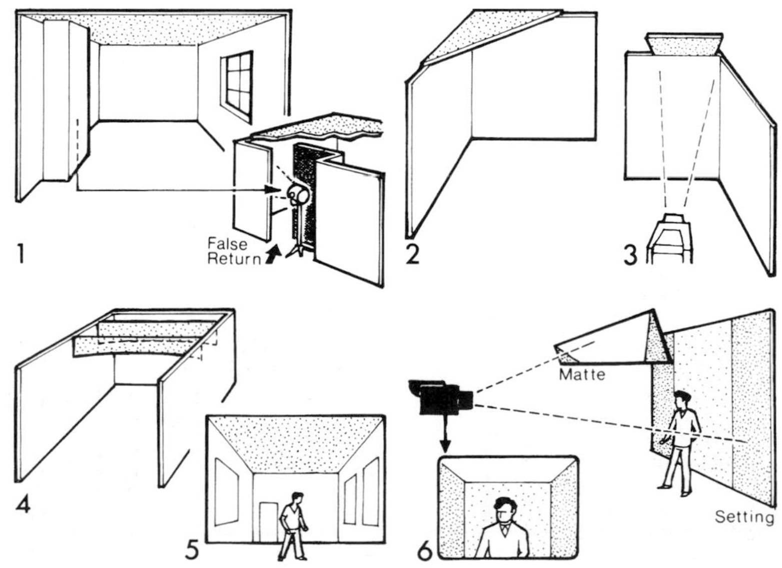

Fig. 10.17 Ceilings
1 Complete ceilings over settings are feasible, provided appropriate lighting can be introduced (through windows, doors, lamps behind furniture, false returns, etc.). Translucent ceilings can help but light may be hot or patchy.
2,3 Partial ceilings in corners or localized areas may prevent shoot-off.
4 Cutting pieces suggesting beams, vaulting; and suspended lamps (chandeliers) suggest a ceiling.
5 A scenic background (cloth, photo, chroma-key insert) may contain a ceiling.
6 A foreground camera matte simulates a ceiling on the studio setting.

the viewer simply assumes the ceiling, just as he does the non-existent fourth wall of a setting. Where ceilings are essential (in very low or long shots) and where high walls or a void (black drapes) would be unrealistic, various subterfuges are used.

Height and depth in floors

Fig. 10.18 Height and depth in floors
Covered platforms (parallels, rostra) can be used to build up floor levels where height or depth are required.

Vari-height platforms (parallels, rostra) are used where you need elevated floor areas. Any irregularities are built up with blocks, additional framework, tightly packed sawdust, or sandbags.

To create 'holes in the ground' (graves, bomb craters, trapdoors, wells) it is best to build up the overall floor level and leave the required 'hole'. This flooring must be suitably reinforced, and where heavy loads of scenery, people, or equipment are involved, tubular scaffold structures are essential. Where cameras are to move around on the elevated areas, surfaces must be level, flat, and non-skid.

To prevent unnaturally resonant flooring, platforms are best surfaced with felt, flexible urethane foam (foam-plastic sheeting), carpeting, or similar sound absorbants, plus internal packing where necessary.

Space economies

In most studios there comes a time when there is insufficient room for the sets you need in a production. Apart from cutting items, or restricting action to smaller sets, one can often improve matters by

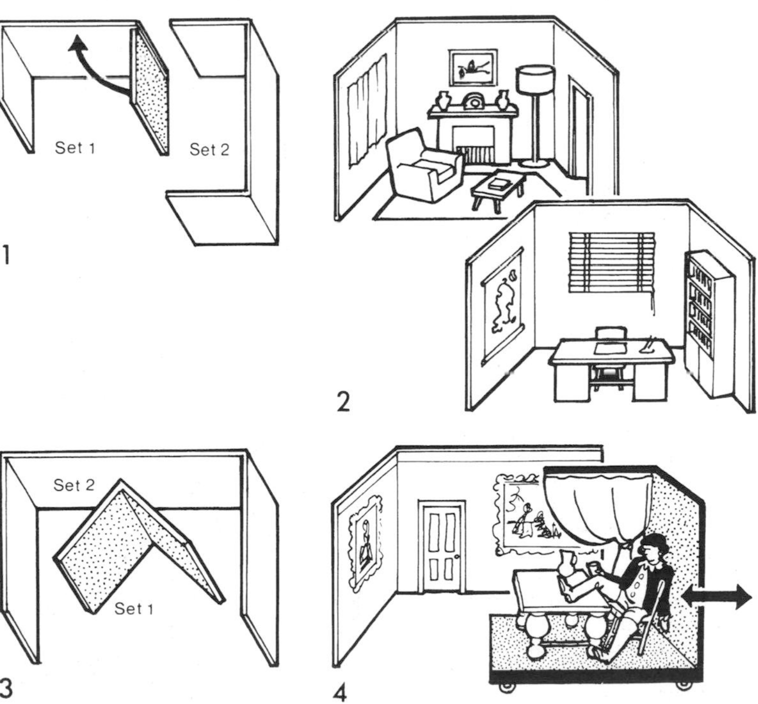

Fig. 10.19 Space economies
1 Where congestion is acute, flats may be moved aside for camera access (hinged folds, wheeled, man-handled, or hung).
2 Settings' appearance may be changed by re-vamping (retain structure, alter dressing), rearranging scenery, and changing lighting.
3 Nesting sets, where the inner unit is used and struck to give access to the second set.
4 Part of a setting can be built on a low wheeled platform (stage wagon, truck, float) and moved aside for access. Combined with chroma-key backgrounds (Chapter 21), considerable flexibility is possible.

imaginative mechanics such as those we see in Figure 10.19. They include move-aside flats, revamping sets, nesting sets, and wheel-away sections.

Alternatively, you can record discontinuously (altering or striking sets during recording breaks), use prerecorded inserts (on videotape or film), or chroma-key processes to provide backgrounds.

Multi-plane techniques

Our impressions of *scenic depth* are comparative. They come from our relating the appearance of progressively distant planes, overlapping, scale, and a series of similar visual clues. The more planes visible between our viewpoint and the horizon, the stronger is the illusion of depth. When there are few spatial clues in a shot (e.g. an open stage), the picture seldom conveys a convincing three-dimensional effect.

Fig. 10.20 Multi-plane techniques
Foreground planes enhance the impression of depth.

1 They may arise naturally from the camera viewpoint.
2 Items can be deliberately positioned in the foreground.
3 Even an artificially introduced foreground object can appear natural in the picture.

These impressions of depth derive primarily from the foreground and middle distance. So you can arrange your staging techniques accordingly. Foreground pieces particularly enhance the feeling of depth and dimension. These can be such diverse objects as tree branches, furniture, tracery screens, and columns; all used to provide progressive scenic planes.

When carefully organized, foreground planes come into shot quite naturally as the camera moves around. But the effect can appear contrived, particularly when the viewpoint is unfamiliar. Overdone, this technique could leave cameras continually weaving among foreground obstacles, with the viewer failing to get a clear view of the action.

Partial settings

Why build more than the camera needs to see? Although some production situations require a total overall viewpoint or extensive construction, many shots need only a sectional view – *partial setting*. Two deliberately restricted staging approaches are widely used. The first implies the whole by showing a *complete but localized part* – the doorway shot suggesting that the rest of the building is there – if we could see it. Audio effects help to create the illusion. The second method creates an impression by *judiciously placed foreground pieces* suggesting that the staging is more extensive than it really is, e.g. shooting through a foreground bookshelf, you imagine an entire library.

Fig. 10.21 The illusion of four walls

1 The fourth wall is usually assumed to be at the camera's position. Where the foreground wall must be seen, a mobile scenic piece (door, window) is often used. Designed as a *break-through piece* if camera dollies 'through' it.

2 Cameras can shoot over a low four-walled set for group discussions. (Beware of reverse cuts!)

Fig. 10.22 Partial settings

An environment can be implied by building a complete but abbreviated section.

Admittedly, such restrictions may not allow the director much latitude to change his mind, but the economies achieved in cost, space, and materials are considerable. The resultant effect can be totally convincing for short, relatively static scenes, and provide greater elaboration and scenic variety than would otherwise be practicable. Although, when unskilfully used it can lead to a cramped, restricted quality in the staging.

Realism

The artificiality of theatrical scenery is generally unacceptable in television wherever realism is intended. Yet paradoxically, where artificiality creates a genuine-looking effect, deception can go to any lengths. You may successfully use a fishline-activated curtain to suggest billowing winds, or have a leafy branch shadow indicate a nearby tree. Yet a genuine tapestry may look less realistic than a dye-painted canvas replica.

Realism can derive from quite subtle touches. A living room set must look lived in. Too tidy, too pristine, and it loses conviction. Surreptitious *dirtying up* (*antiquing*, *blowing down*) with a fine film of dark water paint can suggest wear, grubbiness, and discoloration around switches and door handles. Hand-sprays are useful for rapid localized treatment; although for large-scale effects (a slummy tenement) broad spraygun work becomes necessary.

Deception must be discreet. You must not expect photobackgrounds with foaming breakers that never move to fool anyone. Occasionally still backgrounds containing motionless trees, even static people, will be acceptable, but sooner or later they look suspiciously inert; particularly when accompanied by sounds of associated movement.

Sometimes the most convincing results come from using the real thing (e.g. real turf, tall grasses) while at others, grass matting (suitably discolored) and plastic flowers and foliage would be preferable to natural growth wilting under hot lights. Real water pools may be no more realistic on camera than clear plastic sheeting.

Scrim (scenic gauze)

Scrim or gauzes consist of thin cotton or synthetic net with a mesh of around 1.5–3 mm (1/16–1/8 in.) diameter, in white, light gray, or black. Although it can be used in draped form, the material is generally stretched taut without visible seams or wrinkles. It needs to be of sufficiently open weave to prevent excessive light absorption or obscuring subjects beyond, yet robust enough to stand handling and stretching.

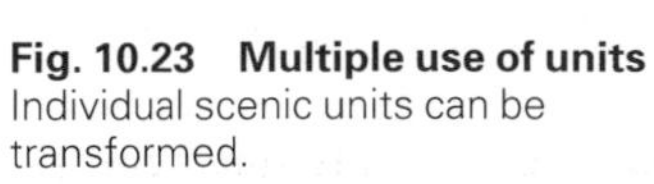

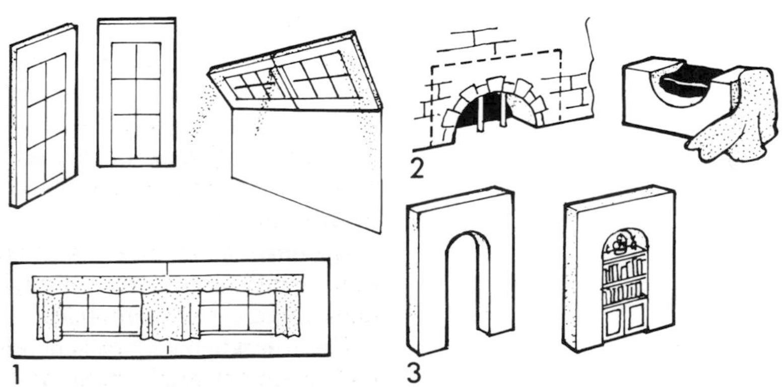

Fig. 10.23 Multiple use of units Individual scenic units can be transformed.

1 Two glazed doors become a long window, or a ceiling light.
2 A low window can be turned into a throne.
3 An arch becomes book-shelves.

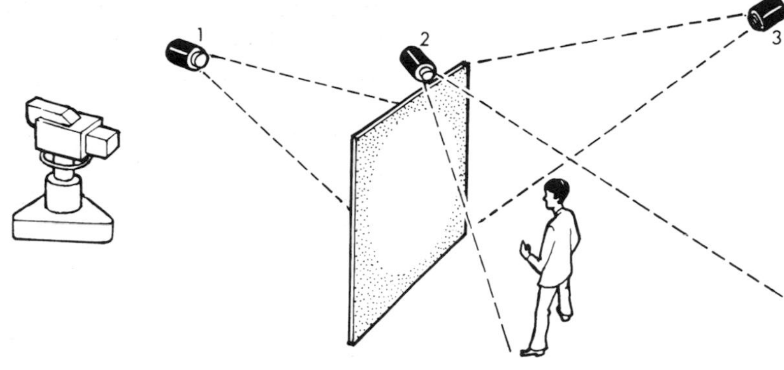

Fig. 10.24 Scrims/gauzes
Lit from the front alone (1) the scrim appears a solid plane. Surface painting or decoration shows up brightly against a plain white or black background. Unlit subjects behind the scrim are invisible.

By reducing brightness of front illumination (1) and lighting the subject (2) (behind scrim), the subject and setting are revealed with outlines and contrast softened, surface painting having almost disappeared.

A third lamp (3) added to rear-light the scrim, increases the mistiness over the scene, while silhouetting details on the surface of the scrim.

Stretched before a light-toned cyclorama, a scrim diffuses and obscures irregularities, and enhances the impression of spaciousness. Over a scenic background a scrim reduces contrast and artificiality. The material may be used as a glass substitute in scenery; it is safer, lighter, and gives no reflection problems. Lettering or decorative shapes can be attached to 'window panes' of scrim.

By adjusting its lighting you can alter the appearance of the scrim in several ways. When frontally lit, the scrim will look like a flat 'solid' surface. Lit from the rear, it becomes translucent with surface details silhouetted on it. Unlit, the scrim appears transparent, softening the distant scene.

Mobile scenic units

Mobile vehicles

To create a convincing illusion that a studio vehicle is moving you need to introduce a variety of 'clues': moving passing backgrounds; parts of the vehicle shaking; people being swayed or jogged; lights or shadows passing over them; perhaps wind, or dust clouds; sounds of progress (engine noise, hoofbeats, wheel noises, etc.); and the sounds of other passing subjects.

You have to interrelate these various features carefully, and above all ensure that there is compatible action between the subject and its background scene. If the vehicle stops, the background must stop too! This requires close coordination. Where moving film or videotape backgrounds are used (rear projection or chroma key) their timing and duration should be anticipated to prevent run-out or incompatibility.

A *sprung platform*, when suitably, handled, can provide realistic movements for a variety of application – from rowboats, buggies, hansom cabs to automobiles.

For a large structure such as a ship you may need to imitate movement by gently tilting the camera, introducing moving light

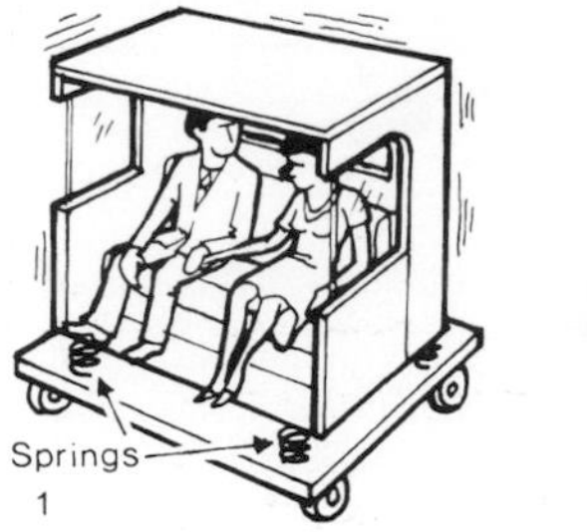

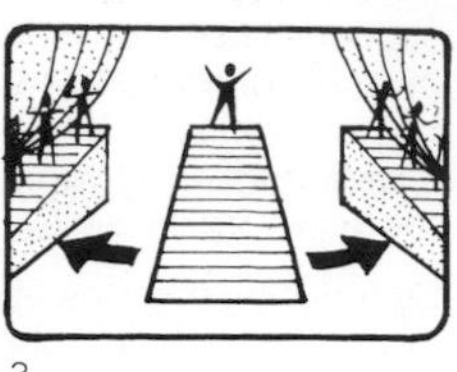

Fig. 10.25 Movable units
1 The movements of a vehicle can be imitated by mounting it on a sprung platform or truck.
2 Using movable scenic sections, the large staircase splits to leave the soloist isolated, 3.

(e.g. a key light rising and falling), and even having people sway in unison.

Movable scenic sections

When you want to move around a subject and space is restricted, or to reposition staging to form new composition arrangements, you can often do this by using movable scenic sections. These may be flats or solid units on wheels, low wheeled trucks (floats, stage wagons), turntables, and similarly adaptable staging; see Figures 10.19(4) and 10.25(2,3).

Set dressing

Dressing is the process of furnishing and decorating the built setting . . . the arrangement of furniture, ornaments, drapes. This is the treatment that personalizes an environment.

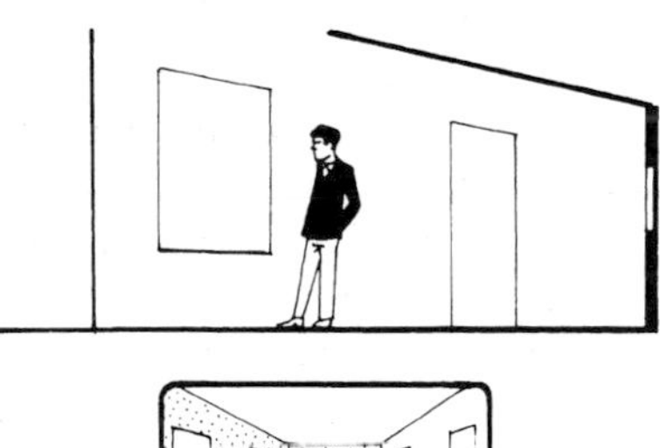

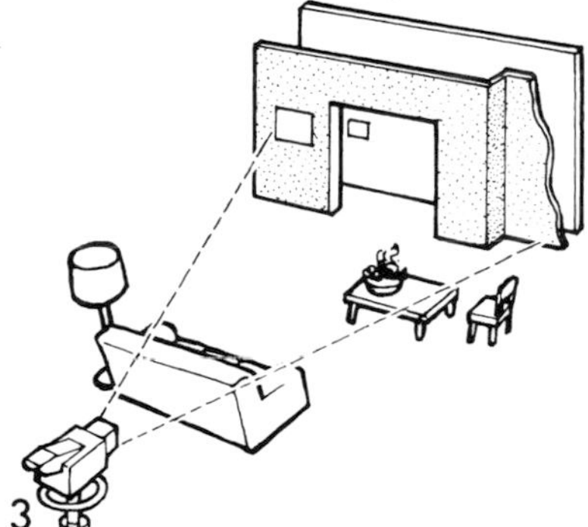

Fig. 10.26 False perspective
The background can deliberately convey a false impression of space.

1 A flat background (photographic, painting, chroma-key) may contain an illusion of depth. But give-away shadows, wrong scale, or wrong foreground-background perspective can destroy the effect.
2 The whole setting may be built in false perspective (exaggerated size-reduction with distance), but then action must be kept downstage.
3 By deliberately arranging to have large objects in the foreground and progressively smaller items further from the camera, perspective can be cheated.

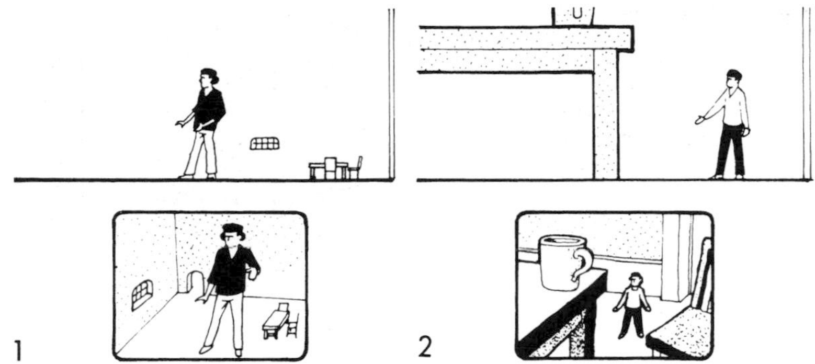

Fig. 10.27 Scale changes
1 Where the set is built with everything proportionately scaled down, people assume gigantic proportions.
2 If everything is scaled up, people are dwarfed.

These properties (props) are of several categories:

1 *Dressing props* used solely as decorative features.
2 *Action props* used in the course of plot action; e.g. a newspaper or telephone.
3 *Personal props* used or worn by specific performers; eyeglasses, wallet.

Where the item is *non-practical* it is not functional; for instance, a revolver that cannot fire or is simply not loaded, a *fully practical* article is completely working – the revolver is loaded, and used in the course of the action.

A setting soon acquires a filled-up look, cluttered with bric-à-brac that never registers on camera. So appropriate selection rather than profusion is the aim (Figure 10.28).

Where foreground space has been left clear for performers and cameras you may need to introduce (*set in*) extra props or furniture there for longer shots, removing (*striking*) them for camera moves. Although camera cranes can extend over foreground furniture to some degree, even slight obstacles impede pedestal dollies.

Furniture should not only be environmentally suitable but physically practical. Deep well-sprung armchairs, for instance, can encourage people to slouch, to look leggy when sitting, and to have difficulty in rising. Cushions may help where unsuitable design is unavoidable. So, too, seats that allow guests to swivel round, or that perch them uncomfortably, are best avoided.

If there can be said to be any specific tool for set dressing it must surely be the *staple hammer* or the *staple gun*, which can shoot wire staples through prepared board and soft wood up to 12.5 mm (½ in.) thick. These versatile tools can attach pictures, drapes, posters, foliage, wall coverings, plastic moldings to flats; felting to flooring . . . A close runner-up is *double-sided adhesive tape*, which prevents articles from slipping or being moved out of position, attaches decorative motifs, holds arranged drapes in place, and fixes graphics. Adhesive gray *Duct tape, Gaffer tape*, too, is a tough many-purpose adhesive gray plasticized cloth, sticking firmly to many surfaces yet removed without marking them. Its main purpose is to attach lightweight lampfittings or cables to walls on location.

Technical problems

Production treatment and the camera's idiosyncracies place a number of restrictions on set design. Occasionally you can disregard them – but only occasionally.

The final effect

It is important to remember that the audience only sees what the camera *shows*. Many a delightful skeletal setting has resolved itself into just a series of 'pole-through-the-head' shots as the director has concentrated on close viewpoints. Many a setting has looked fine in an establishing long shot but quite ineffectual in closer shots, or from other camera positions.

Color and tonal proportions in the picture can vary considerably with the shots selected. There may be only one small area of bright red in the set; but this could totally dominate and distract in a close-up.

Various hues are quite distinct in color, yet may merge indecipherably in monochrome; and for graphics (titles, graphs, maps) this can be a real embarrassment.

Tonal values

Marked tonal contrasts give a long shot a more definite emphasis than subtle pastel shades. But when you pan in closer shots over sharply contrasting background tones, or intercut between them, pictorial quality and visual continuity can be badly upset.

Conversely, if subject tones are too similar to their backgrounds the overall effect is unsatisfyingly flat or confused. So the tonal contributions of the setting, lighting, costume, and make-up need to be coordinated for optimum results.

To ensure good tonal reproduction it is best to work within a fairly restricted scenic contrast range for most purposes – around 10:1 to 15:1 (40–60 per cent reflectance) is sometimes quoted. Unless lighting is diffused, it will usually extend this effective contrast to the system's limits.

Surface detail

Plain surfaces, unbroken by detail or modeling, have limited pictorial appeal, but they can be considerably enhanced by lighting (shading, dappling, color variations).

Fig. 10.28 Visual detail
1 Excessive scenic detail is distracting, confusing, fussy.
2 If all but essentials are excluded, the result can be meager, cheap, empty; although suitably applied it becomes open, expensive.
3 Coordinated shape and line produce a stimulating arresting effect.

Bold details such as a strong pattern or elaborate motif are attractive as long as they do not draw attention from the action. They are most likely to do this if isolated within a plain background, or appearing unexpectedly in isolated shots.

Very small detail easily becomes lost in longer shots, or defocused where depth of field is restricted. So an attractive pattern that is quite clear in closer shots may dilute to an unexciting overall gray background at a distance. Consequently, where action moves to and from such a background we find pattern prominence altering as the focused plane changes.

Very close vertical or horizontal stripes are best avoided at all times – whether they derive from distant coarse patterns or close fine ones – for they can produce violent line beating (strobing).

Surface brightness

Bright surfaces leave the TV camera at a disadvantage where a full tonal range is to be reproduced. Even if no technical defects arise, the effect is generally distracting. So it is a good working principle to avoid overlight or shiny surfaces, unless for a specific effect.

Whereas in a *monochrome* picture excessive highlights simply reproduce as white areas within grays, in *color* they block off to become white blotches on colored surfaces – and are therefore more prominent.

Highly reflective materials such as decorative aluminium foil or shiny plastic are notorious for causing troublesome hot spots, flares, or trailing. Providing any defects are not obtrusive, their attractive sheen can introduce vitality to a shot. But the borderline between pictorially attractive effects and disturbingly eye-catching blobs can be very slight.

'First-aid treatment'

Exposure is normally adjusted to achieve the most realistic *face* tones. If there are any disproportionally brighter surfaces in the shot they will block off to a detailless white. The result may be quite unobtrusive. But if it is unacceptable, the only solutions are to modify the lighting, remove the offending subject, or apply 'first-aid treatment'.

Although there are times when excessive lighting has aggravated the situation (as when strong back light burns out the shoulders of light-toned garments), such problems are more often due to high reflectance or smooth surface textures.

The obvious way to improve any overbright surface is to reduce or cut off the light falling onto it. But this may be impractical, especially where it robs adjacent areas of light. Flares or strong reflections (speculars) from a shiny surface can usually be cured by re-angling or tilting it, or changing the camera position slightly, or even by masking it with another subject.

Various aids can be applied to reduce such reflections (on automobiles, glossy paint, plastics), including dulling spray/anti-flare (wax spray), water paste, latex spray, putty, and modeling clay. Spurious reflections in glass or clear plastic can be similarly treated, although we may well obscure the surface by doing so.

Sometimes the only way to reduce overbright surface tones is to spray or spatter the surface lightly with black water-soluble paint or dye. Overdone, though, this can produce a dirty lifeless result, and destroy surface pattern.

Overdark surfaces may be improved similarly by light-toned treatment, picking out (edge painting) molding or detail, or perhaps by increased localized lighting.

Care is needed, too, in avoiding white or near-white set dressings; clothing, drapes, table coverings, papers, bed sheets, etc. You may substitute cream or light gray materials, or lightly dye them, or have them strategically sprayed or powdered down. Carefully done, the results on camera are well-modeled light-toned surfaces, reproducing as white. Overdone, though, you may finish up with people in dirty shirts reading gray newspapers!

Although modern cameras can handle wider tonal variations it is best to avoid tonal extremes as far as possible.

Using color

We tend to take *color* in the world around us for granted, but for the set designer it presents both opportunities and problems. In excess, color can become visually distracting and tiring to watch. On the other hand, if color is too subdued, a picture can lack vigor.

When staging with color, we meet two extremes:

- Situations in which the persuasive potentials of color can be fully exploited; where color adds visual excitement, enchantment, arrests the attention – e.g. when presenting singers, music groups, dance.
- Situations where unless carefully controlled, color can inadvertently distract the viewer, create false associations, appear tawdry, overglamorize. Color harmonies may be inappropriate, or create too strong a background for the action or the ambiance of that particular production.

For many kinds of presentation such as newscasts, talks, demonstrations, the colors of the surroundings are deliberately restful and supplementary, rather than forceful or dramatic.

For various psychological and physiological reasons, the TV screen can often exaggerate – even caricature – reproduced color. Certainly the general practice is to underplay color, rather than have color emphasis.

As a good working principle it is best to choose the surrounding décor to match the unalterable objects in the scene. Strong color is easily achieved; but subtle, sensitive color staging without simply resorting to gray-scale neutrals requires interpretive skill. Somber, slummy, drab surroundings can be particularly difficult to stage realistically in color.

Large areas of even, unrelieved color are best avoided, preferably being broken up with lighting, scenic elements, or set dressing.

Emphasis is generally achieved through the use of color in costumes, key props, and furnishings rather than in the set walls or drapes. Strong background hues easily dominate.

Table 10.2 Costume problems

White shirts, blouses, etc.	Details and modeling lost where surfaces block off to white.
Glossy materials – satin, etc.	High sheen, especially from shoulders, blocks off to white or reflects color of incident light.
Light tones	These emphasize size, but if loosely cut, light garments can appear formless.
Dark tones	These minimize size, but modeling is easily lost in reproduction; particularly with dark velvets.
Strong, vibrant colors	Usually appear oversaturated and reflect onto neck and chin.
Fine stripes, checks, or herringbone patterns on clothing	Pattern strobes causing localized flicker, or produce blue-colored fringes (cross color), or color break-up. Color detail is liable to be unsharp and lost in longer shots.
Shiny, sequinned, or metallic finishes	Blocked-off highlights. Reflects onto nearby surfaces.
'Noisy' jewelry or ornamentation – e.g. multi-string beads	With a personal mike these cause extraneous clinks, rattles, or rustles.
Rhinestones and other highly reflective jewelry	Reflects bright spots of light onto chin, neck, face; and flashes obtrusively, especially when using star filters.
Very low necklines	In close shots can create a topless look.
Color fidelity	Certain colors can become emphasized or distorted (blues, magentas, deep reds) due to deficiencies in electronic or film processing.

Fig. 10.29 Costume problems
1 Avoid costume tones merging with the background.
2 Beware detailed or fussy patterns in both costume and background.
3 Close stripes and checks in costume flicker (strobe) at certain distances.
4 Low necklines appear topless in close shots.

Finally, we need to remember that *it is the effect on camera that counts*. Even a relatively small area of strong color may appear very pronounced in a long shot if surrounded by neutrals. Take a close shot of someone standing in front of it and that color patch can fill the entire screen!

Costume (wardrobe)

Costume effectiveness is strongly influenced by its background. In larger TV organizations, performers' clothing (costume, wardrobe) is the responsibility of a specialist. But for many productions people wear their own clothing, and diplomatic guidance may be necessary to ensure that unsuitable attire is avoided.

You need to be sensitive to talents' feelings and taste when suggesting changes; particularly when you want them to wear an item from stock (off-white shirt, or a different necktie) to replace their own. Experienced talent may bring along alternative garments for selection on camera.

A costume that looks attractive full-length may be less successful when seen as a head-and-shoulders behind a desk. Color matching that looks good to the eye, can reproduce quite differently; for example, 'reds' that differ due to their having dissimilar brown or blue proportions. Colors that have a strong bold appeal in long shots can seem harshly crude in closer views.

11 Make-up

The television camera is a critical tool, and facial characteristics that pass unnoticed in daily life can appear surprisingly exaggerated or distracting on the screen. Most of us can benefit from the enhancement that skilled make-up treatment provides. Whether this needs to be slight or elaborate must depend on the type of production and the role of the talent. But even where someone is already wearing an apparently effective street make-up, results on camera can usually be improved.

Forms of make-up

Television make-up treatment follows three general forms: *straight*; *corrective*; and *character* make-up.

Straight make-up

Straight make-up is a basic compensatory treatment, affecting the performer's appearance to a minimum extent.

Skin-tone adjustment

This provides a good tonal balance in the picture: darkening pale faces and lightening swarthy complexions.

Routine improvements

These subdue blotchy skin tones, shiny foreheads; strengthen lips and eyebrows; remove beard-line (blue chin); darken overlight ears; lighten deep-set eyes; and lighten bags under eyes.

For many TV productions, performers require little or no make-up, with minimum correction and brief last-minute improvements often being sufficient. Regular performers may do their own.

Corrective make-up

Corrective make-up seeks to reduce less pleasing facial characteristics while enhancing more attractive points. Actual treatment can range from slight modifications of lips, eyes and nose, to strapping sagging skin or outstanding ears, or concealing baldness.

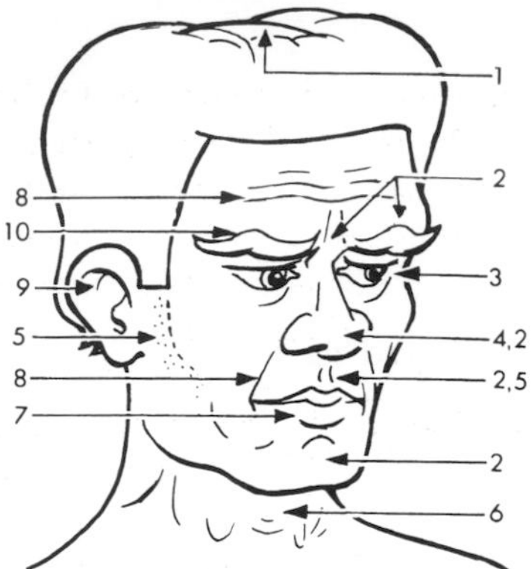

Fig. 11.1 Corrective make-up
Make-up can improve or disguise various effects that may appear emphasized on camera.

1 Shiny bald head; untidy hair; scalp showing through thin hair; hair too light, dark, dense, to show well.
2 Perspiration shine.
3 Deep eye sockets; eyes appear too prominent or small; eyes lack definition.
4 Shiny nose; nose coloration prominent.
5 Beard-line prominent (blue chin).
6 Neck scrawny.
7 Lips need definition or shaping; normal lipstick too dark or light on camera.
8 Age-lines; wrinkles over-prominent.
9 Ears too prominent; different color from adjacent skin.
10 Eyebrows barely discernible. over-prominent, untidy.

The general aim is to treat the person without their appearing 'made up'. Skin blemishes and unattractive natural color must normally be covered; preferably by using several thin applications of increased pigmentation, rather than trying to obscure with heavy mask-like coatings. Arms, hands, necks, ears may need blending to an even tone (body make-up).

A person's skin quality will modify the make-up materials used. While coarser skin textures provide more definite modeling, finer complexions tend to reveal veining or blotches that the camera may accentuate. In color, ears can appear reddish and translucent. Complexions become flushed with exposure to heat (or hospitality). Make-up can become disturbed in the course of action (e.g. lip colors 'eaten off'). Also, bleached hair can exhibit alarmingly greenish shading, while blue-tinted white hair can look startlingly overcolored, only improved by corrective rinses.

Character make-up

Here, emphasis is on the specific character or type that the actor is playing. By facial reshaping, remodeling, changes in hair, etc. the subject may even be totally transformed; for example, Frankenstein's monster. But most character make-up involves less spectacular, subtle changes. Theatrical make-up treatments appear rather too broad and crude under the camera's scrutiny, except for such stylized characters as clowns, ballet, pierrot.

Conditions of television make-up

The principles and practices of television make-up are almost identical with those of motion pictures, except that in television the tempo and continuous performance usually prevent the elaboration or shot-by-shot changes that are possible in film.

A long shot ideally requires more defined, prominent treatment than a close-up. A similar situation, in fact, to that found in lighting techniques. But such refinements are seldom possible under typical conditions. You may not even be able to do anything about such distractions as perspiration, or disheveled hair, when the actor is on-camera for long period – except to correct them for any retakes, where time permits.

For the very exacting demands of television drama, careful planning and presentation are essential. At a preliminary meeting with the program's director the supervisory make-up artist will discuss such details as character interpretation, hair styling, special treatments, and any transformations during the program (aging, etc.). Actors who need fitted wigs, or trial make-up, are then contacted.

Camera rehearsal

For camera rehearsal either of two approaches is common. In the first the performers are made up beforehand as experience suggests. When seen on camera this treatment enables the make-up artist to judge more exactly the eventual detail work and tones needed. It also allows the lighting director and video control operator to assess tonal balance, contrast, and exposure.

While watching camera rehearsals on a picture monitor the supervisory make-up artist notes any changes that seem desirable, to guide the individual make-up artists handling the performers. The other make-up approach (especially for straight or corrective forms) is to see performers on the screen first, treating them as time and facilities allow.

Make-up treatment

Generally speaking, a straight make-up for men may take around 3 to 10 minutes; women require 6 to 20 minutes on average. Elaborate needs can double or even treble these times.

After a few hours, cosmetics tend to become partly absorbed or dispersed through body heat and perspiration. Surface finish, texture, and tones will have lost their original definition, and fresh make-up or refurbishing becomes necessary. Apart from on-the-spot retouching and freshening (mopping off and applying astringents), performers are normally treated in make-up rooms near the studio. Miracles of makeshift quick-changes have been achieved on the studio floor amidst the turmoil of production. But unless time limits or body position necessitates this (as with wounds), a more leisurely procedure is preferable.

There will always be problem occasions. Some performers cannot have make-up, owing to allergy or temperament. There are times when make-up has to be done immediately before air time, without any opportunity to see the performer on camera beforehand – a situation that the wise director avoids.

Varying conditions

Apart from artistic considerations, many technical factors affect make-up treatment:

1 Lighting – intensity, balance, direction, etc.
2 Scenery – relative face/background contrasts (simultaneous contrast effects).
3 Video adjustment (picture control) – exposure, gamma, black level, color balance.
4 Costume – relative to face/costume tonal contrast.

Such variations help to explain why the same performer's treatment may need to alter from one show to the next. Sometimes an astringent and light powdering may suffice, while at others more particular make-up becomes necessary.

Principles of make-up

The broad aims of facial make-up and lighting are complementary. Make-up can sometimes compensate for lighting problems, lightening eye sockets to anticipate shadowing cast by steep lamps. But whereas the effect of lighting changes as the subject moves, that of make-up remains constant. This distinction is important when we consider corrective treatment:

1 Large area tonal changes – making the entire face lighter.
2 Small area tonal changes – darkening part of the forehead.
3 Broad shading – blending one tonal area into another.
4 Localized shading – pronounced shading to simulate a jawline.
5 Drawing – accurately lineated lines and outlines.
6 Contour changes – built-up surfaces.
7 Hair work – mustaches, wigs, etc.

Localized highlighting by slight color accents will increase the apparent size and prominence of an area, while darkening reduces its effective size and causes it to recede. By selective highlighting and shading, therefore, you can vary the impression of surface relief and proportions considerably. But you must take particular care to prevent shading looking like grime!

You can reduce or emphasize existing modeling, or suggest modeling where none exists; remembering, though, that the deceit may not stand close scrutiny.

A base or foundation tone covers any blotchiness in the natural skin coloring, blemishes, beard shadows, etc. This can be extended, where necessary, to block out the normal lips, eyebrows, or hairline before drawing in another different formation.

Selected regions can be treated with media a few tones lighter or darker than the main foundation, and worked into adjacent areas with fingertips, brush, or sponge. After this highlighting and shading, any detailed drawing is done using special wax lining pencils and lining brushes. Lips are color outlined with a lip brush, then filled in with the lip color.

Make-up materials

The make-up media used in television and motion pictures include:

1 A dry matt cake of compressed powder (pancake).
2 A non-greasy base of creamy consistency, in small stick-containers (Pan-Stik) or jars.

3 A greasepaint foundation, contained in tubes.
4 Powder and liquid base.

Before applying a foundation (base) the skin is first prepared by thoroughly working it over with a cleaning cream or lotion (or cold cream) to remove any traces of existing cosmetics. Wiping this off with tissues, an astringent (e.g. eau de cologne) is patted on, to close skin pores, reduce absorption and perspiration, and generally freshen. On dry skins, a highly emollient cleanser/moisturizer (preferably oil based) is used to prepare a non-absorbent surface. This prevents oils in the make-up from being absorbed and causing a patchy finish. But for oily skins, a cleanser with an astringent freshener is needed to remove excess oils.

Following an after-transmission clean-off the skin is cleansed with special removers and washed with soap and water.

Which of the various make-up media is used depends on the effect required, the degree and nature of the treatment, and personal preferences. Each material has its particular features.

The pancake foundation

This base is worked up with water-moist sponge and applied thinly over the whole face. Its covering power (ability to overlay other tones, blemishes, etc.) is excellent. Its finish is predominantly matt. When too thickly applied, it can produce a mask-like appearance, flattening out facial modeling. Highlights and shading can be introduced with a sponge edge, using shades two or four tones different from the foundation color.

Cream base

This is dabbed onto small areas and worked by fingertips evenly over the regions being treated. Localized highlighting and shading with different tones is pat-blended or merged with flat-topped sable brushes. Surface finish depends upon any subsequent powdering to set the foundation. Unpowdered, the skin has a soft sheen. Powdering reduces shine leaving a smooth, satin finish. The cream has reasonable covering power and may be retouched easily. Leaving the skin's natural texture visible, it permits lighting to reveal more subtle half-tone modeling.

Greasepaint

This is similarly spread from small dabs. Although it has little covering power and may need refurbishing sooner than a heavier foundation, it is easily worked and retouched (by brush or fingertips). Powdering modifies its distinct shine to a silky gloss.

Such after-powdering, when applied to any completed make-up, softens contrasts and binds the materials. Any excess can be

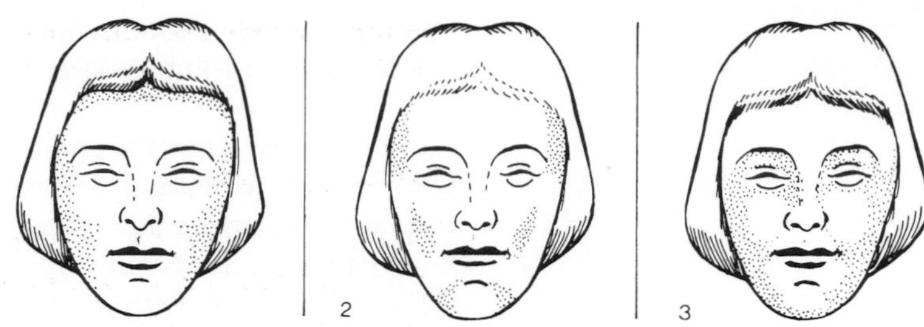

Fig. 11.2 part 1 Basic make-up techniques – general treatment
1 Hard hairline, forehead lowered by shading, face width reduced, cheeks depressed.
2 Softened-off hairline, forehead width reduced by shading, deep-set eyes lightened, cheek and chin modeling increased.
3 Hairline reshaped and extended, forehead height reduced, chin made to recede, 'apple-cheeks' highlighted.

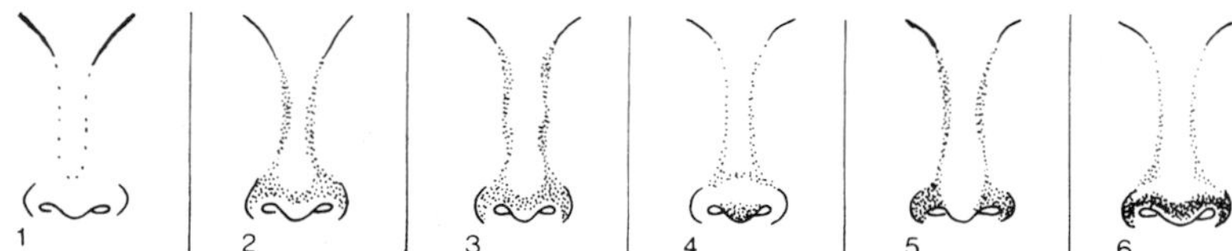

Fig. 11.2 part 2 Basic make-up techniques – nose treatment
Variations in nose shape achieved by shading (side shading, ridge highlighting).

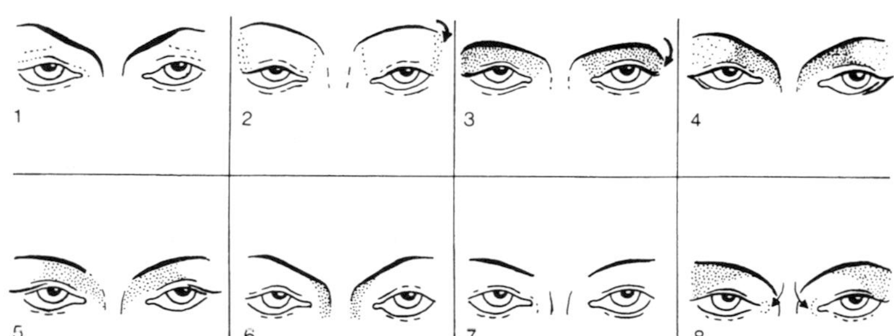

Fig. 11.2 part 3 Basic make-up technique – eye make-up
1 Untouched.
2 Area above eye protrudes as a a result of lightening, eyebrows raised and thinned, making eye seem smaller.
3 Eyebrows thickened and lowered, and area above eye shaded. This opens up the eye and makes it appear larger.
4 Method of lengthening eyes.
5 Method of broadening eyes.
6 Distance between eyes reduced by shading.
7 Distance between eyes increased by shortening brows.
8 Detailed example of eye treatment: base of top lashes underlined thinly from center to just beyond outer corner, end being upturned. A short upturned line is occasionally drawn under lower lashes, but this tend to reduce the eye size. Eye shadow light towards the inner corners, slightly heavier at outer corners. A white penciled line along inside edge of lower lid.

removed with a powder brush. A *beardstick* using a grease base can reduce a prominent beard-line.

Powder bases

These are supplied in compacts and resemble reinforced face powder. Applied with a puff, their covering power is moderate. They have general use for broad shading and tonal improvement, emergency repairs, shiny foreheads, and the like. Most liquid-type media have poor covering power, and tend to become streaky and patchy.

Any powdering, whether to 'set' a foundation, reduce shine, or to absorb perspiration, must be applied judiciously. This is because the powder often tends to change color in use, or obscure base coloring.

Several accessory preparations are common to the beauty salon and the make-up room alike, e.g. mascara, eye shadow, and false eyelashes. A few, like rouge, have a less value on-camera and are better simulated by other means; while materials such as tooth enamel (to blacken or whiten teeth) or artificial blood capsules are more suitable to the television and film studios.

The make-up artist's tools range from brushes (for modeling, lining, applying lip color, etc.), sponges, wax pencils to palette knives. But for many workers their fingertips are their most-used aid, with which they blend foundation media into a homogeneously molded complexion.

The actual color tints and tones used for foundation powder, lipstick, rouge, and eyeshadow will vary according to personal assessment and the subject's skin tone. Some make-up artists work to a broad classification – e.g. fair, medium, dark complexion, but careful selection is necessary to avoid unwanted graying, dirtying, or the distortion of normal skin tones.

Refurbishing

With time, most make-up needs refurbishing, due to perspiration and wear. Blot up perspiration with tissue or a chamois leather lightly dampened with eau de cologne before powdering. Lip color may need renewing, as may localized highlighting or shading. To avoid hands appearing overlight, they may be treated with a darker pancake; which may also require fresh applications from time to time.

Surface modeling (prosthetics)

Manipulation of the subject's own skin or by sticking on new formations can change the physical contours of the flesh.

Manipulation

To produce scars, ridges, etc., *non-flexible collodion* may be brushed onto the skin. This mixture of proxylin, alcohol, and ether contracts the flesh; the painless contraction increasing with successive layers. Although readily removed, collodion can irritate sensitive skins. In such cases, quick-drying, liquid-plastic sealers may be preferable.

Fish skin can be used to contort the flesh within limits. The selected area of flesh is drawn into its new position, and the fish skin spirit gummed to hold it in place. Apart from imparting an oriental slant to eyes, this material is mostly used to emphasize or flatten out folds of superfluous flesh.

Surface contours

Surface contours such as warts, eye bags, wounds, nose modeling can be built up by several methods. Wax nose putty, mortician's wax, and modeling clay can all be molded into shape and stuck on. A latex rubber-base solution, *flexible* collodion (resin, caster oil, ether, alcohol), or various plastic equivalents, can be coated over a selected area until it is sufficiently extended. For larger protuberances, pads of absorbent cotton wool or sponge can be attached first by spirit gum. Surfacing is then carried out over this substructure. Because normal foundation media do not take to these surfaces, plastic sealers are finally brushed over to key them on and prevent any interaction.

For more drastic changes, partial or complete latex masks are molded and attached. They provide us with anything from double chins to grotesques. The advantage here is not only that more extensive alterations are possible but that they can be prepared beforehand, and the fitting/removal process is quicker and easier. All prosthetics are best camera tested to ensure color and textural suitability.

Hair

Hair may be treated and arranged by the make-up artist, or by a separate specialist. Such hair work includes: alterations to the performer's own hair; the addition of supplementary hair pieces; and complete wigs covering existing hair.

Hair alteration

In television, a certain amount of restyling, resetting, or waving may be carried out on the performer's own hair, but where extensive alterations such as cutting or shaving are needed, complete wigs are more popular. Hair color is readily changed by sprays, rinses, or bleaches. Hair whitener suffices for both localized and overall graying. Overlight hair can be darkened to provide better modeling on-camera, while dark hair may need gold or silver dust, or brilliantine, to give it life.

Supplementary hair pieces

Where the performer's natural hair is unsuitable for treatment, hair pieces or full toupees can be attached to the scalp, and unified with existing hair. Where staining of the scalp with masque cannot hide baldness, these made-up hair pieces may be necessary. For women, postiche work (pinned-on hair) may provide flowing tresses, buns, ringlets, etc., augmenting a short coiffure.

Beards, mustaches, side-burns (side-boards), stubble, and the like may be 'home-grown', preformed by using prepared hair goods, or built up from cut hair lengths. Prepared hair goods are, undoubtedly, most popular. These are obtained prefabricated by wig specialists. Here, hair has been tied strand by strand to a fine nylon silk or nylon netting (lace), and can be dressed to suit beforehand. This method is less demanding of the time and skill of the make-up artist.

On the other hand, treatment built up from cut hair is a lengthy and skilled business, but more versatile. Human and yak hair are the most-used materials. (Crepe hair has limited application.) Such hair may be laid in spirit-gummed sections until the required area has been covered. The result is trimmed, waved, and fixed (laquer sprayed), as necessary.

Wigs

These cover the performer's own hair entirely and are again formed from hair tied to a shaped foundation net. The front and sides of this net may be stuck to the forehead and temples and, where necessary, hidden by overlaying it with the base medium.

12 Audio

It is easy to treat sound pick-up casually. A desk stand, a tie-clip microphone, or the ubiquitous baton microphone seem to meet most needs. We adjust audio amplification so that the reproduction is loud enough. Where is the problem? We can hear what people are saying.

The trouble with casual sound pick-up is that we often cannot. The audio quality alters so much it does not sound like the original. It becomes amazingly sibilant, muffled, distorted, volume varies, we hear random noise and distracting background sounds. The scale or proportions of the audio do not match the picture (close-up sound for a distant shot). Voices can become inaudible or confusingly jumbled together. The result is unrealistic and tiring to listen to. Little wonder that the professional audio specialist takes so much trouble to achieve the 'obvious'.

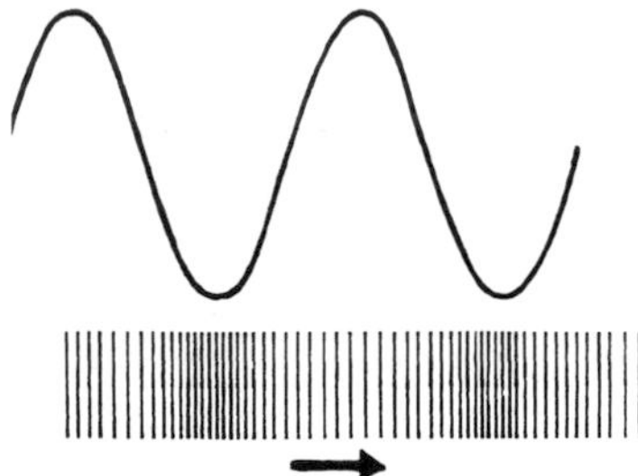

Fig. 12.1 Sound wave
When any material vibrates, its movement creates compressions and rarefactions in the surrounding air. In its simplest form, the air-pressure fluctuates at a sinusoidal rate. Sound in this pure form (*sine wave tone*) is emitted by certain sources.

Sound quality

The simplest sound vibrates regularly in a sinusoidal fashion. Its oscillatory motion traces a *sine wave* of a certain frequency. Some sources (tuning forks, flutes, oscillators) can produce such pure tones. But most emit more complex sounds comprising a main note (the *fundamental*) accompanied by a mixture of multiple tones

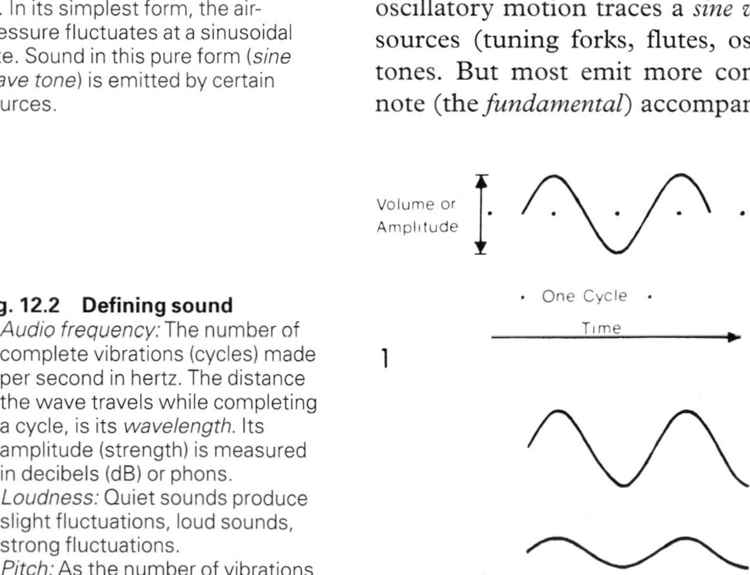

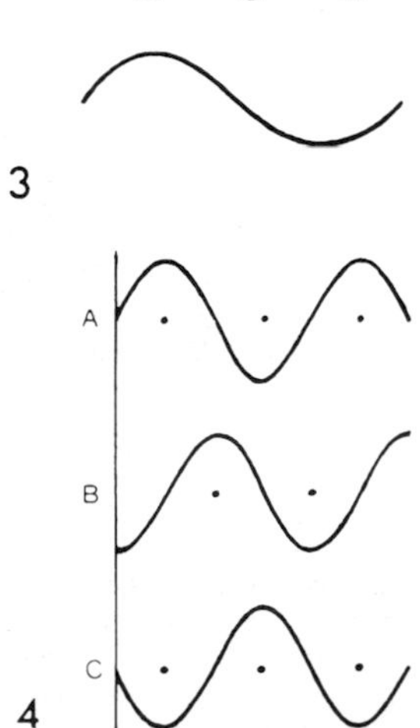

Fig. 12.2 Defining sound
1 *Audio frequency:* The number of complete vibrations (cycles) made per second in hertz. The distance the wave travels while completing a cycle, is its *wavelength*. Its amplitude (strength) is measured in decibels (dB) or phons.
2 *Loudness:* Quiet sounds produce slight fluctuations, loud sounds, strong fluctuations.
3 *Pitch:* As the number of vibrations increases, the sound's pitch rises – from low to high frequency.
4 *Phase:* The relative time displacement between two sounds in degrees. (One cycle = 360°).

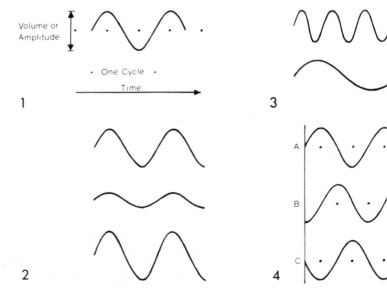

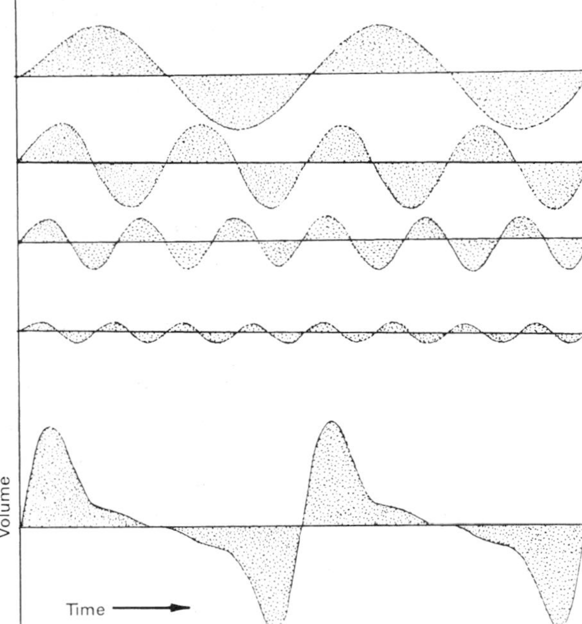

Fig. 12.3 Complex waveforms
The sounds from individual sources combine to form a single complex waveform. This is traced by the microphone, which generates a corresponding electrical waveform – the *audio signal*.

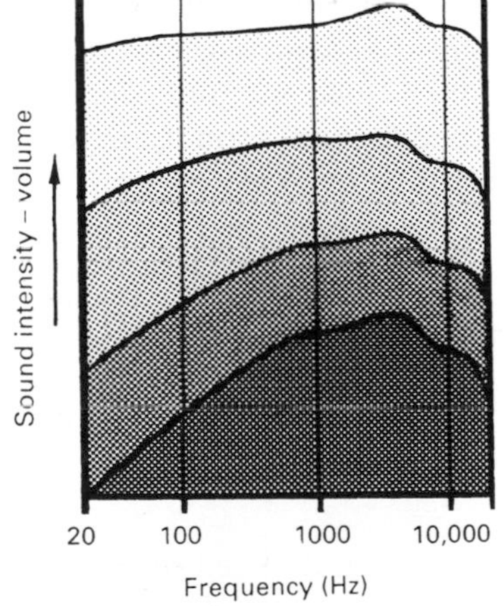

Fig. 12.4 Audibility
The ear's response to sounds varies noticeably with their volume and pitch. At lower sound levels, we are less able to hear the highest frequencies, and there is a considerable loss of bass.

(*harmonics, overtones*). Their proportions alter with the source; e.g. the type of instrument, its design, how it is played. Sometimes, as with the oboe, these harmonics may even be louder than the fundamental note. Transient sounds, on the other hand (clicks, crashes, bangs), contain a broad random mixture of frequencies.

We come to recognize the characteristic ratios of fundamental and harmonics from various sources as their particular *quality*. Ideally we want to reproduce the original proportions exactly – but that is only possible within limits. Most audio systems modify quality due to their emphasizing or reducing parts of the audio spectrum, or adding spurious frequencies that are heard as various forms of *distortion*.

Paradoxically, while our brain is astonishingly tolerant and can interpret even wild travesties as substitutes for the original sound (as small radios continually demonstrate!), yet we remain quite critical of certain distortions – sibilance, overload distortion, severe loss of higher notes (top loss), strong resonances.

Reproduced sound

TV audio is predominantly *monaural* or '*mono*' (one-eared), and like a two-dimensional picture, lacks the ability to convey spatial information directly (although this is possible in stereophonic and quadraphonic systems). Mono sounds can only be segregated by volume, pitch, and quality differences.

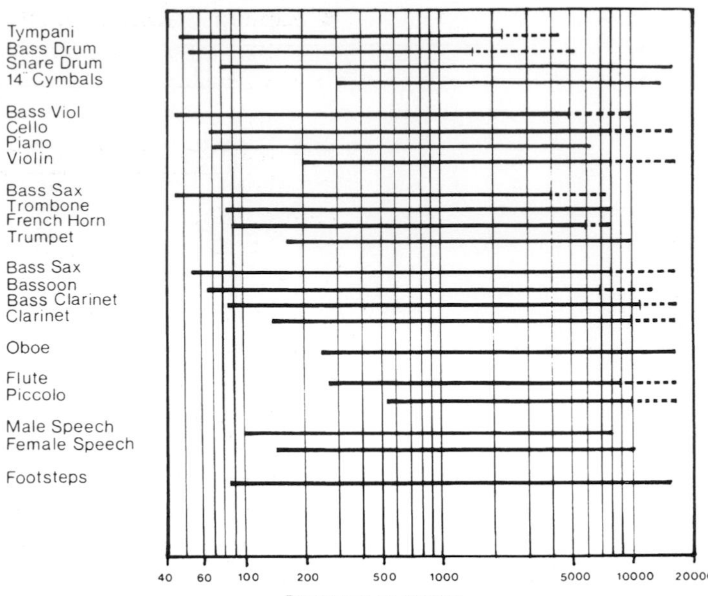

Fig. 12.5 Frequency range
Here the audible frequency range of various sources is compared.

Monaural problems

Our ears demand a wider frequency range for mono-sound reproduction than is necessary to achieve similar fidelity in stereo. Also, we become more aware of (and confused by) reverberation in monaural reproduction.

The audio signal produced by a *mono* microphone cannot indicate the *direction* of sounds within its pick-up range; only their *relative loudness*. Where, for example, one instrument is louder than another it is liable to mask or modify the quality of the weaker sound; even where these sources are located at quite different angles to the microphone. In mono reproduction, sounds can seem to merge, instead of retaining the individuality of stereo reproduction. That is why you need to position the microphone carefully, to provide a clear and appropriate balance between different sound sources, and to avoid picking up extraneous reflections from nearby walls.

Stereo sound

Although *stereo* sound seems so 'natural', you do need to look out for some important practical problems.

- Microphone placement can be quite critical, especially where the subjects are some distance apart.
- Reverberation (reflected sounds) generally seems more pronounced in stereo.

- Random environmental sounds such as footsteps, passing traffic, wind noise, ventilation, tend to become more prominent in stereo.

You may encounter problems in matching a stereo sound to its shot, that for some reason, are acceptable in mono reproduction:

- The lens may capture a close shot of a musician within an orchestra, while the accompanying sound is broad and unfocused.
- Although the shot size varies as a camera zooms, the sound perspective often continues unchanged.
- The sound's direction may be incompatible with the subject's position in the frame; sound coming from the left, for someone appearing on camera right.
- Sounds from unseen (or unimportant) subjects, that in mono would have merged as a general background noise, may seem prominent in stereo.
- If the apparent direction of a sound changes as camera viewpoints alters, the effect can become confusing. When intercutting facing shots, a background sound could move on the cuts.
- Avoid moving or turning the microphone to follow action, otherwise the stereo sound image will change, and not match the shot.

To reduce or overcome these kinds of problems it is common practice to mix central *mono* dialogue (speech) with *stereo* effects and music. The illusion is generally convincing, and it certainly does simplify sound pick-up.

The audio system

The *dynamic range* (volume range) that any audio system can handle is limited. When too loud, sounds will cause *overload distortion*, producing spurious discordant overtones. If too quiet, wanted sounds will become merged with background noise of comparable level (volume), such as tape noise, hum and ventilation.

So to avoid exceeding these limits it is essential that you do not overload the microphone itself (too near a loud source), or overamplify the signal (overmodulation, 'overmod'). Conversely, you must prevent the audio signal from becoming too weak (undermodulation, 'undermod') by placing the microphone close enough and using sufficient amplification. But at the same time, as you will see later, you must not destroy an impression of the dynamics of the original sound source.

Acoustics

Although acoustic design is the concern of the specialist, we are interested as users of the studio in how acoustic characteristics can affect audio quality, studio operations, and audio-visual matching.

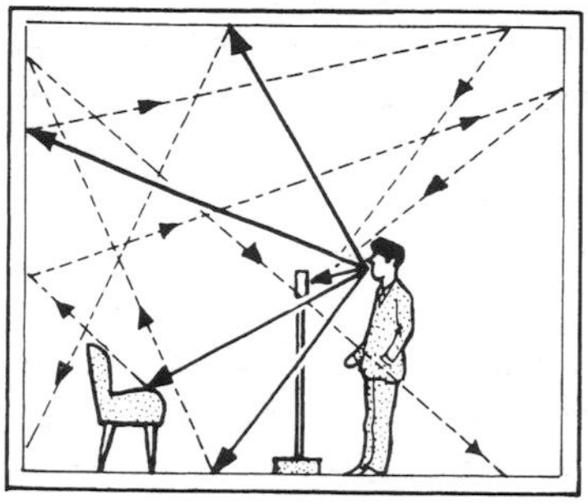

——— Direct Sound
------- Reflected Sound

Fig. 12.6 Studio acoustics
As sound strikes surfaces a proportion is absorbed (frequency selectively). or reinforced by structural resonance. The reflected sound, now modified, adds to the original (augmenting or partially masking it). Some coloration is artistically desirable. The time taken for the sound to die away (decay time; reverberation period) largely depends on room volume, surface materials, shape, and can range from less than 1 second up to about 6 seconds.

Reverberant studios

A *live* (*wet*), highly reflective studio would emphasize all sounds – wanted (speech, music) or unwanted (camera moves, cable drag, footsteps, ventilation, scenery movement). Even using close directional microphones, extraneous sounds would intrude; particularly during quiet scenes.

No staging depicting exterior scenes or small rooms can hope to be convincing if accompanied by echoing sound! It is always possible to *add* simulated reverberation to any sound, but not normally practicable to remove it to deaden the effect.

Strong acoustic reflections can mask the original sound, reducing intelligibility. And, due to quality changes caused by frequency-selective absorption, the overall effect may become hollow, hard, boomy, 'woofy'.

Dead studios

We can only avoid reflected sounds completely in free space, or in special highly absorbent, multi-surfaced *anechoic chambers*. But by using carefully positioned sound-absorbing materials we can suppress most acoustic reflections, and produce non-reverberant (*dead*, *flat*, *dry*) surroundings. Such conditions reduce the pick-up of extraneous noise, and make 'exterior' sets in studios sound more convincing. However, because sound waves do not carry well in such surroundings (reflections help to reinforce sound strength), they can be very tiring to perform in (especially for singers, musicians), and microphones need to be positioned closer as sounds seem weaker.

Practical acoustics

A certain amount of reverberation enriches and strengthens sounds, conveying an impression of vitality and spaciousness. Therefore most studios have quite carefully chosen acoustics; neither too live nor too dead.

In practice, you will find that the amount of sound absorption or reflection within an environment can change considerably if local conditions alter. Sound quality may be dampened or brightened as furnishings are added or removed; there may be a reduction in top ('highs'); the amount of reverberation alters. The difference in a theater's acoustics with and without an audience can be quite remarkable. Moving a large scenic flat can alter local sound quality, making it harsh, hollow, or boxy – particularly if there is an extensive ceiling to the setting.

On location, the audio engineer has to contend with a wide variety of acoustic conditions and encroaching environmental noise, and must rely heavily on selective microphones and careful positioning to achieve optimum audio quality.

Where a performance is taking place in reverberant surroundings (e.g. a string quartet playing in a large empty studio) you can often improve the overall sound by placing *acoustic screens* around the subjects. The sound-absorbent tiles or padding on the screens shield the performers and their microphones from delayed sound waves reflected from the studio walls. Similarly, when an unseen group in the studio provides background music for action seen on camera you can use acoustic screens to prevent the action microphones from overhearing the musicians.

Microphone characteristics

The main thing you want to know before using a microphone concern:

1 Physical features
2 Audio quality
3 Sensitivity and directional properties
4 Installation suitability.

Which aspects are most important to you depend largely on the type of sound pick-up involved and operating conditions. For example, ruggedness may be at the expense of fidelity.

■ *Physical features* While *size* may be unimportant for a slung microphone it can matter where the microphone is to appear in shot or to be handled. *Appearance* then counts, too. *Ruggedness* is a consideration where rough or inexperienced usage is likely. *Handling noise* can also be a distraction for some sensitive microphones. *Stability and reliability* are features that only time and experience reveal, and most high-grade microphones can be relied on if given careful treatment.

■ *Audio quality* Ideally a microphone should cover the entire audio spectrum evenly. Its *transient response* to brief sharp sounds (from musical triangle to jingling keys) should be impeccable. Audio should be accurately reproduced without coloration or distortion. Fortunately, such parameters are less critical in practice!

■ *Sensitivity and directionality* A microphone's *sensitivity* determines how large an audio signal it produces for a given sound volume. Although audio amplifiers can compensate for even the least sensitive microphones, excessive amplification adds spurious hiss and hum to the audio signal.

Any microphone will normally have to work closer to quiet sounds than louder ones, but less sensitive microphones must be positioned that much closer. However, they are less liable to be overloaded or damaged by loud sounds, so that in certain applications (percussion) they may be preferable.

A sound-boom microphone needs to be pretty sensitive, or it would have to work too close to sources (casting shadows); and yet it must not suffer from *rumble* (when racking the boom arm in and out), or wind noise (as it moves through the air). So condenser or dynamic microphones are generally used.

The *directional properties* of the microphone (*polar diagram*) are simply its sensitivity pattern in space. Sometimes you will need an *omni-directional* response, that hears equally well in all directions. At others you require a very *directional* response, able to pick out a selected sound source and ignore or suppress others nearby. Certain microphones have adjustable directionality.

■ *Installation suitability* When you connect together various pieces of audio equipment interfacing problems can arise. Inter-unit cable plugs are not standardized, and you must use the appropriate connectors or adapters. (Types include Mini, phono, RCA, Din, Canon.) As with all audio equipment, the electrical *impedance* of your microphone must match the line or amplifier into which it connects. Although a low-impedance unit may sound fine in a higher impedance input, the reverse is less likely. Low-impedance microphones (50–600 Ω) are most versatile for you can use longer cable lengths without top-loss; unlike high-impedance microphones (2000–10 000 Ω), which are also susceptible to hum/electrical interference pick-up.

In European designs the amplifier input should be at least five times the microphone's rated impedance (typically 200 Ω) to avoid high-frequency distortion.

■ *Choice of microphone* All audio technicians have prejudices about the right microphone for the job and exactly where to place it; for no two situations are *identical*. Listening to a piano performance, we find the instrument's tone varies considerably with its manufacturer, tuning, performer; and even changes with temperature, humidity, and acoustics. While most specialists would agree to use a condenser or ribbon microphone, its positioning is influenced by many subtle factors.

Where there is no 'universal' microphone type, one design may fulfil several different purposes. A certain condenser microphone may well serve for a boom, floor stand, hung, or desk stand. But it would be unsuitable beside a boisterous drummer or as a hand microphone at a remote, due to its susceptibility to overload.

Types of microphone

Dynamic (moving-coil) microphone

A very robust design, the dynamic microphone is not sensitive to handling and has a wide range of applications; baton, fishpole, small boom, desk or stand, slung, and field (location) use. It is often used for less critical sound quality (close singer) or close loud sources (e.g. drums). Small versions are used as lavalier and clip-on personal microphones.

The microphone tends to be unidirectional to higher frequencies, but non-directional to low frequencies. Consequently there is a top fall-off as subjects move off-axis (center line). This feature is useful with sources that are shrill, toppy, or sibilant; when one deliberately positions them off-axis.

This type of microphone works by sound-wave pressure variations vibrating a diaphragm which has a small coil of wire attached. Coil movement within a magnetic field generates audio currents. A typical frequency range is 40–16 000 Hz.

Condenser (electrostatic) microphone

The condenser microphone produces the highest audio quality (typically 20–18 000 Hz), and has an excellent response to transient sounds. It is used for high-grade pick-up (moving or static), especially when some distance from source (e.g. slung over an orchestra). It can be fitted to a boom, stand, fishpole, or slung.

The condenser microphone has the disadvantages that it is relatively large, and, being highly sensitive, it is liable to input overload distortion by very loud nearby sources. In addition, the unit requires a polarizing voltage supply and an adjacent preamplifier.

In the condenser microphone a light flexible metallic membrane is stretched close to a flat metal plate and a polarizing potential (e.g. 60 V DC) is applied between them. Sound-wave pressure fluctuations alter the intervening space and hence their inter-capacity. Varying current continually taken to recharge this changing capacitance constitutes the audio signal.

Electret capsule

The electret capsule is very extensively used as a personal or a concealed microphone, providing good-quality pick-up. This relatively cheap miniature condenser microphone incorporates a plastic film diaphragm with an inbuilt 'permanent' electrostatic charge; thus eliminating the need for an applied polarizing voltage. A tiny associated amplifier (battery powered) is enclosed in the microphone housing.

Performance deteriorates to some extent with aging, resulting in a loss of higher frequencies (top, highs), reduced sensitivity, and increased background noise. Deterioration can be accelerated by high humidity, moisture, heat, and dust. Rapid unexpected failure is not uncommon.

A *pressure-zone microphone (PZM; boundary layer microphone)* is an unobtrusive low-profile, plate-mounted electret capsule with a hemispherical or a semi-cardioid pick-up pattern. Attached to e.g. floor, table, or wall surfaces near the sound source, the rugged PZM combines sensitivity and high-quality output, with considerable freedom from contact noise, or audio overload. It is, however, liable to emphasize ambient reflected noise from surroundings. (*See Digests – Pressure-zone microphone.*)

Ribbon (velocity, pressure-gradient) microphone

This microphone is suitable for static pick-up of speech and music, and for stand and slung applications. It has an excellent transient response and produces the highest audio quality. The ribbon microphone has an even frequency response (e.g. 30–18 000 Hz) over its pick-up field – although there is some top-loss for pick-up oblique to its ribbon. Bass notes are emphasized when the source is very close. Its normal figure-of-eight directional response is often made unidirectional (asymmetrical) by internal design.

On the debit side, the ribbon microphone is not generally robust or compact. It is not normally suitable for mobile boom use (or hand use), being susceptible to wind rumble and wind damage. Also it is subject to overload from close loud sounds.

In the ribbon microphone a thin corrugated foil strip held between magnet poles vibrates with air-pressure differences on either face, so generating an electric audio current in the foil.

Directional characteristics

Whether a microphone responds equally well to sounds from all directions, or only to those over a limited angle, is determined by both its type (electrostatic, ribbon, etc.) and its construction. A microphone's *directional* or *directivity pattern* (*polar diagram*) is normally fixed, but some designs have *adjustable* characteristics that allow you to choose a directional response that suits a particular application.

Omnidirectional

An omnidirectional microphone is equally sensitive in all directions. Quality does not vary with the direction of the sound source. However, because the omni microphone picks up all sounds in its vicinity it cannot discriminate between the subjects you are interested in and unwanted noise. It picks up speech, acoustic reflections, and environmental noises equally well! It is useful, though, for group sound pick-up, or where subject moves are unpredictable.

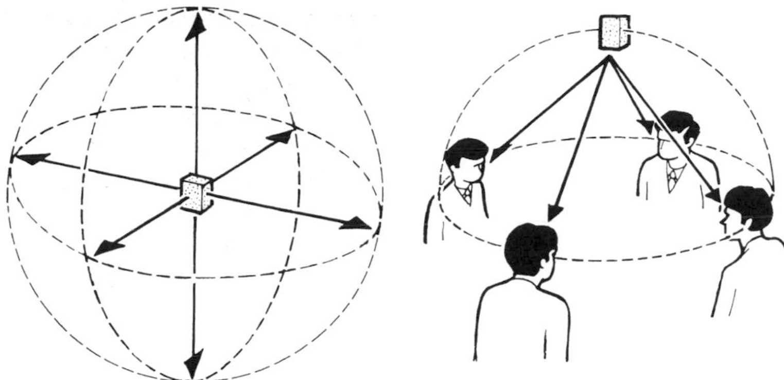

Fig. 12.7 Omnidirectional response
Equally sensitive in all directions
Rugged, generally less susceptible to breath pops or impact shock.

Unidirectional

The unidirectional microphone is most sensitive in a particular direction and relatively deaf in others. This characteristic helps you to concentrate on certain pick-up areas and suppress background sounds, or to favor quieter sounds (weak voices) against louder ones. A boom microphone may be fitted with a unidirectional microphone, so that it can work further away from subjects without extraneous pick-up.

However the microphone's response is not generally constant through the audio range. It is often more directional at higher frequencies than at lower ones. Consequently, if the microphone is not pointed directly at the subject, or a person moves to one side, the audio can lose *definition* (*brilliance, highs*) as the high-frequency response deteriorates.

Cardioid

This broad, heart-shaped unidirectional pattern covers some 160°. Used for general-purpose sound pick-up, it readily accepts spaced sources, unlike a half-eight pattern, which is more restrictive at close distances. Rear pick-up is limited; although some designs are more *omni*directional at lower frequencies.

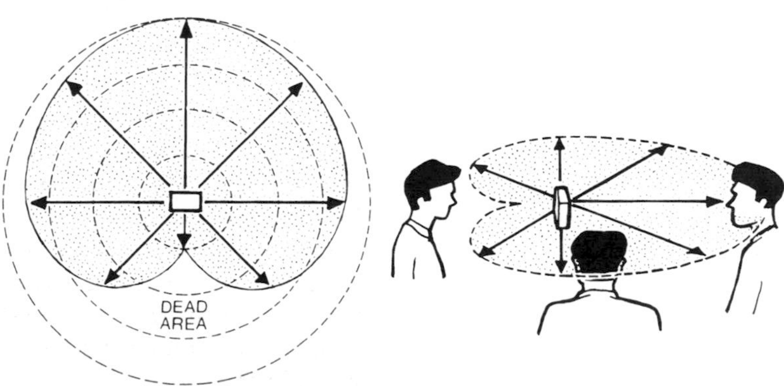

Fig. 12.8 Cardioid response
A broad heart-shaped pick-up pattern, insensitive on its rear side.

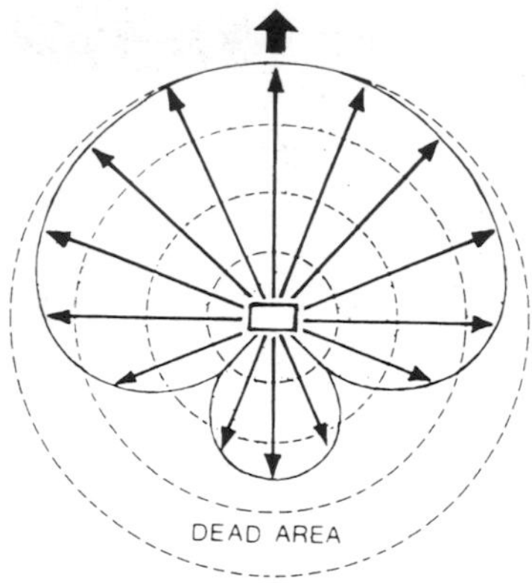

Fig. 12.9 Hypercardioid response A modified cardioid response – more directional with a prominent rear sensitivity lobe.

Hypercardioid (supercardioid)

This has a modified cardioid response with a narrower frontal *lobe* (pick-up pattern) and a weaker rear pattern. Generally considered as providing the best balance between incident and ambient sound.

Bidirectional

Both faces of the microphone are live, providing a two-directional figure-of-eight pick-up patterns of about 100° each. To either side are two dead (deaf) areas. A typical traditional ribbon-microphone characteristic, this pattern is occasionally used for musical set-ups.

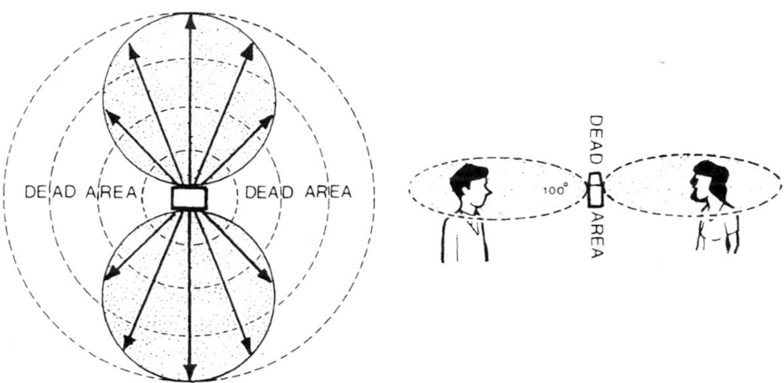

Fig. 12.10 Bidirectional response Sensitive on either face, but deaf to sound pick-up at the sides.

Highly directional microphones

These have two applications:

- Wherever you want to pick out a particular subject from a group.
- In situations where subjects are some distance away, and increased audio amplification would make both the subject and environmental sounds much louder, the very directional pick-up reduces unwanted sound reflections and noise.

Line microphones use a slotted interference tube(s) with an attached electrostatic microphone. The smallest version is the familiar *shotgun* or *rifle* microphone. This is around 0.54 m (22 in.) long, and has a coverage of about 50°. It is very adaptable. It can be hand-held with or without its windscreen (windshield), fastened to the top of a camera to pick up atmospheric sound or single speakers. It can be used in a sound boom, and can be fixed to a fishpole (fishing rod). The shotgun/rifle microphone is widely used for ENG and EFP applications and other work in the field.

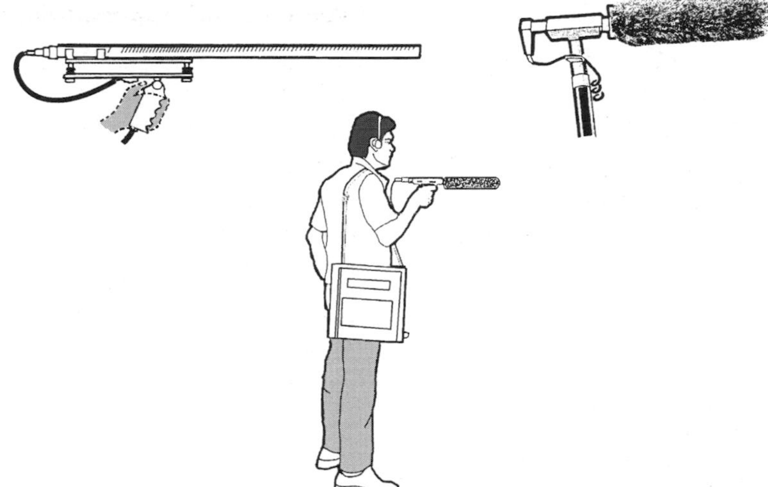

Fig. 12.11 Shotgun (rifle) microphones
A type of highly directional microphone. The popular shotgun (rifle) form is shown here, with and without its windscreen (windshield) of cloth, foam plastic, or artificial fur.

The largest *machine-gun* versions, 2.5 m (8 ft) long, use combined tubes of varying lengths and are tripod mounted. Although rather cumbersome and producing inferior quality (particularly off-axis), the device is useful for isolating individuals in a distant group. Because directivity worsens below 2000 Hz, a bass cut is often introduced to reduce noise pick-up.

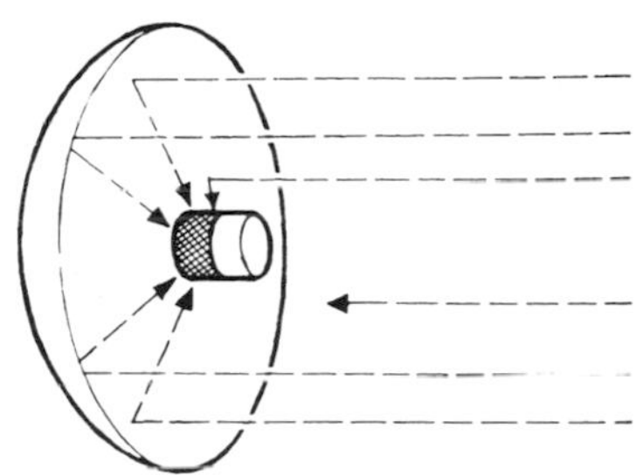

Fig. 12.12 Parabolic reflector
Extremely directional and sensitive, sound is focused by the reflector into the central microphone.

Parabolic reflectors provide a sensitive highly directional system (10–40°) in which a parabolic-shaped metal reflector 0.6–0.9 m (2–3 ft) in diameter focuses sound into a central cardioid microphone. Ineffective below about 300 Hz, the reflector is bulky and liable to wind rock unless firmly mounted. Whereas the *line microphone's* directionality is achieved by rejecting sounds outside its pick-up angle, the *parabolic reflector* actually concentrates sounds by acoustical reflection, and so has increased sensitivity.

Using the microphone

Personal microphones

One of the simplest and most convenient ways of picking up sound is to clip a personal microphone onto a person's clothing; a lapel or their tie. The audio quality is generally good, even under fairly noisy conditions. (This form of microphone is often called a *lavalier*, but strictly speaking, that is a small microphone hung on a *lanyard* cord around the neck – particularly useful on the beach.)

Where the microphone is worn *underneath clothing* such as a sweater, blouse, or dress it is less obtrusive – apart from the giveaway bump. However, there can be disadvantages. Apart from the chore of threading its cable beneath the person's clothing to a connecting cable or a belt wireless transmitter there is the likelihood that the sound will be muffled. There may be contact

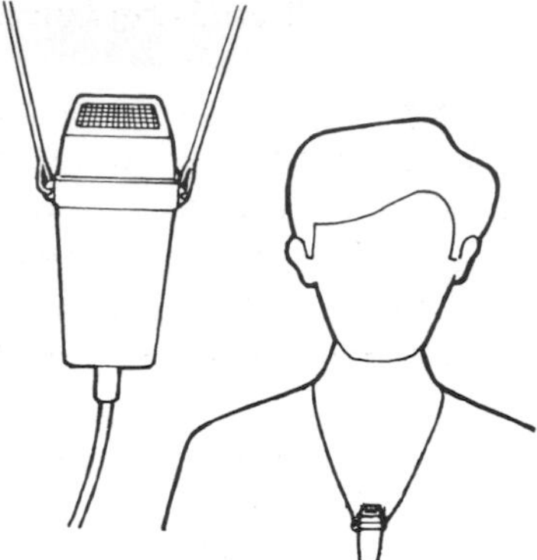

Fig. 12.13 Lavalier (lanyard, neck)
This microphone is slung on a neck cord 15 cm (6 in) below chin. Although less used today, this technique remains useful where a *clip-microphone* cannot be fitted, e.g. where clothing is unsuitable or absent.

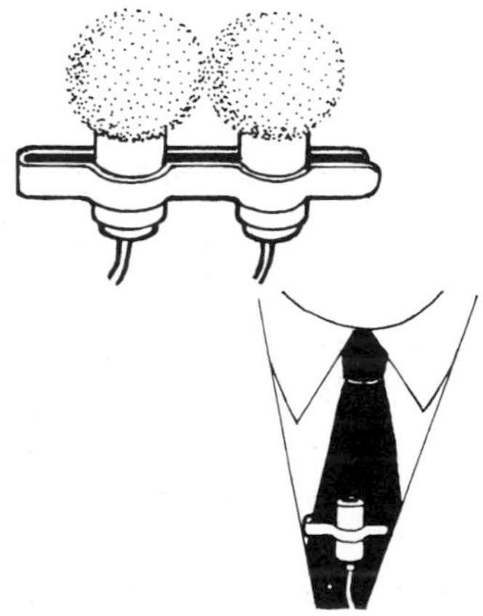

Fig. 12.14 Miniature capsule microphone
Known variously as a *clip microphone, tie-tack microphone* or confusingly as a *lavalier.* Both electret and dynamic versions are used. The microphone is clipped to the necktie, lapel or shirt, in single or *dual-redundancy* form (live plus stand-by microphone). Presence filters may improve sound quality. Plastic-foam windscreens/windshields can be fitted to reduce wind noise.

Clip microphones are often worn *upside down,* to reduce sound level variations caused by head movements, and to avoid breath noise, etc. Results vary, but there is some loss of top (reduced definition). and extraneous sounds from clothing. footsteps, etc., may be more pronounced.

noises as clothing or personal ornaments rub against the microphone. And the wearer may need to be warned against handling the microphone or holding any objects against the chest during a demonstration. Lovingly cuddled pet animals can wreak havoc with the sound!

Unwanted sound pick-up can be a problem too; from other people speaking nearby or from noisy machinery in the vicinity. (If you are using personal microphones on several speakers in a group make sure that these are all *in-phase.*)

To avoid the rumble of wind striking the microphone it is advisable to fit a small foam *windshield* when working in the open air; or even leave it permanently attached.

Because an electret microphone is small, there is a tendency to use it casually. But remember that its leads and connections are particularly vulnerable, and need to be checked regularly. Where a speaker is seated, the microphone cable can be attached to a nearby floor outlet. But if someone is going to move around, any cable is going to drag along behind them. Some people quickly accept the idea, others feel tethered, others foul up the cable on any obstacles . . . To overcome this, a personal *wireless microphone* can be used instead. In either case, of course, you always need to remember to recover the microphone and cable before the speaker can leave.

Wireless (radio) microphone

In this arrangement a miniature microphone (e.g. an electret type) is plugged into a small pocket or belt transmitter. Its signal is picked up by the nearby antenna (aerial) of a sensitive receiver and routed into the audio mixer. Although modern units are themselves very reliable, there can be problems in transmission pick-up.

Radio black-out (dead spots; drop-out), fading, distortion, or interference can arise from multi-path reception or screening due to metal structures or equipment. Diversity reception using multi-antennae arrangements can improve reliability. The system's range is often limited to around 400 m (440 yd) and the transmitter's battery should be regularly checked (life about 4 to 6 hours).

Each microphone needs its own transmitter/receiver system. Particularly where several production production groups are working in the vicinity and using the same FM frequencies, there can be interaction. For long-distance reception in the field a more sensitive antenna array may be essential. So it is wisest wherever possible to carry out a preliminary site survey to check for potential problems, rather than assume that it will all work on the day.

Earpiece

In most live presentations the newscasters, anchors, commentators, regularly wear an *earpiece* fed from a small pocket radio receiver (or in some situations a trailing cable). This arrangement allows them to have continuous contact with the production group, and hear instructions, up-to-the-minute information, editorial guidance, prompting where necessary.

This earpiece may be supplied with regular *production intercom (talkback)*, and/or *program sound*. But where this information would be an unnecessary distraction it can be fed instead with a switchable source; a technique known variously as *interruptible foldback, interrupted feedback (IFB), program interrupt, switched talkback (STB)*. This may be a private wire, or a single selected audio source; e.g. the voice of a distant interviewee.

Where a commentator is roaming around at a news event, a conference, or an exhibition, for example, a combination of a *wireless microphone* (to pick up their speech) and an *earpiece* guide to provide them with intercom gives the wearer considerable freedom of movement.

Hand microphone (baton, stick)

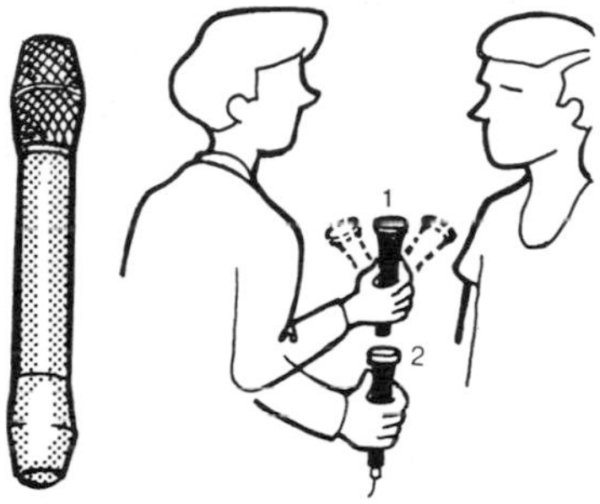

Fig. 12.15 Hand microphone
The baton microphone is widely used for interviews. Directional response (cardioid) reduces extraneous noise pick-up. *Techniques*:

1 Held just below shoulder height. Pointing at speaker improves quality but can be daunting, and microphone may then be too close. Avoid omnidirectional microphone which needs closer use (23 cm/ 9 in.).
2 Avoid low microphone position (it picks up background noises).

If a visible microphone is unacceptable, use a personal, fishpole, or shotgun/rifle fitting.

The hand microphone, which is usually of the omnidirectional type, must be rugged, permit free handling, and have an efficient *windshield (wind gag, blast filter, pop filter)*. This cloth or foam-plastic shield suppresses the rumbles and thumps from wind noise or close explosive sounds.

Many hand microphones are fitted with a *spherical ball mesh*. This permits very close positioning when used outdoors in noisy environments (to exclude extraneous sounds), or to avoid *howl-round (audio feedback)* where the microphone feeds a PA system (public address, studio address loudspeaker) for a studio audience. It is a safeguard, too, where singers traditionally '*mug the mike*', holding it close to the mouth to add presence to their performance. A close directional microphone exaggerates bass, so often needs filtering.

Although the sound quality from a hand microphone is usually very satisfactory a lot depends on the skills of the person using it. There is always the risk of the microphone being badly positioned. Some experience is needed, too, in handling the microphone cable. This is best held in one hand while directing the microphone with the other. As it trails behind, the cable is liable to be caught up, stepped on, tripped over, unless the user takes care. The cable should never be pulled along by the microphone or allowed to become knotted or kinked.

The cordless *wireless microphone* overcomes that particular hazard, for it incorporates a tiny radio transmitter, with an internal or 'hanging tail' antenna.

Lip/noise-canceling microphone

This specially designed hand-held microphone is invaluable for off-camera commentaries in noisy surroundings. Its mouthguard is held against the upper lip.

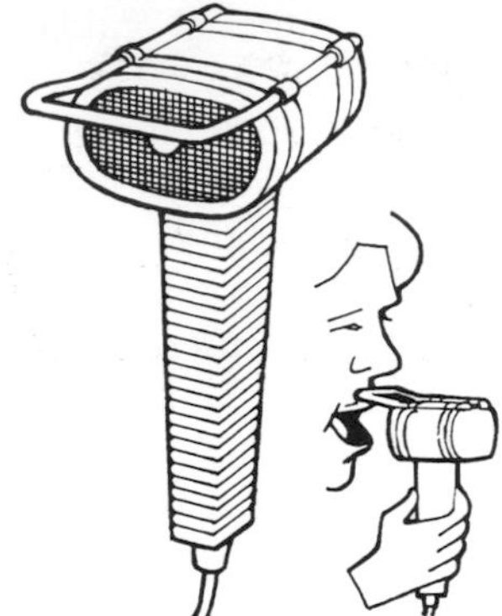

Fig. 12.16 Lip microphone
Used under high-noise conditions: the bar is held against upper lip to maintain constant mouth distance. All noise-canceling microphones are susceptible to breath noises, and microphone-to-mouth distance can be critical.

Equalized for close speech (attenuating its normal bass excess), the environmental noise becomes inaudible. Because it obscures the user's face, the lip microphone is seldom used in shot.

Stand microphone

Made in various sizes and of adjustable height (0.3 to 1.5 m (1 to 5 ft)) the stand microphone is used for soloists/speakers and for instrumental pick-up in orchestras, groups, etc. Various offset tubes (swan-necks) permit precision positioning and small slim fittings prevent the stand from being obtrusive. A quick-release top-clip enables the microphone to be removed and hand-held where necessary.

The main disadvantages of the stand microphone are that the performer (talent) may kick it, causing loud resonant noises, or displace it, and its cable can prove a hazard (floor tape it if necessary). Remember, too, that it is essentially a *static* pick-up arrangement and people may easily move 'off-mike'.

Fig. 12.17 Stand microphone
Floor stands are height-adjustable and may be fitted with angled extensions. Microphone clips into quick-release head. Heavy base prevents instability.

Desk microphone

Microphones can be clamped into small supports to enable them to stand on tables or desks. Formerly used to give an 'authoritative air' to a broadcaster, today the microphone is small and unobtrusive, or sometimes hidden. A foam-plastic pad may prevent table-thump pick-up. Some audio engineers prefer to use stand microphones, hidden by a false table-front or through table-top holes, to circumvent this noise (Figure 12.18).

When audio pick-up is difficult a desk microphone is sometimes used in drama productions to augment other microphones – hidden at a vantage point within staging, furniture props.

Desk discussions

Although clip-on personal microphones can be used for this situation, desk microphones offer better quality and are preferred by some audio engineers. Microphones should be positioned in the direction of head movement. Directional microphones reduce unwanted pick-up of acoustic and environmental noise or audience loudspeakers, but placement may be more critical. Do not intermix different types of microphone because quality will be inconsistent. Cables should be concealed, tidied, and taped (to desk and floor). Never run them alongside power cables and only cross them at right angles.

Prerehearsal checking includes: connections, microphone routing to the audio control board (scratch microphones, never blow on

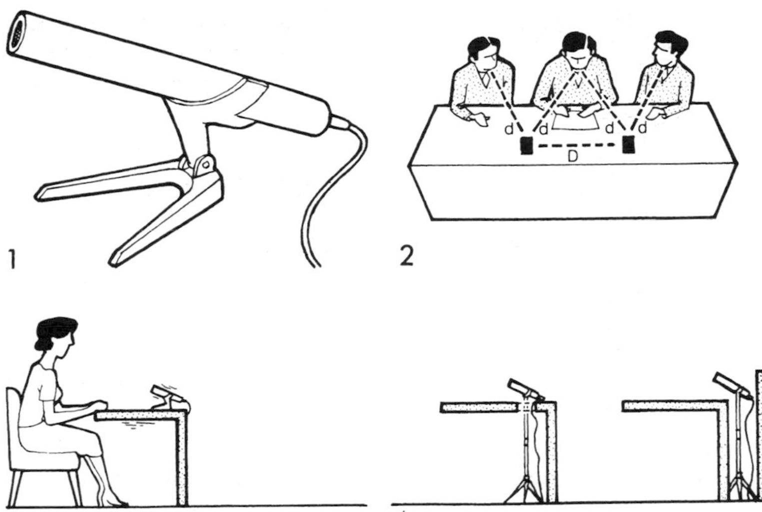

Fig. 12.18 Desk microphone
1 For desk discussions, microphones in small fittings are often used.
2 Careful positioning is essential for good sound pick-up; typical distances D = 0.9–1.2 m (3–4 ft) and d = 0.3–0.6 m (1–2 ft).
3 Desk-top microphones may be vulnerable (desk thumps, displacement).
4 Alternatively the microphone may be isolated on a floor-stand, either using holes in desk-top or behind false desk front.

them when identifying), and *phasing* (connections). If microphones are not all similarly connected, the quality will change when their outputs are mixed together (bass loss).

Slung microphone (hung, hanging)

Where space is restricted, or other mountings cannot be used, you can suspend a microphone over the performance area. The slung microphone is useful for broad group sounds such as sections of an orchestra, or to pick up audience reactions. It is less successful when used to pick up speech from individuals within a seated group; especially when they are being shot in close-up. The microphone is high above their heads, particularly when raised to be kept out of long shots, so that they are speaking across or away from the microphone. The audio gain has to be increased, and the background noise can be very audible.

In a limited-access area (e.g. a narrow hallway) a slung microphone may be effective providing the performers play to the microphone and there are not excessive reflections from nearby walls. Sometimes the microphone can be disguised as a light fitting.

If a *directional* microphone is used, you can reduce pick-up of acoustic reflections and environmental noise, but run the risk of people moving 'off-microphone'. A non-directional (omni) pattern is less restrictive but needs to be closer to avoid reflected sound.

A slung microphone must be rigged securely with safety lines and placed to avoid distracting shadows or overheating by nearby lamps.

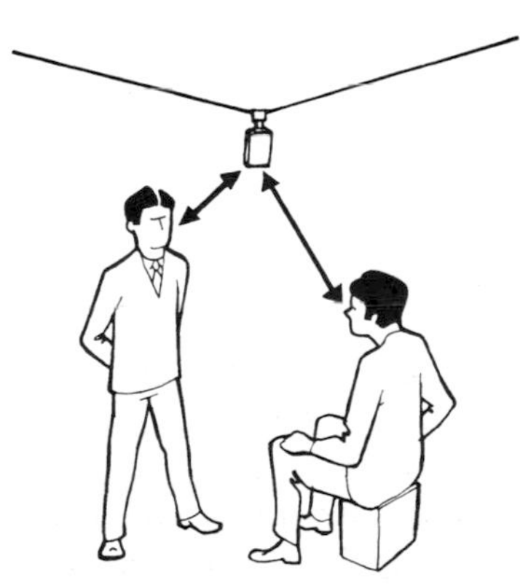

Fig. 12.19 Slung microphone
Suitable for area pick-up or nearby sounds. Problems arise when people move, or are at different distances, or are seated.

The shotgun (rifle) microphone

The *shotgun* or *rifle* microphone is a form of *line* microphone. Unlike the very sensitive, highly directional *parabolic reflector* we met earlier, the *shotgun* or (*rifle*) microphone does not concentrate the sound pick-up into a narrow beam. Instead, it has a cardioid response at middle and lower frequencies, but is very directional at upper frequencies. So it is excellent when we want to give prominence to a particular person, picking them out from others nearby; e.g. a reporter in a crowd. It is less effective, though, in live surroundings.

Table 12.1 Hints on using the shotgun (rifle) microphone

In a sound boom
When faced with the problem of picking up a singer surrounded by a choir, or individuals within a group, a shotgun microphone is often fitted to a large sound boom to help isolate subjects. But it is important to remember that because the microphone is directional, 'top' can vary when the person or microphone moves (*off-microphone*) if it is not pointed accurately.
Hand-held
When working in the open air, a hand-held shotgun microphone has several advantages. Although it is sensitive to low-frequency noise from all directions (e.g. traffic), a bass-cut reduces this considerably. The slotted tube with microphone attached is fitted into a shock-mount, which you hold with a pistol grip. A windscreen is usually clipped on to protect the unit and suppress wind noises. Take care not to cover the tube's slots (e.g. with clothing), or to handle the tube itself. Keeping as close to the subject as you reasonably can, and making sure that the microphone has an unobstructed view, you point the shotgun at the subject while checking the audio on earphones and adjusting the microphone's position for optimum quality. (The operator's earphones are usually split, so that one ear receives the program sound while the other is fed with intercom (production talkback) or private wire (audio control sound).)

The fishpole (fishing rod)

The *fishpole* or *fishing rod* is widely used for sound pick-up on location, and in smaller studios where there is insufficient space for a sound boom. A *shotgun/rifle* type of microphone is attached via a rumble-insulating cradle to the end of an adjustable lightweight aluminum tube. Preset tube lengths are typically around 2–2.5 m (6–9 ft).

The microphone is usually enclosed in a *windshield* (*wind-gag*; *windjammer*; *wind muffler*), which is made of a synthetic fur-type fabric with 'hairs' around 3 cm long. This can very effectively

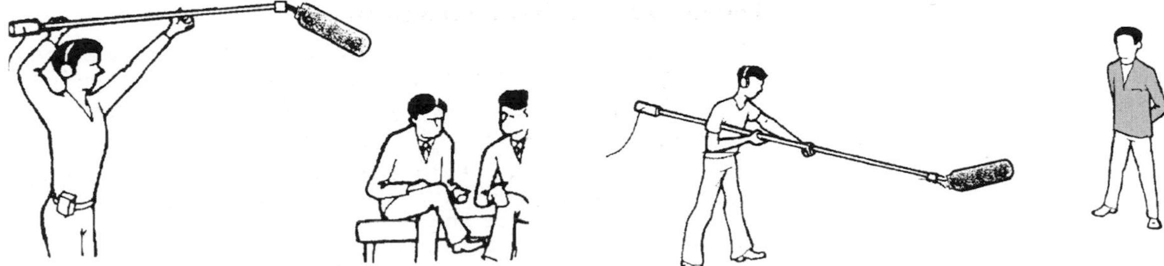

Fig. 12.20 Fishpole operation
The fishpole is fitted with the microphone (preferably in shock-proof cradle) at one end, and a counter-balancing audio cable connector-box (intercom to operator, audio to console) at the other. The fishpole can be held well-balanced above head or tucked under arm. 'Pole-in-belt' methods are unbalanced, particularly tiring, and hazardous.

suppress obtrusive wind noises. Alternatively, the microphone may be fitted with a tubular plastic-sponge or a fabric-tube wind-filter; although these materials are really inadequate in all but the lightest breeze.

The fishpole is a very adaptable device, for it can be held above or below head-height, and angled to suit the action. However, it can be very tiring to support in position for long periods, particularly when held above the head or when it is unbalanced (i.e. all the weight at the microphone end). Because the operator needs to be quite close to the action, it may not be easy at times to keep out of the way of the camera or to avoid getting into a cross-shooting camera's picture. Because the microphone's angle is fixed or preset (often at right angles to the pole), its positioning is usually rather approximate, compared with the precision possible with the regular sound boom.

Table 12.2 Hints on operating the fishpole (fishing rod)

- First check out the microphone in its shock-proof mount, making sure that it is secure and not rubbing against the mounting or the pole.
- Extend the pole to its working length. Avoid long extensions wherever possible (an unsteady microphone is difficult to position and turn accurately). Check and secure the cable (and its connections); whether the cable runs within or outside the pole.
- Discuss with the camera operator whether you are going to position the fishpole microphone above, under, or to the side of the picture's frame.
- Decide how you are going to hold the pole. If people are going to move around, anticipate your own moves or turns. (Otherwise they might walk away from you or get too close for you to follow!)
- Angle the microphone towards the action, turning the pole as necessary to cover the person speaking. Position it ahead of them as they move. Do you have a clear unobstructed path to follow them? Check that you have enough cable, and that it will not become trapped.

Sound booms

Small sound boom (small giraffe, tripod boom, lazy arm)

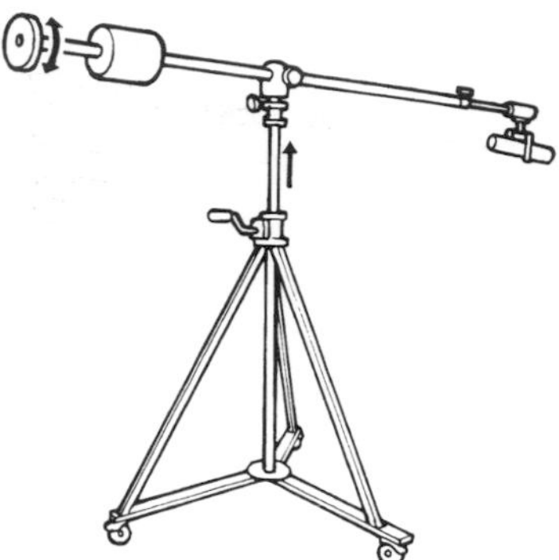

Fig. 12.21 Small studio boom
The pre-adjusted telescopic arm (counterweighted) is pivoted on a column of adjustable height in a swivel-castered tripod dolly. The boom arm can be tilted and panned, the stand wheeled around, and the microphone can usually be turned and tilted. Boom stretch is typically 3–4.5 m (10–15 ft).

Extensively used in smaller studios, this lightweight supplementary sound boom is used for static pick-up or limited movement over a smooth floor. Due to its fixed (preadjusted) arm length, the mounting must be pushed around to follow action; an operation that can be cumbersome and preoccupying.

As its central column height is raised the assembly becomes increasingly top-heavy and less stable (particularly during moves), so you normally tilt the boom arm for higher microphone positions, keeping the column low. The boom's closeness to the subject makes it correspondingly more difficult to keep out of shot. Even where the microphone can be turned and tilted by an extension control at the end of the boom arm, the small sound boom is best regarded as a stationary mounting. In some studios, it has earned the nickname of '*the menace*' due to its instability when moved around fully extended!

Cable guards on wheels prevent accidental cable overrun. Pushing over floor cables can be hazardous. The microphone's cable is laid along the floor away from cameras and lamp cables. The boom operator often plugs a headset into a nearby camera's auxiliary outlets for program and intercom.

Large sound boom (big boom, perambulator boom, big studio)

Operationally, the large boom provides the most flexible method of audio pick-up, for you can easily follow movement and favor selected sources. This ensures optimum sound quality while keeping just out of shot and avoiding boom shadows.

The boom's microphone is held in a swiveling cradle at the end of its long, telescoping, tubular arm. This counterweighted arm is pivoted on the central vertical column of the wheeled boom perambulator (pram).

With the left hand the standing operator controls microphone tilt and direction (gripping and turning respectively) and swings the boom arm, while extending/retracting the boom with the right (hand crank). The platform's operational height is adjustable – useful for seeing action past cameras. The microphone cable may be suspended or run along the floor to a wall outlet.

The large boom's main disadvantage for the smaller studio lies in its size. Also, unless the operator descends and moves the boom around, a second person is needed to reposition it. Boom tracking (moving the pram while in use) is only normally necessary for large-area working, to follow widespread action, to move aside for cameras, or for fast relocation.

Efficient boom operation requires considerable skill, particularly where action is wide-ranging, and there is the danger of casting boom shadows across performers and the set.

Fig. 12.22 part 1 Large sound boom (Fisher)

1 Three-wheeled base (1.1 × 1.6 m/3 ft 9 in × 5 ft 3 in).
2 Brake (B) and gear change (G).
3 Control to hydraulically raise/lower operator's platform (moves with column), max column height 2.4 m (7 ft 10 in), pump handle (P) to recharge cylinder. Operator's seat (S) for stand-by periods.
4 Pan and tilt lock screws (pans over 360°).
5 Right-handed crank (max microphone height 4.5 m/15 ft).
6 Script board. (a) Intercom/program *junction box*.
7 Left hand-grip (squeeze for microphone tilt, turn for microphone turn).
8 *Steering wheel.*
9 *Operator's platform*: *On Fisher-type* boom, circular to allow operator 360° movement. On *Mole–Richardson-type* boom, rectangular, collapsible sides, allows 180° movement.

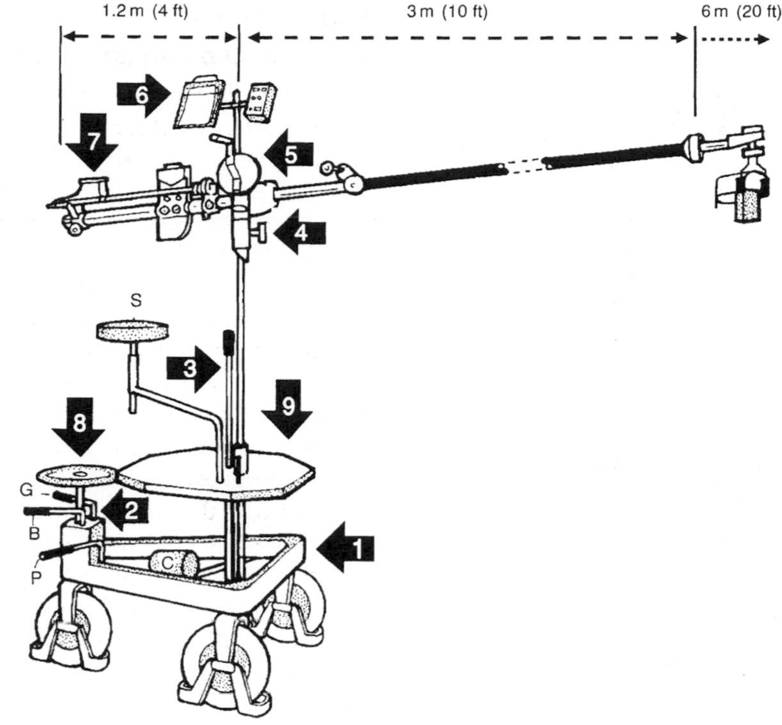

Fig. 12.22 part 2 Typical boom operations

1 *Microphone position* is adjusted to suit shot, remaining just outside frame limits. Boom arm is raised/retracted as shot widens. Operator must anticipate cuts to longer shots.
2 *Head turn*: Either a swing and microphone turn (slight arm-length change), or a static compromise position with microphone turn.
3 *Reverse turn*: Extend and swing arm, with microphone turn. Aim to avoid over-reaching subjects and turning microphone back (any face shadows cannot be seen by operator).
4 *Ascending*: Boom arm tilts up and extends, microphone tipping down during walk.
5 *Split sound*: Boom can accommodate separate sources up to about 2 m (7 ft) apart, by turning microphone and/or swinging boom. Otherwise sources must move closer together, or use a second microphone.

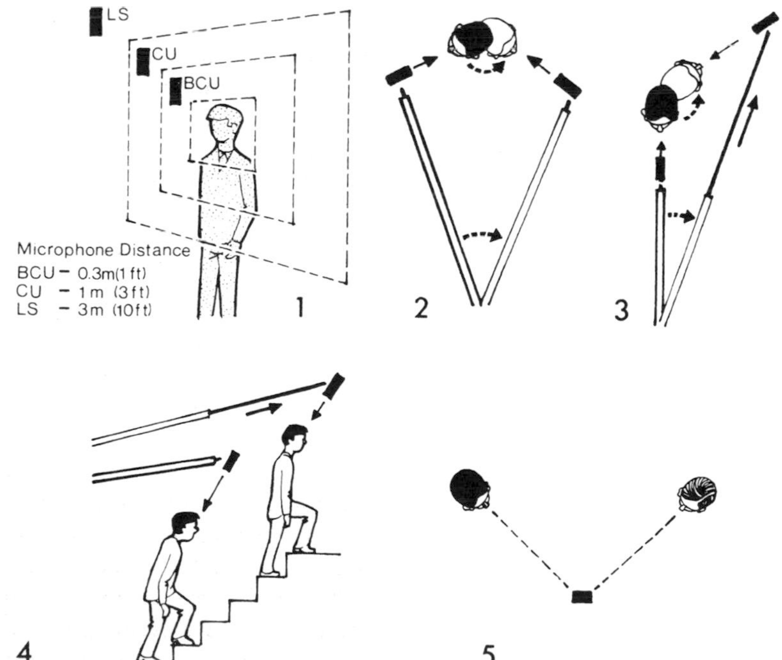

Table 12.3 Checking out the sound boom

Microphone	Speak to the audio engineer to identify microphone and check audio quality. *Phase* the microphone if necessary, with others. Place the microphones close together. If there is a bass loss, reverse one set of connections.
	Check microphone connector is secure (waggle cable end).
	Check microphone cradle. Suspension OK? Free movement?
	Turn and tip microphone. Operating strings taut and free moving?
Boom arm	Extend/retract boom arm (racking in/out). Any rumble? Controls and movement smooth? Is arm balanced throughout movement? (Adjust weights to suit microphone weight.)
	Lock off the arm's pan and tilt.
Pram (perambulator)	Raise/lower platform (hand crank or hydraulic pump).
	Check wheel brake, lock, and steering.
	If steering mode is adjustable (steer/crab) check action.
	Tires OK? (Not overinflated, no stuck-on floor tape?) Check the seat.
Cable	Check plug into wall outlet.
	Is cable routing satisfactory? *Slung cable* – avoiding lamps, anticipating moves. *Floor cable* – not obstructing, sufficient available, free for boom moves.
Additional	Check intercom/talkback and private line (reverse talkback) to audio engineer.
	Check script board is secure and script available.
	Check picture monitor being used by boom operator (fixed to boom, or slung).
	If a loudspeaker is attached to boom (for foldback of effects, music, talkback instructions, etc.), check cables, connections, and reproducing levels.

Table 12.4 Sound-boom operation

	Preliminaries
	Check the boom is in the planned floor position relative to lighting treatment, and angle it to provide maximum use.
	Check platform height to give good viewpoint over cameras, but avoid hanging lamps when operating.
	Check boom arm at max/min reach relative to area coverage, obstructions, accommodating possible action spread.
	Note key-light positions, look for potential shadow problems.
	Operation
Microphone position	Positioning depends on several factors: microphone sensitivity and directivity, acoustics, ambient noise, source loudness, and shot size. Closeness varies with the ambience required; a close microphone minimizes studio acoustics, provides deader sound, and has better presence. It also avoids extraneous sounds. Very close microphone positions coarsen sound quality, reveal breath noises, etc. Close microphones come into shot and cast shadows.
	When the microphone is further away, the distant sound quality and increased background noise may not be acceptable for the shot.

Table 12.4 (cont.)

A steady boom	For a stationary situation, hold the boom arm still and the microphone location steady towards the speaker. Avoid overhead positions – except when an omnidirectional microphone covers random groups.
Swiveling the microphone	A directional boom microphone may be turned successively to favor each person speaking (gunning the microphone), but someone can inadvertently be left *off-microphone* unless the show is scripted. Benefits with closely positioned people are arguable.
Anticipate action	Lead rather than follow talent as they move around. Do not rely on script memory, or instructions alone, but watch people for preliminary signs (e.g. before they rise or sit).
Locking off	Beware locking off the boom arm (tilt and pan) except for a static subject, or when leaving or moving the boom. People may unexpectedly move away, get up, or sit!
Fully extended	Despite counterweighting, the boom arm becomes less manageable when extended. Swinging (arc) and raising the arm is less controllable, particularly when done quickly. By retracting during wide swings it is easier to move and avoids causing shadows.
	Divide your attention between:
Performers	What performers are doing – are going to do.
Headset	The audio is 'split' on your earphones – one ear has *program sound*, the other has *intercom* from director and audio engineer. You can only judge audio quality and balance approximately, so be guided.
Shots	Be aware of picture monitors showing line (transmission) picture; check shot size. Camera tally lights show which is switched on-air. Monitors are usually too distant to detect whether your microphone is appearing in shot. If in doubt, during rehearsal carefully dip it into shot; and when told of the shot limits remember these for subsequent microphone positions.
Boom shadows	Watch for microphone shadows on people or backgrounds. Move the microphone and check if sound quality is still acceptable. If not, indicate that it cannot be cleared. (Have the performer speak up, alter the shot, or relight.) During transmission (or a 'take'), hold the shadow still, or creep it out stealthily, or slowly raise the boom, or try to hide it, or wait until off-shot before repositioning.
Repositioning the boom	Boom moves to a new floor position may require a separate operator's aid (*tracker*) under instruction Coordinate boom moves with cameras; watch for cable or boom arm catching in lamps. Take care when running over cables (damage, noise, instability).
Script or show format	Keep up to date on deleted or extra shots, or moves. Mark *take-over points* where action is to be covered by another boom.

Techniques and fashions change, and many types of productions that would once have used a boom regularly for sound pick-up now use personal microphones, wireless microphones (clip-on or baton type), and fishpoles with shotgun microphones instead.

Audio control

Located at the *audio control console* (board, desk, mixer panel) the *audio control engineer* (*sound mixer, sound supervisor*) selects and blends the various program sound sources.

Attention is divided variously between:

1. Selecting and controlling the outputs of various audio sources (microphones, discs, tape, film, VT).
2. Keeping the volume indicator within system limits by adjusting appropriate channel faders (amplifier gains).
3. Following the program audio and pictures (script, breakdown sheet), and the director's intercom (talkback) information.
4. Checking audio quality on high-grade loudspeakers.
5. Scrutinizing picture monitors showing line and preview shots, to check sound perspective, warn against microphones coming into shot, and boom shadows.
6. Guiding (and cueing) operators on booms, studio floor, audio disc, and tape repro.
7. Perhaps operating audio disc/tape equipment.
8. Liaison with other production team members.

Before rehearsal begins, the audio engineer plugs up the circuits to be used at a *patch panel*. Each of the various audio sources (e.g. Mic-1, Mic-2, Mic-3, audio tape, disc, cart, VTR, film, etc.) has an outlet socket (*jack*) on the panel. Using *patch cords* (short cables with *jack plugs* at either end), each source is routed to an appropriate *channel input* socket on the patchboard, which is permanently tied to the audio console. Now, each source is individually connected to an audio channel on the console, and can be separately controlled.

The outputs of audio equipment vary from a few millivolts (requiring a *low-level/microphone level* input system) to higher signals from audio tape or cartridge machines, film, and VT channels. Having already been amplified to e.g. 1 V, these are fed into *high-level/line-level inputs*. Each audio channel includes a *pre-amplifier (pre-amp)* to boost weaker sources and/or *attenuators (pads)* to reduce strong audio signals. Comparisons of average volume are made during rehearsal (*level tests*) to match their relative levels (volumes).

The gain (amplification) of the *program/channel amplifier* for each source is adjusted with a channel fader or 'pot' (potentiometer).

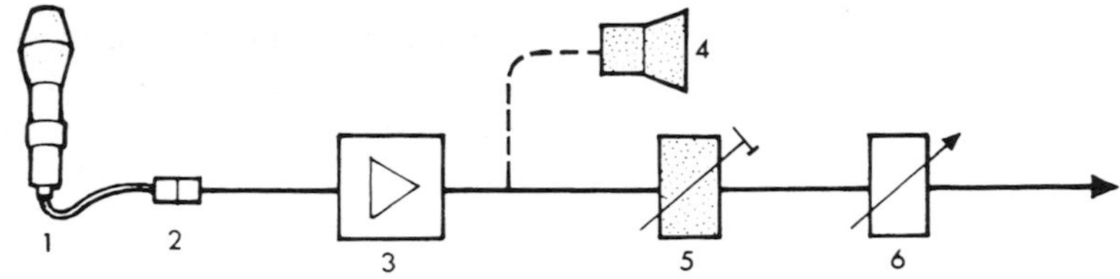

Fig. 12.23 part 1 Basic audio control
Microphone (1) plugs into studio wall outlet (2) and the audio is amplified (3). A side-chain *audition/pre-hear circuit* provides check-point before further processing. A preset *attenuator/pad* (5) adjusts channel amplification (gain) and a channel fader (slide, quadrant or knob) (6) controls it overall.

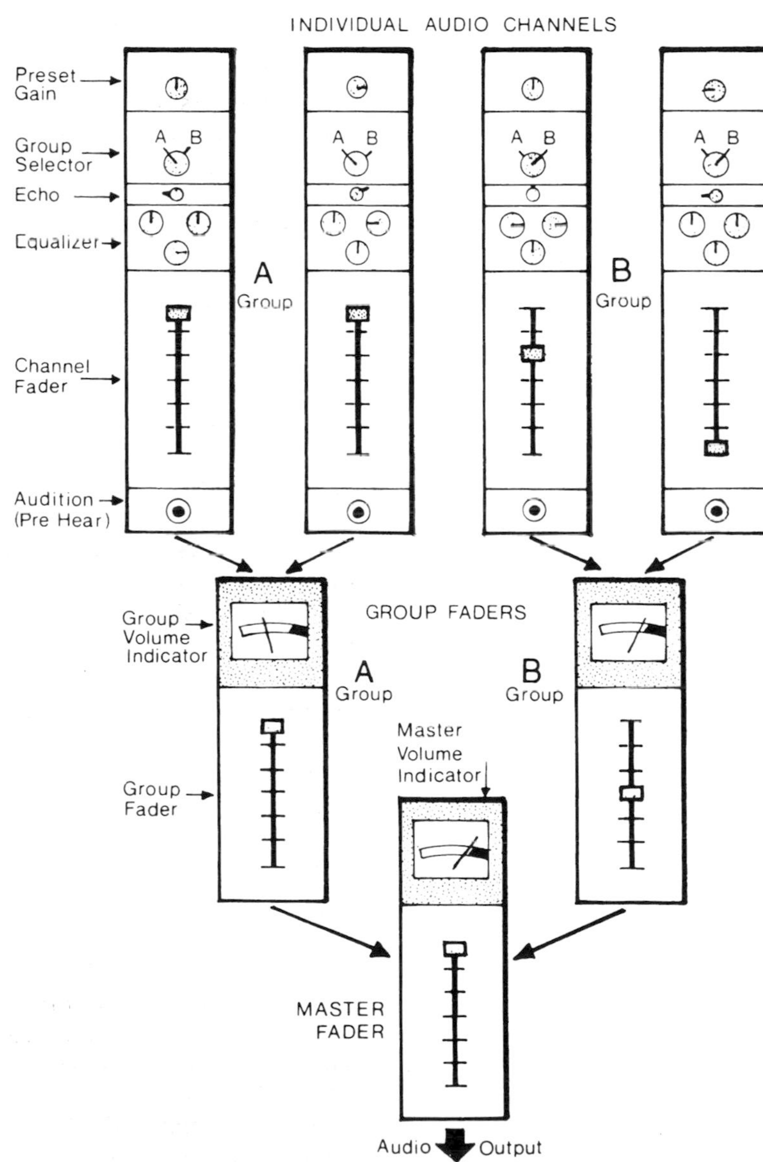

Fig. 12.23 part 2 Audio console

Preset gain Adjusts audio channel gain (amplification) to compensate for variations in levels from sources.

Group selector. Switches a sound channel to a group fader (A or B).

Echo (Reverb). Adjusts the amount of artificial echo added to an individual audio channel.

Equalize (E.Q.). Adjustable tone filters altering sound quality by boosting/reducing/cutting high or low notes, or part of audio spectrum.

Channel fader. The main control adjusted to suit the volume of an individual source (e.g. quiet voice, loud instrument).

Audition/cue/pre-hear. A switch enabling the audio engineer to check-listen (earphones or loudspeaker) to a channel that is faded out; so not audible on the main audio output.

Group fader/group master/sub-master. All sources switched to that group (here labelled A or B) will be faded in/out simultaneously. The audio signal's strength (amplitude) is monitored by a local indicator.

Master fader. The outputs of the group faders are routed to this master control, which adjusts the overall program level, as shown on the master volume indicator.

Audio-control desks are made as completely integrated units, or in modular form as above (plug-in sub-units).

Additional facilities include: audio limiter/compressor; audio batons; echo devices; program monitoring level adjustment; control or audience address/foldback/playback system; panning (left/right); balance (relative loudness of groups: *prominent/ pullback*.)

This may be a rotating knob, or slider/quadrant control. (The latter has the advantages that several can be operated simultaneously with one hand, and their relative positions are obvious.) These channel faders can be used to fade individual sources in/out ('pot in/out') as well as control their average level. One some consoles you can switch to a preset pot setting (*keying in*); but there is always the danger of clipping the start of the incoming sound through a *late cut (upcutting)*.

Having adjusted their relative strengths with individual *balance* faders, these sources (e.g. several choir microphones) can be linked to a single *group fader*, and are controlled simultaneously. The outputs of all group faders are controlled by a *master pot (line/main-channel control)*. At selected points in the control chain, volume indicators show the strength of the audio signal there.

Dynamic range control

We need to control the system's amplification (gain) to keep the audio signal within its volume limits (*dynamic range*). This is done both manually and by automatic limiter/compressor circuits.

Manual control

Although our ears are tolerant of a wide volume range, tensing to very loud sounds and relaxing to receive quiet ones, straight audio systems do not have this property. If you keep audio amplification down to prevent peak overloads, quietest sounds will be inaudible. Increase amplification to hear these, and even fairly loud sounds now reach upper system limits and distort.

You can overcome this dilemma by imperceptibly altering the audio gain manually, to compensate for these volume peaks and troughs. Some sound sources need little or no control, while others (symphony orchestras) require continual sensitive readjustments. The trick is to anticipate, and to make any changes gradually, so that the listener is unaware of the subterfuge. You must not 'snatch back' peaks, or boost quiet passages, destroying dynamics completely through overcontrol (riding the gain).

VU meters and PPMs show the audio signal's strength relative to the system's available range (Figure 12.24). (*See Digests – Volume indicators*.)

Audio processors

Automatic circuits can be used to adjust audio amplification; restricting the volume range, controlling unanticipated peaks (*finalizer*), or wildly varying sound levels. They can substitute for manual judgement – but electronics make no artistic evaluation and can create unnaturally strangled crescendos, or inappropriately

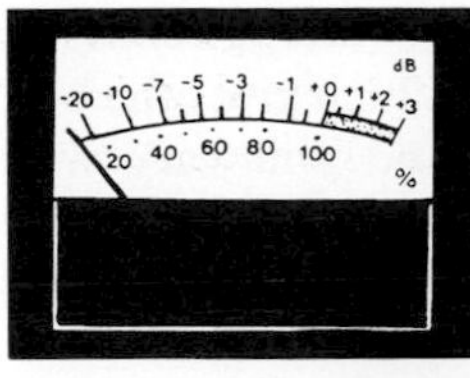

1

2

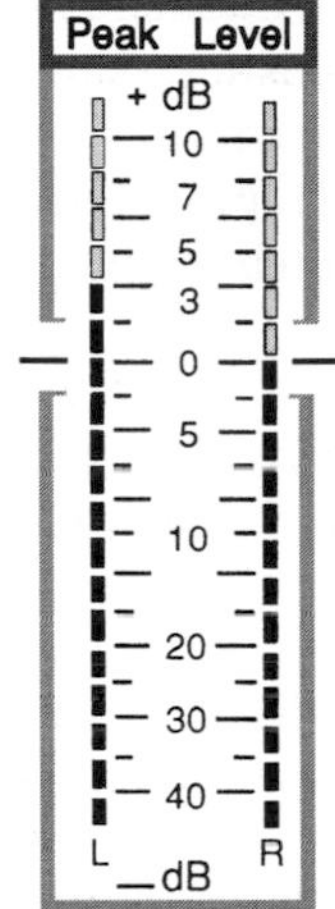

3

Fig. 12.24 Volume indicator

1 *Volume Meter* (*VU Meter*). The upper scale, marked in decibels (dB), is for calibration and line-up purposes (using steady tone). The lower scale shows percentage modulation, where 100% is system's max limit.
2 *Peak Program Meter* (*European*). Designed specifically to indicate sound volume peaks. The PPM has fast-rise/slow-return characteristics, so its needle fluctuates less than VU meter. Its easily read seven section logarithmic scale is akin to ear's loudness response (unlike VU meter).
3 Instead of a meter dial, the volume indicator is often in the form or a bargraph of *LEDs* (*light emitting diodes*), *gas-discharge devices*, or *plasma displays*. In this example, both channels of a stereo system are monitored, showing the *peaks* of the audio signals. In a more complex arrangement, twin bargraphs are used to indicate separate *VDU* and *PPM* displays.

boost quiet sounds. Most audio operators regard such equipment as a useful safety facility for the unexpected moment rather than an artistically viable control method (compressors; limiters).

While both variable gain systems prevent peak overloads above a selected volume the compressor also increases amplification of quieter passages, and can be used to compensate for unwanted volume variations, e.g. fading as a vocalist's hand-microphone position changes. In radio, DJs deliberately use (misuse?) such facilities to make quiet background music surge in whenever they stop speaking. Similarly, the surging beat of *peak-limiting* is used as an audio effect. (*See Digests – Ducker.*)

Sound balance

When you *balance* various sound sources you are adjusting their relative volumes, clarity, quality, scale, perspective, and the ratio of direct to indirect sound. The audio operator is concerned in practice with two forms of program balance, that we can consider as *continuity balance* and *internal balance*.

Continuity balance

Here, the operator controls a succession of sources; ensures that one person is not disproportionately louder or quieter than another; that the background music or effects are proportional to the dialogue; that other audio sources (film) match with studio sound. (Preliminary *level tests/voice levels* assess typical audio control settings needed.)

Microphone arrangements

A number of different factors can affect the apparent quality of a sound source:

- The characteristic sound quality of many instruments will vary, depending on whether they are being played loudly or softly. (An instrumentalist playing in dead surroundings may instinctively play louder and produce a harsher sound quality.)
- Local acoustics can modify the apparent sound quality, as some parts of the instrument's audio spectrum are reflected and reinforced, while others are absorbed. So results can vary, depending on the subject's position relative to nearby structures.
- Other nearby sound sources may mask your sound source.

So obviously it can make a great difference where you place your microphone relative to the subject and its surroundings. You can approach the problem of sound pick-up in several different ways.

You can use a *single* microphone or a *group* of microphones, or *individual* microphones for each sound source. Which gives the best results will always be a matter of opinion, and will vary with circumstances. And, of course, it will depend on whether you are working with a mono or stereo sound system.

■ **Single microphone balance** – You can place a single sensitive microphone (often non-directional) in what appears to be the optimum position overhearing the action area; e.g. to pick up an entire group, choir, orchestra, etc. However, remember that what you hear on the spot, and the way the microphone interprets the sound, can differ considerably in practice.

On the face of it, this method is simple; but a lot can depend on the layout (grouped or spread) and the acoustics. Single-microphone pickup is invariably a compromise, and in a mono system can produce merged sound with unreliable perspective. Some instruments or performers may be overprominent, while others are barely audible.

■ **Multi-microphone balance** – Where you have various kinds of instruments with different quality and attack, a single microphone position is unlikely to suit them all – especially if they are spread over a wide area and shot from several camera angles. Particularly where the acoustic conditions vary from one spot to the next, it is better to use a series of carefully positioned microphones.

It is easier and quicker to blend a multi-microphone set-up than to move a single microphone around empirically, hopefully seeking optimum results – particularly when time is short, and you need to anticipate before the performers arrive for rehearsal. Using a multi-microphone approach, you can either build up a fixed overall balance, or vary the sound balance during performance; emphasizing certain instruments (or groups) while backgrounding others.

There are limitations, though, when mixing several microphones' outputs:

- Where microphones which are at different distances away pick up the same instrument their combined outputs may blur its attack, due to *phase distortion* (i.e. self-cancelling at some frequencies).
- Varying the gain (amplification) of microphones selectively during performance can upset the internal balance of a group, as sections or soloists are 'brought forward' or 'backgrounded' in various musical passages. There is always the danger that you might lose overall perspective, so that instruments which normally provide an unobtrusive accompaniment become disproportionately prominent.

■ **Close balance** – The *close balance* techniques that are now widely used when recording musical groups are virtually a 'sound-processing' operation. Each instrument's (or subgroup's) output is recorded on a separate track of a multitrack audio tape (16, 24, 32 parallel tracks on a 2 in wide tape; 4, 8 tracks on 1 in tape). Instrumentalists or singers (using earphones) may perform together, or to prerecorded tracks. Individual tracks can be *lifted off* (*dubbed*), replaced, treated selectively (adjusting volume, quality, reverberation, pitch), synchronized, and blended with the others to achieve exactly the required combined sound. This complex *track-laying* or *mixdown* process can be computer assisted in the *dub-down* to a final track!

Sound perspective

At first it seems self-evident that the sound's proportions should match its associated picture. Close-up sound for a close-up shot; more distant sound for a long shot. This is a good working maxim. But there are exceptions where it is preferable to cheat this relationship and deliberately introduce nearer or more constant perspective than the actual shot suggests.

For example: the scene intercuts between shots of a bedroom where an old lady is dying and shots of a street parade showing her long-lost soldier son's band returning from overseas. Audio cuts from the quiet death bed to the blaring military band. Should we avoid the rapid volume jumps that would actually take place – and either reduce the differences or spread the same sound over both scenes? The optimum treatment is a matter of taste, the effect you want to achieve, and the need to avoid ambiguity.

If a singer wanders around a spacious set, moving from close to long shots, do we really want the volume to vary? Can the microphone maintain a constant relationship to the singer? It may be necessary to prerecord the song and have the performance mimed on camera to its playback.

We normally adjust sound perspective within a scene by altering the microphone distance to suit the shot size by boom movement or intermicrophone mixing. As closer sounds tend to seem louder, with stronger bass and top than more distant pick-up, *presence filters* (*dialogue equalizers*) may be introduced to simulate or emphasize differences between close and remote sound quality.

Sound quality

Although high fidelity is our normal aim, there are good technical and artistic arguments for using audio filters to modify the system's frequency response when necessary:

1 Cutting low bass to reduce boom rumble, hum, improve speech clarity, improve the hollow or boomy quality in boxy scenery; reduce background noise/atmosphere (e.g. ventilation).

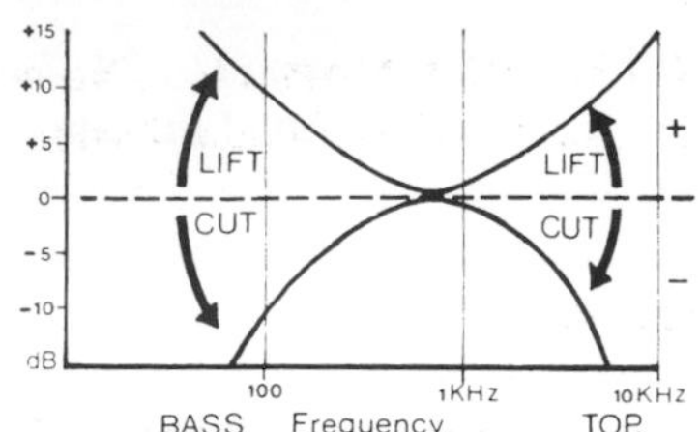

Fig. 12.25 part 1 Equalizers, audio filters, response selection amplifiers (RSA)
Filter for compensatory or dramatic effect. Progressive accentuation or reduction of top or bass. Bass and top roll-off are widely used, e.g. to remedy boomy reproduction, reduce air-conditioner noise, wind, traffic noise.

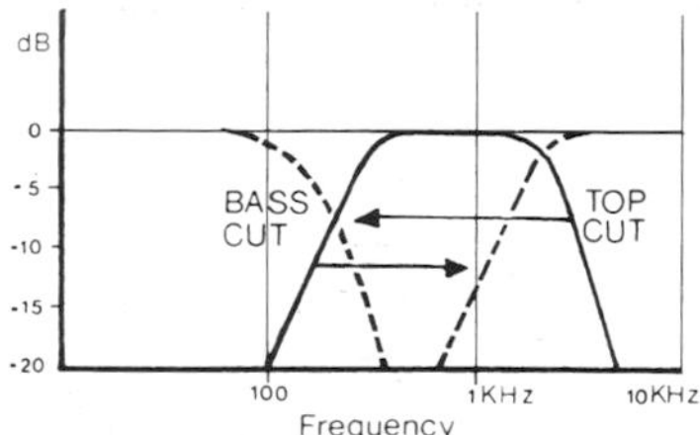

Fig. 12.25 part 2 High and low pass filters
Suppress rumble, hum, and high-pitched noises respectively.

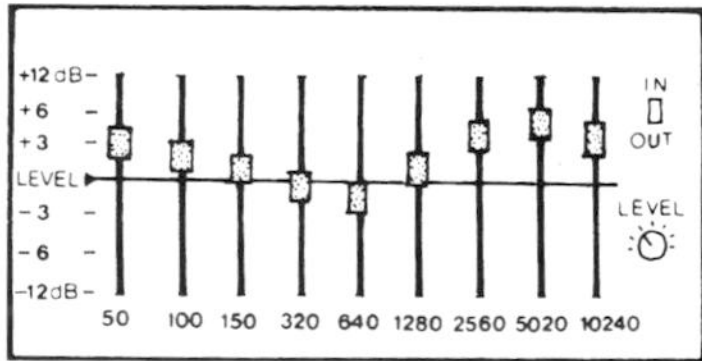

Fig. 12.25 part 3 Audio baton, octave filter, shaping filter, graphic equalizer
A series of slider controls boost or reduce chosen frequency segments in the audio spectrum. Slider positions show effective response.

2 Cutting upper parts of the audio spectrum to reduce sibilant speech or S-blasting, quieten studio noise, reduce disc reduce disc, tape, or other background noise.
3 Cut bass and top to enhance the illusion of exterior settings.
4 Slightly accentuate bass to increase the impression of size and grandeur of vast interiors.
5 Effects filters to simulate telephone (300–3000 Hz) intercom, public announcements. Phone filters (*distort*) are often controlled by the video switcher equipment, to provide automatic *audio-follow-video* switching as the picture intercuts between the two ends of a phone conversation.
6 By matching different types of microphones' frequency responses, we can reduce audible quality differences.
7 Quality matching between different sound sources (e.g. studio and film) can be improved.

Filtering can provide better audio continuity, and helps you to remedy such defects. Where the director is using *electronically inserted backgrounds* (e.g. by chroma-key), or studio settings have inappropriate acoustics (e.g. a 'cave' constructed of timber and plastics), the audio quality can be made much more convincing by audio filtering and reverberation treatment.

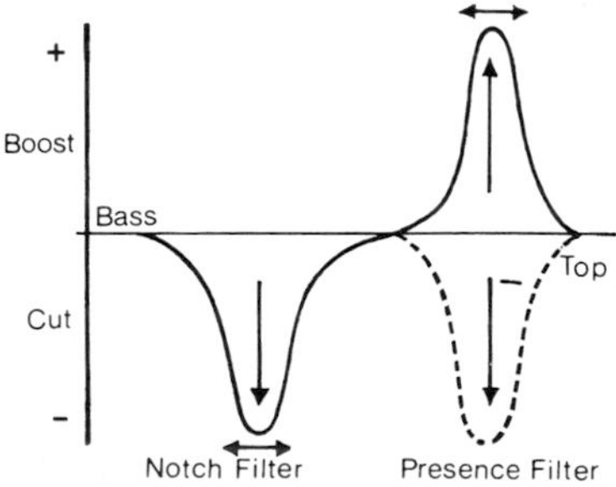

Fig. 12.25 part 4 Notch filter, presence circuits
Notch filter puts very steep localized dip into audio spectrum to diminish interference (e.g. hum) without substantially affecting overall quality.

Presence circuits (*mid-lift*) provide boost or cut (up to 6 dB) around selectable frequencies (2 to 6 kHz) to improve clarity and audio separation, improve sibilants lost with distance, or bring sounds 'forward' (presence) from others.

Equalization

When disc or audio tape recordings are made, the frequency spectrum is automatically modified (top is boosted, bass is reduced). This anticipates or overcomes various technical difficulties such as background noise. There are several 'standards' in use. Strictly, therefore, a disc or tape should always be reproduced with compensatory equalization matching the standard used for recording (*Audio tape*: NAB, NARTB, CCIR, IEC, DIN, *Disc*: RIAA,

Standard Spectra, ANSI, BSI, DIN, IEC, ISO, NAB, etc.). Some reproducers have selectable filters to suit a variety of standards.

Audio tape (recording and replay)

Operationally, audio magnetic tape recording is simplicity itself. You have only to avoid over- or undermodulation, and many recorders have automatic recording-level circuits (AGC; automatic gain control).

Audio tape

There are several types of audio recording tape: ferric, chrome (and 'pseudo-chrome', i.e. cobalt-treated ferric), ferrichrome, metal. For minimum background noise, least distortion, and best

Fig. 12.26 part 1 Typical layout of a reel-to-reel tape recorder
1 Supply spool.
2 Erase head.
3 Record head.
4 Replay head.
5 Capstan roller.
6 Pressure idler roller.
7 Take-up spool.

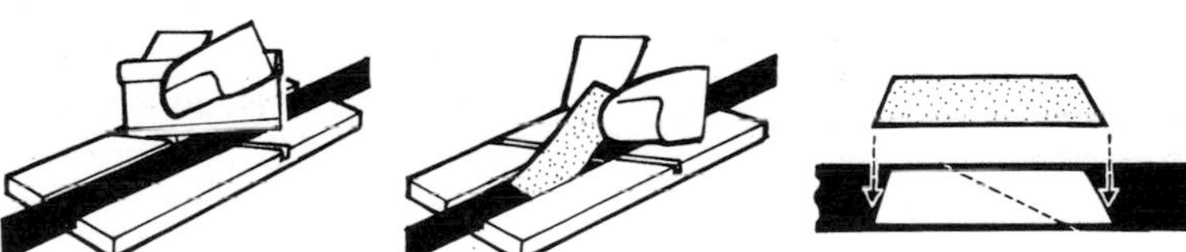

Fig. 12.26 part 2 Splicing audio tape
Play through to the *in* and *out* edit points. At each, stop the tape, and mark it with a felt-tip pen or wax pencil exactly at the *replay head gap*. Lay the tape in the splicer groove, with the recording surface downwards, and the marked tape at the editing groove.

Take the section of tape containing the other edit point, and lay it over the first tape (again face down). The marks should coincide.

With a sharp razor blade cut across at 45° using the splicer groove. Remove the unwanted tape ends, to leave the required sections exactly butted together. Fix a patch of special adhesive *jointing tape* to the splice (i.e. on the *back* of the tape). Cutting both edit points simultaneously produces a more accurate butt join than cutting the tape ends separately and pushing them together.

Editing audio cassettes. It is better to dub off passages, rather than try to physically edit 3.5 mm wide tape.

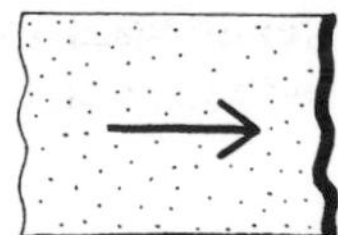

Fig. 12.26 part 3 Audio tape tracks

Mono (monophonic) full track. The single track audio covers the full tape width. The tape is full after one pass.

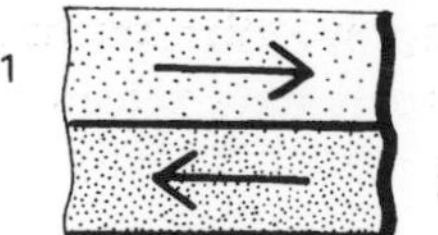

Mono half-track. The audio signal is recorded across half the tape width. During the first pass, the tape winds from the left-hand (supply) spool onto the right-hand (takeup) spool. At the end of the tape, the cassette is turned over ready to record/replay the second pass. In reel-to-reel systems, the full takeup spool is removed after the first pass, reversed, replaced on the supply spool and re-laced.

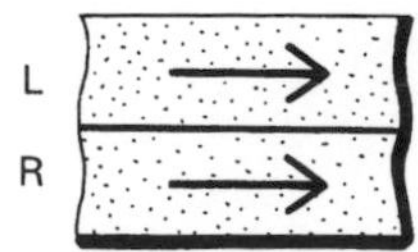

Half-track stereo. The audio from the left-hand channel is recorded on one half of the tape, while that from the right-hand channel is recorded alongside. The tape is full after one pass.

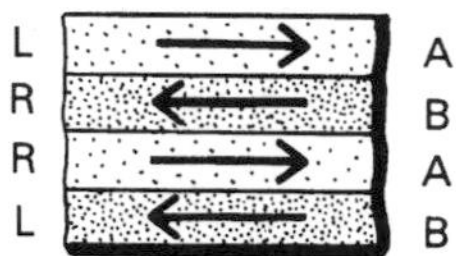

Quarter-track stereo. During the first pass (A), the left and right channels are recorded on tracks 1 and 3. After turning the tape over for pass (B), tracks 2 and 4 are used Most stereo cassette systems use this format.

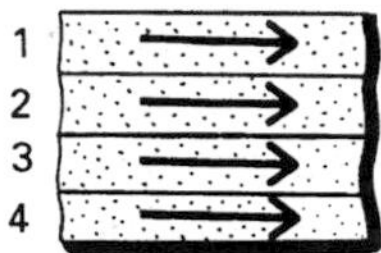

Multitrack systems. Using audio tapes up to 25 mm (1 in) or 50 mm (2 in)) wide, from four to 24 parallel tracks may be recorded/reproduced simultaneously.

Audio tape (like video tape) may be *bulk erased* with a large electromagnet to completely neutralize the tape's magnetic state.

Audio tape speeds are typically 7½ or 15 inches per second for reel-to-reel systems, and 1⅞ i.p.s. for audio cassettes.

top response the appropriate bias setting and equalization should be switched in on the recorder/reproducer, to suit the type of tape used. Longer-play tapes are thinner, less rugged, and liable to print-through between adjacent layers (echo; pre-echo).

Recording

Before recording, the tape must be magnetically neutralized (wiped, erased). This can be done initially by a bulk electromagnetic eraser (bulked), but is usually a regular part of the recording process. In the recording mode the tape first passes an *erase head* where strong ultrasonic currents eliminate any previous recording. The result when played would be a barely audible rustling – *tape noise*. This *clean* tape passes against the *record head*, which is fed with the audio signal you wish to record. As each particle of the tape contacts the head's gap it becomes magnetized in proportion to the audio at that instant. The modulated magnetic pattern is invisible. To assist this recording process the record head is also fed with an ultrasonic *bias current*, which substantially reduces distortion and background noise.

Replay

The tape can be replayed (monitored) during recording and subsequently reproduced (and/or recorded on) several hundred times. To reproduce the tape, it is passed over a *replay head* (playback, reproducer); the tape's magnetic pattern inducing weak electric currents in the head, corresponding with the original audio. An interlock mechanism usually prevents your activating the recording circuit accidentally and wiping the tape during replay.

Audio cassettes (and also video cassettes) have a breakaway tag at the rear which, when removed, automatically prevents you from recording over the existing material. If you really want to record over the present recording, simply attach an adhesive tape strip to substitute for the safety tag.

Tape speed

The tape must be reproduced at the recording speed, or you will get a marked pitch change; fine for chipmunk effects, but otherwise to be avoided. Higher tape speeds provide a better high-frequency response, lower background noise, less obvious *drop-out* (momentarily silent gaps due to tape surface irregularities or damage), easier audio editing (the audio pattern is more spread out), but it uses more tape per minute.

Editing

You can edit 1/4 in. (6.35 mm) magnetic tape by physically cutting (45° diagonally, with an unmagnetized razor blade) and joining sections with an adhesive patch on the back of the tape. This quick, flexible process produces a silent joint but disrupts the original recording, particularly if it contains several parallel tracks. Instead, you can re-record (*dub, dub-off*) sections onto a new tape; but this can result in cumulative distortion, hum, background noise, etc. Colored non-magnetic tape is often interspliced as lace-up *leader*, or as mute *blanking* between sequences for identification.

Production use of audio tape

1 Providing a premixed track of music, effects, background, to simplify handling during the show.
2 Bringing back sounds from location shooting, to provide audio background to studio action.
3 To suggest that there is an unseen speaker (e.g. at the other end of a phone, outside a door).
4 Providing taped commentary while a lecturer moves to another exhibit, or is out of microphone range.
5 Providing total prerecorded commentary to film or videotape (voice-over, voices off, VO; sound over vision, SOV).
6 Preselected effects or music dubbed from disc for cuing or treatment.
7 Recording atmospheric sounds (*room tone*), or other non-synchronized sound (*wild track*) for use when laying audio tracks during subsequent videotape editing. To provide overlays (bridging sound) between scenes.
8 Checking what was said during impromptu discussion (to guide editing).

Building the soundtrack

Most TV programs contain not only speech but also a proportion of music and effects. These vary with the type of program. While a chat show is only likely to have music at the start and end, to 'top and tail' the production, and give it a 'packaged' feel, a dramatic presentation may well be strewn with a variety of carefully selected atmospheric effects, and musical passages (bridges, stings, mood music).

While some sounds are prominently in the *foreground*, others are carefully controlled to provide an appropriate *background* to the action. Some may be crept in, and are barely audible, yet add an atmospheric quality to a scene (e.g. the quiet tick-tock of a grandfather clock). Others may be deafening, even drowning dialogue.

Some sound effects are continuous while others rely on split-second cuing to exactly match live action (e.g. the 'boing' sound as a clown's watch disintegrates).

Types of program sound

When a production is running smoothly one easily overlooks the complexities that lie behind it. That is particularly true of its sound component. The person controlling the program sound often has to work simultaneously with a diversity of sound sources. Some of these are live and therefore liable to vary unpredictably; others may have been prerecorded specifically for that show, or selected from stock libraries.

Contributory sounds can include:

1. *Dialogue* – Direct pick-up of the voices of people in the picture.
2. *Voices off* – The voices of people who are out of shot (*off-camera*); e.g. an unseen bystander, on a radio in the background, a public announcement (e.g. in a train station).
3. *Voice-over (VO)* – The voice of a commentator or announcer (with introductory or explanatory information).
4. *Sound effects* coinciding with action in the picture.
5. *Background or environmental effects* – General atmospheric sounds, such as wind, seawash, traffic, birdsong.
6. *Foreground music* – Someone playing an instrument in shot (or miming to playback).
7. *Background music* – Atmospheric mood music. (Usually recorded.)
8. *Special effects sounds* – Treated sounds, electronic music, synthesizer, etc.

Sound effects

We may want to introduce sound effects into a program for a variety of reasons:

- To *substitute for the real thing:* a sound effect to accompany a mute library shot, or when there was no suitable sound pickup during shooting.
- To *'correct' the original:* producing a more convincing noise than the recorded version.
- To *compensate*: When shooting the country scene, there were passing aircraft. We omit these and introduce birdsong recordings.
- To *augment the original sound:* A small group in the studio seems like a large mob when their sounds are reinforced with multiple copies or added recorded library effects.
- To *add realism:* e.g. In the studio – close shots of a jogging cart accompanied by the noises of a horse and cart wheels. A stationary car with recorded sounds of its engine and passing traffic.

Manual sound effects (Foleying)

Manually created sound effects have been used in film, TV (and radio) production for decades. These *spot effects* have the great advantage that they can be precisely synchronized and tailored to the action in a way that is often extremely difficult with *prerecorded* sounds.

A great deal of skill and ingenuity goes into producing convincing substitute sounds. Some effects are *direct imitations*; e.g. an operator walking in a gravel tray to exactly replicate the ineffective sounds of a person on the screen. Other are *simulated effects* which can be made to sound much more convincing or dramatic than the real thing – and safer too! – e.g. blows during a fight scene (a cabbage hit with a baseball bat); the noise of a battering ram striking a door (a box thrown onto the floor). In practice, where a sound effect has to coincide with action in the picture (e.g. the noise of a door closing synchronized with a mute film shot) the sound needs to be timed exactly or the result is ridiculous. In real life we see a rifle fire, and as sound takes longer to travel, we hear it a moment or two later (depending on its distance from us).

Recorded sound effects

The main advantages of a *recorded* sound effect is that you can check out its quality, volume, reverberation, duration, and general suitability beforehand. The problem lies in finding exactly the right sound for your particular purpose. You can often modify an existing sound effect by changing its quality (equalization), add reverberation, alter its speed. Particularly when several effects are mixed together, even the most critical listener would not recognize them as 'stock effects'.

There are many libraries on disc, CD, audio tape, film that would seem to cover any possible occasion. But in practice, there are often subtle differences that can draw attention to the trick.

Where you have a series of effects to play at the same time (e.g. seagulls, seawash, children playing on the beach) you can often simplify operations in the studio by '*mixing down*' the separate tracks beforehand, dubbing them onto a single audio tape. However, it is best to omit any critically cued effects (e.g. a cued shout), in case there are any later changes. This technique is particularly useful when your playback facilities are limited.

When you are using a recorded effect, there are several points to look out for:

Cued effect – a sound effect that has to be played at a particular moment; e.g. a telephone rings on action or dialogue.

Synchronized effect – where a sound effect has to coincide with action in the picture; e.g. the sound of a bat hitting a ball to accompany a mute picture. It needs to be synchronized exactly, or the result is ridiculous. Where possible, it may be better to omit the effect altogether.

Foreground effect – i.e. prominent; loud environmental noises. The *scale* of sounds needs to be matched to the shot. As a shout does not become a whisper simply by playing it at low level, so the scale of backgrounds needs to be chosen appropriately. If the recorded sound was relatively quiet or distant it cannot be made to seem loud or close by amplifying it. The sound character will be quite different.

Background effect – i.e. sound that is only heard quietly as an incidental accompaniment. Again, we must consider the scale of the effect. While the quality of recorded sound can be important if it is used as a foreground effect, even a poor quality sound effect may be quite usable as part of the background. If you are adding sound effects to a mute library shot, picture and sound details need to match reasonably well. Where, for instance, we hear a crowd cheering as the troops march by, we may accept that there is an unseen crowd if the shots are pretty close. But if the shot shows us a distant isolated group of men this will stretch our credulity!

Forms of sound effect

Sound effects have several basic forms:

- *The single event.* When a sound effect is brief (e.g. a cannon being fired) it usually needs to be set up and cued very accurately.

Check the channel gain beforehand to ensure that it is not going to overload the audio system.

- *Regular rhythms.* Where the effect has a pronounced rhythm take care not to interrupt it during editing. It requires patience and luck to match effects of e.g. footsteps to a mute picture of soldiers marching.
- *Repeated sound patterns.* Even when a sound effect is successful it may be too brief for your purpose. If you have only a few seconds' track of a dog barking you cannot usually repeat it conveniently more than a couple of times. Some sounds have distinctive recognizable features. It may be a shout from the audience during applause, someone coughing in a crowd, the toot-toot of a car horn within street noise . . . If you replay such an effect several times behind the action it will become recognizable, and seem quite false.
- *Continuous sounds.* Provided there are no easily recognized features, you can extend background sounds such as seawash, wind, applause, crowds, traffic by joining copies together without a break. Playing two copies of the effect can reinforce it, particularly if they are differently equalized.
- *Acoustics.* The surroundings in which an effect was recorded can limit their use. 'Footsteps', for example, come in endless variety; echoing, on pavements, gravel, squelching mud, moving through grass . . .
- *Extraneous sounds.* Many an effect has others intermixed with it. Birdsound may be accompanied by the other sounds of the countryside (e.g. sheep, tractors). Such mixtures cannot be used as *cued effects*.
- *Defects.* It is wise to check sound effects recordings for defects; particularly discs, which may have high surface noise, clicks, and scratches.

Music and effects (M&E track)

If a show is live, or live-on-tape, performance is continuous. The dialogue, music, and effects are all introduced as you go.

But what happens if you decide to *edit* this videotape with its *composite soundtrack (married track)*? Suppose the program needs shortening, or you cut out some boring 'business'? On replay, you could find that there is a distracting change in the accompanying background music where you made this edit cut!

So where you anticipate detailed postproduction editing it may not be a good idea to add all music and effects during studio taping. Instead, to avoid these editing disruptions in the soundtrack you could record all the *dialogue* on the videotape during performance, but add the *music* and *effects* later at a separate editing/re-recording (*dubbing*) session away from the studio.

When the action is shot in brief takes out of sequence you have no option but to build the program soundtrack in this way. Any effects or music played during individual takes would not carry through between the shots when they were edited together. There would be a poor continuity matching.

Another advantage of compiling the final soundtrack at the *postproduction stage* is that you can augment or modify the original track (e.g. remove or replace faulty material; insert censor bleeps) as well as adding title music. Where it was not practicable to perform a comedy show in front of a studio audience it would be legitimate to invite the public to watch a copy of the tape on large-screen replay, record their applause/laughter, etc., and add this to the final videotape soundtrack.

By keeping the dialogue separate from the accompanying *music and effects (M&E) tracks* you have the additional advantage that it can make your program a very saleable product for foreign-language markets. They can add dialogue or commentary in their own language based on the original script, and mix this with the M&E track.

Anticipating sound editing

When shooting on location you can make eventual editing and audio sweetening a lot easier if you habitually follow certain practices:

- *Level continuity.* Aim to keep the level and quality of successive shots in the same scene reasonably similar. Particularly in location interiors, you may find longer shots with lower sound levels and strong reverberation, while closer shots are louder and relatively dead acoustically.
- *Wild track.* It is good practice to make supplementary recordings of general 'atmosphere' (background noise) from time to time. Even in the studio, there is always a low-level background sound of air conditioning/ventilation. On location this 'atmos' may include wind in trees, passing traffic, etc. When editing the program there will be occasions where the soundtrack has been cut, or a sequence is mute, and this covering 'atmos' can be introduced to avoid distracting lapses into silence, and to give a feeling of continuity to the edited shots.

Incidentally, when recording on location keep an alert ear for any potential 'sound effects' that arise when you are not actually shooting yet might be integrated into the final soundtrack. Even unwelcome intrusive noises (e.g. passing fire wagon) might prove useful in your sound library for another occasion!

Extra audio taping is useful, too, when shooting *interviews* on location. Typically, the camera and microphone concentrate on the guest, and separate shots of the interviewer are cut in during editing. At the end of the interview the extra audio tape recording can be replayed to remind the interviewer, who repeats the questions to camera, or in an over-shoulder shot behind the guest.

Finally, this technique is widely used to ensure good speech continuity for *pick-up shots*. These are situations where you have someone speaking to camera, then the shot changes to show them continuing in another location. For example, the guide speaks to camera in a shot taken from a church tower ('She is buried down there beneath those trees . . .'): cut to a shot of the guide beside the grave ('. . . and you can see this inscription on the tombstone').

Audio sweetening

The process of working on the program sound after studio production is called *audio sweetening* (*dubbing session*; *track laying*). Although it is obviously a lot cheaper to record a show *live-on-tape* and have a complete production ready for use at the end of the session, audio sweetening is both necessary and preferable where extensive videotape editing is involved.

Audio sweetening can be carried out at various levels:

1 *Additional material*. Adding extra material to the finished edited program; e.g. playing in title music, adding a commentary.
2 *Corrections*. Improving the sound within a scene. One might, for example, readjust varying levels between speakers' voices. Careful filtering could reduce sibilance, hum, rumble, ventilation noise, etc.
3 *Enhancement*. Modifying sound quality to improve realism or to achieve a dramatic effect; e.g. by adding reverberation, or changing its tonal qualities (equalizing).
4 *Blending*. Adjusting the relative strengths of effects and music tracks to suit the dialogue and action.
5 *Continuity*. Ensuring that the sound levels, balance, etc. are consistent from one shot to the next when various shots are edited together.
6 *Bridging*. Adding bridging effects or music that will run between shots. An *overlay* track can be played throughout an entire sequence to ensure that the same background sound levels continue without level jumps or changes in quality. It may be kept down behind dialogue and made more prominent during action.
7 *Added effects*. Where video effects have been introduced into a program after the studio action (e.g. laser beams, explosions, disintegrations) suitable sound effects can be added during sound sweetening.
8 *Overdubbing*. Replacing unsatisfactory sections of the soundtrack spoiled, for instance, by passing aircraft or other extraneous noise.

As you can see, there are very practical reasons to rework the soundtrack after production. Now that television makes increasing use of short takes and sophisticated videotape editing, it promises to become a regular part of the production process on complex shows, as in film making.

Typical postproduction methods

It is often quite practicable to introduce all the sound effects, music, commentary, etc. for each sequence while shooting the action. The end result would be a fully developed soundtrack. After all, that's exactly what you have to do when presenting a *live* show! But this leaves no opportunity to correct errors or have second thoughts. Where possible, when taping a show it is far better to just record the basic dialogue and add all audio refinements later during a postproduction session. Particularly where taped sequences are shot out of final order, and there are retakes to correct faults, or alternative versions of the action for later selection, the resulting tape material will need to be edited. If you include all the effects and music initially while shooting the action, it is almost inevitable that the sound continuity between scenes will be disrupted when those original tapes are edited. To avoid this dilemma, and to provide greater flexibility, many organizations use a different approach when taping more complicated productions.

First, the videotape is picture-edited. All shots are selected and arranged in their final order in a *rough cut* with appropriate transitions (cut, mix, supers), and any postproduction video effects in place. During the original taping session the precise time at which everything happened was continuously recorded along with the picture and dialogue on the videotape. This *time code* serves as a reference point throughout all subsequent editing and sound treatment.

Now you either make a copy of the picture-edited videotape's dialogue soundtrack or take a corresponding ¼-in. audio tape derived from the original taping session. Using a *multi-track audio tape recorder*, you copy this *dialogue track* together with the matching *time code track* onto two of the 16 or 24 parallel audio tracks available on its 2-in. tape. Typically, the '*lifted-off*' (dubbed) program dialogue goes onto Track 1, with the corresponding time code on Track 16. (See Table 12.3.)

The next step is to develop a '*combined working tape*' during the postproduction *sound sweetening session* by adding all the required sound effects, music, commentary on separate tracks. This process allows you to cue and time each track independently, adjusting relative balances, modify audio quality (filtering, reverberation,) and so on, without affecting the rest of the composite.

You might reserve the empty Tracks 2–5 for *sound effects*; wherever possible, keeping them separate, so that you can intercut/

Table 12.5 Multi-track log

PRODUCTION TITLE:	TOMORROW'S PEOPLE	MIX-DOWN DATE:	SEPT 15	DIRECTOR:	ABLE
REFERENCE No.:	123-4	VT CHANNEL:	VT 3	AUDIO ENGINEER:	BAKER
STUDIO/DATE:	A/ SEPT 3	DUBBING CHANNEL:	2	TRANSMISSION DATE:	OCT 9
MULTI-TRACK:	A/12				

Time code	1	2	3	4	5	6	7	8	9	10	15	16
	VTR TRACK	FX	FX	FX	FX	MUSIC	MUSIC	V/O		MIX		MASTER
	DIALOG	DISC Ch.1	DISC Ch.2	TAPE Ch.7	TAPE Ch.8	CD Ch.3	CASS Ch.5	CASS Ch.4		DOWN		TIME CODE
15:20:03 15:20:07 15:02:09 15:23:17 16:02:11 16:07:00 16:07:02 16:18:09 16:50:11 16:53:04 16:55:13 17:02:19 17:42:12 17:47:20 18:32:01	15:20:07 → 16:02:11 16:18:09 → 18:32:01 Dialogue track from original videotape recording	HEAVY WAGON (VH 820) BAND 4 15:20:03 → 16:07:00 EXPLOSION (EXP 31) 16:50:11 → 16:53:04	THUNDER (WS 27) BAND 6 15:21:09 → 15:23:17 SCREAMS (HN 15) 16:55:13 → F/O 17:47:20	HEAVY RAIN (WS 32) SECN 3 15:20:03 B/G → Continuous sound of rain in background throughout	MOB SHOUTING (HN 16) 17:42:12 F/I →	'PARIS - OVERT' (CD 294) BAND 3 15:20:03 → 16:07:02 X-FADE →	MOOD MUSIC 'OMINOUS' SECN 4 →	CAS 27A 17:02:19 → Narrator's voice; other sounds in background	Unused track available for alternative mix-down	Mix-down of tracks 1–8 recorded on track 10	Unused track available for alternative mix-down	00:00:00 → Time code during mix-down used on final master

Information from off-line editing. Time code from original VTR recording

Abbreviations

F/I	Fade in
F/O	Fade out
X-FADE	Cross fade (mix over) between channels
B/G	Background (less audible)
Effects are identified by tape track numbers (i.e. FX2, FX3, FX4, FX5)	
CH. no.	Audio channel number on board

mix/ cross-fade between. Tracks 6–7 may be reserved for any *music* inserts, and Track 8 for any *additional dialogue* (e.g. voice-over commentary, narration, etc.). The final *mix-down* can be dubbed onto e.g. Track 10.

The actual arrangements will depend on the complexity of the production. The idea, in principle, is to record the various missing sounds in their respective tracks so that their time slot coincides with the correct point in the picture/dialogue sequence. If someone presses a doorbell in the shot at time code point 10 h.30 m.05 s to 10 h.30 m.08 s (3 seconds' duration), then this sound effect must be inserted in Track 2 at that position. Sound and picture will then be synchronized.

Each track on the multi-track tape can be independently recorded, reproduced, wiped. When you have finished *laying down* these tracks they will all be played simultaneously and blended together to be recorded on a new synchronized tape. This combined track is then dubbed onto the *master edited videotape*, exactly in sync with the pictures there.

If you wish, you can lay down just *one* track at a time. While the edited videotape is playing the picture sequence through, the multi-track is running in sync, ready to record on the selected track when you fade up the required effect or music at the right moment. (The effect or music comes from a separate audio tape machine, disc, cart, or CD player.) If the inserted sounds are to be *faded* in or out, you will need a long enough sequence to cover the head and tail fades. After rewinding, you can replay the videotape plus multi-track, to check that the result is successful.

However, this is a time-consuming method, and usually unnecessary. Instead you can adopt either of two methods: 'on the hoof' or 'laying tracks'.

The simplest technique is to treat the session as if it were a live show; cuing and controlling the dialogue, effects, music passages, narration, etc. as you go. You run a copy of the edited videotape and, following the script, play in the effects/music at the appropriate moments, recording them on their respective clean (unused) multi-track tape channels. If any feature does not work first time (e.g. the bell effect was too loud) that particular track can be re-recorded at that point.

Another way of approaching the sweetening session is to work from a *track log*. You prepare this in advance. The log consists of a series of vertical columns (one for each multi-track channel), with the time scale running vertically. Watching a copy of the edited videotape with a *burned-in time code* visible at the bottom of the screen (Figure 14.4) you are guided by a prepared *track log* (Table 12.3). This may be worked out beforehand in collaboration with the director. This identifies all of the contributory audio sources, listing '*in and out cues*', probable in and out times. We see, for example, that sounds of rolling thunder from a CD effects disc come in at 15:21:00 and are taken out at 15:23:17. This sound is dubbed off at the allotted points; usually at a standard loudness (*zero level*).

When all the tracks are complete with the various contributions on their respective tracks, it is time for the *mix-down*. You play the multi-track audio tape, adjusting the output from each track, blending and adjusting the sounds to suit the associated picture. This balanced and controlled composite is recorded as a *master soundtrack* on an unused track of the multi-track. (On two tracks if you are working in stereo.) This *master track* (*final mix-down*) is then *laid back* (*dubbed*) onto the soundtrack of the master edited videotape; and thanks to the time code, will be exactly in sync with its pictures.

Where *computer-aided* dubbing systems are used, all variations of fader positions, equalization, reverberation you make during the mix-down rehearsal are stored. When you are satisfied, the system will run the VTR and audio multi-track, and perform all these adjustments exactly as rehearsed – unless you decide to override it at any point.

Playback (foldback)

Where someone in a drama needs to react to a particular sound – e.g. an arriving car, or a ringing telephone, or a distant baby crying – it may be sufficient for the floor manager to give them a hand cue and to insert the sound effect later during a postproduction session. But where it is preferable for them to hear the actual effect, or where they need to synchronize their actions – as when dancing – portable *playback* or *foldback* loudspeakers are placed near the action area. This method has disadvantages. Sound reproduced over a loudspeaker can become colored by the acoustics of the setting or the studio. Fire a gun in the studio, and the accompanying echo reveals that the 'open-air' scene is a phoney! In addition, if music or a sound effect is played over the studio loudspeakers and overheard by the main action microphones you will find that it develops a falsely hollow quality.

Miming and postsyncing

There will be occasions when good sound pickup is simply not possible, or conditions are too unfavorable for a good performance. The action may be too energetic, or too far away, or in very noisy surroundings. A regular solution is to prerecord the sound (e.g. a singer with full orchestra) and to reproduce this track over nearby loudspeakers or an earpiece, while the person synchronizes action, miming to this *prescored* playback. This has been done where a pop group relies on heavily processed sound and multi-takes to achieve their particular effects – treatment that cannot be replicated during a live TV performance. So on air, they mime to their commercial disc.

Another approach is to shoot the action with its sound (however unacceptable) and afterwards have the performer (or someone else!) record the required song or dialogue in time with the reproduced pictures. This *postsyncing* process is widely used in film making to improve sound pickup quality or overcome poor shooting conditions.

Whatever method is used, it can be extremely difficult to sustain *lip-sync*, with the lip movements exactly matching the accompanying sound. In the past, the regular solution was a process called *looping (dialogue looping)* in which brief sections of film were played over and over while the performer attempted to speak or sing in unison. This enabled remarkably effective results when dubbing foreign language films.

Much of this tedium and uncertainty is overcome by using electronic *time compression* techniques, in which the soundtrack is recorded digitally and displayed on a monitor as a continuous sound-strip, which can be edited to fit the picture action – i.e. paused, stretched, compressed, extended or abbreviated. (*See Digests – Time compression techniques*.)

The simplest and cheapest solution, where it is possible, is to avoid shots that show clear mouth movements. Use more distant shots, point-of-view (POV), or over-shoulder shots, and reaction shots, which do not reveal any lip-sync errors, and add a separate voice-over track recording to the picture later!

Treated sound

There will times when you will want to alter the character of sound to make it more convincing, more dramatic, or to create a novel effect. You might, for instance, want to simulate telephonic speech, or suggest a public address system, or create an echo effect. Then there are a number of clever techniques. Some require quite simple tonal changes; others involve ingenious electronics and computer software programs.

■ *Quality changes* Using *audio filters*, *graphic equalizers*, *notch filters* (Figure 12.25) you can increase or decrease bass or top, introduce a peak or dip at a chosen frequency. So by emphasizing or reducing parts of the audio spectrum the sounds can become bright, dull, shrill, edgy, thin, tubby, harsh, brittle, etc.

■ *Distortion* When you need to simulate the distorted sound (e.g. from shortwave radio reception or an intercom system) this can be done electronically. But ironically, it may be a lot easier and quicker to use such crude methods as holding an earphone or earpiece near a microphone, putting the microphone in a box, bowl or pipe, and then add filtering and reverberation!

■ *Feedback* If the amplified audio from of a sound system is fed back into its input and reamplified over and over, this *feedback* build-up produces noises ranging from a whistle to the loud oscillatory howl-round familiar with sound reinforcement (public address) systems, when the microphone overhears nearby loudspeakers. (When howl-round occurs accidentally, the remedy is to reduce the loudspeakers' outputs, reposition the microphone, or use more directional microphone and loudspeakers.) As an *effect*, you may deliberately introduce a controlled amount of acoustic feedback to produce a hollow, echoing sound quality.

■ *Audio tape feedback* On an audio tape recorder there is a brief delay between the moment a sound is recorded and its reproduction from the replay head further along the tape path. So if you mix the incoming audio with a little of its delayed repro, you can create various effects, from a drawn-out hangover effect, to distinct echo, stutter effects, or flutter echo.

■ *Speed changes* If you replay a recorded sound at a *slower* speed than when recorded, its pitch is lowered, its tempo reduced, and the apparent reverberation increases. This can produce some interesting effects. Most sounds take on a deliberate, sinister character. Percussive sounds from bells, drums, gongs, xylophones, as well as thunder, cart wheels, become strikingly powerful. Other sounds are unrecognizably transformed (e.g. slow speed wind or waterfalls), and can be used to create 'synthetic' or atmospheric effects.

Replaying at a *faster* speed than normal raises the pitch and tempo. At about one-and-half to twice speed, sounds become 'miniaturized', appear perky and comic – the audioland of singing mice, insects, household utensils, etc. of cartoons.

The speed of some audio disc and tape players can be varied. But there are also tape systems with special rotating multi-head turrets that can provide pitch changes while the tape runs at a normal speed. (These can also be used to correct speed inaccuracies during recording.) Digitally recorded sounds can be lengthened or time-compressed during subsequent editing.

■ *Reversed sound* When sound is reproduced backwards the effect will vary with the character of the sound. While percussive or transient sounds develop a strange 'indrawn-breath' quality, sustained sounds may seem little altered. The simplest method of reversing sound is to take a normal audio tape recording and feed it into the player tail first.

■ *Repeated sound* Very occasionally one wants to repeat a sound over and over again, e.g. to heighten tension, imply hysteria or mental derangement. You can either take a secion of audio tape, join its head to its tail, and reproduce this loop or digitally record the sound which is repeat-played for as long as required.

■ *Fading* Interesting fading effects can be created by playing two identical recordings slightly out of step.

■ *Reverberation* TV studios are relatively non-reverberant ('dead'); so we often want to enhance program sound – particularly for musical performances – by adding a certain amount of *artificial reverberation*. Most sound control desks have a control fitted to each channel, which enables you to mix a proportion of the original audio signal with a treated '*echo*' or '*reverb*' version. Increase the mix, and you simulate larger echoing surroundings.

Techniques for creating this reverberant sound have developed over the years. The oldest and simplest approach was to place a loudspeaker in a live empty room (*echo room*) – even a cellar, bathroom, or corridor – and pick up the multi-reflected sound with a nearby microphone. Ingenious devices evolved to simulate reverberant sound. In *spring delay systems* the audio signal to be treated was fed to a transducer head which vibrated a coiled spring. A second head at its far end picked up the sound plus resonances within the spring, converting them into a 'reverberant' sound effect. A *multi-headed tape player* produced a succession of replays that could be added to the original audio or reproduced over loudspeakers within the studio. In a *reverberation plate* system sound waves from a transducer head travel through a large suspended steel sheet, are reflected within the sheet, and detected by a further pickup head.

Today, *digital reverberation units* offer a wide range of coloration effects. The sound is stored in digital form, to be read out selectively, according to the effect you require. It can provide variable reverberation, echo, doubling (close repeats), delays, chorus, hollowing, etc. In addition, various sound effects may be produced, including sweep effects, doppler effects (pitch changes), feedback, flanging (original with delayed version of changed strength and phase), as well as time compression and expansion.

Synthetic sound

There are many fascinating program opportunities for synthesized sounds, including abstract background noises, voices for the inarticulate or mute, newly created sounds for monsters and science fiction.

■ *Modulated sounds* You can use one audio signal to control another, modulating its volume or pitch by using voltage-controlled amplifiers, ring modulators, hybrid coils, etc. So you can articulate sound effects; a locomotive whistle cries 'All aboard', or an organ sings its own lyrics.

■ *Fragmented sounds* You can create an entirely 'new' sound by taking brief excerpts from a number of different sound effects and restructuring them: rearranging them in different orders, reversing, repeating, modulating them . . . The resulting *musique concrète* effect may be amusing, imitative, sinister, arresting, shocking . . .

■ *Dissociated sounds* Many sounds lose their identity when divorced from their original context. Some are unfamiliar anyway (straining pack-ice, roaring gas flames, insect noises). You can often transpose sounds for dramatic effect – jet engine noise to accompany typhoon scenes. Some take on an entirely new significance – a crushed matchbox simulating a collapsing barn.

Musical instruments can be used to produce a fantastic range of sound effects – disembodied waverings from a musical saw; squeaks, grunts, whines, and creaks from a violin. These noises can in turn be treated and modified. Such devices are more than audio stunts. They enable you to stimulate the imagination, often improve on available sounds, and to materialize the unknown or the impossible.

■ *Synthesized sounds* Entirely synthetic sounds can be created electronically by an *audio synthesizer*, which enables a keyboard or interconnected control circuits to manipulate specially generated and processed sounds. Oscillations of various shapes, frequency, repetition rate can be selected and treated; volume can be varied (*vibrato, crescendo, diminuendo*); build-up and die-away adjustments can be used (attack and decay times); quality can be modified (selective filtering), and so on. The resultant synthesized sounds may deliberately simulate recognizable sources, or provide a new audio impression.

■ *MIDI systems* A simple method of creating some quite unusual sounds is to play the instruments of a computer's MIDI system, way outside their normal scale range; e.g. very high-pitched timpani; very low-pitched tubular bells. By altering the attack and decay times of an instrument, you can change its sound characteristics further. Standard MIDI sounds that are less familiar (such as 'goblins', 'echoes', 'calliope', 'new age') can be combined to produce a selection of 'Space Age' sound effects at the press of a key.

Noise reduction

As you know, the strength of the audio signal has to be controlled, to prevent its exceeding the system's limits. (A loud sound can overload and create unpleasant distortion. A very quiet sound can be lost among background noise.) This control of the volume range flattens the sound's dynamics. Particularly where a sound is re-recorded several times in the course of preparing a program, relative dynamic ranges can be noticeably reduced.

The simplest method of reducing high-pitched background noise is to boost the upper part of the audio spectrum during recording (*pre-emphasis*) and reduce it correspondingly during replay (*de-emphasis*); but this is only partially successful.

A number of ingenious *noise reduction* (*NR*) circuits have evolved which considerably reduce background noise, permit quieter sounds to be reproduced, and so extend the effective dynamic range. Unfortunately these systems are not mutually compatible, and it is as well to realize this when reproducing a recording using a particular NR system.

Although designs differ, NR systems fundamentally aim to automatically compress the dynamic range during recording, and expand it (in a mirror image) during reproduction. (*See Digests – Noise reduction*.)

13 Film

Distinctions between film and television program making continue to blur. Here we shall be looking at the basics of film making, and seeing how film contributes to today's TV production techniques.

Film versus video

For many years the *film camera* offered a high picture quality and productional flexibility that the television camera could not rival. But video technology developed steadily. Nowadays it can take a keen eye to discern whether the TV picture you are watching is photographic or from a video camera. The TV camera has become a 'go-anywhere' device.

Shooting film – The high costs of using a 35 mm motion picture format (theatrical movie standard) preclude its general use in TV production. Super-16 mm film is used to some extent, but because the video camera has the increasing advantages of lower costs, immediate results, and greater adaptability, many TV stations use little or no film for program making; although they have facilities for showing 16 mm film.

Reproducing film – Both program material and commercials are distributed on 16 mm film. But to simplify operations, and to overcome the problems of coping with a variety of film formats (from 8 mm to 70 mm wide, with different image aspect ratios), many TV stations have any film copied onto a convenient in-house *videotape* format by a specialist organization (*postproduction house*).

Film in television production

You can use film material in several ways in television production:

- *Reproduced directly* – Simply play the film through a film chain while a telecine operator controls picture quality.
- *Transfer and correct* – Copy the film onto videotape while a video control operator introduces any corrections necessary to improve picture quality. All or part of the tape may be transmitted. Limited changes (e.g. censoring) can be introduced.

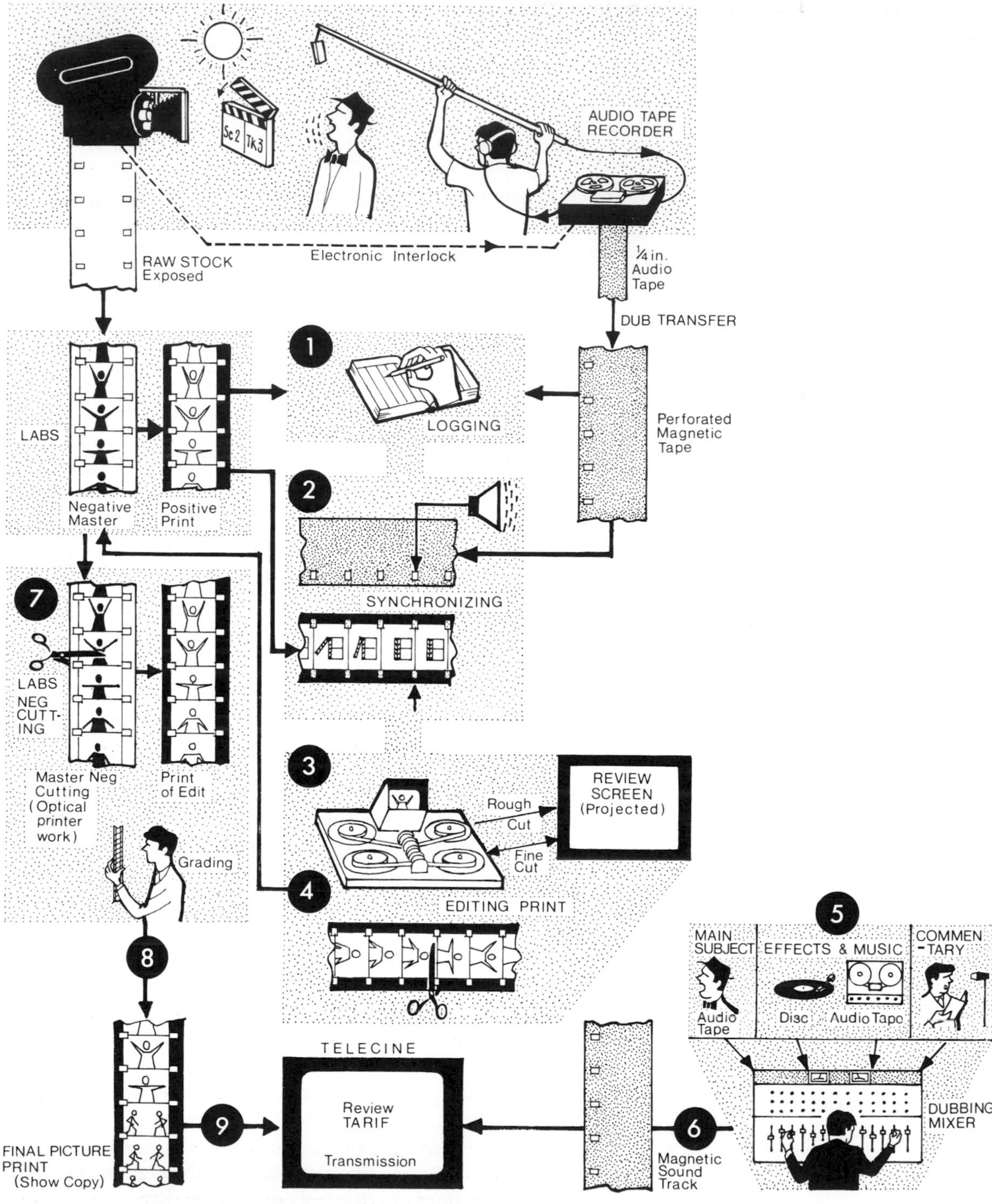
AUDIO TAPE RECORDER
Sc 2
Tk 3
RAW STOCK Exposed
Electronic Interlock
¼ in. Audio Tape
DUB TRANSFER
1
LOGGING
Perforated Magnetic Tape
LABS
Negative Master
Positive Print
2
SYNCHRONIZING
7
LABS
NEG CUTT-ING
Master Neg Cutting (Optical printer work)
Print of Edit
3
REVIEW SCREEN (Projected)
Rough Cut
Fine Cut
4
Grading
EDITING PRINT
5
MAIN SUBJECT
EFFECTS & MUSIC
COMMEN -TARY
Audio Tape
Disc
Audio Tape
8
TELECINE
Review TARIF
Transmission
9
6
DUBBING MIXER
FINAL PICTURE PRINT (Show Copy)
Magnetic Sound Track

Fig. 13.1 (opposite) Basic sound filming process

Picture. Film is shot in a series of separate camera set-ups (re-takes, multi-versions); clapper-board being shown at head or inverted at the tail of each take (for identification and sound/picture sync mark). Potentially usable takes are processed and a *master negative* is obtained. An uncorrected positive check print is made (*rushes, dailies*). This is used for review and, later to devise editing *cutting copy*.

Audio. Location sound is recorded on 1/4-inch magnetic tape. It is later dubbed selectively onto full-coat sprocketed magnetic film, to correspond with cutting-copy picture selections.

Editing development

1 All information on material is logged (edge numbers, take numbers, descriptions, lengths/footages).
2 Picture and sound-track is then synchronized.
3 Sections are selectively assembled (rough cut, work print).
4 Revision, exact cutting points and transitions are chosen (cutting copy, fine cut).
5 Various additional sound tracks are prepared or assembled (commentary, music, effects).
6 All sounds are then dubbed (using *dubbing mixer*) onto one mixed master soundtrack to match the edited picture.
7 Master negatives are prepared by the laboratory which correspond to editor's cutting copy (with a wax-pencil code marking the transitions required). Master negatives edge-numbers are used for section/frame identification.
8 Specimen test-strip print-sections supplied by laboratories (timing, grading, cinex), for approval of processing color balance, exposure variations. corrections, etc.
9 Final print: This show print is either a *combined print*, which has the picture united with optical or magnetic sound track; or is *double-headed*, having separate picture and magnetic track, which are run synchronously.

- *Transferred and edited (excerpted)* – Short sequences (*clips*) from the original film or from a videotaped copy are inserted into a television program at selected points. They may be used for various purposes:

  To extend studio scenes
  For location scenes
  To provide illustrative material (e.g. archive film)
  To introduce atmospheric stock shots (*library shots*)
  To provide promotional material.

- *Transferred and treated* – The original film may be copied onto videotape and its pictures then modified: titling or subtitles added; sign language inlays introduced; video effects added (e.g. lightning strikes), etc.

The basic filming process

As far as the director is concerned, there are important distinctions between the TV and film media. In most *television* productions the TV director has two or three cameras (or more) in use, continually selecting and checking shots, and guiding cameras while watching picture monitors.

The *film* director, on the other hand, usually works with a *single camera*; except for those '*once-only*' situations, where a multi-camera set-up is used to shoot the action simultaneously from several angles (e.g. for special effects and spectaculars). The film director cannot assess final results until the film stock has been processed and screened, so has to explain what is required, and rely on the camera operator (*Director of Photography*) to interpret these instructions.

A *film camera's* viewfinder may have a small auxiliary video camera attached which provides a television picture of the film shot. This facility can be an invaluable guide for checking the shot's coverage, performance, continuity, etc., when the video is taped and reviewed on a nearby monitor. (Without this facility, only the camera operator would know, for example, whether the microphone dipped into shot; perhaps overlooking this distraction while preoccupied with the action.) Unfortunately, the quality of the actual filmed shot can still only be judged after processing.

Action is rehearsed and filmed in brief *takes*; being reshot wherever necessary. Additional *cover shots (protection shots)* may be taken 'just in case'. As a result of *retakes* to anticipate or correct productional and technical problems, and later selective editing, only about 1/10 to 1/20 of the overall film that has been exposed is finally used – a *shooting ratio* of 10:1 to 20:1. (To reduce processing costs, obviously faulty takes (NG) are not printed.)

At the start of each take an *identifying head slate* is held in front of the camera, giving all reference details to assist editing. By matching up the sound and picture as this clapper-board closes (*sync marks*) we ensure that picture and soundtrack are in step when reproduced. '*Automatic slating*' is sometimes used in which a frame is 'flashed' and an audio bleep sounded simultaneously. When a head slate has been omitted, an upside-down *tail slate/end board* is usually shot at the end of a scene.

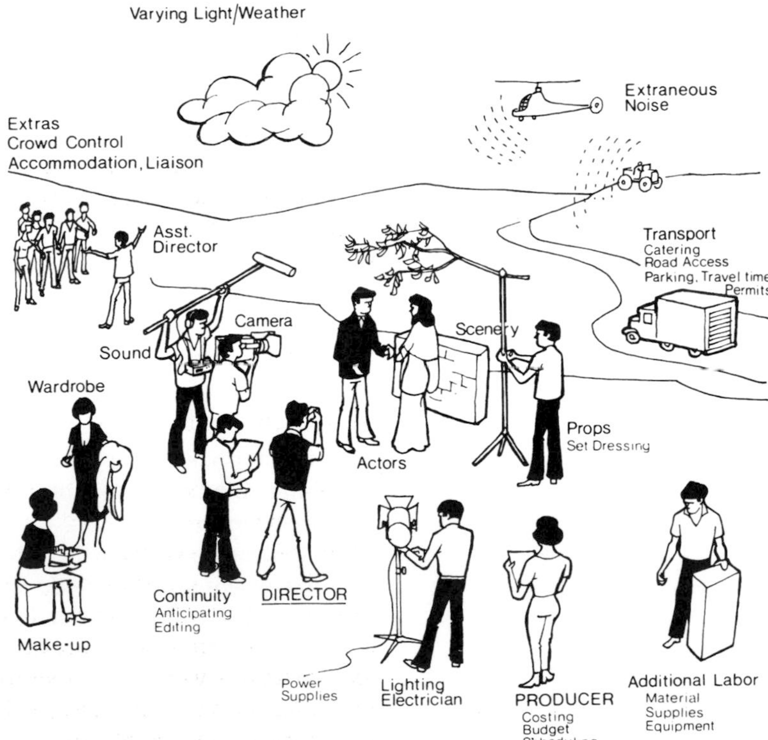

Fig. 13.2 Location filming
The location film team needs to be self-sufficient anticipatory, well organized and adaptable.

The single original camera negative is very precious and a positive print is made from it (*dailies, rushes*), which the film editor separates into shots. Using various information, from a *script or brief, cue-sheet, continuity-report* (giving details of action, slate numbers, etc, identifying each take), the editor joins individual clips of film into a cohesive and appropriate sequence – which becomes the *cutting copy.* (To simplify and speed up editing, this film copy may be transferred to *videotape* and/or *hard disk.*) Picture quality is then evaluated technically and artistically to guide the film labs' *grading or timing process* (controlling the print density and color balance by adjusting the relative exposures given when printing the pictures' red, green and blue components).

So now the editor has a *rough-cut* in which the order and duration of shots, the action cutting points, and the types of transitions have been arranged, and this is submitted for the director's approval. After any further revisions, a final version (*fine-cut*) is produced.

Later, the processing labs will match the stored master negatives produced in the camera, to this print, using the edge-numbers or the time code printed along the film's edges to guide them. An optical print is then made by the labs, in which transitions between shots follow the editor's wax-pencilled code marks drawn on the cutting copy.

Now the final *soundtrack* is compiled (*laying tracks*) and the *dubbing mixer* skilfully blends dialogue, commentary, effects, and music. A *rock-and-roll* facility enables picture and sound tracks to be run synchronously forward/backward for rapid correction during dubbing.

So we see that film making is a segmented process, usually taking place over weeks (even months), which *theoretically* at least, allows us to examine and reconsider at each step and to remedy or improve results. Quite unlike most television production, where immediate judgments have to be made, and there is often too little opportunity to correct or improve results.

Sound on film

The sound track

Although film is sometimes shot *mute (silent)*, and suitable sound added later, it is more usual to record synchronized sound while shooting. For maximum editing flexibility, film picture and sound may be recorded separately (*double system*). But whatever the process used, it is essential that the film camera and the audio recording system remain precisely synchronized; particularly where any variations would be obvious (e.g. *lip-sync*). The cumbersome interconnecting sync-pulse cable formerly used to accurately match motor speeds of camera and sound systems is now replaced

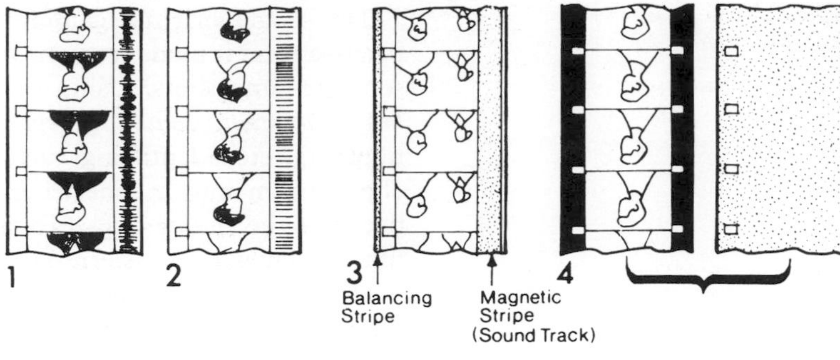

Fig. 13.3 Film sound
Optical track – combined (married) print:
1 Variable area track.
2 Variable density track.

Magnetic track:
3 Magnetic stripe. Balancing stripe facilitates flat, smooth roll wind.
4 Mute picture, separate 16 mm perforated magnetic film.

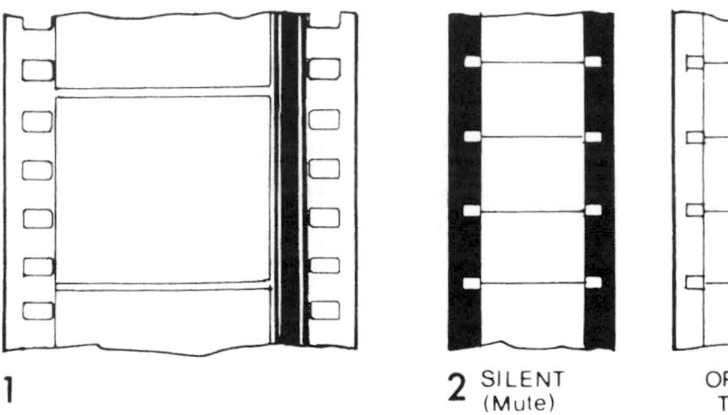

Fig. 13.4 Film formats
1 35 mm gauge.
2 16 mm.
3 Super-8.

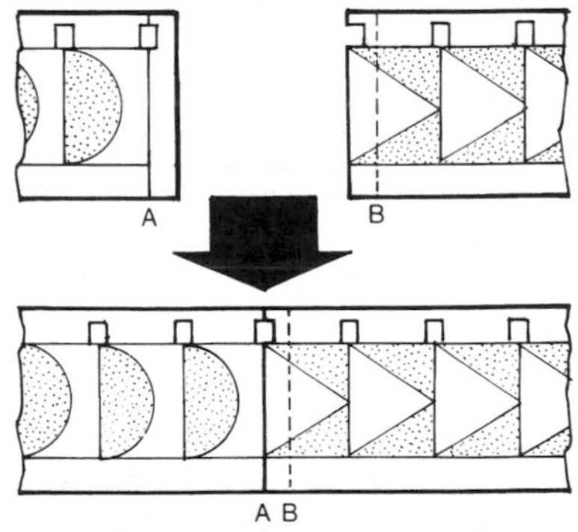

Fig. 13.5 Joining film
The two shots to be joined, are cut in the splicer and connected by: a *temporary splice* using translucent adhesive splicing tape (butt join), or a *permanent overlap weld* using film cement (scraping off film emulsion for overlap join), or a *heat butt-welded splice* along frame-line (used for negative editing). Unobtrusive splices require checkerboard (A/B roll) cutting.

by crystal controls or wireless interlocks. Alternatively, a reference time code may be used.

■ **Optical and magnetic tracks** Two forms of soundtrack are used with film – *optical* or *magnetic*.

Optical recording – Optical soundtracks may be recorded alongside the picture in the film camera, or preferably, on a separate photographic film roll in a 'sound camera'. As the audio fluctuates, a *light valve* varies the area or intensity of a small slit of light falling onto the passing film. After processing, this *variable area* or *variable density soundtrack* can be edited to match the corresponding pictures. Later it is printed photographically along one edge of the released show print, to form a *combined* or *married* print. As the photographic soundtrack passes over a constant-intensity slit of light from an *exciter lamp* it produces light fluctuations which are picked up from its reverse side by a light-sensitive cell, and amplified as an audio signal.

Magnetic recording – Some cameras use a *single system* in which the audio is recorded on the film as a separate *magnetic edge track* running alongside the picture area. Although compact, this combined arrangement does complicate editing. Cutting the film to edit the picture will disrupt the soundtrack. And because the magnetic audio recording head in the camera is located in advance

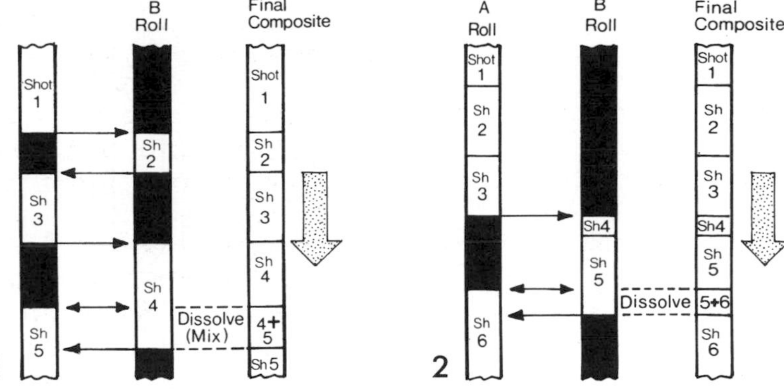

Fig. 13.6 Checkerboard and A/B roll assemblies
When printing narrow-gauge film, material is usually distributed between two rolls A and B, interspaced by blanking (black leader). By inter-switching/dissolving between rolls, optical combinations (dissolve, wipe, etc.) and invisible splices (not intruding into picture area) become possible. The system avoids intermediate duplication stages for combined effects.

1 For *checkerboard assembly*, the output changes between A and B rolls at each cut; except where an overlap is required for a combined effect (dissolve, wipe, etc.).
2 For *A/B roll assembly*, shots are spliced consecutively on one roll, until an overlap is required for a combined effect. The output then remains with the other roll for successive shots until the next combination is required. These techniques are also used for rapid excerpting from complete programs (film and VT).

of the *picture gate* (by 28 frames), the reproduced soundtrack leads its corresponding picture by about a second.

Double-headed process – Here instead of combining picture and soundtrack on the same film they are recorded and *reproduced* separately. The film camera uses regular photographic film stock to shoot the picture. The associated soundtrack (mono or stereo) is recorded magnetically in another unit on 16 mm or 35 mm perforated film material which has a full-width magnetic coating. In *double-headed* systems the *picture print* on one roll of film and the *sound film* with its magnetically recorded soundtrack on the other roll are laced in the telecine machine, and reproduced in synchronism. This arrangement can simplify and speed up editing, particularly for urgent news items.

The mechanics of film reproduction

The film chain

Film is universally shot at a standard rate of 24 frames or pictures per second. But in the NTSC *television* system 30 pictures are transmitted a second. To rationalize these differing standards, a sampling process is used during projection, such as that shown in Figure 13.8. For other TV systems such as *PAL* or *SECAM*, in which the television frame rate is 25 pictures a second, program makers have the option of either shooting at a special TV rate of 25 film frames per second or simply projecting any 24 fps films directly, and ignoring the imperceptible 4 per cent speed-up.

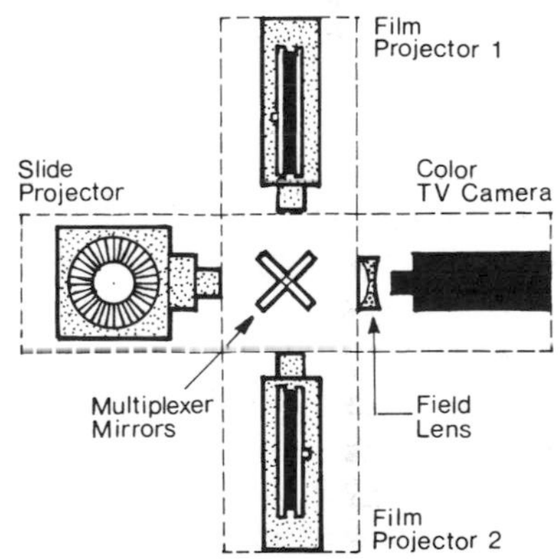

Fig. 13.7 Multiplexed telecine
A mirror or prism system enables one TV camera to selectively shoot a slide projector or either of two film projectors. The assembly is mounted on a film island.

Film island

In this widely used arrangement a single standard video camera points at a mirror system which reflects the outputs of a pair of

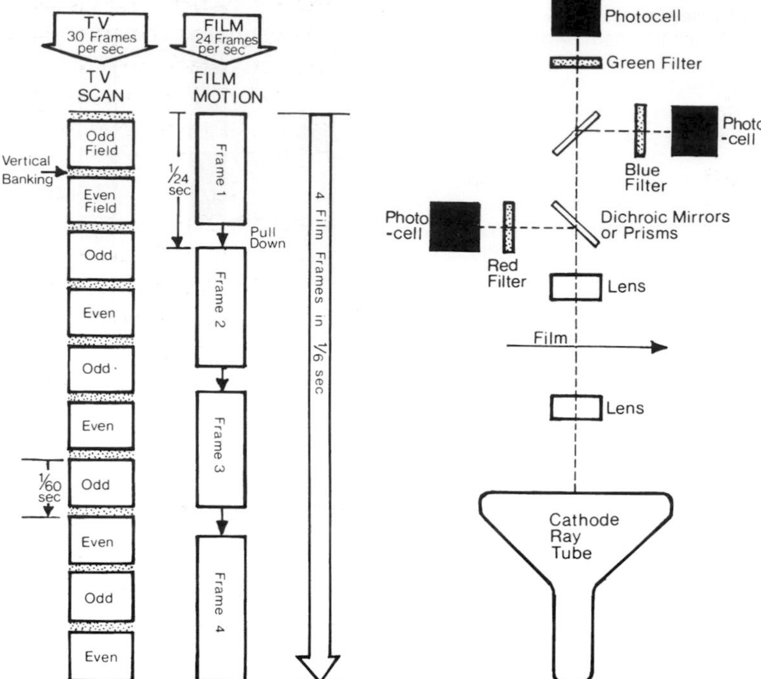

Fig. 13.8 Picture-rate conversion To relate the standard film projection rate (24 frames per second) to TV standards of 30 pictures (USA) per second, several sampling methods are used (e.g. project one film frame 3 times, the next twice; fast film pulldown with light-source pulsing 5 times per film frame/4 times per TV picture).

Fig. 13.9 Color flying-spot scanner A plain white raster traced on the cathode ray tube focused onto the moving film. This exploratory light spot is focused through color filters into corresponding photo cells or CCDs. Their outputs as each point is scanned, constituting red, green, blue video signals. To compensate for film movement, twin displaced rasters, twin-lens systems, or a rotating polygonal prism are used.

16 mm film projectors, and a 2 × 2 in photo-slide projector. Simply by adjusting the mirrors or prisms that divert the light path in the enclosed multiplex system, you can select any of these picture sources.

- *Projector* – To provide continuous operation, two 16 mm film projectors are usually fitted. To compensate for the discrepancy between the standard film frame projection rate (24 fps) and the TV picture rate of a 30 pps TV system (USA), each film frame is exposed for the duration of 2½ TV fields (see Figure 13.8). The projector's intermittent mechanism moves the film in rhythmic 'pull-and-hold' jerks to freeze each frame momentarily as it passes the projector's picture gate; so giving the TV camera time to register successive pictures clearly. The color quality, brightness, contrast, of the camera's video is then adjusted/corrected as necessary; either manually or automatically. The maximum 16 mm film reel typically holds 1220 m/4000 ft (51 cm/20 in) diameter) which lasts for 1 h 51 min at 24 fps.

- *Slide* – Two systems are widely used for televising 2 × 2 in slides in film islands: a regular slide projector with a horizontal rotatable drum or a special vertical dual-drum arrangement (each holding 18 slides). Slides can be selected remotely in any order although it is preferable to arrange them in the sequence required. To avoid the danger of buckling, it is advisable to mount slides in plastic, glass-faced supports, rather than use vulnerable thin card mounts.

Flying spot scanner

Flying spot scanner systems are capable of extremely high quality film reproduction. Because the film travels at a constant speed through this type of equipment (*continuous motion*) it avoids the film wear and the unsteadiness of intermittent-motion designs. To convert the photographic images into a video signal a special high-intensity picture tube is used. Its phosphor screen is continually scanned to create a plain white rectangle of light (*raster*), which is focused onto the moving film. As light from the scanning spot passes through the film image, the amount falling onto photo-cells behind the film fluctuates with changes in its density, and is transformed into a corresponding *video* signal. (To achieve *interlaced scanning* the tube screen displays *two* scanning rasters; one above the other. The second *re-scans* each picture as it passes, to provide the alternate TV frame.)

Digital telecine system

This is the highest grade method of televising film. Three full-line CCD sensors (red, green, and blue) scan the continuous motion film as it passes. They analyze its light variations, and the resulting charges are held in a digital frame store to be read out as the video signal. This system provides flicker-free slow motion, frame-by-frame jog, and still-frame pictures.

Another advantage of digital telecine systems is that they enable dirt and scratches to be concealed to a remarkable degree. A beam of infrared light passes straight through the film, unaffected by the color images, and falls onto a fourth CCD sensor. Any dirt, defects, or scratches that interrupt this beam cause circuits to switch momentarily, inserting earlier picture information instead at that point – a form of *drop-out compensation*.

Non-standard projection

Some designs of telecine equipment are extremely versatile:

- *Freeze frame* – Any film frame can be selected and held; although any blemishes, grain, scratches, or other defects in the film will be more obvious than when it is running.
- *Inching* – Allowing one still frame to be dissolved slowly into the next.
- *Run up from still frame* – Starting with a freeze frame, the film can be run up to full speed (mute!) without frame-roll or flicker.
- *Non-standard speeds* – Running at a constant non-standard speed (e.g. between 16 and 60 fps), forward or backwards.
- *Fast wind* – Ability to wind-on (run on) and rewind rapidly.
- *Cuing* – Facilities for *remote manual cuing* (from the production switcher) or *automatic cuing* using attached cue tags or tape strip, or computer selection.

Transmitting negative film

The original film negative is normally far too precious to risk damage or defacement through handling, dust or scratches. But to save the cost and time involved in printing, a negative may very occasionally be transmitted by electronically reversing tones. Any video control adjustments to compensate for color and exposure variations would need to be made in reverse – either manually or using programmed electronic correction.

Reversal film

The emulsion of *reversal film stock* is designed to produce a *positive picture image* with natural colors and tones instead of the usual negative version. So no print is needed, and a processing stage is eliminated. The advantages also include improved sharpness, finer grain, better color reproduction. However, there are limitations, including a reduced exposure range and less opportunity to correct exposure and color errors. Because this positive print is the *original* film it may be necessary to copy it anyway, to facilitate editing.

Video control for telecine

Film is capable of superb color reproduction, but it is not an entirely consistent material. We shall find some variations in color balance between different batches of the same film stock; and between different types of color film. Moreover when filming, exposure or color temperature may not have been accurate or consistent. Where film has aged, or is a copy of the original print (dupe), further changes arise. So in printing, film labs adjust the intensity and color balance of their printer lights to compensate empirically for discrepancies (grading).

However, when televising a film such errors are more apparent than in theater viewing, where eye adaptation and subjective effects tend to compensate. Consequently, a film that may appear satisfactory when theater-reviewed beforehand often requires further compensations when televised. Where the film has not been finely graded, these may be considerable.

By adjusting video gain, black level (sometimes gamma), color balance, and saturation considerable improvements become possible. Color correction may also be introduced by *electronic masking circuits*, compensating for film dye deficiencies and certain *analysis errors* arising when television color film. Video gain and gamma adjustments to the RGB color channels ('TARIF' operation) provide good correction for various errors. Similar correction can be applied to slide (transparency) scanners.

Exposure and color-correction adjustments may be made 'on the fly' by an operator during replay; either empirically or to settings found during rehearsal. Some systems enable corrective settings to be filed, selected, and activated; automatically or by push-button.

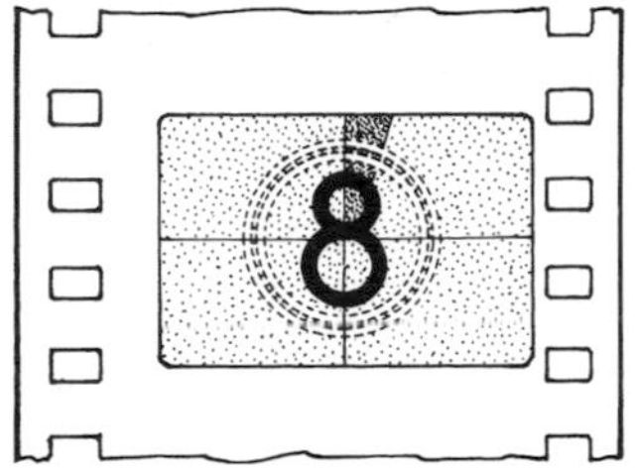

Fig. 13.10 TV film sync leader
Several types of film leader are in use. In the American National Standard leader shown (35 and 16 mm motion-picture theater, and TV studios), a *start identification frame* ensures exact picture sync with the sound-head. A series of numbers from 8 to 2 (seconds) appear (a black background then a dark wedge moving clockwise in series of 15° steps) provide a visual count-down.

Cuing film

Most telecine equipment cannot provide an instantaneous start for picture and audio. A brief run-up period is necessary for audio to stabilize. By attaching a time-scaled *sync leader* (e.g. SMPTE universal leader) to the head of a film you can ensure that the first picture frame with fully stabilized audio will appear a predictable time after switch-on. The required picture sync marker is positioned in the projector's picture gate, the director giving an anticipatory run cue 4 (or 8) seconds before cutting to film channel output. This avoids inadvertently switching to a stationary or unstable channel. To ensure that the film reproduction is neither clipped at its beginning nor runs out immediately after action finishes, a few *buffer (safety) frames* of the scene are included at the head and tail of each section.

Fig. 13.11 Changeover synchronizing
At the appearance of a white (or black) circular dot in the top right corner of the picture area, the second projector is started (motor cue). After 7 seconds, a similar dot cues the changeover switch-point. This mark is printed or punched in the print (during processing, or editing).

Where several film lengths are conjoined, you can:

- Use timed lengths of blanking between them; leaving the machine running while cutting away to studio (*roll-through*).
- Introduce a series of sync leaders; re-cuing each section.
- Cue the film at any time, switching to it when it appears.

Having previously ascertained the exact 'timing' (duration), the *in-cue* (first words) and *out-cue* (last words), precision insertion into the program becomes practicable. Occasionally, the exact entry/

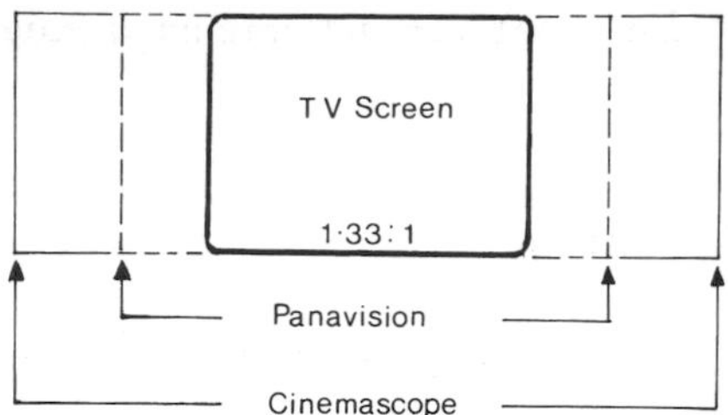

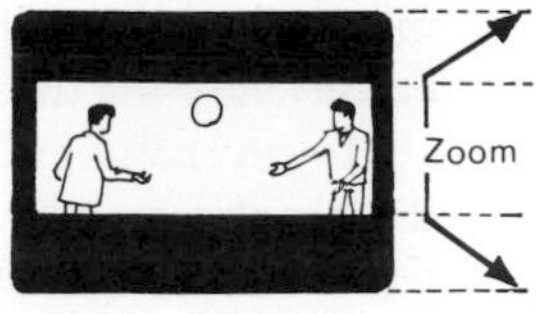

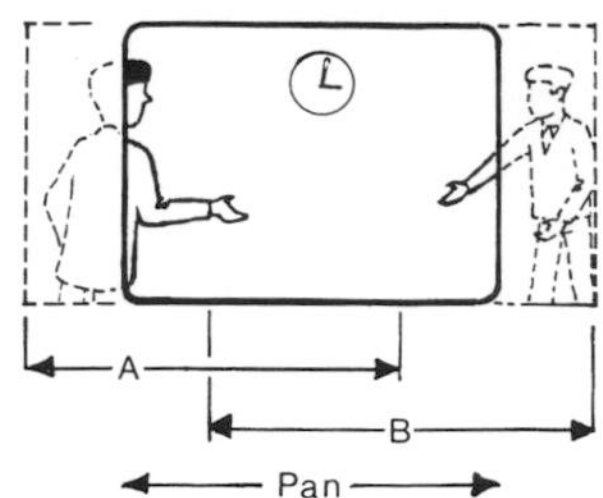

Fig. 13.12 Wide-screen films
Wide screen motion pictures do not use the TV screen's aspect ratio (4 × 3 shape; i.e. 1.33:1). If the picture is fitted to frame side-edges, so seeing all of film. Overall picture size is small and areas are wasted at top/bottom of TV screen. If the *top/bottom* of the frame is fitted to the TV screen, then the sides of the film picture are lost. Solutions to this problem include zooming to full height, panning left/right to follow main action (top-fit) as shown (A to B). These *'pan and scan'* operations involve scanning circuit adjustments (on-air or pre-coded), or compensated film prints.

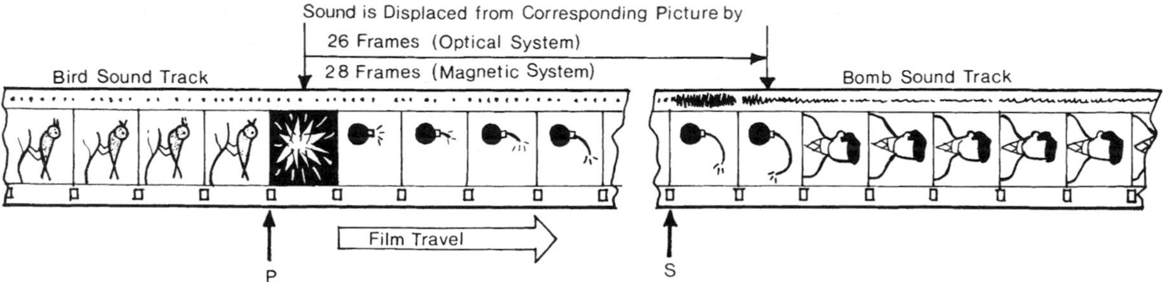

Fig. 13.13 Cutting combined prints – problem
In a combined print (optical or magnetic stripe) the sound is displaced ahead of its corresponding picture (to suit the picture-gate to sound-head separation distance).

Physically cutting this combined print creates a dilemma: if the sound track is cut at a specific point (S), then over a second (26–28 picture frames) of unwanted picture is included in the selected film. When editing continuous speech, this can result in *lip-flap* before the wanted action. i.e. silent mouth movements left from the previous material, without any accompanying sound.

In the above example, cutting at the end of the picture sequence (P), will spuriously introduce sound from the next shot; while cutting after the explosion sound (S) will lose the picture of the event.

The problem can be overcome by intercutting a mute shot (e.g. cutaway), or re-laying the sound track.

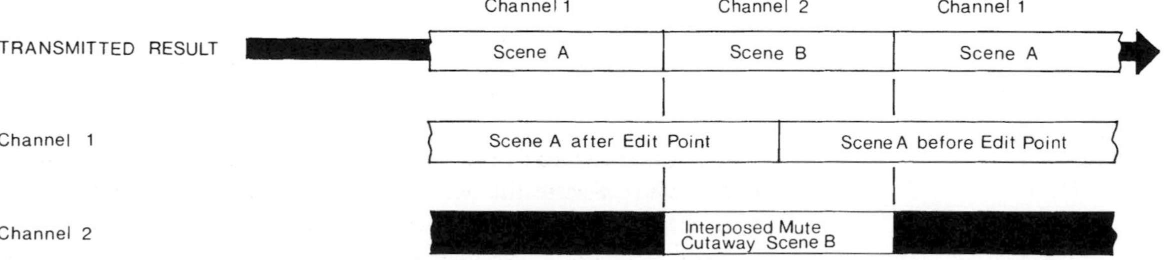

Fig. 13.14 Cutting combined prints – solution
A standard method uses a double chain or A/B system. A brief silent cutaway shot (reaction shot) is interposed to hide any lip-flap, jump-cut etc., by strategically switching away.

exit points for a videotaped film insert are determined during subsequent VT editing.

Film aspect ratio (picture shape)

As motion picture technology has developed over the years the shape of the picture area has undergone various changes. So we may encounter film prints with picture proportions from *1.33:1* (i.e. *4 by 3*), to *wide-screen* 1.85:1, and the 2.35:1 standard of *CinemaScope*. The more recent introduction of the 16:9 *high definition television (HDTV)* format adds both opportunities and complications.

All current color TV systems derived from NTSC have a regular aspect ratio set at 4 by 3. If you televise film which has been shot in any other format – assuming that your telecine will run this format – its picture shape will not fit the TV screen. (And that includes the special format of 1.66:1 for *Super 16 mm* film.) If you adjust the telecine's horizontal or vertical scans to fit larger formats into the 4 by 3 transmitted picture everything in the shot will become correspondingly distorted!

There are really only two practical solutions when showing wider film formats on a 4 by 3 screen:

- '*Letter box*' transmission – In which you adjust the telecine system so that the film picture's *width* will fit to the TV frame's *side edges*. That will leave large black areas at the top and bottom of the television receiver's screen, and the overall image is correspondingly smaller than normal. But at least the viewer sees the entire film image.
- '*Pan-and-scan*' technique – Here the telecine is set up to scan the entire *height* of the film picture. That results in the left and right edges of the original film image being lost on transmission due to overscan. To compensate, the telecine's scanning system is continually adjusted to pan left/right across the film image (or zoomed) to follow the main action. This 'pan-and-scan' operation can be carried out manually on-air. But it is preferable to use an automated process, in which the film is reviewed beforehand and all the necessary panning and zooming adjustments coded. When the film is transmitted, these changes are carried out automatically.

Unfortunately such '*pan-and-scan*' subterfuges have major drawbacks. They disrupt the film makers' original composition and the film's editing. Important action or reactions can be lost outside the transmitted frame. Comedic timing may be upset; especially during rapid intercutting sequences. At times, the effect can even be disastrous; e.g. where the scan is centered and important subjects at the edges of the original shot cannot be seen! There are artistic judgments to be made too. Someone organizing the maneuvers has to decide whether to concentrate the restricted shot on the character who is speaking or on the reaction of their listener at the other side of the frame. The film maker included *both*! However, many viewers prefer the result, rather than a 'cut-down' display with large black borders on their TV screens!

With the new 16:9 (1.77:1) wide TV screen shape, complications arise when you display pictures recorded with the standard 4 by 3 format. Transmit these pictures to fill the screen *width*, and the shot will be cut off at the top and/or bottom. Fill the screen *height* and large black panels are left at the sides. Later TV receivers and monitors may have adjustable screen formats, but remember, there will always be those viewers who still have the receivers with the earlier picture shape.

Recording video on film

Several methods have evolved for transferring video pictures to standard color film stock. Each has its particular advantages and limitations. At best, results are excellent. Film recordings have advantages in certain markets. They overcome incompatible TV standards that frustrate the world distribution of videotape

Table 13.1 Film running times

	35 mm (16 fr per ft)				*16 mm (40 fr per ft)*				*Super 8 mm (72 fr per ft)*			
	24 fps		*25 fps*		*24 fps*		*25 fps*		*24 fps*		*25 fps*	
	ft	*fr*	*ft*	*fr*	*ft*	*fr*	*ft*	*fr*	*ft*	*fr*	*ft*	*fr*
Seconds 1	1	8	1	9	0	24	0	25	0	24	0	25
3	4	8	4	11	1	32	1	35	1	0	1	3
5	7	8	7	13	3	0	3	5	1	48	1	53
7	10	8	10	15	4	8	4	15	2	24	2	31
10	15	0	15	10	6	0	6	10	3	24	3	24
30	45	0	46	14	18	0	18	30	10	0	10	30
Minutes 1	90	0	93	12	36	0	37	20	20	0	20	60
5	450	0	468	12	180	0	187	20	100	0	104	12
10	900	0	937	8	360	0	375	0	200	0	208	24
15	1350	0	1406	4	540	0	562	20	300	0	312	36
	Seconds											
Feet 1	0.7		0.6		1.8		1.6		3.0		2.9	
3	2.0		1.9		5.0		4.8		9.0		8.6	
5	3.3		3.2		8.3		8.0		15.0		14.4	
7	4.7		4.5		11.6		11.2		21.0		20.2	
10	6.6		6.4		16.6		16.0		30.0		28.8	
15	10.0		9.6		25.0		24.0		45.0		43.2	
20	13.2		12.8		33.3		32.0		1 min 0.0		57.6	
30	20.0		19.2		50.0		48.0		1 min 30.0		1 min 24.0	
50	33.2		32.0		1 min 23.0		1 min 20.0		2 min 30.0		2 min 24.0	

1 foot = 0.3048 meters

Table 13.2 Displacement of picture and sound

	35 mm	*16 mm*	*Super 8 mm*
Magnetic track	28 frames behind pic.	28 ahead of pic.	18 ahead of pic.
Optical track	21 frames ahead.	26 ahead.	22 ahead.

recordings. Film prints permit large-screen projection, have wider educational and library applications, and are more convenient for certain field work.

Several major films have been shot with video cameras and then transferred to film stock, for theatrical release. The main advantages here have included: the opportunity to monitor while shooting, immediate playback checks, more convenient and economical videotape editing, the opportunity to use digital video effects, and image enhancing. And all this has become possible due to the high image-transfer quality now available.

Methods of image transfer

You can transfer video onto film in several different ways:

1 A special film camera (using color film) shoots a color TV picture tube.
2 A similar set-up, filming a monochrome picture tube which displays in three successive runs the red, blue, and green component images from a videotape. The three separate monochrome recording of the color information are combined to full color during laboratory printing.
3 *Laser beam* recording, in which three separate video-modulated lasers (RGB) combine optically on *color* film.
4 Electron beam recording (EBR) produces three separation negatives (RGB) on black-and-white film, scanned by electron beams akin to those in picture tubes. These records are combined during laboratory printing, using corresponding red, green, blue light sources.

14 Video recording

For the audience, *live* television can be exciting! Anything can happen – and often does! But from the director's point of view, transmitting a program as-it-happens has major hazards. You can't correct errors, improve, or augment. If anything goes wrong, your audience sees it too! There are no second chances; no afterthoughts. Consequently the strain on performers and the production team can be extremely high. There are inevitably compromises. It can be difficult to introduce finesse. Complicated visual and sound effects take time to develop and build up; time that may not be available in a live show. The coming of the videotape recorder or '*VTR*' changed all that, and added an extra dimension to TV production techniques.

Until relatively recently, the director had two options: to shoot on film, or to record on *analogue* videotape. Film is expensive, and has its drawbacks (e.g. no immediate checks; processing is needed). Like film, *analogue* videotape recordings cannot be copied and re-copied without severe deterioration in the picture quality – and yet, multi-copying is unavoidable where you are developing complicated visual effects.

Now *digital* videotape recording is available which allows extensive copying and manipulation without appreciable losses. Disk-based digital systems are also developing which use magnetic *hard disk* or re-recordable optical videodisc. Solid-state techniques are emerging, which store date in a computer's *RAM* memory. Each offers its particular advantages.

Recording formats

When studying video recording it's easy to become bogged down in technicalities; although most users are really only concerned with the characteristics of the particular equipment *they* are using. So we shall concentrate here on basics. (You will find more details of typical recording formats in the *Digests – Videotape recording methods.*)

It is important to realize that several VTR designs or *formats* have evolved over the years and that these systems are *incompatible.* A tape recorded on one format will not replay on another. (There are dissimilarities in the ways the picture and sound are recorded, as well as differences in the videotape's magnetic characteristics and in tape widths.) However, where various manufacturers' equipment uses *the same format* (e.g. all are S-VHS systems) recordings should be interchangeable.

Does it really matter which recording format you use? Well, there are a number of practical differences:

- In the picture quality: definition; color fidelity; whether there are any noticeable defects (*artifacts*) such as picture noise, edge effects around subjects, unmodelled highlights, etc.
- Whether you can make several generations of copies (i.e. a copy of a copy) without detectable deterioration. (Digital systems are greatly superior to analogue in this respect.)
- The video tape required; the types available, and their durations.
- Whether the form of video (i.e. composite or component; analogue or digital) matches the rest of the video equipment you are using.
- The facilities the recorder provides (i.e. the number of audio tracks, the type of tracks, the kinds of equipment outputs, controls, etc.).
- The ease with which the recording can be edited. (And the equipment needed.)
- How readily you can replace the *sound* on the original tape without disrupting the *picture*.
- The portability of the video recording system.
- Its suitability for developing complex video effects; for post-production work.
- Can a tape recorded on your equipment be played by the people for whom it is intended (e.g. your client)?

The advantages of videotape recording

Videotape recording offers the program maker a number of opportunities:

- **Operation** – Videotape recorders are quite straightforward to operate.
- **Quality** – At best, the quality of the videotaped program is indistinguishable from the original pictures and sound.
- **Immediacy** – You can replay the tape immediately; and in some equipment monitor off-tape during recording (using confidence playback) to check quality.
- **Long life** – Videotapes can be reproduced many times without deterioration. Properly stored, the recording will last for years.
- **Selective replacement** – You can erase (*wipe*) all or part of the recording, and replace it with new material.
- **Editing** – The videotape's picture and sound can be edited or modified separately. Faulty, ineffectual, or unwanted sections can be removed or replaced with retakes (to replace distractions, redundant shots, ambiguities, censor cuts, etc.). You can adjust the overall duration or the pace of the presentation by making cuts or introducing cutaway shots.
- **Sectional compilations** – You can record the program in sections and replay the tape as a continuous performance. Similarly you can compile a new program by copying sections from other recordings (tape or film) made at different times and places.
- **Off-line editing** – By making a copy of the videotape recording with a displayed time code the director can make off-line editing judgments before the final postproduction on-line editing session.

- **Video effects** – Any video effects can be taped and checked immediately to check their effectiveness. If necessary, the effect can be re-recorded or augmented with further effects. Complex sequences (e.g. multi-layer video effects, complicated animated graphics) can be prepared separately, and subsequently edited into the main program.
- **Scheduling** – Programs can be recorded when convenient and replayed when required; to suit transmission arrangements, fit time zones, training schedules, etc. So educational programs can be transmitted during the night for home-taping in educational schemes.
- **Excerpting** – It is simple to copy selected sections from the complete program for publicity trailers, study or training purposes, etc.
- **Extend apparent facilities** – By taping the action in a series of sections (changing camera angle, shot sizes, lighting changes) and then editing these together you can create the illusion of far greater facilities, more extensive studio space, etc.
- **Overcome staging problems** – By recording the show in sections you have time to introduce changes in costume and make-up, and to move scenery (e.g. reposition wild walls, refurbish settings, re-light). This may be difficult or impracticable in continuous performance.
- **Instant replay** – Videotape provides the opportunity to replay action again, immediately afterwards; e.g. to show the winning goal, or to demonstrate a golfing stroke in slow motion.
- **Duplication** – Videotape is easily copied for archiving or multi-copy distribution – either in real-time (which takes as long as the original tape's duration) or on special copying VTRs operating at several times the original recording speed. To avoid any possibility of tape damage or loss it is a good idea to make protection or back-up copies; either by copying the original (edited or unedited) or by recording on two machines simultaneously during the taping session.
- **Multi-use** – The videotaping process is very adaptable. It lends itself to a wide range of applications from study to surveillance.
- **Archiving** – Videotaped programs are easily stored – in their entirety or as excerpted sections. This library can contain a range of material from complete programs awaiting later reruns, to reference items used to illustrate future programs (copyrights permitting!). A sequence within one program may be excerpted and stored as a library shot; to be re-used in various other productions. Detailed cataloguing and computer search programs enable you to rapidly select, retrieve, and copy (*dub off*) any topic. Archives can also include stills (*freeze frames*). These are copied from newscasts, sports events, interviews, etc., to provide portraits of personalities, film stars, actors, etc. These are held in a central still-store or server; typically for instant selection in a news item, or to identify a player during a game. (Although it is possible to use a 'frame-by-frame' recorded videotape as a still-store, it can be difficult to rapidly locate and retrieve specific frames.)
- **Copying film** – Motion pictures are often copied onto videotape for television transmission. This protects the original print and also gives opportunities to add subtitles (explanatory; language translation; identifying titling). Music and voice-over commentary may be added to films which were originally mute or had inappropriate soundtracks. Film material that is valuable, damaged, or non-standard, or prints that need to edited or excerpted can be transferred to videotape.
- **Distribution** – Because tape is compact it is easily mailed. Alternatively it can be transmitted by cable or satellite to other organizations and copied by them on a local VTR.
- **Speed changes** – The apparent speed and direction of the action in a shot can be altered during videotape replay. By jogging the tape forwards or backwards at selected constant speeds you can speed up or slow down action. Action may be frozen at any point by replaying the same frame over

and over. Some VTRs have the facility for recording events at a very slow regular rate (e.g. one frame per hour). When replayed at normal speed this results in a greatly speeded-up effect (time lapse); used to show plant growth, traffic flow, changing cloud formations.

- **Animation** – By shooting a single frame or two at a time, and readjusting the subject a little between each shot, you can produce animation (*stop-motion recording*). The subjects appear to be moving when the complete tape is replayed at normal speed.

Videotape recording basics

Of course, you do not need to know how a video recorder works to use it successfully. But if you understand the principles involved you will find it lot easier to sort out equipment differences and to appreciate problems that can arise.

The tape support

Depending on its purpose and design, the tape may be wound onto *open-reels* or housed in a cassette:

- *Open reel (reel-to-reel)* – Here the tape is unwound from a full *supply reel*, laced manually through the tape path (transport system) and secured to an empty *take-up spool*. You must take care when handling the tape to avoid damage (creasing, scrape, edge crushing) or contamination (finger-marks, grease, dust).
- *Cassette* – This is the familiar tape housing which incorporates both supply and take-up spools, used in audio and home videotape systems as well as most professional formats. The cassette consists of a plastic box which almost entirely encloses the tape except for a section under a hinged shield – which is automatically raised as the cassette is inserted into the VTR. Because the tape is self-lacing it is entirely protected from handling problems.

  To avoid accidentally wiping a wanted program, the cassette is fitted with a *safety device*. With some tapes (e.g. oxide) this is a break-out tag which you remove – similar to that used on *audio tape cassettes*. If the tag is missing and you want to make a new recording on this cassette, stick a piece of adhesive tape over the opening. Alternately, the cassette may be fitted with a small movable knob or plug, which is pushed in to prevent re-recording.

The magnetic tape

Magnetic media have the great advantage that they can be used, erased, and reused many times. The surface does wear or become damaged in time (causing *dropout* or picture disturbance), but it is a very economical medium with a potentially long storage life. Although all videotape systems use a thin polymer-based plastic tape with a magnetic coating, the tape's width, type, and length need to be appropriate for your VTR system. Tape widths include 8 mm, ½ in, ¾ in, (housed in cassettes) and 1 in and 2 in (open reel). The magnetic coating may consist of a high-density *metallic oxide* or a pure metal coating in *particle* or finely *evaporated* form. The last provides improved packing density, coercivity, and physical structure. Although 'metal' tapes are more expensive, they produce recordings with greater detail, less video noise, improved tonal contrast. However, they are generally thinner, and so more vulnerable to damage. While all video recorders using magnetic tape are called *VTR*s (*videotape recorders*), those with tapes in cassettes are often referred to as *VCR*s (*videocassette recorders*).

Neutralizing the videotape

To make sure that your tape is completely *'clean'*, i.e. all previously recorded program totally eliminated, you should pass it through the strong fluctuating magnetic field of a *bulk eraser* (*degausser*) beforehand. That prevents any possibility of interference or background effects between the old and new recordings. (You can neutralize audio tape similarly.)

But for most everyday purposes, you will probably rely on erasure carried out within the VTR during the recording process. As the tape moves through the machine it passes *erase heads* which locally demagnetize (*wipe*) previous tracks, neutralizing the tape, ready to take fresh magnetic information.

The videotape recording process

As you can see in Table 14.4, there are a number of different video recording formats in use today. When you operate the VTR in a *record mode* several kinds of magnetic signals are laid down on the tape simultaneously. The actual form they take will depend on the VTR system you are using.

Helical scanning

The amount of detailed information you can record on the passing magnetic tape depends partly on the magnetic characteristics of its coating and partly on the speed at which the tape passes the recording head(s) – i.e. the *writing speed*. The faster the tape moves, the more detail you can record. But fast-moving tape causes mechanical problems and faster wear. Unless the storage reels are

Fig. 14.1 part 1 Typical helical scanning arrangement
The tape is wrapped in a slanting path round a drum. Within the drum a disk head-wheel supporting recording (and erase) heads rotates, pressing heads against the tape at an acute angle as it slides past. (Designs include rotating upper drum, or slot scanner with narrow rotating center section.) Each head-drum revolution records one video track.

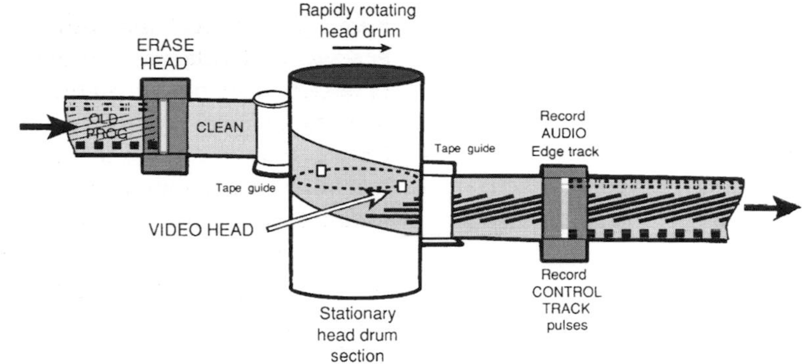

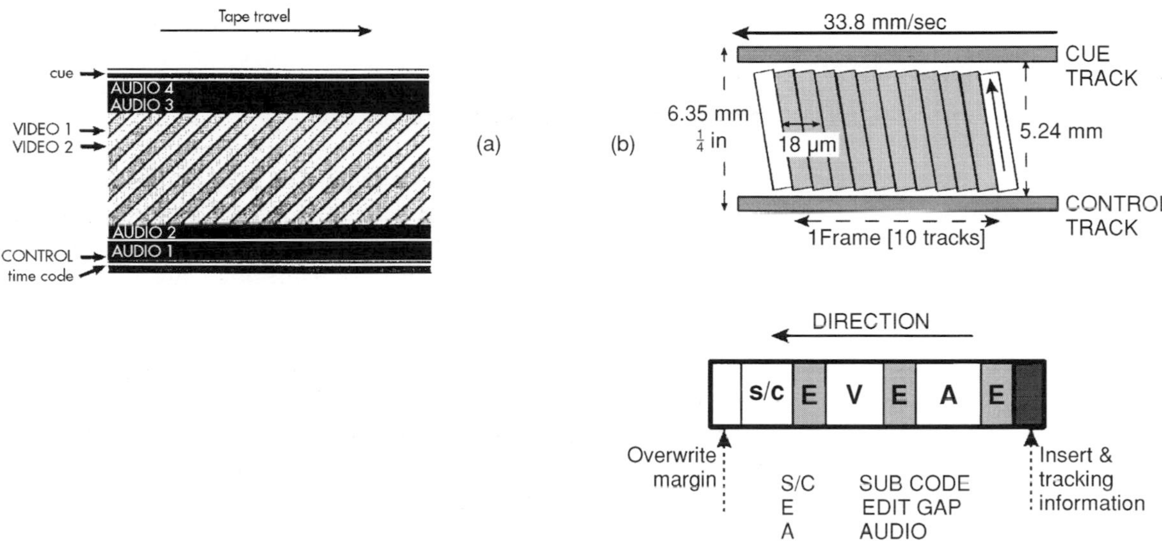

Fig. 14.1 part 2 Videotape tracks
The ways in which tracks are arranged on the tape, vary considerably with different videotape recorder systems.

(a) A typical helical scan *analogue* system showing: the video slant tracks, longitudinal audio tracks, control, cue, and time code tracks.
(b) In this *digital* VTR system the slant tracks are subdivided into a series of sections, containing the digital video and audio information, as well as coding data. Two longitudinal tracks carry the cue track, and the control track.

large, the recording/replay time is very limited. So designers developed another approach. Instead of the tape moving quickly past stationary recording heads (as in the regular *audio recorder*), the video recording heads are mounted in a rotating drum. Now the *combined head* and *tape movements* result in a very high *effective writing rate* while the tape itself is moving at a very economical speed. The result is a series of parallel sloping magnetic tracks (*slant tracks*) across the tape width. On a single-headed scanner two rotations of the scanning drum are needed to lay down a complete frame (i.e. the odd and even fields) on the moving tape. A two-headed scanner records both fields in one rotation.

Let's look at this technique more closely. The tape travels from the supply reel on the left, past a fixed *erase head* which demagnetizes ('wipes') the entire width of the tape. The 'cleaned' tape then moves up at an angle to a cylindrical *head drum* or *scanning drum*, and wraps round most of it, to form a path shaped like the Greek letter omega (Ω) – an '*omega wrap*' of e.g. 190°. (A few VTR systems use a more enclosed, *alpha* wrap path (α).) Half-way down the drum is a slit from which two or more tiny video *record/replay heads* protrude. (They may be attached to the drum's rotating upper half, or on a separate revolving central disk.) As they turn, the heads rhythmically press against the passing tape sliding over the drum's surface ('tip penetration'). Because the tape is wound round in a helical path, this process is termed *helical scanning*. It is used in all modern videotape recording systems and in audio *R-DAT* digital tape recorders.

So not only is the effective *writing rate* considerably increased by using this scanning method, but the oblique tracks are much longer than would result from simply scanning across the tape (as in the old *Quadruplex* system). There are interruptions, of course, as each track approaches the tape edge and continues again on a new parallel path slightly further along the tape, but these gaps in information can be hidden. For example, a gap can be made to coincide with the retrace period at the end of each field; i.e. falling outside the picture area of the TV screen. If, however, a VTR's *tracking control* is not correctly adjusted on replay (particularly when playing tapes recorded on another machine) we shall be able to see the *noise-bar* or picture disturbances caused at each track end. But again, a lot depends on the system you are using.

Replay – When you play the tape, the slant tracks are read either by additional *replay* heads on the scanning drum, or by reusing the re-routed *recording* heads.

Longitudinal tracks

While the slanting *video tracks* are being recorded across the tape, several *fixed heads* are recording other tracks along its length at the upper and lower edges. Again, the actual arrangements vary with different videotape recording systems. As you will see, these *longitudinal, linear* or *edge-tracks* have various uses: providing an *audio track*, a *control track*, and a *cue track/ time code*.

The recorded signals

Although track details vary considerably, and can be very complex, two aspects of video recording are common to all VTRs:

The video is recorded as a succession of narrow parallel slant tracks across the tape.
The video is not applied directly to the *video head* but is used to control a frequency-modulated (FM) carrier, which creates the magnetic changes in the tape.
The sound track(s) are recorded separately.

There are two methods of recording the video and audio signals on the tape:

- *Analogue* – In which all the fluctuations of the original continuous signal are recorded. This is the simplest method, but has the disadvantages that the recorded signal is easily distorted or corrupted, and each copy is of lower quality.
- *Digitally* – Here the original analogue signal goes through a sampling process, which examines its strength at regular intervals and interprets the results as a numerical pattern of pulses. Although more complex, this method has the advantage that the final signal is not readily degraded, and copies without distortion.

■ **The video signal** – *Video signals* can be organized in three different forms: *composite* – *component* – RGB.

- **Composite signals** – In the standard NTSC, PAL, or SECAM systems the picture is transmitted as a '*composite*' TV signal. This is used in broadcast and single-wire cable systems, and includes:

  All the picture's brightness/detail information (*luminance* – Y).
  The color information (*chrominance* – C).
  And the scanning and color *synchronizing pulses*.

  This technically ingenious arrangement involves various unavoidable compromises: e.g. the picture displays mutual interference between chrominance and luminance information, which worsens each generation (copy).
- **Component signals** – Picture information can also be conveyed as '*component*' video. Here the video information is *encoded* into its *luminance* (Y) or brightness component and its *chrominance* (C) or color component. These are routed separately so require a two-wire system throughout. The separate signals may be combined (but not always) when recorded on the tape. This technique avoids *cross-color* and *cross-luminance* interference.
- **R.G.B. signals** – Some systems convey the picture's red, green and blue signals (*R.G.B.*) as entirely separate components throughout. Although this seems the most obvious method, there are practical disadvantages: the need for triple-routing and the possibility of *phase errors* (altered hues) as color components get out of step.

■ **Audio tracks** – The audio may be recorded in several ways; as stereo pairs or as single mono tracks. Where edge audio tracks (*linear; longitudinal*) are used, the audio quality is limited by the tape speed and the fact that the grain orientation of the magnetic material layer is optimized for the slanting video tracks. Several VTR systems now include a very high quality stereo recording facility, in which the audio signals are integrated with the video signal track in various ways (*multiplex FM* or *segmented digital*). In general, the quality of audio edge-tracks is not as high as that of the faster slant tracks.

■ **Control pulses** – A series of regular pulses recorded every 1/30 or 1/25 second are used to accurately adjust and synchronize the tape speed, the speed of head-drum rotation (i.e. scanning rate) and tape tension. They are usually recorded on a longitudinal track, and ensure that the video heads re-scan the existing tracks correctly on playback (particularly if the tape has been recorded on another machine), and aid color frame identification. (In some VTR formats, *sync signals* are recorded instead at points within or at the end of each slant track scan.)

■ **Cue track (timing)** – To identify each frame of the video recording one of the audio tracks is normally used to record a special *time code* (*address code*). (*See Digests – Time codes*.) Where the more reliable time code system is not available some systems rely on counting the control pulses to locate points on the tape during editing processes. Otherwise this track may be used to record production information, commentary, or a second language, or cue tones.

■ **Edit signals** – To indicate a chosen place in the tape, to assist editing, or to select a passage during playback a brief identifying pulse may be recorded on a longitudinal track. This pulse may be inserted automatically (e.g. at the start of each recorded scene) or manually (e.g. at a certain action point).

Practical VTRs

Videotape recorders are available in several forms, depending on their purpose and how robust they need to be.

- *Larger VTRs* (such as Types B and C 1-inch systems) are generally located in edit suites, central videotape recording departments in broadcast organizations (VTR room), facility houses.
- *Medium-size portable* VTRs (typically ¾ in. and ½ in. systems) are widely used in ENG/EFP production (in a van or support vehicle); for small-studio production; in postproduction suites; in corporate, industrial, and educational video.

Table 14.1 Typical videotape recorder controls

SP/LP	Recording speed selection; *standard play and long play*. The latter allows twice the normal recording duration for a given tape length but at lower definition.
Standby mode	'Standby' automatically withdraws the tape from the cassette and laces it along the tape path, holding it stationary in readiness, without its making contact with the rotating video heads. This facilitates 'instant start' when you press *record* or *replay*. (Without this facility there is a delay on starting while the machine pulls the tape from the cassette and threads it through the tape path.)
Pause	If you press *pause* during **replay** the action will '*freeze*', holding a *still frame*. (The tape stops moving, and the heads continually re-scan the same video track(s).) However, although some tape surfaces are more resilient than others, this inevitably wears the tape at that point; eventually causing surface damage and permanent drop-out. The loosened surface material can clog the heads. Most VTRs have an automatic cut-out system, that switches off the repeat-scanning after the tape has been stationary for about 2 minutes. If you pause while **recording**, the tape stops, but remains laced up, re-scanning the same small path. Press the pause button again, and recording continues. If you stop and restart the VTR during recording this can cause momentary disruption of the syncs at that point, and/or delay as the tape relaces. To avoid this, some people use *tape pause* during recording.
Fast forward, fast rewind	Running the tape at high speed, to reach a point further along the tape, or to fully rewind to the start of the tape.
Fast scan	Running the tape fast forward or in reverse while reviewing the pictures. With some VTRs you can still see pictures sufficiently well at quite high speeds (e.g. × 9) to follow action in color.
Jog	Playing the tape frame by frame; usually after selecting a still frame.
Shuttle	A variable rotating dial or ring, allowing the tape to be played/searched at selected speeds; forward or reverse. Alternatively, a series of preselected constant speeds may be selectable for continual jogging, slow motion, or fast motion effects.
Index search	This runs the tape on to an *auto-mark* introduced automatically at the start of each new recording. Alternatively, you can manually key in an electronic tag to identify a chosen section in the program.
Introscan	This winds the tape on to the next index marker tone and plays a few seconds of the program in order to let you identify that section. Unless stopped, it proceeds to fast-run on to the next marker.
Blank tape search	A facility for locating the next blank unrecorded section on a tape.
'Go-to' search	A fast-wind facility, taking the tape rapidly to a point which is a certain playing-time, or tape length, from the beginning of the reel.
Tracking control	Adjusts the accuracy with which the replay heads trace the recorded slant tracks by very slightly altering the tape tension and head drum speed. Mainly used when reproducing tapes made on another machine. Tracking errors only occur on replay, and include *skewing hooking/flagging* (in which the top of the frame curves left and right), picture tearing, picture breakup. Some VTRs include self-corrective auto-tracking systems.

Table 14.1 (cont.)

Connections

Videotape recorders (and cameras) provide a range of input and outputs, using several types of connection. Although video and audio cable connectors are 'standardized', a considerable range of types includes *BNC, BCN, UHF, F-type, S-video, Scart, 'RCA'/phono, DIN,* mini-plug, phone plug, XLR/Canon plug. The best advice is to check what *your particular equipment* is fitted with and ensure that you have spares! To cope with those embarrassing situations where the equipment socket and your cable connector are dissimilar, *adapters* and cables with dissimilar types of end plugs (or sockets) are available. Devices called *splitters* allow a single cable to diverge and provide two outputs or to accept two inputs. But beware! Problems can arise, such as reduced signal, reflections, phasing errors (double termination).

Consumer videotape recorders

Those (e.g. *S-VHS*) include a *modulator (RF generator)* unit. This is virtually a tiny TV transmitter, sending the VTR's NTSC (or PAL) composite signal along a cable as a *modulated RF* radio wave to the antenna (aerial) socket of a TV receiver. The modulator is tuned to a channel that can be selected on the receiver like a regular off-air transmission (e.g. Ch. 32–40). Professional VTRs do not include a modulator, for their output is intended to be fed directly to video equipment (including monitors,) with minimum loss of quality. In addition, consumer VTRs' facilities include *TV station selection* and a *timer/programmer* for off-air recording.

The picture may be output from the VTR in separate *Y* (luminance) and *C* (color) components in composite form, or in certain cases, as separate RGB signals.

- *Lightweight VTRs* range from consumer products (home recorders) to compact professional units using S-VHS, Hi-8, DVC-Pro, etc. In the field, the VTR may be carried in a shoulder-pack, a trolley-pack or a cart.
- *Camcorders* incorporate a videotape recorder so that the system can be virtually self-contained. The actual VTR unit may be built-in to the camcorder or be made as a separate *dockable* unit that can be detached and used separately. So the same camera system may have quite different videotape recorders attached (e.g. M-II, Betacam- SP, S-VHS, or Hi-8) to suit postproduction editing equipment, etc.

Practical editing

In Chapter 8 we discussed the principles, the aims, and the art of editing. Let us now take a look at the mechanics involved in the videotape editing process. These must vary to some extent with the type and design of the equipment you are using.

Table 14.2 Tape care

Here are some tips for prolonging the life of your tape, ensuring good recordings, and avoiding embarrassing tape snarl-ups inside the machine. Many are very obvious, but we all get caught out at times!

- Store your tape at around 18–20°C (64.5–68°F); not above 40°C (104°F) or below about –10C° (14°F). The humidity of storage should be around 45–55% RH; not exceeding 85% RH. (Check the humidity indicator on a camera or VTR before loading the cassette.) Very low humidity can result in strong static charges which attract dust and produce permanent drop-out. Very high humidity causes stiction (i.e. tape tends to stick to revolving head-drum and become displaced). Tape surface deteriorates (heads clog). Avoid rapid temperature/humidity changes (e.g. moving from a cold exterior to a warm interior) and allow both tape and equipment to become acclimatized before use.
- Before loading a cassette check that you have an appropriate cassette and tape type, and that it has not been *protected against recording.* (Reposition the safety knob or tape over its tag opening.) Does the tape contain wanted program material?
- Before using a cassette check in its window that it has been rewound and that its tape has not been left slack from previous use. Insert a finger to gently turn the takeup spool a little clockwise to take up the slack. But do not *over*-tension.
- Clean the VTR's tape path, heads, and tape transport periodically, using a commercial head cleaner tape. This removes particles of coating and avoids head-clogging. (Fabric tape with *isopropyl alcohol* is preferable. Abrasive cleaning tapes wear heads unduly.) For maximum performance, it is advisable to clean the heads after each run; particularly for equipment such as digital VTRs, which uses faster tape speeds and multi-headed scanning drums.
- Store cassettes in their protective boxes to avoid damage and dust.
- It is best to rewind tapes to their start if they are not going to be used for some time. However, remember that if every new recording begins at the start of cassette, the early tape will become worn while the 'tail' remains unused.
- If a tape is frequently stopped, started, and run back and forth it is liable to stretch, wind unevenly (cinching), and even develop edge-wear. (Preferably keep a 'straight-wound' original recording, and use a copy for shuttling during review/editing.)
- Even when treated carefully, all tapes wear in time; coating particles clog heads, drop-out causes visual defects. Check tapes before important recordings. Keep well-used tapes for off-line editing copies.
- Make sure that each recorded tape is clearly identified on the label (e.g. shot/scene numbers), use its safety device, and seal box (adhesive tape) to avoid accidental reuse.
- Remember that if a camera's battery voltage is allowed to fall too far there may not be sufficient power to withdraw the loaded cassette.

Manual editing during replay

In this arrangement you play a tape on one VTR, copying selected parts of it onto another. This is done empirically by watching the tape as it runs and making the editing switch 'on the fly' at the right moment.

- The MASTER VTR has the program tape to which the new scenes will be added.
- The SOURCE VTR has the videotape that includes the new scenes.

On a ½ in. helical VHS VCR this simple editing approach is quite straightforward:

- Connect the SOURCE VCR to a suitable video input on the MASTER VCR recorder.
- Play the program tape on the MASTER VCR up to the edit point, and *PAUSE* the tape. (The tape stops moving, but the head-drum continues to turn.) You see a freeze frame.
- While still in 'PAUSE', you switch the MASTER VTR to the *RECORD* mode. You now see the source VTR's output.
- Next, you run the SOURCE machine, watching the new scenes, until you see the moment you want the copying to start. At the edit point you immediately release the 'pause' button on the MASTER VTR and the dubbing begins.
- On replaying the MASTER VCR, the picture on the original program tape should show a clean cut to the new shot.

Suppose that, instead of this maneuver, you simply play the MASTER program tape up to the edit point then stop. You run the SOURCE machine, and at the right moment you begin recording on the MASTER machine. What happens?

The probability is that when you press the *RECORD* button to begin recording, the MASTER VCR will automatically backspace for a few seconds, run forward, and, when up to speed, begin recording. If this happens you will lose the last few seconds of the previous program shot, interruption of the control track pulses will cause picture disturbance, and you will probably be slow cuing into the new shot. So be warned.

Computer controlled copying

This is a regular method of editing videotape today. As in the second method, you replay tapes on one or more VTRs, while re-recording on another, to form a new compilation *Edited Master tape*. But this time, operations are computer-controlled with precision.

The videotape editor

Comparison with film editing

Broadly speaking, a *film editor* runs through a *cutting copy* of the material on an editing machine, snips out wanted shots, and hangs them separately on nails over a bin (trim barrel). These are then selected, joined into lengths, and reviewed. The separate sound-track is compiled and matched up to the edited pictures later.

The *videotape editor* cannot cut the tape at all. Physical editing is impracticable with helical-scan systems. Apart from ruining the tiny video heads, any cut will interrupt several tracks, and at best produce a crude vertical picture 'wipe' at the join. Also the physical displacement of the audio and video tracks prevents their being cut simultaneously.

Instead, the VT editor has to *copy* (*dub-off*) each wanted segment onto a 'master tape' to build up the final program. Much or all of the program sound was recorded on an audio track on the original videotape, so may have to be dubbed off and handled separately.

The raw material

Videotape editors receive program tape in several different forms:

- A *continuous recording* in which most intershot transitions have already been made with a studio switcher. In this case the editor is mainly concerned with *corrective* work; removing faulty sections and inserting retakes, rearranging the sequence of scenes (e.g. from 'recording order' to 'program running order') adjusting the program running time, introducing detail shots that were recorded separately, making censor cuts, etc.
- A tape which has been recorded *discontinuously*. The scenes will probably have been shot out of sequence, the tape will include faulty takes, alternative versions, unwanted material, intermixed with the required takes.
- Several tapes recorded simultaneously on *dedicated VTRs*. Each has the output of a single camera. The required shots from that camera's tape have to be selected and joined to those from the other cameras shooting the same action.

Electronic splicing

We now come to some technical niceties that may appear only to concern the technician. In fact, there are real practical advantages in your knowing the differences between the two main editing processes.

When you record on a helical VTR, a series of special pulses are generated and continuously recorded on the *control track*. These stabilize the motor system and ensure constant speed replay. If these pulses are interrupted for any reason, picture stability will be affected at that point.

When you are dubbing material onto a master tape you can use either the *assemble* or the *insert* mode.

- The *assemble* (or *assembly*) *mode*. This does the obvious thing, and adds the new picture sequence onto the end of the previously recorded shots. Using this method, the VTR records new video, audio, *and new reference pulses on the control track*.

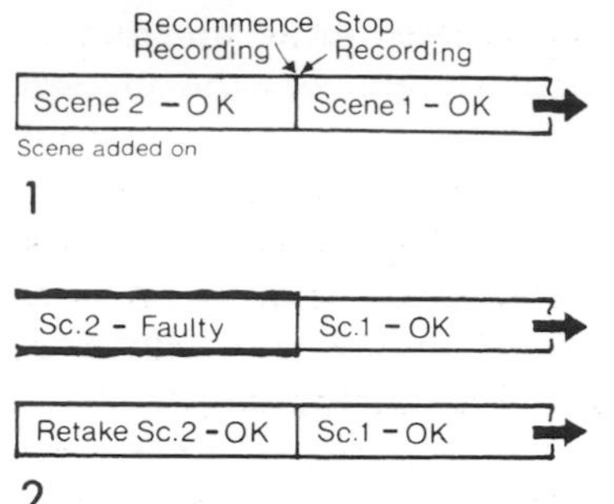

Fig. 14.2 part 1 Electronic editing – assemble mode
Program is built up either (1) a scene at a time or (2) shot continuously, retaking any faulty scene immediately from its opening point. Assembly involves switching from replay (of Scene 1) to *record mode* at a chosen cue point (manually or automatically). As assemble mode automatically lays down a fresh control-track for each take, sync pulses change at joins, thus disturbing replay.

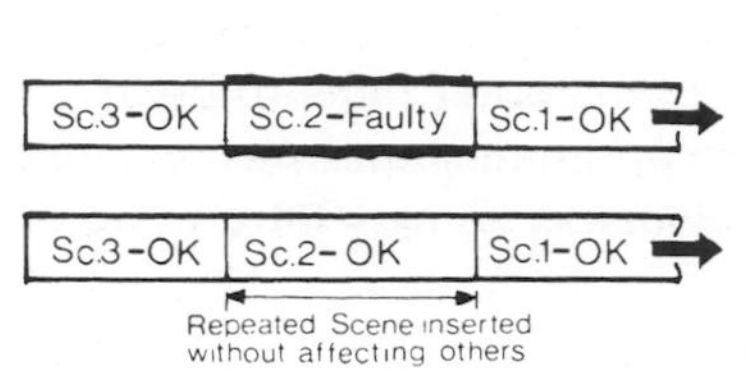

Fig. 14.2 part 2 Electronic editing – insert mode
If new material is to be inserted precisely between existing wanted shots, the 'in' and 'out' points must coincide with original, unwanted program. The original control track is not erased during the insert process, so no sync disturbances occur at the electronic splice.

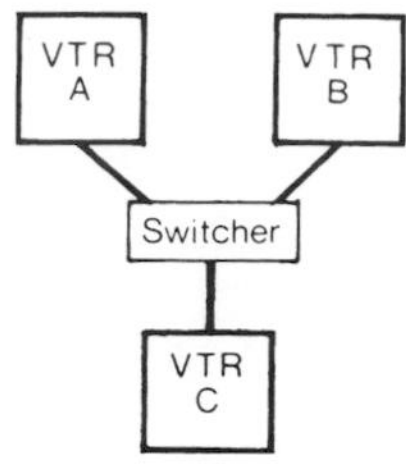

Fig. 14.2 part 3 A/B dubbing
Here duplicate copies of the program are used on VTRs A and B to permit quicker search for sections, than by shuttling a single tape to and fro for selection. A simple production switcher can be used to cut/mix/super during transfer to VTR-C.

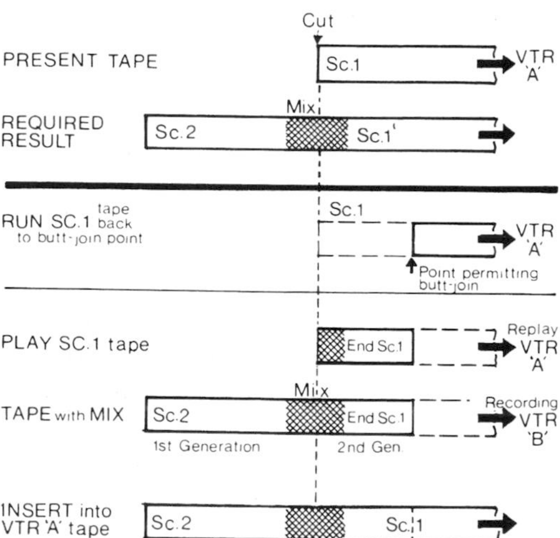

Fig. 14.2 part 4 Roll back and mix
Problem: Scene 1 has been recorded. You now wish to *mix* from Scene 1 to Scene 2 live in studio. Two VTRs available.
Solution: Roll back Scene 1 on VTR 'A' to convenient cutting point before mix. Recording on VTR 'B', replay VTR 'A' tape, mixing to studio when required. VTR 'B' tape now incorporates mix. Result can be inserted within original VTR 'A' tape at the earlier butt-join.

But there is a problem here! When you use the *assemble* dubbing mode these control pulses begin afresh *every time* you start to record. That's fine when making a fresh recording, but if you are adding another sequence to an existing tape there will be an interruption, however slight, in these all-important pulses. Consequently, on reproducing the master tape there could be a frame-roll or line tearing at each edit point!

- The *insert editing mode* records in a different way. In this case the VTR only replaces the video and audio, but leaves the *original* references on the master tape's control track. So the control track is uninterrupted, and on replay there is no break-up at each edit point!

The original purpose of the *insert mode* was to allow the user to slot new pictures within an existing recording; to record the new scene in place of the old faulty section. It does that well – provided you position your insert *very accurately*! (Otherwise you will be left with a bit of the faulty scene, or clip an adjoining shot!)

To overcome this dilemma of an interrupted control track it is a common practice to use a little trick. You take the clean master tape before the session and record on it a *continuous control track throughout* – with a picture black and no sound (*assemble mode*). Then all editing is done using the *insert mode* (irrespective of whether you are actually going to add or insert pictures). The result is that you have a completely uninterrupted control track and optimum sync stability.

The disadvantage of this technique is that if you have an hour-long recording session ahead it takes an hour to prepare the tape's control track! So it is usual practice for VTR channels to stockpile a supply of prepared 'crystal-black' tapes for when they are required.

Postproduction editing

Let us turn now from the basic mechanics of editing to the realities of an editing session. The tapes invariably contain both wanted and unwanted shots, which can be in any order. They may be on several reels or cassettes. You now have to find the required material and dub it off onto the new master tape, in the right order, with the appropriate sorts of transitions between the shots.

Editing equipment provides straight cuts between shots. For mixes, wipes, supers you need to use a production switcher; while for more elaborate effects digital video effects (DVE) equipment of some kind is necessary.

Time code

(*See Digests – Time code.*) If you are cutting together pictures of general action which have uncritical 'heads and tails' you may need no more than a general description, or a shot number, to identify sequences. But where a production is at all complex, or editing is to be precise, a more specific technique is necessary that allows you to identify *individual frames* in the recording. (In film making this is done by 'edge numbers' printed on the master negative.)

For precise identification, a *time code* system was introduced (*time address code, digital frame address system*). This is basically a

Fig. 14.3 Time address code
Monitor display shows the precise time at which the recording was made – hours, minutes, seconds, frames – to facilitate identification, cuing and editing. (For special applications such as time-lapse recording – day, month, year may be indicated.) Time-code may be seen *burned in* to the picture as above, or as a separate display. Many studios time-code to actual *clock time*, so that any notes made during production can be coded simply by glancing at an accurate clock nearby. Some organizations use *zero start* (*lapsed time*) coding, i.e. zero time at the beginning of each reel or session; using the hour digit position to denote the reel number.

continuous 24-hour digital clock showing the instant at which each moment of the videotape was recorded. This information is recorded on the tape's *cue track* or on a secondary audio track, in the form of binary pulses. A digital code provides four sets of figures: hours, minutes, seconds, frames (0–29 SMPTE, 0–24 EBU) plus 32 *user bits* of extra information. Although recordings made on different *days* will normally have similar coding, the time code allows you to identify any sequence at a glance, right down to the individual frame.

Normally this time code is laid down while recording. This is a particularly useful technique for you can look at a digital clock at any time (or the time code readout displayed on a nearby monitor) and log when something happened, how long it took, the available or elapsed time. With this knowledge you can say 'We'll use the retake recorded at 15.25.30 not the one at 15.20.10' in anticipation of later editing.

If you are unable to include the real-time code while recording (e.g. when on location) you can record code on the tape later to serve as identification markers; although it will not, of course, be related to clock times of the original taping session.

Some organizations do not use the time code in real-time but prefer *zero start* (*lapsed time*) coding. They set the clock to zero at the beginning of each reel or session and use the 'hour' digit position to denote the reel number.

On-line editing

One approach to the editing session begins with carefully prepared notes made when recording the program. These could, for example, include a marked-up script and a *take sheet* showing the Reel No.; Scene No.; Shot No.; brief shot descriptions; possible 'in-and-out points', durations, etc.

You look through the recorded tape(s), choose the shots you want, then dub each in sequence onto the master tape. However, for anything other than the simplest situations this *on-line* editing approach usually proves to be a time-consuming business.

Off-line editing

In a large organization *on-line* editing can tie up costly facilities and personnel for considerable periods. So a far more effective method is now universally used, called *off-line* editing. Here you make an *identical* copy of the program tape(s) on a small-format VCR during the studio taping or by transfer afterwards. This *copy-tape/workprint* has the program's time-code/address code *burned in*, i.e. visible in picture (Figure 14.3), that identifies every frame of the recorded material.

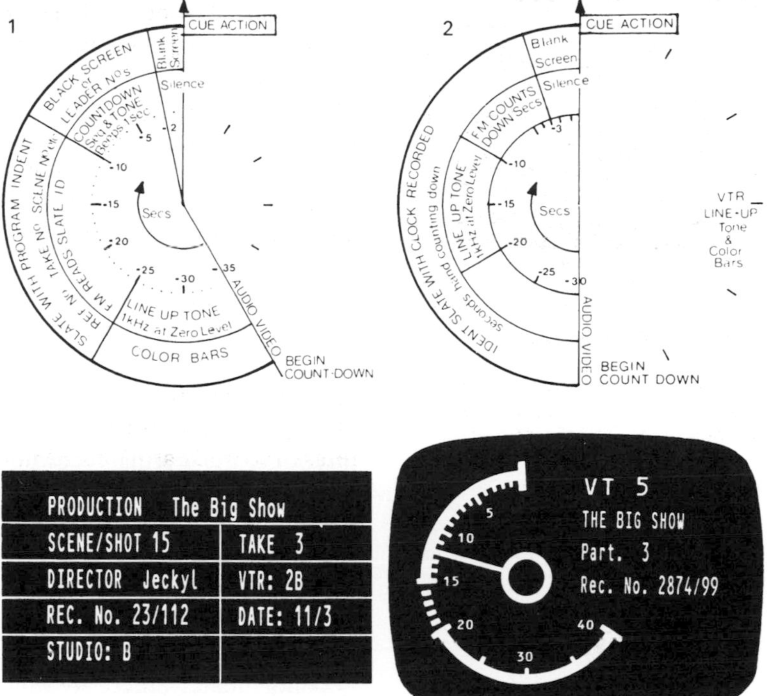

Fig. 14.4 part 1 Video tape leaders SMPTE standard
A video equivalent of the film leader, providing program identification details, technical alignment, and synchronizing information. The diagram shows the time sequence.

Fig. 14.4 part 2 Video tape leaders – typical British practice
Color bars and tone are recorded in prerecording line-up period. One-minute clock with seconds sweep-hand provides visual countdown. Retakes are identified by taped FM announcement (e.g. Retaking Shots 20–34, Take 3).

Fig. 14.4 part 3 The 'slate' and 'VTR clock'
An identifying *slate* or *board* is held in front of a camera during videotaping (after color bars and tone), to identify each take or scene, and provide information to assist editing. Erasable details may be added using chalk, china pencil (wax pencil) or dry marker. Some slates include a battery-powered stop clock. (TV slates are not fitted with clappers.)

Alternatively, an electronic 'slate' is often introduced at the start of a videotape recording. This also serves as a timed 'leader' and assists *preroll cuing* where the VTR requires several seconds to reach full speed on playback (e.g. 5 or 10 seconds). Many VTRs are now cued and run up from a freeze frame. Additional information may be included from a character generator.

Referring to a *take sheet* or a detailed script made during the production, you can play this copy tape 'at leisure', running at normal or slow speeds, freezing frames, to list the editing treatment you require – the exact edit points, transitions, etc. Later, at an editing session, your list of time-coded edit points will guide the VT editor, who uses it to develop an *edit decision list*.

In certain circumstances, particularly when shooting on location, there are advantages in checking through the copy tape at the end of each day (*rough editing*) to judge whether any retakes or extra shots are needed to improve final editing.

Editing problems

How complex the editing process becomes is influenced, of course, by the number of takes involved, their lengths, their order, how many NG (no good) takes there are, etc. But much depends, too, on systematic note-taking while shooting, and on the editing facilities available.

Even routine postproduction editing is very time consuming. A typical finished half-hour program can involve some 150 to 200 cuts. You may find that you can make around six to ten straight cut edits an hour; but combined-shot video effects can slow you to only one to four. Even to run straight through a 1-hour tape on a 3/4 in. VTR can take about 12 minutes, so shuttling/searching for shots (especially with tape changing) and arranging the edit points can be quite a lengthy process.

Both in audio and video recording, the original tape made of a 'live' event is known as the *first-generation* take. If we dub that tape, the copy – which is the *second generation* – is inevitably somewhat inferior to the original recording (in an analogue system). There will be imperfections, such as greater background noise, a loss of definition, distortions of various kinds. Hopefully, they are not obvious. But if we go on to make a copy of that copy (*third generation*) – for distribution perhaps – quality will be further degraded. Consequently, it is as well to keep such dubbing to a minimum; not going beyond the third generation if possible.

Unfortunately, there are times, particularly when creating special chroma-key effects, when one cannot avoid doing so, and has to accept any deterioration, for the sake of the effect.

One of the appeals of *digital videorecording* is that there is negligible deterioration of this kind at each dubbing, and copies of up to the twentieth generation may still prove satisfactory! But in the meantime most systems are analogue, and care is needed.

Quality losses on *dubbing down* from larger tape formats (e.g. 1 in.) to smaller ones (1/2 in.) are less severe than when *dubbing up*, or when dubbing between *color-under* helical systems. You will find similar degradation when copying film (*duping*; e.g. library shots for program inserts). These copies of copies show increased graininess, color errors, and loss of definition that cannot be remedied.

The edit controller

Here, we come to the heart of the VT editing process – the *edit controller*, which provides a computerized control center for the entire system. It remotely controls the *RECORDING* (*Master*) VTR and the *SOURCE* VTRs. This control process involves not only switching them on and off at the right moment but allowing for the exact time they take to run up to speed (*run-up time*), stabilize, and synchronize. Having done this, the controller then makes the edit at precisely the right instant; copying the exact section you have chosen on the *SOURCE* VTR tape onto the correct section of the *MASTER* tape.

The edit controller does all this 'housekeeping' automatically, to your prearranged instructions! It counts off the tape's recorded control-track pulses (and/or time code) relative to your chosen edit point, and times operations accordingly.

Two monitors are used with the edit controller; a line monitor showing the input and replay of the *MASTER VTR* and a preview monitor showing the *SOURCE* picture.

Using the edit controller

Single-source editing

Let us look first at a *single-source editing system* using just two machines: the *MASTER* VTR to record and the *SOURCE* VTR providing the shots to be edited in. If all the required program material is not on one cassette you will need to change the *SOURCE* cassette from time to time. You can, if necessary, introduce titling or graphics from supplementary sources (character generator, slide scanner) via a small switcher unit.

Designs vary, but typically you enter on a keypad the *time code number* or the *control track pulse count* – depending on which method you are using. The simpler process of counting pulses can be quite accurate, but it has the disadvantage that, unlike the precise time code method, the edit point can become displaced or lost during operations.

The keypad entry directs the system to a specific place on the tape. You can then use the handwheel/joystick to *shuttle* the tape forwards/ backwards at vari-speeds and examine the program material. *Jogging* will advance the tape frame by frame, and *freeze frame* allows you to stop temporarily to check an individual frame for precision editing.

Imagine that the shot on the *MASTER* tape shows someone opening the door of a safe (as in Figure 8.8(4)). We see them walk up and reach forward to grasp the dial. Having roughly selected this *outpoint*, you can *frame trim* (i.e. add or cut frames to get exactly the right moment for a cut). You then cue in the indicated time code or pulse count. The new shot to be added after the one on the master tape shows a close-up of the hand about to turn the dial. Following the same search process as before, you run the *SOURCE VTR* tape and select the frame for the editing *inpoint* on the replay tape and enter that indicator reading.

You can then instruct the controller to *simulate* the edit without performing the actual dub-off. It will automatically back the master tape to its 'pre-roll' position, stop, roll, then switch the preview picture over to the *SOURCE* tape at the edit point. If you have second thoughts, the point is adjustable. If you accept this review, it will then repeat operations, and, making a real edit, go on to copy the *SOURCE* shot.

Multi-source editing

The most sophisticated computer-assisted edit controllers enable you to use two or more *SOURCE VTRs* from which to select material (usually identified as A, B, C). Even where scenes were shot out of order on different tapes, *multi-source editing* allows you to rapidly excerpt and copy them in sequence. And, of course, less time is lost in running tape to selected points, for while one sequence is being copied, another machine can spool to the next sequence.

This system allows you to choose edit points anywhere in the tape, and then, using a *list management* facility, to arrange these filed edits in a logical sequence. Your editing decisions entered at the keyboard can be displayed as an *edit-decision list* (*EDL*) either on a monitor screen or as a hardcopy printout sheet. This provides you with both a current guide and a record of how you have used the available material. You can remove all irrelevant or cancelled data with a *list-cleaning* program.

Advanced systems will check when you have accepted the workprint version of the editing and automatically create a *final edited master tape* to match (*see Digests – Automatic assembly*).

You can edit the picture and its accompanying sound separately (*split edits*) using *layover/layback* techniques – i.e. dubbing off the soundtrack, treating it, then re-recording it on the VT soundtrack in place of the original audio. Audio mixing between soundtracks on the same tape may be possible.

At faster or slower speeds the sound can still be sufficiently identifiable for you to select sections. If the system is fitted with an audio *time compressor/expander unit* this will allow you to hear normal speech even when running tape above or below standard speed.

The system can be interfaced with:

- A production switcher – to make mixes, wipes, etc.
- Audio recorders – e.g. to add pre-recorded commentary on cue.
- Inserting photo stills from an electronic still store.
- Introducing video effects.
- Switching a character generator.

The entire dubbing process can be automated to follow prescribed editing instructions and produce a continuous, correctly assembled master tape.

A/B editing

In this dubbing system the program material to be copied is arranged on two or more separate *SOURCE* VTRs. The main benefit of doing this is to allow more rapid interselection of shots on the tapes, and to enable pictures to be combined for effects. There are several variations.

1 Two *SOURCE VTRs with identical copies of the program.*
2 One *SOURCE VTR* contains the main program, while tape on a second *SOURCE VTR has shots to be inserted into (or replace) those within the main program.*

3 Each *SOURCE VTR* has a collection of shots that are to be intercut or combined.

1. The first technique is used when e.g. excerpting shots from long-duration events, such as sports meetings, speeches, processions, where you have recorded the entire action yet only want to use highlights. While shots on reel A are being copied an identical copy on reel B runs on to the next high point. At an appropriate point you switch to reel B, and fast-run A on to the next excerpt. Using this principle you can even excerpt from tapes on-air! At a large sports meeting, for example, where several events are taking place, concurrently, one VTR records continuously and two others record and replay highlights, which can be used to recap earlier action or show slow-motion replays. This may be combined with shots from dedicated VTRs, shooting other events.

2. The second technique is to have a main program (usually a talk or demonstration) on *SOURCE* VTR A, while on *SOURCE* VTR B a series of shots have been assembled, to be used as cut-ins, cutaways, illustrative inserts, etc. The audio from reel A is used throughout, while pictures from reel B are introduced at appropriate points.

3. If the shots to be copied are all on the *same* reel or cassette, the *SOURCE VTR* has to continually spool to and fro to find the selected sections. This can waste a lot of time; particularly if you are building up a rapidly intercut sequence, using shots near the start and end of the tape! When the shots are distributed within two or more replay tapes the whole process is speeded up; *and* you can now combine shots in supers, split screens, etc. This method is helpful where scenes are shot out of order on different spools/ cassettes.

Editing ethics

Editing is a powerful tool. And we must not forget that the way a sequence is edited can strongly influence an audience's interpretations of what is happening. Editing can manipulate – sometimes unwittingly – and, particularly in factual programs (newscasts, documentaries), one needs to be aware of the underlying ethics of certain treatment. In the same way that unjustified canned laughter can be added to a poor comedy show, a sequence of pictures can be selective, and mislead an audience:

- One could deliberately avoid showing significant reactions – e.g. cutting out enthusiastic applause, or heckling during a speech.
- Omitting important action or dialogue – e.g. a person rises, turns to another, bows reverently, and slowly leaves the room. This could be edited so that we see them rise, open the door and

Table 14.3 Anticipating editing
However good the pictures are, if they have been shot inappropriately they will not allow effective editing. Here are typical points to watch when shooting.

- Include *cover* shots of action wherever possible, to show the general view of the action.
- Always leave several seconds of *run-in* and *run-out* at the start and finish of each shot. Do not start taping just as the action is beginning or the reporter is about to speak; nor stop immediately action/speech finishes. Spare footage at the beginning and end of each shot will allow more flexible editing.
- Include potential *cutaway shots* that can be introduced when any sequence is to be shortened or lengthened; e.g. crowd shots, general views, passers-by.
- Avoid *reverse shots* (direction reversal). If it is unavoidable (e.g. when crossing the road to shoot a procession from either side). Include head-on shots of the same action.
- Keep 'cute shots' to a minimum, unless they can really be integrated into the program. These include such items as reflections, sunbathers, silhouettes against the sunset, animals or children at play, footsteps in the sand . . .
- Try to anticipate continuity. If there are only a few shots taken in daylight and others at night, it may not be practical to edit them together to provide a continuous sequence.
- Where there is going to be narration behind the pictures allow for this in the length and pace of takes; e.g. avoid inappropriately choppy editing due to shots being too brief. (Editors sometimes have to slow-motion or still-frame a very brief shot to make it usable!)
- Aim to include longer shots and closer shots of action, to provide editing opportunities. For example, where the action shows people crossing a river bridge a variety of viewpoints can make a mundane subject visually interesting; e.g. *LS* – walking away from camera towards bridge; *MS* – walking on the bridge, looking over, *VLS* – shooting up at the bridge from the river below: *LS* – walking from the bridge to the camera on the far side; etc.
- Try to avoid sequences that are straight into the sun in one shot and against it the next. They do not intercut well.
- Remember that environmental noises can provide valuable bridging sound between shots when editing. They can be audio-taped separately as wild track (non-sync sound)
- Where possible, include features in shots that will help the audience to identify the particular location or terrain (landmarks, street names). Too often, the walls and bushes behind closer shots could be *anywhere*.
- Keep an accurate camera log giving relevant shot details that could help the editor (time, place, identify action, indicate if a take is faulty, etc.)
- Wherever possible, use an identifying *board* or *slate* at the start of each shot. Failing that, announce the shot number so that the soundtrack carries identification. If an 'intro-ident' is missed, put one at the end of a take (showing the board upside down).
- If there are pronounced background sounds during a take, in some circumstances they can be cut out (overlaid) during during editing and replaced by neutral sounds (e.g. 'atmos' wild track).

  But this is not always possible. Suppose you have just shot a single-camera interview in quiet surroundings. Finally, you shoot the reporter's questions to camera, but now there is high background noise. When the shots of the guest and the reporter are edited together the noise will mysteriously cut and reappear during the sequence.
- Most one-camera interviews shot while speakers walk around, are taken in three sections as (a) long-shots, (b) closer shots of the people speaking, (c) 'reaction shots/nod shots'. Make sure that mouths cannot be seen moving in (a) and (c). Check that the continuity of the action and positions in each version is reasonably similar.
- For the standuppers, check what is happening in the background behind the reporter. If the piece to camera is shot in several takes the background subjects could change noticeably between takes!

Table 14.4 Video recording formats

The following list of videotape recorder systems is intended to give you a broad idea of the range and variety of types rather than specifics, for there are continual developments as well as obsolescent formats still in use. Format preferences vary between organizations and between countries; with the applications and economics involved. Currently, for example, there are some 13 different tape formats used in archiving, with a further 5 data tape formats in use!

Video recording systems are designated by their American National Standards/SMPTE classifications (shown here as '*Types*') and by their manufacturers' trade names. The following table gives brief details of many systems. (*See Digests for further details – Videotape formats; Video recording methods.*) While some are mainly used as *acquisition formats* (i.e. to record the original material) others are used primarily for *postproduction editing, editing,* and *archiving* work, as multi-generation copying results in negligible deterioration. Some involve signal compression, while others record uncompressed signals.

All analogue systems need to be converted from analogue to digital before they can be digitally edited (*non-linear editing*) or distributed (hence the benefits of direct-to-disk digital recording).

½ in. = 12.65 mm ¾ in. = 19 mm 1 in. = 25 mm

Quadruplex ('Quad')	Obsolete system. 2 in. tape. Open reel (14 in. max); cart; cassette. *Composite*					
U-Matic [Type-E]	¾ in.					
¾ – U-matic (U-format) Low-band (Standard U-format) (CDO) Obsolescent		Analogue	*Composite*	[OX]	280 lines horizontal resolution.	¤ 60 mins
¾ – SP High-band (BVU-Matic)		Analogue	*Composite*	[MP]	340 lines	¤ 60
Type-B	1 in.	**Segmented field** (1 field + 5 (6) tracks, 2 fields per picture)				
		Analogue	*Composite*	[OX]	360 lines	¤ 90
	(Broadcast standard widely used in countries with 625-line TV systems.)					
Type-C	1 in.	**Non-segmented** (1 field per track, 2 fields per picture.)				
		Analogue	*Composite*	[OX]	360 lines	¤ 90
	(Broadcast standard widely used in countries with 525-line TV systems.)					
M-II [Type- M]	½ in.	Analogue	*Component* Y,R-Y, B-Y	[MP]	344 lines	¤ 90
Betacam [Type- L]	½ in. Earlier version	Analogue	*Component* Y, R-Y, B-Y	[OX]	300 lines	¤ +100
Betacam-SP (Beta SP)	½ in.	Analogue	*Component* Y, R-Y, B-Y	[OX/MP]	344 lines	¤ 120
Digital Betacam (PVW)	½ in.	Digital	*Component*	[MP]	800 lines	¤ 120
	(Other versions include **UVW, DVW, BVW. Also Betacam SX**)					
Type D-1	¾ in./19 mm	Digital	*Component* Y, R-Y, B-Y	[CDO/MP]	460 lines	¤ 76/94
Type D-2	¾ in./19 mm	Digital	*Composite*	[MP]	450 lines	¤ 208
Type D-3	½ in./12.65 mm	Digital	*Composite*	[MP]	450 lines	¤ 185/245

Table 14.4 (cont.)

D4 CLASSIFICATION NOT USED						
Type D-5	½ in.	Digital	*Component*	[MP]		
Type D-6	¾ in./19 mm	Digital	*Component*	[MP]		
DVCPro	¼ in./6.35 mm	Digital	*Component*	[MP]	500 lines	¤ 63/120
Type D-9 (DIGITAL-S)	¼ in./6.35 mm	Digital	*Component*	[MP]		¤ 105
HDVS/HDD 1000	1 in.	Digital	*Component*	[MP]		¤ 80
CamCutter	2.5 *magnetic disk*	Digital	*Component*			¤ 20
CONSUMER FORMATS*						
VHS [Type-H]	½ in.		*Composite*	[OX]	240/260 lines	¤ 360
S-VHS (Super VHS)	½ in*		*Component* Y/C	[MP]	400/410 lines	¤ 360
8 mm (Video 8)	8 mm (0.32 in)		*Composite*	[MP]	260 lines	¤ 240
Hi8 (High-band 8 mm)*			*Component* Y/C	[MP]	410 lines	¤ 120

Further developments include: DVCam (Sony). (DV format formerly known as DVC.) **S-VHS ET**

*Also used for broadcast applications.

Abbreviations
Tape types (on e.g. a polyester base):
IO – Iron oxide. CDO – Cobalt doped oxide. MP – Metal particle. EM – Evaporated metal tape.
¤ = Maximum recording time in minutes.

exit – apparently departing abruptly and unceremoniously . . . giving a very different impression of events.

- Introduce misleading or ambiguous action – e.g. during a speech, intercutting shots of people leaving or of a person in the audience yawning or sleeping.
- Introducing false material – e.g. showing enthusiastic applause . . . associated with a speech *different* from the one we have been watching.

Library shots taken from old newscasts may imply that action is occurring currently. (Such material should be subtitled as a 'library shot' and dated.) Particularly where the camera shows extreme behavior or enthusiasm, one has to consider whether this is representative or just a small group playing to the camera.

15 Titling and graphics

First impressions are important! And the first impressions your audience has of your production come from the *opening titles*. They help to set the style and ambiance of the program, they inform, they guide. Well-designed graphics make a direct contribution to the success of any presentation. Poorly designed titles immediately discredit the production itself.

Titling and graphics today

In this chapter we are really concerned with two separate but frequently combined elements:

- *Titling*. The form and arrangement of lettering and numerals.
- *Graphics*. The diagrams, maps, charts, tables, decorative and pictorial illustrations.

The methods we shall be looking at range from less sophisticated techniques that have stood the test of time, to up-to-the minute innovations.

Not so long ago, it needed considerable skill and experience to produce high-grade titling and graphics. Today, modest home computers with low-cost software enable us to produce eye-catching graphics! Even the most ambitious titling can be devised from the thousands of different fonts readily available from software. CD-ROMs of *Clip Art* encapsulate endless symbols and icons. At the touch of a button you can grab video images from a sequence, and manipulate, transform, or combine them in a matter of minutes. You can develop moving titles by inter-frame switching or by using animated features . . .

Instead of designing graphics from scratch it may sometimes be a lot quicker and more convenient to base them on existing artwork or photographs. Rather than painstakingly drawing a map *ab initio* you might trace over and simplify an existing print. You can take a library photograph and electronically process it; changing its colors, modifying details, introducing textures, and so on, until it no longer resembles the original at all!

There are dangers to such creative freedom. It is easy to become self-indulgent and to overdesign. Results can become disproportionately spectacular so that the program material which follows comes as an anticlimax!

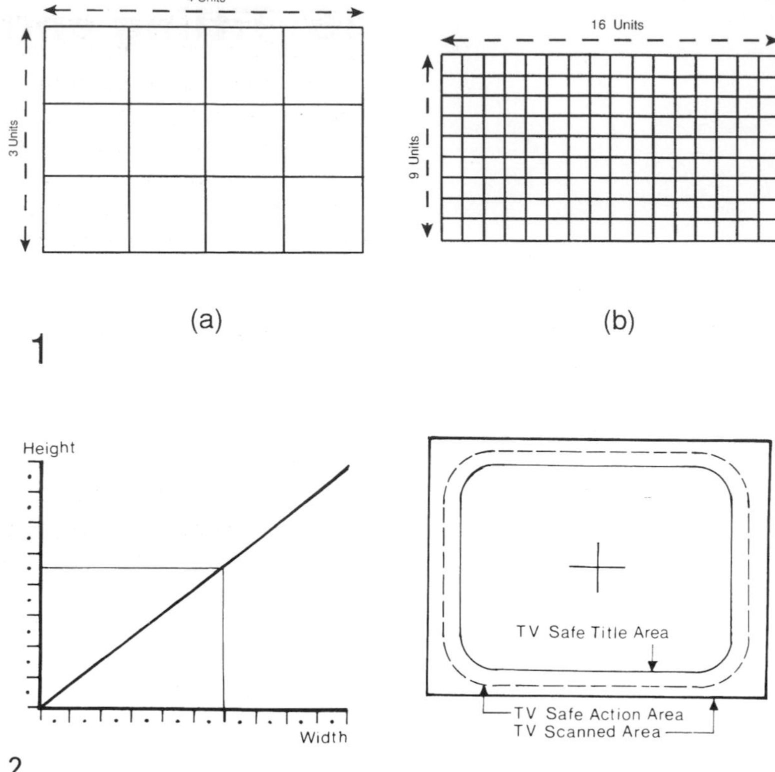

Fig. 15.1 Frame proportions
1 Screen aspect ratios
(a) The proportions of the regular TV screen picture are 4 units across and 3 units vertically. So if a picture is 18 in. (45.7 cm) wide, it is 13.5 in. (34.29 cm) high.
(b) In the later 16 by 9 format, a picture which is 18 in. (45.7 cm) across is 9 in. (22.9 cm) high.

2 Fitting the screen
If a graphic, title card, or a shot of an object is to fill the regular screen exactly, it must have 4 by 3 proportions. This graph shows the relative sizes needed. Draw a line from the width on the horizontal scale, to see the height needed on the vertical scale.

3 Cut-off
To avoid edge cut-off on the screen, important parts of the shot and any subtitling should be confined to the safe title area (e.g. within a 10% border).

Good titling

The principles of effective titling are largely a matter of commonsense. Yet how often have you seen examples of overcrowded, barely readable credits on your TV screen?

Titling is there to *inform* your audience. They should be able to read it quickly, easily, and unambiguously. If they cannot, it has failed in its purpose. None of the lettering should be lost beyond the frame edge. This is particularly true of *subtitling*. How clearly lettering can be read will depend on its size, how elaborate it is, and the background against which it is seen. Readability will be affected, too, by the quality of the picture on the TV receiver, and how far away it is from the audience.

It is advisable to avoid lettering that is smaller than about 1/10 to 1/25 of the picture height. Fonts that look great on the printed page may not appear at all successful on the screen. Lettering should generally be bold and firm. Delicate, elaborate lettering with thin outlines or serifs is likely to break up, while closely patterned striping or cross-hatching is liable to strobe distractingly. If lettering is too condensed, with little space between its members, areas within it are likely to fill in, particularly if the lettering is electronically keyed into a picture, or given an electronic border.

Aim to keep titling information to a minimum, particularly if it is combined with detailed background. A screen full of 'printed information' can be daunting to most viewers, and tiring to read. People are easily discouraged from reading rapid titles. Leave information on the screen long enough to allow it to be read aloud twice, so that the slowest reader can assimilate it. If, for any reason, someone is to read out text that is clearly displayed on the screen, ensure that the reading is *accurate*!

Backgrounds to titles

Choosing a suitable *background* for your titling can be as important as the foreground lettering itself. Where you are using a scenic background, such as the closing shots of a drama, it may actually determine the style and weight of the lettering you can use.

Plain backgrounds can prove very effective, as they are unobtrusive and emphasize the lettering. But they can also be dull and uninteresting. Ornamental backgrounds, which include patterning, texture, abstract designs, may increase the graphic's visual appeal. But they can equally well look fussy and confused. Clearly, background selection requires careful choice.

Lettering against a multi-hue or multi-tone background is invariably harder to read. If you insert titles over location shots (e.g. a street scene) the eye may have some difficulty in discerning information, and may also be tempted to wander around the background instead.

In most cases, by using larger type in light tones (white or yellow) with strong borders (black edged), legibility is considerably improved. But even plain titling can be unclear in certain color relationships (red on green, or red on gray); or in monochrome when gray-scale of lettering and background are similar.

It is good working practice with all graphics work to consider what the result is going to look like in monochrome. Otherwise you are likely to find areas merging together – even disappearing within the surrounding tones!

As a general rule, avoid introducing lettering over backgrounds of similar tones or hues, or over printed matter (e.g. titles over a newspaper page). Obvious enough, but people do! Light lettering is usually more easily read than dark; and pastel or neutral backgrounds are preferable to saturated hues. Unless *superimposed* lettering has a black background (it then appears 'solid'), it is best keyed in (electronically inserted) from white-on-black title cards or

Fig. 15.2 Title positions
Titling is normally localized for maximum impact, avoiding important subject areas (e.g. face).

slides; or in film, by *burn-through* using masking or controlled overexposure. Black lettering cannot be superimposed on a white background.

Forms of lettering

The most effective methods of producing titling use either a *character generator* or a suitable computer with a document processor program. But there are situations where it may be less practicable to use electronically created lettering – e.g. for wall displays, for lettering on articles.

■ **Dry-transfer (rub-on; instant transfer) sheets** These offer a considerable range of rub-off lettering in many styles and fonts. (Some are unsuitable for television use.) Lettering and symbols can be applied to various surfaces. Arrange the titling on a transparent acetate cell overlay, and it can be laid on a background graphic or photograph without damage. The position of the titling can be adjusted; even moved around in vision. And the same overlay can be reused over different backgrounds.

■ **Hot-press lettering** This system uses heated metal type to stamp through a pigment-faced plastic foil. It can provide black, white, or colored characters. Available styles are limited, and tend to become overfamiliar. This method has been used traditionally to prepare camera title cards and crawls (roller captions).

■ **Plastic letters** Standard lettering can be stuck or clipped onto a background with double-sided adhesive tape, magnetic board, felt . . . There are many variations.

■ **Constructed lettering** Arranged from toy bricks; formed in thumb-tacks, toothpaste, rope; finger traced in sand or snow. . .

■ **Decorative effects** Here lettering is seen as shadows, reflected, silhouetted, stencilled.

■ **Handwritten lettering** However neat, handwritten titling tends to look crude, and is best avoided – even when lettering aids are used. It may be successful where results are meant to look inexpert; e.g. on walls, sidewalks, chalkboards, using chalk, crayon, aerosol paint.

Introducing titling

You can introduce lettering or titling into a picture in two ways:

- *Superimposition* by fading up two or more picture sources on the production switcher. There will be tonal interactions between lettering and its local background. Light letters will effectively superimpose 'solidly' on a darker background, but not the reverse. Against a multi-tone background, the lettering will appear 'transparent', but may be difficult to read. When the titling or the background are colored, you will see random color-mixing effects, depending on the hues involved.

- *Insertion* using either *keying* or *non-additive mix* facilities on the switcher provides lettering which is 'punched solid' into a background shot.

The character generator

Character generators have become a regular production facility, providing on-screen text of all kinds; from subtitling to sports scores; identifying captions to weather map data. Anyone who is familiar with handling a *word processor* soon feels quite at home with a character generator.

Alphanumeric characters (letters, numbers, and selected symbols) typed on a standard computer keyboard are displayed against a plain background on a TV screen. You can present the lettering in this form or insert it into a picture; typed progressively letter by letter, or switched in as a complete display. Each '*page*' can be filed for instant recall (manual or cued) from a store on a hard disk or from a solid-state computer memory (RAM – random access memory).

Character generators vary in their complexity. As well as providing a variety of lettering styles, they may include format designs for graphs, tables, charts, etc. Some generate scripts as diverse as Roman, Cyrillic, Japanese, Arabic. There may be prearranged graphics (e.g. station logos, program idents) which can be integrated into the captions.

You can introduce lettering into a picture from any video source: a studio camera, slide store, VTR, film channel . . . So you might, for instance, use a library slide of a map, chart, etc. and add new topical information, directional arrows, or whatever, to suit the current production.

The display is prepared while watching a *preview channel monitor*. A separate *line channel monitor* shows the page being fed to the studio switcher for selection there. You usually begin by deciding on the general formats. Where guests are to be identified by briefly introduced subtitles, you must choose appropriate layout, fonts, backgrounds, decorative borders, etc. for these inserts. These may be selected from a series of in-built choices or from a store of your own 'customized' treatments.

As with regular computers, you locate the various elements of the display in turn with a *cursor* (using a *trackball*) and position them anywhere on the screen. You can correct or revise details instantly, combine screens, select sections. There are facilities for auto-centering, left or right justification, tabulation, size adjustment, and multi-page storage.

As well as moving lettering around the screen, you can change font size and style; alter color, shape, texture, design, add edge effects (black edge, white edge, drop shadow). You can make lettering *roll vertically, crawl sideways, flash, spin, animate, flip, rotate, zoom, wipe, squash, tumble, fade, merge, zip. . .*

Using a *color synthesizer* you can selectively color the lettering and the background (these are normally black-on-white). Words or individual characters may be treated separately.

A *border generator* can introduce an outline or partial outline in black, white, or color around lettering to improve its legibility and impact. Borders are particularly effective when adding titling to multi-tone color picture backgrounds. There are several styles:

- All round the character, or along one edge.
- Along one side and the lower edges, to create *a dropped shadow* effect. This gives the characters a 'solid' look.
- The character is replaced with an electronically generated *outline* of itself.

Both the *color synthesizer* and the *border generator* facilities are also fitted to many production switchers to allow titling from *any* video source to be treated (e.g. camera title cards).

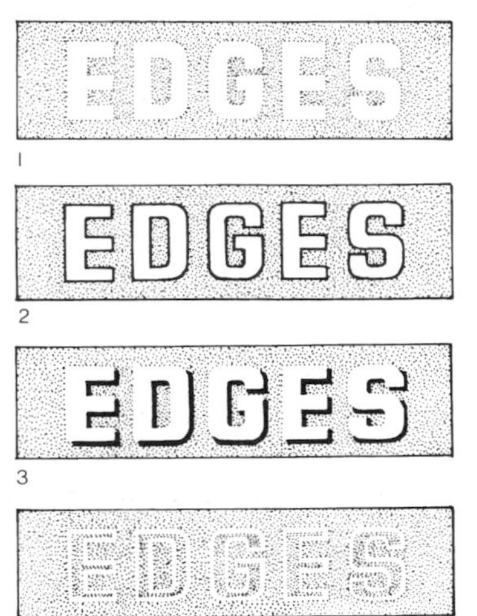

Fig. 15.3 Border generators
1 White solid lettering.
2 Black-edge border.
3 Drop shadow effect.
4 Outline.

Forms of graphics

Graphics can make a valuable contribution to all types of TV program.

- *Statistical graphics in the form of bar graphs and charts* can show, in a moment, information that would be hidden in columns of figures. They enable you to simplify complex data, to compare, to show developments, to demonstrate relationships, etc.
- *Pictorial graphics* can be used to illustrate a children's story, to set the scene in a drama, to explain scientific principles, to provide an atmospheric background to titling, etc.

Graphic display

You can introduce graphics in several ways. The most obvious is to cut to a shot of a screen-filling graphic (e.g. a slide, or a title card). But, in many situations, it can be more attractive to have a graphic within a setting; on a display screen, as a desk chart, or a wall map, or a free-standing panel. Sometimes it may be best to keep a particular graphic out of shot or hidden until it is needed, to avoid it distracting the audience's attention.

You can even introduce titling or pictorial graphics as 'natural features' of a scene; a book title on a shelf, a wall poster, a street sign, a baggage label . . . even displayed on someone's sweatshirt.

You can show simple graphics on an in-shot picture monitor, but it is generally preferable to use a wall display screen (rear-projected, or electronically inserted), for the scale is more satisfactory. That method is particularly useful when you want to show a succession of graphics and VTR or film clips.

As in all aspects of presentation, there are vogues in the types of graphics used. It was once a familiar ploy for presenters to stand beside wall graphics adding and removing labels and symbols. Three-dimensional maps and graphs had their popularity. Many forms are left behind as others prove cheaper and easier to make.

Animated graphics

Animation can bring a graphic to life. Even the simplest movement, such as panning over it from one detail to another, zooming in/out on details, or intercutting between sections of it, can sustain interest in what would otherwise be a static display. Such techniques are an effective and economical way of illustrating children's stories, or a program that relies heavily on graphics or photographs (e.g. maps, photographs, paintings in historical sequences).

You can animate in a number of different ways. For instance, you can build up a graphic on-air by progressively adding details or sections (wipes, insets, supers). The most reliable method of animation is to videotape the sequence beforehand. You record a section, pause and add/remove/blank-out details, then continue recording, and so on. The result on replay is an animated graphic. This type of animation is best done by using overlay cels or attached sections, rather than by actually altering artwork, for if anything goes wrong it is far easier to reshoot the sequence!

Graphics have been enlivened with falling snow, swirling mist (obscuring one title, and clearing to reveal the next), falling rain, traveling light patterns . . . even by setting fire to them! Puppets have 'operated' them or pointed out information. Ingenuity knows no bounds!

Many mechanical animation devices that served well for decades, such as rotating boxes, drum titles, animated cards, have been superseded by electronic methods. But other 'old faithfuls' such as the *title card* have an ongoing value.

Don't despise simple methods. Suppose you want to wipe in the letters of a program title, one by one. You could use a character generator, or a special effects generator, or a digital video effect . . . or you could simply place a sheet of black paper over a title card and move it to one side, to get the same effect!

Table 15.1 Camera graphics

	Advantages	*Disadvantages*
Graphics on stand or easel	Simple method. Camera can zoom, select any section, adjust framing. The original artwork can be used (avoids extra copying stages). Graphics can easily be modified or updated.	Method ties up a studio camera. Graphics require an operator (opportunities for errors, wrong positioning, etc.). Graphics may shake during rapid; operation or changes. If graphics sizes vary, camera may have to refocus and reframe. Positioning may vary, causing glare, specular reflections, or revealing surface unevenness.
Front-projected graphics	Camera can zoom, select frame. Slides provide rapid, predictable changes.	Graphics must be prepared in a standard format (e.g. 35 mm slides). Spill light on screen may spoil image. Color quality variations are not easily compensated for. Apparatus usually requires an operator.
Rear-projected graphics	As above.	As above. Uneven illumination likely (central hot spot). Screen grain may be apparent in close shots.

Table 15.2 Graphics using special equipment

	Advantages	*Disadvantages*
Electronic still store (ESS)	No need to transport and sort slides The equipment is very reliable. Stills can be selected instantaneously from a large library. Slides cannot become damaged through handling or use. You can 'browse-select' from available shots.	Any purpose-designed slides have to be shot and inserted into the general stills library for the occasion. Appropriate slides may not be available. Slides of the required subject may be overfamiliar from use in other programs. It may not be possible to mix between slides.
Caption scanners	Designs vary considerably; slide transport by carousel or vertical drums; tray/box carriers, discs. Slide selection in sequential, random, or programmed order. Flexible color correction facilities included in equipment control. Can be remotely controlled.	Slides must be shot and mounted in proportions and framing required-position and size cannot normally be adjusted. Slides are not readily modified/corrected, and may acquire blemishes, dirt. Equipment reliability varies.
Rostrum camera	An adjustable overhead camera shooting horizontal artwork. Used to record a series of graphics (stills) on film or videotape; in order to simplify a rapid graphics sequence, to record a complex graphics presentation, or to animate a succession of shots. Sequence can be prerecorded, simplifying studio production.	Revision of individual segments requires editing or remake.

Table 15.3 Typical graphics sizes

Smallest size for convenient handling (smallest type size 24–36 pt)	30.5 × 23 cm (12 × 9 in)
Commonly used sizes shooting a 30.5 × 23 cm (12 × 9 in) area	43 × 35.6 cm (17 × 14 in) 40 × 30 cm (16 × 12 in)
Title cards – copy area 23.5 × 18 cm* (9.5 × 7 in)	35.6 × 28 cm (14 × 11 in)
Largest size for elaborate artwork	61 × 46 cm (24 × 18 in)
Thickness of support art board	2 mm (1/16 in) minimum

**Standard board is 71 × 36 cm (28 × 22 in).*

Camera graphics

Title cards

The 'standard' *title card* is printed on a piece of thin plain black board, typically 35.6 × 28 cm (14 × 11 in). *Graphics* are mounted on a correspondingly larger sheet. The board is supported on an adjustable stand or an easel, and shot by the camera (Figure 15.4 and Table 15.1).

Title cards are used for show titles, performers' names, subtitles, and other credits. You can, of course, use many colors, tones, and textures for the lettering and background (although it is best to avoid white backgrounds). And for decorative titling, this is done. But many organizations regularly use title cards that are printed white on black.

These have the advantage that they are easily read, *superimpose* well on other shots, and the white lettering can easily be keyed into other pictures (*luminance keying*). In addition, you can *colorize* and *black-edge* (outline) lettering in the switcher. The background, too, can be colorized to suit.

It is good practice to use an acetate overlay showing the TV safe title area (Figure 15.1) when deciding on the layout of your title cards. Most titling is centered, but it is best to position lettering to suit its final purpose; i.e. slightly nearer the lower edge for subtitles, the upper edge for head titles. But leave sufficient space around for the camera to adjust framing to suit the shot. That, incidentally, is an advantage the title card has over a slide, which cannot be readjusted at the last minute to improve composition.

Try to avoid lettering smaller than about one-fifteenth of the card height, for it will probably appear too small on the screen and the camera will need to take a closer shot to improve proportions. This could emphasize any irregularities in the lettering.

Aim to standardize your title card size. It makes them easier to handle, and the camera does not have to readjust framing to suit individual cards. Where you have a stack of title cards on a stand it is a good idea to attach numbered *card pulls* (*edge tags*), so that it is

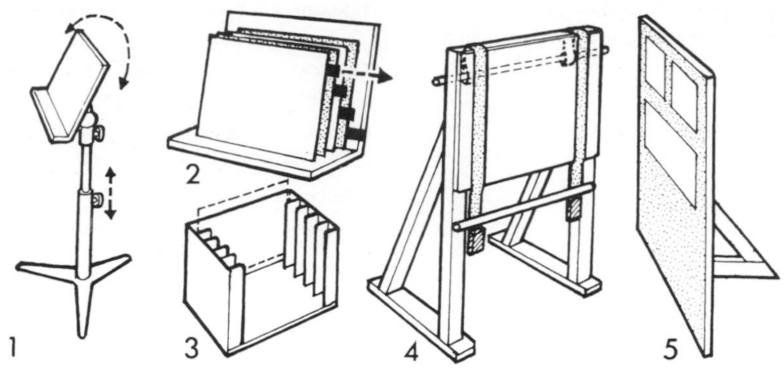

Fig. 15.4 Graphics supports
1 *Caption stand* (tiltable shelf, adjustable height) suitable for title cards.
2 *Card-pulls* attached to edges make removal easier.
3 *Title card box* – top card pulled out to reveal next title.
4 *Strap easel* used for larger graphics. Weighted webbing straps adjust to suit all sizes.
5 *Flat* displays various graphics of different sizes.

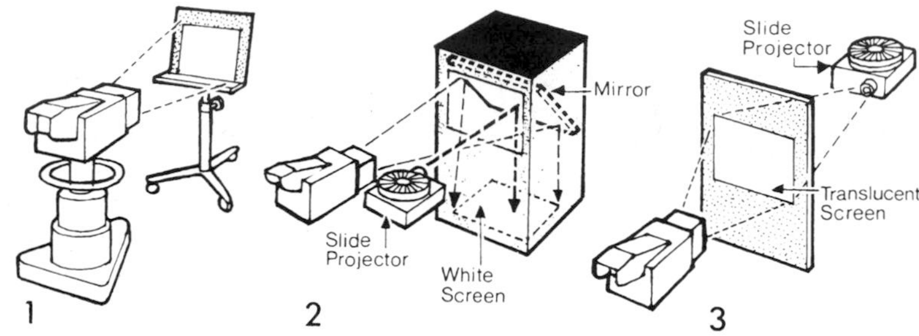

Fig. 15.5 Methods of shooting graphics
1 Studio camera shoots graphic supported on easel or stand.
2 Caption projection unit; Slide is projected onto screen within box, via a mirror. Camera shooting via same mirror, sees and explores the picture.
3 Camera explores picture from rear-projected slides on translucent screen. Slides are usually transmitted using a multiplexed film-island projector (see Fig. 13.7) or a flying-spot scanner (see Fig. 13.9). Opaques may use similar systems.

easier to remove cards quickly, to reveal the next beneath (Figure 15.4(2)).

Where you want to insert a multitone or colored title card into a picture the answer is to use a *chroma-key card* in which the lettering and decorations are against a background of chroma-key blue. If you use such a chroma-key card regularly (e.g. as opening titles over a live show, or an inserted logo) you can make it into a slide. This will avoid tying up a studio camera, which can be used for other shots.

Normally, if you have a series of title cards you would need to use two (or more) cameras for the sequence. But, with a little ingenuity, you can show all the titles on one camera:

- Slide or lift the top card aside to reveal the next underneath (*pull titles*).
- Have the cards top-hinged on a ring binder or tape hinges (*flip-in/drop-in*), or bottom hinged (*flip-out/drop-out*).

The secret is to change cards smoothly without jerking them, and to take care that they do not become displaced.

If lettering on a title card proves to be too large, or needs to be offset, a larger black card placed behind it will enable the camera to take a longer shot or reframe without shooting off. Similarly, a chrome-key title card (usually white lettering on a blue card) can be extended with a large blue backing sheet.

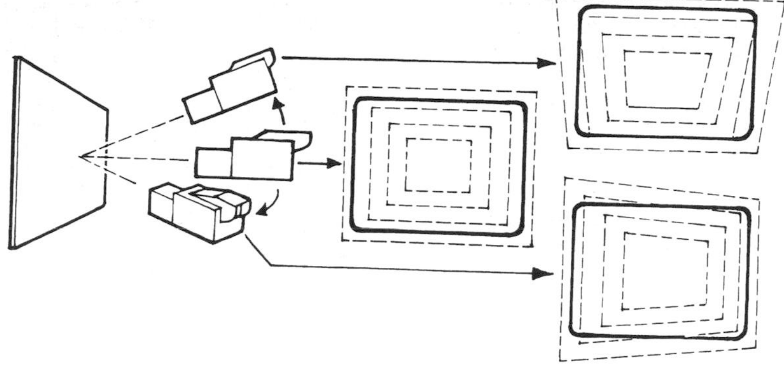

Fig. 15.6 Shooting graphics
Only when shot straight-on, will the image of a flat plane be undistorted. Shooting off-axis produces *keystone* distortion, e.g. when the viewpoint is too high or shot from the side. In geometrical subjects (music, print, diagrams) the effect may be pronounced.

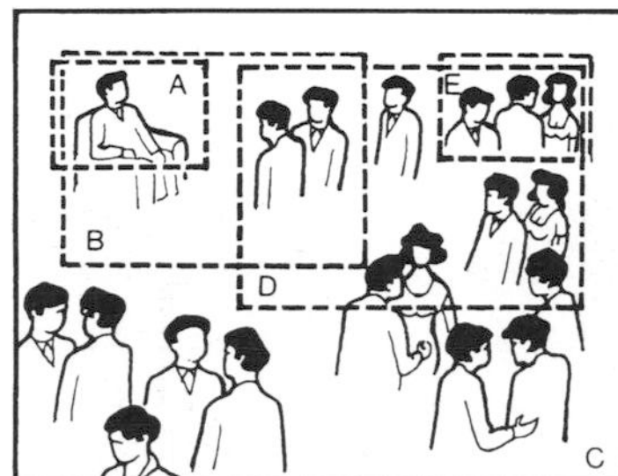

Fig. 15.7 Exploring graphics
A graphic can be 'animated' by exploring it with the camera, so creating continual visual change, e.g. from shot A, zoom out to include B, then to the full picture C, zooming in to select frame D, then E.

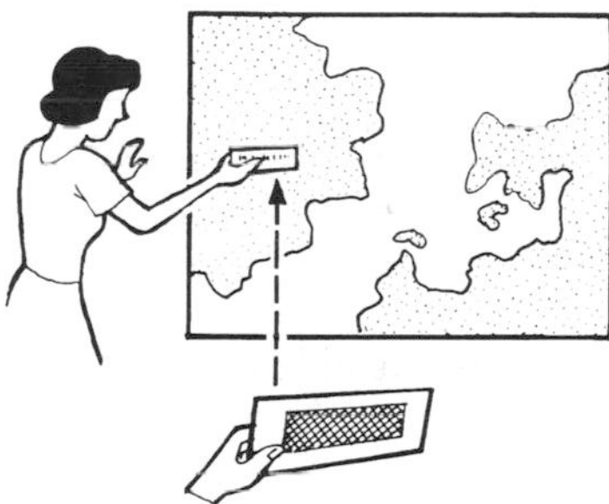

Fig. 15.8 Attached detail
Regular methods of attaching detail, labels, symbols, sections to graphics:

Flannelboard – Both the rear-strip behind shape and the background have surface of felt, baize, flannelette, PVC (plastograph).
Teazlegraph (Velcro) – shape backed with small nylon multi-hook strip; background has multi-loop strip.
Adhesive strip – double-sided adhesive tape behind shape; smooth background.
Magnetic – magnetic plastic strip or small magnets, attached to steel-sheet background.

Transparent plastic overlay sheets (cels) may be used for titling, which is then laid over background graphics. But there is always the danger of light reflections from the surface of the cel.

Although cameras can shoot titling on a foreground glass panel, depth of field is usually too restricted to obtain a sharply focused background scene at the same time. Instead, you would have to pull focus from the titling to 'dissolve' to the action.

Moving titles (Figure 15.9)

When you want to screen a considerable amount of printed information you could present it on a series of intercut *title cards* or *title slides*; remembering to time each carefully, to suit typical reading rates. A better solution, however, is that used at the end of most motion pictures, where a list of those involved in the production rolls continuously upwards over the screen.

You need to adjust the speed at which this *roll title* travels (sometimes termed a vertical *crawl*) to suit the density and complexity of the information. Always bear in mind that fast rolls are frustratingly hard to read! End titles are best timed to match the duration of end-of-show playout music. *Crawl titles* moving from right to left across the screen can be difficult to read; particularly when there are several lines of print. Wording near the left of the screen quickly passes out of frame, allowing less catch-up time when reading, than roll titles.

- *Roller captions* – The oldest form of rolling titles comprised a long strip of stiff black paper with hot-press or photo-printed titling wound vertically between two rollers. (These can be turned by hand, or motorized.) This method still has its applications. It is a useful way of displaying a succession of graphics or artwork showing a continuous process; such as stages in a manufacturing operation. (It is certainly preferable to having a camera trucking past a long strip graphic (*pan card*).)

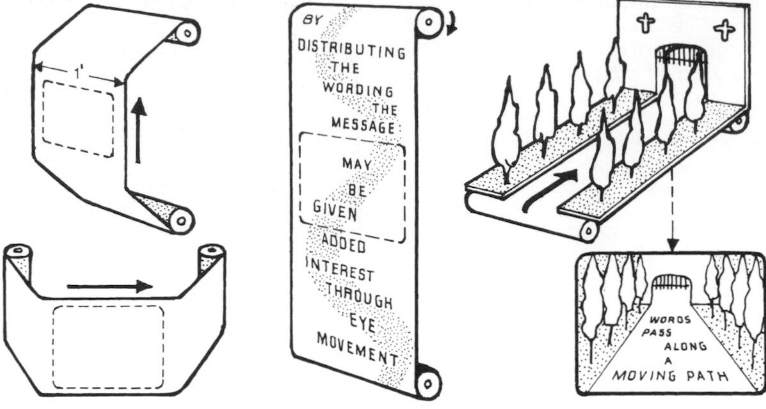

Fig. 15.9 Moving titles
This continuous strip display may be rolled up, or rolled horizontally. Varying the frame position of titling produces a *horizontal crawl title*. It may also be used as a traveling path display.

- *Character generators (CG)* – Moving titles are much easier to prepare on a *character generator* that has *roll* and *crawl* modes. It is simple to make any last-minute changes or corrections, the size and distribution of wording can be adjusted, and the speed and direction of the display are continuously variable. Feed a *CG* copy of the program script into an on-camera *prompter* and the speaker does not need to learn a single line!

Unseen drawing

Seeing a drawing gradually form as we watch has a persuasive fascination. It is a useful method of introducing complex information piecemeal, or making a little material go a long way. However, its extended use can become tedious.

Methods of obtaining unseen writing include:

1 Rear writing in white paint on a clear glass sheet backed by black drapes. The performer is totally dressed in black.
2 Rear writing with a felt-pen on a paper sheet; the camera shooting the bleed-through on the reverse.
3 Drawing on a surface of chroma-key (CSO) hue (e.g. blue) for electronic insertion.
4 Writing on an overhead projector cel.
5 Special electronic 'remote-writing' equipment.

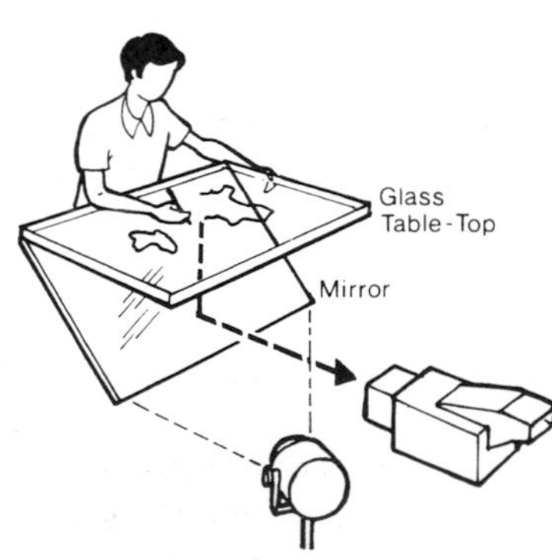

Fig. 15.10 Animation table
The mirror reflects operations on the glass topped table. Sections can be moved, removed, added, animated (in vision or single-frame recorded). It can be used for unseen writing.

Electronically generated graphics

Working with computer graphics is a fascinating process. Even everyday home computer platforms have an impressive range of software packages available, which are capable of producing graphics to the highest standards. Earlier problems such as *aliasing*

Table 15.4 Precautions with graphics design

Always work within 4:3 proportions.
Provide an adequate border for camera framing.
Use matt materials. Avoid spurious reflections from shiny or glossy lettering, paint, plastic tape, overlay sheets, pencil marks, etc.
Avoid buckling, wrinkles, and similar surface unevenness. Attach thin copy to heavy illustration board, which can be re-used.
A large graphic can look the same as a smaller one on the screen. But considerable side reduction will noticeably weaken thin lines; while magnification of small graphics coarsens detail.
Ensure that graphics are evenly lit, and shadows do not disrupt multi-plane captions.
Coarse tonal variations (for example, five spaced gray-scale steps between black and white) provide more dynamic reproduction than subtle half-tones.
Always consider how colored graphics will appear in monochrome.
Color impact in titling and graphics is important. A vibrant hue (red, yellow) may be arresting, forceful, giving emphasis, or disturbing, brash, tasteless, or aesthetically inappropriate.
Simplification of detail, clear symbolism, and unambiguous approaches have maximum effect.
Keep information detail to a minimum for rapid assimilation.
Choose simple structural forms for diagrams, particularly for comparative graphics.
Maps should contain only relevant main features, with good tonal and color contrasts: water areas (sea, lakes, rivers) being shown in darker tones. Name labels may be provided by a plastic overlay, superimposition, keyed in, or manually attached.
Comparative information on a single graph is preferable to a succession of graphics.

(*'jaggies'*; *'staircase'*) which causes curves and diagonals to appear stepped and prominent *pixel* structure on enlargement can now be avoided by *anti-aliasing* software.

When we come to the outstanding 'photographic' quality of advanced computer graphics, the sky is the limit, as is demonstrated daily in television commercials!

You can use computer graphics in several ways:

- *Clean canvas*. Here, the artist works from a blank screen and builds up the final artwork.
- *Tracing*. Existing artwork or a photograph is laid on the graphics tablet and the required elements are traced over with the stylus. These tracings are used as the basis of the new design.
- *Grabbed frames*. A full-color or black and white picture from a video camera is *grabbed* and 'retouched'. The artist can add or reduce details, change textures, add or reduce shading, alter colors, combine picture segments, etc.

Table 15.5 Problems with graphics

	Even quite simple graphics can reproduce badly on the TV screen if they are not prepared, shot, and lit carefully.
Graphic size	*If too small* Close-up details appear coarsened (e.g. texture looks crude, lines rough-edged). When close shooting with a narrow-angle lens, to get big enough detail, any camera movement is exaggerated. No room to pan around (explore or reframe) without shooting off. Camera may not be able to get large enough image due to limited minimum focused distance. Camera may shadow the graphic. *If too large* Camera may not be able to position far enough away to take in the entire graphic. If shot on a wide-angle lens, the graphic may appear distorted. Finer lines may be unclear or merge in a full shot.
Graphic shape	If a graphic is not roughly 4 by 3 horizontal format, it will not fit the TV screen shape. (See Figure 15.11.)
Surface	*Tones too light* Light tones block off. Flare. Loss of detail/gradation in lightest tones and/or darkest tones. *Tones too dark* Picture usually lacks contrast. Lower tones merge. Muddy appearance. *Black tones* Various 'black' surfaces may have such different reflectances (shades, textures) that, when intermixed in a graphic e.g. black card, paint, ink, plastic tape), the picture cannot be set down to crush and unify black areas without degrading other picture tones. *Texture* Shiny surfaces appear either strongly saturated (bright color), or reflect light as unwanted white patches. Surface details and lettering become lost in the glare. (Tilting the graphic, or altering camera height slightly, may clear the reflection.) *Distractions* Graphics are easily defaced by surface wrinkles, finger marks, scrapes, scratches. lettering faults, adhesive, etc. that the casual glance overlooks but which stand out plainly on the screen.
Lighting	*Uneven lighting* Brighter towards the top, or to one side. (Lamp too steep, or far off the lens axis.) *Central hot spot* Lamp spotted: too close: filament image: lamp too close to lens axis. *Multiplane shadows* One surface can shadow another under it. (Centralize and soften the light; use Pepper's ghost device.) *Camera shadows* If lighting is at too shallow angle: or the camera is too close to graphic. (Use narrower lens angle.) Optimize lighting.
Camera angle	*Distortion* If camera is not straight-on to graphic (trapezium distortion): too high, off-center. Wide-angle lens distortion (barrel/pincushion distortion). Graphic not correctly positioned on its support.

The tools

In most equipment the artist 'draws' with a pressure-sensitive electronic *stylus* on a special *graphics tablet*. The results appear on a color monitor screen.

The *menu* through which the artist instructs the system may be shown on the viewing monitor displaying the artwork, or on a separate monitor. In other cases the 'palette' is arranged as a border around the tablet, to be selected at a touch of the stylus. So you have at your fingertips such features as:

- Various drawing 'instruments': pencil, brush, airbrush, spray; in variable thicknesses and densities.
- A wide variety of textures, tones, colors that can be added *specifically* (e.g. a brush using 'spotted paint') or to *fill areas* (e.g. a 'wash' of predrawn bricks).
- Automatically drawn lines and geometrical shapes.
- Color mixing and shading.
- Tonal changes such as posterization (a multi-toned image reproduced in coarse tonal steps).
- Insert lettering from selectable fonts (using an associated keyboard).
- Erase, copy, paste-over (insert sections of other images).
- Invert, mirror (reflections), stretch, magnify, rotation.
- Icons (i.e. predrawn symbols and signs).

You can create effects as diverse as a cartoon or an engineering drawing; make a 'pencil', 'pastel', or 'charcoal' sketch; 'paint' in 'watercolors' or 'oils'; produce virtually photographic images. You can add textural, mist or smoke effects; crispen, soften, or outline objects; introduce distortions. Size, shape, and perspective can be scaled or changed. And if you make an error, or do not like the results, a key press will return your screen to the previous picture. Using *positional* adjustments you can invert or mirror the subject. Areas can be filled with color or design at the press of a button.

Refinements

The objects you produce can appear three-dimensional. Having drawn a skeletal *wire-frame* model which follows the surface contours and main features of the subject, you produce 'solidity' by giving it a 'surface skin' of an appropriate tone, color, density and texture.

When drawing irregular outlines (e.g. broken terrain) or 'growth patterns' (e.g. tree leaves and branches) *fractal geometry* will introduce a realistic randomness to the graphic. Using a *ray tracing program*, you can simulate the effect of light on the subject to enhance the illusion of solidity and surface texture. *Rotational programs* allow you to 'move' the subject around and see it from

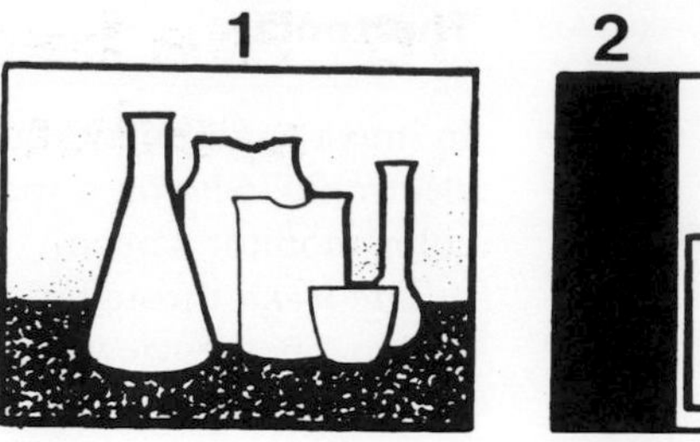

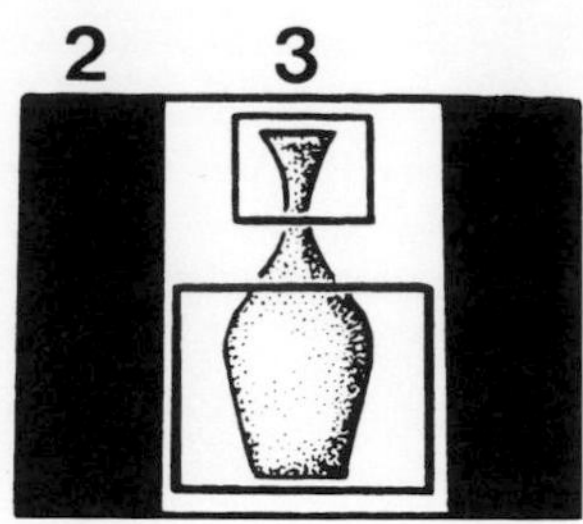

Fig. 15.11 Picture shape
1 Only a graphic in 4 by 3 proportions will fit the TV screen.
2 A tall narrow graphic can be shot as a whole, with black-sided borders.
3 Or it can be shot in selected sections.

various viewpoints. Using a *morphing process*, you can magically transform one subject into another.

Finally, you have the choice of storing the entire screen or selected parts of it or combining it with other material in computer memory in either full or compressed form. It can then be called up or transferred when required, printed out for reference, or photographed off-screen.

16 The background of production

As you would expect, organizations differ in their demarcations between various jobs. In some there are strictly observed distinctions, while in others, people gain by shared experience.

The director's job

The TV director's job can vary considerably within organizations, and the size and type of production. At one end of the scale there are those who initiate the program idea, write the script, even predesign the settings. They cast and rehearse the performers, guide the production team, and, having recorded the show, control the editing. Such all-round craftspeople are rare, but they exist.

At the other end of the scale, some rely heavily on specialists in the production team to provide them with workable staging treatments (settings, lighting, sound, camerawork). They themselves concentrate on directing talent, and on shot selection.

The director may have a *presentational* role. Here a number of separate program items (*stories*) are independently prepared by members of an editorial group (researchers/writers/editors). He or she visualizes production treatment that will coordinate these various contributions. We meet this situation in many magazine programs, newscasts, public affairs (current affairs) programs.

There is a place for all levels of expertise in the wide spectrum of television production. Like other craftspeople in the medium, directors become skilled in their particular field. Someone whose talent lies in drama production would probably lack the edge-of-seat intuition of a good sports director: an almost clairvoyant ability to anticipate action, and take off-the-cuff shot opportunities. On the other hand, someone specializing in sports would be lost in the world of drama. There the director, with painstaking shot-by-shot planning, guides performance and develops dramatic impact. Again, in presenting a symphony orchestra, one needs skills that are far removed from those involved in shooting a documentary on location.

For smaller productions the director may combine the functions of both director and producer. Having been allocated a working budget, the person in this dual role is responsible for the entire business and artistic arrangements: origination, interpretation, casting, staging, and treatment; subsequently directing the studio operations and postproduction editing.

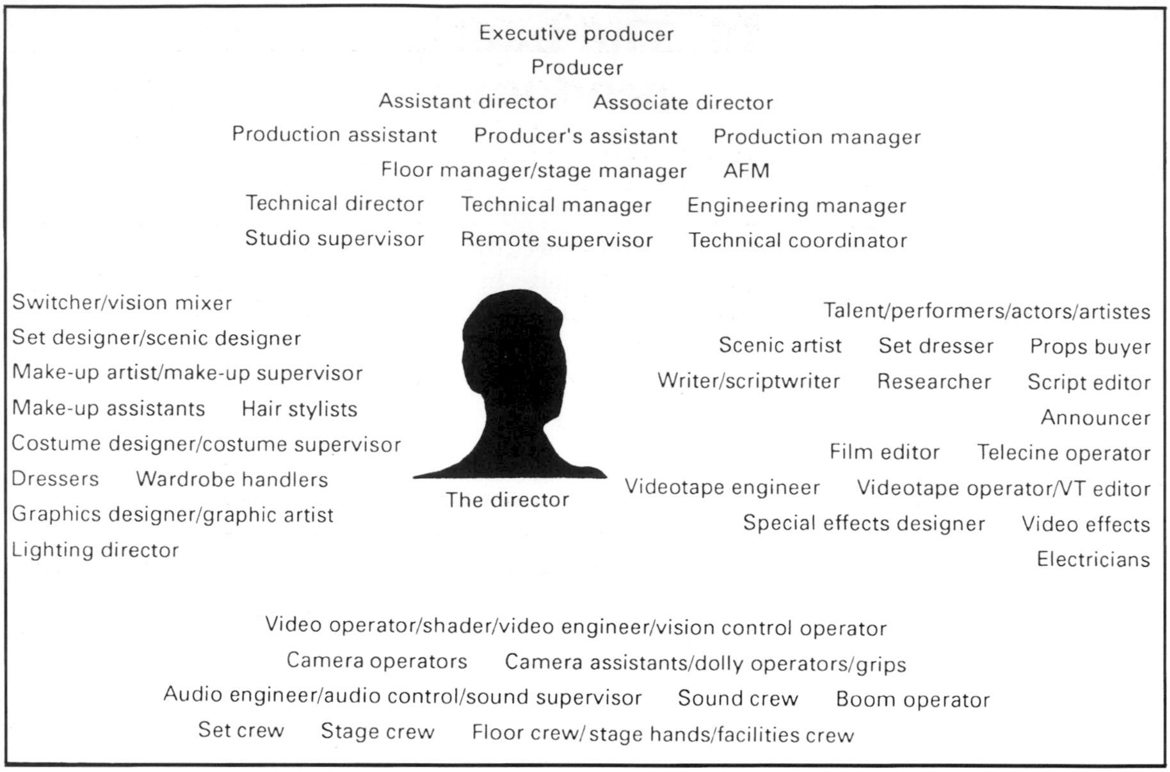

Executive producer
Producer
Assistant director Associate director
Production assistant Producer's assistant Production manager
Floor manager/stage manager AFM
Technical director Technical manager Engineering manager
Studio supervisor Remote supervisor Technical coordinator

Switcher/vision mixer
Set designer/scenic designer
Make-up artist/make-up supervisor
Make-up assistants Hair stylists
Costume designer/costume supervisor
Dressers Wardrobe handlers
Graphics designer/graphic artist
Lighting director

The director

Talent/performers/actors/artistes
Scenic artist Set dresser Props buyer
Writer/scriptwriter Researcher Script editor
Announcer
Film editor Telecine operator
Videotape engineer Videotape operator/VT editor
Special effects designer Video effects
Electricians

Video operator/shader/video engineer/vision control operator
Camera operators Camera assistants/dolly operators/grips
Audio engineer/audio control/sound supervisor Sound crew Boom operator
Set crew Stage crew Floor crew/ stage hands/facilities crew

Fig. 16.1 Production team
Studio production requires the services and skills of a large number of people. Their exact job functions and titles vary between organizations.

More often, a *producer* serves as the business head of a production; responsible for organization, finance, and policy, serving as artistic and business coordinator for several directors. As productions have become increasingly costly and more complicated, the workload needs to be spread. The director is then freed to concentrate on the program's interpretation, the staging and direction of the subject presentation.

Production emphasis

You can use picture and sound to report events simply, undramatically, and unobtrusively. For some types of production the best kind of staging and camera treatment provides a quiet, sympathetic background to the performance – a piano recital, an interview. However, there are program subjects that need as much 'hype' as you can offer: flashing, swirling light effects, arresting color, dominant, unusual sound quality, bizarre camera angles, unpredictable intercutting, to create an extravagant, sensational excitement.

While some productions have a relatively loose format, others require split-second timing, with accurately cued inserts coming from live remotes. There are effective programs based on a

continues on p. 406

Table 16.1 Production personnel

*Executive producer**	Overall organizational and administrative head of production group (e.g. a series of programs devoted to a particular field). He or she controls and coordinates the business management, including program budget, and may be concerned with wider issues such as funding/backing/coproduction arrangements.
*Producer**	Responsible to management for a specific production. Concerned with: choice of supervisory staff and crew; interdepartmental coordination; script acceptance; production scheduling. The producer may select or initiate the program concepts and work with writers. He or she assigns the production's director, and keeps a watching brief on deadlines, production planning, location projects, rehearsals, production treatment, etc. During rehearsal/recording also becomes involved in such specifics as retakes, overrunning scheduled times, craft or union problems, assessing postproduction treatment and the final program format.
Associate producer	Aide to producer. Coordinates appointments, jobs, schedules, etc.
*Director**	Responsible for interpreting and staging the production. This involves advising, guiding, and coordinating the specialists in the production team (scenic, lighting. sound, cameras, costume, etc.) and approving their anticipated treatment. The director may choose and hire performers/talent/actors (casting): envision and plan the camera treatment (shots, movements) and editing, and direct/rehearse the performers during prerehearsals. During studio rehearsals the director guides and cues performance (through the *floor manager*), and instructs the camera and sound crews, and switcher (vision mixer). He or she also evaluates the specialists' contributions (settings, camerawork, lighting, sound, make-up, costume, graphics, etc.). In some situations the director may operate the production switcher (e.g. on location), and guide and coordinate postproduction editing/audio sweetening. For smaller productions, the *producer's and director's* jobs may be combined. The director's job can range in practice from being the sole individual creating and coordinating the production to a person directing a camera and sound crew with material organized by others.
*Assistant director, associate director (AD)**	Director's aide. Functions can depend on size of production. Supervises prerehearsals, location organization, etc. on director's behalf. During rehearsal in the production control room, lines up shots, checks special shots (supers, chroma key), gives routine cues (film and VT inserts), etc., while the director guides performance/cameras. Advises director of upcoming cues. May assist in off-line editing (timings, edit points). Checks program timing and progress. Helps director with postproduction editing routine.
*Production assistant (PA) – (UK)**	Director's aide. Supervises pre-rehearsals, location organization, etc. on director's behalf. During rehearsals/recording, functions similar to those of *floor manager.*
*Producer's assistant – (UK)**	Director's aide. General liaison/secretarial/coordinating helpmate. Checks performance against the script. Checks continuity. May line up shots, prepare inserts, etc. while the director guides performance/cameras. Readies director, crew, VTR, and film channels re upcoming cues. Notes the durations/time code of each take. Keeps director's notes re changes to be made, retakes. etc.

Table 16.1 (cont.)

*Floor manager (FM)/ Stage manager (SM)**	The director's representative and contact on the studio floor. (May be allocated at planning stage, or only joins the production in the studio.) Cues performers. Checks and directs floor crew. Responsible for general studio organization, safety, discipline (e.g. noise), security. Assisted by AFM, who also ensures that talent are present.
*Production manager (UK)**	Responsible to producer/director for maintaining production within allocated budget. Also administrative functions relative to production.
Technical director (TD)†	Crew chief. Coordinates and supervises engineering facilities. Evaluates technical quality. May instruct operational crew during production. May operate production switcher on director's instructions.
Studio supervisor (or Remote supervisor)/Technical coordinator†	Coordinates all technical operations, books facilities, checks technical feasibility, safety, etc.
Switcher/Vision mixer†	Specialist operating the production switcher (and perhaps electronic effects).
Set designer/Scenic designer†	Conceives, designs, and organizes the entire scenic treatment. (Perhaps including graphics.) Supervises scenic crew during setting, dressing, and striking settings.
Make-up artist/ Make-up supervisor †*	Designs, prepares, and applies make-up treatment; aided by make-up assistants and hair stylists.
Costume designer †*	Designs selects performers' costume (wardrobe). Assisted by dressers/*wardrobe handlers*.
Graphics designer/Graphics artist†	Responsible for design and preparation of all graphics and titles (studio cards, titles, displays, computer graphics, etc.)
Lighting director†	Designs, arranges, and controls all lighting treatment, both technically and artistically. (May be responsible for artistic picture quality.)
Vision control/Shader/ Video operator/Video technician/ Video engineer†	Controls picture quality by adjusting video equipment. (Equipment alignment/line-up, exposure, black level, color balance. etc.) Operations are closely coordinated with lighting treatment.
Camera crew†	A team responsible for all camera operations on a production; led by a team head.
Audio control/Audio engineer/ Sound supervisor/ Audio technician†	Organizes and supervises the sound crew, in the studio and control room. Responsible for technical and artistic quality of program sound. Controls audio level, balance, tonal quality, etc, of all sound contributions. (Usually involved in planning, rehearsals, recording, and postproduction audio sweetening.)
Sound crew†	Supervised by the senior audio technician or engineer, and responsible for positioning microphones, operating sound boom(s), and operating all audio equipment.
Set crew†	Group of personnel responsible for erecting (*setting*) scenery.

Table 16.1 (cont.)

Stage crew†	Group of personnel responsible for dressing sets (positioning furniture, props, drapes, etc.). Properties (props) may be arranged by a specialist property man.
Floor crew/Stage hands/Grips/ Facilities crew†	They are responsible for general non-technical studio mechanics: such as resetting scenery, props, etc. during production; setting up title cards, graphics; action cues (e.g. rocking a vehicle), and similar routines. In some organizations, they may initially set up and dress settings.
Electricians†	Crew responsible for rigging and setting lamps, and electrical apparatus (including electrical props).
Special effects designer†	Specialist designing and operating such mechanical illusions as fire, snow, explosions.
Video effects†	Specialist designing and operating various types of digital video effects.
CG operator†	Person organizing and typing on-screen text and titles for a program; either during the production or storing material ready for later cueing. A separate *prompter operator* may prepare text for camera prompter readout.
Studio engineer/ Maintenance engineer†	Engineer responsible for maintenance and trouble-shooting of all camera and sound equipment in a production (or a studio).
Videotape channel†	Engineers/operators recording and replaying videotape machines. Videotape editing may be carried out by a separate *VT editor*.
Film channel†	Operators reproducing film (telecine)
*Announcer**	Concerned with off-screen announcements commentary, continuity, etc.
*Writer**	Person responsible for writing the script. May be freelance or staff. Producer or director may write material. May be assisted by *researcher*, who obtains data/information/references etc. for production team and/or writer.
	Further personnel operate other ancillary equipment, such as *prompters. character generator*, etc.
	Performers/talent
	People appearing on the screen are termed variously:
Actors	Working to an established script, invariably play a role, create a character. Action/performance usually rehearsed before the camera rehearsal.
Performers/talent	Broad term for people appearing in front of the camera as themselves (interviewers, announcers, newscasters, anchor persons, emmcee, etc.), often addressing the audience directly through the camera. (May be scripted, semi-scripted, or unscripted material.) Sometimes *performer* refers to a person providing a specific act (e.g. juggler).
Guests	Invited 'personalities', specialists, or members of the public; usually without experience in front of the camera. (Interviewees, contestants, audience contributors, etc.).

*Personnel rated as *above the line* (non-technical) relative to program budgeting.
†Personel generally rated as *below the line* for budgeting purposes.

compilation of video-tape and film material woven together by commentary and music. Some types of production concentrate on action; others on reaction. Dialogue may be all-important – or quite incidental.

Away from the studio, productions can be anything from a one-camera shoot trailing wildlife to a large-scale *remote (outside broadcast)*, covering a vast area with many cameras. Unforeseen problems are inevitable, and the restrictions of the environment and the weather must affect the director's opportunities.

Selective tools

The camera and microphone do not behave like our eyes and ears but substitute for them. Our eyes flick around with a knowledge of our surroundings, providing us with an impression of unrestricted stereoscopic vision; in fact, we can only detect detail and color over a tiny angle (about 1½°), and our peripheral vision is monochromatic and quite blurred. Also, our ears provide us with selective binaural pick-up, quite unlike the TV audio system.

In daily life we build up an impression of our environment by personally controlled sampling; concentrating on certain details while ignoring others. The camera and microphone, on the other hand, provide us with only restricted segments. And the information provided in these segments is modified in various ways, as we have seen, by the characteristics of the medium (distorting space, proportions, scale, etc.).

Selective techniques

As we saw earlier, if you simply set up your camera and microphone overlooking the action the viewer soon becomes overaware of the small restricted screen and limited detail; prevented from seeing whatever is outside the shot. Go closer for detail and the viewer progressively loses the overall view. Show more of the scene and particular detail becomes indiscernible. In the choice of suitable viewpoint and shot size for a particular purpose lies the concept of guided selection; the beginnings of techniques.

Good production techniques provide *variety*: of scale and proportion; of composition pattern; of centers of attention and changing subject influence. You achieve these things by variation in shot size and camera viewpoint, by moving the subject and/or the camera, or by altering the subject seen.

Although you may sometimes encourage the viewer to browse around a shot, more often you will want him or her to look at a particular feature, and follow a certain thought process. The screen can all too easily become 'moving wallpaper', with our audience seeing – but not looking, hearing – but not listening!

The screen transforms reality

The camera and microphone can only convey an *impression* of the subject and scene. Whatever the limitations or inaccuracies of these images, they are the only direct information our viewer has available. And, of course, interpretation must vary with one's own experience and foreknowledge. Whether you are aiming to convey an accurate account (newscast) or to conjure an illusion (drama) the screen will transform reality.

You could fill the screen with a shot of a huge aircraft, or with a diminutive model. The pictures would look very similar. Yet neither conveys the subjective essentials; i.e. how you *feel* standing beside the giant plane or handling the tiny model. Introducing a person into shot would establish scale, but it would still not include our characteristic responses to such a situation: the way we would ourselves be overawed by size, or intrigued by minute detail.

Use your camera to select detail from a painting or a photograph and your TV screen puts a frame around it, to make this isolated area into a new complete picture; an arrangement that did not exist in its own right within the original; an arrangement that if sustained in close-up can become detached and dissociated in the audience's minds from the complete subject.

When you shoot solid sculpture its three-dimensional form becomes reproduced as a flat pattern on the TV screen. Planes merge and interact as they cannot do when we ourselves examine the real sculpture. Only on the flat screen can a billiard ball become transformed into a flat disc under diffused lighting. In practice, you can continually make use of this falsification of reality. The very principles of scenic design rely on it. But it is as well to appreciate that the camera and microphone do inevitably modify the images they convey; and that these images are easily mistaken for truth.

Interpretative techniques

It is one of those production paradoxes that although your camera can show what is happening, it will often fail to convey the atmosphere or spirit of the occasion. You can frequently achieve more convincing representative results by deliberately using selective techniques than by direct reportage.

Straightforward shots of a mountain climb impart none of the thrills and hazards of the situation. But use low camera angles to emphasize the treacherous slope; show threatening overhangs, straining fingers, slipping feet, dislodged stones, laboring breath, slow ascending music . . . and the illusion grows. Even climbing a gentle slope can appear hazardous if strong interpretative techniques are used.

Sometimes the audience can be so strongly moved by this subjective treatment that sympathetic bodily reactions set in when watching such scenes – dizziness, nausea. Even situations outside the viewer's personal experience (the elation of free fall, the horror of quicksand) can be conveyed to some degree by carefully chosen stimuli.

Making the contrived arise 'naturally'

You can introduce techniques *obtrusively* for dramatic effect, or so *unobtrusively* that the effect appears 'natural' and the viewer is quite unaware that the situation is contrived:

Obtrusive. The camera suddenly depresses from an eye-level shot to a low-angle viewpoint.
Unobtrusive. The camera shoots a seated actor at eye-level. He stands, and the camera tilts up with him. We now have a low-angle shot.

Where situations seem to occur accidentally or unobtrusively they are invariably more effective. For example, as an intruder moves towards camera he becomes menacingly underlit by a nearby table lamp.

Where an effect is blatantly contrived it often appears to challenge our credulity and we tend to reject it. A sinister figure is reflected in the victim's sunglasses; the camera whip pans to show him standing nearby.

As conventions become understood, and accepted by our audience, even flagrant changes become permissible: *flash cut-ins* (lasting ½–2 seconds) to convey 'recognition' or 'recall'; extreme viewpoint changes, close sound on long shots; exaggerated filmic time. But a director who deliberately misuses an established convention, trying to give it a new significance, treads a thorny path.

Many techniques have become so familiar that we now regard them as the normal and natural way of doing things. But they are really artifices that help us to convey particular concepts:

1 'Chipmunk' voices (high-pitched through tape speed-up) for small creatures.
2 Echo behind ghostly manifestations.
3 Rim light in 'totally dark' scenes.
4 Background music.
5 Wipes, supers, etc.

Gratuitous techniques

Skilful presentation blends a carefully selected combination of visual and audio techniques to attract and persuade. But you can too easily use techniques for their own sake.

1 Rapid cutting in time with music – that provides a disjointed dissatisfying jumble of images.
2 Video effects – that leave us preoccupied with how it was done.
3 'Clever' camerawork – focusing on irrelevant foreground objects while main subjects remain unsharp; shooting into lamps or specular reflections.

Such contrived methods have their occasional purpose, but they can quickly degenerate into imposed gimmicks.

Production pressures

Preoccupation with the organization and coordination of production mechanics leaves most directors little time to meditate on the medium's aesthetics. Rehearsal time is limited. The camera and sound crews are meeting the director's brainchild for the first time and need to be guided in the interpretation. If the treatment is elaborate and exacting there is greater opportunity for problems that require immediate solution. If the production is shot out of sequence it becomes that much more difficult to ensure that each segment is coherent, and will provide good continuity when edited together. In such circumstances there is an understandable temptation to substitute effective known mechanics for creative experiment.

Also, when you are closely involved with a production it can be quite difficult to estimate accurately the audience impact of pace, timing, tension, etc. Watching a film clip through *several* times, you will see how the stresses, emphasis, speed, and even its significance can change. A word or gesture can have more or less impact with repetition, while heavily pointed action may appear hackneyed or mannered.

17 Production practices

TV production groups all over the world follow surprisingly similar practices. This is partly due to the nature of the medium's mechanics, partly the result of sharing knowledge and experience.

Single-camera techniques

In the earliest days of television, multi-camera shooting soon became the established practice. It has many advantages. But as cameras and videorecording equipment have become lightweight and more flexible, an increasing number of productions are now being made on location with single-camera units.

As you will see, there are essential differences between single- and multi-camera production techniques.

Scripting

There are several approaches to shooting ranging from the hopefully empirical to the meticulously planned.

In *unscripted* off-the-cuff shooting, the camera tends to record available events: perhaps working from a rough outline (*shooting plan*). Material is selected during editing and compiled into a program format with added commentary. This technique is often used when shooting documentaries and news stories.

Fully scripted productions, on the other hand, are first broken down into their component shots or scenes, and the mechanics involved for each shot or group of shots are assessed. The staged action is then methodically shot out of story sequence (*shooting schedule/plan*) for maximum economy and efficiency. For example, if the story line requires a series of intercut shots between the heroine at the cliff-top and the hero below, you shoot all the sequences involved at one camera set-up, then move to the other viewpoint.

This 'out-of-sequence' shooting prevents unnecessary changes in camera set-up, location, relighting, resetting, and uses actors more economically.

Single-camera shooting

Single-camera shooting is the traditional method of film making. Two or more cameras are only used for situations where repeat action would be impracticable or costly, or simultaneous multi-viewpoints are required; e.g. when derailing a train.

Shooting discontinuously out of sequence often requires performers to repeat their action for each change in camera viewpoint or shot length (and remember, their performance is probably out-of-story-sequence anyway). That introduces *continuity problems.* Action, gestures, expressions, costume, lighting, etc. must match in intercut shots and relate to the story development – although filmed at different times.

Flexibility of viewpoint

After a sequence is skilfully edited, the continuity appears so natural that one can easily overlook that it was originally shot as a *disjointed series of individual set-ups.*

In a typical sequence we may find ourselves close to a man as he walks – yet an instant later see him from a distant viewpoint. The camera is often 'left behind' as he moves away – yet is at his destination as he arrives. Shots intercut from his viewpoint to that of the person to whom he is speaking.

The overall effect here is smooth-flowing and provides a variety of viewpoints. To do the obvious and shoot this entire sequence as *continuous* action would have required several cameras, spread over an appreciable distance – an approach that might not be practical anyway. Usually it would not provide the same effect.

As in film, shots tend to be of briefer duration than those in *continuous* TV production. Watching a well-made film, we see that most shots (the period between picture transitions) last only a few seconds (typically 3–15 seconds). A good serial film unit may achieve as many as 120 shots a day (about 18 minutes' running time), although this is untypical. A live TV production might last 25 minutes, and contain 100–200 shots, edited 'on the hoof'.

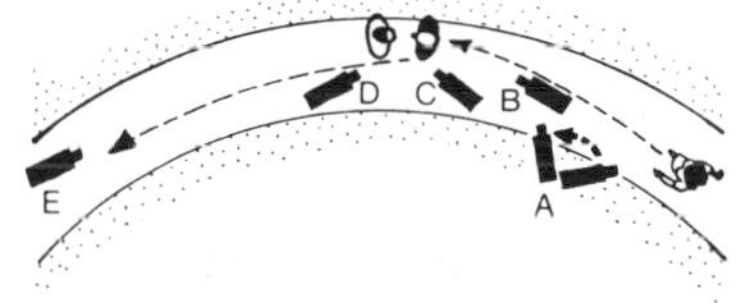

Fig 17.1A Single-camera shooting
To achieve apparently smooth-flowing action with *one camera* a series of camera set-ups are often necessary.

Example.
A. Girl out walking (comes up to camera . . . which pans as she moves past).
B. Cut – she sees friend in distance (over shoulder shot).
C. Cut – CU of friend smiling.
D. Cut – friend's point of view. Girl arrives, speaking (LS to CU).
C/D. Intercut close-shots during conversation.
C. Girl says goodbye (MS).
E. Girl walks on.

The action taken for each camera set-up will be enacted/repeated out of sequence to suit each camera set-up in turn.

Continuous single-camera shooting

Following camera

One approach when shooting *continuous action* 'live' or 'live-on-tape' is to adopt a *following camera* method. The single camera moves around to new viewpoints, following the performers, adjusting the shot size as the situation requires. If well done, the result can be a powerful subjective impression, in which the camera represents the audience's uninterrupted viewpoint. There are no transitions to distract them. Where closer shots are needed, the camera anticipates and moves nearer for that moment.

Continuous single-camera shooting can be so effective that entire plays have been shot live on a single mobile dolly. There are drawbacks to this approach, though. It requires skilled, well-controlled camerawork on a smoothly operated mounting. Mobile hand-held shots can only be sustained over a short period.

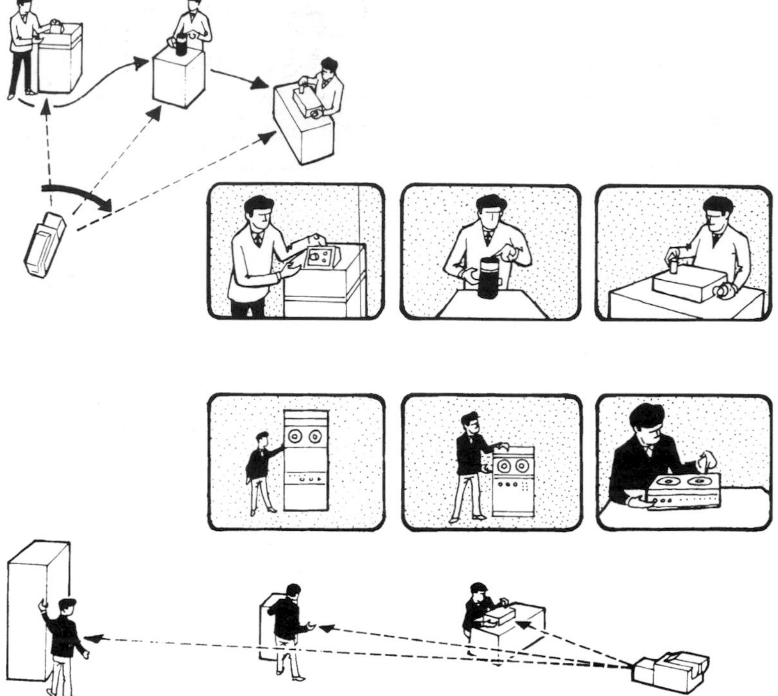

Fig. 17.1B part 1 Subject movement and the single camera – equidistant positions
Items can be arranged equidistant from the camera, to provide a series of similar shots as the talent moves around.

Fig. 17.1B part 2 Subject movement and the single camera – movement in depth
Where subjects of various sizes are involved, the largest can be located furthest away; the smallest closest to the camera.

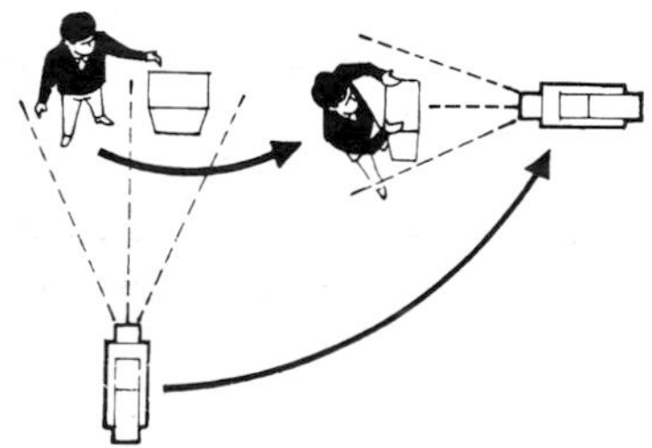

Fig. 17.1B part 3 Subject movement and the single camera – repositioned camera
Here the camera zooms out from a close-up, and arcs round to a new viewpoint as the talent moves to the new subject.

Working to the camera

Instead of having the camera 'work to the subject' in this way, you can arrange action and treatment so that the talent '*works to the camera*' instead. They move around to suit the shot; coming nearer the camera for close-ups and moving further away for long shots. This can be done naturally and unobtrusively, as we see in Figure 17.1. You can place larger subjects in the background, while smaller ones are closer to the camera. A turntable, or even a mirror may help to see an object from various angles. Occasionally, you might pull focus/throw focus from one subject to another to transfer attention.

Even if your camera is on a *fixed tripod*, you can still create an impression of shot flexibility using this technique. Because you must simulate camera movement by zooming, aim to do so gradually and inconspicuously. Wherever possible, try to arrange zooming to coincide with subject movement. Zoom in as the talent turns to point at a wall chart. As they lift up an object we have been studying in close-up detail, zoom out to a mid-shot. Zooming in this way provides shot variety without becoming intrusive.

Stretched facilities

In a *multi-camera* studio you would assume that there would always be a camera or two free to shoot the subject from a fresh angle. Yet

Fig. 17.2 Relocation
During an insert shot, the talent has unexpectedly moved to a new location and is discovered there; often disconcerting the viewer.

Fig. 17.3 Continuity
When retaking shots, inattention to detail can lead to poor continuity during editing, due to items having been consumed, moved, action or positions wrongly repeated, etc.

surprisingly often you will find that you have only *one camera* to work with! In a three-camera studio, for instance, if *CAM-1* is on-air, and *CAM-2* is set up on a title card, that leaves only *CAM-3* available to shoot the action at the start of the next scene.

If, during a demonstration, a geologist is showing us specimens on one camera, and the other two cameras are tied up with a combined illustration (e.g. a map graphic on *CAM-2* and superimposed titling on *CAM-3*), you are back to single-camera techniques.

When you are restricted to a single camera for any reason, you can often add variety and flexibility by cutting to insert material on slides, film, and videotape. This may also give you the opportunity to reposition the camera, or change the shot size. Take care, though, not to create visual discontinuity. Inserts of this sort can show information that the studio camera itself might not pick up – such as hallmarks on silverware.

Discontinuous single-camera shooting

Shooting uncontrolled action

When using a single camera to shoot broad action over which you have no control you have the option of:

- Remaining at a fixed viewpoint and relying on the zoom lens to provide a variety of shots.
- Or moving the camera to a series of vantage points, changing viewpoint and shot size to capture the main features of the occasion.

Clearly, if you are shooting a public event such as a street parade on a single camera the first technique is very limiting. However, if you move around or stop shooting you are liable to lose some of the action, unless you can time your moves to fit in with a lull in the proceedings.

To assist subsequent editing make sure you have plenty of extra general material that can be used as *cutaway* shots. 'Cutaways' tend to be of two types; *active* and *passive*. The 'active' cutaway includes subjects that can only be edited into the program at a particular moment (e.g. shots of the town hall clock showing that the parade is about to start), or the crowd's responses to a particular event. 'Passive' cutaways, on the other hand, can be used at almost any time, and might include reflections, flags, sun through branches.

As with news events, you make the most of available opportunities. You may be able to plan exactly what you are going to do, checking out the route and your viewpoints beforehand. You may even be able to influence events a little; arranging for the beauty queen in the procession to turn and smile to camera as she passes. But, on the whole, you have to take things as you find them. There are no repeats!

Shooting controlled action

When shooting situations you *can* control (e.g. interviews, drama sequences) the situation is very different. Now you arrange the action, the camera set-up, and sometimes the lighting and staging (background, props, etc.) to suit each shot in turn.

If you want to repeat the same action so that you have long shots, medium, and close shots of it to intercut, that is usually quite practicable. Instead of having to select from whatever is happening at the location you may have the option to change things: to have a person leaning over the bridge to improve the composition; to wait for the sun to come out; to pause while loud aircraft pass over.

You will usually take the shots in the most convenient, rational order, then edit them together afterwards to suit the production sequence. If, for instance, you have a series of shots of people either side of a river it is obviously more sensible to shoot all the action on one side and then move to the other, rather than hop to and fro, shooting in script running order.

When shooting discontinuously you have to take care throughout that there are no obvious discrepancies that spoil the *continuity* between these shots when they are joined together. If in our example it happened to have been bright sunshine when shooting on one bank of the river, but pouring rain when shooting the other, the intercut shots could look pretty unconvincing, to say the least!

Segmented shooting

Shooting controlled action with a single camera, you will normally break the action down into a series of quite brief 'action segments'. If part of the action adds nothing to the situation you may deliberately *omit* it altogether. At other times, you may actually *emphasize* the action. Let's illustrate this with a simple situation:

Someone is walking along the street.

- If we are only really interested in what they do when they reach their destination we can omit the walk altogether.
- But perhaps we want to emphasize that they are lame, and every step is taken in agony. In that case, we might follow them in close detail . . . the heavy tread, the hesitant walking stick . . . the uneven paving, in a series of shots taken from different angles.
- On the other hand, suppose the story at that point aims to intrigue us. We wonder whether the person is being followed by the villain. We would probably shoot the sequence quite differently. The entire walk might be taken on a static camera, using a continuous panning shot. We show them walking past the camera into the distance . . . and out of shot. We hold the empty frame . . . and their pursuer moves into the foreground of the shot.

Clearly, how you break up the action must depend on the dramatic purpose of the picture sequence.

As an exercise, run a videotape of any long action sequence from a motion picture or a documentary. It might be showing someone rock climbing, sailing a boat, in a car chase. Analyse the shots that make up this action sequence. Time them. Think carefully about the viewpoints.

In a car chase we might find that at one moment the camera is in the car beside the driver . . . in the next we see a front-on shot of it showing the driver alone in the car. *Cut*, and we are behind the driver's shoulder looking through the windshield . . . and now we are looking down from a high building as the car maneuvers a corner. It moves away into the distance and – *cut* . . . we see it coming up towards the camera.

When watching this treatment we never question the rapidly changing viewpoints, or query why the camera is suddenly located on a helicopter. When shooting in the desert we see the car vanish into the distance . . . without wondering if he is going to come back to pick up the camera operator!

Many types of action are, in reality, very drawn out and somewhat boring to watch. Shoot them continuously, and audience interest will wander. Break sustained action into continually varying viewpoints, and we create pace, and provide continuing interest.

One particular function of editing is that we can create an illusion of continuity between shots or situations where in fact none exists. This is not only a valuable dramatic facility but it enables us to develop action sequences which in reality we could not shoot.

Imagine a scene showing a bird on a branch . . . a close shot as it dives into the stream . . . an underwater shot of fish . . . a fish is caught by the bird . . . the bird sits beside the river eating its catch. These are probably shots of different birds, and of different fish, shot at different times. The separate shots are edited together to form a complete effective action sequence.

We have looked at these examples in some detail, for they epitomize the thinking and the techniques that underlie *single-camera shooting*. As you will see, they are noticeably different from multi-camera treatment.

Multi-camera treatment

Using two or more cameras gives you additional flexibility in the way you handle any situation. Without missing any of the action, or needing action repeated, you can intercut between different shots of the same subject, alter the camera's viewpoint, move to another area.

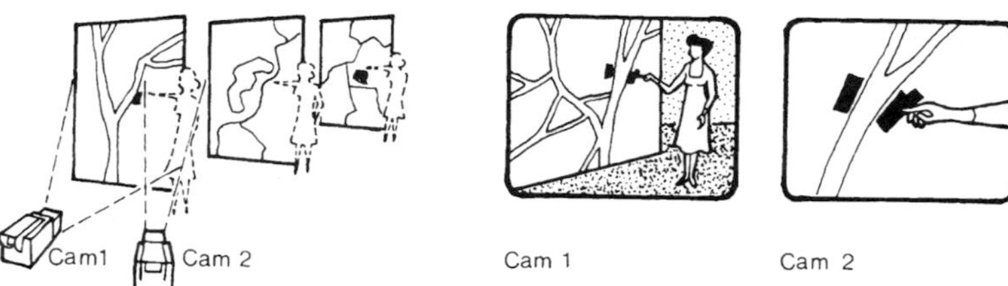

Fig. 17.4 Two-camera treatment Here shots are divided between two cameras. Cam 1 concentrates on long shots. Cam 2 takes close-ups of maps and speaker.

In an instant you can change the significance of a shot. You can provide fresh information, alter emphasis, point new detail, show reactions, shift audience attention, compare relationships, introduce visual variety. And all this while the action continues. Using a single camera, much of this effect has to be contrived.

Using *several cameras*, you can arrange to have one covering the action and another ready to catch the audience's reactions. But if you are shooting with a *single camera* you are unlikely to turn away from the main event to see whether someone in the crowd is responding. You are more likely to shoot some reaction shots later (probably relating to entirely different action), and cut them in for effect at that point during editing!

Multi-camera treatment allows you to *combine* cameras; pictures – for supers, inserts, split screen, or other effects. You can fit one camera with a device (e.g. a periscope mirror), while other cameras provide normal pictures.

If you have only one camera you may need to alter a shot for purely mechanical reasons – e.g. widening a shot to accommodate

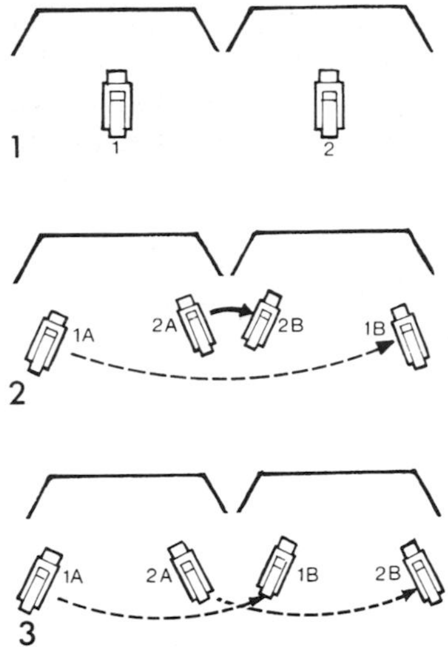

Fig. 17.5 Maximum use of cameras
1 One camera to each set is unnecessarily restrictive.
2 Near the end of a two-camera scene. Cam 2 pans to the next area.
3 Cameras move away successively. Cam 2 moves first (A to B), then Cam 1 joins it.

an extra person. That recessive movement may be artistically inappropriate. It may be better to cut to a wider shot on another camera.

Visual variety

Static shots easily become a bore. So audience interest is encouraged by introducing movement and change. Although, if overdone, the pictures can become a strain to watch. Rapid cutting demands continual viewer concentration . . . that is not readily sustained. Ceaseless action and camera moves lead to pictures that fidget with movement. As always, the aim is a well-balanced blend with variations in pace, tempo, and emphasis.

Performer movement

Most visual variety stems from action within the scene, as people alter positions and regroup. Quite often more meaningful changes are achieved by performer movement than by camera moves or editing.

In a close shot the performer dominates. As he moves away from camera the audience becomes more aware of his relationship to his surroundings. In long shots these surroundings may dominate. So by changing the length of shot you change emphasis and create visual variation.

These moves are motivated in various ways:

1 By *deliberately arranging* subjects (props, demonstration items) so that a performer is artificially 'motivated' to move to them in the course of the production.
2 By introducing a *gesture* (hand pointing) towards a subject – the camera pans over to see.
3 By a deliberate *turn* of the head or body – to initiate a pan, dolly, or zoom to a subject.
4 By a *verbal reference* ('The machine over there') providing a direct introduction to a shot change.

Changes by grouping

Where people are seated (panels, talk shows) you can achieve visual variety by *isolation*; selectively shooting individuals, two-shots, subgroups.

Fig. 17.6 Visual variety
Depending on how a picture is arranged, its centre of attention, emphasis, and even the audience's interpretation can change.

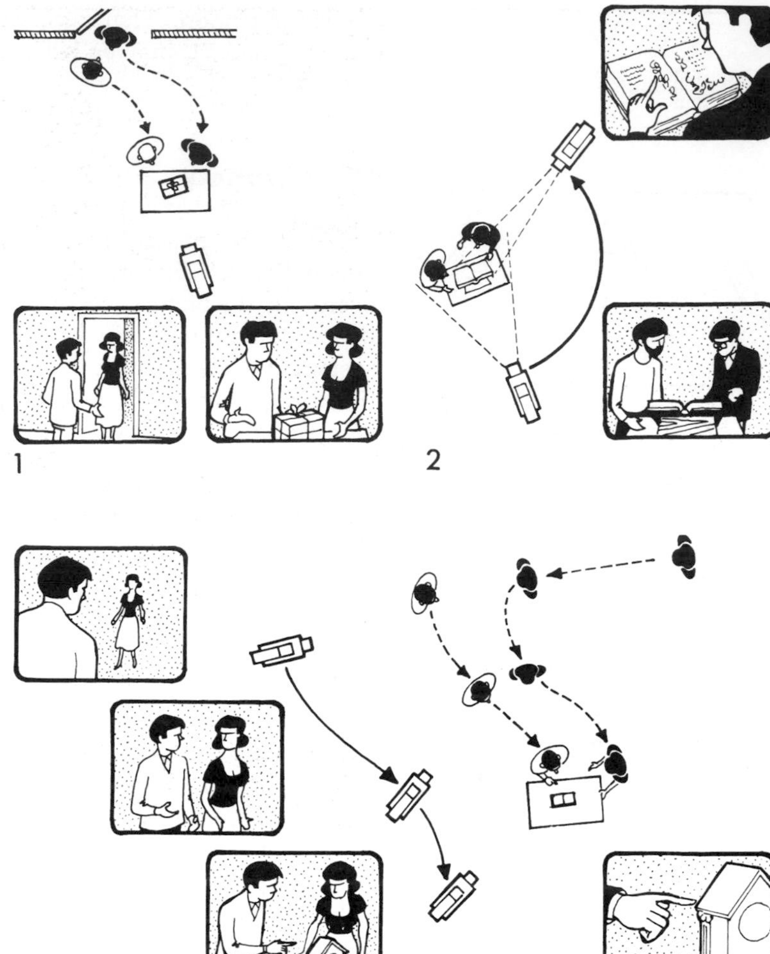

Fig. 17.7 part 1 Subject/camera relationship
1 Here subject and action have been arranged to suit the camera's static viewpoint (playing to the camera).
2 Here the camera moves, relating to the static subject and action.

Fig. 17.7 part 2 Subject/camera relationship
Subjects may be arranged to provide shot opportunities, while cameras are moved or intercut to explore these arrangements.

When people are mobile you can *regroup* them to provide freshly composed shots by introducing 'natural' moves (sitting, going over to pick up a book), or introduce visually motivated cuts (turning as a guest arrives). By varying emphasis and composition balance in this way the movement attracts attention and conceals the deliberate shift of interest.

Shooting static subjects

Visual variety can be introduced into your treatment of non-moving subjects (statuary, pottery, paintings, flowers) by the way you shoot and light them:

1 Camera movements alter the viewpoint.
2 You can selectively pan over the subject, interrelating its various parts.

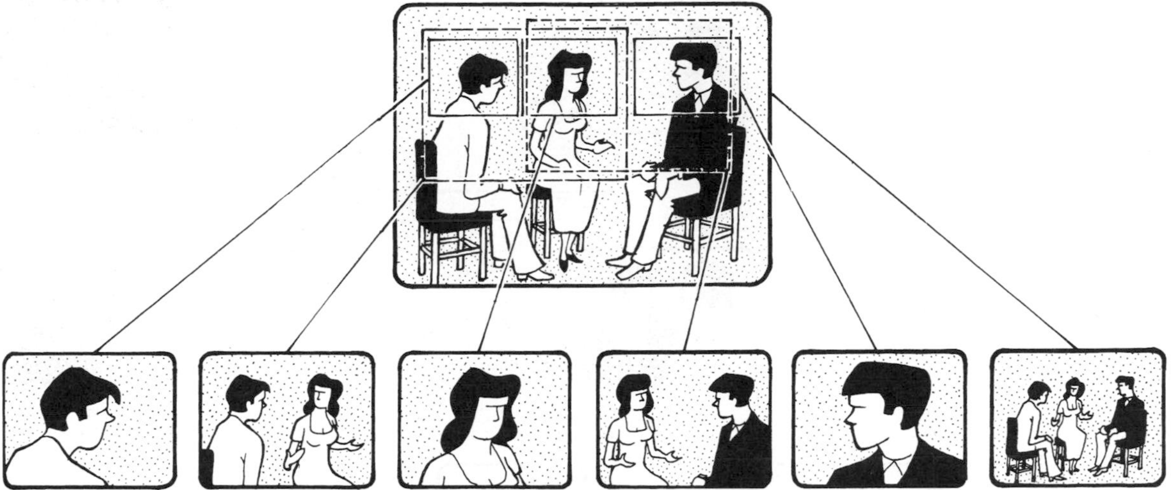

Fig. 17.8 Forming shots by isolation
By intercutting various shots of a group, you can introduce visual variety into a static situation.

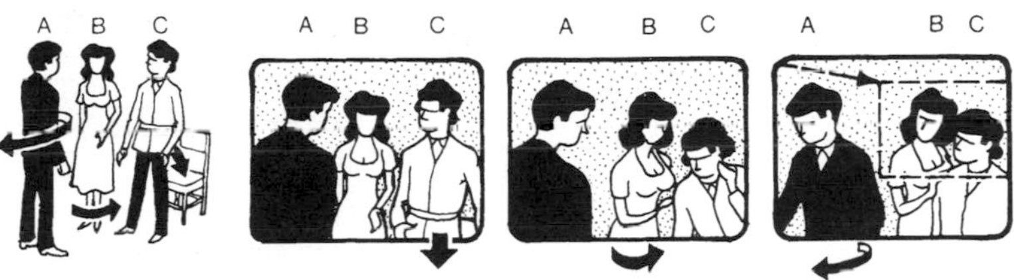

Fig. 17.9 Forming shots by subject movement
By introducing natural moves you can form new groupings. Here *C* sits, *B* turns to him. *A* turns and exits. camera tightens to shot *BC*. A series of compositional changes have moved attention between the people.

3 Changing lighting can isolate or emphasize sections or alter the subject's appearance.
4 Small objects can be handled, turned to show different features, or turntable-displayed.

Variety by décor

The presentation of certain subjects is necessarily restricted (piano playing, singers). They are relatively static and meaningful shot variations are limited. You can prevent sameness between productions by introducing variations in the decor – whether by scenic changes or by lighting. The pictures *look* different, even if the shots and viewpoints follow a recognizable format.

Fig. 17.10 Composition change altering significance
By a single change in the picture's composition you can alter its significance. The girl confronts her father (her frame position gives her strength, even in a rear view). He rises – the strength of his upward move and new position now make him dominant.

Variety by effects

This is achieved by introducing various visual effects such as: combined shots, superimpositions, multi-images, split screens, decorative inserted backgrounds (using chroma key), and synthesized color.

Fig. 17.11 part 1 The imaginary line – intercut facing shots
Shots can be intercut (cross-cut) between cameras located on the same side of the imaginary line: i.e. between 1 and 2, or 3 and 4. But inter-switching between cameras on opposite sides of this line causes jump cuts (1 and 3, 1 and 4, 2 and 3, 2 and 4).

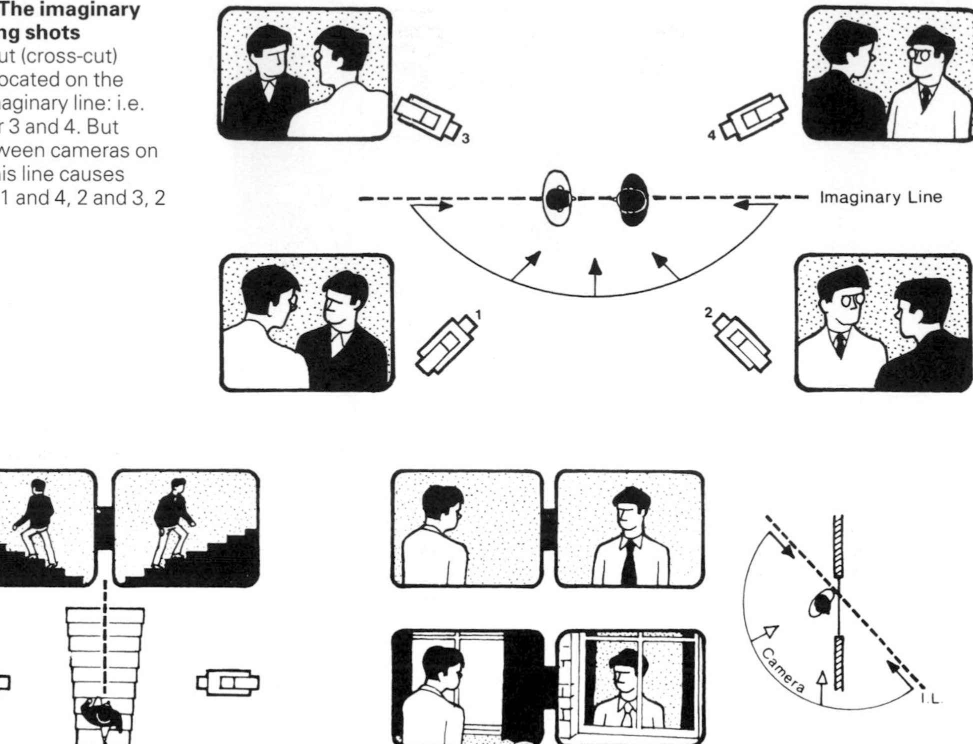

Fig. 17.11 part 2 The imaginary line – reverse-angle shots
1 Direction is reversed on the cut, for cameras have crossed the line.

2 A common scenic unit (doorway, window) usually makes reverse-angle cuts acceptable, providing cameras remain on one side of the line.

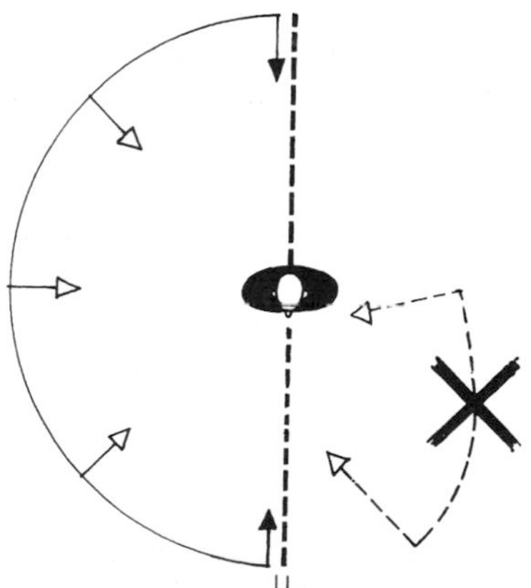

Fig. 17.11 part 3 The imaginary line – forward-facing positions
Whenever someone faces the camera (walking, sitting, singing, demonstrating) it is all too easy to interswitch inadvertently across the line to region X, and reverse direction.

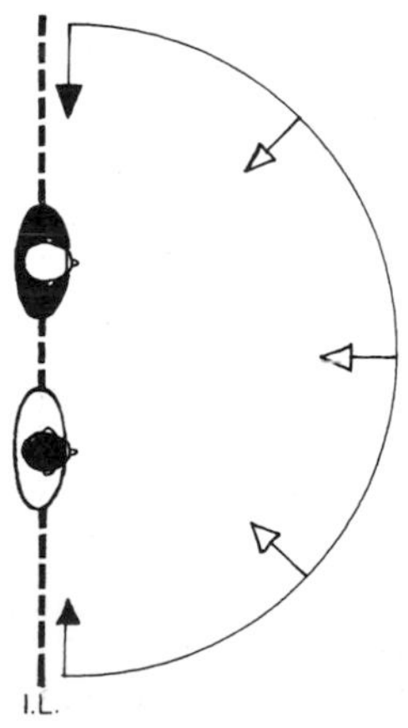

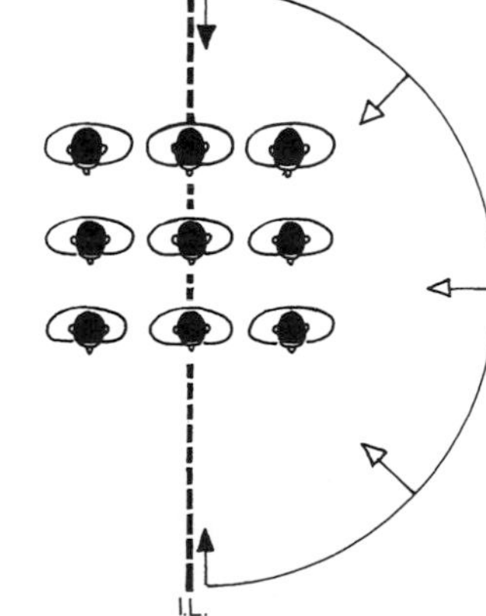

Fig. 17.11 part 4 The imaginary line – aligned positions
1 Where people are shoulder to shoulder (riding, walking) wide viewpoint changes are acceptable.

2 But for a larger gathering (audience, choir, parade) cameras should keep to one side of the front-rear axis when interswitching viewpoints.

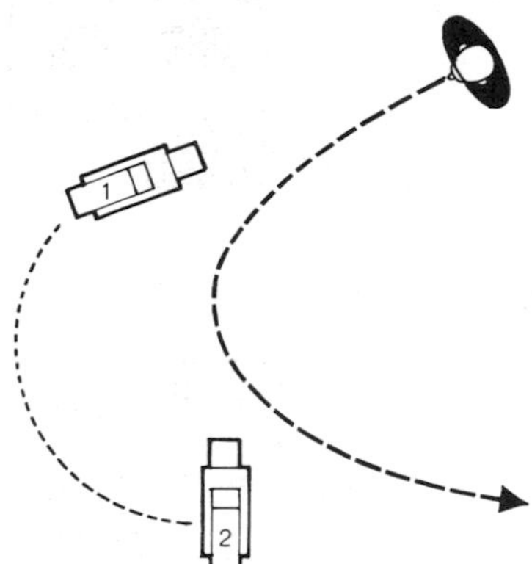

Fig. 17.11 part 5 **The imaginary line – curving path**
Where action follows a curved path, only a head-on viewpoint is reliable if shooting is discontinuous. With continuous action viewpoint changes such as 1–2 are practicable.

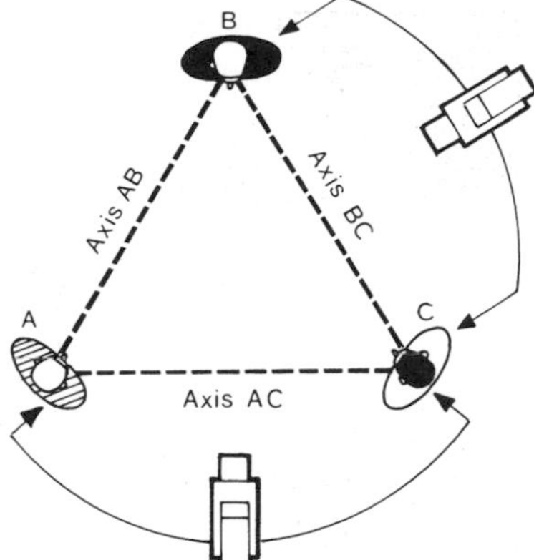

Fig. 17.11 part 6 **The imaginary line – three-way situations**
If you assume that the direction of person A's look has established the axis AC, then you can intercut shots along the AC axis. Now, if he turns towards B, the axis is changed to AB (excluding C from shot) and shots can be intercut along the BC axis. Eyelines can be changed (even cheated) to permit inter-axis cutting.

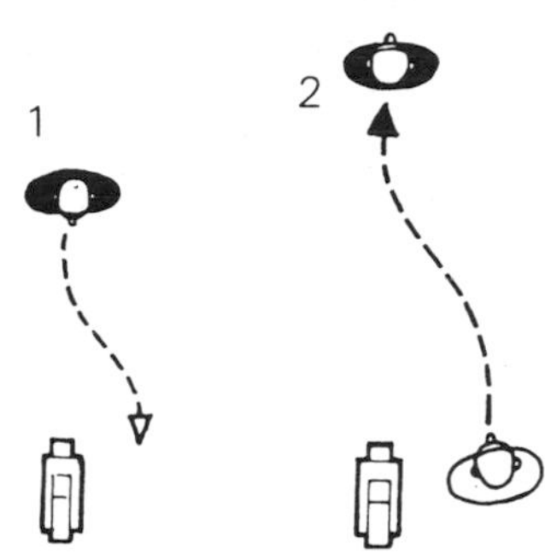

Fig. 17.11 part 7 **The imaginary line – exits and entrances**
If during supposedly uninterrupted action a person exits beside camera-right 1, a straight cut showing action continuation should show him entering camera-right also 2.

The illusion of relationships

As we watch a succession of pictures we build up a mental image of where things are located within the scene. We form these judgements from various visual clues; comparing common features, movements, the relative directions in which people are looking, etc.

If, for instance, we see someone looking screen right and the picture cuts to another person looking screen left we tend to assume that they are facing each other. In reality they might be in quite different places. But we have interrelated and interpreted these shots. Subsequent shots (a more distant view, for instance) will confirm or correct our interpretation.

In a scene where someone says goodbye to their partner and walks out of the shot we usually assume that they have departed. If the camera cuts to another viewpoint, and shows them nearby speaking to somebody else, the audience is likely to be disconcerted.

The camera easily misleads, and unless you actually want to create ambiguity, to make a dramatic or a comic point, it is best to avoid such situations.

Sometimes we deliberately create a *false* impression. We have a close shot of someone speaking towards the camera, with their eyeline slightly to one side, to suggest that they are talking to a person seen in the previous shot. But they are really alone. It is a productional device – quite as much as the actor's earnest telephone 'conversation' with a prop phone.

It is very easy to confuse or destroy spatial impressions the audience has formed. When you change the camera's viewpoint some strange visual anomalies can take place. Something on the left of the screen in one shot . . . appears an instant later over to the right of the screen. Having established where someone is looking in one shot, their eyeline can appear to change direction on the cut.

As you can see in Figure 17.11, these disconcerting *jump cuts* and the loss of orientation arise whenever you *cut* across an *imaginary line (action line, action axis, center line)*. This line has normally been established in our minds by previous camera viewpoints, or by eyelines (the 'direction of look'), or by performers' movements. If the camera *dollies* across the line, or you change the direction of the line by regrouping or moving people, or change the eye-lines, the effect does not arise.

Shot organization

It takes time to experiment, and production time is limited. So directors need a rational plan of campaign. You could distribute cameras around the scene and choose from shots the camera offered – but there would usually be little relationship between these pictures. Subject coverage would be patchy. There would probably be several near-identical shots of the pretty girl guest and none of the chairman! Perhaps several overall views or dramatic close-ups – but who could use them?

Fig. 17.12 part 1 Visual treatment – planned viewpoints
Cameras are placed at vantage points, from which appropriate shots can be selected and intercut.

Fig. 17.12 part 2 Visual treatment – storyboard approach
Following script analysis, treatment is visualized and broken down into key shots, which are sketched to show required camera treatment.

Shots have to be appropriately chosen and interrelated according to a coordinated plan, and only the *director* is in a position to do this.

Planned viewpoints

Using this technique, you begin with the action's mechanics (where people move, what they do there) and arrange strategic camera viewpoints from which to shoot it. Each camera position provides a series of shot opportunities and you select from these available shots as required.

At sports events and other large-scale public occasions this is the only practical approach. Cameras are often widely dispersed, camera movement is restricted, and the director relies on camera operators using their initiative to find appropriate shots. The director's knowledge of actual shot opportunities is mostly derived from what the cameras reveal and on-the-spot assistants. He/she guides selection, adjusts shot sizes, suggests desirable shots, and chooses from the available material.

You can use a similar strategy in *studio* production for certain types of shows with a regular format. For example:

Camera 1 – taking wider, *cover* shots (mid to long shots).
Camera 2 – primarily close-up shots.
Camera 3 – supporting close-ups, close detail, title cards, graphics.

This approach can be particularly useful for unscripted, off-the-cuff situations. But it is also valuable for a demonstrator, who

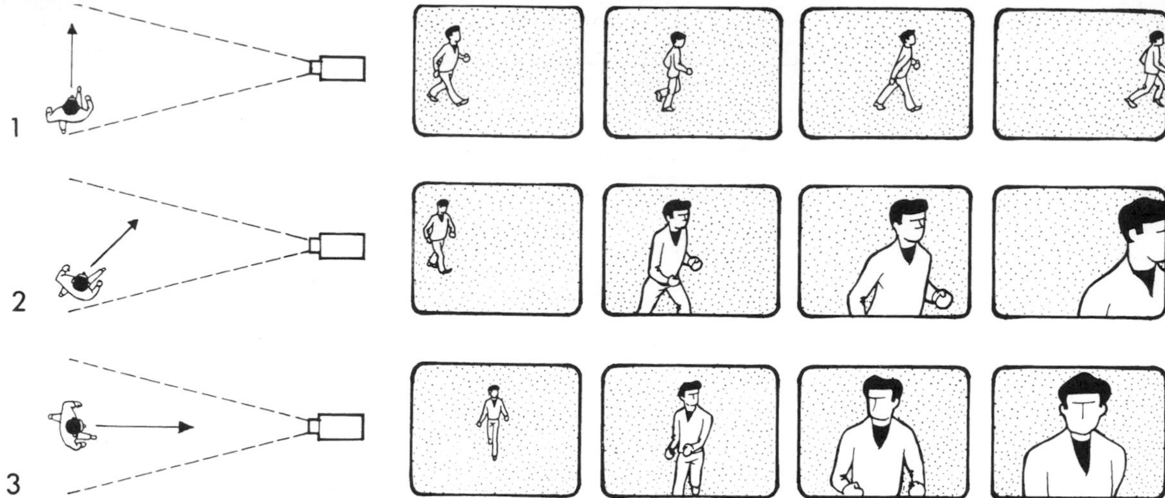

Fig. 17.13 part 1 The moving subject – direction of movement
1 A movement across the screen, quickly passes out of shot.
2 Diagonal moves are preferable, for they are visually more interesting.
3 Moves towards the camera from a distance are sustained longest, but can seem drawn-out.

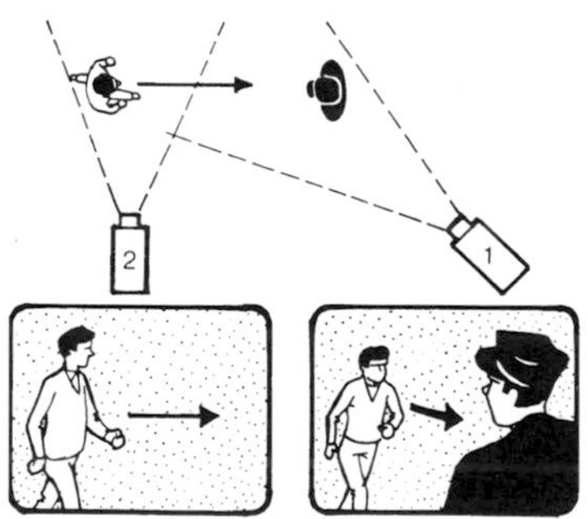

Fig. 17.13 part 2 The moving subject – widely spaced moves
Moves between widely spaced points are best shot obliquely (Cam 1), rather than with a following pan (Cam 2).

Fig. 17.13 part 3 The moving subject – avoid decapitation
1 The camera operator must be warned of a 'rise' or 'sit', to avoid the bizarre effects of a delayed following tilt.
2 Equally ridiculous effects can arise if framing does not follow action.

consequently knows which camera to play to for close-ups at any time. However, you should resist any temptation to apply such a routine where more exploratory camera treatment is possible.

Storyboard approach (Figure 17.12, part 2)

Where systematic planning is practical a director may use a storyboard technique; sketching the required picture treatment for selected *key shots* or for scene-by-scene treatment. Here we are concerned with *shot significance*; ensuring that the shots have the

Table 17.1 Arranging the shot

	In arranging a shot, you should be able to answer such questions as:
Broad objectives	What is the *purpose* of the shot? What is it aiming to show?
	Is it to *emphasize* a particular point or feature?
	Which is the *main* subject?
	Are we *primarily concerned* with: the subject, its relationship to another, or to its background/environment?
The actual picture	Is the shot *too close or distant* for its purpose?
	Is the *attention* reasonably localized – or split or diffused?
	Is the *composition arrangement* appropriate?
	Is the subject suitably *framed*? (Headroom, offset, edge cut-off, overcrowded frame.)
	Are subjects *clearly seen*? (Sharp, unobscured, good background contrast?)
	Is there any *ambiguity* or *distraction* in the shot?
The action	Are we aiming to show what a person is *doing* – clearly, forcefully, incidentally, not at all?
	Does action (movement, gestures) *pass outside the frame*?
	Are any *important features* or action accidentally excluded?
More specific objectives	Is the presentation to be *straightforward* or *dramatic*?
	Do we want to indicate subject *strength* or *weakness?*
	Do we aim to *reveal, conceal, mislead, puzzle*?
	What *effect, mood, atmosphere* are we seeking? (Businesslike, clinical, romantic, sinister.)
	Does the shot *relate successfully* to previous and subsequent shots?

appropriate dramatic value, attract attention to certain features, emphasize a particular point, and engender a mood.

Storyboard methods involve analyzing the script, deciding on composition arrangements, and then working out how to get them. You can use such planning as a general or specific guide. Accurate prerehearsal planning can achieve the highest standards; but it must be *realistic*, taking into account how one set-up needs to be developed from another. Most directors dislike the commitment of such planning methods and prefer a more flexible empirical approach. Although, where complex special effects are involved the storyboard may become essential.

Program opening

Establishing shots introduce the scene and the action, setting the mood, influencing your audience's frame of mind towards what you have to say and show. There are several familiar openings:

1 *The formal start.* Beginning with a 'Good evening' or 'Hello', introduces the show and gets on with it. Whether the presenter appears casual, reverent, indifferent, or enthusiastic can create an ambience directly influencing the audience's attitude.
2 *The teaser.* Showing dramatic, provocative, intriguing highlights from the production, before opening titles. Sometimes this inadvertently gives away the plot before the show even begins!
3 *The crash start.* Takes us straight into the program, which probably appears to have begun already. An automobile screams to a stop outside a store, a figure throws a bomb . . . which explodes, an alarm bell shrills, a police siren wails – the show has begun and titles roll over the chasing vehicles.
4 *The character introduction.* A rapid montage of symbols or shots of the hero in various predicaments provides an introduction to the characters we are to meet.
5 *The eavesdropping start.* The camera peers through a house window, sees a group round a TV screen, and moves in to join them.
6 *The coy welcome.* The camera dollies in to someone who is supposedly preoccupied. Realizing that we have arrived, his welcome of 'Oh, there you are!' provides informality – or nauseating artifice.
7 *The slow build-up.* The camera pans slowly round, arousing curiosity or suspense . . . until we reach a climax point (the bloodstained dagger). It is essential to avoid diminishing interest or anti-climax.
8 *The atmosphere introduction.* A series of strongly associative symbols establish the place, period, mood, or personality. On a mantleshelf: the brass telescope, ship in bottle, and well-worn uniform cap – the old sea captain is introduced long before we see him.

Subjective and objective approaches

You can use the camera either:

Objectively – in which the viewer becomes an *observer*, or
Subjectively – in which we become participants in the action.

In an *objective* role the viewer becomes an onlooker, eavesdropper, an invited audience at a vantage point, or a casual bystander. We are seeing what is going on but never addressed directly.

Subjective approaches are a regular part of TV, as performers speak straight to camera, using the screen as a communicating opening to our home. The *subjective* role can be an extremely powerful one when the camera lens moves within the scene as our eyes – or those of a character. It goes up to see an object. It moves

Fig. 17.14 The developing shot Continuous camera movement may explore the scene where intercutting would disturb the sustained mood, yet you wish to change the focus of attention reveal new information, show various reactions, etc.

among a group of dancers. It follows a guide around a museum. The concept can be used forcefully, linking us closely with the action as the camera 'climbs stairs' or jumps out of a plane. Taken to extremes, it all becomes a visual stunt as we find ourselves punched, kissed, fired at, even drowned!

In *developing (development) shots* the camera moves from one viewpoint to another; helping us to build spatial impressions and to see varying aspects of the action. This requires carefully controlled camerawork, but it can be most effective in *slow-paced* scenes involving tension, expectancy, solemn or romantic occasions.

Provided the viewers realize their intended relationship to the scene, you can change techniques between subjective and objective treatment. At times, the distinction may be very nominal.

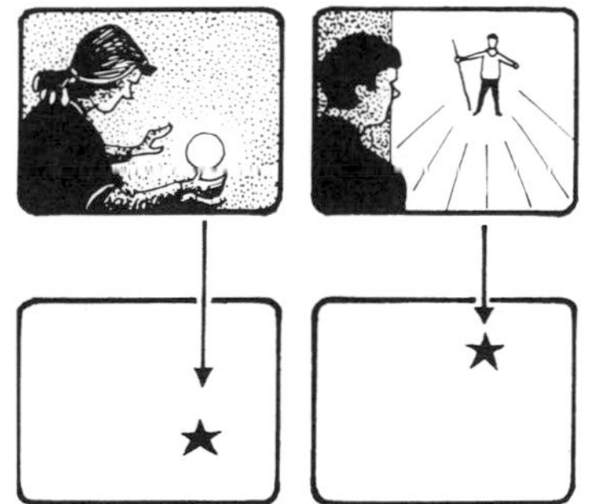

Fig. 17.15 The center of interest You can attract attention to a specific place in the shot, by the way you arrange and present the subject.

Focusing audience attention

It is as well not to overrate how much effort the audience is willing to make to evaluate your picture. You can do a great deal to localize and hold their attention by taking care how you arrange and present subjects.

Audience concentration easily lapses, so you need to continually direct and redirect their attention to hold interest along particular lines. Such redirection implies *change*. But excess or uncontrolled change can lead to confusion or irritation. Pictorial change must be clearly motivated, to allow the viewer to readjust easily to each new situation.

Fig. 17.16 Unifying interest
The eye should normally be led to (1) a single (2) unambiguous center of interest.

Fig. 17.17 Changing the center of interest
1 The eye-lines and attitudes of performers guide the viewer to a particular center of interest. If there are no visual clues; attention is not readily transferred to another point. We must look around to see who is speaking.
2 By introducing eye-line and posture clues, the transference becomes obvious.
3 In moving interest around the picture, you must take care not to draw attention to a focal point where there is no real interest or create ambiguous centers.
4 Avoid leading attention out of the frame.

Varying concentration

You have to strike a balance between *sustained concentration* (where interest soon flags) and *free association* (where minds wander):

1 In some shots you will aim to concentrate attention on a particular center of interest.
2 In others you will encourage attention to move around, on ordered detectable lines.
3 Others of a more general nature encourage free ruminative inspection; concentrating perhaps on the audio (commentary, dialogue, music).

Although you cannot expect to direct an entire audience's attention with any precision you can do a great deal to lead them in their selection and influence their associated thoughts.

Shifting visual interest

It is just as necessary to be able to shift the viewer's concentration to another aspect of the picture as it was to localize his attention originally. You can do this by readjusting any of the influences listed:

1 Having a person stand up within a seated group.
2 Give the first person weaker movements (turn away), strengthening those of the new subject (face the camera).

Fig. 17.18 How to focus visual attention
1 Avoiding spurious centers of interest, e.g. prominent lettering, tonal contrast, etc. in supporting subjects.
2 Compositional lines (real or implied).
3 Tonal gradation. The eye naturally follows gradation from dark to light areas.
4 By deliberate unbalance (tonal or linear), with the subject in the heaviest position.
5 By isolating the main subject in depth.
6 By isolating the main subject horizontally.
7 By body position.
8 By height.
9 Using a stronger part of the frame.
10 With lighting.
11, 12 By similarity between the subject and its surroundings, although too great a similarity can pall or (13, 14) lead to confusion.

3 Transfer the original emphasis (contrast, isolation, etc.) to the new subject.
4 Use linking action; first person looks to camera right . . . cut to new subject on screen right.
5 Weaken the original subjects, having them move to a new stronger subject.
6 Alter the shot size, camera height, etc.
7 Pull focus from old subject to the new.
8 Change the sound source; new person speaks instead.

Creating tension

Tension in a dramatic situation derives partly from the dialogue, story line, and interaction between characters; but it can also be considerably influenced by the way in which you present the subject:

1 Using progressively more powerful shots (intercutting closer and closer shots; lower viewpoints, gradual canting).
2 Using suspenseful music and effects.
3 Presenting ambiguous information – is the nocturnal shadow a bush . . . or prowler?

Table 17.2 Selecting camera treatment

	Mechanical purpose	*Artistic purpose*
Why pan or tilt?	To follow action. To show a series of conjoined parts. To exclude unwanted subjects. To show an area that is too large to be contained in a static shot.	To join separate items. To show spatial relationships. To show cause/effect. To transfer attention. To build up anticipation or suspense. As an introductory move.
Why elevate? (ped up)	To see over foreground objects. To see overall action.	To reduce prominence of foreground. To look down onto objects. To reduce subject strength.
Why depress? (ped down)	To frame picture with foreground objects. To obscure distant action. To obtain level shots of low subjects.	To increase their prominence. To emphasize subject strength.
Why zoom?	*See Tables 6.1 and 6.2.*	
Why dolly (track) in?	To see or emphasize detail or action. To exclude nearby subjects. To recompose shot after one of subjects has respositioned or exited. To change emphasis to another subject. To emphasize an advancing subject.	To underline an action or reaction. To emphasize subject importance. To localize attention. To reveal new information. To follow a receding subject. To provide spatial awareness. To increase tension. To create a subjective effect.
Why dolly back?	To extend field of view. To include more of subject(s). To include widespread action. To reveal new information. To include entry of a new subject. To accommodate advancing action. To withdraw from action.	To reduce emphasis. To show relationship or scale of previous shot, to the wider view (whole of subject, other subjects). To increase tension, as more significance is gradually revealed. To create surprise (e.g. reveal unsuspected onlooker). To provide spatial awareness. To create a subjective effect.
Why truck (crab)?	To follow subject moving across the scene. To reveal the extent of a subject/scene, section by section. To examine a long subject or series of subjects.	To emphasize planes in depth (parallactic movement).
Why arc?	To see subject from another viewpoint, without transitions. To exclude/include a foreground/ background subject. To realign or recompose subject(s) when it moves. To reveal new information or a new (extra) subject. To correct for inaccurate subject positions (actor off marks).	To change visual emphasis.
Why follow a moving subject?	In *close shots* – to keep it in frame. while showing reactions or detail information. In *long shots* – to show subject progress through an environment, or its relationship to other subjects.	To spatially interrelate subjects. To avoid transitions or viewpoint changes; maintaining continuity.

4 Presenting insufficient information – the audience sees the figure in the doorway . . . is it the villain?
5 Withholding information – have the pursuers arrived yet?
6 The audience knows something a character does not – the victim runs to escape . . . we know the route is blocked.
7 A character is suddenly confronted with an insurmountable problem – the stairway collapses on reaching it.
8 We anticipate what is going to happen – surely someone will burst in through that door.

The borderline between tension and bathos can be narrow. An intended climax too easily becomes an *anticlimax*. So you have to take care not to emphasize the trivial, or unintentionally to permit an emotional let-down after an emotional peak.

Pace

We might define *pace* as the rate of emotional progression. While a *slow pace* suggests dignity, solemnity, contemplation, deep emotion a *fast pace* conveys vigor, excitement, confusion, brashness, etc.

A well-balanced show continually readjusts its pace. A constant rapid tempo is exhausting; while a slow sustained one becomes dull. Pace comes from an accumulation of factors:

1 *The script*. Scene length, speech durations, phrasing, word lengths. Sharp snappy exchanges produce a faster pace than lengthy monologue.
2 *The delivery*. Fast, high-pitched, interrupted sounds provide a rapid pace compared with slow, low-pitched ones.
3 *Production treatment*. The rate of camera movement, switching, performer moves.

The eye can maintain a quicker pace than the ear. While the eye can assess, classify, evaluate almost immediately, the ear has to piece together consecutive sounds to interpret their overall meaning.

While a fast *visual* pace is readily assimilated, it is usually at the expense of less attention to the accompanying sound; unless visual changes are so rapid that the viewer ignores the information and just listens! Where emphasis is to be on the sound, visual pace generally needs to be relaxed.

Timing

There are two kinds of timing:

Mechanically – timing refers to duration checks that ensure a program keeps to schedule.

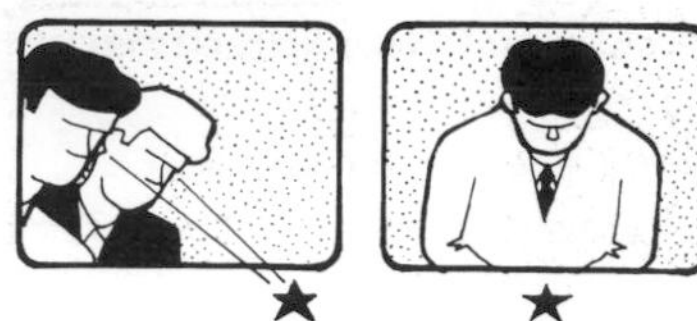

Fig. 17.19 Hidden areas of interest
If an implied center of interest falls outside the frame, or is obscured, you may either intrigue or frustrate the audience. Subtly introduced, the technique may make a change of viewpoint welcome.

Artistically – timing is choosing the right moment and duration for an action – exactly when to cut, the speed of a transition, the pause duration between a comment and a retort.

Inept timing lays wrong emphasis. It can ruin a gag, over-emphasize mechanics, and disrupt continuity.

Visual clarity

If a picture is to get its message over quickly and unambiguously your audience must be able to see relevant details easily and clearly. Aim to avoid confusion, ambiguity, obscured information, restricted visibility, distractions, and similar visual confusion.

Viewpoint

A poor viewpoint can make even the commonest subjects look unfamiliar. Occasionally you may want to do this deliberately. But you should generally aim at clear unambiguous presentation; even if, for instance, it becomes necessary for a demonstrator to handle or place items in an unaccustomed way to improve shot clarity.

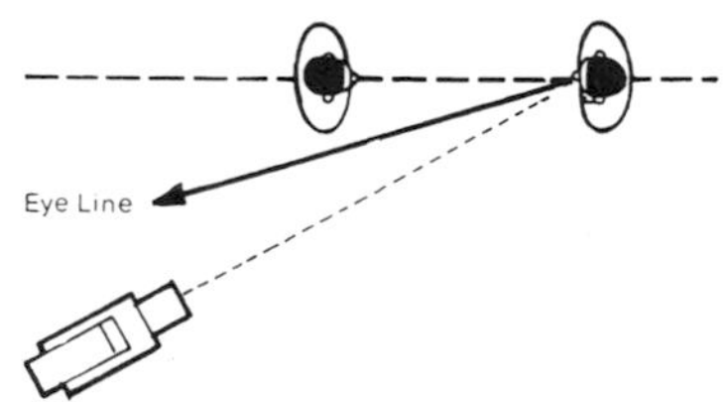

Fig. 17.20 Eyelines
Sometimes a more attractive convincing shot is obtained by having an actor cheat the eyeline. Instead of looking at the other person, turning the eyes/head along an axis roughly bisecting the centerline and the lens axis (using a distant marker). Cheated eyelines may also be used to intercut across the imaginary line (see Fig. 17.11).

Distractions

Poor lighting treatment can distract and confuse, for it can hide true contours, cause planes to merge, and cast misleading or unmotivated shadows (especially from unseen people). It can also unnecessarily create hot spots, lens flares, and specular reflections.

Strong tonal contrasts can distract, as can strongly marked detail. Where someone stands in front of a very 'busy' background the camera may inadvertently focus harder on the background (or

Fig. 17.21 Viewpoint and subject attitude
While frontal viewpoints can suggest alliance, over-shoulder reverse-angle shots can convey conflict.

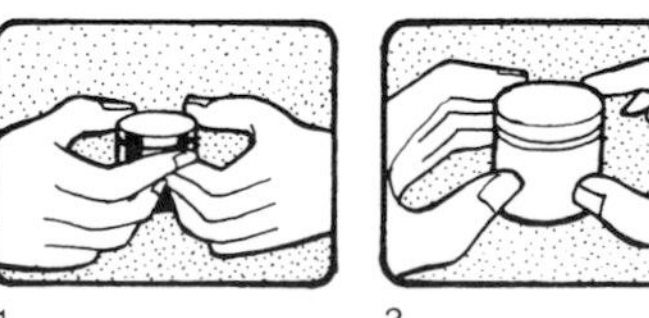

Fig. 17.22 Viewpoint and clarity
A good camera viewpoint can mean the difference between: (1) important parts of the subject being hidden, or (2) a clearly visible demonstration.

Fig. 17.23 Ambiguity
1 In a flat picture, visual ambiguity can arise whenever lines or tones in one plane merge into those of another; as when adjacent patterns of adjacent tone are similar or where scenic lines continue.
2 Take care to avoid items in the set becoming extensions of the performer.

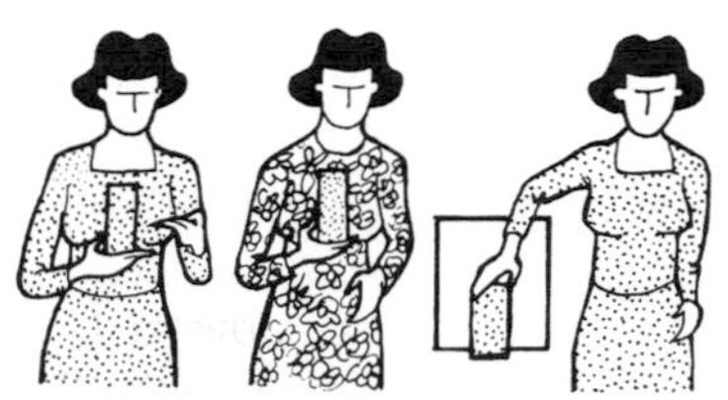

Fig. 17.24 Background contrast
Hand-held items are often shot against clothing. Ensure that this background is not similar in hue and tone, or too distracting. If necessary hold it against a more suitable background.

seem to) than on the subject itself. Close inspection of eyes, necktie, hair, etc. will show us if this is happening.

Slightly defocused details, particularly lettering that we cannot read easily, can sidetrack our attention. For similar reasons, strongly colored defocused background objects are best excluded from shot wherever possible.

Confusing and frustrating techniques

How often, when watching regular TV productions, do you experience total frustration or antagonism at the way the show is being handled? Here is a list of frequent annoyances:

1 Important subjects cannot be clearly seen – they are soft-focused, masked, or shadowed, or merge with the background.
2 Someone points to detail – it is too small or fuzzy to see.
3 An intriguing collection of items fills the table – we are shown only a couple.
4 The demonstrator shows the host a particularly interesting item – the camera never sees it in detail.
5 An item is promised us later in the show – but time runs short and it is eliminated.
6 Titling or graphics are shown – but too briefly for us to read or examine properly.
7 A demonstrator shows us how to prune a tree – but the camera gets a close shot just as he finishes.
8 We are watching interesting action – but it is cut short and now we watch a talking head instead.
9 We can hear the events taking place off camera – but the camera is still on this voluble announcer.
10 The speaker who says to camera. 'I'll be with you in just a moment' – why isn't he ready?
11 The interviewer who asks questions (quoting from notes) but is not really listening to replies.

12 The interviewer who gives the *guest* information about himself!
13 The interviewer who asks the guest questions which require only 'Yes' or 'No' replies.
14 A too-brief glimpse of a subject – followed by the commentator talking about it instead.
15 Someone speaks in a group – but the camera dwells on the previous person. (They have not yet lined up a shot of the new speaker!)
16 Wrongly cued performers – the action has already started, and we feel that we have missed seeing something important. Or the performer has finished, but the camera lingers. The performer with 'egg on the face' wonders what to do.
17 The shot that leaves us wondering what we are supposed to be looking at or where we are now.
18 The lost opportunities when the camera goes to a remote exotic location – but all we see are a few close shots against a nondescript background.

Interest or concentration patterns

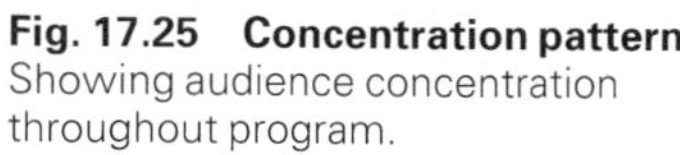
Fig. 17.25 Concentration pattern
Showing audience concentration throughout program.

Throughout any production audience interest and concentration will fluctuate; growing and subsiding. Tension and excitement build up and relax. The trick is to arrange these responses so that they come when you need them most.

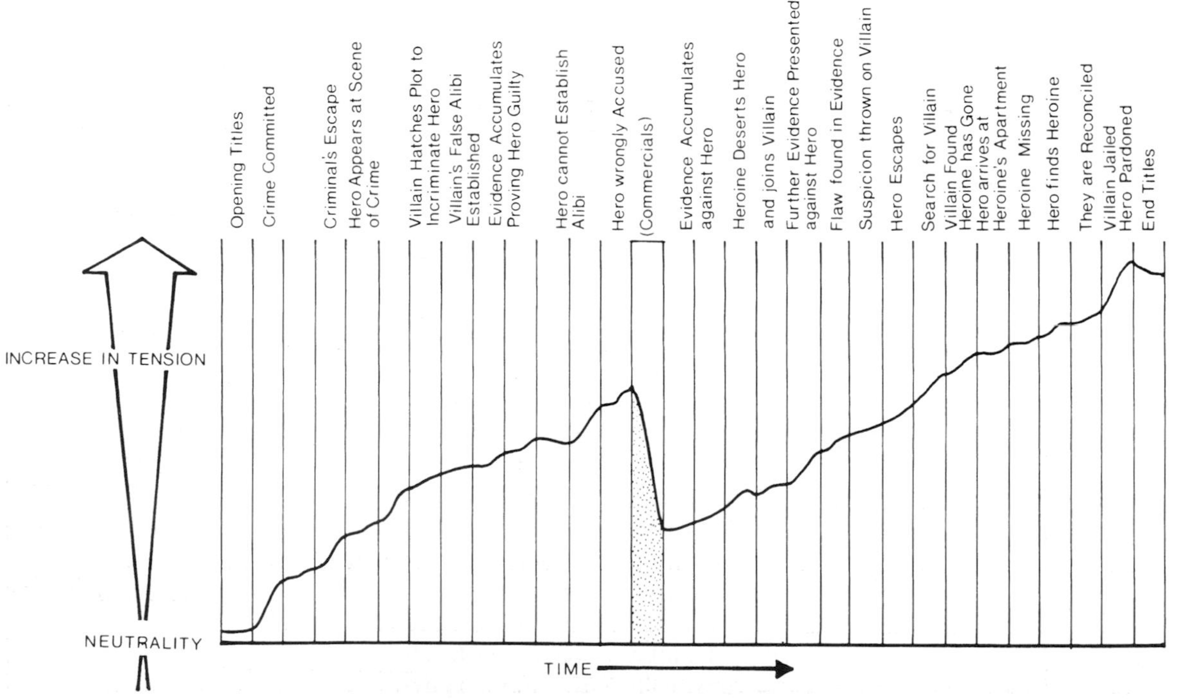

Directors and writers rely on experience and intuition rather than analysis to blend the various contributory factors:

1 *Script construction* – the order and duration of shots, their dramatic strength, plot outline, etc.
2 *Interpretation* – the performance, its delivery, etc.
3 *Production treatment* – staging, camera treatment, editing, audio treatment, etc.

But by outlining this reaction pattern as a rough graph you can see how the overall impact changes throughout the production and how the separate factors combine.

In the well-worn storyline of Figure 17.25 you can see where one seeks to build tension; where it will be allowed to fall. You aim to grip audience interest at the start of the show, introducing suitable variations, and building to an encouraging peak just before commercial breaks. You can see the bid to recapture interest immediately afterwards . . . and so on to the finale.

Both strengthening and relaxing tension require some care. After a lull, a peak appears greater. But after a long relaxed period, a

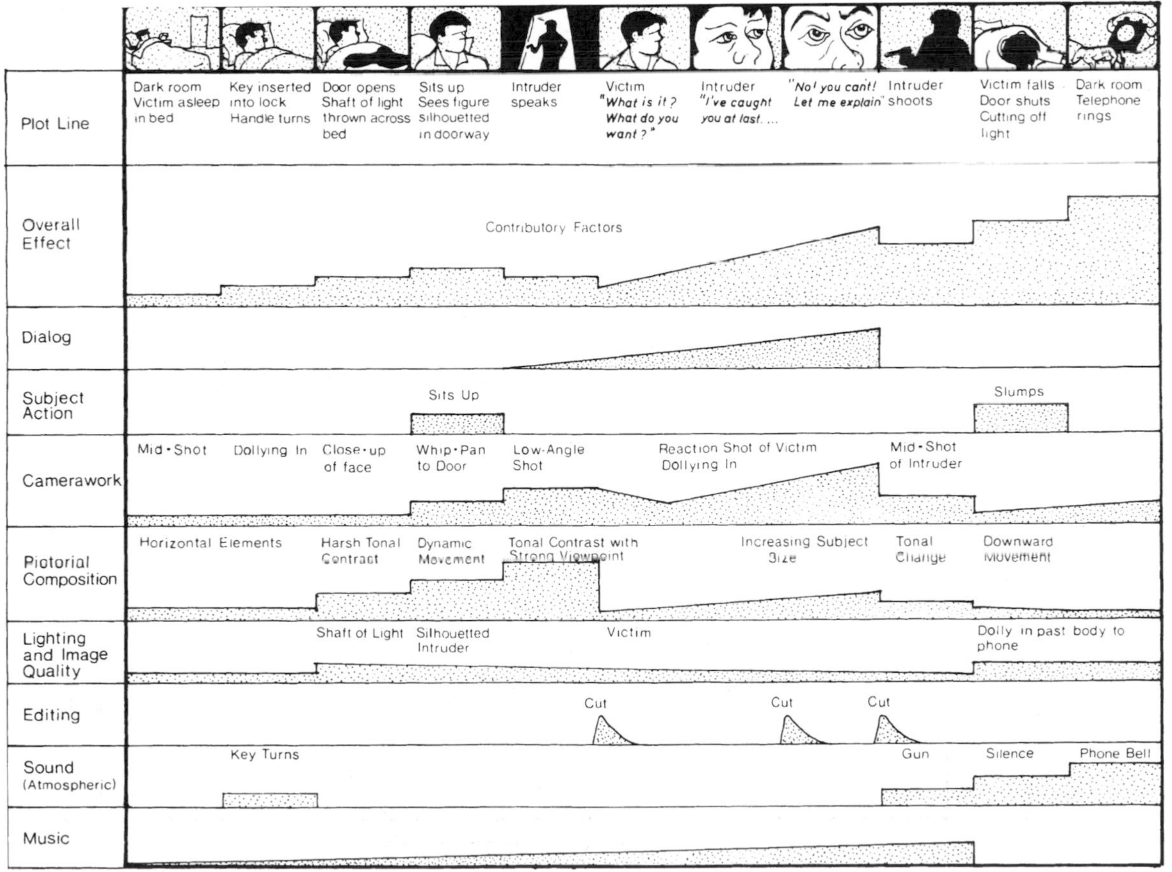

Fig. 17.26 Scene analysis
Various factors contribute to the effect of each scene.

highly dramatic peak can be intrusive, so that the viewers become overaware of their own sudden reactions; responding with laughter rather than shock. A climax may even pass them by, unless they are emotionally preconditioned to receive it.

Preferably, you build interest, concentration, or tension in a progressive series of peaks. But too slow a development can allow interest to wane. Too many climaxes eventually produce no climax at all.

Relaxation after an interest peak can lead to indifference. Again, sudden tension release can precipitate amusement, after the nervous strain of concentration.

Where action or storyline follow a recognizable pattern the viewer may grasp the point before the director has time to finish making it! To avoid this happening you can disguise the obvious

Table 17.3 Methods of focusing attention (Figure 17.18)

Exclusion	Taking close shots. Excluding unwanted subjects. Using neutral backgrounds.
Visual indication	Indication with a finger, inserted or superimposed marker (arrow, circle).
Aural indication	A verbal clue or instruction – 'Look at the black box'.
Color	Using prominent contrasting hues against neutrals or muted (pastel) colors.
Camera viewpoint	Avoid weak viewpoints (side or rear) or weakening angles (high or long shots). Concentrate interest by differential focusing or camera movement.
Composition	Using convergent line or pattern, picture balance, isolation, prominence through scale.
Contrasting the subject with its surroundings	Through differences in relative size, shape, proportions, scale, type of line, movement, association (e.g. elaborate with plain), disposition (e.g. seated with standing), etc. The area of interest might have the lightest tones or maximum contrast in the picture.
By movement	Movement attracts according to its speed, strength, and direction. Change direction during motion, or interrupt and resume, rather than maintain sustained action. According to how it is introduced, a movement can attract attention to itself (a moving hand), the *subject* (person whose hand it is), or the *purpose* of the movement (what the hand is pointing at). Remember, when the camera moves (or zooms) it can virtually create the illusion of subject movement, so drawing attention to it. Synchronizing a movement *with* dialogue, music, effects (especially the subject's own) gives it strength and draws attention to it. Having a person move on his own dialogue emphasizes both action and speech.
By subject attitude	Having performers use strong movements – upward or diagonal, stand up, play to camera, move in front of others or scenic elements.

through careful treatment; or if this is not possible, at least bypass all superfluous detail (using filmic space and time).

Sometimes attention will wander, despite great visual activity. And when quickening pace or high mobility follow a slow episode (e.g. a fast-cutting film clip after slow-speed studio shots) the viewers often find themselves *inspecting* the fast scene rather than stirred by its tempo.

If you present an excess of information or provide facts too quickly the earnest student may feel frustrated and confused at his inability to note them. But a general audience is more likely to absorb a few random aspects and then relax when they have seen enough (not, as some believe, becoming bored when they have grasped its full import).

Visual padding

Although there are occasions when you can make effective use of silence, a blank screen is an anathema! Yet many subjects have no *direct* visual element. Consider discussions, poetry, music – the emphasis is on *sound*. What does the viewer gain from *seeing* people perform! The camera shows shots of their expressions, details of instrumental fingering, etc., but these have nothing intrinsically to do with the significance or purpose of the occasion. In fact, the pictures may actually *distract* the audience, who become preoccupied with the performers' appearance, expressions, and mannerisms.

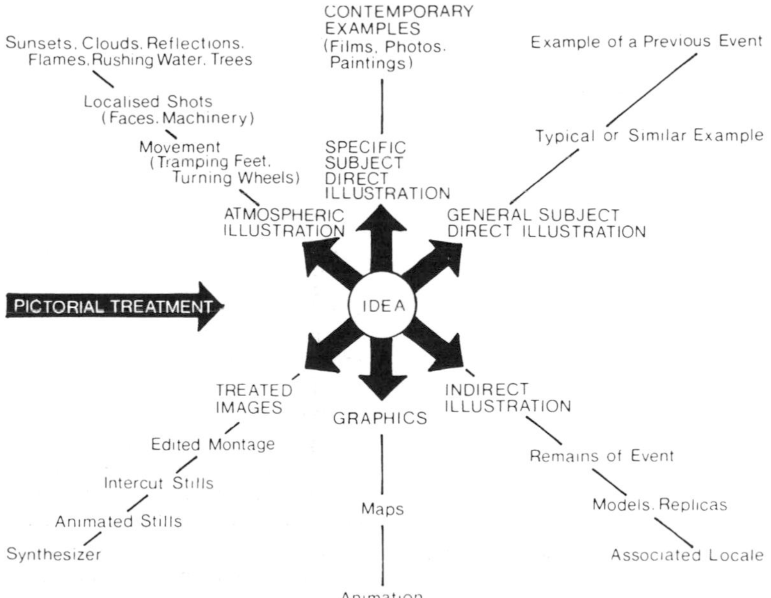

Fig. 17.27 part 1 Subject illustration – pictorial treatment Where pictures are not readily available, or a more imaginative effect is required than the direct approach, various substitutes are possible.

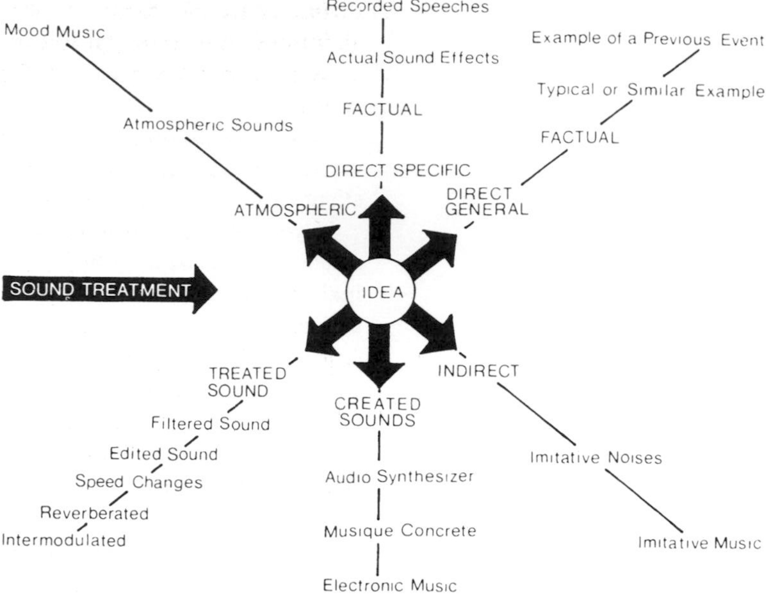

Fig. 17.27 part 2 Subject illustration – sound treatment Some possible alternatives to direct sound.

The visual problem

For some programs, directly appropriate visuals are not obvious:

1 *Abstract subjects* – philosophical, spiritual, social concepts.
2 *General, non-specific subjects* – humanity, transport, weather.
3 *Imaginary events* – hypothetical, fantasy.
4 *Historical events* – before photography, or unphotographed events.
5 *Forthcoming events* – future projects.
6 *Shooting is not possible* – prohibited or subject inaccessible.
7 *Shooting is impracticable* – too dangerous, meaningful shots not possible.
8 *Concluded events* – event now over and has not been photographed.
9 *Appropriate visuals too costly* – would involve distant travel, copyright problems.

Possible solutions

When the director cannot show the actual subject being discussed he often has to provide a suitable alternative picture – a kind of *visual padding* or 'screen filler' ('wallpaper shots').

The most economical solution, and the least compelling, is to introduce a *commentator*; who *tells* us about what we cannot *see*, as he stands at the now empty location (historical battlefield, site of crime, outside the conference hall).

Inserts in the form of photographs, film clips, VT excerpts, paintings, drawings (typically used for courtroom reports) can all provide illustrative material. Occasionally, a dramatic re-enactment is feasible.

When discussing future events you can show stills or library shots of a *previous occasion* to suggest the atmosphere, or show the principles (celebration days, processions).

You may show a *substitute* subject (not the animal that escaped but one just like it), hoping your audience does not mistakenly assume that they are seeing the actual subject.

Occasionally the camera can show the *absence* of the subject: the frame of the stolen painting; where the castle once stood.

Associated subjects are frequently used. We visit the poet's birthplace, often using stock tourist location shots. However, they may not be strictly applicable (wrong period), inaccurate (wrong part of city), or irrelevant (not architecture, but social conditions influenced his poetry). But, apart from family album snapshots or newspaper cuttings, nothing else is available!

When using library (stock) shots or stills there is always the danger that available shots will become overfamiliar through

Fig. 17.28 part 1 Cheated substitutes – the desired sequence
A fugitive climbs a cliff to escape pursuers. The viewer sees the formidable cliff, and his climb – but he dislodges a rock, and they look up.

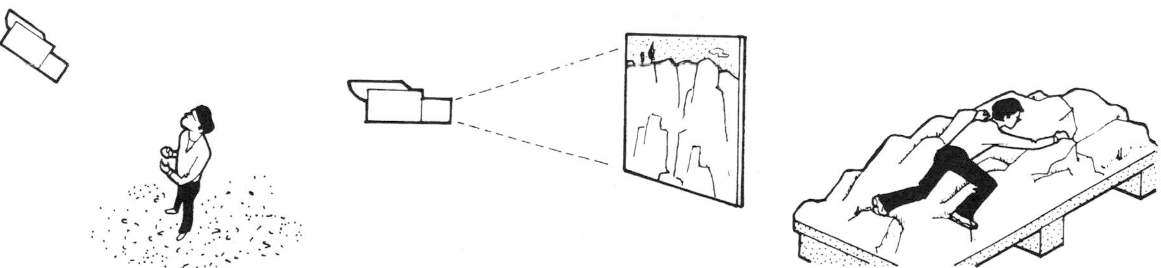

Fig. 17.28 part 2 Cheated substitutes – the studio procedure
The studio set-up is simple: A gravel-strewn floor, a photograph of a cliff face, and a surface-contoured flat over which the fugitive crawls (shot is canted to suggest vertical climbing).

repeated use. This is particularly likely with historic material, or unexpected tragedy (assassination, air crash).

Some forms of visual padding suit a variety of occasions. The same waving wheatfield can epitomize food crops, daily bread, prosperity, agriculture, the war on insect pests . . .

Abstracts can be pressed into service at almost any time! Atmospheric shots of rippling water, shadows, light reflections, into-sun flares, defocused images, shooting up into a tracery of leaves . . . all have very regular use!

Table 17.4 Continuity (Figure 17.3)

	If you are shooting discontinuously, or out of sequence (for later correct-order editing), several kinds of continuity problems can develop.
Technical continuity	The quality of intercut shots of the same action should match: similar color, brightness, contrast, tonal balance; light direction; shot height; perspective.
Pictorial continuity	Atmospheric effect should be consistent; e.g. weather conditions – not raining in one shot, dry in a reverse shot.
Environmental continuity	The location should appear consistent from different viewpoints.
Spatial continuity	The audience can lose their sense of direction, e.g. on reverse cuts. Space and distance can change with varying lens angle.
Physical continuity	The appearance of people and the scene should not change noticeably between successive shots, e.g. clothing, set dressing, props. etc.
Performance continuity/Action continuity	If you repeat an action sequence (to provide different shot lengths or viewpoints for intercutting) performers should have similar expressions and make similar gestures in each version. (Check VTR replay.)
Time continuity	There should be appropriate signs of time passing during scenes. Check how food, cigarettes, clocks, candles, etc. change.
Event continuity	Take care to avoid accidental jumps in time or place, when parts of continuous action are missing. (Use cutaways.) Avoid accidentally duplicated action. Avoid rediscovering people in a scene after they have apparently exited: or having a person unexpectedly relocated after an intermediate shot.
Relationship continuity	Avoid shot mismatches that jump-cut the subject around the screen.
Attention continuity	Make sure that centers of attention are reasonably related between shots.
Audio continuity (technically)	Ensure that audio volume and quality are compatible between successive shots.
Audio continuity (artistically)	Maintain similar atmosphere between shots in an edited scene; reverberation, background noises, effects, room tone, balance, etc.
Dialogue continuity	Uninterrupted speech when shots change during dialogue.

The illusion of time

Motion-picture editing has long since accustomed us to concepts of filmic space and time:

Filmic space – intercuts action that is concurrent at different places. As a soldier dies . . . his son is born back home.

Filmic time – omits intermediate action, condensing time and sharpening pace. We cut from the automobile stopping . . . to the driver entering an apartment.

Where all the intervening action has no plot relevance the viewer would often resent a slow pace stating the obvious.

Time lapses

You can use several devices to indicate the passage of time. Explanatory titles are direct and unambiguous, but other subtler techniques are generally preferable. For short time lapses:

1 Slow fade-out, new scene slowly fades in.
2 Cutting away from a scene, we assume time has elapsed when returning to it.
3 A time indicator (clock, sundial, burning candle) shows passage of time.
4 Lighting changes with passing time (a sunlit room gradually darkens).
5 Dissolve between before/after shots of a meal, fireplace, etc.
6 Transition between sounds with time association – nocturnal frogs and owls, to early-morning roosters and birdsong.
7 Defocus shot, cut or mix to another defocused shot and then refocus.

For longer time lapses:

1 A calendar sheds leaves or changes date.
2 Seasonal changes – from winter snow to spring flowers.
3 Changes in personal appearance – beard growth, ageing, fashion changes.
4 New to old – dissolving from a fresh newspaper . . . to a yellow crumpled discarded version.

Flashbacks

A familiar device, the *flashback* turns back time to see events before the present action for reminiscive, explanatory, or comparative purposes. Typical methods include reversed time-lapse conventions (e.g. the old becomes new again) or explanatory dialogue during 'mist', edge diffusion, ripple, or defocus dissolves. Nowadays, a very brief *flash cut-in* (½–2 seconds long) conveys recognition or moments of memory recall.

Interscene devices

As well as the usual editing transitions (cut, dissolve/mix, wipe) and their derivations (defocus and ripple dissolves), you can use various interscene devices to link sequences.

1 *Blackout.* A performer moves up to block out the lens. He (or another subject) moves away, revealing a new scene. A balloon is used similarly, being burst to show the new scene
2 *Pan away.* The camera turns from the action area to a nearby subject. Panning back, we now see different action (or appearance), for time has passed.

Fig. 17.29 Crowds
Crowds can be simulated by selected viewpoints:

1 Showing part of the crowd.
2 Using foreground (real, dummy, cut-outs).
3 Inserting people electronically into a recorded scene.

3 *Bridging subject.* Associative material interconnects two scenes: shots of wheels turning to imply travel, swirling mists to form an atmospheric transition.
4 *Decorative bridge.* Abstract forms in light or shadow between scenes. Moving patterns – kaleidoscope, spirals, whip pan. Digital video effects are increasingly used here: mosaic tile, posterization treatment, explosions, etc.
5 *Matching shots.* The close-up ending one scene (wristwatch) dissolves to a matching shot (bus station clock) in the next.

Deliberate disruption

The idea of deliberately cutting away from the main action to look at incidental happenings nearby may seem somewhat incongruous. Yet, if appropriately introduced, this disruption offers valuable production opportunities. Provided the viewers do not feel that they are missing vital information or robbed of exciting action, the technique can heighten interest and enthusiasm.

Cutaway shots (intercut shots)

By cutting from the main action to *secondary activity* or *associated subjects* (e.g. spectator reactions), you can:

1 Join shots that are unmatched in continuity or action.
2 Remove unwanted, unsuccessful, dull or excess material.
3 Suggest a time lapse, to compress or expand time.
4 Show additional explanatory information (*detail shots*).
5 Reveal the action's environment.
6 Show who a person is speaking to; how another person is responding (reaction shots).
7 Show what the speaker is seeing, talking about, or thinking about.
8 Create tension, to give dramatic emphasis.
9 Make comment on a situation (cutting from a diner to a pig at trough).

Interviews can be shot using a continuous intercut multi-camera set-up or as a one-camera treatment. A separate series of cutaway shots (*cutaways*, *nod shots*) are often recorded *afterwards*, in which the interviewer and interviewee are seen in singles or over-shoulder shots, mutely smiling, nodding, 'reacting', looking interested. When edited in (to disguise cuts, continuity breaks, or to add visual variety), the subterfuge appears quite natural. Without such intermediates, any continuously held shot would *jump frame* when edited (dissolves may improve the disruption).

Cut-in or *inserts* may also be used when reshooting parts of the action from another camera set-up (different shot size, or angle).

Reaction shots/partials/cut-in shots

By skilfully concealing information you can prime the imagination and arouse curiosity. Instead of showing an event, you demonstrate its effect.

1 *Reaction shot*. The door opens . . . we see the victim's horror-stricken face, not the intruder.
2 *Partial shot*. A switchblade opens . . . is moved out of frame . . . we hear the victim's cry . . . then silence.
3 *Cut-in shot*. We watch the victim's cat drinking milk . . . to sounds of a fight and a body falling . . . the victim's hand comes into frame, upsetting the milk dish.

This technique can provide maximum impact with minimum facilities, conveying information by implication rather than direct statement. It aims to intrigue and tantalize. Ineptly introduced, though, it can frustrate.

The recorded insert

Occasionally during a studio production we may cut away from studio cameras' pictures to show film or videotape instead. There are several reasons why we might want to do this:

- *To illustrate a lecture, demonstration or talk*; e.g. shots of a trip down the Amazon.
- *To imply that the studio setting is in a particular location* (showing stock shots of moorland 'outside the house').
- *To 'authenticate' a setting.* We see a small boarded room in the studio. A stock shot of a ship is inserted, so we accept that this is a ship's cabin.
- *To show environments that could not be re-created effectively in the studio* (e.g. a typhoon).
- *To extend action.* You can have a person walk through a door in the studio set (an apartment) out into the street (on film).
- *To extend settings.* Shooting a *partial setting* in the studio (e.g. a shop doorway) we cut to the complete street location in the film insert.
- *Reducing the number of studio settings.* Where studio space is too limited for the required number of settings, additional scenes can be insert-filmed.
- *Once-only action.* Prefilming or videotaping is essential where action might prove unsuccessful in the studio (for example, involving animals); or take too much time during the videotaping period (an elaborate make-up change); or is too dangerous (fire); or is non-repeatable (an explosion); or is very critical (an accurately thrown knife).
- *Visual effects.* To produce time-lapse effects, reversed action, transformations, etc.
- *Animation sequences.* These may be cartoon or animated still-life.

Fig. 17.30 Staging distractions
Various distractions can appear in shot. Here is a particularly disastrous collection!

1. Unexplained, distracting object in shot.
2. Cable in shot.
3. Visible surface damage on flat.
4. Shadow of someone out of shot.
5. Wall-picture not straight.
6. Light reflection.
7. Camera reflection visible in table picture.
8. Multiple shadows from lamp fitting.
9. Distracting light patch.
10. Wall mirror appears as 'halo'.
11. Wrinkle in background surface.
12. Shooting off the set!
13. Obtrusive foreground prop.

- *To include performers not otherwise available.* Filming persons who could not attend the taping session (e.g. overseas guests).
- *Situations where effective studio staging is impractical.* Recording location exteriors, spectacle, etc. where studio replicas would be impractical or less effective.

Library shots (stock shots)

These are short film (or video) sequences of illustrative material, held in an organization's archives or rented from specialist libraries. *Library shots/stock shots* are inserted into a program where it would be impracticable or uneconomic to shoot new material. These short clips cover a very wide field, including news events, location shots, manufacturing processes, natural history, personalities, stunts, etc. etc. They are widely used to illustrate talks, demonstrations, newscasts, and to provide atmospheric and environmental shots for drama.

The picture quality of library shots can be variable in color, blemishes, and definition – they may not cut into studio shots unobtrusively. Also, available library shots can become too familiar, particularly when they are the only record of an event.

Where only monochrome shots are available and the program content is appropriate, these clips may be tinted (sepia, blue, red-orange). This is achieved by using a color synthesizer, by adjusting color balance, or using 'TARIF' controls. Snow scenes and night shots may still prove convincing in black and white, although transmitted in a color system.

Library shots are often run mute (silent), and new effects or music substituted for any original soundtrack.

The illusion of spectacle

Budgets do not generally permit lavish staging. Yet occasions arise when you want to create an impressive illusion of space, grandeur, and spectacle. Several methods are available.

■ **Library shots (stock shots)** By intercutting existing filmed library shots with limited studio action (often close shots) it is possible to build up extremely convincing illusions. Where highly dramatic spectacle is required, as in battle scenes, hurricanes, volcanic eruptions, mobs, earthquakes, floods, this is usually the only solution.

However, available library shots may not be exactly suitable for your purpose (contents, quality, viewpoint, time of day, unwanted or spurious aspects included). It might even be necessary to reorganize the studio treatment to suit the library shot!

■ **Direct imitation** A complete or *partial* replica of part of the scene (e.g. a stone wall) is intercut with location material or library shots (the actual castle).

■ **Indirect imitations** Here an environment provided by electronic insertion (chroma key, CSO), rear projection, photo backings, or glass shot, etc. is conjoined with a localized studio setting. For example: an automobile in the studio is inserted into a filmed shot of a highway; an impressive ceiling (a graphic) appears to be part of a studio set.

■ **Cheated substitute** Montage can create an illusion by intercutting small representative parts of the action to convey a composite impression. Ingenious, imaginative, and most effective, if properly handled, you must ensure that the component parts are completely integrated. For instance, you can build up a dramatic impression of a battle simply by rapidly intercutting close shots of details in war photographs to an audio background of battle noises.

18 Production organization

As you would expect, in the real world there are a number of ways of tackling a production. We meet at one end of the spectrum, the '*Give us a good shot, Joe*' approach, largely relying on the initiative of the camera team to offer up shots for selection. At the other extreme, there are directors who know precisely what results they want, and arrange performers and cameras to get exactly that. Much depends on the artistic and operational standards demanded and on the production crew's experience.

Fundamentals

Basically, organization must be influenced by three main elements:

- The action.
- The camera viewpoint.
- Limitations/restrictions.

The action

Can you arrange the action, adjusting it to suit the production? In a drama, the actors' positions, actions, moves, will normally follow a carefully rehearsed format that the director has arranged.

On the other hand, when shooting a documentary it may be a matter of grabbing opportunities as they arise. The camera is usually an onlooker, selecting from whatever is available. In some situations (e.g. in a laboratory interview) you may be able to initiate when or where someone moves but local circumstances can dictate one's approach.

The camera viewpoint

Are you free to position the camera wherever you select, and can you move it around? Again, the answers will depend on where and what you are shooting. The camera may be confined to a prearranged position (as at many public events), or able to move freely.

The action may be virtually *static* (e.g. at a public meeting) making it quite difficult to present a succession of interesting shots;

or the situation may be *dynamic* (e.g. a race) in which the subject(s) are traveling quickly and require a fast-moving camera to keep up with them.

Limitations/restrictions

There are also a number of obvious factors that determine what you can do, and how you go about the production, such as: budget restrictions; the amount of time available; the time of day or season; weather; limitations or shortages (of equipment or personnel); the experience and adaptability of the performers/talent/anchors/commentators/interviewers; any local intrusions (e.g. location noises) . . .

Production approaches

Let's assume that you are in a two-or three-camera studio and about to shot the action. How do you arrange the cameras to get the most successful shots, and how do you organize the talent that is going to appear in front of the cameras? Presumably you could just say '*CUE THEM TO START*' and point the cameras at the action! But results would, at the very least, be haphazard and unpredictable! You need a strategy of some kind; a system that enables you to get effective shots that convey the nature and purpose of the show to your audience. There are several methods in regular use, each with its advantages and drawbacks:

Camera

- *Static cameras at strategic viewpoints* – In this approach the director usually places a camera in a central position, accompanied by one or two cameras angled over to the sides, to take oblique shots of the action. The cameras remain fixed, varying their shot sizes by zooming. Using the production switcher, the director intercuts between these shots Particularly where the action is not specifically organized, the off-the-cuff shots may include too many compromises (e.g. one person masking another; ugly or inappropriate composition).

  In another arrangement, the cameras have *dedicated vtrs* (i.e. a videotape recorder attached to *each* camera throughout), and the director edits selected shots together during a postproduction session.
- *Repositioned strategic viewpoints* – Similar to the previous approach, but cameras may move to *new viewpoints* as the show develops. For example, in a cookery demonstration a camera that has concentrated on close-ups of food preparation (while the main camera takes a wider view) now moves over to the oven to see food being removed.

- *Changing viewpoints* – Cameras move around to a series of planned positions as the action varies. This not only conveys a better overall impression of the setting but allows cameras to get clear shots of the action (what people are doing; reaction shots) and to develop consistently effective composition. At the same time, the camera movements, while on shot, can make an important psychological impact on the audience.

  This refined approach requires imagination, foresight, and careful anticipatory planning, and is most likely to be used in drama productions. We shall be looking at this technique in some detail in a moment.

Action

- *Free action* – Here performers 'do their own thing' and the cameras follow the action as the director selects from available shots. When dealing with inexperienced performers, or unplanned action this situation may be unavoidable.
- *Guided action* – Where necessary, the director (via the floor manager) explains to a performer which camera is taking their shots (perhaps told to look for the *tally light*), and shown how to work to the camera (e.g. when holding up an item for a CU shot).
- *Controlled performance* – Here all the dialogue and action is planned and specified. In this situation the talent moves to specific places (accurate marks), looks in arranged directions, and carries out specified action. The performer (actor, host) is usually experienced, and may have learned scripted material (*lines*), or reads from a prompter, or repeats from an earpiece prompt. Because this performance is normally predictable and repeatable, it allows very precise camera treatment.

Unplanned productions

Total unpredictability is not adventurous. It creates needless stress and unreliable results. If people do not have a clear idea of what is happening you must not be surprised if there is no chair for the extra guest, or a film insert for the program is not ready, or the lighting is inappropriate, the camera has a wrong shot, or you cannot hear the speaker.

But what do we do about those situations that *cannot be planned* – where there is insufficient time or we cannot know what the shot opportunities are going to be until we are actually there, on the spot? This can happen in productions as diverse as documentaries or last-minute news breaks. In the studio an impromptu show will quickly resolve itself into a regular format of some sort; but away on location, one faces the unknown. Shooting hopefully and assuming that it can all be '*put together in the edit*' is a recipe for trouble.

Working on an unplanned situation one has to make rapid systematic decisions guided by whatever advice is available. First, you must decide on the most important features of the scene and check out the most appropriate viewpoints. A shot of the village street may be interesting but a vantage point that shows the threatening volcano in the background gives it a very different significance!

Which aspects do you want to emphasize? Are there others to be avoided; e.g. crowds of waving sightseers? How are you going to shoot the main action? Is it best shown from several angles or would that result in missing shots of the event while you move the camera around? This may be an occasion where interviews with eye-witnesses or onlookers are important.

As well as the main event you should also make a point of shooting extra material that will anticipate editing problems and help the program flow. *Cutaway shots* (e.g. of spectators or added people working on the site) will allow taped material to be unobtrusively cut, rearranged or added during editing. (A spontaneous gesture or a change of expression may reveal more in a moment than a whole page of prepared scripting.) A few generalized shots (such as a slow pan around the site) can be introduced into the final edited tape to fill the screen where a voice-over commentary needs time to expand (e.g. explaining a point, outlining background, giving data). These *supplementaries* can also include identifying shots such as a roadside name, a signpost, or any local features that the audience is likely to recognize. *Pickup shots* in which the commentary is continuous as the shot changes may create a better feeling of continuity, and avoid what might otherwise appear as a sequence of disjointed shots (*see Digests*).

So we see that even where it has not been practicable to plan a detailed shooting schedule it is possible to assemble material of the right kind that can be woven into an interesting, even breathtaking sequence.

Regular formats

There are a number of regular formats: interviews, panel discussions, piano and instrumental performances, singers, and newscasts. These are usually familiar to the production team and meaningful shooting variations are limited. What the performer is saying (or playing) is more important than straining to achieve new and original shot development. Consequently, such productions follow recognizable lines, so that the director often starts off with planned viewpoints and then introduces a particular treatment as it becomes desirable.

Planning for regular productions may largely be a matter of co-ordinating staff and facilities, ensuring that film or VT inserts are available (with known timing and cue points); graphics, titles, etc. are prepared, and any additional material organized. The produc-

Fig. 18.1 part 1 Regular formats – piano recital
The basic range of pictorially attractive shots is limited when presenting a piano performance.

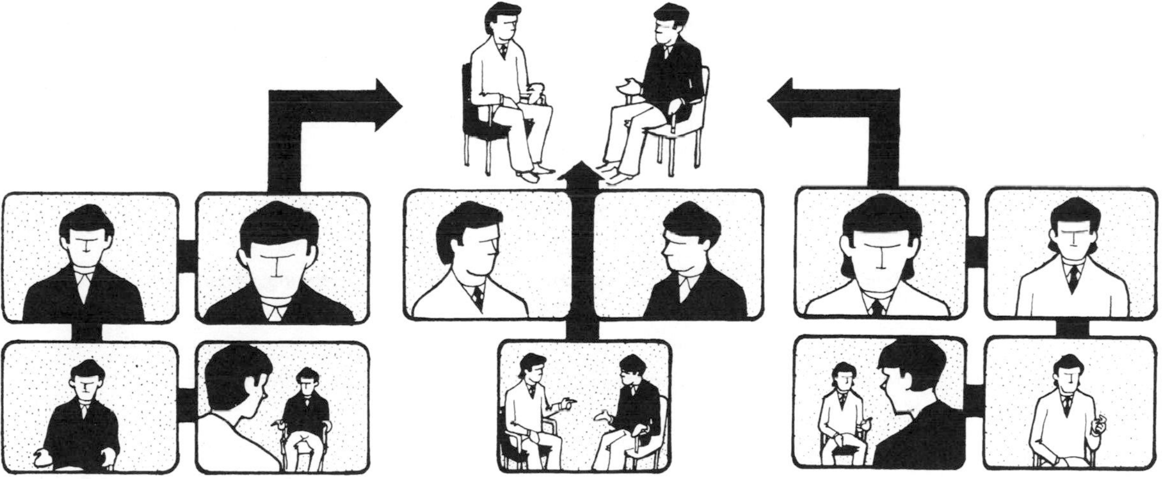

Fig. 18.1 part 2 Regular formats – formal interview
In a formal interview, the number of effective shots is relatively few.

tion itself may be based upon a series of key shots and spontaneous on-the-fly decisions.

Complex productions

Whether you are shooting in the studio or on location, time is money and must be used efficiently. While smaller shows may get by with a preliminary talk-over a few days before the production date, for

Table 18.1 Production organization

Program concepts	Idea potentials, objectives, potential audience, market, saleability, probable duration.
Executive decisions	Selecting *above-the-line* personnel (production: director, writer, etc.). Budget allocation. Production scheduling (deadlines). Preproduction publicity.
Scripting	Theme, coverage, style, research/advisor. Script editing (evaluating content and practicability). Script conference/rewrites. Director's visualization.
Organizing talent	Contacts, auditions, interviews, casting, contracts. Organization/preparation of performers. Read-through rehearsals, costume/make-up preliminaries.
Organization of inserts	Any *pre-studio* photography, filming, taping. (Arrangements for shooting these: copyright clearances, facility fees, access permissions, permits, insurance, scheduling, staffing, editing, etc.) Selection of illustrative inserts (film clips, VT, stills. Graphics and titles, Musical inserts (on disc. on tape, performed live). Any equipment for demonstrations (construction or hire).
Staffing	Coordinating services of *below-the-line* personnel (technical, operational, facilities).
Production paperwork	Requisitions. Scripts (draft, rehearsal, and camera script). Rundown sheet, camera cards, etc.
Organizing artistic services	Staging, costume/wardrobe, make-up.
Organizing technical services	Cameras, lighting, audio, telecine, VTR, special effects.
Organizing facilities	Loan/hire of equipment. Storage, transport, catering, accommodations (dressing rooms). Prompters, audience arrangements (tickets, seating, warm-up).
Pre-studio rehearsals	Rehearsal of dialogue, moves, action; treatment preparation.
Studio rehearsals	Camera rehearsals (finalization of action, video, and audio treatment).
Videotape recording	Straight-through, discontinuous, or compilation recording.
Postproduction work	Off-line selection, organization, and editing of video recording. Audio sweetening.
Review and transmission	Evaluation of recording.
Follow-up	Logs/reports. Publicity/billing/promotion. Correspondence, ratings.

Table 18.2 Typical considerations in technical planning

Talent	Cast discussed, re costume and make-up requirements (styles, fitting, etc.).
Staging	Style, treatment of sets. Staging plan: details of set structures, scenic changes, storage, audience seating. Special visual effects (physical, video, lighting). Special props. Safety precautions, regulations, etc.
Action	Director indicates possible performer positions, action, business.
Cameras	Number of cameras, types of mountings, main positions for each scene, probable moves. Any camera accessories (special lenses, etc.). Specialists estimate feasibility of anticipated treatment (checking sufficient working space for cameras/booms, time for moves, cable routing, etc.).
Lighting	Discussion of lighting treatment feasibility, relative to: scenic design, action, sound pick-up, time/equipment/manpower availability. Discussion of pictorial effects, atmosphere, etc. Discussion of picture matching to inserts (film or VT).
Audio	Similar discussion to '*Lighting*'. Considering audio pick-up methods, potential problems. Audio inserts discussed (prerecorded library effects, spot effects, music).
Effects required	Special effects, staging effects, lighting effects, optical effects, chroma key (CSO), video effects, special sound effects, etc.
Artwork/graphics/titles	Displays, graphics, maps, charts, models, etc.
Further technical facilities	Equipment organization, re filming or pre-studio videotaping. Technical resources required: telecine, videotape, video disc, slide scanner, picture monitors, prompters, cuing facilities, etc.
Scheduling	Pre-studio/recording. Experimental sessions.
Pre-studio rehearsals	Read-through, block action, dry run (technical run).
Studio rehearsal/recording	Production approach: live, live-on tape, rehearse/record, scene-by-scene, etc. Camera rehearsal (times and arrangements, meal breaks). Technical periods (camera line-up, relighting, resetting scenery). Recording schedule.
Editing	Scheduling and facilities. Audio sweetening. Postproduction video effects.

more complex projects comprehensive planning is essential. The team must be briefed and organized, and this requires discursive agreement; for there are sundry factors to consider, such as time estimates, costing, manpower, safety, union agreements, etc.

Planning preliminaries

Planning begins with *script study*; the director reading and visualizing with his budget, facilities, and personnel in mind.

Some directors rely on the set designer to produce an environment for action and then arrange performers within this setting. Others indicate the strategic features or staging format they require, and from that briefing the designer interprets and builds workable arrangements.

After preliminary discussion, the designer produces a rough scale plan of the various settings; often on separate pieces of overlay (tracing) that can be moved around the studio staging plan for optimum layout. This may include sketches, reference photographs, and preliminary elevations.

Those responsible for studio operations, including technical organization, cameras, lighting, audio, make-up, costume, etc., may be involved at these early stages.

Treatment breakdown

This is the point at which directors' techniques diverge. For many shows, the action is predetermined by the program format – the talent is going to enter down a staircase and sit in prearranged chairs to be interviewed; then move over to a table, to talk about the collection of widgets displayed there. The shots are straightforward enough. The director checks over the studio plans, and with an eye to the program script, places cameras in regular positions that will suit typical treatment (cover shots, group shots, singles, reaction shots). Any variations can be worked out during rehearsals.

But if you are directing a more involved production, planning will need to be more detailed. You begin by reading through the script, with the agreed staging arrangements in mind (i.e. the sets, and their layout in the studio). As you read, you visualize each scene in turn, and consider such matters as *whether talent is going to make an entrance or exit; what they are going to do; where they will be doing it; whether they will need props (e.g. a map). Are they going to speak to the camera? Are other people in the scene, and what are they doing? Are they going to move around (e.g. up to a window in the set)? . . . and so on.* All very obvious, but it will not just happen. Everything has to be planned, arranged, and learned.

The next step is to systematically block out the action. '*Would it, for example, be better if the hostess is seen entering the room and moving over to the desk, or should we discover her already seated? As the show is*

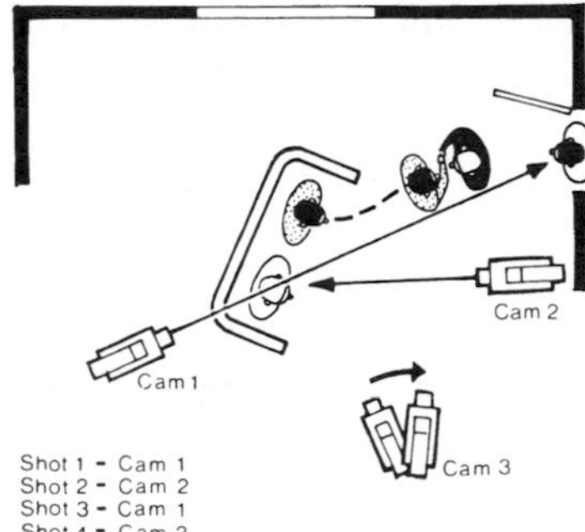

Fig. 18.2 Action treatment
The plan summarizes the camera treatment for a brief scene (see text).

about dress design, would it be preferable if the audience saw her fashionable ensemble as she enters rather than opening with a 'head and shoulders shot' at the desk? Is the idea of a desk too formal anyway? Would an easy chair be preferable?. . .'

Having considered the action, what sorts of shots would be appropriate and where would the cameras be to get them? If Camera 1 moves into the setting to get a close shot of the item they are discussing, is it now going to be in Camera 2's shot? Would it be better to tape the item afterwards, and edit in an *insert* shot during 'post'? And so one builds up a continuous succession of shots, noting them in the script margin, either as abbreviated reminders or as tiny scribble sketches. The same situation can often be tackled in various different but equally successful ways. Let us look at an example for a dramatic production:

Returning husband enters door, wife has unexpected guest.

This could be broken down as:

1 Husband enters door, hangs up hat . . . MLS shows who it is, yet orientates audience.
2 Wife looks up, greeting him . . . Medium two-shot showing her with guest.
3 Husband turns and sees guest . . . CU of husband's reaction.
4 Guest rises, walk to greet husband . . . From medium two-shot; pans with guest, dollying in for tight two-shot of guest and husband.

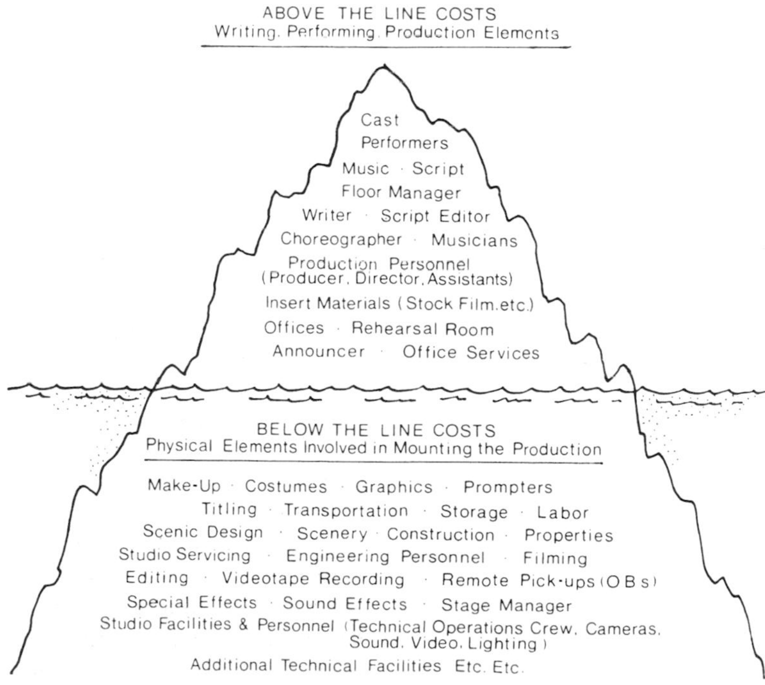

Fig. 18.3 Budget
Accurate cost estimation and accounting are essential in TV organization, despite the great diversity of the various contributions. Budgets are usually related to the concepts of 'above' and 'below' the line. These differentiate between the 'writing, performing, and production elements', and the various 'back-up' services and physical elements involved in mounting the production.

The interpretation could have been simpler. Its impact would have been different.

1 Husband enters door, hangs up hat . . . Over-shoulder long shot between wife and guest, showing entrance. Watch husband's reactions, tightening shot as he walks to guest.
2 As guest stands . . . Cut to frontal two-shot of guest and wife greeting him. Zoom in to guest. Intercut CU of guest and husband.

Developing the camera plan

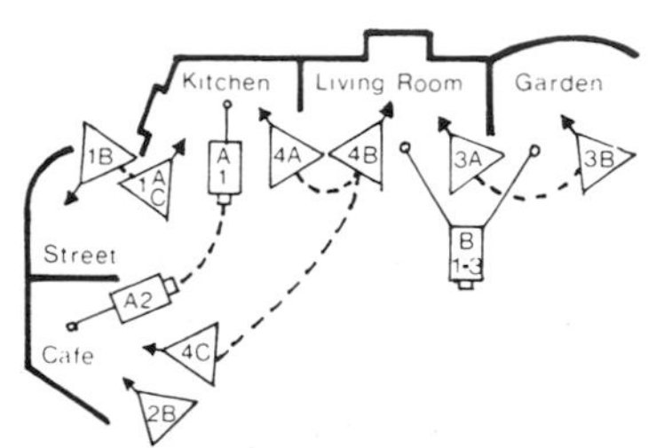

Fig. 18.4 The Camera Plan
Position of cameras 1, 2, 3, 4 are successively marked (1A, 1B). Positions of sound booms A, B, are successively marked (A1, A2).

Now comes the moment when you have to transform program ideas into the mechanics of reality. To plan the camera and sound boom's positions we need the scale *staging plan (floor plan, ground plan, setting plan*) provided by the designer. Our main aid here is a triangle of transparent plastic marked with typical camera lens angles (often called a '*shot plotter*') – or a protractor. With its apex placed in the planned camera position you can see how much of the scene is covered by different lens angles. You can also judge the types of shot (CU, full-length, etc.) a certain lens angle will give – but more of that later ('Calculating shots'). You then mark these camera positions on the plan as, for example, 1A for Camera 1), 2A–2B (to show Cam 2's position move)

There will usually be a sound boom, which may be central or to one side; positioned to follow the action without obstructing nearby cameras (marked as A1).

The resultant *production plan (camera plan)* together with margin action notes or sketches will form the basis for all technical planning and subsequent rehearsals. Even the biggest productions can be analyzed into shots or sequences in this way.

Production planning meeting

Whether the various specialists involved in the studio operations meet with the director and the set designer at this stage or beforehand, depends on the complexity of the production. They examine the staging proposals and production treatment; evaluate, discuss, anticipate practical problems, and so on. They outline their own proposed contributions – lighting treatment, audio effects, costume details, etc.

Following this meeting, they then carry through their own organizational procedures (documentation, costing, manpower, scheduling, equipment selection), and the designer issues the agreed *version of the staging plan (floor plan, ground plan, setting plan*).

The production planning meeting forms the basis for efficient economic teamwork. Problems anticipated and overcome at this stage prevent last-minute compromises. Camera cable routing, for example, is a typical potential hazard. Cables get snarled up, can impede other cameras, or drag around noisily. So directors may move around scale card cutouts of cameras (perhaps cord-attached to simulate cables) when devising their camera plans.

Much depends, of course, on the type of show you are working on, how it is to be recorded, elaboration of treatment, any special set-ups (chroma key), rehearsal time, editing facilities, etc.

In a *live* or live-on-tape show you must allow time for people, cameras, and sound booms to move between situations; time to cover any costume or scene changes, and to reposition equipment or furniture. Discontinuous shooting overcomes such problems; although continuity and editing factors then arise.

The script

Semi-scripted show

For ad-lib shows, discussions, interviews, variety, compilation shows, and demonstrations it is normal to use *outline scripts*. This script lists the talent involved, facilities being used, graphics (slides), film and VT inserts (identifying sections, giving durations). Dialogue is only included in detail for introductory announcements, and commentary containing cue-lines (for cuing inserts, editing breaks, or redeploying cameras).

Fully scripted show

Here the script develops in several stages:

1 *Preliminary script/draft/outline script/writer's script*. Initial submitted full-page script (dialogue and action) before script editing.
2 *Rehearsal script*. Script prepared for TV and used for pre-studio rehearsal. Script details the locales (settings), characters, action, talent directives, dialogue (Table 18.3).
3 *Camera script*. A revised script for camera rehearsals, augmented with details of production treatment: cameras and audio, cues, transitions, stage instructions, set changes (Table 18.4).

TV scripts follow several 'standard' layouts. The preferred version uses two vertical columns, with picture treatment (cameras, switching) on the *left*, action and dialogue on the *right*, together with stage instructions and lighting/effects cues. Some studios prefer a *single-column* cinematic format, with transitions in a left margin, and all video and audio information in a single main column. Directors often hand-mark this version with their own

Table 18.3 The rehearsal script

SCENE	INT./ EXTR	LOCATION	TIME OF DAY
3.	INT.	LOUNGE	NIGHT

(GEORGE ENTERS. WALKS TO TABLE SWITCHES ON LAMP.)

GEORGE: (CALLS) The lights are OK in here. It must be your lamp

(GEORGE TAKES GUN FROM DRAWER.)

SLIPS IT INTO HIS POCKET: PULLING OUT TELEGRAM. HOLDS IT UP.

'SORRY CANNOT COME WEEKEND, BRIAN SICK, WRITING . . . JUDY.'

(HAND SCREWS IT UP AND THROWS INTO FIRE.)

(DOOR OPENS: EILEEN ENTERS.)

EILEEN: Really, these people are too bad. They promised to be here tonight. Look how late . . .

GEORGE: It's probably the storm that has delayed them. They'll be here all right.

(EILEEN SITS ON COUCH: GEORGE JOINS HER.)

EILEEN: If Judy knows you're here, it'll take wild horses to keep her away.

GEORGE: How many more times do I have to tell you . . .

EILEEN: Why do you keep pretending?

LIGHTNING FLASH

GEORGE: I've warned you. You'll go too *far*.

instructional symbols indicating transitions and shots. But for more complex productions this is less easily followed than a two-column format.

The *full script* is not, as some people believe, an artistically inhibiting document that commits everyone concerned to a rigid plan of procedure. It can be modified as the need arises. It simply informs you about what is expected at each moment of the production. Studio rehearsal time is too precious to use up explaining basic mechanics as you go. Far better to have a detailed script that shows the exact moment for the lighting change, to cue the film, or introduce the superimposition. The full script is a plan of campaign, that has details added to it as the production develops.

For some types of show the outline script is quite sufficient; in fact, any attempt to include 'pseudo information', such as the entire dialogue for a film insert, would usually be pointless. (The duration and 'in and out cues' would suffice.)

Table 18.4 The camera script

SHOT	CAM.	(POSITION)	SCENE / INT./EXTR. / LOCATION / TIME OF DAY	F/X
			CAMS. 2A, 3A, 4B. SOUND BOOM B1	
			3. INT. LOUNGE NIGHT	TAPE:
10.	F/U 2.	A		WIND RAIN
		LS PAN/ZOOM on GEORGE to MS	(GEORGE ENTERS. WALKS TO TABLE. SWITCHES ON LAMP.)	
			GEORGE: (CALLS) The lights are OK in here.	
11.	3.	A.	It must be your lamp. /	
			(GEORGE TAKES GUN FROM DRAWER.)	
12.	2.	A	/	
		MS	SLIPS IT INTO HIS POCKET: PULLING OUT TELEGRAM. HOLDS IT UP.	
13.	4.	B	/	
		BCU of telegram	'SORRY CANNOT COME WEEKEND. BRIAN SICK. WRITING . . . JUDY.'	
		PULL FOCUS on fire as he throws.	(HAND SCREWS IT UP AND THROWS INTO FIRE.)	
14.	3.	A	/	
		LS	(DOOR OPENS: EILEEN ENTERS.)	
			EILEEN: Really, these people are too bad. They promised to be here tonight. Look how late . . .	
			GEORGE: It's probably the storm that has delayed them. They'll be here all right.	
		DOLLY IN to MS as EILEEN X's to couch.	(EILEEN SITS ON COUCH: GEORGE JOINS HER.)	
			EILEEN: If Judy knows you're here, it'll take wild horses to keep her away.	
			GEORGE: How many more times do I have to tell you . . .	
			EILEEN: Why do you keep pretending?	
			LIGHTNING FLASH	
15.	2.	A	/	
		CU	GEORGE: I've warned you. You'll go too far.	DISC: THUNDERCLAP

When is it necessary to fully script a production?

1 When the dialogue is to follow a prescribed text, that is to be learned, or read from a prompter or script.
2 Where action is detailed, so that people move to certain places at particular times and do specific things there. (This can affect cameras, sound, and lighting treatment.)

Table 18.5 TV script abbreviations

Many organizations duplicate the *rehearsal script* on white paper. Operational information is added to the original to provide the *camera script* on yellow paper.

All *camera shots* are numbered in a fully scripted show. *Inserts* are not numbered (film, slides, VT, titles, graphics), but are identified in the audio column. Where possible, cutting points are marked in the dialogue with a slash mark ________/ underlining back to the camera number.

Various abbreviations are widely used.

Equipment	CAM	Camera.	CG	Character generator.
	MIKE; MIC	Microphone.	Title; TC	Title card.
	BOOM	Sound boom.	G	Graphic.
	F/P: FISH	Fishpole.	PIC	Pictorial graphic.
	VT; VTR	Videotape.	PIX	Photo-caption (on camera).
	F	Film.	ESS	Electronic still store.
	TC; TK	Telecine.	SL	Slide.
	PROJ	Projection unit.	CP; CAP	Caption.*
	RP	Rear projection.	BP	Back projection.*
	DVE	Digital video effect.	ROLLER	Roller caption (crawl).*
			CPU	Caption slide.*
			TJ	Telejector (type of slide scanner).*
Position	L/H, R/H	Picture left-hand, right hand	B/G, F/G	Background, foreground
	C/S	Center stage	X	Move across.
	U/S, D/S	Upstage, downstage	POV	From the point of view of person named.
	P/S	Prompt side (RHS facing stage)	O/C	On camera.
	O/P	Opposite prompt (LHS facing stage).		
Cuing	Q. I/C, O/C	Cue, in cue, out cue.	ROLL; RUN	Start cue for film (telecine) or VT.
	Pull, flip, animate	Graphic (caption), animation.	C/S	Change slide.
	S/B	Stand-by.		
	FX	Cue effects.		
Cameras	BCU, CU, MCU, MS, MLS, LS, LVS (*see Chapter 6*).		D.I.	Dolly in
	2-S, 3-S	Two-shot, three-shot.	H/A, L/A	High angle, low angle.
	AB	As before, i.e. shot as previously.	N/A, W/A	Narrow angle, wide angle.
	O/S, X/S	Over-shoulder shot.	P/B, D/B	Pull back, dolly back.
	FAV	Favor (make the named subject more prominent than another).	FG/BG	One person foreground; another background.

Table 18.5 (cont.)

Switching (vision mixing)	CUT	Not marked, but implied unless other transition marked.	LOSE 2	Cut out Cam. 2 from a super or key
			FI, FO	Fade in, fade out.
	MIX (DIS)	Mix (dissolve).	T	Take. (Moment for a transition.)
	WIPE	Wipe.		
	SUPER (S/I)	Superimpose.	S/S	Split screen.
	KEY (INSERT)	Electronic insertion (chroma key, CSO).	CK	Chroma key.
Audio	F/UP	Fade up audio.	Spot FX	Sound effect made in studio.
	FU	Fade audio under.		
	P/B	Playback.	STING	Cue strong musical chord emphasizing action.
	FB	Foldback (audience address).	OS; OOV	Over scene, out of vision (audio heard where source not shown).
	DISC CART CASSETTE S/TAPE; A/TAPE GRAMS	Recorded audio insert	REVERB	Reverberation added
			B/G	Keep audio in background.
			OPT; MAG	Film audio; optical; magnetic.
	ANNCR	Announcer.	SOF	Sound on film.
	ATMOS	Atmosphere (background sounds).	SEP MAG	Separate magnetic film track.
			SOT	Sound on tape.
			SIL	Silent.
General	TXN	Transmission.	POS, NEG	Positive, negative.
	SEQ	Sequence.	MON	Monitor.
	P/V	Preview.	ID	Station identification.
	ADD	An addition (to a story).	MOS; VOX POP	Man-on-street interview
	PBU	Photo blow-up.	EXT	Exterior.
	PRAC	Practical.	INT	Interior.
	PROP	Property.	LOC	Location.
	RT	Roll titles		

** UK term.*

3 When there are carefully timed inserts (film, videotape) that have to be cued accurately into the program.
4 When the duration of a section must be kept within an allotted time bracket, yet cover certain agreed subject points. (The speaker might otherwise dwell on one point, and miss another out altogether.) Even where postproduction editing is available, it is not always possible to remedy uneven subject coverage.
5 Where there are spot cues, e.g. a ‘lightning flash’ and an effects disc of thunder at a point in the dialogue.

So you will find fully scripted approaches in newscasts, drama productions, operas, comedy shows (situation comedy), documentary-type presentations, and major commercials. Where dialogue and/or action are spontaneous, there can be no script; only an outline of routine (e.g. discussions). A formal talk is scripted.

The more fragmentary or disjointed the actual production process is, the more essential is the script. It helps everyone involved to *anticipate*. And in certain forms of production (rehearse/record; total chroma-key staging) anticipation is essential for tight scheduling.

In a complex production that is videotaped out of sequence the production crew may be unable to function meaningfully without a full script, which makes it clear how shots/sequences are interrelated, and reveals continuity. The lighting director may, for example, need to adjust the lighting balance for a scene so that it will intercut smoothly with a different viewpoint shot yesterday.

So the full script can be a valuable coordinating document, enabling you to see at a glance the interrelationship between dialogue, action, treatment, and mechanics. During planning, of course, it helps the team to estimate how much time there is for a camera move, how long there is for a costume change (perhaps a recording break will be necessary), whether re-arranging shooting order will give the necessary time for a make-up change, the scenes during which the 'rain' should be seen outside the windows of the library set (i.e. the water spray turned on and the audio effects introduced) . . . and the thousand and one details that interface in a smooth-running show.

The full script is used differently by various members of the production team. For the director the script has two purposes: as a reference point when developing treatment, estimating the duration of sequences, planning camera moves, etc., and to demonstrate to members of the team what he or she requires. The director's assistant(s) follows the script carefully during rehearsals and taping, checking dialogue accuracy, noting where retakes are needed, timing sections (their durations; where a particular event occurred) perhaps readying and cuing contributory sources, as well as 'calling shots' on the intercom – e.g. '*Shot 24 on 2. Coming to 3*'. The person operating the production switcher follows the script in detail, preparing for upcoming transitions, superimpositions, effects, etc., while checking the various monitor pictures.

Others in the team, for whom a script would be too distracting (e.g. camera and boom operators), use it as a detailed reference point when necessary, but are guided by simplified outlines such as *breakdown sheets* and *camera cards*, as they memorize their operations.

Auxiliary information

In addition to the script, various supplementary summaries may be necessary.

■ **Synopsis** An outline summary of characters, action, plot. Appended to a dramatic script; particularly when shot out of sequence, or to coordinate a series.

Table 18.6 Breakdown sheet/show format/running order

EXAMPLE 1: DRAMA PRODUCTION

Page	*Scene (sequence)*	*Shots*	*Cameras/audio (layout across set)*	*D/N Day/night*	*Cast*
1	FILM – 1 (40 sec) OPENING TITLES (20 sec)		SOF (SEP. MAG.) 4A. S. TAPE (RAIN)		
1	1 INT. DINING ROOM	2–9	1A, 4A	N.	GEORGE EILEEN
3	2. INT. LOUNGE	10–27	4B, 2A, B1, 3A.	N.	GEORGE EILEEN
			RECORDING BREAK		
10	3. EXT. GARDEN	28	B2, 3B	D.	JUDY GEORGE
10	4. EXT. STREET	29	1B. Slung.	D.	BRIAN
11	5. INT. CAFE	30–43	2B, 4C, A2	Eve.	BRIAN JUDY GEORGE
			ETC . . .		

EXAMPLE 2: DEMONSTRATION PROGRAM (TOTAL DURATION: 15 MINS.)

Sequence no.	*Item (sequence segment)*	*Cameras/F/VT*	*Seq. dur.*
1	OPENING TITLES – SIG. TUNE.	4A, 1A.	07 sec
2	PROG. INTRO.	2A, 3A.	30 sec
3	TIMBER FELLING	VT.	24 sec
4	PREPARING WOOD.	1B, 2B.	2 min 30 sec
5	CARVING DEMO.	1C, 4B, 3B.	8 min 00 sec
6	TIMBER IN BUILDINGS.	FILM.	2 min 58 sec
7	CLOSING LINK.	3A.	22 sec
8	END TITLES – SIG. TUNE.	4A, 1A.	09 sec
			15 min 00 sec

■ **Fact sheet/run-down sheet** Summarizes information about a product or item for a demonstration program; or details of a guest for an interviewer. Provided by a researcher, editor, or agency for guidance.

■ **Breakdown sheet/show format/running order** Lists the events or program segments in order, showing allowed durations, participants' names, cameras and audio pick-up allocated, setting used, video and audio inserts, etc. (Sometimes ambiguously called a run-down sheet.)

Invaluable for unscripted, semi-scripted, and scripted shows that contain a series of self-contained segments (sequences, scenes). Also as a summary of a complex dramatic script to show at a glance: shot numbers for each scene, operational details, inserts, VT breaks for major resetting (clearing props, redressing set, moving scenery), costume/make-up changes, etc. (See Table 18.6).

■ **Camera card/shot card** A sheet provided for individual cameras, showing their successive floor positions (perhaps with a layout sketch) and their allocated shots (shot numbers, type of shots), camera movements, action.

Table 18.7 Camera card

CAMERA THREE		'DEATH COMES ONCE'	STUDIO B	
SHOT NO.	POSN.	(LENS ANGLE*)	SCENE/SETTING	
11	A	13°	SC. 2. LOUNGE	
				CU GEORGE pockets gun from drawer pulling out telegram.
14	A	35°		LS EILEEN enters DOLLY IN to MS as she X's to couch.
19	A	20°		BCU GEORGE'S eyes.
23	A	13°		BCU EILEEN screams.
25	A	20°		CU GEORGE puts gun in drawer.
		QUICK MOVE TO GARDEN		
28	B	35°	SC. 3. GARDEN	
				MLS follow GEORGE carrying body: tightening, depressing to L/A shot: ZOOM IN to hand as he stops.
		MOVE TO RHS LOUNGE		
44	A	50°	SC. 4. LOUNGE	
				LS DETECTIVE enters. PAN with him into MS as he goes to phone.

* *Optional*

The camera card is not to be confused with a *shot sheet*, which carries brief details of *all* cameras' shots and is used as a summary list when preparing a treatment framework for an unscripted show. (See Table 18.7).

■ ***Requisition forms*** Essential for interdepartmental organization, requisition forms are legion. There are no standard approaches. Each station has its own procedures for booking studios, equipment, facilities, services, manpower, etc. The director may become involved directly in ordering props, graphics, titles, etc., or simply inform specialists. Various requisitions concerning costume, make-up, staging, lighting, video, audio, VTR, filming, editing are normally handled by the specialists.

Calculating shots

Many directors prefer to work empirically, from mental concepts, rough notes, and experience. They make 'guesstimates', or wait until they can guide the cameras and see which shots are practical. They improvise instinctively and draw inspiration from the occasion. This is fine, as long as time is available to experiment, improvise, and coordinate the production team. But as a general practice it is preferable to plan as fully as possible; modifying, correcting, and improving during camera rehearsal and subsequent editing.

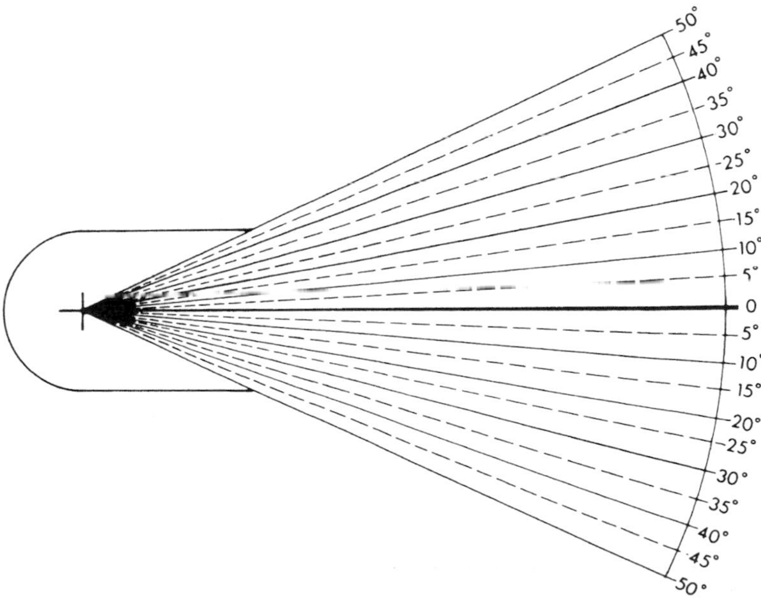

Fig. 18.5 The 'shot plotter' The horizontal lens angles are marked on this protractor. Laid on a scale floor plan, they show the shot coverage for any angle. (Vertical angles for use on elevations, are ¾ horizontal angle.)

20° coverage, for example, is between the 20° markings either side of the central axis (0).

Why measure?

Preliminary planning can provide you with the answers to a lot of your camera problems long before even preliminary blocking:

What shots are available on this immobile camera?
Am I going to shoot off the set?
Can I get the shot from here?
What will relative sizes (proportions) be?
How large must we make the graphic in this setting?
Where do I position people for this chroma-key effect?

Why *guess* whether it will work on the day when you can check it out now?

The tools are simple enough: a scale floor plan and a transparent triangle or protractor representing the horizontal lens angle. Wherever you place this 'shot plotter' on the floor plan it shows what the camera sees from that viewpoint. If the angle falls outside the marked-out setting you are shooting off (Figure 18.6).

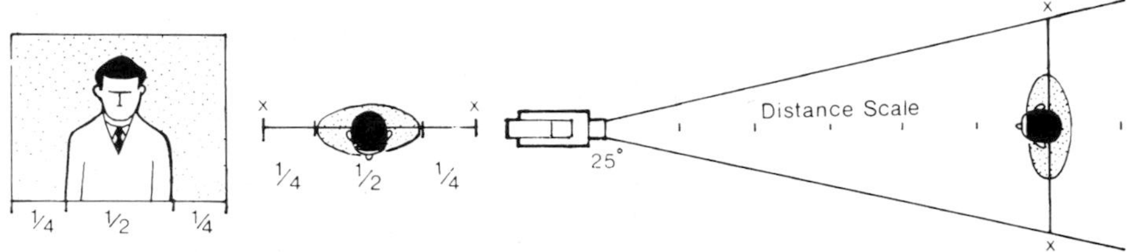

Fig. 18.6 part 1 Shot planning – required camera distance
You can find shots by *trial and error* or calculate them from a *graph* (Fig. 18.7), or measure the set-up needed as follows.

Q: What camera distance is needed on a 25° lens, to have a person fill half the screen width?
A: Person is $\frac{3}{8}$ in across on a $\frac{1}{4}$ in = 1 ft scale (1 cm across on a 1 cm = 0.5 m scale). So draw a line × 2 this length (i.e. person is now *half* the line length). Fit this line exactly across the lens angle, and check the distance on scale from camera to subject.

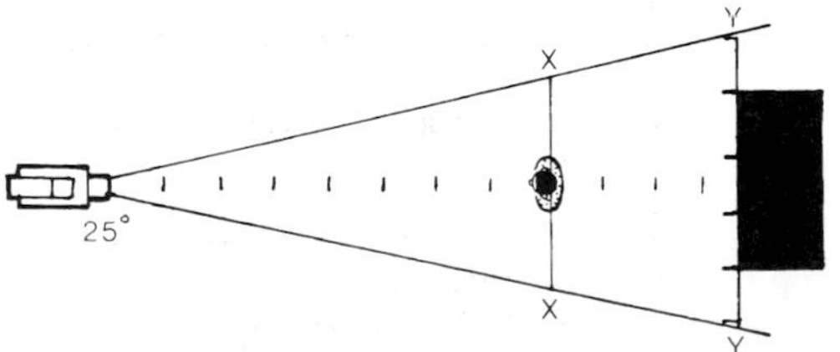

SHOT	BCU	Cu Head & Shoulders	MCU Chest	Mid-Shot Waist	3/4 Shot Knees	Full Length
Meters	1.0	1.25	1.75	2.0	4.0	+6.0
Feet	3.3	4	5.7	6.5	13	+20

Fig. 18.6 part 2 Shot planning – shots available from a particular layout
First measure the person's distance. In the example he is 4 m (14 ft) away. (A 25° lens would provide a $\frac{3}{4}$ shot/knee shot – see table.) Draw a line across the lens angle at that point and you see that he occupies about $\frac{1}{5}$ screen width. The object behind him is 1.5 m wide at Y–Y (shot width 2.5 m) = $\frac{3}{5}$ of screen width. So now you have the shot's proportions.

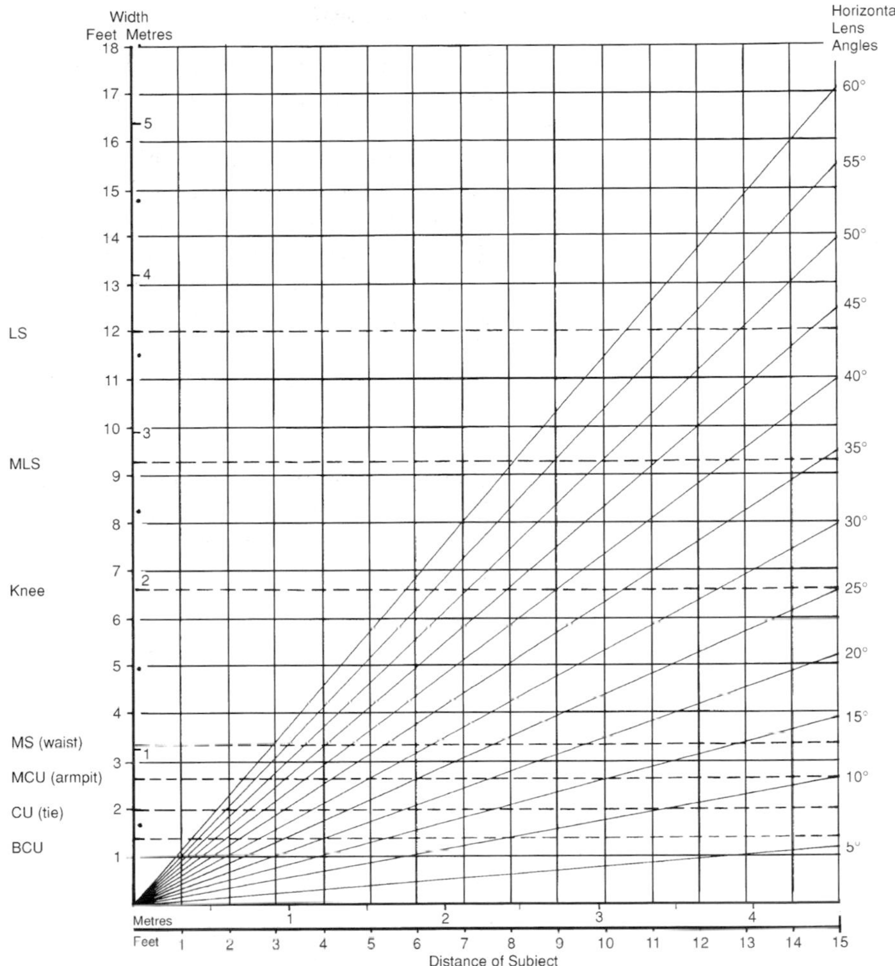

Fig. 18.7 Camera set-up graph
The graph shows how much any lens sees at various distances. (The *height* of the area seen is ¾ of the *width*.)

1 **How far away does the camera have to be to get a certain type of shot**? Select type of shot you want on vertical scale . . . look across to the lens angle you are using . . . then down to the *distance scale*.
2 **What lens angle is needed for a certain type of shot?** Trace a line across graph, from the *shot* you want (vertical scale) . . . draw another line, up from camera's distance on the bottom *scale*. Where they cross, shows the best *lens angle*.
3 **What type of shots will I get from here?** Draw a line up from the *distance scale* to the *lens angle(s)* you have available (max and min zoom angles). Then across left, to the *shot scale*.
4 **How much will the camera see from here?** As 3, but read the scene *width/height scales*.
5 You can get the **same shot size at different distance** by altering lens angle. Trace a line right from the shot needed (e.g. CU) and note the distances at which it cuts various lens angles.
6 **To make a subject fill a certain proportion of screen width** (e.g. ⅓). Measure the subject width; multiply this by 3 for ⅓ width (4 for ¼, etc.). Look up this screen width on the left vertical *width scale*. Trace across to the *lens angle* used, then down to the *distance needed*. The subject will now fill ⅓ screen width.

Lens Angle

Horizontal	Vertical
5°	3·75°
10°	7·5°
15°	11·25°
20°	15°
25°	18·75°
30°	22·5°
35°	26·25°
40°	30°
45°	34°
50°	37·5°
55°	40·25°
60°	45°

Fisher Boom
Mole Boom
Pedestal
Max
Min
Min
Max
Camera jib arm
Scale 1 : 50 (300 mm units)
3 meters
6 meters
9 meters

1

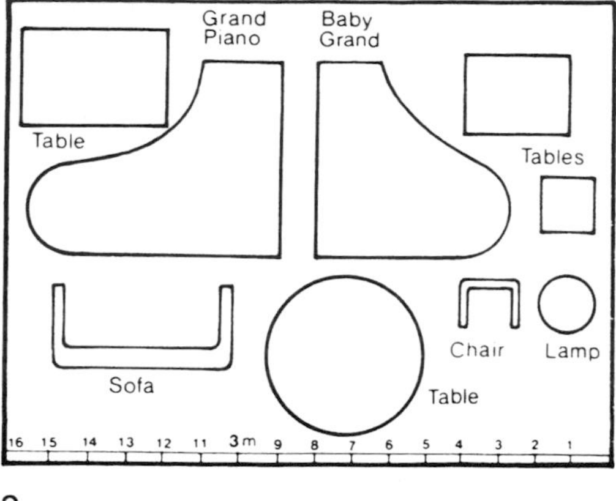

2

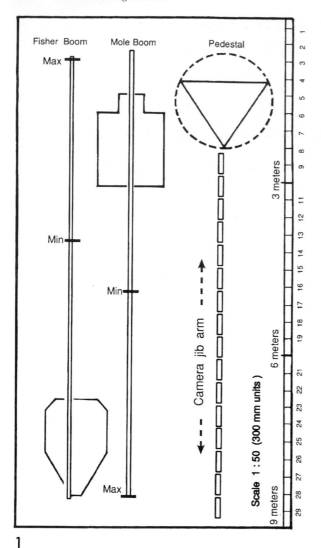

Fig. 18.8 Equipment stencil
Scale stencils are used to mark the floor plan, with equipment positions.

1 Camera/sound boom stencil.
2 Typical furniture stencil.

Shot proportions

The edges of the lens angle represent the left- and right-frame edges. Any object that touches both lines fills the screen width – whether a small close item or a large distant one.

To make a subject fill one-third of the screen width just mark on a paper strip a length *three times* the subject's width. At the distance this marker fits across the angle the subject will exactly fill one-third of the screen width. Conversely, if a subject is a known distance away, measure the scene width there and divide this by the subject width to find proportions.

In Figure 18.6 you have a quick shot-check table showing the distances for 'standard' shots on a 25° lens. For other lens angles, distances are inversely proportional:

$50° = {}^{25}/_{50} = \times 0.5$ table distance.

$10° = {}^{25}/_{10} = \times 2.5$ table distance.

$40° = {}^{25}/_{40} = \times 0.6$ table distance.

For a useful formula that you can apply to your particular zoom lens system, multiply its maximum focal length (in millimeters) by the corresponding horizontal lens angle at that setting (e.g. 110 mm × 5° = 550).

Then, when you want to find the lens angle given by a particular focal length (e.g. 55 mm), simply divide this 'standard factor' by that figure (e.g. 550 ÷ 55 = 10°). When you need a certain lens angle (e.g. 25°), divide the factor by 25, and you will find that you need a focal length of 22 mm.

19 In production

Here we shall be exploring several well-established methods of preparing and taping productions. Which you use depends not only on the type of show but whether it is a live or videotaped, the facilities, and the amount of time available.

Unrehearsed formats

Any production benefits from rehearsal before being taped or going on air. But what do we do when the talent is going to arrive at the last minute, or even while we are on air? If it is a live show with long filmed or videotaped inserts (a magazine program, for instance) it may be possible to *outline-rehearse* a short item in the studio during these inserts. Otherwise we may have to accept that the action will have to be aired or taped '*raw*'.

Fortunately, as we saw earlier, a number of regular television productions fit into familiar routine formats. Consequently, even when it is not possible to rehearse the action beforehand you can still prepare a set-up that will work successfully when the talent does arrive. *Interviews*, for example, have regular layouts so you can line up appropriate chair positions and locate cameras. Using available people as stand-ins, you check the lighting and sound arrangements. When the talent appears you can quickly preview them on camera to check over their voice levels, makeup, lighting, and costume.

Where the unrehearsed action is less defined – such as a late-arriving dance group – you will have to rely on cameras arranged strategically in frontal and cross-shooting positions. Rather than grabbing shots at random, you can allocate cover shots (broad views) to one camera, have another concentrate on localized shots (e.g. footwork), while another takes shots of small groups or individuals. Before they begin always explain to the performers the floor area limits within which they must work or their action may spread uncontrollably. Production treatment is largely a matter of recognizing effective shots as they are offered by the cameras; taking care to dwell on any special features; such as *action detail* in the footwork of a flamenco dance or *grouping shots* of a chorus.

Pre-studio rehearsal

Camera time is expensive, and there are seldom opportunities during studio rehearsals to experiment, to try out variations, or to work out half-formed ideas. Even a demonstration at a bench will often gain by practising with the equipment beforehand, discussing alternative methods of presenting an item, making sure that the ideas work. This is sometimes done in a *preparation room* set aside for that purpose.

Certainly, when it comes to the complexities of larger productions, preparatory work needs to be completed long before camera rehearsals. It is essential to work out their mechanics, practice dialogue and action, and coordinate performance. So a drama or a comedy show is often rehearsed in a hall or rehearsal-room some two or three weeks before the studio date. Meanwhile, the studio is scheduled for other programs.

Let's go in our imagination to the *pre-rehearsal* of a typical drama production. It begins with a *briefing (read-through, line rehearsal)*. The director goes over the play, indicating particular points about style and presentation that will help to familiarize the cast with their parts. They read their lines from the script, becoming more accustomed to the dialogue, the other actors, and their characterizations.

The rehearsal hall's floor is taped or chalked with a full-size layout of the studio setting(s). Doors, windows, stairways, etc. are outlined. Stock rehearsal furniture substitutes the actual studio items, and action props (telephone, tableware) are provided. Rehearsing in this mock-up, actors become accustomed to the scale and features of their surroundings; vertical poles, chairs, dummy doors, marking the main limits of each setting.

The director arranges the action, the actors' positions, and their groupings to suit the camera treatment. Rehearsing a scene at a time, the cast is learning their lines, practising performance, until their moves and business flow naturally and the entire show runs smoothly, ready for its studio debut. The durations of segments are checked and adjusted. (In calculating the overall timing, allowances are made for the time taken by later inserts such as film or videotape sequences.)

During rehearsals the director scrutinizes action through a hand viewfinder from planned camera positions, adjusting them and rearranging compositional details as necessary.

A few days before the studio date, the specialists concerned with the technical operations (cameras, sound, lighting) watch a complete rehearsal (*technical walk-through; technical run*), checking for potential operational problems. Following this meeting, facilities bookings are finalized, and the lighting plot prepared.

Studio rehearsal

Before a studio rehearsal the staging crew, supervised by the set designer, erects and dresses the settings. Lamps are rigged and adjusted under the guidance of the lighting director, to cover their plotted areas. Camera and sound equipment are positioned. The

Table 19.1 Prerehearsal blocking hints

Timing	A preliminary read-through gives only a rough timing estimate. Allow time for business, moves, recorded inserts, etc. Anticipate potential script cuts if an overrun is evident. Many productions include sequences that can be dropped, reduced, or expanded to trim timing.
Briefing performers	Ensure that performers have a clear idea of the program format, their part in it, and their interrelationship with other contributions. Ensure that performers have a good notion of the setting: what it represents, where things are.
Props	Provide reasonable substitutes where real props are not available. Sometimes only the actual item will suffice. Where unfamiliar costume is to be worn (cloak, hoop skirt, space helmet), a rehearsal version is preferable to dummy motions.
Directing performers	Maintain a firm attitude towards punctuality, inattention, background chatter during rehearsals, to avoid time wastage and frustration. Check that performers' positions are consistent and meaningful (they do not stand 'on' a wall). Avoid excessive revisions – of action, grouping, line cuts, etc. Wrong versions can get remembered, new ones forgotten. Warn performers where they are in close shots, to restrict their movements; perhaps indicating which camera to play to.
Shot arrangement	Use a portable viewfinder to arrange shots. Even a card cut-out frame or a hand-formed frame is better than unaided guesses. Always think in terms of *shots*, not of theatrical-styled groupings, entrances, exits, business. At script stage, form ideas about shots rather than arranging 'nice groups' and trying to get 'good shots' during rehearsal. When setting up shots in a rehearsal hall do not overlook the scenic background that will be present in the studio. Check shot coverage with plans and elevations. Consider depth of field limitations in close shots or deep shots (close and distant people framed together). Think in terms of practical studio mechanics. You may rapidly reposition your viewfinder, but the move may be impossible for the studio camera.
Audio and lighting	Try to bear audio and lighting problems in mind when arranging positions and action. For example: where people are widely spaced, a sound boom may need time to swing between them, or have to be supplemented.

performers arrive, seeing the staging for the first time. The show is ready to begin.

Directors organize their studio rehearsals in several ways, according to the complexity of the production, available time, performer experience, and criticality of results. Given the opportunity, you might like the luxury of:

1 *Dry run (walk-through)*. Actors perform, familiarizing themselves with the studio settings, etc., while the studio crew watch, learning the format, action, and production treatment.

Table 19.2 Effective studio rehearsal

Unrehearsed or briefly rehearsed studio production	*Director's assistant* checks that available production information is distributed (breakdown sheet/running order). Also checks that contributory graphics (titles, slides, floor graphics) and film/VT inserts are correct. The assistant has details of all word cues, for inserts, announcements, etc. and their timings. Director with floor manager, technical director, lighting director, cameras and sound crew, arranges basic performer and camera positions (floor is marked). Even a basic plan aids coordination. The director outlines action or moves, and shot coverage. Lighting is set. If talent is available, line up shots and explain to them any shot restrictions, critical positions, care needed in demonstrating items, etc. (Otherwise use stand-ins for shot line-up and brief talent on arrival.) Check that performers, crew, and contributory services (prompter, film channel, etc.) are ready to start. If full rehearsal is impractical, carry out basic production checks: rehearse 'tops and tails' of each segment with intermediate links (e.g. announcer's in-cues/out-cues, to cue film or VT inserts); check any complicated action or treatment. Check any errors or problems.
Intercom and the director	Remember that the production team is interdependent. A quiet, methodical, patient approach is as infectious as an acrimonious one. Be firm but friendly. Avoid critical comments on intercom. How detailed intercom instructions need to be depends on the show's complexity and crew experience. Aim at a balanced information flow, avoiding continuous chat and comment. (A mute key cuts the circuit when necessary.) Preferably call cameras by numbers, guiding all camera moves (and zooms) during rehearsal, warning the crew of upcoming action and movements. Examine each shot. If necessary, modify positions, action, movement, and composition. Consider *shot continuity*. Alterations may affect earlier shots, too.
	Remember, the crew and performers are *memorizing*. Their aids are the production paperwork and your intercom reminders/instructions. Do not be vague. Make sure that your intentions are understood. In correcting errors, explain what was wrong and what is wanted. Not 'Move him left a bit' but 'He is shadowing the map'. Do not assume performers will see and correct any problems. Avoid excessive changes or revisions, or there will be hesitations and mistakes. Correct operational and performance errors, even in early camera rehearsal. Misjudgements and inaccuracies should be noted directly they occur (e.g. camera in shot, shooting off, late cue, wrong lines, wrong shot, wrong microphone). But avoid an overinterrupted rehearsal, or timing and continuity will be lost. If a camera operator offers alternative shots (e.g. to overcome a problem), briefly indicate if you accept or disagree, and why. Where practicable, at the end of each sequence ask if there are any problems, and whether anyone wants to rehearse that section again. Remember, various staging and lighting defects may be unavoidable in early rehearsal. Certain details (set dressing, light effects) take time to complete. Some aspects need to be seen on camera before they can be corrected or finally adjusted (overbright lights, lens flares). Shot readjustments during rehearsal often necessitate lighting alterations.

Table 19.2 (cont.)

Never repeat a segment without indicating whether it is to be *changed* (move faster next time), or is to correct an *error* (late cue), or to *improve* the performance/operations.
Ensure that everyone knows when shots have been deleted or added (e.g. Shot 2A, 2B, 2C).
At the end of rehearsal; check timings, give notes to performers and crew on any errors to be corrected, changes needed, problems to be solved. Check whether they have difficulties that need your aid.
At least one complete uninterrupted rehearsal is essential for reliable recording/transmission.
At the end of videotaping, give details (including shot numbers) and reasons for any retakes.

2 *Camera blocking (stagger-through)*. Initial camera rehearsal, co-ordinating technical operations, discovering and correcting problems.
3 *Predress run-through (continuous run-through)*. 'Polishing' rehearsal, proving corrections.
4 *Dress rehearsal* (dress-run). Hopefully, fault-free 'on-air' quality performance.
5 *Videotaping/transmission*. Final optimum performance.

In reality, many productions have little more rehearsal time than the show's running duration, and the second and fifth stages have to suffice. So a continual watch on progress, relative to available rehearsal time, is essential.

Rehearsal procedures

In many types of production we want to prepare and rehearse the entire action and treatment until it reaches a peak, then record the polished performance. In others, we rehearse each small section and record it before going on to the next.

Camera blocking/stagger-through/first run/stopping run

Here, the director controls operations from the production control room, only 'going to the floor' when personal on-the-spot discussion is essential. Otherwise, his or her eyes and ears are the picture monitors and loudspeaker. All communication with the crew is via the *intercom* (*production talkback*) system; the *floor manager* cuing and instructing the talent through intercom guidance.

Many directors use the *whole method*, and go straight through a sequence (segment, scene) in camera rehearsal, continuously guiding until a serious problem arises to require stopping and correction. The director discusses problems, solutions, and revisions; then reruns the sequence with corrections. It should now work.

This method gives a good idea of continuity, timing, transitions, and operational difficulties. But, by skimming over the various shortcomings before the 'breakdown point', quite a list of minor corrections may develop.

Other directors, using the *stopping method*, stop action and correct faults as they arise – almost shot by shot. This precludes error adding to error, ensuring that everyone knows exactly what is required throughout. For certain situations (chroma-key treatment) this may be the only rational approach.

However, this piecemeal method gives the impression of slow progress, and can feel tedious and nit-picking. The continual stopping makes checks on continuity and timing more difficult. Later corrections are given as notes after the run-through.

Floor blocking

Using this method, the director forsakes the production control room and works from a studio picture monitor. Guiding and correcting performers and crew, he or she calls out required transitions to the switcher in the control room, watching results on his monitor screen. This is the luxury of delayed decisions!

This technique is often used by directors who find visualizing difficult, feel remote from operations in their orthodox position, and prefer direct contact to relaying instructions.

The director often returns to the control room to run each floor-rehearsed scene. During videotaping, the show may be shot as segments, scenes, or continuous action.

Where a set-up is particularly complicated or discontinuously recorded, the system may have some advantages. But it has all the weaknesses of the 'stopping method' plus low crew cohesion. When they *all* hear the same intercom instructions, crew members can coordinate more effectively. At worst, this method wastes a great deal of time, and because the director has not been watching channel previews or listening to audio while on the floor, continuity and video/audio relationships may be below optimum.

Rehearsal problems

During the course of rehearsal various problems regularly arise. Here, in summarized form, are typical situations.

The shot

1 *Subject detail not sufficiently visible.* Move subject/camera closer. Zoom in. Shoot subject in a series of close detail shots or

localized insets (magnified view within longer shot). Is greater detail available? (Very close shots of some subjects are confusing or reveal no further information – e.g. close-ups of unsharp photographs.) Is detail defocused? Is the subject shadowed or obscured?

2 *Extreme close-ups of details required.* Problems can arise from the limited depth of field, an unsteady camera, the subject moving in/out of frame. So where possible, locate the item on a firm surface (use position marks). Use higher light levels (intensities) to permit stopping down. The camera may be able to focus closer on a wide-angle lens (closer MFD). Use the *macro* position on the lens. Use a photo-enlargement of detail.
3 *Subject's shape does not fit screen aspect ratio.* Take a long shot of total subject, then pan/tilt over detail or intercut closer shots. If a series of items are involved do similarly or recompose the shot (move them together, arrange in depth, or shoot more obliquely).
4 *Unsatisfactory framing.* Subject cut off by frame edge. Shot too tight or loose. Subject too high in frame or off-center (unbalanced). Unsuitable headroom.
5 *One subject masks (obscures) another.* Reposition subject and mark floor. (Check that this does not spoil earlier shots.) Reposition camera (e.g. arc or truck/crab).
6 *Subjects appear too widely spaced apart.* Move subjects closer together, shoot obliquely, or intercut single shots.
7 *Subject appears too large or small relative to others in shot.* See Table 6.3.
8 *Subject appears too prominent.* Reduce shot size, alter composition, or increase camera height.
9 Background objects or scenic lines 'grow out' of subject. Reposition camera or subject. Move, cover, or remove background items. Reduce their prominence by lighting or defocusing.
10 *Unwanted distortion.* Adjust lens angle to nearer 'normal' (25°) and change camera distance accordingly, reposition subject or change viewpoint.
11 *Colors have similar monochromatic values.* Lighten/darken areas concerned. Change hue or materials (surface texture). Put black outlines round areas of similar tone.

Performers

1 *Out of position.* Check if they have toe marks or location points. Move them and re-mark floor (instructing performers). Reposition camera.
2 *Performer working to wrong camera.* Floor manager signals. Draw attention to tally (cue) light on camera. Switch over to the 'wrong' camera.

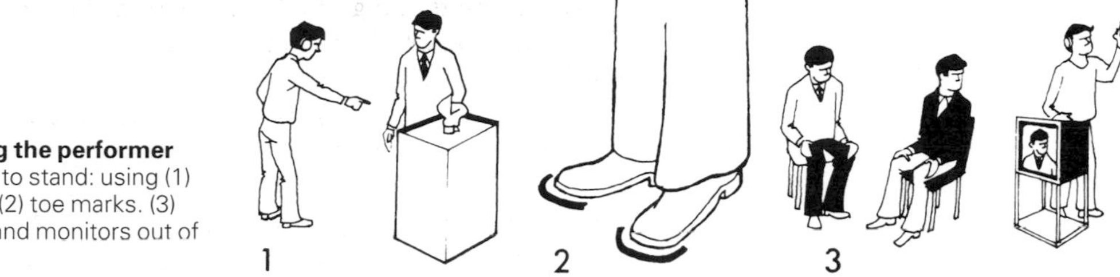

Fig. 19.1 Guiding the performer Show them where to stand: using (1) a locating point, or (2) toe marks. (3) Keep other action and monitors out of their eyeline.

3 *Dialogue errors (cuts lines, dries/fluffs, or freezes and needs prompt, wrong lines)*. Use prompter, cue cards, etc. Give audible prompt. Is prompter working, script OK? Misunderstanding? Retake sequence, or insert cutaway shot and dub audio retake into audio track of VT.

Scenic problems

1 *Check staging for distracting features.* Overbright surfaces or reflections. Can relighting cure? Re-angle, use dulling spray, repaint, cover over, scrim over or remove.
2 *Colors or tones unsuitable* (e.g. subject merges with background). Modify background, lighting or subject (e.g. change costume).
3 *Background blemishes* (dirty marks, tears, scrapes, wrinkles, etc.). Rectify, refurbish, cover over, or relight.
4 *Ugly or distracting shadows on background.* Performers or scenery too close to background? Relight or modify shot.

Operational hazards

1 *Camera shooting off set.* Modify shot, extend scenery, or add foreground masking.
2 *Lens flares.* Raise camera viewpoint, improve lens shade (hood), shield off camera, or raise lamp height. Alter shot.
3 *Unwanted subjects in shot.* Have their positions changed since last rehearsal? Alter framing, camera position, or lens angle. Rearrange shot, remove unwanted items. Mask/cover items. Leave items unlit.
4 *Boom microphone in shot.* Check whether boom operator is aware. Warn him before cutting from close to distant shot. Tighten (reduce headroom) or recompose shot. Alter sound pick-up method.
5 *Boom shadows.* Check with audio/lighting personnel if avoidable. Consider modifying shot – tighter shot or change viewpoint. Alter sound pick-up or lighting.
6 *Cables in shot.* Check for distracting cables in shot – audio, lighting, monitors, cameras.
7 *Graphics/captions/titles.* Check they are straight, level, and undistorted. Can all be seen (no cut-off) and read? Time to read?

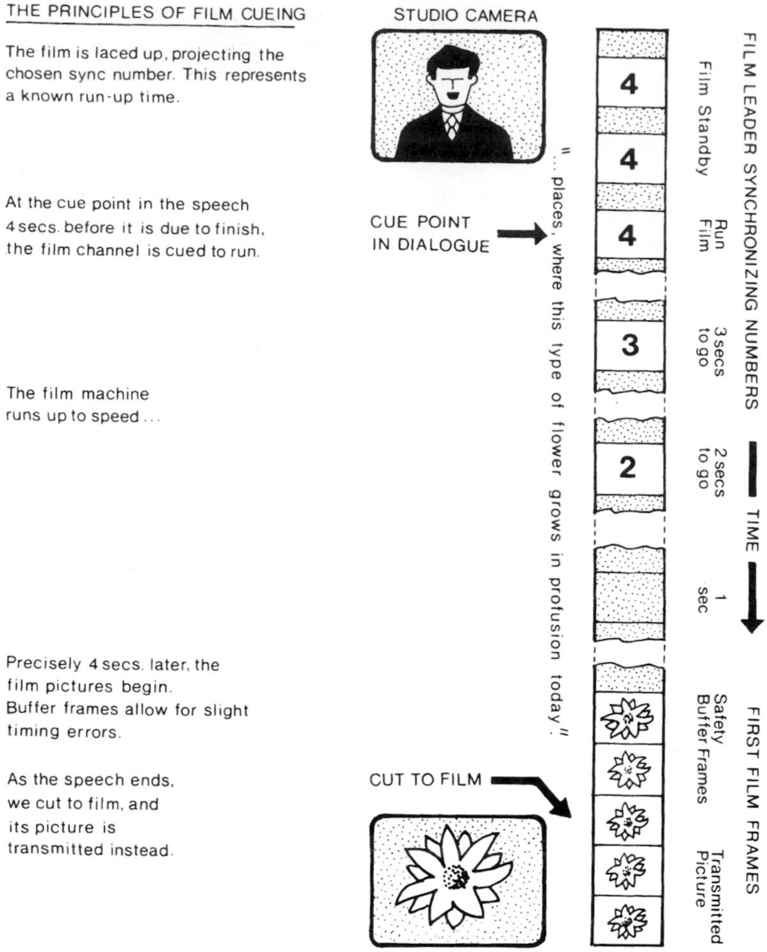

THE PRINCIPLES OF FILM CUEING

The film is laced up, projecting the chosen sync number. This represents a known run-up time.

At the cue point in the speech 4 secs. before it is due to finish, the film channel is cued to run.

The film machine runs up to speed . . .

Precisely 4 secs. later, the film pictures begin. Buffer frames allow for slight timing errors.

As the speech ends, we cut to film, and its picture is transmitted instead.

STUDIO CAMERA

CUE POINT IN DIALOGUE

CUT TO FILM

" . . . places, where this type of flower grows in profusion today."

FILM LEADER SYNCHRONIZING NUMBERS

TIME

FIRST FILM FRAMES

Film Standby

Run Film

3 secs to go

2 secs to go

1 sec

Safety Buffer Frames

Transmitted Picture

4

4

4

3

2

Fig. 19.2 Cuing a film channel Although some telecine channels provide an 'instant start' from a still frame, many take a few seconds to run up to normal running speed and stabilize. A film leader (marked in seconds) is spliced onto the start of the film, and provides an accurate, predictable run-up time when the film is cued.

Some VTR systems similarly require time to reach normal speed, and an equivalent *leader* is recorded at the start of a sequence (a numbered count-down, or visible clock; see Fig. 14.4).

Editing/video switching/vision mixing

1 *Transitions appropriate?* Suitable type? Timing and rate of transitions OK?
2 *Any distractions?* Any reverse cuts, jump cuts, position jumps, instant changes in size, direction, frame height? Any loss of orientation or direction on cuts? Any image confusion during supers or mixes?

The floor manager

The *floor manager (FM)* is a person of many parts. On larger productions, he or she may, with an assistant (AFM), join the show at its onset and assist with organization, local liaison, location shooting, and sometimes substitute for the busy director at pre-studio rehearsals. Alternatively, the FM may join the production in the studio for camera rehearsals.

During studio preparations for camera rehearsal the FM checks all *non-technical* aspects of the show, confirming the team's readiness. Progress checks ensure that there are no staging hangups (i.e. action props work, scenery and furniture are in planned positions, doors do not stick . . . etc.); that no fire, safety or union regulations are being contravened. He guides the floor crew/stage hands, relative to operating graphics, studio/title cards, cue cards, scenic moves, effects cues, etc.

Around this time, arriving performers may need to be welcomed, checked in, and accommodated; and told when and where they are required. Ensuring punctuality and the observation of scheduled times are important aspects of the FM's duties; whether for rehearsal starts, *turnarounds* at the end of a rehearsal (returning equipment, props, scenery, to opening positions), or studio breaks (meals).

Rehearsal

As the director's contact on the studio floor, the FM, wearing earphones, listens to the director's intercom (talkback) and then passes this information on to the talent. The FM anticipates problems, rearranges action and grouping, furniture positions, etc., as the director indicates, marking the floor where necessary; supervising staging and property changes.

Normally, the FM alone will cue and stop all action in the studio on the director's instructions. The director only exceptionally uses the *studio-address loudspeaker (public address, studio talkback, loudspeaker talkback)* to talk directly to performers. (Loudspeaker announcements can be quite disrupting!) The FM talks back to the director over studio microphones, using a miniature 'reverse-talkback' transmitter, or by gestures in front of preview cameras. Being on the spot, the FM can often correct problems not evident to the director in the control room.

A good FM combines calmness, discipline and firmness with diplomacy and friendliness; putting talent at ease. Always available yet never in shot. The FM maintains a quiet studio, yet appreciates that various last-minute corrective jobs must progress; investigates any delay, aiming to clear it; or if rehearsal is likely to be halted, suggests an alternative sequence that is ready instead. Later, the FM may welcome and guide any studio audience, relative to the show format and their contributions.

Taping/transmission

In checking and making ready for 'air time' or videotaping, the FM confirms that all studio access doors are shut, talent and crew standing by in opening positions, the ident slate has accurate details (which is read during the VT countdown), studio monitors are showing pictures, etc.

During the show the FM is cuing talent, keeping a wary eye on all about, listening to intercom guidance, anticipating hazards, and generally smoothing proceedings. At the end of taping the FM holds talent and crew until results have been checked; announcing and preparing any necessary retakes, finally 'releasing the studio' (performers and crew). The floor manager checks on safe storage of any valuable or special props or equipment and ends duties with a logged account of the production.

Guiding performers

How much guidance performers need varies with their experience and the complexity of the production. But you must always ensure that talent realizes exactly what you want them to do and where to do it. A preliminary word may be enough, or a painstaking rehearsal may prove essential.

Inexperienced talent

Having welcomed talent, put them at ease, and outlined their contribution, they are best supported by an experienced host who guides and reassures them. Have them talk and demonstrate to the host rather than the camera, for he or she can steer them by questions and ensure that subject positions suit the shots.

We all feel daunted by unfamiliar conditions, mechanics, and disciplines; self-confidence is essential for good performance. So keep problems to a minimum, with only essential instructions to talent. Avoid elaborate action, discourage improvisation, and have minimal rearrangements.

Even slight distractions may worry inexperienced talent. Sometimes a small cue card or a list of points held beside the camera may strengthen their confidence. However, few inexperienced people read scripts or prompters 'naturally'; but instead have a stilted, ill-at-ease delivery.

The balance between insufficient and excessive rehearsal is more crucial with inexperienced talent. Uncertainty or overfamiliarity can lead them to omit sections during transmission. Sometimes the solution lies in either taping the item sectionally or compiling from several takes.

Professional talent

You will meet a very wide range of experienced professional performers in TV production – actors, presenters, hosts, commentators, demonstrators, anchors . . . Each has a particular part to play in the presentation.

Familiar with studio routines, they can respond to the most complicated instructions from the FM, or an earpiece intercom (*program interrupt*, *switched talkback*) without the blink of an eye, even under the most trying conditions – and yet maintain cool command of the situation. Comments, feed questions, timing and continuity changes, item cuts, ad-libbing padding are taken in their stride.

The professional makes full use of a prompter displaying the full script – this means that cameras must always be within reading distance. The performance (action and positions) is accurately repeatable and he/she will play to particular cameras for specific shots, making allowances for lighting problems (e.g. shadowing) or camera moves.

Cuing

To ensure that action begins and ends at the instant it is required, precise cuing is essential. If you cut to performers and then cue them you will see them waiting to begin or watch action 'spring into life'. Cue them too early before cutting and action has already begun. So '*cue and cut*' is normal practice.

Wrong cuing leaves talent bewildered. If they have finished their contribution and you have not cut away to the next shot they may stand with 'egg on the face', wondering whether to ad lib or just grin! Wrong cuing can mean that film or VT runs out to a blank screen, or we see run-up leaders flashing by on transmission. VT editing may compensate for poor cuing and disguise sloppy direction.

Methods of cuing (see Figure 19.3)

1 *Hand cues*. Given by the FM (or relayed by the AFM), these are the standard methods of cuing action to start or stop. Sometimes a performer cannot watch for cues (during an embrace) and a tap on foot or shoulder may be used instead. Remember, some stations have their own variants on the signals in Figure 19.3 and it is advisable to use these. But make sure that your signals are going to be understood by the talent. Explain any basic cue to them if necessary. Do not assume – especially with inexperienced performers! If you use a hand over the mouth to indicate 'You are speaking too loudly' they may interpret it as a sign to 'Stop talking'! People have been known to *turn round or speed up*, instead of *winding up* when the FM rotated an upward-raised arm!
2 *Word cues*. An agreed go-head word or phrase during dialogue, commentary, or discussion may be used to cue action or to switch to an insert. We note *out cues/out words* (last spoken words) at the end of a recorded insert (VT or film) to ensure accurately timed switching to the next item.

Fig. 19.3 Floor manager signals

1 Stand-by . . . go ahead.
2 Speed up, faster pace, quicker tempo (speed according to increase required).
3 Slow down, slower pace, stretch it out (indicated by slow 'stretching' gestures).
4 OK, you're all right now, it's OK (confirmation signal).
5 Keep talking (open/close beak movement).
6 We're/you're on time, on the nose.
7 FM TO CAMERA. Are we on time? How is the time going?
8 You have . . . time left (illustrated – 2 min and ½ min).
9 Wind up now, conclude action. Some use this sign for *speed up* ('Go faster'), and hold the arm vertically, moving the hand or arm in circles, to indicate *wind up*.
10 Cut it, stop, finish, omit rest of item.
11 You are cleared. You are now off camera, and can move or stop action.
12 Speak more loudly.
13 Volume up, louder.
14 Volume down, quieter (sometimes preceded by 'Quiet' signal).
15 Quiet, stop applause
16 Get closer to mike.
17 Come nearer, come downstage.
18 Go further away, go upstage.
19 Stop, keep still.
20 Turn round (in the direction indicated).
21 Move to camera left.
22 Tighten up, get closer together.
23 Open up, move further apart.
24 You're on that camera, play to that camera (sometimes with turning head gesture).
25 Play to the light indicated. (When actors are shadowing, point to light source and to area of face shadowed.)
26 Commercial break (brush right hand over left palm – spreading butter on bread).
27 FM TO AUDIENCE: You can applaud now (may be followed by louder sign).
28 Stop. (For applause, widespread action, etc.). Some use this sign ambiguously: slow to stop; fast to increase.

Additional signs include:

VTR or film is running – hand turning an imaginary crank.

Walk to the next position – walking movements with index and middle fingers, while pointing direction with other hand.

3 *Monitor cues.* Commentators and demonstrators often watch recorded inserts on a nearby picture monitor, taking a go-ahead cue from certain action. Alternatively, they may use a *time cue*, counting down (e.g. from 10 seconds) from a cue point. Most inserts have a few seconds without strong action or speech as *run-in* (*top*) and *run-out* (*tail*) to cushion/buffer the cuing.

4 *Light cues.* Performers can take a cue from the *camera tally* (*cue*) *light* (illuminated as the camera is switched to line). For announce booths or when cuing actors behind scenery, small

portable *cue lights* are often used, where the stand-by 'flick' is followed by a steady 'action light'.

5 *Intercom cues.* These are given direct to a performer (newscaster, commentator) wearing an earpiece – interrupted (interruptible) feedback, program interrupt, switched talkback.
6 *Clock cues.* A go-ahead at a specific time.
7 *Buzzer cues.* Used in some organizations, for intercom between film/videotape areas and the production control room. (One buzz; 'Yes' or 'Start'; two buzzes; 'No' or 'Stop'.)
8 *Electronic cue dots.* Used by networks at program change points, these small black/white squares in corner frame cue program out time, or give the next source a go-ahead cue.

Prompting

Relatively few performers can be expected to learn a script accurately and deliver it at a repeatable speed. Even the most experienced are liable to deviate from the written script, 'dry' (forget), or 'cut' lines. Whether this is a problem largely depends on the show format, whether live or taped, and if it is spontaneous or strictly scripted.

While a quiet verbal prompt may suffice (perhaps using a muting key to temporarily kill the microphone), more sophisticated methods are generally needed. There are generally two types of

Fig. 19.4 part 1 Prompting – direct methods
1 Handwritten prompt cards usually held near the camera, may contain dialogue or reminder notes. (Cue-cards, idiot board, goof sheet.)
2 Camera flip cards usually carry brief reminders.

Fig. 19.4 part 2 Prompting – video prompters
1 Video prompters use a 45° clear glass sheet at the camera lens, reflecting a picture-tube display of the script from a nearby script-scanner (monochrome TV camera shooting a miniature roller script), or a computer-stored script.
2 The camera lens shoots through the glass sheet at the subject. The reader appears to be looking straight at the lens and the audience. (Other systems can result in an off-camera stare.)
3 Where the speaker does not need to speak directly to the camera, the prompter-script video may be fed to floor video prompters or monitors.

prompters – *reminder notes (aide-mémoires)* that give data, subject heads, or show format; and *continual references* giving entire script or lyrics.

Reminders

These have been written on shirt cuffs or nearby scenery, but more orthodox methods range from small hand notes to the clip boards used by many interviewers, commentators, and anchors. These boards carry their notes, questions, and research information.

For brief information, cards can be held near the camera by floor crew (cue card, goof sheet, idiot card), or smaller *flip cards (flippers)* suspended under the camera head.

Script

A talking head reading a desk script does not make good television. It is dull and lacks 'spontaneity'. But a regular script ensures accurate timing. Consequently, many shows use a *roller prompter* (mechanically or electronically operated) that provides a continuously rolling copy of the script at or near the camera lens.

The vari-speed display is remotely controlled (by the talent or an operator) and typically has some 20 words visible in an eight-line frame. To disguise eye movements or a fixed stare, the performer 'casually' changes their head position while reading. Off-camera prompters can lead to a 'shifty-eyed' presentation, for the speaker has to continually glance away from the lens axis.

Prompters may inhibit shot variations because cameras carrying prompters need to be close enough for comfortable reading. Where only selected cameras have prompters, you must ensure that one of these is always near the speaker.

Earpiece prompts

In a daily soap opera the cast has little time to learn new lines. So some organizations fit actors with earpieces attached to small receivers. As they perform, the actors hear each line in turn being read from the script, which they repeat aloud. This is done so skilfully that the audience is quite unaware of the technique. The actor is completely mobile, and does not have to read visual prompters.

Production timing

Whereas a *closed circuit* program needs only approximate timing, a *live transmission* must fit its allocated time slot exactly. Overruns can result in end cut-off or cause scheduling problems. In live

Table 19.3 On-air intercom

Intercom (talkback) instructions reveal the split-second teamwork involved in efficient TV directing. Although local terminology and personnel vary, the following intercom talk from an actual show certainly reflects the spirit of the occasion.

Director's assistant	*Director*
Stand-by studio. Going ahead in 1 minute . . .	(FM alerts studio and gives countdown.)
Stand-by film. (Acknowledging buzz from film channel.)	Start VT. Show slate (identifying board) on 4.
Stand-by announcer.	
Roll film . . . 4–3–2–1–Zero.	Fade up film. Music (on audio tape).
On film for 1 minute . . . Stand-by 1.	Super 1.
Shot 1.	
On 1 . . . Stand-by 2.	Take music under. Cue Announcer. (Cue light in announce booth.)
Coming to end of film. Counting down . . . 30 seconds–20–10–5–4–3–2–1–0.	Bring up music. Cue Peter (FM cues talent). Take 2 (cut to Cam. 2). Take music under.
On 2. Shot 2 . . . 1 next.	He's going to sit. Go with him . . . Dolly in slowly to CU . . . Hold it there . . . Super slide title (guest's name) . . . take out super. Steady 1 . . . a bit tighter . . . good . . . take 1.
On 1. Shot 3 . . . 2 to graphic.	
Inserting 2 . . . Stand-by disc (grams).	Wipe in 2 . . . fine . . . take 2 out.
Clear 2 (after combined shot).	Go disc. Stand-by Joan (FM alerts talent).
Stand-by 3 . . . Coming to 3.	Music under. Cue her on and cut. He'll exit left.
On 3. Shot 4 . . . Stand-by 2 . . . Extra shot 4A.	
On 2 . . . We're 15 seconds over (overrun).	Coming to 2 . . . Mix to 2 . . . She's going to open the box . . .
On 2 . . . Shot 4A . . . Stand-by VT.	Cue Joan to open it (FM cues) . . . we're tight for time . . . Drop Shot 5.
Shot 5 is *out* (to be omitted).	Give her a wind-up . . . run VT.
Coming to VT . . . 4–3–2–1–0.	Cut to VT.
On VT for 2 minutes 7 seconds.	
1 minute left on VT . . . Coming out of VT in 30 seconds.	
Out words . . . 'on the road'.	
Stand-by 2 for Shot 6.	
Stand-by studio. Coming out of VT.	
20–10–5–4–3–2–1–0.	Hold it 2. Cut to 2.
– – – – – – – –	– – – – – – – –
On 3. Shot 60 . . . Clear 1	He's going to move to the door and wave. Give him ½ minute.
Roll titles.	
Stand-by tape (audio). Stand-by 1 for Shot 61.	(FM signals talent). Wind him up . . . go crawl, go tape.
On 1 and 3 . . . Off the air.	Super 1. Take out 3 . . . Go to black at end of phrase.
– – – – – – – –	– – – – – – – –
Stand-by for retakes.	Right everyone. That was great. We'll just check VT (VTR spot-checked). OK. Thank you very much. We have a clear.

composite productions, where various contributory sources '*opt-in*' or '*opt-out*' (temporarily join or leave) the main presentation to insert their own material accurate timing is imperative.

Scripts may be roughly timed by reading aloud and allowing for any mute action, business, or inserts. Many run at around a minute a full page. During rehearsal each segment or scene is timed, and subsequently adjusted to suit a timed show format/running order (estimated, permitted or actual).

Types of timer

Time can be checked in several ways:

- By referring to an *analogue wall clock*. It is often quicker to calculate an 'out time' by envisioning the repositioning of the clock's hands than to add figures (e.g. 1527 to 1545 = 18 minutes).
- Using a *digital timer* for *forward timing*. The clock counts forwards, showing *real-time* ('clock time'). Or it starts from zero, and shows *elapsed time*. This can be a desktop display or superimposed on a preview monitor.

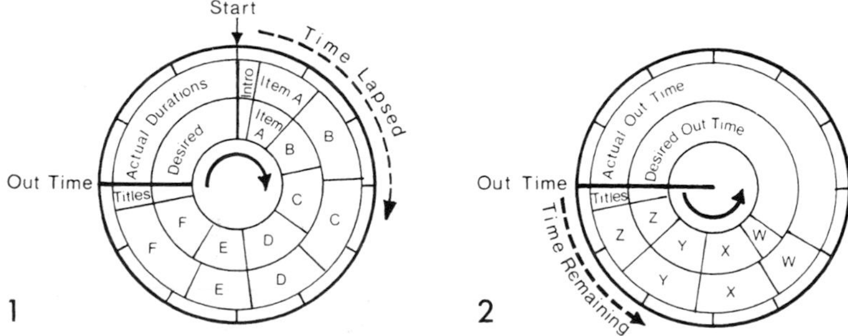

Fig. 19.5 Forward and back timing

1 *Forward timing* (*front timing*): duration timing (estimated and real) as the show proceeds.

Desired durations	*Running stop watch reads (from prog. start)*	*Clock start time*	*Clock end time*	*Item running times (actual duration)*
Intro 30″	30″	19.15.00	19.15.30	30″
Item A 10′	10′ 33″	19.15.30	19.25.33	10′ 03″
Item B 8″	18′ 30″	19.25.33	19.33.30	7′ 57″

2 *Back timing*: a 'remaining time' measurement, showing the amount of time before the production ends.

Item duration	*Clock time (item starts)*	*Remaining time*
Item X 1′ 0″	20.23.00	2′ 0″
Item Y 30″	20.24.00	1′ 0″
Item Z 30″	20.24.30	30″
End titles, Out time	20.25.00	00.00

- Using a *digital timer* for *back timing*. A similar facility, in which the scheduled duration is entered, and the clock counts down to zero. Any *minus* reading represents an overrun of the allotted time.
- Two hand-operated stopwatches, checking overall running time, and running time of individual sections, items, or scenes.

Timing methods

■ **Intermittent timing** When rehearsal is halted for any reason the stop clock time is noted. Rehearsal recommences at a point *before* the fault and the timer is restarted when the fault point is reached. A videotaped production can usually be edited to reduce excess; its associated *time code* providing duration or elapsed time checks throughout.

■ **Shortening inserts** A live transmission needs continual timing surveillance to obviate over- or underrunning – particularly with unscripted material. If one segment *overruns* (*spreads*), another may have to be shortened. Where prerecorded inserts (film or VT) are involved, their durations and *out words* should be precisely known. However, they offer little time flexibility, particularly if accompanied by recorded dialogue. We can only shorten them on the air by omitting their start (a *late-in*) or end (an *early-out*), or even omitting an insert entirely (*dropping*).

To assist cuing when excerpting from existing material (e.g. a complete speech), we should note both the *run-in* (pre-cue) dialogue and the *in-cue* (in-words).

■ **Back-cuing** To ensure that recorded play-out music finishes precisely at program fade-out, time the music from a recognizable cue point to its conclusion (say 1 minute 35 seconds). On transmission we start the music from that cue point at 1 minute 35 seconds before program out-time, fading it up when required. (Dead-pot/backtime.)

Taping the production

Videotape recording has added new freedoms to production techniques, so it is not surprising that today most shows are taped wherever possible. Here we are going to look at the variety of methods that are used; their advantages and limitations.

There are six regular approaches:

- Live-on-tape
- Basic retakes
- Discontinuous recording

Continued on p. 494

Table 19.4 The director's instructions

	Instruction	Meaning
To cameras	Opening shots please.	Cameras to provide initial shots in the show (or scene).
	Let's line up Shot 25.	Adjust that camera's shot and subject, for composition required in Shot 25.
	Ready 2: Stand-by 2.	Stand-by cue for Cam. 2.
	Give me a single: two-shot; three-shot/group shot/cover shot.	Isolate in the shot the single, two or three persons specified./A shot including a group of people./A wide shot taking in all likely action.
	Zoom in (or out).	Narrow (or widen) zoom lens angle.
	Tighten your shot.	Slightly closer shot (slight zoom in).
	Get a wider shot.	Get the next wider standard shot, e.g. from CU change to MS.
	2 match to 3.	Cam. 2 relate to or fit into Cam. 3's shot (using viewfinder 'mixed feeds').
	More (or less) headroom.	Adjust space between top of head and top of frame.
	More (or less) offset.	Adjust space between angled or profile face and side of frame.
	Center (frame-up).	Arrange subject in picture center.
	Lose the hands.	Compose shot to avoid seeing hands.
	Cut at the hands.	Frame to just keep hands in shot.
	Pan left (or right).	Horizontal pivoting of camera head.
	Tilt up (or down)/pan up (or down)	Vertical pivoting of camera head. (Strictly, 'pan' should apply only to horizontal action, but term's misuse is very widespread.)
	Dolly back/pull back/track back.*	Pull camera mounting away from the subject.
	Dolly in/push in/track in.*	Push camera mounting towards the subject.
	Creep in (or out).	Push in (or pull out) very slowly, imperceptibly.
	Truck left (or right)/crab left (or right).*	Move mounting to the left (or right).
	Arc left (or right).	Move mounting round subject in an arc.
	Ped up (or down).	Raise (or lower) column of pedestal mounting.
	Crane up (or down)/boom up/ (sometimes elevate or depress).	Raise (or lower) crane arm or boom.
	Tongue left (or right)/crane/slew/ jib.	Turn crane boom to left (or right).
	Tongue in (or out)/crane/boom in.	Crane positioned across the scene, move boom to and from subject.
	Focus up 3.	Warning to a camera 'standing by' that is defocused.

Table 19.4 (cont.)

	Lose focus on the boy.	Let the moving boy become defocused, remain sharp on other subject(s): *or* deliberately defocus on the boy.
	Pull focus on the girl.	Change focus deliberately from previous subject to the girl.
	Follow focus on the boy.	Maintain focus on moving boy.
	Split focus.	Focus equally sharply between main subjects.
	Focus 2/two, you're soft.	Criticism that Cam. 2's shot is not sharply focused.
	You're focused forward (or back).	Focused at a point too near the camera (or too far away – e.g. background sharp while nearer subject is unsharp).
	Rock focus 2. (Focus check.)	Focus to and from the subject to check optimum sharpness.
	Stand-by for a rise (or sit).	Person is about to stand up (or sit down).
	Follow him over/hold the boy.	Keep subject in shot (well composed) as he moves.
	Let him go.	Do not reframe. Let him pass out of shot.
	Lose him.	Recompose (or tighten shot) to exclude him.
	Cam. 2. you're on lights.	Cam. 2 has lamps or strong reflections in shot.
	Clear on 3/you're cleared 3.	A 'clear', usually after a combined shot (super, chroma key): Cam. 3 can move to its next position.
	Release 3 to captions.	A 'clear' directing camera to next position.
To the floor manager	Opening positions please.	Performers (and equipment) in position for start of show (or scene).
	Stand him by/give him a stand-by.	Alert him in readiness for a cue.
	Cue action/cue 'Bob'	Give sign for action to begin (perhaps name person or character).
	Hold it.	Stop action/performance; to correct an error.
	Freeze there.	Stop movement exactly at that point; hold it quite still.
	Back to the top/take it from the top.	Begin again at the start of the scene; repeat the rehearsal.
	Pick it up from Shot 20.	Recommence rehearsal from Shot 20.
	Would they just walk it?/Go through it	Without dialogue or performance, actors move through their various positions
	Clear 2's shot.	Something/someone is obscuring Cam. 2's shot.
	Tighten them up.	Move them closer together.

Table 19.4 (cont.)

	Move him downstage (upstage).	Move him toward (away from) the camera.
	Move her camera left.	Move her to *left* of the camera's shot (i.e. stage *right*).
	Give him a mark.	Draw a toe mark to show him a location point.
	Give her an eyeline.	Show her the direction in which to look.
	He'll take a word cue.	He will begin action on hearing certain dialogue.
	Give him a light/flash him.	Operate a cue light.
	Have him take a beat (or two) before he moves.	He should delay for a silent count of one (or two) before moving.
	Have him play to his key.	He should face his main light (key light).
	Show David 3/he's on 3.	Indicate to him Camera 3, which is shooting him.
	He's to work to/play to 3.	He should face Cam. 3.
	Ask him for more (less) voice.	To speak louder (more quietly).
	Show him the mike.	Indicate the microphone, picking him up.
	Speed him up.	Tell him to go more quickly (i.e. time is short).
	Stretch him/tell him to spread	Tell him to go more slowly (i.e. there is time to spare).
	Tell him to pad/keep talking.	Tell him to improvise until next item is ready. (Often a hand signal, thumb and extended fingers touch and part.)
	Give him 2 minutes ... 1 minute ... 30 seconds.	He has 2 minutes left (followed by countdown on fingers).
	Give him a wind/wind him up.	Signal him to finish.
	Give him a hard wind/quick wind.	It is essential for him to stop immediately. (Faster signal.)
	Kill him/cut him.	He is to stop immediately.
	Give him a clear.	We have left him. He is free to move away (or relax).
	Lose the flowers.	Remove (kill) the flowers (for the shot or scene; or take them away entirely).
To audio (sound mixer)	Fade up sound/fade up boom.	Fade up from zero to full (general or specific source).
	Stand-by music (disc/grams; taps, effects, etc.)	Warning before cue.
	Cue music/go music.	Go-ahead for music (live, disc or audio tape).
	Creep in music/sneak in music.	Begin very quietly, gradually fading up audio.
	Down music.	Reduce volume (level) of audio.

Table 19.4 (cont.)

	Music under/music to background.	Keep music volume low, relative to other sources.
	Hit the music.	Begin music, at full volume.
	Up music.	Increase volume of music, usually to full.
	Sound up (or down).	General instruction to increase (or decrease) overall volume.
	Kill (cut) the music.	Stop the music.
	Fade sound.	Fade out all program sound.
	Fade tape (disc, film sound, etc.).	Fade out specified source. Usually leaving other sources.
	Cross-fade; mix.	Fade out present source(s), while fading in the next.
	Segue (pronounced 'seg-way').	One piece of music immediately follows another without a break.
	Cue tape.	Start audio tape replay.
To switcher (vision mixer)	Take 1/cut to 1/cut 1.	Switch to Cam. 1's picture.
	Fade up 2.	Bring Cam. 2's video-fader from zero to full.
	Stand-by to fade 2/ ready to fade 2.	Prepare to fade Cam. 2's picture out.
	Fade/go to black/fade out.	Fade selected camera's video fader down to zero.
	Stand-by to mix (dissolve) to 3.	Warning before mixing cue.
	Mix (dissolve) to 3.	Mix from present camera(s) to Cam. 3's picture.
	Supering 3/ready to super 3.	Warning before super cue.
	Super 3/superimpose/add 3.	Fade Cam. 3's picture up, adding to existing sources.
	Take 2 out/lose 2.	Remove (usually fade) Cam. 2's picture. leaving the rest.
	Wiping 3 over 2.	Stand-by for wipe.
	Wipe to 3.	Using prearranged pattern, Cam. 3's picture obliterates present picture.
	Ready black . . . go to black.	Stand-by . . . fade picture to black.
To graphics (captions)	Flip. animate (de-animate). Change caption. Go crawl (Go roller).	Cuing animated graphics. (De-animate indicates 'return to pre-animation position').
To other source	Cue telecine/roll film/run TK.	Start film projector (similarly for *videotape*, although some organizations ROLL film and RUN VT).
	Go ahead PARIS.	Start cue to remote source in PARIS.

*British/European terms.

Table 19.5 Methods of videotaping productions

'Live-on-tape'	Multi-cameras (e.g. 2–4). Single videotape recorder.*
Advantages	• Program is ready for transmission immediately after taping. • No lengthy postproduction editing is needed. (Saves cost, equipment, staff, time.) • Recording period needed is only slightly longer than the length of the show. • No loss of pace or interaction, which can occur when action is continually interrupted. • Performers and team are all keyed up to give their best performances.
Disadvantages	• All shots and transitions are normally unchangeable. • There are no opportunities for second thoughts or alternative treatment. • The production includes any less successful material, errors in performance and treatment (editing, camerawork, sound, lighting). • All costume, make-up changes, scene changes, etc. have to be made in real time during the show. • Any editing is usually nominal, unless insert shots are taped afterwards (e.g. cutaway shots or brief retakes inserted).
Shooting in segments/scenes/ sections	Multi-cameras (e.g. 2–4). Single videotape recorder.*
Advantages	• Opportunities for corrective retakes, alternative treatment, experiments, etc. • Editing within the sequence can be made with the switcher. Where necessary, further editing decisions can be left to a postproduction session. • The performers and production group can concentrate on each segment and get it right before going on to the next. • Recording breaks can be arranged to allow costume, make-up changes, scene changes, etc. • Scenes can be shot in the most convenient time-saving order; in sequence or out of sequence. • Performers who are not required for later scenes can be released (actors, extras, musicians). This can save costs and reduce congestion in the studio. • If a setting is used at various times throughout a show (e.g. a classroom), all scenes with action there may be shot consecutively, and the scenery struck to make room for a new set. This technique virtually extends the size of the studio, and makes optimum use of available space. • Where a set appears in several episodes of a series, all sequences there can be shot in succession to avoid the need to store and rebuild the set over and over. • Similarly, where a program consists of a series of brief episodes (e.g. a story told in daily parts) these can all be recorded consecutively during the same session.
Disadvantages	• Much more time is needed to tape the show. Time lost during breaks can become greater than anticipated. • Retakes and revisions can take so much time that the session falls behind schedule (overrun). This can result in economic and administrative problems. There is a continuing pressure to save time and to press on. • Extensive postproduction editing is essential. At the end of the taping session you have no show until the separate segments are sorted and edited together. • All extended transitions between segments (mixes, wipes, video effects) must wait until postproduction. Similarly, music/effects/dialogue carrying over between segments must be added during audio sweetening. • In a complicated production, recording out of sequence can lead to confusion and to continuity errors in a fast-moving taping session.

Table 19.5 (cont.)

Multi-camera with ISO camera	All cameras are fed to the switcher, and program taped by the main VTR.*
Advantages	A separate ISO VTR can record continuously the output of any chosen camera: ● Provides slow-motion replay for inserts into the program. ● Provides extra shots for postproduction editing.
Disadvantages	● The arrangement ties up another VTR. ● Most of the material on the ISO recording is not used.
Multi-cameras with dedicated VTRs	Action is shot: live-on-tape, or in segments/scenes/sections.
Advantages	● All material from all cameras is recorded. ● No shots are missed. ● Alternative shots are available throughout the show. ● No irrevocable editing was carried out during the performance. ● Unexpected action, unrehearsed action, is recorded and available. ● Postproduction editing can be adjusted to suit the final performance. ● Camera treatment can need little planning. ● Normally, ad lib unplanned shots can upset planned production treatment (e.g. may delay a camera from moving to a new position). This is less likely when using dedicated VTRs.
Disadvantages	● The entire show requires total postproduction editing. ● The total program sound may need to be recorded separately from the pictures and laid down, with effects, music, applause, during postproduction editing. ● The arrangement can lead to poor mechanical production treatment; off-the-cuff shooting. Concentration on action rather than visual development. ● Camerawork may degenerate into semi-static cameras zooming in and out to vary shots.
Single camera	Single videotape recorder.* Taking brief shots or continuous sequences.
Advantages	● An extremely flexible, mobile method. ● One camera is easier to direct than a multi-camera crew. ● There are advantages in working with a small unit. ● The director can concentrate on the action and treatment. ● No switching is involved. ● No cuing of film or videotape inserts.
Disadvantages	● All the strain of camerawork falls on one operator. ● The production process is much slower than multi-camera treatment. ● There is a temptation to shoot retakes for better performance, or extra 'just-in-case' shots that might be used. These extra shots can absorb allotted shooting time. ● All material requires sorting and detailed editing. ● Production flow is continually interrupted (unlike multi-camera treatment). ● Away from the studio, various extra problems arise when shooting on location (weather, traffic, public, etc.). ● All film or videotape inserts in the program have to be introduced during postproduction.

*Usually a duplicate with backup VTR, in case of recording faults.

- Dedicated VTRs
- Isolated camera (ISO)
- Single-camera recording.

Live on tape

The program is recorded continuously in its entirety, as if it were a live transmission. The videotape is used here as a straightforward recording medium to provide more convenient scheduling of facilities and transmission, repeat transmissions, later analysis, etc. All editing is carried out on the studio production switcher during performance, and the show is ready for transmission at the conclusion of the recording session. A single videotape recorder (VTR) may be used; perhaps with a parallel VTR channel recording a duplicate version, in case of recording faults (*back-up copy, backing, insurance copy*). A very worthwhile practice, particularly when repeats are not possible!

Basic retakes

Here the production is recorded continuously as for transmission, but any errors (performers, production, technical) are re-recorded and the corrected sections substituted. *Duration trimming* may require some editing cuts – often covered by introducing *cutaways/nod shots/reaction shots*. As most programs can be improved by such editing, this method is widely used.

Discontinuous recording

We meet two types of discontinuous recording: *sectional* and *rehearse/record.*

Sectional

Using this method, the director goes through the *entire* production during the *camera-rehearsal* period, rehearsing each sequence or scene in turn. Any problems or revisions needed to correct or improve the action, camerawork, sound, or lighting are noted; and, if necessary, that section will be rehearsed again.

During a later taping session, each sequence or scene is recorded as the rehearsed version is repeated. If necessary, recording stops at the end of each to check whether a retake is necessary for any reason (e.g. '*Did a microphone come into shot*?). If using a single VTR, it may be advisable to *spot check* the tape to confirm a good recording; but preferably, the show would be taped simultaneously on two VTRs (*in dup*) 'just in case'.

The tape recorded during this period is subsequently edited during a postproduction session. Although a production switcher was used within each sequence, the takes need to be edited together to form the final 'transmission' version. The original taped material may include rerun scenes (to allow the preferred version to be selected later). Scenes may need to be shortened. Action may be removed. The original order of shots may be changed.

In addition, various postproduction work may be needed, such as *audio sweetening* (adding music and effects, sound quality adjustments, etc.), video effects, subtitling, picture quality treatment, etc.

Rehearse/record

This is really a form of 'floor blocking', in which the director sets up a sequence, rehearses it, then immediately records the corrected result. Each sequence may need to be relit, cameras repositioned, and scenery reset or cheated. The separate videotaped sections are later edited together with appropriate transitions and bridging sound.

Ideally, this pseudofilmic technique could provide optimum results for each shot. But in practice, the process can be extremely frustrating and time consuming. Normally the effectiveness of lighting, scenery, make-up costume, etc. is checked on camera, and improved or corrected while another scene is being rehearsed or during a studio stand-down. In a *rehearse/record* situation such changes have to be made immediately, so that the scene can be shot – and this leads to many compromises. To save time, a director may even record the first camera rehearsal with all its imperfections, in case it can be used! A videotape channel is continuously tied to the studio. Themes and variations are shot for later selection, and repeat action may be necessary to ensure editing continuity. Considerable post-studio videotape editing is necessary. Audio sweetening becomes a major consideration.

Dedicated VTRs

Here each camera's output is separately recorded on its own dedicated VTR. No production switcher is used during recording; all transitions and selections being made during a postproduction dubbing session to form a composite tape.

Videotape editing is carried out using complex computer-controlled facilities incorporating digital editing techniques, all guided by time-code shot identification. As a one-hour program may involve 300–400 individual edits, the operation clearly requires systematic organization of sophisticated postproduction facilities.

Isolated camera (ISO)

Here the production, which may be live or 'live-on-tape', is edited 'on the hoof' with the studio production switcher, and taped by the *main VTR*. However, throughout the show, pictures from one of the cameras are *also* being recorded on a separate isolated VTR. (The camera chosen for the 'ISO' can be varied at any time.)

Pictures from the ISO camera can be selected on the switcher whenever they are needed, but all its shots (on-air and off-air) are taped on the isolated VTR. This arrangement provides several useful opportunities:

1 *Replay inserts.* A regular use for the isolated VTR is to provide *instant replay in slow motion* during a live or live-on-tape production. At any chosen moment (e.g. after a goal has been scored in a game) the ISO tape is stopped, rewound, and replayed into the program. (This tape may also be used for later videotape editing.)
2 *Cover shots.* If the *ISO* camera concentrates on one particular aspect of the scene (e.g. the goal area) there is no danger of important action there being missed while the director is using other cameras' shots.
3 *Stand-by shots.* When a production switcher is used on a multi-camera shoot, the resulting program tape contains all the shots of the event you have available. So if you subsequently need to modify this tape (e.g. to lengthen the overall timing, or to excerpt sections), all you can do is to reuse portions of the original; perhaps copying and inserting them as 'repeat shots'.

However, if there is an ISO camera recording separate *additional* shots during the event (e.g. crowd shots, an overall view, or action seen from a different viewpoint) this unused material can be edited into the program tape wherever necessary as 'cutaways', to allow changes or corrections to be made.

Single-camera recording

In this situation, a single portable camera with its own videotape recorder shoots the action:

- As the *main production camera*, recording material in any convenient order.
- As a *mobile camera* supplementing a series of fixed cameras.
- As a *'freelance' unit*, exploring for shot opportunities which can be edited into the main multi-camera operation.

The postproduction process (the 'post')

As TV equipment became more sophisticated and productional aspirations grew, directors often found that there was insufficient time during scheduled studio periods to add the polish to their shows that they were striving for. So the practice grew of working on a program afterwards in a separate *postproduction* (*'post'*) session.

At first this involved an extended *videotape editing* process, but with time it also embraced such areas as:

- *Sound sweetening* (e.g. quality/reverberation adjustments; the introduction of music and audio effects).
- *Picture treatment* – Slight *corrective changes* in a picture's brightness, contrast, or color balance to improve the visual continuity between intercut shots. Similarly, adjustments to create or improve *atmospheric effects* – e.g. to enhance a candlelit, moonlit, or sunset scene. To provide image softening.
- *Titling and subtitles* – Title insertions may be elaborate, or require critical positioning.
- *Video effects* – Whether a video effect is prepared beforehand or carried out during the studio session will depend on several factors, including its complexity. Setting up video effects can be very time consuming. They might be of:

  A *general* nature (e.g. an electronically inserted background panel)
  A *specific cued effect* (e.g. lightning striking a tree on cue)
  A *layered* (*built-up*) treatment
  Or even *frame-by-frame rotoscoping* changes in which each picture frame involves hand-worked alterations.

Postproduction sessions also give the director opportunities to correct, to augment, to change, to modify, to refine editing, to introduce supplementary features such as sound effects and music . . .

- There may have been insufficient time to complete the program during the taping session. (Perhaps things went wrong, or took longer than expected, overrunning scheduled time.)
- Previously overlooked errors may need to be corrected (cut out a microphone in shot; tighten a shot to avoid an *overshoot (shoot-off)*.
- Maybe insert material was not ready in time (e.g. film was still being processed or edited).
- Certain complex video effects may make use of material shot during the studio taping session. (For example, morphing a man into a monster, and re-inserting this into the original scene.)
- Excerpts from the program may be needed for promotions.

So in practice, postproduction processes can involve anything from routine editing, to a major transformation of the original material. One can even use the studio taping period for recording basic visuals in front of chroma-key backdrops, leaving all other decisions, including *background insertions*, until busy *postproduction sessions* at a later date!

20 Style

There is no 'correct method' of presenting any subject. Directors have tried most approaches over the years. Some of these have become regular practice; others just passing whims. Techniques that have been used adroitly by some (e.g. background music) have been crudely overdone by others, and become distractingly intrusive. Certainly, if you choose an *inappropriate* technique you are likely to find your audience becoming confused, distracted, resentful . . . or simply losing interest!

Production approaches

Appropriateness

So what is *appropriate*? Well, in practice, it is largely a matter of custom, fashion, and convention.

- *Informal presentations* usually take the form of 'natural' situations. We chat with the craftsman in his workshop, or at the fireside, or while on a country walk.
- *Formal presentations* often follow a very stylized artificial format. We see people in carefully positioned chairs, sitting on a raised area in front of a cyc. They are often behind desks. There may be a chair-person, and 'rules of procedure'.
- *Display* is an unrealistic, decorative way of presenting your subject. Emphasis is on effect. We meet it in game shows, open-area treatment (e.g. choirs, music groups, dance), in children's programs.
- *Simulated environments* aim to create a completely realistic illusion. Anything breaking that illusion, such as a camera coming into shot in a period drama, would destroy the effect.
- *Actuality* is a revelatory style. We make it quite clear to the audience that we are in a studio by deliberately revealing the mechanics. On location, the unsteady hand-held camera and microphone dipping into shot supposedly give an 'authenticity' or 'veracity' to the occasion. We meet this approach in '*vox pop*' street interviews.

Routines

Some production techniques have become so familiar through convention or suitability that it could seem strangely unorthodox if we presented them in any other way – e.g. a newscaster sitting in a lounge.

Certain approaches have become so stereotyped that they enter the realms of cliché; routine methods for routine situations. The sheer extent and repetition of TV productions has thrown up a number of such formats: newscasts, studio interviews, game shows, chat shows, etc. If we analyze such productions we usually find that styles have evolved as the most effective, economic, and reliable ways of handling their particular subjects.

If we regard such a packaging as 'a container for the goods', then these routine treatments can free the audience to concentrate on the event. If, however, we consider the presentation treatment as an opportunity to encourage interest and heighten enjoyment, then any 'routine' becomes unacceptable.

Clearly, any dramatic or emphatic treatment would be quite gratuitous for many types of TV production. Instead, it is best to aim for pictorial variety, coupled with clear, unambiguous visual statements that direct and concentrate attention, rather than introduce any imposed 'style'.

Many non-dramatic subjects are *inherently* limited in their potential treatment. How many sensible meaningful shot variations can you take of people speaking to each other, or driving an automobile, or playing an instrument, or demonstrating an article? The range is small.

For certain subjects the picture is virtually irrelevant. What a person has to *say* may be extremely important; while what he *looks* like is immaterial to the message. It may even prove a distraction or create prejudicial bias. 'Talking heads' appear in most TV shows, but unless the speaker is particularly animated, the viewers' visual interest is seldom sustained. Changing viewpoint helps – but can appear fidgety.

Motion pictures inform us through continual illustration and commentary. Television's more economic but less enticing approach is for people to tell us about matters instead. They sit in the studio with graphics or film clips, or stand at the scene of activities and talk directly to us, instead of using the camera itself to demonstrate. Here the difference in approach is not inherent in the medium but the way it is being used.

Ambience

From the moment a show begins, we are influencing our audience's attitude to the production itself. Introductory music and titling style can immediately convey a serious or a jokey feeling towards what is to come.

We have only to recall how the hushed voice, quiet organ notes, slow visual pace, impart a reverential air to proceedings, or the difference between a regal and a 'show-biz' opening fanfare, to realize how our expectancy changes.

Surroundings can also directly affect how convincingly we convey information. Certain environments, for example, impart authority or scholarship: classroom, laboratory, museum, study. A plow shown at work on the farm will not only be more readily understood but will carry a conviction that is lacking in the studio demonstration.

The illusion of truth

As you've seen, even when we are trying to present events '*exactly as they are*', the camera viewpoints, lens angles, picture composition, the choice and sequence of shots, etc. will all influence how our audience interprets what they are seeing. But the way we set about making a program can also have an important bearing on the end product. Where we lay emphasis, what we leave out, even the weather conditions (gloomy, stormy, harsh or sparkling sunlight, heavy rain) will all modify its impact.

Let us consider for a moment, the initiation of a documentary program. The audience invariably *assumes* that they are seeing a fair and informative account. But that can depend on how the program maker tackles the subject:

1. There is the hopeful approach; a 'voyage of discovery' in which the director points the camera around with extemporized comments, giving a 'tourist's-eye' view' of events. This invariably results in a rag-bag of disjointed and unrelated shots. Sometimes, by adding commentary over, graphics, music and effects, it is possible to develop a coherent program theme, but such an empirical approach is uncertain, to say the least.
2. More often, the director begins by having the subject researched and making a plan of campaign. There are great advantages in anticipating and organizing beforehand. However, having found out about potential locations and local experts, the director develops a schedule, arranges transport and accommodation, obtains permits . . . and so on. There is the danger that preconceived ideas will dominate, so that you develop a thesis even before you arrive, and reject whatever does not seem to fit in with it when you actually get there!
3. Occasionally we encounter the *contrived* approach, in which the director has really *staged* what we are seeing – arranged the action, edited selectively. Dressed in their best, the participants put on a show for the camera – and the television audience assumes that this is a peep into reality!

Leaving aside *ethics*, even these brief (but real) examples are a reminder of the power of the camera, and the director's responsibilities in the way it is used.

Pictorial function

Most pictures are factual, showing subjects in a familiar undistorted fashion, without any predominating emotional appeal. Yet, by judiciously arranging these same subjects, by careful composition, and a selective viewpoint you can modify their entire impact and give them quite a different implied *significance*. You *interpret* the scene.

You can deliberately distort and select reality so that your presentation bears little direct relationship to the actual situation; you may do this to create a dramatic illusion . . . or to produce an influential force (advertising, propaganda).

Abstracting further, you can stimulate emotions and ideas simply by the use of movement, line, form, etc., which the viewer personally interprets.

Most TV production aims at the direct reportage of events. But there are occasions when we seek to stimulate the audience's imagination; to evoke ideas that are not conveyed directly by camera and microphone. In this chapter we shall examine these concepts and how they can be used.

Picture applications

Because so much television program material is explicit, it is easy to forget how it can be. We can use pictures for a number of different purposes:

- *To convey information directly* (e.g. normal conversation)
- *To establish a location* – e.g. Big Ben to imply that the location is London, England.
- *To interpret a situation* – Conveying abstract concepts (ideas, thoughts, feelings) through associative visuals; e.g. plodding feet suggest the weariness of a trail of refugees.
- *To symbolize* – Symbols that we associate with particular people, places, events, etc.
- *To imitate* – Pictures that appear to imitate a condition (e.g. the camera staggers as a drunk reels; defocusing to convey losing consciousness).
- *To identify* – Showing features such as icons, logos, trademarks, associated with particular organizations, events, etc.
- *To recapitulate* – Pictures that remind us of subjects met earlier (flashbacks).
- *To couple ideas* – Using pictures to link events, themes, etc. (e.g. panning from a boy's toy boat . . . to a ship at sea, on which he becomes captain).
- *To create a visual montage* – A succession of images interplay to convey an overall impression; e.g. epitomizing war.

Productional rhetoric

Rhetoric is the art of persuasive or impressive speech and writing. Unlike everyday conversation, it stimulates our imagination through style and technique, by inference and allusion, instead of direct pronouncement, by appealing to our inward ear and eye. The rhetoric of the screen has similar roots that film makers such as Alfred Hitchcock have explored over the years to great effect.

The analysis that follows is more than a concise list of facts. It is a distillation of production techniques with exciting persuasive potentials, techniques that have moved audiences to tears, of laughter and of pity; that have held them in tense expectation. Translate these principles into living illustrations and we see how the camera can, without a word of dialogue, convey the whole gamut of human responses.

An example, A veteran performer ends his brave but pathetic vaudeville act amid gibes and cat-calls. He bows, defeated . . . we hear hands clapping . . . the camera turns from the sad lone figure . . . past derisive faces . . . to where his aged wife sits applauding.

Summary of devices used

Regard this analysis as a series of fingerposts, pointing the opportunities to build up original situations of your own. The summary outlines the principles involved. The examples that follow show those principles in action.

1 Making a *direct visual contrast.*
   (a) Of the picture quality – brightness, clarity, tonal contrasts.
   (b) By editing, contrasting the shot duration, transitions used, cutting rhythm.
   (c) Contrasting camera treatment – shot sizes, viewpoint height, camera movement, composition.
   (d) Through the subject itself. Creating a change that reveals new information, altering the picture's significance, e.g. by introducing a subject movement (the blonde turns . . . to reveal it is a man in drag); by cutting to a new viewpoint (the formally dressed butler . . . is wearing sneakers); by lighting. Contrasting the movement of one subject with another (contrasting energy with langor). Contrasting subject associations, i.e. the mood, qualities, properties, state of one subject with another (new with old). Contrasting subject form (building construction with its subsequent demolition).

2 Making a *direct audio contrast.* Contrasting the sounds' relative volume, pitch, quality, reverberation, speed, rhythm, duration, methods of transition, composition, sound movement, association.

3 We can *directly contrast the picture and its sound.* By comparing any aspect of (1) with another in (2) (e.g. a picture of starving children singing *Pennies from Heaven*).

4 Similarly, we can make a *direct comparison* between two ideas, situations, etc. for visual comparison, audio comparison, picture and sound compared.

5 Showing identical subjects with *different associations.*
   (a) Identical or similar subjects having different purposes, values, significances, etc.
   (b) The original purpose (or associations, etc.) of a subject has become changed.

6 Linking a variety of subjects, through *common association*.
7 *Juxtaposing apparent incongruities*.
8 *Implication*. Hinting at a situation without actually demonstrating it. Examples range from filmic time to censorable innuendo.
9 *Unexpected outcome*.
   (a) Climatic build-up to an unexpected outcome.
   (b) Anticlimax, following a build-up.
10 *Bathos*. A fall in significance; from the sublime to the ridiculous.
11 *Deliberate falsification or distortion*. 'Accidentally' causing the audience to misinterpret.
12 *Imitative interpretation*.
   (a) Between subjects.
   (b) Between mechanics and subjects;
13 *Associative selection*.
   (a) Direct, using part of a subject to represent the whole.
   (b) Recalling a subject by referring to something closely associated with it.
   (c) Symbolism – using a symbol to represent a subject.
14 *Deliberate overstatement*. Excessive emphasis on size, effort, etc. for dramatic strength.
15 *Deliberate understatement*. Preliminary underemphasis, to strengthen the eventual impact of size, effort, etc.
16 An *unreal effect* seeming to evolve naturally.
17 A *natural effect* introduced through *obviously contrived* means.
18 *Repetition*.
   (a) Of sound.
   (b) Of picture.
19 *Sequential repetition*.
   (a) A series of sequences, all beginning with the same shot, associations, etc.
   (b) A succession of similar circumstances.
20 *Successive comparison*.
   (a) Showing the same subject in different circumstances.
   (b) Showing the same subject in different manifestations.
21 *Pun*. Play on a subject's dual significance.
22 *Irony*. A comment with an inner sardonic meaning, often by stating the opposite.
23 *Modified irony*. An ironic modification of the real significance of a subject, situation, etc.
24 *Dramatic irony*. The audience's perceiving a fact that the character involved is unaware of.
25 *Personification*. Representing an inanimate object as having human characteristics.
26 *Metaphorical transfer*. Transferring the properties of one subject to another.
27 *Flashback*. Jumping back in time, to a point earlier than the narration has reached.
28 Referring to *future events* as if *already past or present*.
29 Referring to *the absent as if present*. Usually relating concurrent events by montage.
30 Referring to *the past as if still present*.
31 *Cutaway*. Deliberately interrupting events to show concurrent action elsewhere.
32 *Fade-out on climax*. Fading at the crucial moment in action:
   (a) To leave the audience in suspense.
   (b) To prevent the climactic peak being modified by subsequent action.
33 *Double take*. Passing by a subject casually . . . then returning to it quickly, having suddenly realized its significance.
34 *Sudden revelation*. Suddenly revealing new information that we were not previously aware of . . . immediately making the situation meaningful.
35 *Incongruity*. Where a character:
   (a) Accepts an incongruous situation as normal.
   (b) Exerts disproportionate effort to achieve something.
   (c) Displays disproportionate facility (i.e. exaggerated speed, etc.).
   (d) Is unable to perform a simple act.
   (e) Imitates unsuccessfully.
   (f) Does the right thing – wrongly.
   (g) Caricature.

These are, of course, only the bare bones of opportunity. You can take any of the devices listed and apply them in many quite different ways. For example, let us take (10) *Bathos*. Here is the basis of the 'banana-skin' and 'custard-pie' jokes, and our reactions when the tattered hobo dusts off the park bench before sitting. In the following examples you will see how readily these ideas can be introduced.

Examples of productional rhetoric

1 (a) A suddent mood change, by switching from bright gaiety . . . to macabre gloom.
Contrasting a soft-focused dream-like atmosphere . . . with the hard clear-cut state of harsh reality.
Contrasting the airiness of a high-key scene . . . with the restrictiveness of heavy chiaroscuro treatment.
(b) Contrasting the leisurely pace of prolonged shots . . . with fast-moving short-duration shots.
Contrasting the peaceful effect of a series of fades . . . with the sudden shock of a cut.
Contrasting the jerky staccato of rapid cutting . . . with the deliberation of a slower cutting rhythm.
(c) Contrasting the size of a giant aircraft . . . with its diminutive pilot.
Contrasting an individual's dominance in close-up . . . with his relative insignificance within his surroundings.
Contrasting the subject strength from a low-angle shot . . . with its inferiority from a high-angle viewpoint.
Contrasting a forward aggressive move . . . with a backward recessive move.
Contrasting the restriction of limited depth of field . . . with a spacious deep-focus shot.
Contrasting the normality of a straight-on shot . . . with the instability of a canted shot.
(d) The only refuge on a storm-swept moorland is revealed by a lightning flash . . . as a prison.

2 Contrasting the busy crowds' noise by day . . . with the hush of the empty street at night.
Contrasting realistic . . . with unreal sounds.

3 A hippopotamus lumbers along, in step with delicate ballet music.

4 A pair of lovers embrace . . . and the camera tilts up to show a pair of lovebirds.
A soprano's high C . . . merges into the scream of a factory siren.
A helicopter hovers . . . to the sound of a bee buzzing.

5 A favorite record which has been played at a party is later used to cover the sounds of a murder.

6 Shots of sandcastles, rock pools, beach ball; sounds of children's laughter, sea-wash, suggest the seaside.

7 Shots of a massive French locomotive . . . end with the shrill, effeminate toot of its whistle.

8 Suspecting that he is followed, a fugitive leaves a café . . . the sound of feet joins his own in the empty street.

9 A thief grabs a valuable necklace . . . it breaks . . . the pearls scatter. It is spring. Migrant ducks arrive and land on a lake . . . but skid on its still-frozen surface.

10 After ceremonial orders, a massive gun is fired . . . producing a wisp of smoke and a pop.

11 South American music, a striped blanket on sun-drenched stone, a bright straw hat, cactus . . . but only a sunbather in a suburban garden, listening to the radio.

12 Someone is speaking to a deaf person . . . we see his lips in close-up, but without sound.
An upward movement . . . accompanied by rising-pitch sounds.

13 (a) The name on a ship's life-belt identifies the vessel – *Titanic*.
(b) The guillotine used to epitomize the French Revolution.
(c) A shot of the Golden Gate bridge to represent San Francisco.
14 A close shot of an auctioneer's gavel descending.
15 A smoker casually throws aside a cigar-butt. A fire starts . . . which develops into a devastating forest blaze.
16 As we watch a moving picture . . . a large hand appears and turns it over like the page of a book.
17 Watching a street fight as a distorted reflection in the chromium wheel-trim of a nearby automobile.
18 A searcher shouts the lost person's name . . . it echoes and re-echoes. An angry crowd closes round a central figure. Close shots cut alternately between the accused and individuals in the crowd.
19 A successful concert tour is symbolized by the artist taking a series of similar curtain calls.
20 A succession of shots show the same policeman in a variety of situations; directing traffic, guiding a sightseer, rescuing a would-be suicide, making an arrest . . .
21 A parrot at an open window whistles for food . . . a passing girl turns at the 'wolf whistle'.
22 It is a power blackout. The lost traveler strikes a match . . . and sees a poster – 'Save Energy'.
23 A newspaper advertisement shows extraordinary bargains . . . then we see it is an old copy, used to line a drawer.
24 A mountaineer climbs . . . unaware that his rope is fraying.
25 An animated coffee-pot describes the great coffee it makes.
26 An elephant that flies ('Dumbo').
27 An old woman tells of her childhood . . . brief shots showing her life as a girl.
28 Looking at the projected plans of a ship . . . we hear the launching festivities.
29 A superimposed montage showing a missing man surrounded by headlines; radio announcers telling of his disappearance.
30 A derelict ballroom echoing to the sounds of bygone dances.
31 The fugitive escapes down a side alley. But just as we see that his way is blocked the shot changes to show his pursuers.
32 A little man arrogantly challenges a person sitting nearby . . . who stands and towers over the challenger. The picture cuts to another scene.
33 Walking past a poster of a wanted robber, a man suddenly stops, reacts, and returns to it. He realizes that its picture looks like himself.
34 Entering a room, we see someone reading . . . a close viewpoint reveals the dagger-hilt protruding from his back.
35 A man takes off his hat . . . and eats it.

Imaginative sound

Although the aural memory is less retentive it is generally more imaginative than the eye. We are more perceptive and discriminating towards what we see. Consequently, our ears accept the unfamiliar and unrealistic more readily than our eyes, and are more tolerant of repetition. A sound-effects recording can be re-used many times, but a costume or drapes design may become familiar after a couple of viewings.

In many TV shows the audio is taken for granted, while attention is concentrated on the visual treatment. Yet without audio the presentations can become meaningless (talks, discussions, interviews, newscasts, music, game shows, etc.): whereas without video the production would still communicate.

Audio can explain or augment the picture, enriching its impact or appeal. Music or effects can suggest locale (seashore sounds), or a situation (pursuing police heard), or conjure a mood (gaiety, foreboding, comedy, horror).

A non-specific picture can be given a definite significance through associated sound. Depending on accompanying music, a display of flowers may suggest springtime, a funeral, a wedding, or a ballroom.

Sound elements

■ **Voice** The most obvious sound element, the *human voice*, can be introduced into the presentation in several different ways:

1 A single person addressing the camera, formally or informally.
2 An off-screen commentator (voice-over) providing a formalized narrative (e.g. travelogues); or the spontaneous commentary for a sports event.
3 We may 'hear the thoughts' of a character (reminiscive or explanatory narration) while watching his silent face, or the subject of his thoughts.
4 Dialogue – the informal natural talk between people (actual or simulated), with all its hesitance, interruptions, breaking off, overlapping; and the more regulated exchanges of formal discussion.

■ **Effects** The characteristic sound picture that conjures a particular place or atmosphere comes from a blend of stimuli: from action sounds (e.g. footsteps, gunfire), from environmental noises (e.g. wind, crowd, traffic), and from the subtle ways in which sound quality is modified by its surroundings (reverberation, coloration, distortion).

■ **Music** Background music has become near-obligatory for many programs. It can range from purely melodic accompaniment to music that imitates, or gives evocative or abstract support. You can even use musical instruments to create audio effects (creaks, clicks, whines, etc.).

■ **Silence** The powerful dramatic value of *silence* should never be underestimated. However, silence must be used with care, for it may too easily seem to be just a loss of audio.

Continued silence can suggest such diverse concepts as: death, desolation, despair, stillness, hope, peace, extreme tension (we listen intently to hear if the marauders are still around).

Sudden silence after noise can be almost unbearable: A festival in an Alpine village . . . happy laughter and music . . . the tumultuous noise of an unexpected avalanche engulfing the holiday makers . . . then silence.

Sudden noise during silence creates an immediate peak of tension:

The silently escaping prisoner knocks over a chair and awakens the guards (or did they hear him after all?)

Silent streets at night . . . then a sudden scream.

Dead silence when the audience has been following action that would logically lead to a tremendous noise can give a scene a taut unreal quality: To a crescendo of sound, intercut shots of two locomotives traveling towards each other at speed on the same track . . . they crash in silent slow-motion.

The explosive charge has been set . . . the detonator is switched . . . nothing happens . . . silence.

Sound emphasis

You can manipulate the relative volumes of sounds for dramatic effect; emphasizing particular sources, cheating loudness to suit the situation. A whisper may be amplified to make it clearly audible, a loud sound held in check.

You may establish the background noise of a vehicle and then gradually reduce it, taking it under to improve audibility of conversation. Or you could deliberately increase its loudness so that the noise drowns the voices. Occasionally you may take out all environmental sounds to provide a silent background – for a thoughts sequence, perhaps.

You can modify the aesthetic appeal and significance of sound in a number of ways.

For *factual sound* you can use:

1 *Random* natural pick-up (e.g. overheard street conversations).
2 *Selective pick-up* of particular sources.

For *atmospheric sound*:

1 By choosing certain natural associated sounds you can develop a *realistic illusion*. (Cockcrow suggests it is dawn.)
2 By deliberately distorting reality you create *fantasy* to stimulate the imagination. (A Swannee whistle's note suggests flight through the air.)
3 By *abstraction* the pitch and rhythm of sounds can evoke ideas and emotions without direct reference to naturalistic phenomena. (Film music, cartoon soundtracks, musique concrète.)

Sound applications

As we saw relative to pictures, sound can be used for a number of different purposes:

- *To convey information directly* – Normal conversation.
- *To establish a location* – e.g. traffic noises, that imply a busy street scene nearby.
- *To interpret a situation* – Conveying abstract concepts (ideas, thoughts, feelings) through associative sounds; a slurred trombone note as a derisive comment.
- *To symbolize* – Sounds that we associate with particular places, events, moods, etc. (e.g. an air-raid siren denoting an attack).
- *To imitate* – Sounds that appear to resemble, mimic, parody or mock; e.g. music copying a cuckoo's call.
- *To identify* – Sounds associated with particular people or events; signature tunes, leitmotif.
- *To recapitulate* – Sounds recalling others heard earlier.
- *To couple ideas* – Using music or sound effects to link events, themes, etc; e.g. a musical bridge between scenes; aircraft noise carried over between a series of shots showing its stops *en route*.
- *To create a sound montage* – A succession or mixture of sounds arranged for comic or dramatic effect; e.g. a bassoon and piccolo duet; combined sound effects that build up an overall impression (e.g. separate sound effects of explosions, gunfire, aircraft, sirens, whistles . . . create the illusion of a battle scene).

Off-screen sound

When someone speaks or something makes a sound it might seem logical to show the source as a matter of course. But it can be singularly dull if we do this repeatedly: she starts talking, so we cut and watch her.

You can use *off-screen* sound in many ways, to enhance program impact:

1. Having established a shot of someone talking, you might cut to see the person they are speaking to and watch their reactions, or cut to show what they are talking about. The original dialogue continues, but we no longer see the speaker. So you can establish relationships, even where the two subjects have not been seen together in the same shot.
2. Background sounds can help to establish location. Although a mid-shot of two people occupies the screen, the audience interprets that they are near the seashore, a highway, a sawmill.

3 Off-screen sounds may be chosen to intrigue us, or arouse our curiosity.
4 A background sound may introduce us to a subject before we actually see it, informing us about what is going on nearby or is going to appear (e.g. the wheezy spluttering of an approaching jalopy).
5 Tension can build as a character recognizes and reacts to a sound that the audience cannot interpret. Again, tension grows when a character hears a sound (that we also hear) but cannot understand its significance. Alternatively, we may realize the significance of a sound that the character has not heard or understood.
6 Off-screen sounds can exaggerate or emphasize our impressions of a scene (a crowd, traffic); perhaps indicating them even where none exists.
7 By deliberately *overlapping* sound you can create a linkage between scenes; introducing the next scene's audio before you cut to it. For example, an old man reminiscing at dinner: 'In those days, Vienna was a city of wonderful music.' While watching him, we hear a waltz in the background . . . the picture dissolves to show a soirée.
8 The background sound may create audio continuity, although the shots switch rapidly. Two people walk through buildings, down a street . . . their voices are heard clearly throughout at a constant level.
9 An audio montage of several different sources, may be used to suggest thoughts, dreams, etc.

Substituted sound

Surprisingly often, instead of reproducing the *original* sound we shall deliberately devise a substitute to accompany the picture. There are several reasons for this approach:

No sound exists. As with sculpture, painting, architecture, inaudible insects, prehistoric monsters.

Sometimes the actual sounds are *not available*, *not recorded* (mute shooting), or *not suitable*. For example: absence of birdsong when shooting a country scene; location sounds were obtrusive, unimpressive, or inappropriate to use; a location camera may obtain a close shot of a subject (using a narrow-angle lens) that is too distant for effective sound pick-up.

The sounds you introduce may be just *replacements* (using another lion's voice instead of the missing roar), or *artificial substitutes* in the form of effects, music, synthesized or treated audio.

Background music and effects should be added cautiously. They are easily:

1 Disproportionate (too loud or soft).
2 Hackneyed (too familar).
3 Over-obvious (imitating every action – 'Mickey Mousing').
4 Obtrusive (surging into slight gaps of silence).
5 Out of scale (overscored music).
6 Inappropriate (have wrong or misleading associations).

Controlling sound treatment

Various working principles are generally accepted in sound treatment:

1 The scale and quality of audio should match the picture (appropriate volumes, balance, audio perspective, acoustics, etc.).
2 Where audio directly relates to picture action it should be synchronized (like movements, footsteps, hammering, other transient sounds).
3 Video and audio should normally be switched together. No audio advance or hangover on a cut.
4 Video cutting should be on the beat of the music, rather than against it; preferably at the end of a phrase. Continual cutting in time with music becomes tedious.
5 Video and audio should usually begin together at the start of a show; finishing together at its conclusion, fading out as a musical phrase ends.

Audio analysis

We all recognize that some sounds seem exciting, martial, happy . . . while others are melancholy, soporific, wistful. Is this entirely fortuitous, or are there working principles to guide our audio selection? Experience suggests that there are.

If you analyze a series of sounds creating a particular emotional impact you will find they have many common features. Table 20.1 shows some 42 sound characteristics and typical associated responses. These effects can, of course, combine in various complex ways. For example, from Table 20.1, it is obvious that a sound containing the features 1, 4, 9, 10, 13, 15, 19, 20, 23, 24, 26, 27, 31, 33a, 35, 39, 42 must necessarily produce an exciting, vigorous impact. On the other hand, one containing features 2, 5, 8, 11, 14, 16, 18, 21, 22, 28, 32, 34b, 36, 41 must be a sad, peaceful, sound.

Table 20.1 Analysis of sounds and their effect

	Sound characteristics	Associated with
Volume	1 Loud sounds	Big, strong, assertive, powerful, energetic, rousing, earnest.
	2 Soft sounds	Small, soothing, peaceful, gentle, subdued, delicate, little energy.
	Against a quiet background	Alerting, persuasive.
Pitch	3 Pitch	Often suggests physical height.
	4 High-pitched sounds	Exciting, light, brittle, stirring, invigorating, elating, attractive, distinct, sprightly, weak.
	5 Low-pitched sounds	Powerful, heavy, deep, solemn, sinister, undercurrent, depression.
Key	6 Major	Vigor, brightness.
	7 Minor	Melancholy, wistful, apprehensive.
Tonal quality	8 Pure, thin (e.g. flutes, pure string-tone)	Purity, weakness, simplicity, sweetness, ethereal, daintiness, forthright, persuasiveness.
	9 Rich (possessing strong overtones, harmonics)	Richness, grandeur, fullness, complexity, Confusion, boisterous, worldly, vitality, strength.
	10 Edgy, brassy, metallic	Cold, chill, bitter, snarling, vicious, forceful, hard, martial.
	11 Full, round tone (e.g. horn, saxophone bowed basses)	Warm, rich, mellow.
	12 Reedy (e.g. oboe, clarinet)	Sweetness, nostalgic, delicate, melancholy, wistful.
	13 Sharp transients	
	(a) High-pitched (e.g. xylophone, breaking glass)	Thrilling, exciting, horrifying.
	(b) Low-pitched (e.g. timpani, thunder)	Dramatic, powerful, significant.
Speed and rhythm	14 Slow	Serious, important, dignified, deliberate, ponderous, stately, somber, mournful.
	15 Fast	Exciting, hopeful, fierce, trivial, agile.
	16 Simple	Uncomplicated, deliberate, regulation, dignity
	17 Complex	Complication, excitement, elaboration.
	18 Constant	Uniformity, forceful, monotonous, depressing.
	19 Changing	Vigorous, erratic, uncertainty, elation, wild.
	20 Increasing (accelerando)	Increasing vigor, excitement, energy or force, progressive development
	21 Decreasing (rallentando)	Decreasing vigor, excitement, energy or force; concluding development.

Table 20.1 (cont.)

Phrasing	Repetition of sets of sounds:	
	22 Regular repetition	Pleasurable recognition, insistence, monotony, regulation, coordination.
	23 Irregular repetition	Distinctiveness, personality, disorder.
	24 Strongly marked accents	Strong, forceful, emphatic, rhythmical.
	25 Unaccentuated sounds	Continuity, lack of vitality.
	26 Interrupted rhythm (syncopation)	Character, vigor, uncertainty. unexpectedness.
Duration	27 Brief, fragmentary	Awakening interest, excitement, forceful, dissatisfaction.
	28 Sustained	Persistence, monotony, stability, tiredness.
	29 Staccato	Nervous vitality, excitement.
Movement	30 Movement pattern	Movement pattern of sound suggests corresponding physical movement, e.g. upward – downward – upward – glissando pitch changes suggesting swinging movement.
	31 Upwards	Elation, rising importance, expectation, awakening interest, anticipation, doubt, forceful, powerful.
	32 Downwards	Decline, falling interest, decision, conclusion, imminence, climatic movement.
Pitch changes	33 Sudden changes	
	(a) Rise	Increasing interest, excitement, uplift.
	(b) Fall	Force, strength, decision, momentary unbalance.
	34 Slow changes	
	(a) Rise	Increasing tension, aspiration, rising motion.
	(b) Fall	Saddening, depression, falling motion, reduced tension.
	35 Well-defined pitch changes	Decision, effort, brightness, vitality.
	36 Indefinite pitch changes (e.g. slurs, glissando)	Lack of energy, indecision, sadness.
	37 Vibrato	Instability, unsteadiness, ornamentation.
Volume changes	38 Tremolo	Uncertainty, timidity, imminent action.
	39 Crescendo	Increasing force, power, nearness, etc.
	40 Diminuendo	Decreasing force, power, nearness, etc.
Reverberation	41 Dead acoustics	Restriction, intimacy, closeness, confinement, compression.
	42 Live acoustics	Openness, liveliness, spacious, magnitude, distance, uncertainty, the infinite.

The effect of combining sounds

When we hear two or more sounds together we shall often find that they *interrelate* to provide an emotional effect that changes according to their relative loudness, speed, complexity, etc.

Overall *harmony* – conveys completeness, beauty, accord, organization.

Overall *discord* – conveys imbalance, uncertainty, incompletion, unrest, ugliness, irritation.

Marked *differences* in relative volume, rhythm, etc. – create variety, complication, breadth of effect, individual emphasis.

Marked *similarities* – result is sameness, homogeneity, mass, strength of effect.

Focusing attention

Audience attention is seldom divided equally between picture and sound. One aspect usually dominates. However, you can transfer concentration between ear and eye. For example, a movement will emphasize a remark made immediately afterwards. Dialogue before a move gives it emphasis.

The ear is particularly drawn to certain types of sound:

1. Loud sounds, increasing volume.
2. High-pitched sounds (around 1000 to 4000 Hz).
3. Sounds rich in overtones (harmonics); edgy, metallic sounds; transients.
4. Fast sounds, increasing speed or rhythm.
5. Complex rhythms.
6. Briefly repeated phrases, syncopation, strong accents.
7. Short-duration or staccato sounds.
8. Aural movement.
   (a) Especially increases in volume, pitch, etc.
   (b) Clear-cut, unexpected, violent, changes.
   (c) Interruption, vibrato, tremolo.
9. Reverberant acoustics.
10. Marked contrast.
    (a) Between the principal and background sounds.
    (b) Between the sound and the picture (i.e. their associations, composition, etc.).
11. Marked similarity.
    (a) Between sounds (e.g. one source echoing another).
    (b) Between sounds and picture (e.g. simultaneous upward movements in both).

We can transfer aural attention to another subject by:

1. Giving the original subject's sound pattern (rhythm, movement, etc.) to the new source.
2. Weakening the original subject's attraction and strengthening the new source.

3 Linking action, e.g. having the pattern of the original sound change to that of the new subject, before stopping it.
4 Transferring aural movement through, e.g. by carrying over a solo sound while changing its background.
5 Cutting to a shot of the new source alone.
6 Changing the original composition lines, e.g. whereas upward sounds lead attention towards high notes, downward sounds lead attention towards lower notes.
7 Dialogue attracting attention either to its source or to its subject.

Selective sound

In recreating the atmosphere of a particular environment the trick is to use sound *selectively* if you want the scene to carry conviction, rather than try to include all typical background noises. You may deliberately emphasize, reduce, modify, or omit sounds that would normally be present; or introduce others to convey a convincing sense of location.

The selection and blend of environmental sounds can strongly influence the interpretation of a scene. Imagine, for example:

The slow, even toll of a cathedral bell accompanied by the rapid footsteps of approaching churchgoers.

In developing this scene, you could reproduce random typical sounds. Or, more persuasively, you might deliberately use audio emphasis:

1 Loud busy footsteps with a quiet insignificant bell in the background.
2 The bell's slow dignity contrasted with restless footsteps.
3 The bell's echoing notes contrasted with the staccato impatience of footsteps.
4 The booming bell overwhelming all other sounds.

So you can use the same sounds either *environmentally* or *atmospherically*; to suggest hope, dignity, community, domination . . . simply through selection, balance, and quality adjustment.

As you saw earlier (*substituted sound*), instead of modifying a scene's natural sounds you might augment them or replace them by entirely fresh ones.

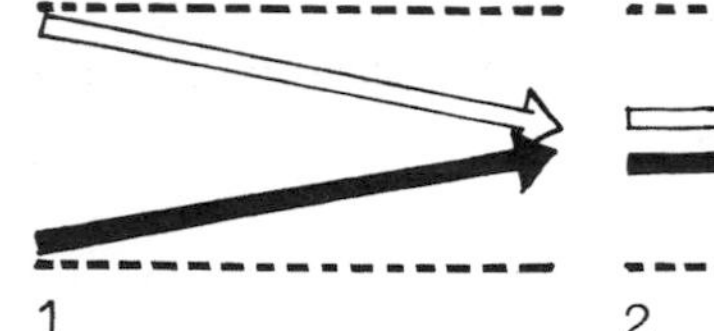

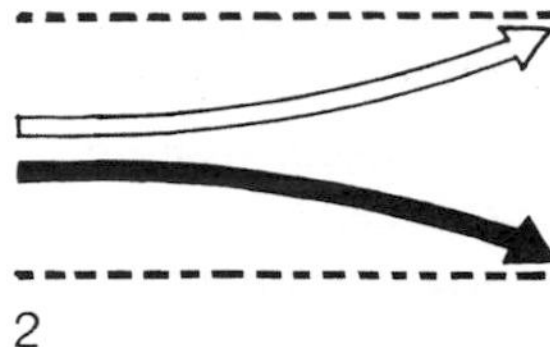

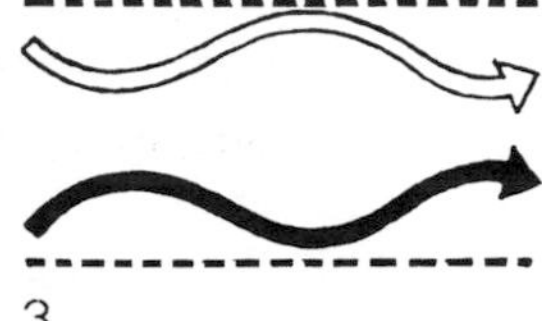

Fig. 20.1 Interaction between sounds
1 Towards a common focal point – suggesting conflict, concentration.
2 Away from a common focal point – suggesting divergence, broadening.
3 Contrasting sound movement – suggesting diversity, variety, interdependence.
4 Parallel sound movement – suggesting similarly, unanimity.

Table 20.2 Selective sound treatment

Scene: After a long hopeless day seeking, work, a cripple returns through emptying streets.

Sound selection	*Interpretation*
All sounds audible – of subject and background.	His footsteps sound amidst traffic and crowd noise.
The subject alone is heard.	His stumbling footsteps echo through quiet streets.
The subject plus selected background sounds.	His slow tread contrasts with the brisk steps of passers-by.
General background sounds alone.	Traffic noises. Passers-by.
Significant background sounds alone.	The laughter and gaiety from groups he passes; contrasting with his abject misery.
Interpretative sounds, not directly originating from the scene.	His echoing footsteps become increasingly louder and distorted. By progressively filtering out the higher audiofrequencies his labored tread becomes emphasized.
Significant selected sounds from another scene (providing explanation or comment).	Voices of people refusing him work echo in his brain.

Audiovisual relationships

The picture and its audio can interrelate in several distinct ways:

1 *The picture's impact may be due to its accompanying audio.* A close shot of a man crossing a busy highway. . .
   (a) Cheerful music – suggests that he is in lighthearted mood.
   (b) But automobile horns and squealing tires – suggest that he is jaywalking dangerously.

2 *The audio impact may be due to the picture.*
   (a) A long shot of a wagon bumping over a rough road . . . and the accompanying sound is accepted as a natural audio effect.
   (b) But take continuous close-ups of a wheel . . . and every jolt suggests impending breakdown!

3 *The effect of picture and audio may be cumulative.*
   A wave crashes against rocks . . . to a loud crescendo in the music.

4 *Sound and picture together may imply a further idea.*
   Wind-blown daffodils . . . birdsong, lambs bleating . . . can suggest spring.

21 Visual effects

We use 'effects' to create an illusion. They may be simple and unobtrusive, or elaborately impressive. In more extreme applications our audience will realize that there must have been some subterfuge, but many effects are subtle and their methods undetectable.

'Effects' are used for very *practical* reasons too: for convenience, economy, safety, reliability – and when a particular visual impact is not possible in other ways.

Pictorial effects are achieved by various means:

1 *Special effects* such as fire, explosions, fog, are a specialist craft, and best left to the expert. In amateur hands the results can be uncertain, unconvincing or dangerous.
2 *Staging effects* include scenic illusions such as false perspective, scale changes (Chapter 10).
3 *Lighting effects* range from environmental impressions such as sunsets to illusory effects – passing vehicles, water ripples, firelight.
4 *Mirror effects* to reposition the camera viewpoint or multiply images.
5 *Projection effects* using front- or rear-projection images.
6 *Camera effects* using optical attachments.
7 *Foreground effects* in which the camera shoots through a foreground device.
8 *Electronic or video effects* resulting from manipulating or controlling the video signal.
9 *Temporal effects* involving the speeding, slowing or freezing of time.

Mirror effects

When you want to provide a particular visual effect there are often several ways of going about it. Supposing for instance, you want a high shot:

- You could do the obvious, and take your camera up to a *high viewpoint*. (But is there a safe spot? Will the camera take long to reposition?)
- You might use a *crane jib* for the shot. (Will its jib be long enough, and can it be set at a steep vertical angle?)

Fig. 21.1 Basic laws of reflection
1 Light is reflected at an angle (R) equal to the angle of incidence (I). The *normal* is a line perpendicular to the mirror surface and starting from where the beams meet. The *incident* and *reflected rays* and the *normal* lie in the same plane.
2 The reflected image appears laterally reversed and as far behind the mirror as the subject is in front. The camera focuses on the subject image, not the mirror surface.

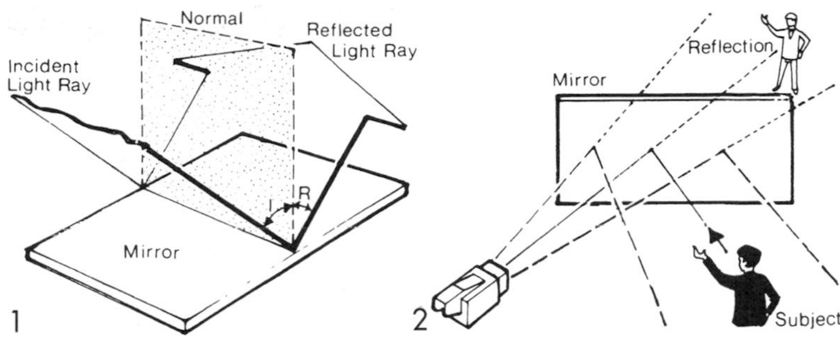

- Why not shoot via a *suspended mirror*? This would allow you to tilt your camera up for a reflected overhead view, then pan away in a moment, to resume normal working.

Quite often, a simple mirror shot provides an effect more quickly and with less effort. Which method you choose, will depend on your facilities, and on the time and space available. Although vulnerable to marking, surface-silvered mirrors are preferable to

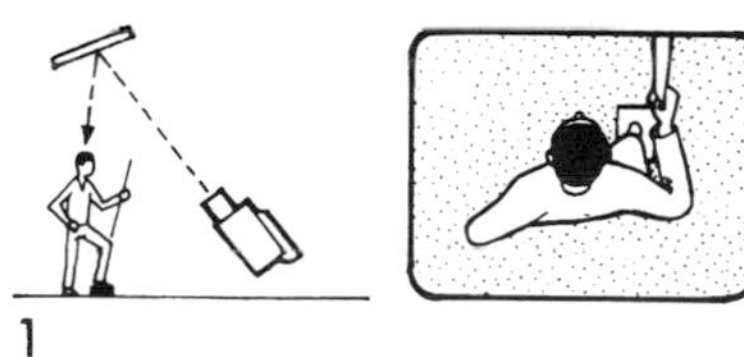

Fig. 21.2 part 1 Changing the viewpoint with mirrors – using a single mirror
1 Overhead (top) shot – image inverted and laterally reversed.
2 Reverse-angle top shot.
3 Very-low-angle shot (inverted).

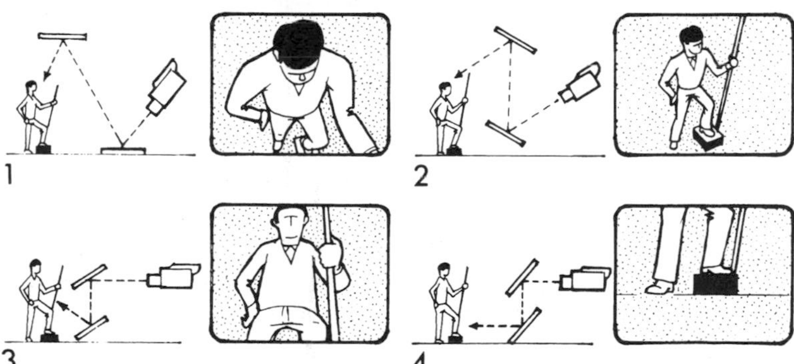

Fig. 21.2 part 2 Changing the viewpoint with mirrors – using two mirrors
1 Overhead shot.
2 High-angle shot.
3 Low-angle shot.
4 Low-level shot (mirrors may be mounted separately, fixed in a portable periscope stand, or attached to the camera mounting).

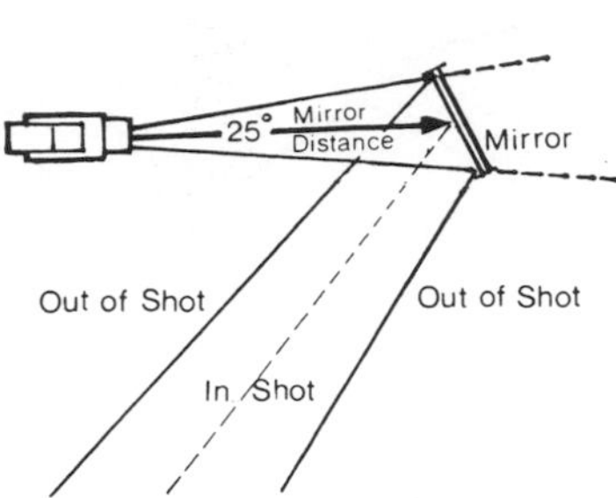

Fig. 21.3 Area seen in a mirror
The easiest method of planning a mirror position and judging what it reflects, is to cut out a paper triangle of the lens angle (e.g. 25°), folding it at the anticipated mirror position and placing this on a scale floor plan. This indicates mirror size and distance required. (The smaller the mirror, the closer it must be to the camera.)

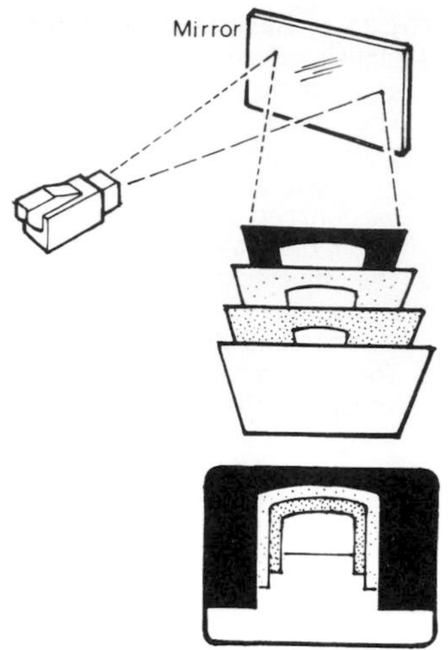

Fig. 21.4 Mirrors to extend space
The camera's effective distance can be increased, to obtain a longer shot than studio space permits.

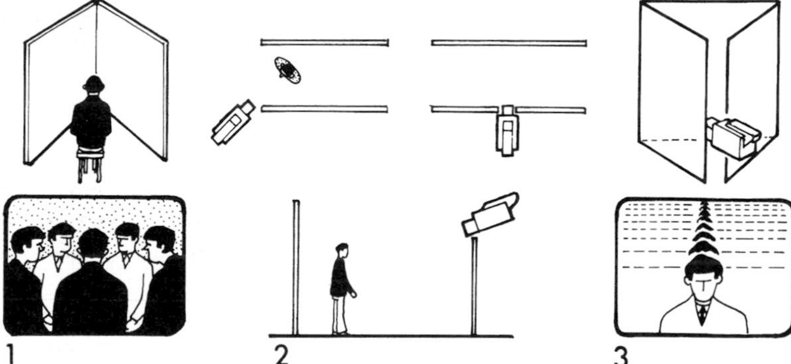

Fig. 21.5 Multiple images
For multi-reflections, you can arrange mirrors:
1 Angled – the smaller the mirror-angle, the more the images (number = 360/angle).
2 Parallel mirrors.
3 Triple mirrors.

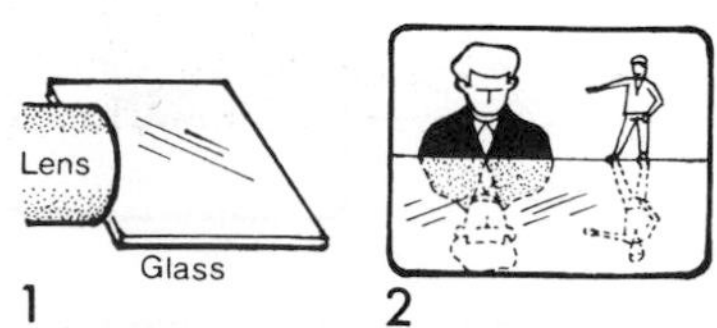

Fig. 21.6 Split screen reflection
A horizontal reflector (foil, mirror, clear glass) across the lens can provide reflected images, mirage or water-reflection effects.

Fig. 21.7 Mirror shot
Here a subject is shot together with a background mirror. The result is a combination of the direct and reflected images.

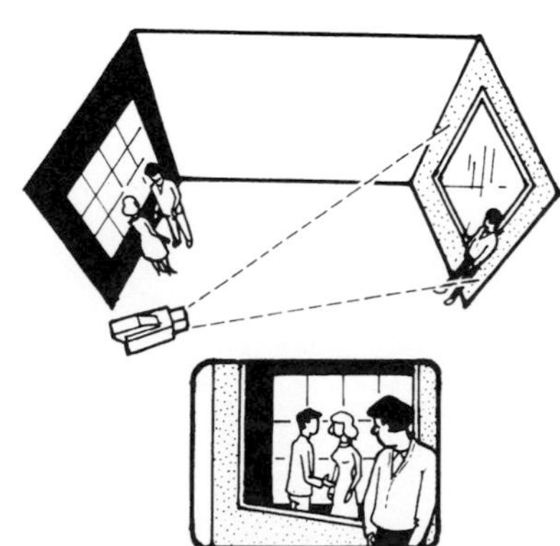

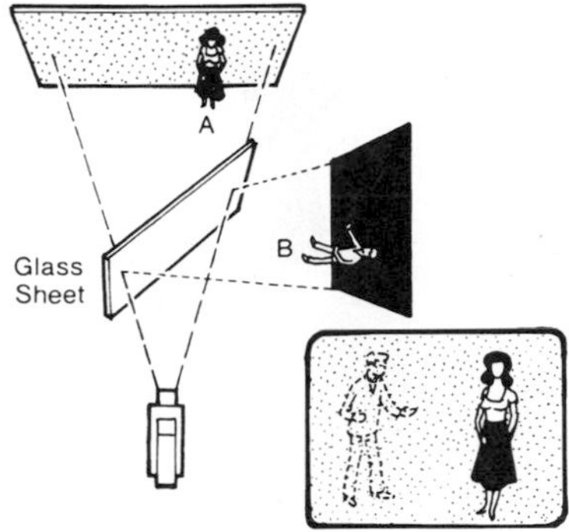

Fig. 21.8 Pepper's ghost
While shooting through an angled glass sheet at one subject (A), the camera also sees another subject (B), reflected from a side position. Depending on the relative strengths of their respective lighting, we see subject A, or B, or both (B ghostly). The device can also be used when we need shadowless ('straight-on') lighting, or to provide the background picture in a *reflex projection* setup.

Fig. 21.9 Two-way mirrors
The thin reflective coating on this two-way mirror makes it appear transparent (with a considerable light loss) from the rear unlit side (Cam 1); but as a normal mirror in the brightly-lit scene (Cam 2).

rear-silvered types, which produce a tinted, less sharp image. Mirror-plastic, ferrotype, or chromium sheeting are successful for less critical applications where distortions can be tolerated or are required.

Mirrors are mostly used for overhead shots (demonstrations, piano, dancers) and for low-angle (periscope) shots. They can be time consuming to adjust and usually permit little camera movement. The mirror size needed increases with the camera/mirror distance and when using oblique mirror angles. Large mirrors are heavy and expensive items.

Having adjusted any mirror set-up during rehearsal, ensure that camera, mirror, and performer positions are clearly floor marked.

Where the lateral reversal (mirroring) is unacceptable a further intermediate mirror or reversing prism can be introduced to correct the effect. While monochrome cameras can be either laterally or vertically reversed electronically, only the latter is possible directly with most color cameras. (Digital video effects systems, where available, may provide lateral or horizontal reversal.)

Rear (back) projection (see Figure 21.10)

Here the camera shoots action against a translucent screen of 'frosted' plastic; a film or slide being projected onto its rear side.

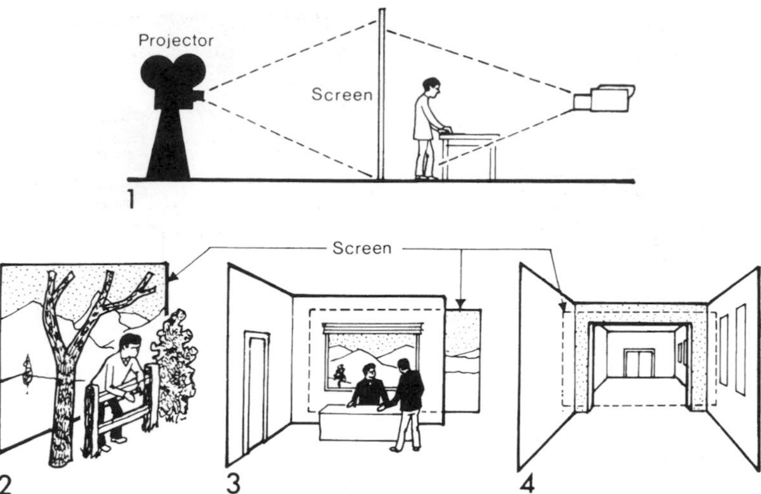

Fig. 21.10 Rear projection
1 A slide or film image is projected onto one side of a matte translucent screen. On the reverse side, a camera shoots action for which the screen image provides a background.
2 The rear-projected image can be used as a complete scenic background with foreground set-pieces, furniture, etc.; or (3) used to supplement a built set (e.g. window backing); or (4) to extend a built set.

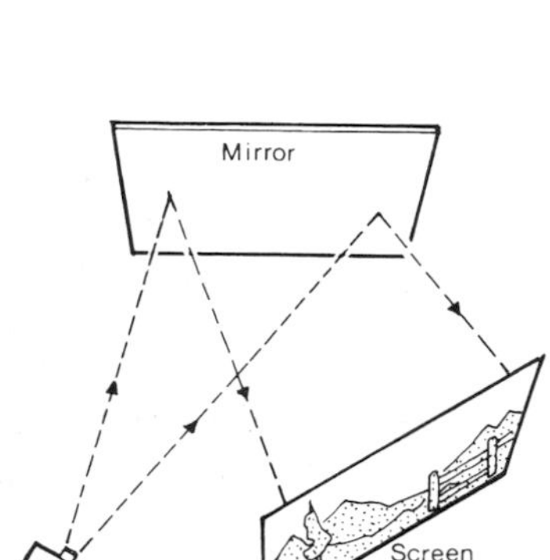

Fig. 21.11 Folding the light path
By folding the light path with a mirror, floor space can be saved. Using a second mirror even greater compactness is possible, but with a further loss of clarity.

Once used extensively in motion pictures and monochrome TV, rear projection has been largely replaced in film by process work (matting during optical printing), or reflex projection; and in color TV by electronic insertion (chroma-key, CSO).

However, rear projection still has some useful applications in TV studios. As well as being used for pictorial rear projection, the translucent screen can be used to display silhouettes, shadows, or pattern effects.

Front projection

We can project still or moving images directly onto a light-toned background, or even onto action for decorative or scenic effect.

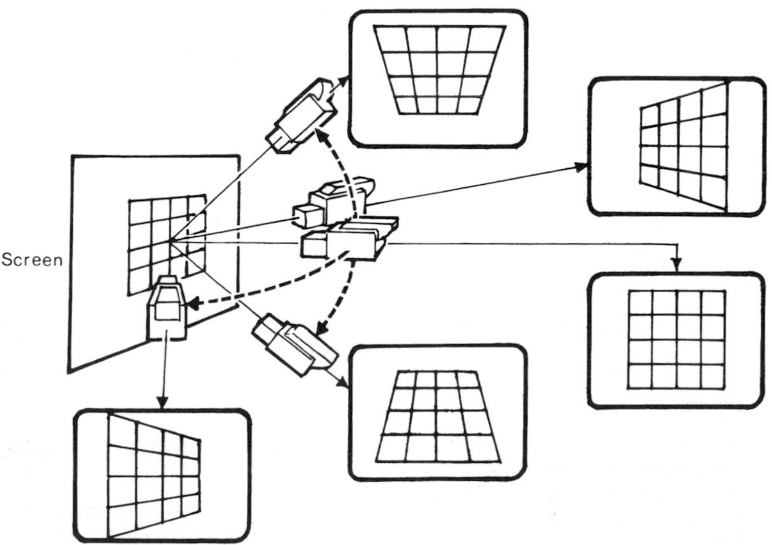

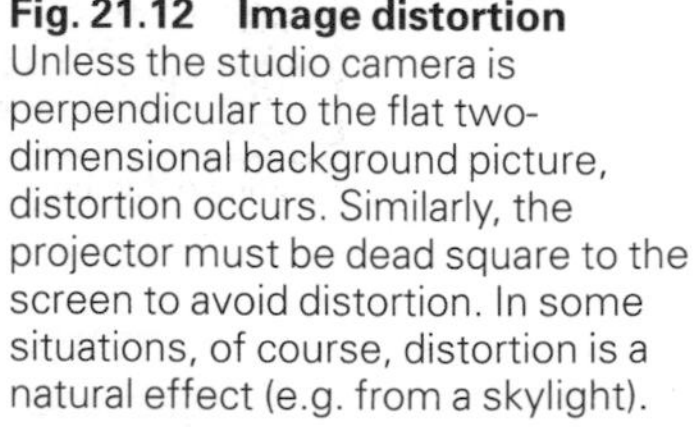

Fig. 21.12 Image distortion
Unless the studio camera is perpendicular to the flat two-dimensional background picture, distortion occurs. Similarly, the projector must be dead square to the screen to avoid distortion. In some situations, of course, distortion is a natural effect (e.g. from a skylight).

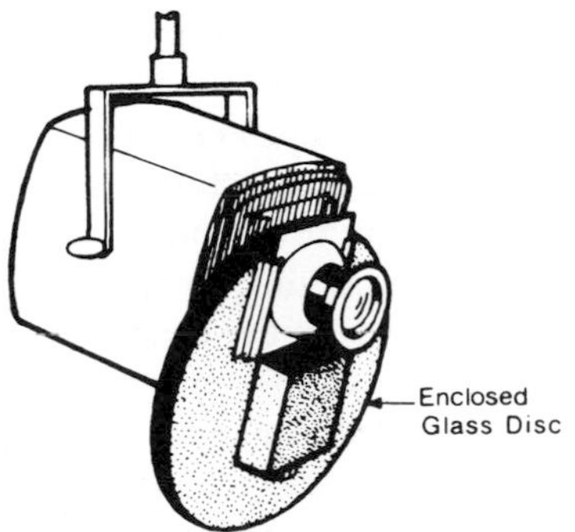

Fig. 21.13 Scenic projector
An enclosed glass disc with painted or photographed patterns is rotated at an adjustable speed by a small motor. This device is attached to a projector spotlight and focused onto a background to simulate moving clouds, snow, water patterns, etc. The low image-intensity usually restricts the usable image-size.

Basic light patterns (from metal stencils) are most effective, but under typical full-lighting conditions subtle half-tones and low-key images may be disappointing. Geometric patterns and shapes, clouds, etc. are regularly projected onto cycloramas, and used to simulate natural light and shadow effects (window shadows). Scenic projectors can provide certain moving images (flames, sea-swell, snow) that are effective enough under favorable conditions. See Figure 21.13.

Given *sufficiently sensitive* cameras and no spill light to dilute the image (so reducing its clarity and contrast), further interesting effects are possible, e.g. an announcer with newsprint projected onto his face, dancers against black drapes who are illuminated only by striped lighting.

Reflex projection

In this system (also called *front axial projection* or simply *front projection*) the background is projected directly along the TV camera's lens axis via a half-silvered mirror onto a special background screen material. The secret lies in this *highly directional* surface, comprising millions of minute glass beads, each reflecting nearly 92 per cent of the projected background image back to the camera. (The principle of this *Scotchlite* sheeting is identical to that used in many reflective traffic signs and night-safety clothing strips.) See Figure 21.14.

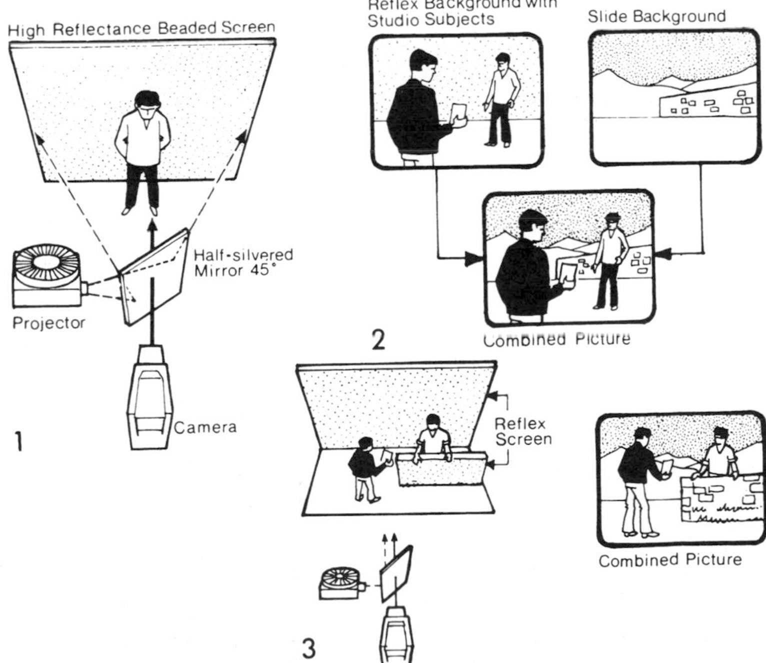

Fig. 21.14 Reflex projection
1 In Reflex (axial) Front Projection, the background scene is projected along the lens axis, via a half-silvered mirror, onto a highly directional glass-beaded screen. Actors' lighting swamps the image falling on them.
2 People appear *in front* of the background scene.
3 If people move behind a surface covered with beaded material, they will appear *behind* corresponding areas of the background scene (walls, trees, etc.).

Normal subject lighting cannot dilute the background image (unless placed near the camera) thanks to the screen's directionality. Where the front projected *background* image falls onto the performer or foreground subjects it is swamped by action lighting and so is not visible on camera. Shadows from it are cast directly behind subjects and so are unseen by the camera, providing the system is accurately aligned and the lens angles of the camera and projector are comparable.

Although not a foolproof system, it can provide near-miraculous effects for both film and TV cameras. Its limitations include: mirror light losses; light subject tones can be reflected in dark screen areas, causing edge haloes; the system must be aligned to avoid dark subject edges; and the studio camera must be *static* in most applications.

If pieces of reflex screen material are cut out and positioned to match objects or planes in the background picture (e.g. wall, tree, couch, archway) the studio performer can seemingly walk 'behind' them very convincingly.

Table 21.1 Rear projection/BP

Advantages	The system is adaptable and simple to use.
	The background image is visible to performers.
	Compact screens can provide backgrounds outside small scenic openings (e.g. automobile windows).
	Rear projection can provide display panels in settings to show graphics, titles, microscope shots, film clips, etc.
Disadvantages	Studio space is wasted due to the projector-to-screen distance (*throw*) required, especially for large screens.
	Projectors occupy floor space.
	Projector noise may be audible.
	Subject illumination may spill onto the screen, diluting its image. (A black scrim layer over the screen may improve matters.)
	The projected image may be insufficiently bright, have a central hot spot or edge darkening.
	Only slides or film can normally be projected. (Film is susceptible to vertical hop and horizontal *weaving*.) Projected TV images are seldom of suitable quality when shot by the studio camera.
	The rear-projected picture's apparent sharpness will vary with the studio camera's focusing and depth of field.
	Matching of the projected background and foreground subject/scene may pose problems: perspective, scale, light direction, contrast, color quality, etc.
	Problems can arise in matching audio perspective and quality to varying projected backgrounds.

Camera lens filters

Filters of various kinds can be clipped over the front of the lens or inserted in a *filter-wheel* holder within the camera.

■ **Neutral density filters** These have various light transmissions (Chapter 4) and are used to prevent gross overexposure when working under strong sunlight.

■ **Corrective filters** When there are changes in the color temperature of light sources these filters can be used to compensate, e.g. when moving from daylight to tungsten-lit areas.

■ **Star filters** These are clear disks with closely scribed grid patterns. Diffraction effects produce multi-ray patterns (typically 4, 6, 8) around highlights from flames, specular reflections, and lamps. Sunburst versions may have some 60 rays! The rays' directions change as the filter is turned.

■ **Diffusion disks** Available in various densities, these filters provide general image softening through fine surface scratches or dimpling on a clear disk. Nylon or muslin net or hose may be similarly used. Sharp detail is reduced and highlights develop glowing haloes. To produce localized softening or distortion, a clear glass disk can be lightly smeared with grease or oil where required – usually round the edges. The effect can be ethereal, or woolly and irritating. But never treat the actual camera lens, for this would damage its special surface coating!

■ **Low-contrast filters** When used, these desaturate and mute colors, while softening contrast.

■ **Fog filters** Made in different densities, these create image diffusion from slight mist to dense fog, with strongly haloed highlights.

■ **UV (haze) filters** Clipped over a lens, the UV filter reduces haze blur (due to ultraviolet light) when shooting daylight exteriors; and protects the lens surface.

■ **Night filters** These are graded neutral density or blue-tinted filters (denser at the top) used to simulate night or evening scenes. By heavy filtering (particularly the sky areas) and considerably reducing overall exposure it is possible to shoot 'night scenes' during daylight ('day for night' shooting) – thereby saving money and avoiding lighting problems.

■ **Color filters** These are rarely used on *color* TV cameras, as hue changes can be introduced electronically. In monochrome, they facilitate lightening/darkening the tonal reproduction of parts of the spectrum. Color sky-filters can be used for dramatic effects.

■ **Polarizing filters** These are occasionally used to reduce strong reflections or flares from smooth or shiny surfaces such as glass or water. (They have little effect for rough materials.) Polarizing filters can be used to darken an overbright sky without affecting overall color quality; although light loss is inevitable (e.g. 75 per cent loss). The filter's properties derive from its crystalline structure, which enables it to discriminate against light reflected at around 35°. By rotating the filter, you can selectively reduce or suppress particular reflections.

Lens attachments

A variety of add-on devices can be attached to the lens to modify the image:

■ **Multiple images** These can be produced by prismatic or multi-faceted lenses. One form splits the screen into a series of repeat-image strips. Another has a static central image facet surrounded by a series of repeat versions, while a further form provides a ring of merging images. Their image patterns can be repositioned or rotated about the center by a small handle (or motor control), the images remaining upright; unlike those from the simple *kaleidoscope* mirror tube.

■ **Image distortion** Methods available for distorting the image include shooting through molded ripple or patterned glass, via a

Fig. 21.15 Prismatic lenses
The number and position of images is determined by the facets on the lens. The peripheral images move round as the lens is turned but remain upright.

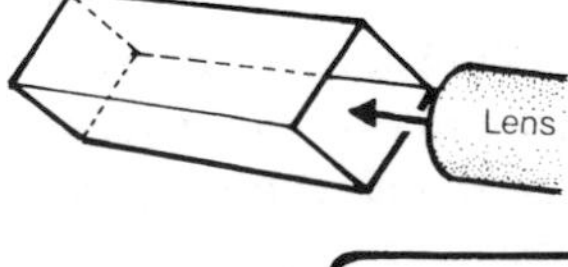

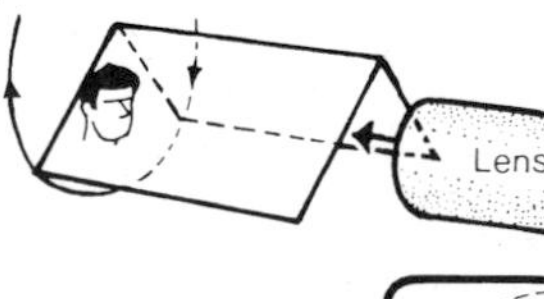

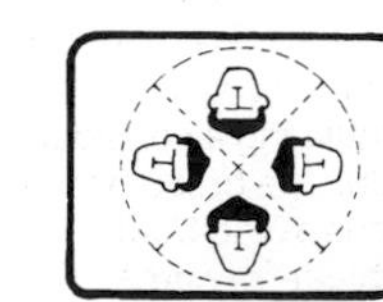

Fig. 21.16 The kaleidoscope
1 Shooting through a three- or four-sided mirror-tube produces an upright central image surrounded by angled reflections, which move round as the tube turns.
2 Two angled mirrors provide multiple converging images. (Number of images equals 360 divided by angle of mirrors.) Surface-silvered mirrors are needed to avoid spurious ghost images.

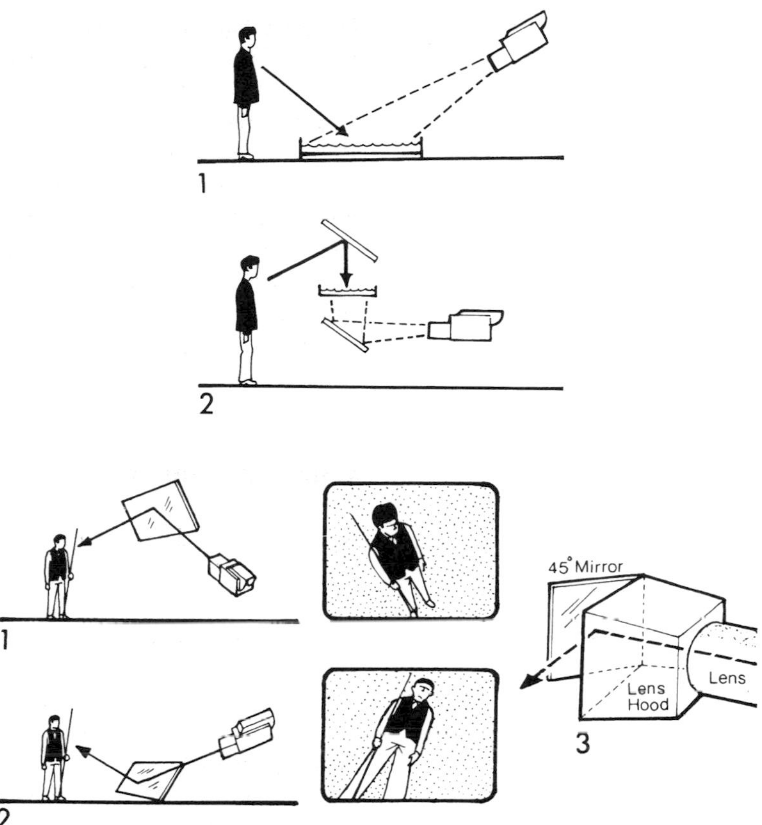

Fig. 21.17 Ripple distortion
1 The camera shoots into a shallow mirror-bottomed water tank, giving an inverted ripple image.
2 The camera shoots into a mirror periscope containing a water-filled glass tray. Ripples can be made to flow across the picture, finally breaking it up altogether. If an opaque liquid is poured into the tray, the picture blots out with a fluid wipe.

Fig. 21.18 Tilting the picture using mirrors
Tilted shots can be obtained from (1) elevated or (2) depressed angles using canted mirrors. Shooting via a 45° mirror (3) attached to the lens system, causes the scene to cant as the camera tilts.

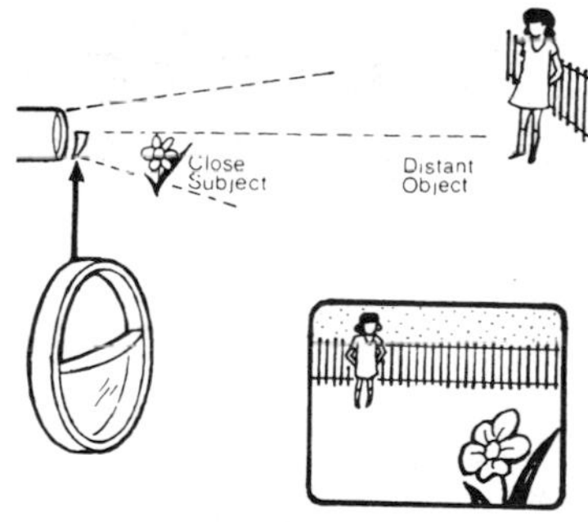

Fig. 21.19 Split-field close-up lens
A half-lens (½ to 3 diopters) provides a sharp image of a close object, although the main lens is sharply focused on a distant subject; so simulating a considerable depth of field. The broad band of confused focus at the border, is arranged in a subject-free area.

flexible mirror, or water dish, or a foil tube giving peripheral effects. Fisheye lenses cover a wide angle of view (e.g. 100–360°), providing extreme geometrical (curvature) distortion.

■ **Image rotation** Several mirror or prismatic attachments enable you to rotate, invert, or tilt the picture. Apart from ceiling walking, you can simulate floating in free space, flying, cliff climbing, and other feats – the easy way. The most frequent use, however, is for *canted* (*dutch angle*) shots in which the picture is horizontally tilted for dramatic effect. If the image is to be rotated continuously this must be done smoothly and at a suitable speed. Digital video effects allow images to be tilted, reversed, inverted, or rotated.

■ **Split-field close-up lenses** These are used to overcome extreme depth-of-field problems, for they can provide sharp images of both close *and* distant subjects simultaneously (Figure 21.19).

Camera mattes (gobos)

For many years, solid or transparent foreground devices have been used in motion-picture making to create composite visual effects.

Although often replaced in TV by electronic insertion methods, they still remain a useful facility. These *mattes* (masks) or *gobos* ('go-between') take several forms. The term *gobo* is also used for a black surface that masks off lights or cameras appearing in shot; *and* for the metal stencil used in effects projection lamps.

Foreground matte

At its simplest, this is just a plain surface with a hole in it, through which distant studio action is seen. Painted black, it provides a soft-edged isolating *vignette* (stencil) selecting part of a scene for example:

To superimpose or insert somebody's head into another shot.
To create a shaped border, simulating a telescope, binoculars, keyhole. See Figure 21.20.

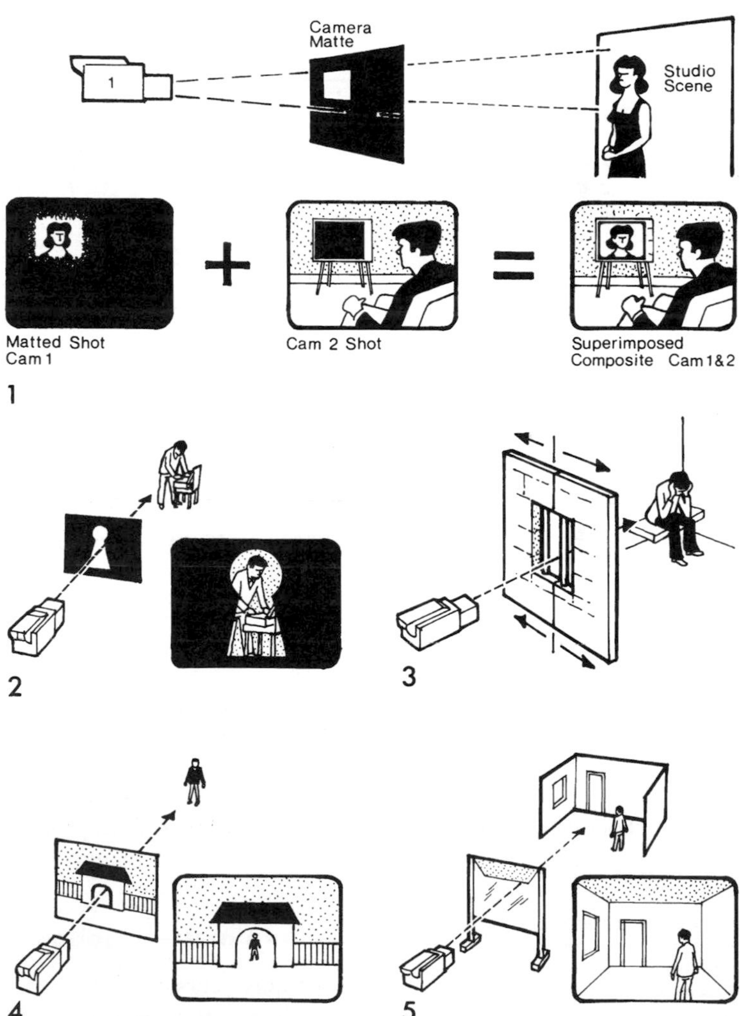

Fig. 21.20 Foreground mattes
This is a foreground surface (plain or decorated), through part of which the distant scene is visible. It has several purposes:

1. Selectively isolating an item, e.g. for localized superimposition.
2. A pattern vignette, e.g. keyhole effect.
3. Scenic foreground, e.g. a window through which camera shoots. A breakthrough frame parts to enable the camera to dolly 'through' the foreground.
4. *Camera matte.* A studio subject is apparently inserted into an area within a foreground graphic.
5. A glass-shot, e.g. positioning a foreground painted ceiling 'on' a studio setting.

To provide localized *chroma-key* insertion, a colored foreground matte board (e.g. blue) is used. See Figure 21.37.

The foreground matte may be used to introduce a *decorative border*, or a *framed opening* (picture frame), or a *realistic* scenic effect (window). Often the camera dollies forward and 'enters' the scene as it loses the matte. *Cartoon gobos* are 'funnies', where the performer appears behind the cut-out section of a comic drawing, or pokes his or her head through a hole.

Insertion matte

Sometimes the foreground matte is intended to merge imperceptibly with the background scene, e.g. a foreground photograph with a cut-out area, or a painted *glass-shot* putting a matching ceiling 'onto' a studio setting. The scale, perspective, lighting, colors, tones, etc. of 'foreground' and background must be matched accurately to be really convincing and action must not normally move behind the matte opening (or it will disappear). When using insertion mattes, we must have considerable depth of field or overall sharpness may not be feasible.

Foreground miniatures (models) are occasionally used to extend the scene, but these are usually rudimentary – foliage, saloon swing doors, drapes, pillars, arches. *Transparent mattes* can provide a decorated foreground plane showing titling or graphics (a world map, show window sign, patterns, etc.); the camera throwing focus from the foreground to the background scene.

Electronic effects

The pictorial opportunities that electronic effects can provide are endless. The more you use them, the more will you discover fresh applications for both realistic and abstract picture treatment. They combine practical economies with fascinating magic that never palls.

Superimpositions

As we saw in Chapter 8, when two picture sources are faded up together their pictures intermix. The relative strengths of their images are *additive* and can be adjusted, but:

1 Where *black* appears in either shot, the other shot's detail appears firm and solid.
2 Where *white* appears in either shot, the other shot's detail appears diluted, paled out. A peak white can burn through another shot's detail.

3 Where different hues appear in both shots, they form a new color mixture (e.g. R + G = Y).

Black level adjustment

By electronically darkening the lowest picture tones until they crush to a solid overall black (batting down on blacks, sitting down) you can:

1 Ensure that 'black' materials (black drapes, black title cards) reproduce as a firm black without wrinkles or shading.
2 Prevent slight tonal variations and construction being seen in hand-animated graphics – e.g. to make a black strip (with white titling) merge with its black background card.
3 Make parts of a subject disappear – e.g. a black-gloved hand against black drapes will disappear while light-toned objects that are held, remain visible.

To make a near-*white* tone merge with a white area you increase exposure so that lightest tones merge (burn-out, clip off) at white-clipper video limits.

Normal Weave

Fig. 21.21 Electronic weave/ ripple effects
An S-distortion (of variable strength and speed) is created electronically by varying the line-trigger pulse.

Picture weave (electronic ripple)

Many switchers include a device that introduces a sideways ripple into a picture. Its rate and strength are adjustable. Straightforward picture weave is used to simulate flashbacks, or in transformations. But combined with multiple wipe patterns (Figure 8.12, part 4) you can break the picture up to provide a variety of undulating, decoratively shaped transitions.

Negative picture

Electronic switching enables you to reverse picture *tone* (reverse polarity) so that they become *negative*. White reproduces as black, black as white. This is a useful facility for changing standard white-on-black titling to black-on-white (to improve clarity on light backgrounds). It can also be used to produce negative images or to reproduce negative monochrome film.

Complementary picture

Color can be transformed into its complementary hues – red, green and blue become cyan, magenta, yellow. This system enables us to directly transmit negative color film. Reversal can be used dramatically, too: transforming smoke, clouds, steam; creating black highlights glistening in a white sea; black lightning in a white sky.

Camera channel adjustment (see Chapter 23)

The color TV camera channel requires careful adjustment for optimum picture quality. But, by making certain changes from standard line-up, you can obtain some interesting visual effects:

- Altering the *exposure* will brighten or darken the picture overall; revealing or crushing out tonal gradation in the highlights or shadows.
- Adjusting *black level* will cause all tonal values to lighten/darker. (Lower tones may crush.)
- Adjusting *video gain* will brighten or darken the picture overall; without affecting exposure or revealing more shadow/highlight detail.
- Adjusting the color balance can give the picture a color cast that would otherwise require extensive colored lighting (suggesting moonlight, firelight, candlelight).
- Adjusting *gamma* will alter the tonal coarseness or subtlety.

Video feedback

TV camera operators soon discover that by shooting a picture monitor showing their own output they can obtain interesting repeat-image effects. When you mix this camera's repeat-video with that from *another source* (in the studio switcher) and feed this combination back to that picture monitor, all manner of interesting multi-effects develop. (Two or more cameras can be used.) This technique can produce a variety of dynamic patterns, transformations, and surround images.

Interesting effects are obtainable, too, if you take a defocused shot of a subject on a picture monitor and superimpose it on the original picture. The resultant halo creates a convincing aura round 'supernatural' beings.

If positive and negative images of a subject are intermixed, a strangely 'solarized' image results that can be further processed by video feedback.

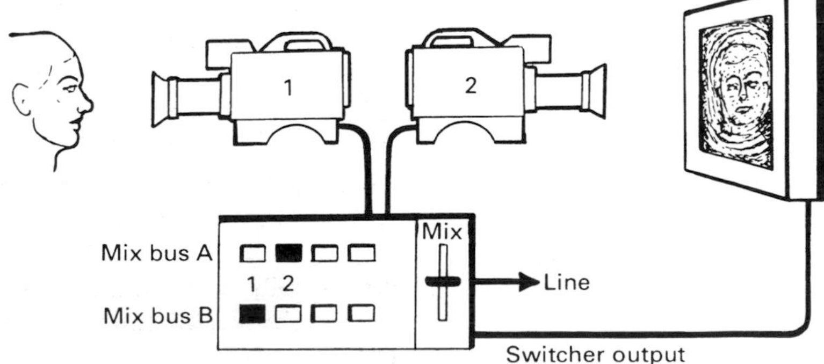

Fig. 21.22 Video feedback
Point a camera at a monitor showing a picture of its *own* output, and a random feedback pattern develops if you momentarily interrupt the shot (wave a hand over the lens, pan the camera, snap-switch a picture onto the screen).
For a more elegant controlled effect, mix the picture into the feedback loop, using a switcher.

Keyed insertion (electronic matting)

There are endless ways in which we can alter or transform the television picture by electronic trickery. Some are eye-catching gimmicks; others are methods of creating scenic effects that would otherwise be impracticable. Some are simple and relatively foolproof; others need experience and expertise to be totally convincing.

How it works

Electronic insertion is an ingenious interswitching process used to selectively combine different picture sources. It is virtually a process of 'cutting a hole' in one picture and inserting exactly a corresponding piece of another picture. (Seldom putting one picture *over* another.)

As you know, a TV picture is normally formed by scanning the scene's image in a series of horizontal lines. The switcher selects which source is sent to line. However, suppose we had an instantaneous electronic switch available, so that the system switches itself between sources *during* this scanning process. We might, for instance, begin *each* scanning line by showing Cam. 1's picture but half-way through that line switch to Cam. 2's shot instead. (Switching back to Cam. 1 at the end of each line.) Because of this interswitching, the resultant transmitted composite would show the left half of Cam. 1's picture and the right half of Cam. 2's picture. (You will recognize this particular example as a split-screen effect.)

Altering the exact switching moment repositions whereabouts the division appears in the frame. If we *gradually alter* the switchover moment, a *moving* division (a *wipe*) is produced; in this example, horizontal wipe movement. So by carefully controlled switching we can create a combined or composite picture, selecting parts of two or more separate shots.

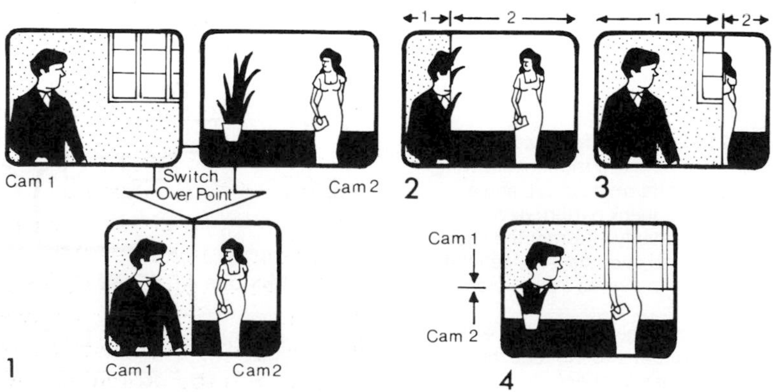

Fig. 21.23 Inter-source switching

1. If an electronic switch changes from Cam 1's picture to Cam 2's output halfway through each line period, the resultant *split screen* combines those parts of the shots.
2. If the switching moment is earlier in the line, the division is displaced left.
3. Occurring later in the line, the division is displaced right. The shots may be composed to suit the division being used; or the division located to suit the composition.
4. If the apparatus is arranged to select the top half of Cam 1's picture, switching to Cam 2 for the remainder of the frame, the result with these particular shots is nonsensical.

Methods of creating the keying matte

So far, we have been talking about large area switching. But what if we want to insert a *small* part of one picture into another? The principles here are surprisingly simple. We supply a special *keying amplifier* with a *matte* (mask) corresponding to the screen area we want to treat. Then wherever this keying system detects the *matte*, it automatically switches from one picture source to another. For example, where there is *no masking*, it may show Cam. 1's picture (e.g. a wall area). But as the scan continues, it detects the *matted area*, and switches over to Cam. 2's picture instead, to show the corresponding section of that shot (e.g. a window). In this case, their combined pictures provide the illusion of 'a window within a wall'. (Anything falling *outside* the matted area in Cam 2's shot is unseen.)

You can use a number of techniques to produce such a *matte key*. Each has its advantages:

- An electronically generated waveform from a *special effects generator (SEG)*.
- An area of a selected *tone (luminance keying)*.
- An area of a selected *color (chrominance keying)*.

The actual keying process can be activated in two ways:

- Some systems rely on an *external key* ('*separate key*') method.
- Others use an *internal key* (*self-keying*) process.

We shall be looking at these wonders in some detail, for they are the basis of many electronic effects widely used in productions today.

External key

All *external key ('separate key')* methods of insertion have to be *prepared* in some way. You need to select a mask pattern from a stored selection or actually make a physical mask of some kind which will trigger the keying device to produce a *matte key* which initiates switching.

Special effects generator (SEG)

The most familiar type of *external keying device* is the *'special effects generator' (SEG)*, often fitted to *production switchers (vision mixers)*. That system would be used to create the *wipe* patterns we were looking at in Figure 21.23.

The SEG provides a selection of waveforms (i.e. voltage variations) to interswitch between picture sources. The shape and frequency of the pattern we select will control the wipe pattern produced. If this switching waveform is constant, the wipe pattern

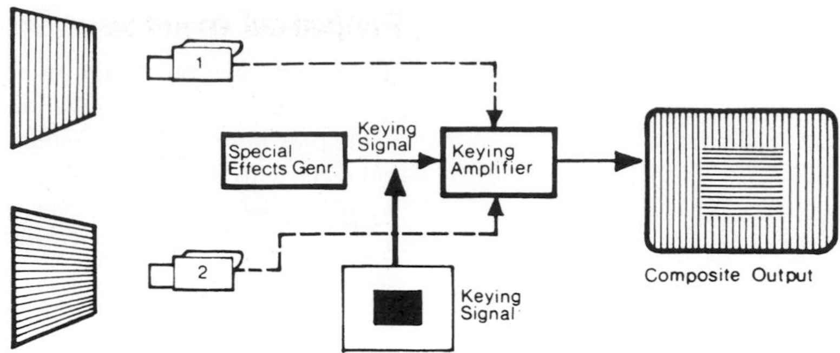

Fig. 21.24 Special-effects generator (SEG)
The SEG provides voltages of variable waveforms (square, parabolic, triangular, etc.). These control the exact switching pattern of the keying amplifier, so producing a series of geometrical matte shapes.

on the screen appears stationary. Gradually alter it, and the pattern will move or change shape. The effects the SEG produces are quite independent of the pictures involved.

Although the results are always *geometrical* you can change them in several ways:

- You can adjust the pattern's *size*; expanding or contracting it.
- You can adjust the pattern's *shape*. A square can be made rectangular, a circle can become an ellipse.
- The pattern can be moved around the frame; up/down, left/right, diagonally.
- It can be moved to a fixed position within the frame; e.g. to form a static *insert* (*inset*).
- You can control the *speed* at which the pattern changes or moves, using a fader lever, or *autowipe* button.
- The *symmetry* of the pattern can be adjusted.
- The pattern *edges* can be made hard (sharp) or soft (diffused). If sources are interswitched *instantaneously* there will be a sharply defined division. If the insertion circuits *mix* between the two sources they will merge at their borders, to provide a soft-edged effect.
- A border can be placed around a pattern insert; in black, white, or color.
- The pattern can be made to *weave* or *ripple* at adjustable speed and strength.
- A spotlight pointer, or magnifying glass effect, can draw attention to a particular feature (Figure 21.34).

There are literally dozens of wipe patterns, but some typical examples are shown in Figures 8.12 and 21.25.

Fig. 21.25 Wipes
Wipes can be controlled in various ways: (1) direction; (2) position; (3) symmetry; (4) edge sharpness. Changes can be made at any speed.

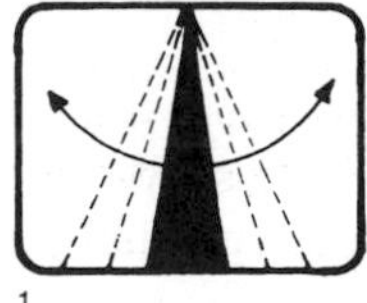
1

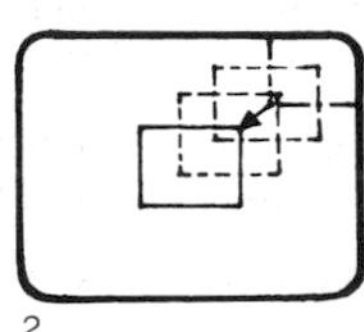
2

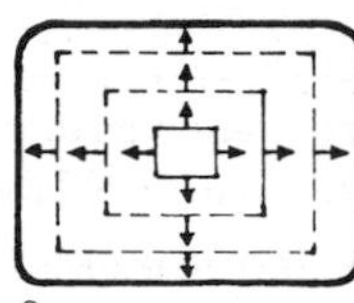
3

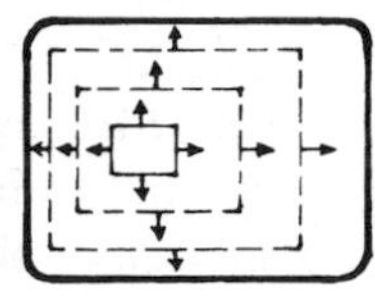

4

Prepared mattes

The most flexible matting technique uses a *prepared image* of a black silhouette on a white background (or vice versa), which is fed into a *keying amplifier*. As we saw earlier, this switches to one picture source as the white area is scanned and another when scannng the black area. This matte can follow any shape or size, and if necessary be fragmented into a series of separate 'sub-mattes'. (Remember, this matting signal is only a utility, and is not seen.)

Fig. 21.26 Camera matte
The graphic in front of the matting camera (3) results in a video signal which interswitches Cam 1 (flowers) with Cam 2 (girl) in a heart-shaped mask form. Wherever complex, non-geometrical matte shapes are required (e.g. tree-branch patterns, flower shapes, decorative screens, etc.), camera mattes are used

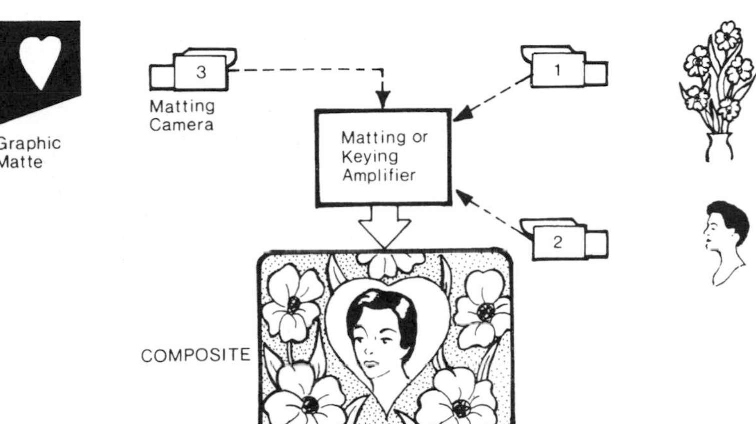

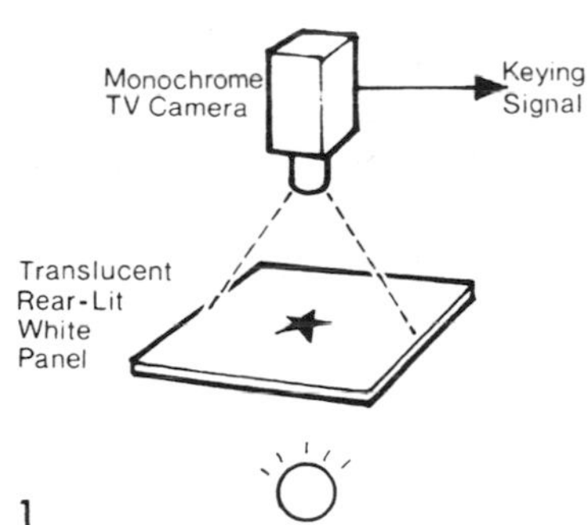

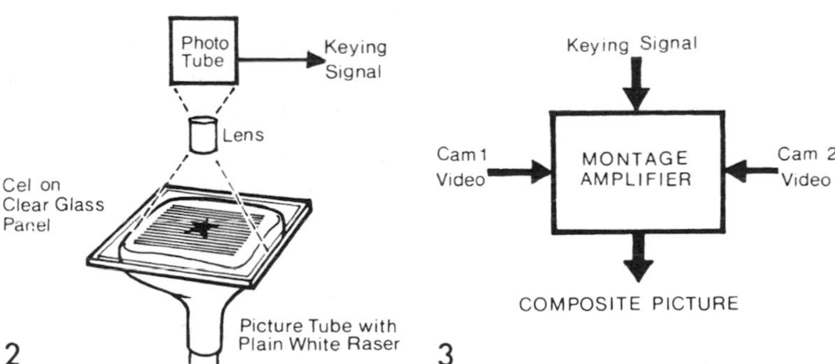

Fig. 21.27 Rostrum camera (inlay desk)
Using this external keying apparatus, even elaborate masks are practical.

1 TV camera – the overhead monochrome TV camera shoots a back-lit white panel. Cut-out card, inked or painted shapes, provide a matte for the keying signal.
2 Picture tube – the matte is placed or drawn on a *cel* (clear plastic sheet) or glass, over a picture tube displaying a plain white picture (raster) – a flying-spot scanner. The phototube picks up a constant scanning output (i.e. peak white video) except where interrupted by the matte. Adjustment of the scanning width or height alters the effective matte shape. Zooming produces matte size changes.
3 Keying signal – this is fed to the montage amplifier, where it interswitches between the cameras' outputs.

The black and white matte used can come from a variety of sources:

- A *camera matte* – A camera shooting a graphic (Figure 21.26).
- A *photo slide* – e.g. of a map silhouette.
- *A character generator (CG)*
  CG – Solid black lettering.
  Cam. 1 – Shoots a brick wall photograph.
  Cam. 2 – Shoots a striped surface.
  The matted result: Lettering in striped paint on a brick wall.
- A *rostrum camera* – See Figure 21.27.
- A *studio silhouette* (e.g. a camera shooting action behind a back-lit screen):
  Cam. 1 – Silhouette of a dancer used as a matte.
  Cam. 2 – A cloud scene
  Cam. 3 – Glittering reflections (e.g. defocused tinsel).
  The matted result: A glittering shape dancing among clouds.
- *Computer graphics* can provide silhouette mattes of any degree of complexity, and be used to initiate switching. (Simply draw the matte outline and *fill* this area instantly in black.)
- A *recorded matte* on film or videotape can be used as an external key:
  E.g. A taped sequence with a show's regular opening titles can contain *tonal* or *chroma-key* patches into which pictures of current guests or topical items can be inserted.

Internal key (self-keying, self-matting, common key mode)

This outstanding method of keying does not require prepared mattes. Instead, it automatically detects a chosen *keying tone* or *keying color* within the foreground shot and switches to precisely that area of a second picture instead.* There are two systems:

- *Luminance keying* (which is activated by black or white areas in the picture) and
- *Chrominance keying* which is triggered by a selected color.

Luminance keying

Luminance keying systems (*Inlay*) are triggered by a black or white *keying tone* in the *subject/foreground shot*. Whichever tone you select must not appear in the *subject* shot; otherwise there will be

* Terminology varies here. The picture containing *the subject* which is to be inserted is variously called the *subject* or *foreground* shot, or the *master* scene (sometimes the *fill signal*). The picture into which it is to be inserted is called the *background shot*.

Table 21.2 Keying methods compared

	Advantages	*Disadvantages*
External key (using SEG, camera matte, slide matt)	Simple to operate and adjust.	Complex scenic mattes (ceiling insert) may require accuracy in construction and adjustment.
	Reliable and definite in action.	
	No spurious breakthrough between pictures.	*The camera set-ups for recording must usually be identical to rehearsed version.
	Any tones/colors usable in foreground subjects and background shots.	*Normally, foreground and background cameras should remain static. Any film must be free from hop or weaving in static scenes.
	Only the matted area is inserted into the composite.	
	No mutual degradation of picture quality (unlike *superimpositions*).	*In pictorial insertions, foreground and background shots should match in perspective, proportions, scale, lighting, etc.
	Studio area required for insertion may be confined.	*The whole of one picture source cannot normally be inserted into part of another shot (*see Figure 21.31*).
	Sharp matte edges keep edge ragging to a minimum.	But appropriate or accidental cut-off or disappearances can arise.
	Subjects disappear behind matted areas. Appropriate when moving *behind* walls, objects . . .	
Self keying/self-matting (using chroma key, CSO)	Operation is automatic.	Similar to *external key* disadvantages above marked*.
	No mattes/masks have to be prepared.	The keying/matting tone or color must only be present where 'background' is required. Shadows or reflections may cause spurious breakthrough.
	Subject movement is not confined (but may need restriction, to suit background scene).	Edge ragging and color fringing arise.
	Various tones or hues can be used, for differential keying.	When inserting into long shots a large studio area may require chroma-key background and floor unless keying foreground matte/gobo is used.
	Foreground subjects always move *in front* of background and cannot be cut off by matte or inadvertently disappear . . .	But the effect may not be appropriate and foreground matting flat or external matte may also be necessary.

embarassing background breakthrough in the wrong places! The *background shot* itself may contain any tones.

Most systems allow you to control whether the edges of the inserted subject appear firmly defined (*hard-edged*) or diffused (*soft-edged*). Soft-edged subjects may blend more successfully with the background picture, where a hard-edged insert might have a 'cut-out' look.

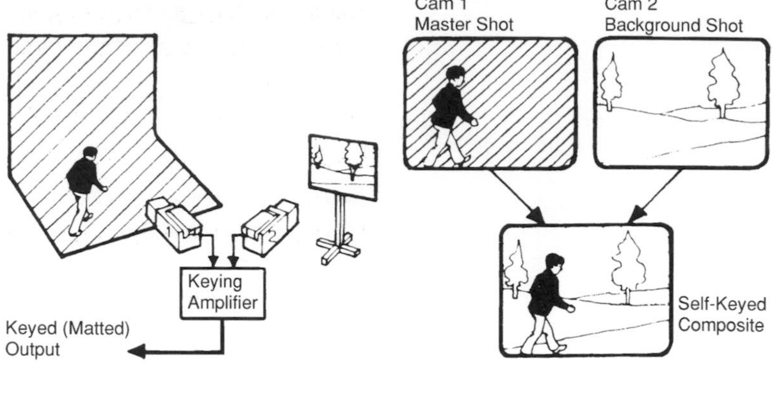

Fig. 21.28 Self-keying/self-matting
Wherever a selected tone (or *hue* if you use *chroma-key/CSO*) appears in the *master shot* (the subject or foreground shot), a corresponding part of the background shot is seen instead. The system switches back to the master shot for all other tones (or hues) in that scene. *Background* scene tones or hues do not affect keying in either system.

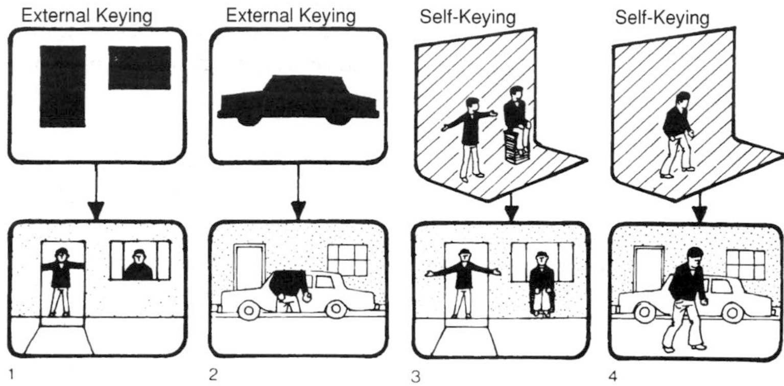

Fig. 21.29 Choice of system
External key. Here switching is controlled by a separate matte. It does not normally allow foreground subjects to move *in front of* features in the background picture. The subject disappears when it moves outside the matted area.
1 This is appropriate when people are to move behind walls, trees, etc.
2 But it is incongruous if, for example, they get out of a car matted in by external key. *Any tone or color* may be used in the foreground and background scenes.
Self-keying. This relies on hues (or tones) within the foreground shot (master shot/subject) to operate the keying. Chroma key is the commonest form of self-keying used in color TV. Subjects cannot normally moved *behind* background features.
3 The process can at times produce incongruous effects. People may appear to stand or sit in mid-air!
4 Where appropriate, self-keying is completely convincing. The *subject and foreground scene* should not contain or reflect the keying color. The background scene may contain *any* colors or tones.

Some facilities also enable you to adjust the *transparency* or the *opacity* of the subject. You can use luminance keying in both *monochrome* and *color* TV/video systems.

Chrominance keying (chroma key; chromakey; chroma-key. CSO – color separation overlay)

Chroma-key processes – which can only be used in a color system – rely on a selected *hue* to trigger the insertion. Wherever that *keying hue* (*usually blue or green*) appears in the foreground scene, a corresponding area of the *background* is switched into the composite instead. The foreground and/or background shots can be changed independently at a button press.

Using keyed insertion

Inserting titling

In Chapter 15 we mentioned the idea of electronically inserting *titling* into a picture for various purposes; e.g. subtitles, credits, data information, etc. Now we can look at title insertion in greater detail. The titling itself can come from camera title cards, a character generator, or photo-slides etc. and be inserted in several ways:

- *Superimposition.* This is only really successful against a dark even-toned surface. Where the background tones or hues vary, the lettering may be locally affected, or appear 'transparent'.
- *Non-additive mix* (*NAM*). Using this facility on the production switcher, the source, with the lightest tones (usually white titling) inserts 'solidly' into the other picture (Table 21.3).
- *Keyed insertion.* This technique allows lettering of any tone or hue to be solidly punched into a background picture without interaction effects. (It may be done through *external luminance keying* or lettering on a *chroma-key* blue backing.)

A *clip control (key level)* adjusts the brightness level at which the titling is keyed in. If set too low, the outline will be unsharp or show tearing. If set too high, finer parts of the lettering are liable to become lost.

Even well-inserted titling cannot be read if its tone or color proves to be similar to the background. If you are faced with this dilemma there are several solutions:

- *Border generator.* Here *edge keying* electronically creates an edge shadow outline around lettering. This can be black ('black edge'), white, or of any selectable color. The width of this border

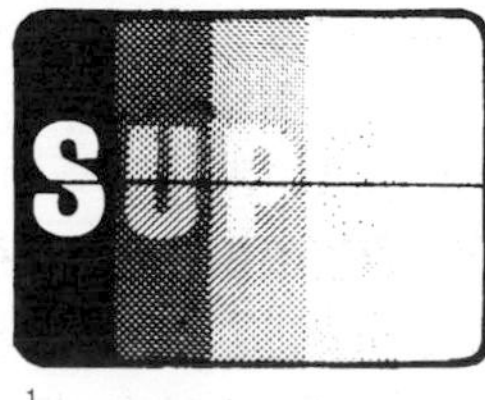

1

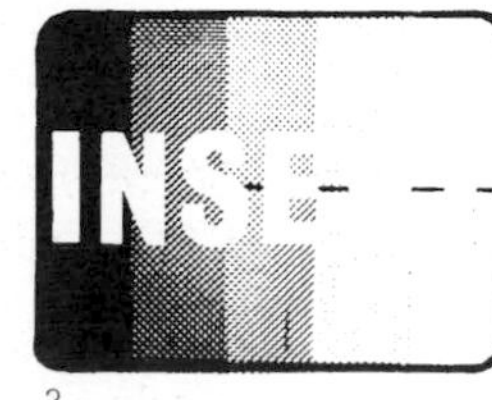

2

3

Fig. 21.30 Title insertion
1 Titles introduced by *superimposition* are satisfactory against plain backgrounds (preferably white letters against black), but otherwise mutual interaction reduces evenness and clarity.
2 *Inserted* letters cut through all picture tones; but for titling against similar tones (white on white, gray or gray) black-edging is desirable.
3 Sometimes an *inset area* (mid-gray presenting black or white titling) is more distinctive. It does not require a border. But the overall effect may be intrusive.

Continued on p. 541

Table 21.3 Keyed insertion terms

Background	The picture into which the foreground subject (master shot) is electronically inserted. It can usually contain any tone or color.
Black edge	Facility putting an artificial black border round titling, to improve readability. Border generator.
Blink; flasher	Blinks keyed-in titling or symbols at an adjustable rate.
Border generator; edge key; black edge generator; outline	Facility introducing a black, white, or color border around a keyed-in subject. It may also derive outlines.
Character generator	Computer-generated lettering, numerals, signs, widely used for inserted titling and graphics.
Chroma-key process	Facility for inserting a subject with a single-color background (e.g. blue) into another video picture. Several systems exist, including: 1 Fast-switching chroma key, using encoded composite video signals (e.g. video coded into NTSC form with syncs). 2 Similar system using direct RGB (decoded) video signals. More precise, less noise or spurious switching. 3 *Ultimatte*, which derives separate black matted images that are then superimposed in an additive mix.
Chroma keyer	Equipment controlling chroma-key operations. 1 Selects hue of the keying color. 2 Selects the input for chroma-key treatment. 3 Selects edge switching (hard, soft, color).
Clip control; clipper; clipping level; key level; threshold level	Adjusts the precise brightness (luminance) level at which switching takes place, when keying in a subject. Adjusted on preview to suit each shot. If incorrect, tearing or spurious breakthrough occurs.
Color synthesizer; colorizer; color field generator	Equipment generating color synthetically by applying proportional voltages to the RGB channels. Can be used to artificially color black and white pictures, either with an overall hue or with different hues for selected tonal values. Can also substitute different colors in a color picture.
Cycling	Facility for progressively changing the hue of synthesized color through the spectral range. *Also* to flash the luminance level (brightness).
Digital video effects	Images produced by storing color and detail information about a picture in digital form, then selectively reading out those data to produce visual effects.
Downstream key; title key	A facility that allows titling to be inserted when the main effects banks are already in use (e.g. for chroma key). It inserts *titles* or an *external key* into the switcher's *line output*. It may also be used to fade a program to black.
Drop shadow	An artificial black contour added to the side and lower edge of lettering, to create a pseudo-three-dimensional effect.
Double re-entry; cascade re-entry	The output of one *mix/effects bus amplifier* (*A/B*) can be re-entered into another *M/E bus* (*C/D*). So we can mix to or from combined shots (e.g. keyed-in titles, split screen, supers, chroma-key). *Also* a key from an external matte source may be used to create a matted area in one shot that is filled in by another camera's background picture.
External key	A prepared matte shape, that virtually punches a hole in the background picture and inserts the corresponding part of *another* picture source in the matted area. (E.g. creating silhouetted lettering, and filling it with a shot of texturing.)

Table 21.3 (cont.)

Foreground	The subject inserted into the background shot. In chroma-key setups it contains the keying color.
Hard key	Keying process *switching* from foreground to background, producing sharp-edged matting. Imperfections (tearing, crawling, jitter) can be very visible at subject edges (see *Soft key*).
Hue control	Control adjusting the actual color used for chroma-key insertion (usually blue, sometimes green or yellow).
Insert in/out	Switches selected matted picture in/out of the program picture.
Insert key	Where the key source exceeds a particular brightness level (selected by clipper adjustment) its subject is inserted into the background picture. Used to insert white-on-black titling into pictures, from camera title cards, slides, character generator, computer.
Insert program fader	Control used to fade inserts in/out of program picture.
Insert source	Selects which picture source fills in the matted area, produced by the key source.
Internal key; self-keying, self-matting	A particular color or tone in the foreground shot actuates an automatic switch, which inserts a corresponding part of another source picture in that area instead (E.g. *TONE* to insert white lettering: *COLOR* for chroma-key insertion.)
Key fill	Selects the source or color of infill for insert titling.
Key invert	Allows the output of a *mix/effects bus (M/E)* to fill external key subjects, and pre-set wipes.
Key mode	Mattes in lettering, giving it black edge, drop shadow, or border/outline treatment.
Key source	Selects the picture source used to matte out part of the background picture (see *Insert source*).
Linear keying; transparent matte, proportional keying	Circuits controlling the keying amplifier gain, for chroma-key insertion. It allows *transparent materials* (e.g. glass, smoke, water) or *finely edged subjects* (e.g. feathers) to be inserted while permitting the background to be seen through them. The linear keying mode can also be used to transform a normal picture input – to provide *color to monochrome mixes, tinting effects* (e.g. sepia tints), and negative pictures.
Luminance	Control adjusting the brightness level (in monochrome) or saturation (in color).
Luminance key; tonal key; inlay	A self-keying/internal-keying process in which a selected tone (black or white) in the foreground/master shot is replaced in the composite picture by a corresponding portion of the background shot.
Matte; mask; key	A specially generated signal supplied to a keying amplifier, causing it to it switch from one source to another in the matted area. It can be derived from a silhouette (painted, inked, or cut in card) as in a *camera matte* or *rostrum camera*, from a picture, from titling (e.g. character generator), from specially generated waveforms (wipes, SEG) from computer graphics.
Matte key	A system for infilling keyed outlines with tone or color (e.g. titling, maps).

Table 21.3 (cont.)

Mode	The *bank fader lever* on some switchers can be made to do several quite different things, so avoiding the need for separate controls. 1 *MIX/LAP DISSOLVE* between banks/buses. Its regular purpose. 2 *MASK KEY* to move wipe patterns. 3 *MIX KEY* to fade in a matte (key) signal. 4 *PATTERN TRANSITION* to provide a pattern transition between A and B buses.
Non-additive mix (NAM); peak mix mode; insert key; white insert mode	A circuit facility in which the lightest tones of one picture are inserted solid (opaque) into another picture. Used for title insertion.
Overcut	Switching in which the main subject is changed, appears or disappears, while the *background* picture remains constant throughout (see *Undercut*).
Pattern direction	Selects the direction in which a wipe/pattern moves when the control lever is operated.
Pattern edge	Adjusts pattern's edge sharpness (hard, soft) or width.
Pattern generator	Control selects interswitching patterns used for wipes and insets.
Pattern limit	Pre-sets the final size or extent of a wipe pattern; e.g. limiting a rotary wipe angle.
Pattern modulator; pattern weave	Causes the wipe pattern or the overall picture to ripple from side to side (adjustable rate and extent) to create a dynamic decorative effect.
Polarity; key reversal	Reverses the picture's tonal scale, so producing a negative image. *OR* it toggles (alternates) whether white or black tones actuate the keying.
Position	Joystick positioning a pattern in the frame.
Preview (P/V) bus key	The source selected on the *preview bus* mattes a hole in the picture on *Bus A* and fills it from the picture on *Bus B*.
Quad split	The screen is divided into four sections, simultaneously displaying separate images. The proportions of the divisions are adjusted with *VAR* or *SPLIT* controls.
Sequential effects amplifer	Matting carried out in a series of steps to produce a complex composite.
Shadow keyer	In chroma-key systems, subject shadows falling on the blue keying surface are normally not seen in the composite, and cause spurious 'tearing'. Special shadow-keying circuits can insert apparently 'natural' shadows.
Soft key	The keying system virtually mixes between the keyed subject and the background shot, producing diffused-edged matting (adjustable softness). Keying imperfections at edges are less visible. Images can be blended together at borders.
Special effects generator (SEG)	Equipment generating a series of electrical waveforms (e.g. square wave, sawtooth, triangular, parabolic) at line and field rate. From these waveforms, switching patterns are derived to provide wipes and inserts.
Spotlight	The background brightness is darkened around a disc matte (joystick positioned) to give a spotlight effect.
Undercut	Switching in which the main subject picture is retained while the background picture is changed; a performer's background switches to a new scene while we watch (see *Overcut*).

may be adjustable. It is usually possible to switch to a *drop shadow mode* or an *outline mode* in which the border replaces the original lettering (Figure 21.30).

- *Infill.* The lettering tone or color can be altered by infilling it with a separate source. A *colorizing generator (color synthesizer)* produces color signals artificially, which can be used to color lettering and/or backgrounds. A *cycling* mode can make the coloring self-change throughout the spectral range.
- *Double re-entry.* This switcher facility enables you to introduce texture or patterning into lettering (see Table 21.3).
- *Negative switching.* White lettering may be switched to black, or black lettering to white, if you find them coinciding with background tones. For example, when using standard white lettering on black camera titles they can be 'phase reversed' to insert them into a snow scene.
- *Flashing/blinking.* It may help at times to flash the lettering rhythmically, to draw attention, or make it more visible against its background.

Display screens

Surprisingly often, we want to accompany a shot of a person speaking to camera with a supplementary background picture showing what they are talking about. We find this regularly in newscasts, where the display screen introduces pictures of the upcoming story, or shows us the person the newscaster is speaking to. In talks, the screen can show us illustrations, photo-enlargements, maps, etc.

The most obvious way to obtain a screen of this sort is to bring a large picture monitor into the shot. If you have a rectangular hole in a flat the monitor can be placed behind it and appear as a wall screen. This can work quite well, especially if the monitor has a

1

2 Subject Cut Off

3

4

5

6

Fig. 21.31 Display screen
1 A 'wall display' screen can be simulated by self-matting (chroma key).
2 External keying can only be used when nothing moves into this area.
3 A 'screen' may be used to include a distant guest in a studio interview.
4 This is achieved by using a corresponding chroma key area in the main shot.
5 Care must be taken that the person to be inset is in proportion and position for the display screen.
To insert the whole of one picture into part of another, a picture monitor must be used (or a digital effects unit). Monitors should be shaded from reflected or spill light, color-adjusted (yellow bias), preferably using a dark screen (black matrix) tube. Quality unavoidably deteriorates.

tinted screen. (Sometimes a neutral gel or black net over the screen helps.) But there may be problems with lights reflected from its screen.

In addition, you will usually find that when you switch from the direct picture of the display subject to the studio shot showing it on the monitor screen, the display subject's color quality changes. You can usually improve matters by altering the color balance of the studio monitor (reducing blue), so that it looks right on camera.

An alternative approach to display screens is to have an opening in a flat behind the subject covered with a translucent sheet. You can then *rear project* slides onto this screen.

Another regular method is to use electronic insertion, to *simulate* a screen in the background:

- Use a *box wipe* or a *camera matte* to insert a picture of a monitor screen. Performers must not move in front of the matted area or parts of them will disappear!
- Have a blue panel or blind, or a patch of blue light on the background, and chroma key the display into this 'screen' area. People in the foreground will not be cut off if they move in front of the 'screen', but edge-ragging problems can arise.
- Using digital video effects, you can reduce the size of the display subject's picture and insert it into the background of the main shot. Again, performers must not move into the matted area.

Localized inserts

■ **Insert/inset** You normally introduce a *detail insert* into a wider shot by wiping in and holding the required shape (e.g. to show a close-up soloist within a full orchestra long shot, a box or iris wipe is positioned in the selected part of the screen). A hard-edged inset is usually preferable, to prevent image confusion – perhaps with a colored border to emphasize demarcations. Occasionally a soft (diffused) edge is unobtrusively effective – for a dream montage or a 'think' bubble (Figure 21.25).

■ **Vignette/surround matte** You can use keyed insertion to provide decorative surrounds or borders to an insert subject, or to form symbolic shapes (keyhole, telescope, binoculars, heart). Geometrical patterns are available on the SEG.

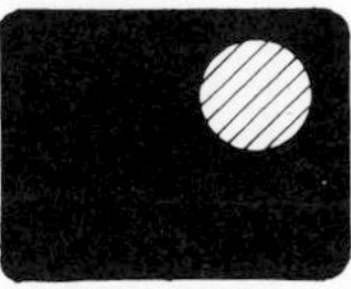

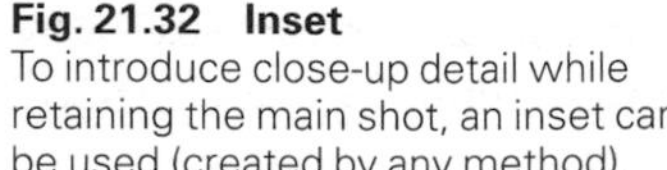

Fig. 21.32 Inset
To introduce close-up detail while retaining the main shot, an inset can be used (created by any method).

1 2

Fig. 21.33 Surround matte
Mattes can be used: (1) to mask off unwanted material in the shot, or (2) to simulate a vignette.

By blanking out parts of the shot you can exclude unwanted subjects. The support stand of a world globe could be matted out, so that it appeared in 'free space' – perhaps inserting a skyscape into the now-black surround.

■ **Indicators** Many switchers include facilities for inserting indicators that draw attention to specific information – in maps, charts, diagrams, photographs. Arrows, surround-rings, spotlight effects (a lightened disk on darkened background) are widely used, and located by joystick positioning; often with a 'blink' option.

■ **Appearance/disappearance** This is simply achieved, by switching or fading the insertion in and out.

Fig. 21.34 Indicators
Visual indicators in the form of an arrow, ring, spotlight (devised electronically or by any matting method), can identify specific detail.

Multi-split screen

This is a method of showing information from several shots simultaneously, by dividing the screen into two, three, four or more sections (with or without border lines).

Individual segments may show:

1 *Different views* of the same situation (reactions and prize giving at a game show).
2 A *montage* of concurrent events (different rescuers moving to the disaster area).
3 *Sequences* (steps in the development of a product).
4 *Groupings* of subjects with a common significance (all members of the team).

This multi-split screen effect (Figure 21.35) can be achieved by:

1 *Sequential insertion* (quad overlay). The switcher treats pictures in turn; matting out a chroma-key area, passing the matted result on to combine with the next source (with its chroma-key area), matting from this combination, and so on. (Each insertion could use a different keying hue if required.)
2 *VT build-up.* Recording a split screen pattern; then reproducing the tape and matting in a further segment(s).
3 *Digital video effects.* Capturing a frame, reducing the image size, and positioning it beside other frozen images, in a multiframe store.

Fig. 21.35 part 1 Type of split screen
Several forms of divided screen are widely used:
1 Split screen.
2 Triple split.
3 Quad split.
4 Multi-split.

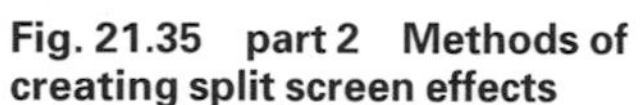

Fig. 21.35 part 2 Methods of creating split screen effects
Several methods are used: *sequential switching* – the system selecting each source in turn for a certain period.
Sequential insertion – after the first picture has been treated, part of a further picture is matted in. The next source is inserted into that composite . . . and so on. Other techniques include VT build-up (see Fig. 21.43), or digital image-processing.

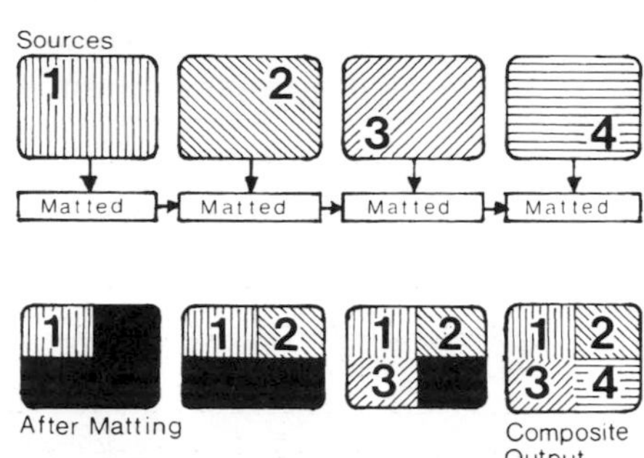

Chroma-key insertion techniques

Chroma-key has endless applications; especially when combined with other video effects. You can simulate total reality or create magical, stylized, decorative displays. The opportunities are endless, the economies considerable. But you need to apply chroma-key carefully, keeping in mind its problems and limitations, if you are going to achieve convincing, accurate results. Forethought and careful planning can save a great deal of rehearsal time. So we shall look in some detail here at many of its potentials and its pitfalls.

Check the chroma-key area

When you are preparing a chroma-key set-up, begin by checking that the chroma-key area and subjects are suitable.

- Is the color of the background appropriate? Ideally, the blue background (and floor if necessary) should be of an even overall tone and cobalt blue. Some systems are more color-critical than others. Check that blue-painted chroma-key flats have a dull, even finish. Blue background or floor cloth should be stretched, without folds or wrinkles.
- The blue keying surfaces should be evenly lit. If they vary in brightness, it will be difficult to adjust clipping levels correctly. Shadowy areas can cause poor clipping. So look out for *deep shadows* falling on the chroma-key blue surfaces (particularly from the performers or furniture).

Table 21.4 Typical chroma-key errors

Although chroma-key insertion, even in its simpler forms, can seemingly perform miracles, it does have important restrictions that we cannot ignore.

Effect	*Cause*	*Remedy*
Breakthrough	Areas of background scene break through into the foreground scene.	Blue areas in the foreground (actual or reflected) cause spurious triggering. Chroma-key backdrop of wrong hue. Shadows of foreground subjects falling onto blue backdrop or floor, reducing its local brightness.
Spurious effects	Ragged edges around inserted subjects.	Incorrect clipping level. Readjust.
Scale errors	Subject appears too large or small relative to its background.	Alter lens angle or camera distance.
Errors in perspective	Subject's size appears to alter as it moves 'within' the background.	Incorrect lens angle. Adjust zoom.
Incompatible viewpoint	Subject camera height obviously differs from that of background shot.	Adjust subject camera to suit the background, or change background.
Floating effect; shadowless	The subject casts no shadows on the ground and surroundings.	Inherent in basic chroma-key systems. Disguise with items in shadow area. (Use ***shadow chroma-key*** system.)
False shadows	Subject shadows are incompatible with planes in the background picture.	As above. Include false blue planes (Figure 21.41).
Incongruities	Subject is misplaced relative to background (e.g. appears to be standing in mid-air).	Reframe subject to an appropriate position on the screen.
Incompatibility	The brightness, tone, color balance of the subject do not match that of the background scene. The direction or character of the light (soft; high-contrast) are noticeably different from that in the background.	Modify the ***subject*** picture's quality (adjust gamma, color balance, black level), and/or lighting to match the background picture. Occasionally adjust ***background*** picture quality.
Blue light spill	Blue light illuminating a chroma-key backdrop spills onto subject.	Restrict blue light coverage. Place subject further from backdrop.
Bizarre changes in subject	Subject camera pans, causing subject to appear to slide sideways. Subject camera ***tilts***, causing subject to appear to slide vertically. Changing lens angle causes subject to appear to grow or shrink.	Inherent in basic chroma-key systems. Foreground and background changes must be synchronized. (This requires a special servo link between foreground and background cameras.)

Fig. 21.36 Background insertion

1 **Internal keying.** The person stands in front of a chroma-key blue surface, and a new *background* is inserted. This can be plain tone or color from a color synthesizer, black level, pictures from any video source.

2 **External keying.** Using a prepared matte part of the studio scene is matted out, and a background picture inserted in its place (from a graphic, slide, VTR or film).

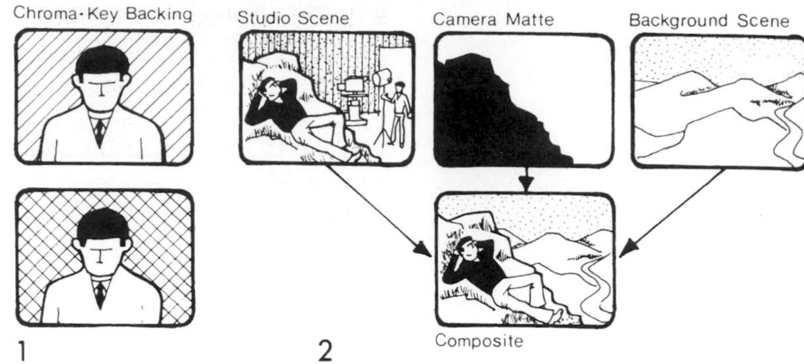

1
2
a
b
3
Studio Scene
Camera Matte
Background Scene
Composite
4

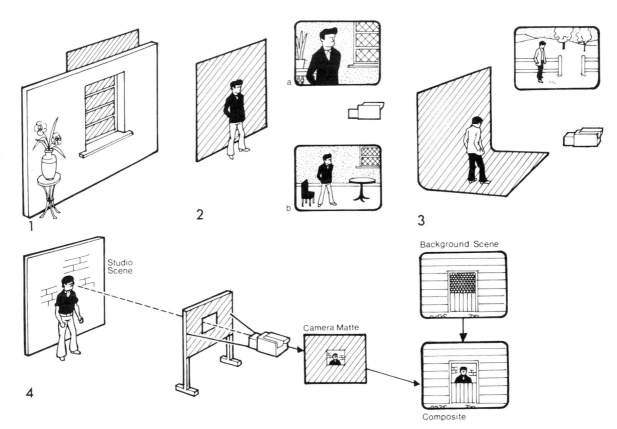

Fig. 21.37 Typical chroma-key set-ups

1 You can insert a photographed 'exterior' outside the window, by using a chroma-key blue backing.

2 Only a simple chroma-key blue flat is needed, if (a) the floor is not in shot, or (b) if the studio floor will appear natural in the composite.

3 When people are to appear *within* the background picture, or where the studio floor would look incongruous in the composite, you must use a *continuous* chroma-key blue surface, behind the subject and on the floor.

4 Here the camera shoots through the hole in a blue matte-board. Particularly useful for long shots, this camera matte masks off most of the studio, so prevents the camera shooting off into lights etc. It also avoids the need for large keying areas in the studio. All blue keying surfaces must be evenly lit to a similar level, free from shadows, etc., to give good overall clipping.

- Spurious breakthrough will occur if there are any *accidental* blue areas in the foreground subjects. So check clothing, objects, props, furniture, scenery, etc.
- Check that there are no shiny surfaces (e.g. mirrors, glasses) likely to reflect nearby chroma-key color from the blue floor or backdrop.

Clipping level

Adjust the *clipping level* to obtain firm, clean edges around inserted subjects. There should be no tearing, ragged edges, or bleeding around edges.

You will need to adjust the clip control continuously for optimum effect. If the clipping levels are set too low the inserted subject will show severe edge ragging around its borders. Set too high, and you will lose parts of the inserted subject itself.

How critical this adjustment is in practice will depend on the system design, how it is set up, and the subject to be keyed in. If lighting is uneven, or there are odd shadows, you will find clipping is successful in some parts of the insert but not in others. Overall firm clipping may not be possible.

At best, the insert will be perfect and undetectable. At worst, there will be discernible tearing, breakthrough, edge ragging within and around the subject.

Technical note: Ideally, for clear-cut insertion one should use the *separate* red, green, and blue signals from the keying source to actuate the chroma-key circuits (*RGB keyer*). However, this is often impracticable, and you will have to use a *composite* video signal from the keying source instead (i.e. the complete NTSC or PAL signal: video waveform plus all color and syncs information). Some sources only output a composite signal; e.g. VTRs, telecine, ESS, external sources and remotes, and some studio cameras. Chroma-key inserts using this *encoded keyer* are more difficult to adjust; edges are less clean as switching is not so accurate. Some chroma-key systems can be switched to either *RGB keyer* or *encoded keyer* to suit the incoming keying source.

Aiding performers

- In a total chroma-key situation (blue backdrop and floor) place blue disks on the floor to give talent *location marks.*
- If action requires an actor to look directly at something in the background shot (which he or she cannot see!) place a dim colored lamp in a corresponding position in the studio to give an *eyeline* to work to.

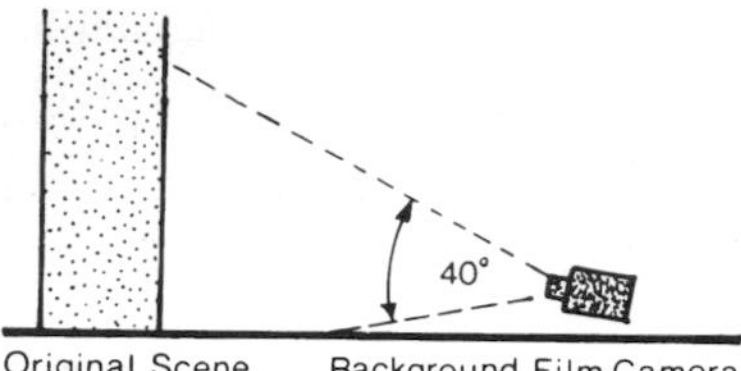

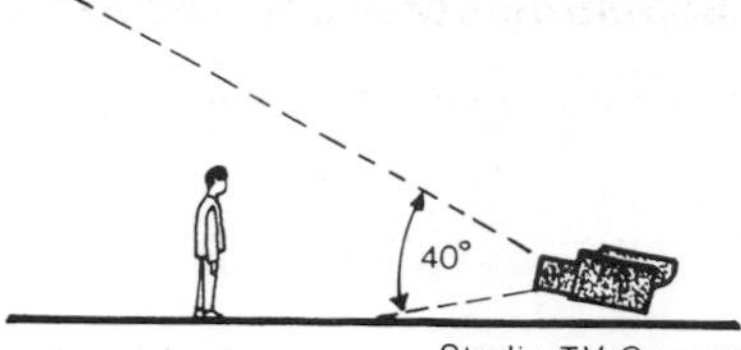

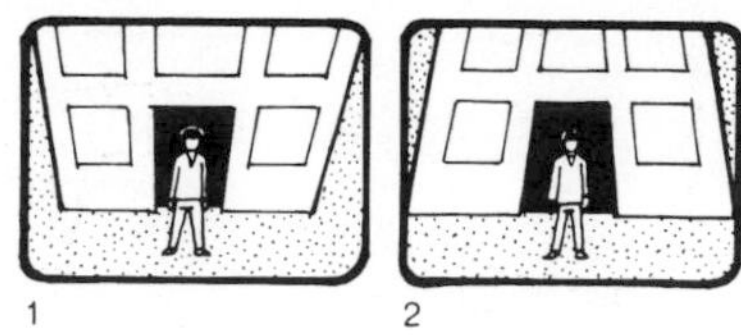

Fig. 21.38 Matching camera height
The height, angle of tilt, and lens angle, of the studio camera should be identical to that used to photograph the background scene, if distortion is to be avoided. Often the errors are not obvious.
1 Unmatched viewpoints.
2 Matched viewpoints.

Matching

For *pictorial* inserts the foreground and background usually need to match reasonably well. The scale, perspective (lens angle, height, eyeline), color quality, contrast, light direction, etc. should be compatible.

So when a person is to be inserted into a background picture we must take care to check proportions, and use a camera height that suits the background viewpoint.

- Check that the person's feet are rationally placed within the background; that he or she does not appear to be standing in mid-air, or in an incongruous position (e.g. on a pond).
- Check that the person can move across the screen, and a short distance forwards/backwards, without creating visual problems. If an actor is apparently to 'walk around within the background', the scale and perspective should appear to be consistent throughout the action.
- People should not seem to grow taller or shrink as they move nearer or further from the camera (wrong lens angle).
- Nor should they rise or fall (wrong camera height).

Much depends on whether there are many visual clues to perspective in the shot. In open background scenes (beach, landscape) even gross errors may not be obvious. But scenes including architectural subjects (rooms, buildings, streets) can be very critical.

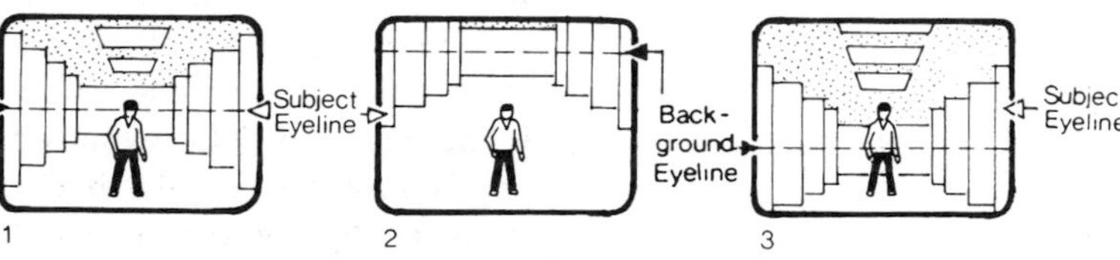

Fig. 21.39 Matching eyelines.
1 The foreground subject matches its background's perspective only when the television camera's eyeline coincides with the eyeline of the background.
2 Background eyeline *above* subject eyeline.
3 Background eyeline *below* subject eyeline.

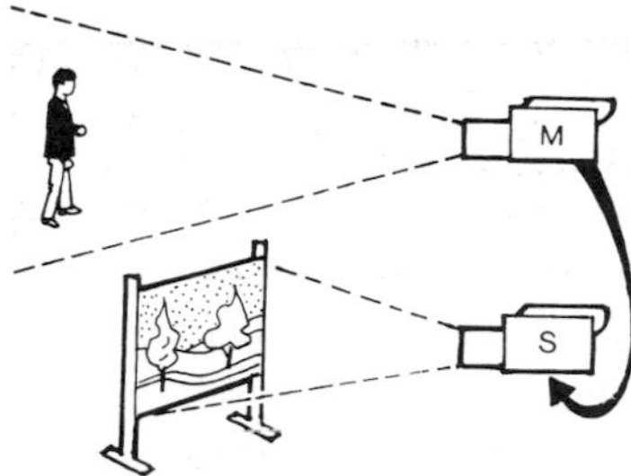

Fig. 21.40 Ganged backgrounds By using a servo-controlled interconnection ('ganging') between the subject (master) camera and the background (slave) camera, the latter pans, tilts, and zooms automatically as the subject camera follows the action. Alternatively, the background graphic itself may be moved vertically/horizontally by servo systems using a static slave camera.

Adjusting scale and perspective

Lacking detail of the lens angle and height of the original camera shooting the background photograph, you can use the following empirical technique to avoid strange scale or perspective effects:

- Display the shot of the background picture on a monitor. If you are using a background photograph set up in front of a camera, lock off that camera's panning head. (If a drawing or painting is used as a background, its perspective might not be correct, so adjustments are a matter of luck!)
- Check the background shot on the monitor and choose points where you can make reasonably accurate guesses about the sizes of subjects; e.g. doorways, cars. (Avoid choosing indefinitely sized objects such as bushes or fences.) At these points, using a wax pencil or a felt-tipped pen, mark vertical lines to scale on the picture-tube, representing the performer's height. (If there are no true clues you will have to make guesstimates.)
- Take a long shot of the studio chroma-key area on a normal lens angle. Insert the performer into the scene. Adjust the clipping level.
- Position the person to coincide with the 'nearest' marker in the background picture. Adjust the camera distance to fit their height to the marker.
- Holding that camera and lens position, move the performer further away from the camera to coincide with a 'distant' marker position in the picture. If perspective is correct, he/she will appear reasonably similar in height to the distant marker. If the person looks disproportionately shorter, zoom in a little and dolly back to compensate. If the person looks too tall at the distant point, zoom out and dolly in. A reasonable compromise is usually possible.
- If the subject camera is now overshooting the chroma-key area, or seeing cameras, boom, lights, place a chroma-key matte in front of the camera (blue card with a 4 × 3 rectangular central hole). Otherwise use a localized wipe pattern to cut off unwanted areas.

Further practical problems

Having set up the chroma-key shot, there may be two obvious defects:

- Depth of field.
- Color fringing.

If the depth of field is limited in the foreground scene, yet depth appears limitless in the background, you have a problem. Occasionally, slightly defocusing the *background shot* will help. Otherwise, more light will be needed on the *foreground scene* so that the subject camera can stop down.

Blue color fringes can develop round the borders of keyed-in subjects. Chroma-key blue lighting may have spilled onto it, or be reflected onto it. It may be due to optical flare. It can be due to the system's inherently poor color detail (restricted bandwidth). The often-recommended 'remedy' of using yellow backlight (minus blue) may occasionally alleviate the problem but is more likely to tint the subject yellow!

Some systems are more susceptible to color fringing than others. Soft-edge keying can diminish the effect, but for total suppression, special circuits (*hue suppressors*, *fringe eliminators*, *exclusive hue matrix*) are often necessary. Unfortunately, these may modify the reproduction of certain color mixtures.

When inserting finer detail (e.g. hair, lace, fur, feathers) or vague, unsharp subjects (e.g. smoke, glass, water, steam) edges will normally tend to break up or become noticeably blue-fringed, due to indecisive switching action. You can often improve the situation by using *soft-edge keying*. But the real solution is to use *linear keying* (*transparent matte; proportional keying*) which allows such subjects to be inserted without any visible side-effects.

Keying surface and hue

Strictly speaking, the color you use in the foreground scene to key the chroma-key insertion should closely match the color for which the system is designed. This is usually a highly saturated blue (approximately *cobalt blue*); chosen because it is chromatically most distinguishable from flesh colors and least likely to arise in foreground scenes. If you try to key with a greenish blue, a fairly dark blue, or some impure mixture you may find it difficult or even impossible to achieve clean sharp keying. Some systems are much more critical than others.

In practice, chroma-key set-ups often deviate from the ideal. Using a variety of colored cyc cloths, cycs lit with blue light, blue-painted flats, stretched blue-painted cloths, blue-painted floors, the brightness and spectral distribution of these various sufaces can vary considerably! Although the system usually works, clipper adjustment can be unreliable.

Chroma-key systems can be adjusted to key on *any chosen color*, but, as you know, this color must not be present (or reflected) in the foreground or master shot. Otherwise there will be serious breakthrough at that point. When using blue keying hue, for instance, any performer wearing blue slacks would appear legless when keyed into the background shot! Similarly, the background would be seen through a hole in the chest when wearing a blue tie!

Where you cannot avoid having blue in the foreground subjects, the system can usually be adjusted to key on *green* or *yellow* instead.

Then, of course, you have to prevent this new keying hue appearing in the subjects.

Refinements

Later design developments have now considerably advanced chroma-key techniques. The *Ultimatte system*, for example, relies on a *color comparison process* rather than the direct color-keying method of regular chroma-key, and so is less susceptible to break-through problems. It can create completely realistic composite images, even where the foreground or subject shot has shadowy areas, reflections, transparent subjects, very fine detail, soft-edged subjects, or shades of the keying color. Consequently it becomes practicable to chroma-key through running water or smoke, without spurious artifacts (e.g. 'chroma-key crawl').

Shadow chroma-key

One of the main weaknesses of the normal chroma-key process is that any shadows falling onto the blue keying surfaces are lost. (Not only that, but if they are dense enough they will spoil the clipping.) If you are using a blue floor then the inserted subject will appear to stand without the natural floor shadows, apparently *suspended* above the ground. The result is very artificial.

This happens because the chroma-key process removes *all* blue and near-blue areas from the picture. As far as the system is concerned, any subject shadows falling on the blue keying surface are normally removed with the rest of the blue areas.

Without floor shadows, however, inserted people may appear to 'float' and the illusion is spoiled – particularly where shadows are evident in the background scene. With shadow-key circuitry a natural shadow can be *simulated*. It detects the lower brightness (luminance) of the shadow on the keying surface, deriving a matte from it of adjustable sharpness and density, and introduces it

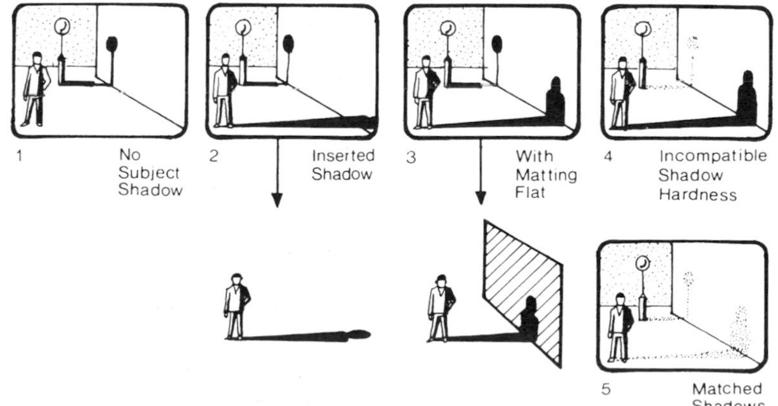

Fig. 21.41 Shadows

1. Chroma-key insertion relies on color to actuate switching, but does not normally differentiate between different intensities of the keying-hue (i.e. shadows on the chroma-key surface). So subject shadows are not inserted.
2. Special extra circuitry permits 'shadows' to be produced (actually luminance-derived mattes), but the shadow falls along the floor and may be inappropriate.
3. If a carefully positioned matting flat is used in the chroma-key set-up, so as to coincide with planes in the background picture, the subject shadows falling on it seem to be on the photographed wall.
4. The inserted shadow's sharpness must be comparable with that of the photo background.
5. Given compatible shadow direction, contouring and hardness, a totally convincing illusion is possible.

transparently over the background scene. Extremely convincing, even its position can be relocated to match the background by including keying surfaces in the foreground scene.

Moving backgrounds

Where a photostill is used for the background scene you should avoid any 'frozen' features (waves, smoke, people) drawing attention to the falsity. When keying into moving backgrounds from film or VT you should make sure that sequences last long enough for the foreground action and are suitably synchronized (e.g. a 'moving' automobile's background).

Foreground pieces

With care, you can arrange the foreground subjects in the studio chroma-key set-up so that they appear totally integrated into the background scene. Furniture, pieces of scenery (pillars, walls, bushes) blend with the overall effect. If there is an unwanted feature in the background shot (perhaps a hovering seagull in a beach-scene photograph!) you might hide it with a foreground tree-branch.

Virtual settings

For decades, chroma-key has been used to insert studio action 'into' photographs, graphics, stylized illustrations, computer graphics. We have seen it in a multiplicity of productions: from interviews to opera; from 'soap' to musical extravaganza; from 'kids' shows' to serious discussions; from newscasts to weather-casting. The opportunities seem boundless. Yet chroma-key has mainly been used as an incidental technique – or to provide 'magical tricks'. There were a number of reasons for that.

Some directors feel uncomfortable when confronted with a studio comprising blue backdrops and floor, odd scenic pieces, and a scattering of furniture. They prefer 'solid settings' that allow them to stand and see potential shots. Working with chroma-key and virtual settings requires imaginative anticipatory planning if it is to be wholly successful. Ineptly handled, chroma-key production can consume rehearsal time, as incongruous effects arise. Detailed planning and methodical set-up methods pay off. Completely convincing results are assured, and the time taken is nominal.

Synchronized movements

As you have seen, when using *basic* chroma-key systems we must take care to avoid spurious effects such as side-slip or hop from camera movements or size changes through zooming.

To allow the subject (foreground) camera's head to turn freely, with corresponding changes in the background shot, requires some form of servo link to ensure that both operate in exact synchronism. Then, although its *mounting* must remain stationary, as the camera pans, tilts, or zooms, we will see proportional changes in both subject and background pictures. The combined results in the composite are completely realistic. Using this ganged system, you can follow a person over an arc, so that they appear to be moving past a photographed scene, a graphic, or a miniature (model).

A *motion tracking (auto key tracking)* facility automatically coordinates changes you make to the foreground shot, with corresponding alterations in the background scene. But remember, there are two separate situations here:

1 If, for example, someone walking across the screen is followed by a panning subject-camera, you will want the *entire background scene* of the street to move past 'behind them' at a corresponding rate.
2 On the other hand, suppose you have a foreground shot of a room with a dummy window, through which we appear to see an exterior scene with a prominent tree – inserted via a chroma key window backing (Figure 21.37(1)). Then we want the scene visible through the window to remain locked in position, even if the subject camera moves or zooms.

Mobile camera

The next step is to give the subject/foreground camera *unrestricted freedom*, so that it appears to move around 'within' the *scene*. To do this, precise information about its floor position, height, shooting angle, lens angle must be fed into a computer, which correspondingly adjusts the background source. Even slight changes in the subject camera require the entire background picture to be instantly recalculated and redrawn to correspond if the composite is to be compatible. No easy task! And here we come to the basis of the newest form of *virtual settings*, where entire scenic environments are created artificially. The background can be derived from a camera shooting a photographic display or a three-dimensional scale model. Alternatively, computer generated backgrounds can be used.

The subject's camera (which may even be shoulder-mounted) moves around shooting action against a blue (or green) background in the studio. Whether features such as steps, parallels, furniture, are actually provided in the studio or substituted with blue-painted items corresponding to those in the background picture will depend on the situation.

The amount of space and the expanse of chroma-key backdrops needed in the studio will vary. It may be quite nominal; but where the action involves a long continuous walk, or subjects are spaced some distance apart, you will generally need studio space comparable with that in the background scene. There are ways round this, of course. Where studio space is limited, you can have the performer walk just a short way, then cut to another camera viewpoint. If you want someone to appear to be standing a considerable distance away, you can shoot them on a wide-angle lens. You might use multi-layer inserts.

Tracking camera movements

There are several ingenious methods of tracking the subject-camera's operations:

- *Motion sensors* attached to the subject (foreground) camera send data on the camera head's actions and position to the computer controlling the background shot.
- A *remote joystick* which controls the positions of both the motorized subject-camera's mounting and the background shot.
- Highly sophisticated *pattern-recognition computer software*, which continually interprets the video output of the subject's camera, and so judges its exact position. From this data, the corresponding section of the background scene is selected.
- A *small supplementary upwards-pointing camera* fixed to the side of the subject camera detects the precise camera position (as well as pan, tilt and roll) by reading circular barcode targets of highly reflective tape in the ceiling. These are illuminated by a ring of yellow light-emitting diodes (LEDs) on top of the camera. The chroma-key backdrop is of special reflective cloth (viewable over 85° off axis) illuminated by a ring of blue light emitting diodes around the camera lens. (Only in very close shots is there light spill onto subjects visible.)

Complex insertion (see Figure 21.42)

Moving 'behind' background subjects

When you want people in the foreground scene to 'move behind' subjects in the background picture you can use either *keying areas* or *external mattes*. If you exactly align an area of keying hue (e.g. blue) in the foreground scene with a subject in the background shot you effectively 'detach' that item in the background picture. Make a blue matching flat in the studio correspond with a wall in the background photograph and a performer can paste a bill on it, or walk behind it in the chroma-keyed composite! Wherever there are features in the background, such as stairs, platforms, rocks, you place an equivalent-sized blue-painted structure in the foreground scene.

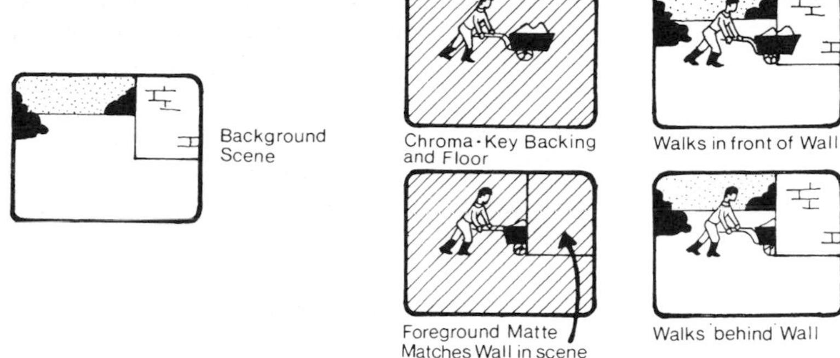

Fig. 21.42 part 1 Foreground mattes – matting flat
A flat of chroma-key hue can be positioned within the chroma-key set-up to coincide with a wall in the photo background, so enabling a performer to 'move behind' it.

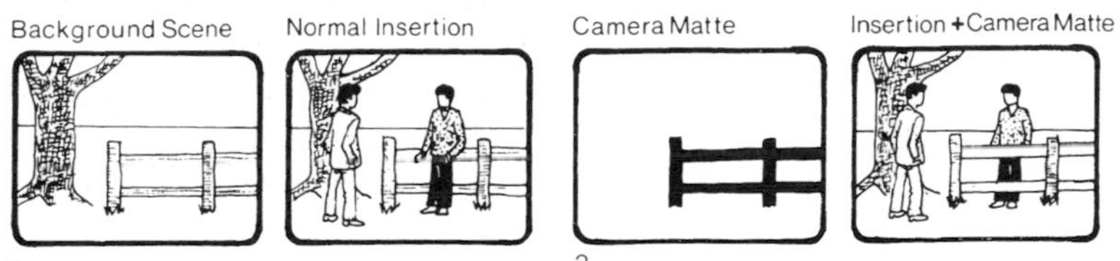

Fig. 21.42 part 2 Foreground mattes – camera matte
Normally, when subjects are chroma-keyed into a scene, they appear in *front* of the background. But by introducing an *additional matte* (e.g. a silhouette camera matte as an external key), to suppress the chroma-key insertion in that area, you can make subjects 'move behind' parts of the background scene. Such matting can be switched in and out to allow moves in front and behind background objects.

Fig. 21.42 part 3 Foreground mattes – relating to background objects
By appropriately positioning suitable items in the chroma-key set-up (blocks, parallels, stairs, etc., painted in the keying hue), people can apparently sit, lean, climb, or put objects on features in the background shot.

Where your performer is to move behind fine detail (tracery, open screens, foliage, fences) in a background photograph you can use an *external matte silhouette* that inhibits the chroma-key insertion, letting the background through instead. A suitable silhouette can be traced from the background picture or the projected image of a background slide. As this inhibiting matting signal can be switched in or out, a person can walk behind (matte in) or in front of (matte out) the background feature at choice.

Practical examples

Let's turn to a couple of examples that show the sort of thing that can be achieved with a little imagination. Built scenery here is minimal, and we have avoided the complications of studio settings or shooting on location:

- *What the viewer saw* – A continuous long shot shows the darkened interior of an ancient church. A cleric walks slowly across the shot from camera left. He is carrying a lighted candle, and passes behind a decorative ironwork grille . . . turning towards the distant altar . . . and moving up the aisle. He lights large candles on either side of the altar . . . and exits.
- *What was in the studio* – A blue cyc and a blue floor cloth. A photograph of a church interior provided the background scene. A silhouette matte had been prepared from a photograph of a period ironwork grille. This was matted in on picture left, over the church interior background shot. Corresponding with the distant altar in the photograph, a blue-painted table, with a couple of regular candles on tall blue blocks.

In another totally convincing example:

- *What the viewer saw* – We are outside a small country store. A girl cycles into shot, stops, and rests her bike against a nearby tree. She bends down to pat a sleeping dog. Reaching up to pick a blossom from the tree, she walks up steps to enter the store.
- *What was in the studio* – A photo slide provided the background scene, complete with store, tree, and sleeping dog beneath it. In the studio (blue cyc and floor) a blue pole on a stand corresponded to the tree in the photograph. (It had a real blossom attached to it by a thread.) The girl patted the air where the photo-dog slept. Blue-painted stock treads were positioned where the store's steps were located in the photograph.

1 2

Fig. 21.43 VT build-up
1 Using chroma-key, extra subjects can be inserted into videotape to provide action build-up e.g. a series of separate recordings (passes) using the same person in different costumes.
2 Multi-camera shooting can be integrated to produce simultaneous multi-images of the same subject.

Video build-up

You can key a person into a background, replay the composite, and then key him into that. So far, he has become twins! You could then continue inserting into composites (with quality deteriorating at each dubbing) to provide any number of different insertions of the same performer; thus generating a barber-shop quartet, choir, or orchestra! One ingenious example showed a man sitting beside himself, taking a tiny figure (of himself) out of his pocket . . . and so on!

Fig. 21.44 Mirror effects
1 A demonstrator stands before a 'magic mirror' displaying a series of changing images. In fact, the mirror reflects a cloth of keying hue, so turning it into a self-matting area, into which subjects are inserted (from slides projected on obliquely angled screens).
2 A person walks through a mirror. In fact, an opening in a blue flat is hung with a curtain of thin blue strips and corresponds to another camera's mirror flat.

You can even insert subjects from videotape (or videodisc) played in fast or slow motion, freeze framed, or reversed, and integrate real-time action and changed time *in the same shot!* (See *Temporal effects*.)

Multi-level synthesis

This keying process switches in a chosen synthesized color wherever a particular tonal level appears in the treated picture. So, for example, in a two-tone system a white-on-black slide can be reproduced as a red-on-yellow picture. Both economical and adaptable, this is a regularly used facility in many studios; titling being prepared in monochrome and then video processed.

Using *multi-level digital synthesis*, greater elaboration is possible. The picture is analyzed into perhaps eight tonal levels, each of which can be colorized to a different hue or tint. So a multi-tone graph becomes transformed into a multi-hue display. A normal vari-toned picture (monochrome or color) becomes strangely posterized in synthetic colors; akin to a colored contour map. The same device may be used to produce *tonal coarsening*, reducing half-tones to three or four gray-scale levels (*posterizing*). It can even reduce the picture tones to solid areas of black and white.

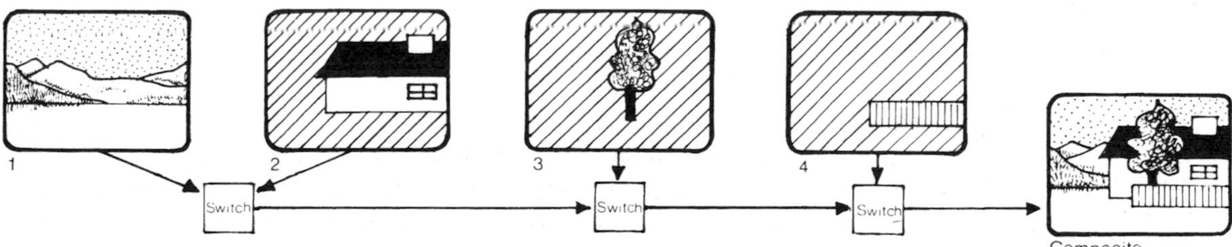

Fig. 21.45 Sequential keying (sequential insertion, cascade insertion, quad overlay)
Each picture is keyed in 'on top of' the previous combination, to build up an overlapping composite; a multi-layering process.

Table 21.5 Chroma-key techniques summarized

Effect	Method
To insert a subject into an open background scene. *Floor not visible.*	Chroma-key backdrop.
To insert a subject into an open background scene. *Floor visible.*	Chroma-key background and floor. Shadow insertion?
To insert a subject into a restricted area within a full background (*Subject will be naturally cut off when moving beyond that area; e.g. by a wall*)	Localized SEG wipe pattern (e.g. box wipe), or localized chroma-key insert (e.g. blue patch), or localized external matte.
Person to move in front of a background subject	Normal effect with chroma-key insertion.
Person to move behind a background subject	Regular chroma-key insertion, with blue scenic elements (flats) in the studio corresponding with wall, tree, etc. in background scene. Or use a localized matte silhouette to inhibit the area of the subject shot which the person moves behind.
Person to sit, stand, walk on a background item (furniture, staircase, table, chair)	Regular chroma-key insertion, with blue scenic elements in the studio corresponding with specific items.
Person to appear abnormally large (e.g. giant)	Adjust size of subject shot relative to background scene. (Zoom in.)
Person to appear abnormally small (tiny; Tom Thumb)	Adjust size of subject shot relative to background scene. (Zoom out.)

Digital video effects

When a sound wave impinges on the diaphragm of a microphone it produces a continuous fluctuating voltage corresponding to these vibrations – the *audio signal*. As a video camera scans its lens's image it produces a varying *video signal* corresponding to the light and shade. *This is the world of analogue technology.* But analogue processes have inherent drawbacks. It is difficult to avoid introducing distortions that degrade reproduction. Even an excellent analogue recording introduces distortion, however slight. Make a copy (dubbing) and this distortion worsens. The quality of further dubs progressively deteriorates until it becomes quite unacceptable.

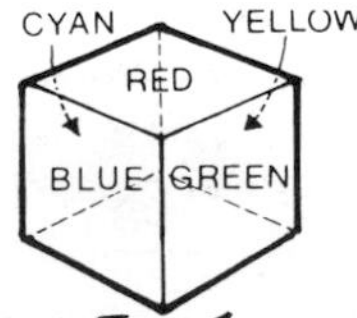

Fig. 21.46 Multi-hue chroma-key Several keying hues are used in turn, each keying in a particular video source. So different pictures appear on this rotating multi-colored block.

It is not surprising, therefore, that as technology advanced and *digital* methods of transmitting data evolved, these began to replace the older analogue systems, for they were not only more 'robust' (i.e. much less likely to become distorted) but they opened up ways of correcting and manipulating picture and sound that hitherto were not feasible. It now became possible to enhance sound and picture quality (*image enhancement*), reduce noise (*'snow removers'*), improve apparent definition (*edge enhancement*), stabilize picture synchronism, permit multi-generation dubbing without quality deterioration. Digital techniques advanced equipment design throughout the entire medium.

The principles of this digital process are not hard to explain. In a digital system the strength of the continuous analogue video (or audio) signal is rapidly sampled at regular intervals and stored away in coded numerical form. The *binary code* used just consists of groups of on–off pulses. (Rather like the dot and dash patterns of Morse code; except that each number has permutations of eight on–off samples.) These pulses are easily stored magnetically. (They are the basis of computer data, CD disc recordings, CD-ROM and many other data storage processes.)

Now instead of the continuous subtle variations of *analogue* waveforms we have a store of numbers representing the brightness and color of each tiny area (pixel) of the video picture or the fluctuations of the sound signal. These 'quantized' digitally coded signals are readily reconstituted into the original analogue picture and sound. This may all sound pretty tortuous, but now we have independent access to *each stored element of the entire picture!*

Normally, we shall want to read out the stored data in the order in which it was recorded. But there are other opportunities if we wish to use them. We can manipulate digitized video in various ways:

- *Altering features* – Instruct the system to change the numbers filed in particular data areas; so causing the picture to become diffused or sharpened, converting hues, etc.
- *Editing features* – We can pick out and change particular sections of coding: adding, replacing, omitting, copying, duplicating, etc.
- *Varying the readout* – We can change the rate and the order in which the filed data is read out: altering replay *speed*; reading out *selected parts* of the data (i.e. reproducing only part of the picture); reading it in reverse order, to mirror or invert the picture.

In practical terms, this all means that by selective processing we can alter the appearance of the digitized picture in many different ways – by pasting one feature onto another; altering color and shape; intermixing and editing . . . It becomes possible to edit and to modify a soundtrack, to alter audio quality, reverberation, attack and decay times . . . In short, we have reached the magic of computer graphics and digital effects!

Using video effects

As you can see from Table 21.6, an increasing range of visual effects is available. Some have a direct productional value, some add an

Table 21.6 Digital video effects

DVE systems manipulate the visual image in many ingenious ways. Terms are not universal, and like the effects themselves, are continually being invented. Many results are obtained by combining several separate effects.

1 *Aspect ratio*	The picture height and or width can be changed independently, to alter the picture shape. Images are deformed, being correspondingly squashed or stretched.
2 *Aspect ratio change*	Picture holds its non-standard shape, as it is zoomed or positioned.
3 *Audio activation*	Effects change at an audio rate.
4 *Auto freeze*	Picture freezes at selected frame intervals, producing a strobe effect.
5 *Auto key tracking/key follow*	Automatic adjustment of the keying area's size and position in a chroma-key insertion as the foreground subject picture is adjusted. (Zoom on a camera shooting a simulated wall screen, and the amount of the background picture visible in the insert would alter. Using auto tracking, it remains constant.)
6 *Auto sequence*	Stores a selected effects sequence to run automatically on cue.
7 *Border*	This puts a color border around a small picture that has been inserted within the frame.
8 *Bounce*	Combined 'flys, zooms, swings'.
9 *Breakthrough/videomelter*	One picture dissolves (in tonal order) into another.
10 *Burns*	Feedback (output back to input) creating swirling, flaring, multi-layering, etc.
11 *Composite*	General term for a picture created by electronically inserting one or more separate images to provide an overall effect.
12 *Compression*	While the picture shape remains constant, the picture contracts from a full-screen size down to a point. This can be done as a continuous movement to provide shrinking, or to readjust the image to a different size for insertion. (See *Expansion*.)
13 *Cover*	One picture moves over, or overlaps another.
14 *Crop*	Moves picture frame edges in selectively, to mask the picture.
15 *Cube*	Rotating cube with different picture on each face.
16 *Curves*	A plane surface (e.g. a flat picture) is made to appear concave or convex.
17 *Cylinders/roll-up*	The picture wraps round to form a cylinder. It may have another picture on the reverse side.
18 *Decay*	Picture contrast/brightness reducing at adjustable rate.
19 *Drop shadows*	Transparent drop shadows trail behind the moving object.
20 *Echo*	Multiple-layered repeats of an image.
21 *Effects dissolve*	Smooth vari-timed transitions between two dissimilar effects.
22 *Elastic sheet*	Differential shape changes.
23 *Expansion*	While the picture shape remains constant, the picture expands from a point to full-screen size. This can be done as a continuous movement to provide growth or to readjust the image to a different size for insertion. (See *Compression*.)
24 *Explosion*	Picture breaks into many diverging fragments.
25 *Flip/flip-over*	Vertical or horizontal reversal. Used to compensate for the image having been reversed when shooting via a mirror. Or to provide more satisfactory composition (lateral reversal). Or reversal may be carried out in vision, as a dynamic effect (rate adjustable).
26 *Fly*	Picture zooms up from nothing to any position on screen while spinning.
27 *Fold*	The left and right edges of the picture fold inwards until the image becomes a vertical line. It may fold out again to reveal a new picture.
28 *Freeze frame*	A single picture selected from a sequence and held.
29 *Globe*	The 4×3 picture contracts to form into a globe shape. (Still or turning.)
30 *Glow*	A glow effect created around key signals.
31 *Hall of mirrors*	Repeated overlapping images of diminishing size, resembling the repeat images seen in facing mirrors.
32 *Image positioning*	Places the image anywhere in the frame.
33 *Image size changes*	Overall image compression, expansion.
34 *Image trail freeze ('Teletrak', 'Action Track')*	Composite shot, showing path of subject movement, by freezing images at regular intervals.

Table 21.6 (cont.)

35 *Key pattern*	Picture shape changes to conform with an external matte: e.g. a star.
36 *Layering*	A process in which a series of separate framed pictures are presented, one on top of the other, each slightly overlapping the image beneath. They may appear to grow smaller with 'distance' *Also*: Picture compositing with a series of planes.
37 *Magnifying glass*	Localized area of picture enlarged; 'false zoom-in' effect.
38 *Matrix wipe*	The picture resembles a jigsaw puzzle of square sections. As pieces are removed at *random* corresponding parts of the new picture 'beneath' are revealed until it is finally complete.
39 *Mirror image*	Horizontal and/or vertical reversal, inversion.
40 *Morphing* (from 'meta*morphosis*')	Progressive transformation of one subject into another, (e.g. a man's face into a bear's head) as selected points merge)
41 *Mosaic*	The screen is divided into a pattern of small equal-sized squares. (Similar to a crossword puzzle.) In each square the tones and colors of the original picture are averaged. The more squares are used (adjustable), the closer the image's resemblance to the original picture. This technique is often used to prevent a speaker's face being recognized.
42 *Motion decay/motion smear*	The moving image trails a smearing image behind it.
43 *Multi-move*	Series of segments or frames moving.
44 *Multi-image freeze/multi-freeze*	Array of frozen images from one input.
45 *Multi-segment*	A checkerboard of frames showing different subjects, or different stages of the same subject's action.
46 *Negative polarity*	Luminance or color, changed to negative version.
47 *Non-linear movement*	Slow start . . . accelerate . . . slow down.
48 *Ooze*	Change picture frame to amorphous shapes; e.g. circle creates fisheye effect.
49 *Orbit*	Circular, elliptical, corkscrew image movement around the screen.
50 *Page turn*	Picture appears to turn over like a page.
51 *Pan/tilt*	Total picture moves horizontally/vertically around screen.
52 *Perspective changes*	Pseudo perspective effect, introducing trapezium distortion along horizontal and/or vertical axes.
53 *Pong*	Reduced frame bounces around as it reaches screen edges.
54 *Posterization/solarization*	Picture tones are coarsened and reduced to just a few levels (adjustable). Tonal gradation is lost and areas appear even toned. (See text: *Multilevel synthesis.)*
55 *Push-off*	Frame moves off the screen.
56 *Push-pull wipe*	A new frame pushes the present picture off the screen.
57 *Rotate*	Image appears to turn around X. Y. Z axes.
58 *Shape*	Forms the flat picture into a geometrical shape (still or revolving): e.g. sphere cylinder (barrel roll), cone, cube. Perhaps with a different image on each face.
59 *Skew*	Partial rotation.
60 *Slide*	Push-off, push-over wipe.
61 *Snapshotting*	A combined display of a succession of four to 16 reduced freeze frames: progressively updated.
62 *Sparkling trail*/star trail	A cloud of small dots ('stars', 'sparkles') trails behind moving objects. (Random pixels.)
63 *Spin*	Continous rotation clockwise or anti-clockwise at variable speed
64 *Split*	Splits the screen into segments, which independently wipe to new sources.
65 *Split wipes*	Picture breaks into two, three, four segments, wiping them off the screen (horizontally, vertically, diagonally).
66 *Squeeze/compression*	Vertical or horizontal reduction of image size, compressing the image
67 *Strobe title*	Flashing image.
68 *Swing*	Image moves to and fro in a curved path.
69 *Swoop/scoop*	Curved path movement.
70 *Toroid*	The picture wraps round into a doughnut shape.
71 *Trail*	Moving video frame passes over a frozen frame, creating a three-dimensional effect.
72 *Tumble/roll*	Similar to continuous flip.
73 *Video outline*	All luminance values changed to e.g. white, with all edges black.
74 *Zig-zag*	Series of reduced pictures move around, collide, overrun, explode from frame center.
75 *Zoom*	Image expands/contracts from full frame to zero on screen.

interesting new (for now) dimension to presentation, and others are just fun! Like wipe patterns, some are rarely used, others have become a regular part of productional techniques.

It is not always obvious that an *effect* is being used. You might, for instance, use a digital effect to fill the screen with just a section of a photo-slide, or to trim off the edges of its picture. A perfectly normal-looking map could be a DVE composite. A 'graphic' showing a series of portraits could be displaying slide images from an ESS, combined by digital effects. A high-angle shot might actually be a digitally reversed mirror shot.

Although terms are still developing, and there may be several names for the same action, most are evocative of the effect they describe.

Technically speaking, when describing movement –

- Horizontal movements (left/right; right/left) are along the X axis. Anything rotating around the X axis is said to *tumble* or flip over and over.
- Vertical movements (up/down; down/up) are along the Y axis. Anything rotating around the Y axis is said to *spin* or *rotate* round and round.
- Where features appear to be moving towards and away from the viewer they move along the Z axis. (The illusion of depth actually comes from their growing larger/smaller; from expansion and compression.)

Adjusting time

Once *real time* has been recorded, you can control the speed at which this action is reproduced; using film, VT, videodisc, or digital processing.

■ **Fast motion** Fast-motion effects can be introduced for various reasons:

1 Speeding up subject movement and time scale.
2 To exaggerate energy for comic effect, pixillation, or dramatic force (fast-moving clouds).
3 To shorten an action's normal duration.
4 To reveal the development of a slow process – time-lapse shots speeding plant growth.

In film this is achieved by shooting at less than 24 fps and reproducing at normal projection rate of 24 fps; or by regularly omitting frames.

■ **Slow motion** The uses of slow motion include:

1 Slowing subject movement and time scale.
2 To exaggerate movement, form, or pattern.

3 To allow rapid movement to be discerned (humming-birds' wing-beats).
4 To emphasize movement, giving it force and importance (emphatic body movements).

In film, slow motion is achieved by shooting at more than 24 fps and reproducing at normal speed, or repeat printing alternate frames (stretch/skip frame). In television, slow motion is achieved by magnetic videodisc, slow replay of helical VTRs, or slow readout of stored digital data.

■ **Freeze frame** Stopping action during its course; to show development, or to prevent its completion. Achieved on VTR or magnetic disc by stopping tape travel and re-reading same part of track over and over. Repeated readout of stored digital data. Repeat-printing required film frame.

■ ***Reverse motion*** Reproducing action backwards for comic, magical, or explanatory effect – a demolished building reforms, articles wrap themselves up, scattered lettering arranges itself. There are several regular methods of obtaining reverse motion:

- Magnetic videodisc.
- VTR with reverse-play facilities.
- Some telecine equipment will provide normal pictures while running backwards at standard or adjustable speeds.
- Certain telecine machines will allow you to feed the film in tail first and electronically invert the picture.
- Film labs can *reverse-print* the selected sequence.
- Reverse readout of stored digital data.

■ **Animation (single frame, stop frame**) Achieved on film or VTR by recording a single frame at a time and changing the subject a little for each. When reproduced in quick succession, the shots develop a group significance – usually creating apparent movement. Thus you can animate cartoons, puppets, still-life.

Photo-animation uses a series of photographic prints as the basis for treatment, re-photographing them after progressively adding titling, retouching, sectional movement, etc. Thus various process effects can be achieved economically, including complex wipes, spins, phantom sections, and explosions.

Video rostrum cameras are increasingly used for animation treatment (often combined with digital video effects) for promotion material, advertisements, graphics.

■ **Cyclic motion** Recurrent repetition of an action; achieved by a film loop or conjoining a series of identical copies of a sequence. Repeated digital data readout.

■ **Extended and contracted time/space** By editing-in a repeated part of an action sequence (from another viewpoint, to avoid an obvious jump cut) we create the impression that space or time are extended. Similarly, by editing-out action (with a viewpoint change or cutaway shot) we contract space and time.

■ **Transformations** By animation; or by stopping action during recording (with locked-off cameras), then modifying the scene and continuing recording. When the sections are joined together we can, for example, make trees burst into bloom and a man turn into a mouse!

22 On location

Today the television camera can go virtually anywhere. In forms ranging from the heavyweight 'studio camera' to super lightweight versions, it is equally at home in the studio and in the field. No longer are productions essentially studio-based. It may, for example, be cheaper, quicker, and more convenient for the camera to shoot an interview on location than to stage a studio set-up.

Shooting on location

There are important differences between making a program on location and using a regular TV studio; differences that directly affect productional opportunities and techniques. Whereas a television studio provides the director with an established package of facilities, and back-up close at hand, the production team on location can have to face many kinds of difficulties, ranging from weather to crowd control. The crew on location has to be very self-sufficient, and to anticipate needs to a degree that their colleagues in studios are spared.

Instead of a convenient overhead lighting rig from which to select any lamp from any angle, the lighting director on location may have difficulty in finding anywhere to place light fittings, without either damaging the surroundings or having a lamp come in shot. A camera operator may need weatherproof clothing when standing for long periods isolated on a rain-swept camera tower. The audio engineer often has to cope with unsuitable acoustics and intrusive environmental noises.

Even the best-organized shoot on location involves a deal of anticipation and improvization – and an element of luck. So it is not suprising that a high proportion of TV shows are still made in the controlled conditions of a studio.

Most program making away from the studio takes two forms:

- The single- or two-camera unit with a small production team.
- A multi-camera crew with full production facilities; using a mobile control center or converting the location point into a 'studio' for the occasion.

On location with the single camera

Even a brief list reminds us of the flexibility of the single television/video camera on location.

1 *Electronic field production (EFP)*
Drama. From isolated shots or scenes to complete drama productions.
Program inserts. To record short sequences for insertion into studio-based programs; e.g. illustrating talks, children's programs.
Documentaries. Material ranging from dedicated (one-topic) nature programs to multi-topic science magazine programs.
Training. On-site surveys of jobs and processes.
2 *Electronic journalism (EJ)*. An increasingly widening field, including investigative journalism, background material to current news stories.
3 *Electronic news gathering* (*ENG*). News features over a wide spectrum, from planned public events to unforeseen disasters.
4 *Electronic sports gathering* (*ESG*). To supplement a regular camera crew, e.g. at a sports event.

Lightweight camera techniques

Typical set-ups

Several different arrangements are used for single-camera units:

- In a two-person team one operator concentrates on handling the *portable camera* while the second operates associated video and sound recording equipment – as well as directing the microphone and a small hand-held spotlight.
- Or a single unassisted operator has an integrated *camcorder* fitted with a camera light and microphone. Alternatively, the camera may be cabled to a portable videotape recorder in a shoulder-pack or in a trolley-pack.

Fig. 22.1 Portable cameras
Mobile camera designs include:
1 Shoulder-mounted (battery belt supply).
2 Hand-held camera cabled to a back-pack. Cameras with microwave transmitters may work up to e.g. 1500 meters from the base unit.
3 Body-brace support for camera cabled to control equipment on a trolley-pack (transmitter or VTR).
4 Small hand-held camera attached to shoulder pack VTR
5 Camcorder.

A single-camera unit is often accompanied by an on-the-spot director/reporter; but at other times it may work independently to an '*outline brief*' which indicates the kind of material required; leaving it to their own initiative to bring back appropriate subject matter (e.g. environmental shots). Where the camera is fitted with a small microwave radio transmitter (or attached via a fiber-optics cable) picture and sound are continuously relayed to a nearby base vehicle where they are recorded, and a production team may be located.

Camera care on location

The old scouting motto of 'Be prepared' is certainly apt when you are working with a portable video camera on location. A moment's oversight can ruin a day's shooting. There is usually no video engineer to provide aid and advice. You are on your own.

When you have been working for some hours, particularly under trying conditions, it is very easy to lay your camera to one side, forgetting what a vulnerable bit of equipment it really is. Any list of dont's is really a matter of common sense. The odd thump, jolt, or vibration may seem nothing at the time, but careless handling stores up trouble.

It is pretty obvious that rain, dust, sand, grit, seawater, snow, strong sunlight, heat, strong magnetic fields can ruin your equipment. But under typical conditions you may well find yourself shooting in the rain, by a waterfall, beside the sea, or where wind-blown sand is unavoidable. Then all you can do is to keep its exposure to a minimum and use waterproof protective covers – even if you have to improvise. But take care, for excess wrapping can cause overheating. Check regularly that your lens is clean and dry.

Unexpectedly high temperatures can build up in strong sunlight, and enclosed places such as the trunk (boot) of a parked car are to be avoided. Make sure that you do not leave spare batteries, tapes, etc. stored there. Nickel–cadmium batteries lose their charge rapidly in hot surroundings.

Cold weather, too, brings its problems – apart from slippery ground underfoot. Condensation can form in the lens and within the equipment when it is brought into warm surroundings. (Internal circuitry includes moisture checks that prevent a video recorder from functioning.) In cold weather, batteries are less efficient, and some camera operators wear their NiCad battery-belt underneath a jacket to keep it warmer.

Whenever you stop shooting make it a practice to put the lens cap on your lens to protect its coated surface. At other times, to protect the image sensor against bright light (sunlight, strong specular reflections) it is advisable to turn the filter-wheel to a blank cap-up position. With certain lenses a '*cap*' position entirely closes the iris, but do not rely on this.

A shoulder-mounted camera can seem to get heavier and heavier through the day! (A good reason for using a tripod where practicable.) Mind how you put it down to rest. The viewfinder, microphone and camera light are easily wrecked.

Damaged cables or connectors are a regular source of trouble, and if you are using a separate VTR there will be less wear and tear if you leave them connected.

From time to time, look over your gear and recheck the security of cables, battery, microphone, etc. so that all is ready to use.

At intervals, and whenever changing location, reset the white balance. Point the camera at 'standard' white-level material you carry with you. (Roll, do not fold it.) Cards are cumbersome and easily damaged. They can, however, be double-sided (white on one side, metal foil on the reverse) and used as a reflector. Never use just any 'white' that comes to hand on location (e.g. handkerchiefs, tissues, scarves)! Results will vary. With some cameras you clip a white translucent cover over the lens and point it towards a light source to adjust the white balance.

Power supplies

Professional video cameras normally require a 13.2 or 14.4 volt DC power supply. This can come from:

- An on-board camera battery pack (internal or clip-on unit at the rear).
- A battery-belt holding a series of rechargeable cells. [NiCAD/ NiCD (nickel–cadmium); NiMH (nickel–metal hydride); Li-Ion (lithium-ion)
- The battery used to power the videotape recorder.
- A separate heavy-duty battery in a shoulder pack.
- A separate heavy-duty battery in a trolley or cart (trolley-pack).
- A car battery's supplementary power outlet (cigar-lighter point).
- An AC power adapter used when working near regular utility supplies (mains supplies). It converts the supply voltage (e.g. 120 or 230 volt AC to 13.2–14.4 volt DC).
- Power supplied by an electrical generator driven by the vehicle's engine.

On many occasions you will be relying on batteries to power your camera. Don't take batteries for granted. Carelessly used, they can be unreliable. Correctly used, they will give excellent service. In Table 22.1 you will see typical points to bear in mind. Always have spare batteries with you. How many depends on the nature and duration of your project and your opportunities to recharge exhausted cells.

The single camera in action

So the equipment is working, you have set up the camera, and are ready to shoot.

Handling the camera

If you are using the camera shoulder-mounted make sure that it is comfortably balanced before you begin. Try to use the camera as an extension of your body; turning with a pan, bending with a tilt. With your legs comfortably braced apart, turn to follow movement – preferably from a midway position between the start and end of the pan.

Learn to shoot with one eye looking through the viewfinder and the other *open*, seeing the general scene. (With practice, it's not as difficult as it sounds.) You stand a better chance of walking around without accident than if your attention is glued to your viewfinder picture.

Table 22.1 Battery care (*See Digests*)

A lot of dos and don'ts here, but remember, when batteries fail, everything may come to a halt!

Batteries power your ***camera viewfinder***, the ***VTR***, ***lamps***, and ***picture monitor***... So switch off (or use the stand-by mode) and conserve power whenever possible. If you are not careful, time taken reviewing tapes and lighting can leave you with low power for the take.

- Handle batteries carefully. Dropping, or excessive flexing of connections (particularly interwired cells in power belts), can cause breakdown.
- Always check a battery's voltage while it is actually working.
- Do not leave equipment on until a battery is completely exhausted. This can ruin a new battery.
- Recharge batteries as soon as possible.
- A battery-pack or battery-belt is made up of several cells connected in series. Its poorest cell will limit the battery's overall performance, so never mix old and new cells.
- Avoid storing batteries in very cold or hot places.
- Stored batteries tend to discharge themselves to a noticeable extent.
- If you partly discharge a battery for e.g. half an hour then recharge it fully; it can develop a 'memory'. Instead of delivering its full change, it will regularly drop after half an hour. (It requires a careful charging/discharging cycle to remedy this state.) To avoid this, use a battery fully but not to exhaustion. Rather than leave it partly charged, discharge it periodically with a lamp and recharge fully.
- *Portable lamps* are typically 30 V: 150, 250, 350 W; and fed from a battery-belt worn round the waist. (Do not sling the belt around your neck or shoulder, it damages connections.) The voltage of a freshly charged battery is higher than normal, and may burn out a bulb. Let the battery-belt stabilize for a while before use.
- In addition to the main battery that powers the camera, there may be 'keep-alive' batteries for memory circuits within the camera and VCR system that should be checked regularly. The camera microphone is probably an electret type, using a small pre-amplifier battery.

Table 22.2 Be prepared – the system check-up

	As with the studio camera, preliminary checks before shooting can anticipate and prevent problems later. If you do not have access to a color picture monitor as you shoot, you are relying on the small black and white viewfinder for all picture checks. So if, for example, you forget to white-balance the camera it will not be apparent until the picture is reviewed at base!
The camera	• *Viewfinder.* Check controls, and adjust for a good tonal range. Check over the various indicator lights, and *always* be guided by them when operating the camera. • *Lens.* Lens cap fitted? Lens clean? Lens firmly attached? • *Focus.* Check both manual and auto-focus systems over the full range. • *Aperture (f-stop).* Manually adjust over range, and check exposure changes in viewfinder. Check auto-iris movements on panning over different tones. • *Zoom.* Operate manual zoom over full range; checking focus tracking. Operate power zoom in and out over full range. • *Microphone.* Test both camera microphone and hand microphone. Check cable and sockets by gently shaking and listening for crackles, breaks in sound. Check the audio output through an earpiece. The sound is not off-tape but confirms that the microphone is working. Replay the tape to confirm the audio recording. Some cameras have an inbuilt loudspeaker against which your right ear presses while shooting. (Useless when supporting the camera in other positions!) • *Genlock.* For multi-camera operation, check genlock system (communal synchronization). • *Subsidiary* controls. Looking at a color monitor, check filter-wheel positions, white balance, black adjust video gain, etc.
VTR	Make check recordings of camera test chart and multi-tone scene. Examine playback in viewfinder and on a color monitor.
Power supplies	Check all batteries. Confirm that all spare batteries are fully charged. Are AC cords/mains cables, AC adapter, car-battery adapter, etc. OK?
Cables	Don't leave cables attached to equipment during storage. Never be casual about cables; they have a will of their own, and tangle easily. Loop-coil them neatly, and secure them with a quick-release plastic cable fastener or tie.
Lamps	*Examine any portable camera light or hand lamp.* Check the condition of its bulb, lamp reflector, cable, plug, while powered from a battery.
Separate audio recorder	Used for continuity checks; to record wild track, sound effects, background, etc. Check its tapes and operations. Monitor all audio on an earpiece or headphones.
Spares	Always a personal choice. There are unarguable essentials, though, such as spare lamps, batteries, cassettes, audio tapes. • Examine all VTR cassettes. Are they the *right types*? Do they have protective tags intact? (Otherwise you cannot record on them.) There should not be excess tape slack within the cassette. If there is, run and rewind the tape. Beware tightening by hand-turning the reels; it leaves the tape under tension. Have fresh labels for all cassettes. • Are the spare *lamp bulbs* and *fuses* good ones? (Broken versions can inadvertently be left as 'spares'.) Take a spare microphone. Include diffuser material and dichroic filter or color medium for the hand-lamp.

Table 22.2 (cont.)

	● Avoid field maintenance and cleaning unless you are experienced and equipment is in need. 'Helpful cleaning' often makes things worse, and can clog heads! Protective covers prevent problems. If it ain't broke, don't mend it!
Tools	Small and medium screwdrivers and pliers; electrical insulating tape; masking tape; gaffer tape; cord... Head-cleaning fluid (isopropyl alcohol), cotton-tipped cleaning sticks. Compressed-air can.
Accessories	Flashlight (with spare bulb and batteries). White material (or card) for checking 'white balance'. Small reflectors (white, silver foil). Again a matter for personal preferences. There are circumstances where mosquito repellant, sunscreen preparations or waterproofs can be more essential than a comprehensive took kit! Much depends on where you are working.

Even though its image is magnified, you need to look carefully at the viewfinder picture to detect exact exposure adjustments. You can overlook something intruding into the frame that will be very obvious on a large-screen TV receiver. Distracting brightly colored items can pass unnoticed in the black-and-white viewfinder.

Keep walking to a minimum while shooting. If you must move, slightly bent legs produce smoother results than normal walking. (Practice to see what you find comfortable and effective. And critically examine the resulting tape.)

Lens angles

Generally speaking, avoid extreme lens angles. A wide-angle lens makes camerawork easier, and slight jolts are less noticeable. But everything looks so far away. Closer subjects appear distorted. You imagine that you have much more space to maneuver than you actually have, and are liable to trip or walk into things in the foreground.

Narrower lens-angles produce unsteady shots, and focusing can be difficult. On hand-held cameras they are only suitable for brief stationary shots, while holding your breath. A little wider than 'normal' is probably the best compromise.

If you have an assistant, walking around while shooting can be guided by a hand on your left shoulder; particularly when moving backwards. Walking backwards unguided is at best hazardous, at worst foolish, unless you are on an open flat area without obstructions. People can move towards you a lot faster than you can hope to walk backwards.

Low light levels

In the studio, light levels are controlled. Elsewhere, you have to adapt to local conditions. Your camera lamp will provide you with a limited main light source (key light), or reduce tonal contrast in nearby subjects, but don't expect too much of it.

Shooting under low-light conditions, the picture will probably be underexposed; i.e. dim and showing signs of lag and smearing, with pronounced picture noise. The real remedy is to open up the lens to a larger aperture (smaller *f*-stop number; e.g. *f*/1.8) to try to expose the shot more accurately. Unfortunately, this inevitably reduces the depth of field, and makes focusing more difficult.

Switching in extra *video gain* will not compensate. It will result in a *brighter* but still underexposed shot. It cannot correct for underexposure defects, and video noise will usually increase. Nevertheless, this is the only solution when working under conditions where one cannot improve the lighting.

Automatic controls

Automatic controls such as *auto-focus* and *auto-iris* are a 'safety net' when you do not have the opportunity to control your camera accurately by hand adjustments. But remember, automatic controls are far from foolproof.

Audio

You can adjust the audio system manually, or switch it to *AGC* (*automatic gain control*). In the *manual mode*, watch the volume indicator for sound *peaks*. If they are way below the upper level (100 per cent modulation/0 VU) increase the audio gain until peaks reach this limit. But remember, if anything louder comes along, it will *overmodulate*, and probably distort. Switching to *AGC* instead will protect against unexpected overloads, but may bring up background sounds, and 'iron out' audio dynamics.

Cables

If you are working with another person, who is handling a microphone, a lamp, or a VTR, always be aware of the cable between you. Forget for a moment, and you are likely to find yourselves either side of a post, or with a fully stretched cable, or caught up on an obstruction. Fast moves can be particularly hazardous.

Shooting from vehicles

When shooting from vehicles, resist the temptation to rest the camera on anything. If possible, shoot through an open window.

With tinted windows, white-balance through the glass for optimum results, and make sure that the glass is as clean as possible.

Logs

Always keep an accurate log with information about all shots: times, observations, tape-indicator reading, etc. Give each video and audio tape an identifying label as it is used. If you are not using *time code* for shot identification (*see Digests*), written details now may save hours later when editing. If your camera has a built-in title generator this can be used as a 'slate' to identify shots (with clock time, date, location, shot number).

Clearing up

When you have finished shooting, camera care comes first: cap up the lens (lens cap, filter wheel, close iris).

Switch off all equipment. Remove camera light, camera mike. Remove and wind up cables.

Disassemble and store the camera in its case.

Remove video and audio cassettes and store safely (insert fresh ones if necessary).

Later clean off and check all items at base before storing. Replace burned-out lamps or fuses, any worn or damaged items. Check and recharge batteries. Check over the log to augment or correct it if necessary while details are fresh in your mind.

Multi-camera units

The single-camera team has some important advantages. It is extremely mobile and is easily relocated. It can be surprisingly unobtrusive. It is largely independent of its surroundings. It is economical.

On the other hand, there are many productional situations where a single camera has little hope of capturing much more than a glimpse of events, and multi-camera treatment is the only answer:

- Where coverage from different viewpoints is to be continuous and comprehensive.
- Where action is spread over a large area; e.g. a golf course.
- At a public event, where there is no time or no opportunity to move cameras around to different viewpoints.
- Where there is to be a 'once-only' event (e.g. demolition of a bridge).
- Where the location of action continually changes; e.g. between various parts of a sports field.

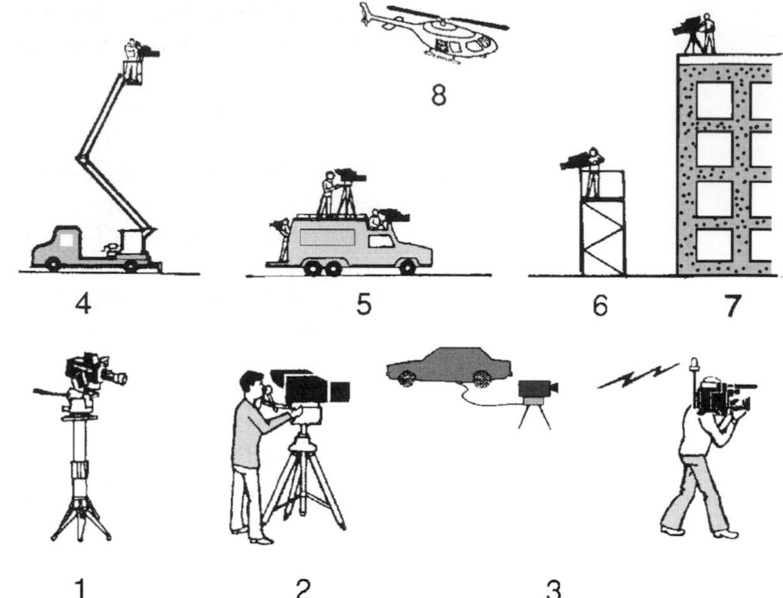

Fig. 22.2 Field camera mountings
Some typical methods of mounting the television camera in the field.
1 Lightweight pneumatic pedestal.
2 Lightweight tripod. (1 and 2 may have wheeled bases.)
3 Portable shoulder-mounted camera, with radio or infrared transmission, or cable link (multi-core or fiber optic) to a support vehicle.
4 Hydraulic camera platform. (Remotely controlled camera on a telescopic mast is also used.)
5 Van with roof platform, hatch, and rear-platform camera positions.
6 Camera on demountable frame (camera tower).
7 Tripod camera at high vantage point.
8 Helicopter or blimp (balloon).

- Where cameras could not move to new viewpoints; e.g. because of obstructions.
- Where cameras must be concealed, or located in fixed places.
- Where rapidly intercut viewpoints are essential (e.g. at a horse race).
- When you cannot accurately anticipate where action is to take place.

Location vehicles

The facilities one needs will depend partly on the scale of coverage and partly on the nature of the event. For example, a 'treasure-hunt' program that dashes around the countryside searching for clues may be based on a couple of helicopters; one to house a single-camera unit that 'hops, lands, and explores', while the other provides a communications support and relay facility. For a museum visit, the same crew could carry their equipment in a car.

Large mobile control room (multi-camera remote unit; MCR)

The biggest vehicles used for remotes usually take the form of a large custom-built truck or trailer. The unit provides a full broadcast standard production control center handling up to six cameras, with complete video and audio facilities. As well as a stack of preview monitors, line monitor, associated switcher, etc., equipment can include comprehensive audio and lighting boards, audio and videotape recorders, character generator, special effects unit, multi-speed VTR for inserts, VT editing facilities, full intercom (wires and radio), etc. The unit also carries a range of cables (camera, audio, lighting), camera mountings, microphone mountings, etc.

The unit may be used in several ways:

- Parked *within* the action area (e.g. in a public square) with cables extending to cameras at various vantage points.
- As a *drive-in control room* parked outside a temporary 'studio' (e.g. a public hall, theater, large tent).
- Control equipment may be removed from the vehicle and installed within a building. This is often done at major indoor events (e.g. at a conference center, or a sports stadium).
- Sometimes a small mobile studio or stage is taken with the unit to the location site and serviced from the mobile control room.

The program may be recorded (and edited) on board the control vehicle. Or it may be relayed to base by microwave links (telescopic mast, or parabolic dish) to be transmitted live, or recorded and edited at base.

For large-scale telecasts in which on-site control is essential this traditional *remotes (outside broadcast)* approach has considerable merits.

Remotes van

A lightweight remotes van provides a small-scale mobile control room with full broadcast-standard equipment, handling two or three cameras. Complete with a bank of small picture monitors, its equipment includes a basic production switcher, character generator, still-store, video recorders (typically Beta-SP, M-II, S-VHS, Hi-8, DVCPro), comprehensive audio and intercom facilities, etc. Although compact, the unit can handle quite large projects in the field; e.g. for EFP documentary or drama programs, ESG, and some ENG.

The program material may be videotaped (perhaps edited on-board) or relayed live to base via a microwave antenna on a central retractable mast (range with uninterrupted line of sight, e.g. +20 miles). Where the terrain is unsuitable for point-to-point transmission because of dead spots or reflected multi-signals from to hills or high buildings, it may be necessary to direct signals to a repeater station instead, which relays them to base. Alternatively a mobile satellite dish (roof-mounted or on a hitch-on truck) may be used as an earth station.

Unlike the large mobile control room, which may require its own power generator unit, the smaller remotes van can usually be powered from utility (mains) supplies at the site.

Lightweight truck (small van units)

This is a very adaptable facility. To provide varied camera viewpoints, it often includes fixtures for a roof-mounted camera, a cab hatch, and perhaps a rear platform. Its equipment may be inbuilt, or off-loaded as needed. Typically, it houses two broadcast-standard lightweight cameras, a videotape recorder, and basic sound gear. Its output is relayed to base via a microwave unit or a satellite dish. This type of vehicle can be used to shoot action while traveling at speed (e.g. around the periphery road of a racing circuit), transmitting to a nearby mobile control room – then sometimes referred to as a '*satellite unit*'.

Station wagon (small van units)

Designed to meet the demands of rapid news-gathering techniques, this unit carries one or two 'broadcast ENG' cameras and a small-format video recorder. The cameras may feed audio/video to the support vehicle by cable or small microwave transmitter. The program is videotaped and/or transmitted to a central relay station (at a high vantage point) from which it is retransmitted to the news center. There the signals are processed (time-base correction, image enhanced, color corrected, noise reduction) and edited.

Auxiliary systems

Motor cycle unit For certain kinds of program material a motor cycle carrying a backwards-facing camera operator provides ultimate flexibility. Following a cross-country cycle race, a marathon run, or a similar cross-terrain/off-road event, this technique has provided continuous on-the-spot reportage throughout; with a greater sense of involvement for the audience than overhead helicopter shots can achieve. Its picture and sound signals are continuously transmitted via battery-powered microwave link, to a nearby van (range e.g. 1 mile) or to an airborne link (helicopter or blimp) which relays to a central control point. The particular advantage of aerial relay is that its footprint can easily accommodate the moving transmitter, and provide a hop of over 150 miles under good conditions to the nearest pick-up or relay point.

Earth-station uplinks This approach uses systems ranging from small portable 'flyaway' earth-station uplinks with a small satellite dish to larger uplink trucks (mobile communications vehicles) with roof or trailer dishes. Portable units provide particularly flexible satellite earth terminals that can be quickly relocated, providing broadcast quality material (picture, sound and intercom) transmitted directly to a communications uplink center, or long-haul repeater centers.

The system provides a two-way communication link between the unit and base or studio. An *earpiece* (*earphone, earplug*) supplies the field reporter with *interrupted/interruptible foldback (IFB)* and/or program sound, enabling conversations with the studio anchor.

Primarily used for *satellite news gathering (SNG)* this technique has also proved invaluable for other field operations.

News techniques

Techniques can vary, according to the occasion. Some news situations are predictable, even routine, while others are unexpected and have to be tackled off the cuff. It may take a great deal of persistence to get good coverage of a news event; as well as the knack of being in exactly the right place at the right time.

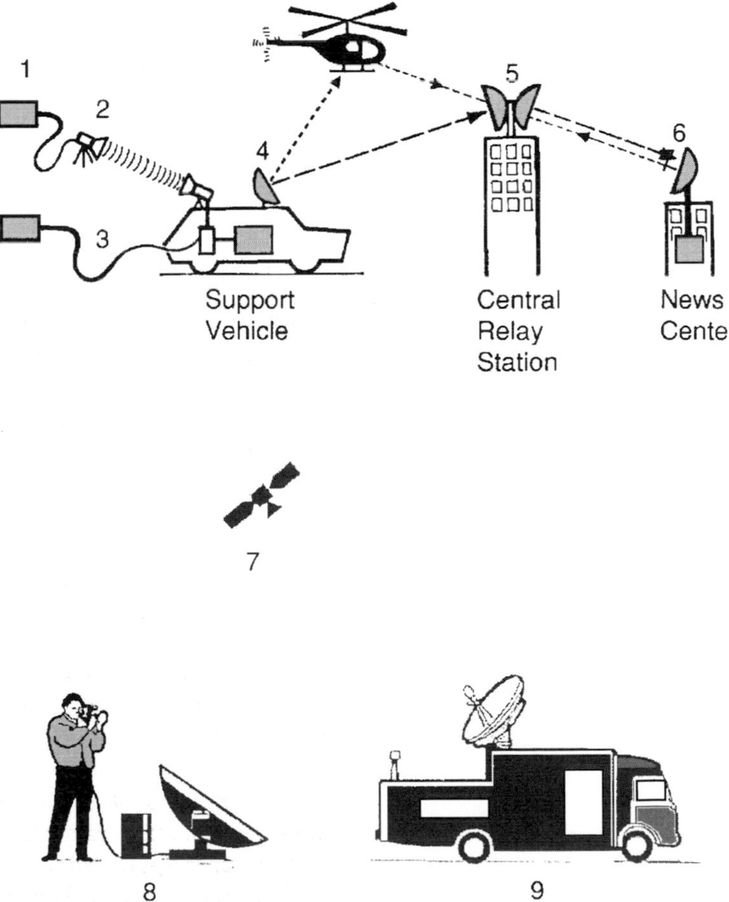

Fig. 22.3 Field transmission

1 *Camera* may be hand-held or tripod mounted, its video being fed to a 'window unit'. Local mike connects to camera's audio pick-up socket.
2 *Window-unit* is a lightweight battery-operated transmitter. Range 1–8 km (1–5 miles) in line of-sight contact (infrared or radio) with support vehicle
3 Coaxial or fiber-optic cable from camera to support vehicle.
4 Portable dish reflector of 60–120 cm (2–4 ft) diameter, or microwave antenna (telescopic mast) transmits audio/video from support vehicle to central relay station. Range is 16–24 km (10–15 miles). (In certain situations a helicopter may serve as a relay point.) Satellite up-links are increasingly used between the remote unit and production center for live ENG.
5 Remote signal is picked up on 4-horn remotely controlled 360° dish antennae system on a distant high building. The signal from the uplink receiver is up-converted for transmission to news center.
6 At news center, signal correction is introduced (digital timebase correction, image enhancer).
7 Two-way communication system from news center (program and engineering coordination) to field unit
8 Portable flyaway system or link package; a small earth terminal for satellite news gathering (SNG).
9 Satellite earth station; mobile satellite uplink truck.

Production teams develop regular approaches to particular situations. In broad terms, news stories fall into the three time categories of 'Before', 'During', and 'After' the event. Obviously, when the camera is able to be present *during* an event it will usually have the best visual opportunities – whether it is covering a highway-opening ceremony or a volcanic eruption.

But there are those other occasions where there is little to see; either because the actual event has not yet taken place or because it is all over by the time the cameras arrive! Many subjects do not lend themselves to visually interesting treatment. Quite often, there is nothing significant to shoot. We can only look at the outside of the bank that has been robbed or the water in which the ship sank.

On such occasions news reportage has to speculate, rather than recount. Quite a lot of news coverage resolves itself into shots of the location, followed by a reporter providing 'sound bites' to camera (*stand-upper*), some cutaways to allow for later editing, and interviews with witnesses or victims.

Routinely, location interviews consist of continuous shots of the interviewee, with later cutaways of over-shoulder 'nod shots' (mute) and frontal shots of the interviewer (perhaps asking the questions).

ENG editing

The production demands of ENG are considerable, and special organization has evolved to meet its particular needs. In some systems, the mobile crew (reporter/director, engineer/operator) is closely coordinated from the news center through two-way ratio communication. The center provides news evaluation, late-breaking information, updating, talent cues, production timing, and interrupted feedback. The editorial co-ordinator serves as field producer, continually examining story progress and giving editorial guidance.

The program material is transmitted from site to the base news center (via a relay point), where it may be continuously taped; both as a 'work-print' copy for editorial purposes and a master reference copy storing the material.

Although time code is widely used for editing (single-frame accuracy), some organizations count VT control track pulses instead (6–8 frame accuracy) for technical convenience.

In one system, an *editor* reviews the 'work-print' copy, assessing edit-decision points, logging in-out times, and audio cues. An *assembler* using this edit decision list enters the precise frame numbers into the VT editing equipment. Computer-controlled VT equipment locates these points in the master reference tape, dubbing off the selected sequences for broadcast – perhaps with a corresponding back-up version. During this dubbing session

Fig. 22.4 Typical ENG organization

1. The *News Coordinator* controls/advises the ENG unit, and scrutinizes the incoming program material.
2. The incoming pictures and sound are videotaped on both a *master VTR*, and a separate VTR making a time-coded workprint. The latter will be used for off-line editing decisions.
3. In a decision booth, an *Editor* (with writers, reporters) examines the workprint, logs in/out times of shots (time-code), selects the excerpts required, notes audio cues for edit points, etc.
4. An assembler dub edits from the master tape, to the editor's instructions. Commentary, graphics, slides (ESS), titles are added. (Computer-controlled selection may be used.) The assembled 'show copy' recording may be arranged on one or more VTRs for stop/start cuing during the newscast, or as a series of separate cassettes that can be loaded into an automated cassette player: 1 in 19 mm (¾ in), and 12.7 mm (½ in) systems.
5. Automated cassette player with edited stories (segments).

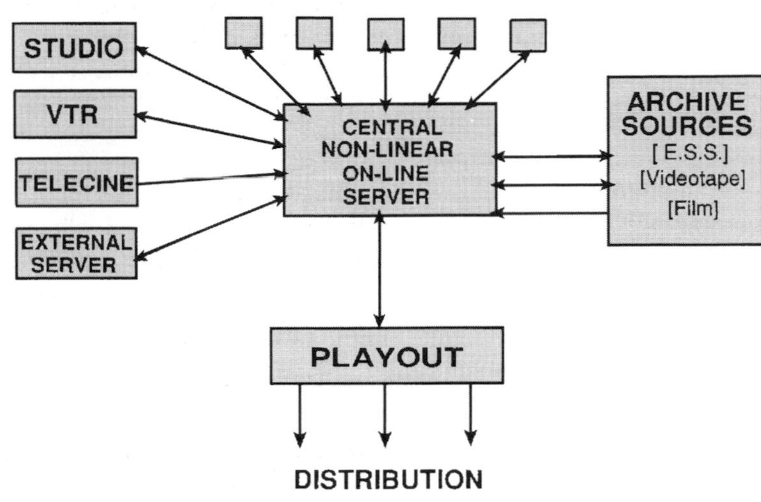

PICTURE		SOUND
Original Video/Film image reviewed		Original sound reviewed
Picture selection Order arranged		Sound selected Order arranged
Additional material obtained		Additional material obtained
Add Graphics	Image combinations	Commentary/Text written
Add Text	Image manipulation	Running order prepared
Add Subtitles	Image improvement	Prompter text prepared

For further bulletins } UPDATING / REVISION/CHANGE EMPHASIS / SUPPLEMENTING

ARCHIVING

commentary may be added from an adjacent announce booth; titles can be inserted (character generator); stills or graphics can be added (ESS, server, rostrum camera); video effects can be introduced (e.g. insets, split screen).

These edited copies of the stories may be videotaped on reel-to-reel or cassette systems. Cassettes offer greater flexibility for they can be loaded into an automated player for push-button selection in any order. This allows items to be revised, updated, or dropped during transmission.

The original *unedited master reference tape* remains unaffected, and is available for any revised editing or revamping for later newscasts or archives.

23 Video engineering

Understandably, most program makers are content to leave technicalities to those who install the equipment and keep it working. But in these days of multi-tasking there are advantages in having at least a nodding acquaintance with these mysteries. So let's take a look here, at the underlying processes.

Behind the scenes

The work of television engineers falls into three general fields: *Maintenance/servicing – Set-up/line-up – Vision control/shading.*

Maintenance/servicing

This is usually a daily routine, in which the video and sound equipment undergoes a series of standard tests to ensure that everything is working to specifications. When necessary, units are replaced and repaired.

Camera set-up (line-up)

If you want consistent high-quality pictures it is necessary to keep camera channels adjusted to within very close technical limits. Even top-grade systems drift to some extent during use, and it is advisable to make periodic checks both before rehearsals begin and before videotaping. Drifting picture quality may not be obvious when working with a single camera (until intercutting various shots during editing!), but in a multi-camera studio, differences can be very evident.

Set-up/line-up involves readjusting preset controls within the camera channel's circuitry. How often the camera chain needs checking and correcting depends on its design and stability.

Currently there are two forms of camera systems:

■ **Analogue designs** Each *camera head* is cable-linked to its *camera control unit* (*CCU*), where most of the circuitry involved in generating and processing the picture video and its associated sync pulses is centralized. The CCU's main electronic adjustments are made manually, using precision test equipment at a master console. A series of geometric patterns, tonal step wedges, color bars, and test pictures are scrutinized and measured on waveform monitors, vectorscopes, etc. and the *CCU*s circuits adjusted to conform with established standards. These checks range from engineering specifics (precise timing, amplitudes, phasing of signals) to very subjective judgements (such as the color balance of monitor pictures). This *set-up/line-up* process is time consuming, and results may depend on individual skills.

As you would expect, there are essential technical differences between camera systems incorporating pickup tubes and those using solid-state CCDs. For instance, while camera tubes require *re*-adjustments to color registration (alignment of the RGB images), geometry (accuracy of shapes), these parameters are consistent in CCD systems, which are more stable, and require fewer adjustments.

Video controls – As we saw earlier, *lightweight cameras* are generally designed to be self-contained, relying in many cases on auto-circuits to maintain picture quality. But when used in a studio, certain of its controls may be extended to an operator at its CCU or a central control point, who continually monitors picture quality and adjusts for optimum effect. This is the regular arrangement for larger studio cameras where pictorial standards are high.

■ **Digital designs** In this system the camera is connected to a *base station unit (BSU)* or *camera-processing unit (CPU)*. The camera's picture, intercom, and audio from the camera microphone are relayed digitally to the base station. In return, it receives a variety of signals in digital form, including: program sound, viewfinder feeds of program and other cameras' pictures, camera prompter information, etc. There are also technical signals including remote-control adjustments, camera circuit corrections, lens-distortion corrections, sync pulses. All this control information and data is continually updated or corrected. The base station includes other facilities such as power supplies, cable-length compensation, genlock.

Computer-aided systems allow various adjustments to be checked and corrected automatically. Set-up is much quicker and requires less experience. To ensure consistency between the camera channels, a standard *alignment card* may be inserted to activate the process.

Video controls – There are several different configurations for camera control:

- A *remote-control unit (RCU)* for each camera, which provides standard operational controls (Figure 23.1) as well as facilities for autoset-up.
- A *set-up control unit* which contains all the operational channel controls for multi-camera working.
- A *set-up panel* which is removable, and can be used for either single- or multi-camera working. The video engineer can choose to make various checks and adjustments manually or use this autoset-up appliance for standardized settings.

Fig. 23.1 Video control
The main operational controls for each camera channel can be centralized at a video control (vision control) position. A single control knob is used to adjust:

- *Exposure* (to and fro). The iris/diaphragm varies ± ½ stop.
- *Black level/lift* (rotate knob). This raises/lowers all picture tones simultaneously.
- *Preview.* Pressing the knob allows the channel's picture to be compared with the shot currently on line from the switcher (to match picture quality).

Further sets of controls may provide:

Gain adjustment (amplification) for the camera's red, green and blue channels. (To adjust color bias.) This may be in the form of separate knobs, or a combined '*paintpot*' joystick control.

Gamma variation. This adjusts tonal coarseness or subtlety. It allows lightest and/or darkest tones to be modified. You can improve their clarity or merge them, to adjust the overall effect.

In an extended multi-camera system when more than e.g. six cameras are used, arrangements become rather more complex, and additional units are needed.

Each camera head contains a memory system (powered by an internal backup battery) which retains all the correct adjustment settings; even when the camera is switched off or disconnected. During operation, self-checking circuits ensure maximum stability of crucial synchronization and timing.

Because the camera cable no longer has to carry as many as 80 separate conductors for the different circuits, its thickness and weight can be greatly reduced for digitally controlled cameras. Consequently the cable is less bulky and easier to handle, and longer reels can be carried on remote trucks. As effective cable losses are low when using digital systems, the camera can work further from the CCU than with large analogue multi-core (e.g. 1.8 km (1.1 miles)).

Adjusting picture quality

Vision control/shading

Although scenery and lighting can build up an atmospheric effect, how successfully this is conveyed by the camera will depend on the video equipment and how it is adjusted.

It is really a matter of standards. The very act of producing pictures *at all* may be sufficient for some purposes – e.g. surveillance. But to produce pictures that are consistently attractive and persuasive requires forethought, skill, and patience. To obtain optimum picture quality you must do more than just point a camera at a scene. Appropriate control is necessary, otherwise shadows can become clogged and detailless; the lightest tones may merge; successive pictures may jump in brightness; and some shots may look 'washed out' while others are overcontrasty.

In the studio you can help to ensure good picture quality by carefully selecting tones, and lighting, wardrobe, and so on. But on location, where the situation is less easily adjusted, it may be necessary to avoid shots that produce unacceptable results, such as an overexposed exterior seen outside the window of a room. Alternatively, you may be able to introduce compensatory lighting.

'Picture processing' in the form of video control (shading) is necessary to get the most from the TV system. Ideally, all video sources (cameras, film, slides, tape) should be continuously monitored and their pictures suitably adjusted. But this is often neither practical nor economic, so three basic approaches to the control of TV picture quality have evolved:

- *Pre-set adjustments.* Here the system is adjusted and left.
- *Automatic control.* With this method we rely on auto-adjustments.
- *Manual control.* An operator monitors pictures and adjusts picture quality.

Pre-set adjustments

In this arrangement the equipment is *set-up (lined up)* manually or using *autoset-up* to adjust its working limits. Thus the lens aperture has been set for a typical working *f*-stop exposure checked against a standard tonal chart, black level set.

From then on, it is up to the production team to adjust lighting, setting tones, costume and make-up for optimum results. They must work within the system's limits.

Lighting under these conditions does not *have* to be *flat* and uninteresting, but it generally needs to be consistent and of low contrast. This technique can be quite adequate for simpler presentations (e.g. newscasts) and where staffing is kept to a minimum.

Automatic control

In this method, after aligning the video equipment, the cameras are switched to *auto-iris, auto black*. During production they will self-adjust, avoiding over-exposure by stopping down and ensuring that the blackest area in the shot is reproduced as 'picture black' (*black level*).

Although this control approach avoids gross errors it has inherent weaknesses. As we saw earlier, automatic systems can be fooled.

A person's face should appear of similar tone when seen on intercut cameras. But automatic controls react to *all* picture tones, whatever their significance. With light backgrounds in one shot, and dark backgrounds in another, face tones would not match. Have another person move into shot wearing a much darker or lighter costume, and the picture may change as the lens opens up or stops down.

Even if the lowest tones in the shot are not really black, but of some dark value, the system can electronically, *set down* the tonal scale so that they appear black, and shadow detail could be lost.

Dynamic contrast compression circuits can help to control highlights and to stretch blacks, so that we can see tonal gradation in shadows. But their performance is necessarily arbitrary, and can modify other picture tones.

When adjusting a camera channel's controls manually we can anticipate, and make allowances. We can make *artistic* judgements.

Manual control (Figure 23.1)

Way back in the early days of television the iconoscope camera tube's pictures were regularly marred by spurious light and dark patches, which varied with picture tones. By introducing specially generated electrical waveforms (known as 'tilt' and 'bend' in Britain) it was possible to cancel out this '*shading*' to a large extent. The patient and dexterous engineers who continuously made these adjustments earned for themselves the title '*Shader*', which has been used in the USA ever since – although this operation has long since vanished!

There are two approaches to manually controlling picture quality. In the first, the video engineers who service and align the camera channels sit at the *camera control units (CCUs)*, *remote-control units (RCUs)*, and adjust them to suit each shot. Adjustments include:

- *Lens aperture/f-stop* (remotely controlled).
- *Black level (lift; sit)*.
- *Video gain*.
- *Color balance*.
- *Gamma*.

In the second system all the camera's operational controls are extended to a central console (usually near the lighting board). Here a *vision control operator*, who is continually in touch with all video sources (cameras, film, ESS), can control picture quality.

Each channel has a combination control knob:

- Forward/backwards to adjust lens aperture or 'iris'.
- Twist to adjust black level.
- Press to compare the channel's picture with the shot on-line at that moment.

The operator also has a set of controls which independently adjust the *gain* (amplification) and the *black level (lift; sit)* of the red, green, and blue channels of each source. A *TARIF* control adjusts the color balance of pictures from telecine film and slides.

Why is video control necessary?

Many TV production groups rely entirely on pre-set adjustment or auto-control methods. It might be reasonable to ask, therefore, how necessary manual control really is today. The answer is a qualitative judgement; rather like comparing the results of automatically processed color film with those achievable by a specialist film laboratory.

Exposure control

As we saw earlier, 'correct exposure' can be very subjective. The exposure suitable for one camera position will not necessarily be appropriate for another. Subtle changes in the *lens aperture* or *iris* can readjust all picture tones.

- Unless a surface is rough, its brightness can alter appreciably as we shoot it from various angles.
- Flat lighting produces uninteresting pictures, and skilled lighting directors avoid it. However, the light and shade that create depth and atmosphere can emphasize tonal contrast and produce uneven light levels for multi-camera viewpoints. Anticipatory vision control can compensate for these variations.
- Similarly, where scenic tones exceed the system's limits, by carefully adjusting exposure, gamma, and black level they can often be accommodated. It is a lot easier (and cheaper) to adjust the system than to change the staging.
- Where we want to see detail or tonal gradation in very light or very dark-toned subjects appropriate video adjustments can show them more clearly. When taking a close-up of a page in a book, for instance, a combination of reduced exposure and lower black level can improve clarity. Otherwise the page would probably block off and appear blank!
- Video is usually adjusted so that the peak whites in the picture meet the *reference white level*, while the blackest tones in the shot

meet the *reference black level*. This makes full use of the system's tonal range. Beyond these limits, any tones are 'clipped off' electronically, and reproduce as solid white or black.

But there are times when we *deliberately* allow white or darkest tones to be clipped off for artistic effect; to make a cyc appear totally white, or a black background to merge into solid black tone. (A regular practice with black-background title cards.)

To lift *all* picture tones we can 'set up/sit up' the video (raise black level). The darkest shades will 'gray out' and can help to simulate a misty day, or enhance an ethereal effect. (You cannot use this idea to reveal any more detail in shadows. Only increased exposure, extra lighting, or reduced gamma will improve shadow detail.)

- *Deliberately 'undermodulating'* a shot by *under*exposing it will help to suggest a dull overcast day or improve a dingy scene. Controlled *over*exposure, on the other hand, can simulate dazzling sunlight.
- Our impression of a subject's brightness can vary considerably with the background tones; particularly where these are very light or very dark. In these circumstances intercut shots can appear mismatched, as the amount of background tone varies. Again, judicious control can compensate for this subjective effect.
- Distant shots generally appear more dynamic if tones are strongly contrasted. Closer shots appear coarsened by excess contrast. When shooting is continuous it can prove more practical to emphasize tonal values in the long shots by setting down the picture a little rather than by lighting adjustments.
- Slight changes in a camera's color balance can help to compensate for unwanted subjective color effects; e.g. for the way faces can appear warmed or paled against strong background hues.

Sometimes a slight color bias will enhance an atmospheric effect: a warmer cast for fireside or sunset scenes; a colder bluish cast for moonlight, or gaslight effects. You would normally achieve this color shift by adjusting the RGB channel gains.

But in a camera that is fitted with *compensatory color filters* (used to match the camera to different lighting color temperatures) you can use a false Kelvin setting to give the picture a color cast. A filter setting that is too high will warm the picture, while a setting that is too low will cool it.

Synchronizing the system

As we saw in Chapter 3, the TV scanning process is kept in step from camera to picture-tube by specially generated *synchronizing (sync) pulses*. A color system is particularly critical, and requires

Table 23.1 Inherent picture defects

Line beating (strobing)	Localized flickering regularly encountered with close horizontal stripe patterns in clothing, fabrics (checks, stripes), line engravings, close mesh, etc. Can be reduced by altering the shot size or by slight defocusing. Effect is due to subject lines coinciding with picture scanning lines. Interference effects (cross-color) can arise too, producing a color-fringing effect on fine stripes.
Stroboscopic effects	When the movement of rotating wheels or pulsating light coincide with the TV picture scanning rate of 60 per second USA (50 per second Europe) they will appear stationary. Slightly faster or slower speeds can cause wheels to apparently rotate forwards or backwards.
Interlace break-up	When viewed closely, a TV picture's interlaced line structure breaks up as we look up or down the frame. Line structure becomes coarser and vertical definition halves. Evident on fast crawl titles and extensive titling ('panning-up') shots.
Horizontal break-up	During panning or fast horizontal movement, strong vertical lines or detail break up into displaced sections. Due to the inherent time lag between scanning the odd and even fields of the picture (1/60 or 1/50 second
Highlight flicker	Sometimes visible on very bright highlights, particularly when viewed in dark surroundings; although the picture repetition rate is too fast to be detected under normal conditions.

stable precise sync pulses (for scanning accuracy), and *color burst* signal (for hue accuracy) for optimum reproduction.

Complete synchronism is essential if TV pictures are to be transmitted and reproduced without color errors: or even total loss of color and picture displacement.

A master SPG (sync pulse generator) supplies these pulses to the entire video equipment in studio or station. So all the equipment is *synchronous* (scanning in unison). Your switcher can accept any synced source (camera, film island/telecine, caption machine), and intercut, mix, superimpose, insert, chroma key between their pictures.

External video sources (remotes) on the other hand, operate from their own synchronizing generators. Although these are producing identical types of pulses they will not be exactly in step with the station's pulses (*out of phase; wrong timing*). If you feed such a *non-sync source* into most production switchers you will get totally unacceptable pictures (having displacement, tearing, break-up, roll, extreme color errors).

Where the production switcher design permits, you can *cut* to non-sync sources (*hot cuts*), but still cannot mix or combine their pictures with other local video sources. Only certain switcher designs (digital systems) allow you to combine 'sync' and 'non-sync' sources.

Table 23.2 Spurious visual effects

	Certain picture defects are created or aggravated by unsuitable lighting or staging or by video operation; while others are inherent. As CCD image sensors have largely superseded camera tubes, some problem effects such as *after-images, comet tails, lag (trailing)* have disappeared; but others remain.
Background	Any constant blemish, spot or patch that remains visible on the screen although the shot changes. Apart from dirt or damage on the lens system or optical path, it may be due to defects in the light-sensitive surface of the CCD, or in the display screen (e.g. faulty LCD element).
Blooming	Term originally used to describe areas of severe overexposure in camera tubes' pictures which blocked-off to detailless white. Still sometimes applied to crushed-out over-bright surfaces.
Burn-in ('burnt-in')	Term originally described a camera tube defect in which light sources or bright reflections remained 'stuck on', defacing all that camera's subsequent shots. Now usually refers to the practice of electronically inserting plain white titling, subtitles, time code or other information into a selected picture.
Color response	Ideally, reproduced colors should be completely accurate. However, apart from design compromises, inaccuracies inevitably arise (analysis errors, unbalance, drift) throughout the system, from camera lens to picture tube. Many are corrected during the set-up/line-up process.
Cross-color	A 'rainbow' interference effect seen on fine stripe or check patterns. Caused by luminance information intruding into the chrominance signal. Inherent in standard NTSC, PAL, SECAM systems. Prominent in helical scan VTR systems, but noticeably reduced when luminance and chrominance are recorded separately.
Cross-luminance	Bands of crawling dots seen at sharp color transitions, due to chrominance information intruding into the luminance signal.
Definition (resolution)	Maximum resolution of detail is not generally possible over the entire screen. Away from the central area, it gradually deteriorates due to limitations in lenses, sensors, and picture tube, but remains well within required standards.
Doming	An effect found in all 'spherical' shadowmask color picture tubes. In bright areas of the picture the tube's shadowmask screen deforms temporarily (local overheating) causing misalignment. Spurious color patches develop, destroying local color fidelity. More evident on large *flat square tubes (FST)*. Significantly improved in nickel–iron (Invar) shadowmask designs.
Edge effects	A false black edging around high-contrast borders; even crispening distant detail that would naturally be soft-focus. (Does not sharpen low-contrast borders.) Usually due to excessive electronic compensation (crispening) on soft pictures.
Exposure time	The inability of the standard television system to capture fast movement accurately; reproducing it instead as a blurred image. An *electronic shutter* on the CCD camera results in sharper images of moving subjects (but reduces exposure).
Flare	An overall or local reduction in contrast due to internal reflections (light scatter) within the lens system. Similarly, spurious light streaks or patterns arising from the camera shooting into strong lights or speculars.

Table 23.2 (cont.)

Geometric distortion (non-linearity)	Cramping, stretching, or bending of the picture due to electronic or optical shortcomings. Includes S-curvature, trapezoid, barrel, and pincushion distortions.
Microphony	Strong horizontal streaks arising when the camera is jarred, vibrated, or near strong sound sources (explosions, gunshots, singers, trumpets).
Performance stability	Equipment such as color monitors may take some time to warm up and stabilize (drift in color balance, geometry, convergence). Errors may only be obvious when comparing a bank of monitors, or when editing shots recorded at different times(!).
Picture noise ('snow')	An overall fluctuating grain; particularly noticeable in darker tones. Always present to some degree, the effect is due to random electronic disturbances or variations, low signal strength with excessive amplification. Usually minimal and unnoticed. (Video equivalent of background noise on audio discs.)
Registration	When the separate red, green, and blue images comprising the color picture are combined they should coincide exactly over the entire picture frame area. However, *registration* errors can arise in the camera – usually at edges or corners. (In *CCD systems*, mainly due to lens/prism imperfections; in *camera tubes*, through scanning inaccuracies.) Known as *convergence errors* on a picture-tube. *Note*: if the error (which usually takes the form of color fringes) disappears on cutting to another source it is faulty camera registration. If the error remains in pictures from all sources, it is a monitor convergence error.
Sensitivity	When there is insufficient light to expose the picture correctly, and the lens aperture is fully open, video gain may have to be increased (often switchable on camera). This will improve video strength and the picture's overall brightness, but video noise will also increase, and any picture defects arising from lack of light will become more pronounced.
Shading	Localized lightening or darkening, or color shading of parts of a picture; from optical or electronic causes. Reduced by compensatory electronic shading signals.
Streaking	Black or white streaks extending across the picture beside high contrast areas (stair treads, blind slats). Usually due to overload, or low-frequency losses in video channels.

Synchronizing sources

To match two independent video sources' synchronization, several ingenious electronic systems have evolved. The earliest and simplest was *Genlock*; which adjusts the timing of the local pulses to get them into step with the remote (non-sync) source. This system of slaving works well as long as the remote's syncs are not interrupted or distorted, for then, *all* local equipment run from these genlocked pulses would 'lose syncs'.

VTR sources present another allied problem. Although the original sync pulses were recorded along with the picture, on replay these syncs become irregular and distorted. This is particularly true

Table 23.3 Picture monitor checks

	Picture quality can only be judged on correctly adjusted, high-grade monitors, without spill light or reflections diluting the picture. Here are general methods of checking performance. Allow time for warm-up before adjustments.
Gray scale (all picture monitors)	Feed a *gray scale* (from camera, slide, or electronic generator) to all monitors. Adjust BRIGHTNESS (BRILLIANCE) to ensure *black* merges with blank screen-face. Adjust CONTRAST for maximum white brightness without line defocusing and good half-tone reproduction. Ensure all monitors' pictures are similar. Replace gray scale (tonal step wedge) with a monochrome picture containing good tonal variations. Compare all monitors' gradations and highlight brightness.*
Color monitors	As above. Examine gray-scale reproduction for traces of color cast throughout tonal range. They should be neutral grays (good color tracking). Circuit adjustments may be necessary. Recheck using same color picture on all monitors. The picture should should contain facial tones and pastel hues (desaturated) and not primary colors, or color bars.*
Picture size/shape	Check that the screens show *all* of the TV picture (no edge cut-off) in correct 4×3 or 16×9 proportions.
Focus	Scanning lines should be sharp over entire picture, reproducing maximum detail on camera test chart.
Linearity	The picture should not show serious geometric distortions (cramping, stretching, bends). Check the linearity with a cross-hatch generator (grille). This produces a lattice of thin white lines on a black background.
Color defects	Check reproduction of cross-hatch for color fringing (*convergence errors*) along pattern. In practice some spurious color edges may be unavoidable. Check overall for: *color balance* (warm or cool?), *desaturated color* (washed-out, low contrast?), *oversaturated color* (overstrong color, high contrast?), hue shift (predominant overall color), and color shading (*purity errors*).
Black level	Picture *black* should be constant; not varying with picture tones, or reproducing as gray in low-key scenes or when faded to black. (Variations are due to equipment design or fault condition.)
Off-air pictures	Probably appear noisier and less sharp than direct off-line pictures. They may have displaced multiple images (ghosts, reflections) and ringing, due to multi-path reception of transmission; and/or interference patterns (herringbone, stripes, edge tearing).

* Electronic devices are available, which attached to a monitor screen guide set-up uniformity while adjusting controls.

on small-format VCRs, due to minute random speed fluctuations arising from tape travel and mechanical imperfections. Although pictures will appear quite satisfactory on a picture monitor (which adjusts itself to varying sync pulses), if we tried to use such an unstable source with a precisely synchronized TV system it would cause color loss and image break-up. Particularly when editing or using picture combinations (supers, insertions), some form of synchronizer is needed that will accept these randomly changing syncs and adjust them to match local pulses.

A range of *time-base correction* equipment is available that provides automatic compensation for synchronizing inaccuracies on replay or imperfect sync pulses from mobile cameras.

Digital time-base correctors store up the video information from the VTR (notwithstanding the incoming variations) and clock it out of store again at precisely timed intervals in perfect synchronism with the station sync-pulse rate. (If the incoming video is interrupted the system may hold a still frame of the action, and recommence when the signal is re-established; so preventing picture break-up on air.) These units often offer additional facilities, such as: freeze frame, digital enhancement, drop-out compensation, noise reduction, color correction . . .

Standards converters (*transcoders*), which are used primarily to convert TV signals from one system to another (e.g. NTSC to PAL), may also be used to ensure source synchronism.

Composite signals – and switcher operation

A *composite signal* consists of the total video (picture) information together with inserted sync pulses at the end of each scanned line and field. Depending on local facility design, the video system may be supplied with either a full composite signal or a *non-composite* version (video information only, no sync pulses).

Certain production switchers are self-compensatory, accepting composite and non-composite inputs. Others only permit you to *fade to black* by sliding split A-B faders to out, when controlling *non*-composite video. If this fade-out is attempted with *composite* signals the switcher loses color. In such designs, you must select a *black-level button*, and mix to this 'non-channel' to simulate a fade-out.

Some switcher designs present severe video overloads when peak-white or light-toned areas are combined through mixing or superimposition. If your switcher does not incorporate protective circuits (processing amplifiers), you must avoid fading up channels fully in such circumstances.

Table 23.4 Video engineering terms

	Synchronizing pulses Sync pulses from the master control sync pulse generator (SPG) keep the entire TV system in step – from camera to receiver (preventing picture tearing, roll, etc.).
Line (horizontal) drive pulses	Initiate the horizontal scan, and synchronize the *line* scanning rate (horizontal sweep). At 525 (625) lines per second.

Table 23.4 (cont.)

Field (vertical) drive pulses	Initiate the vertical scan, and synchronize the *field* scanning rate (vertical sweep). At 60 (50) lines per second. Two *fields* provide one complete interlaced *picture (frame)* at 30 (25) lines per second.
Mixed syncs	The total, combined sync pulse information used to synchronize the system.
Composite video signal	The complete video waveform, together with synchronizing pulses.
Blanking	Special pulses used to suppress video output from the camera to enable sync pulses to be inserted. The scanning process retraces to the beginning of the line or field during blanking.
Timing	Video signals take a measurable time to travel along distribution cables within a building. If various sources (e.g. film, VTR, ESS channels) are at different distances from the studio (or master control) their pictures would arrive at slightly different times. Any attempt to combine these sources' pictures (e.g. mixing/superimposing/insertion) would show some pictures horizontally displaced (or cut off) due to their different path lengths. To avoid this situation, each route needs suitable compensation to ensure identical *timing* at the destination.
	Color information
Color subcarrier	A constant carrier frequency that is modulated to encode color information.
Reference color burst	A brief burst of the above subcarrier, introduced into the synchronizing information to stabilize color reproduction.
Coder (encoder)	Circuitry (matrix) converting a camera's red, green, and blue video signals into a single luminance/chrominance encoded form (NTSC, PAL, or SECAM) for distribution and transmission.
Decoder	Circuitry (matrix) converting the coded video back into separate RGB video to drive the receiver or monitor circuits.
	Equipment
Distribution amplifier (DA)	Video amplifier used to isolate and distribute video signals. (Zero gain, or amplifying signal strength to compensate for subsequent losses.)
Processing amplifier/stabilizing amplifier	Corrects errors developing in the video signal. Used to reshape, reinsert, or separate sync pulses from the composite signal (i.e. video plus syncs).
Image enhancer (IA)	Circuitry used to improve apparent picture definition, reduce video noise. (*See Digests.*)
Termination	To match a picture monitor to its video cable a termination resistance is introduced at its video input. This avoids signal losses, distortions, and reflections. Only *one* termination is required for a succession of looped-through monitors.
Color bar generator	An electronically generated color test pattern, comprising vertical bars displaying white, yellow, cyan, green, magenta, red, blue, and black. Used for video system checks.
Standards converter	Electronic equipment used to enable pictures televised by one TV system (e.g. 525-line NTSC – USA, Japan) to be reproduced by another incompatible system (e.g. 625-line PAL or SECAM).

Digests

Many who are studying *television production* find details of various technicalities beyond their needs. Others want to know more about the processes they are working with. So to avoid interrupting the general flow of the main text with detailed explanations, these digests have been designed to give you maximum flexibility and convenience.

They aim to help you in several ways:

- Explaining or defining points that would otherwise interrupt the flow of the main text.
- Providing technical details of important topics.
- Outlining additional terms.

Acoustics (*see Figure 12.6*) Higher frequency sound waves travel in straight-line paths. So they are easily deflected and reflected by hard surfaces; and are absorbed by porous fibrous materials. Lower frequency sound waves (below 100 Hz) spread widely, so are not impeded by obstacles and are less readily absorbed.

As sound waves meet nearby materials they are selectively absorbed and reflected; the reflected sound's quality being modified according to the surfaces' nature, structures, and shapes. Studios are carefully proportioned and their walls covered with suitable absorbent materials (fiber panels, rockwool, mineral wool, seaweed quilting) to prevent unwanted sound coloration and to reduce reverberation (small TV studios 0.3–0.5 second; larger TV studios 0.7–1 second). The acoustic characteristics of scenery, furniture, drapes, people, further modify audio quality.

AGC *Automatic gain control (automatic volume control; AVC)* circuitry automatically reduces a system's amplification when the strength of a signal exceeds a preset maximum level. This avoids system overload and subsequent distortion. In some equipment the amplification of weaker (lower amplitude) signals when they fall below a minimum limit avoids their being masked within background noise. There is always the danger with automatic regulation of this kind that the program's dynamics will be compressed, creating a 'held-back' or 'strangled' effect on louder peaks or 'surges' as background sounds momentarily grow in strength during quieter moments. (See *Ducker*.)

Animation Creating an illusion of movement by intercutting stills, using graphics with movable sections, using step-by-step changes in a static subject (objects, models, drawings, photographs, etc.), or control-wire activation.

Announce booth A small acoustically isolated cubicle within some studios from which announcements or commentary can be read *off-camera* (*out-of-vision*) while watching a picture monitor. Cue lights and intercom facilities are fitted.

Anti-aliasing Limitations in the horizontal resolution of computer-generated lettering and graphics can result in diagonals and curved lines appearing jagged or even flickering. This effect is particularly noticeable in enlarged lettering and line diagrams. To remedy this *aliasing* (*'jaggies'*) and improve effective detail, *anti-aliasing* software inserts extra pixels of different luminance/chrominance values at each step to create a blend between the line and its background so that these inaccuracies are not noticeable.

Aspect ratio The long-established standard TV picture shape (*aspect ratio*), has a height three-quarters of its width (4:3 or 1.33:1). With the introduction of *High Definition Television* (*HDTV*) came a new format – 16:9 (i.e. 1.77:1). These new proportions are a compromise that more readily accommodates televised wide-screen films. TV cameras can be designed to transpose between these two standards; using a smaller portion of the light-sensitive area of the camera's 16:9 proportioned image sensor when shooting in the 4:3 mode. While the lens *height* coverage remains the same, the horizontal angle of view is reduced. (The effective horizontal resolution changes correspondingly.) (*Computers* use a variety of selectable aspect ratios, resolutions, color and tonal ranges.)

Audio enhancement We can often enhance program sound through careful after-treatment: making it more intelligible, reducing unwanted or distracting features, improving its subjective quality, creating a more dramatic impact, or adjusting its characteristics to match the situation portrayed on the screen. You may improve sound in various ways: by reducing background noise (tape noise, disc surface noise); eliminating unwanted sounds (e.g. hum); increasing/decreasing parts of the audio spectrum (e.g. increasing bass; emphasizing top); enhancing sound balance (i.e. the relative prominence of instruments); adding or increasing reverberation.

Digital sound can be processed to produce new, startling, or unusual effects. For example, by selecting soundtrack segments, which are then repeated, emphasized, reversed, inverted, rearranged, substituted. More complex treatment includes: variable *reverberation, echo, doubling/double tracking* (close repeats), *delays, chorus* (multi-source effects from a single source), *chords, tunnelling, phasing, Haas effect* (shifting stereo images), *hollowing, sweep effects, Doppler effect* (pitch changes), *arpeggio, vibrato, spin* (feedback), *flanging* (original with delayed version of changing strength and phase), *time compression and expansion* (shortening or lengthening its duration) . . .

Audio sources The craft of *sound mixing* involves controlling (volume and quality), cuing, and timing a wide range of sources; particularly during postproduction treatment:

SPEECH *Production dialogue* – Impromptu speech; scripted speech.

Background (off-camera dialogue) – E.g. party chatter, audience or crowd noises; overheard speech from telephone, nearby radio or television, public announcements.

Voice-over (VO) – Narration, explanatory dialogue, commentary from unseen speaker. Voice translating the language of a heard on-screen speaker.

Replacement dialogue (ADR) – Looped dialogue to a mimed performance; synchronized actors' voices substitute those performing in a foreign language; dialogue to replace faulty or censored passages.

MUSIC *Live performance* – Sound and picture of musician(s) performing.

Background performance – Overheard music (e.g. radio in the background).

Atmospheric music – program (mood) music.

EFFECTS *Direct sound effect* – We see the action, hear the actual sound.

Simulated direct sound effect – We see the action, but hear a substituted sound (imitated or simulated (e.g. Foleying)), or from a sound effects library.

Locational background sounds – Actual, recorded, or simulated sounds from wild track or library sound effects. Introduced to convey, establish or reinforce location. (Typically wind, traffic, sea, crowds.)

Atmospheric background sounds – Sounds added to create emotional ambience (e.g. birdsong, choir, children at play.)

Audio synchronizer A facility for computerized automatic editing of audio tapes and VT soundtrack. An audio stereo tape is prepared with *time code* on one track (from a *timecode generator* or the *cue track* of a videotape), and program audio is recorded (in mono) on the other. The push-button programed unit can automatically stop/start and synchronize both audio tape and VT machines. It can locate edit-point addresses, and then

(1) dub-off code-selected sections from one audio tape onto another, or
(2) transfer sound segments from audio tape to VT soundtrack.

Audio tape formats Over the years a number of audio tape formats have developed. The original 1/4 in. analogue tape format using *open-reel (reel-to-reel)* tape transport is still widely used in both studio and location production. (3 in. to 11½ in. reels.) Digital audio tape (*DAT*) cassette-based systems with two tracks are increasingly used, as well as the *Nagra 4D* open-reel system with four digital tracks. There are practical advantages in keeping audio and picture separate – particularly during postproduction, when the audio (*dialogue track*) is dubbed and augmented (music and effects added, etc.). Picture and sound are readily synchronized through time code. Non-linear *digital audio workstations (DAW)* provide optimum flexibility, and precision editing of dialogue (*audio-conformed*) during production and postproduction while working from a video-based *edit decision list (EDL)*. Digital audio tape (DAT) or multitrack recording can be used to provide audio mastering that is finally transferred to the master video tape during *lay back*.

Autofocus The automatic focusing systems fitted to many video cameras provide a very useful facility, but they do have design limitations that you need to bear in mind (*Chapter 4*). Some cameras include *autofocus check* which allows you to check how the autofocus system will respond, while the lens remains in manual focus mode.

- *Infrared* – Infrared light from near the camera lens is pulsed, and the time taken to travel and reflect from the subject to its sensor is measured. It needs no light to operate, so is effective even in lower light levels. However, it has a slow reaction time (1.5 to 3 seconds). Its range is limited. The subject must be in center frame. It cannot focus beyond foreground obstructions such as glass. When shooting small objects, it can be misled by some surface colors (especially black), and by shiny angled surfaces.
- *Piezo (ultrasonic) control* – When you focus a lens for maximum sharpness on a selected area the brightness and contrast of that part of the image rises to a maximum. With this system, you position a *focus frame* within the camera viewfinder display over to the subject to be kept in optimum focus. (A large rectangle for fast action; a small frame to focus on a localized area.) A tiny motor vibrates a special lens element in front of the CCD at a constant rate, while a microprocessor monitors the signal. When the signal reaches maximum, the subject is in focus and the motor switches off. This method is fast and effective, even with very close objects, and is less easily confused.
- *Digital AI* (*Artificial intelligence*) – Here the piezo-controlled vibrating focus element is located *within* the lens system, adjusting it for sharpest focus in the selected area.
- *Auto-tracking system* – A further type of piezo system locks onto the selected subject as it moves within the frame.
- *Fuzzy logic* (*contrast control system*) – This ingenious system searches for maximum brightness/contrast in an expanding central zone until sufficient data is stored to optimize focus. Unlike the previous systems, this type will not search around (hunt), looking for a plane to focus on in an unsharp picture.
- *Operator-directed autofocus* – Here an IR beam scans the scene while another beam in the camera viewfinder scans the *operator's eyeball*. The system, guided by the position of the bulge of their *eyes*, measures the distance of the corresponding subject being detected by the front beam. Ideally, whatever the operator looks at, the lens focuses on! However, '*eyeball focus control*' can be confused by random eye movements! A similar technique can be used to activate other adjustments from viewfinder indicators (e.g. white-balance).

Auto iris (auto exposure) The intensity of the image falling on the CCD adjusts the lens aperture (diaphragm; iris). Many metering systems are balanced to concentrate on the frame center (less influenced by the periphery). More sophisticated systems are less sensitive to the frame top, where bright skies could result in underexposed pictures. The best systems sample all areas of the viewfinder and provide overall optimum exposure.

In certain designs, *both the aperture and the shutter speed* are altered to control exposure; a questionable technique, where high-speed shutters produce jerky broken-up effects on action. When moving from bright to dark surroundings, the lens-stop opens itself up arbitrarily, reducing the depth of field and impairing focusing. Further facilities include an **exposure lock** which overrides auto-iris changes, and holds a selected *f*/stop; a **backlight compensator switch** which reduces the auto-iris setting by an arbitrary amount, to avoid under-exposure of subjects against a very bright background (*'silhouetting'*).

Auto knee (highlight compression) Automatic (or manual) adjustment of the camera's exposure curve (gamma) to increase or decrease the subtlety with which lightest tones are reproduced. Overprominent highlights may be made less distracting by compressing highlight gradation (*white compress*) and allow fuller exposure of lower subject tones. Subtle modeling in light-toned subjects can be revealed by tonal expansion.

Automatic assembly The VT editing process is time consuming, and several methods have developed to assemble the program automatically from instructions. In *auto assembly* the computer-aided editor, guided by time code, files edit decisions, translates, and carries out edits and effects, in sequence.

Linear assembly (Mode A) performs the edits in the order of the *edit list*. As the unedited material is usually shot out of order (execution order), this can involve several reel changes and VTR set-ups.

In *reel sequential assembly (Mode B)* the edit list is scanned, and those sections available in the reels currently loaded on the VTRs are carried out (no overlaps or overlays are permissible).

In *look-ahead assembly* any VTR not actually being used readies itself (i.e. finds the next edit point, pre-rolls ready to run-up and record), so saving preparation time.

Automatic tracking A system on some VTRs for ensuring that the replay head (which is mounted on a deformable piezoelectric element) accurately retraces the recorded video track when replaying a helical recording; particularly when replaying a tape recorded on another machine of the same type. This avoids picture quality variations (of detail, chrominance, saturation), noise bars (due to playing guard tracks), or disturbed synchronism. Video playback head position is automatically adjusted as the recorded track is sampled for maximum signal. This arrangement also allows full color at varying tape speeds; avoiding picture break-up during stop action, jogging, fast/slow motion. (*Ampex* – AST: automatic scan tracking. *3M* – ATF: automatic track follow. *Sony* – dynamic tracking.)

Auto white balance A system for automatically readjusting the color balance of a camera system to match the prevailing light's *color temperature*. Otherwise it would be necessary to manually measure the light's color quality and readjust the camera to avoid *color bias* – e.g. yellowish-orange or bluish pictures. For many applications, fully automatic white balance has proved very reliable but systems can be fooled in closer shots (especially where a single color predominates) or in colored lighting. So cameras usually include some form of manual override, and a *white balance preset/lock* or *'hold'* which maintains the auto-adjusted balance as the camera moves around. (The camera is pointed at a white card or shoots through a white translucent lens cap under the light source, and *'lock'* pressed to fix the setting.) Many cameras have built-in presets which adjust the system to predetermined color balances suitable for daylight, tungsten, or fluorescent light sources.

Azimuth Magnetic recording/reproducing systems (audio and video) use heads that scan the passing magnetic surface with a fine slit. In audio systems the head's slit is at right angles to the tape edge. If the slit of the reproducing head is not at exactly the same angle to the track as the original recording's (i.e. the same *azimuth*) there will be a corresponding reduction in the audio output. Azimuth checks (like cleaning and demagnetizing) should be a regular part of recorder maintenance.

Helical VTR systems deliberately *angle* a pair of video heads (e.g. ±6°) so that two separate tracks can be recorded on the same portion of tape without mutual interference. Neither head reproduces the other's track signals, because their azimuths are different. This principle has been taken further in a VHS system with hi-fi audio (*depth multiplex recording – see Consumer video formats*). Here high-quality stereo sound (in FM form) is recorded along exactly the same track as the *video*, with ±30° heads, angled at 120° to the video record, so providing independent outputs! (The standard audio edge-track is also recorded; lower-quality mono sound.)

Backing track A prerecorded track providing musical accompaniment for a performer who, listening on earphones (or a playback loudspeaker), is recorded on his or her individual microphone.

Banding Can occur on quad or segmented-head recorders, dividing the picture into a series of wide horizontal bands if head responses are uneven (e.g. a head clog) or are not automatically compensated.

Bands In a videotape recorder an FM carrier is generated which is then modulated with the video signal. It is this modulated carrier that is recorded on the tape; the video component itself being recovered during replay. However, spurious interference effects can arise in the process (close bands or stripes, noise effects) depending on the FM carrier-frequency band being used. A *low-level* 2.5 MHz is suitable only for monochrome. A *high-band* 3.58 MHz is suitable for color, but liable to a fine moiré pattern in colored areas, especially red. *Super high-band* 8 MHz considerably reduces the problem.

Batteries Because so much video and sound equipment is battery powered there are practical advantages in understanding their basics. A higher 14.4 volt supply is now specified by all major equipment manufacturers to eliminate previous problems with 12 volt standards. Fundamentally, batteries take two forms. In *primary cells (dry cells)*, expendable chemicals are used up (exhausted) while delivering power. In *secondary cells*, chemical components are transformed during discharge but can be reversed to their original condition during a *recharging* process. Where very compact batteries are essential (e.g. in watches, hearing aids), primary cells are generally most convenient.

But rechargeable cells are more economical for larger equipment.

In selecting a type of battery the manufacturer is concerned with a number of factors: Its terminal voltage (*TPD*); how long it retains this voltage in use (*holds its charge*); whether it degrades when left unused or during rest periods between use (*shelf life*). How does the voltage fall during use (gradually or suddenly)? How much current can it deliver in use (its *capacity*); how long will it supply current before needing to be recharged? Will its terminal voltage return to the original value (*full voltage*) when recharged, and how many times can it be recharged successfully?

Voltage – Any particular type of cell has a maximum voltage output. If you need a higher voltage supply you join several cells in a string, one after another, in a *series* arrangement (+ of one cell to the – of the next).

Capacity – The capacity of a battery is indicated by its rating in *ampere-hours (Ah)*. The higher the rating, the longer the battery will function before recharging or replacement is necessary. A typical *on-board* battery of 2 Ah fitted to a camera may last for e.g. an hour. But when powered from a battery of larger capacity – e.g. a *battery-belt* (*power belt*) of 4–7 Ah – that supply could last 2 to 3.5 hours. Where a cell does not have sufficient capacity for the power required it may be coupled *in parallel* with another (i.e. their + connections joined and their – connections joined). It is inadvisable to combine cells which are of different voltages or at different degrees of discharge.

- *Sealed lead-acid cells (SLA)* which are used in cars are the cheapest, toughest, and the most tolerant of extreme temperatures. However, they are bulky and heavy, and liable to leak electrolyte – a water/sulfuric acid mixture. (*Gel cells avoid this problem.*) They should not be left fully *dis*charged but stored in a fully charged state. The 2 V per cell maximum falls to 1.65 V minimum in use.
- *NiCad (nickel–cadmium) cell* – This very widely used type of portable battery is fairly small, rugged, and with proper attention quite long-lived. It delivers 1.2 V per cell maximum, falling to 1.1 V minimum during use. A NiCad cell works best at 65–75°F (18–23°C), and when being discharged quickly under high-current conditions (as in battery belts used for lights and video camera). It should be stored at 68° to 22°F (20° to –6°C). The cell retains its charge well in cool storage, but loses it rapidly in hot surroundings. When a charged NiCad battery is left for a long time without being discharged, crystals form within it, which can cause high self-discharge or even a dangerous internal short circuit. Discharging stored cells monthly (to 1 volt per cell) and fully recharging minimizes this effect. Otherwise *reconditioning* (deep discharge and full recharging) is needed. Unfortunately, the NiCad (nickel–cadmium) cell suffers from a *cyclic memory effect*. If you recharge this type of battery before it has been completely drained it will not return to the original *fully* charged voltage! Instead, it 'remembers' the depleted level, and progressively deteriorates each time it is recharged. Only *totally drained* cells will fully recharge for maximum performance. So you should either use a cell until it is exhausted (*flat*) or a *battery discharger* unit to drain the battery (to 0.9 volt per cell) before recharging. Alternatively, the charging system may apply a series of brief *discharge pulses* to the battery while charging it, promoting the recombination of gases formed during quick charging. Used regularly, this *burp* or *reverse-load* charging method can add as much as 15 per cent to life of NiCad battery. Chargers that are regulated by temperature control during the charging process tend to 'cook' the battery. 'Smart chargers' adjust the charge to suit the batteries' condition and capacity.
- *Nickel–metal hydride (NiMH)* cells are more expensive than a NiCad types. But they have a higher energy density, suffer less from memory effect, and have up to 40 per cent more run times. However, they do have a high self-discharge rate, so lose their charge quite quickly; e.g. by 10 per cent in 24 hours.
- *Lithium ion (Li-Ion)* cells are even more efficient, and have no memory effect. However, they do *self-discharge* (i.e. their voltage falls off, even without use) when left on the shelf for a while. *Lithium cells* maintain a constant voltage for longer, and are better in extreme hot and cold than other types. Other recent developments in battery design include *Lithium solid polymer* types (which can be moulded into shape), and *zinc–air* forms.

Beam splitter An optical device used to derive three identical images from the camera lens's image. The natural-color lens image passes through a pair of dichroic mirrors that split it into its red, blue, and green light components, respectively. The color images are reflected onto their corresponding sensors (CCDs) via compensatory relay lenses. Additional 'trimming' color filters exactly adjust the spectral spread of each light path.

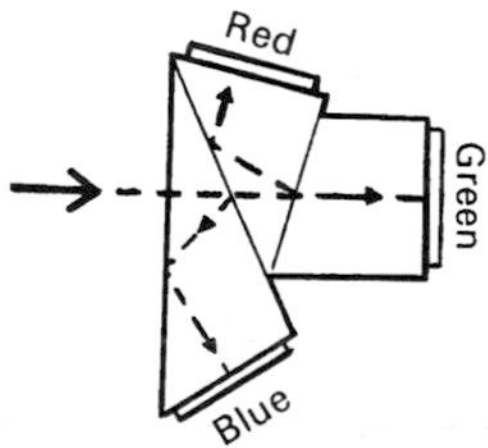

Beeper An identification audio signal sometimes used at the start of a recorded section (videotape, audio tape, or disc band) to aid sound cuing.

Bias current An ultrasonic current (e.g. 75–120 kHz) is combined with the audio in the record head; this effectively linearizes the tape's magnetic characteristic. Its strength is adjusted to suit particular tape materials. The bias setting is a compromise between distortion and high note response.

Black compression An electronic process that reduces noise at low light levels but can upset the color balance in low-key pictures.

Blooming A transparent microscopic anti-reflection coating is deposited on the surface of lenses to reduce light scatter, internal reflections, and flare within the lens system. The result is improved light transmission and overall contrast in the picture. The coated surface must be treated with care to avoid scratching, pitting, or wear. You should use special lens-cleaning tissue, or a soft lens brush to clean the lens surface, and, exceptionally, special lens-cleaning fluid.

Bridge Words or music introduced to tie together two dissimilar items. *Also* the shorting together of RGB channels on a picture monitor to produce a black and white picture.

Bulk eraser A large electromagnet which demagnetizes an entire tape spool, ensuring that any previously recorded program is completely wiped.

Camera cables TV cameras can be connected to video equipment by various means: coaxial cable, triaxial cable (coax plus outer screen), multi-conductor/multi-core cable, fiber-optic cable, radio mini-link, laser link, infrared link. Each method has its advantages, but typical factors to be considered include: cost, bulk, weight, damage vulnerability, interference pick-up. Whereas *multi-core* may have a length limit for a particular camera of e.g. 1800 ft (550 m) with *triax* the camera could be 6500 ft (2000 m) from base, and with *optical fiber* 7000 ft (2150 m) away. Fiber-optic cables weigh only around 5 lb per 1000 ft (2.3 kg per 300 m). Switchable *cable compensation* circuits correct for the definition losses that increase with cable length.

Camera lens The camera lens is a precision optical system, so it is extremely important to protect it from water, shocks, grit, moisture, heat, etc. if it is to maintain performance. The lens system consists of a series of individually designed lenses (*elements*) exactly set within a tubular metal barrel. Various optical inaccuracies can arise that cause the lens image to have uneven brightness, varying sharpness, distortions, color fringes, etc. These *aberrations* can be reduced by including extra compensatory elements within the system.

In earlier camera-tube systems certain inaccuracies (*e.g. geometrical distortion* which causes the picture to be misshapen) could be corrected by compensatory electronics. But in CCD cameras this is impracticable, so the lens itself needs to be designed to a higher specification.

A variable diaphragm or iris within the lens system adjusts the overall amount of light passing through it. So the image brightness can be altered for exact exposure. Its adjustment also affects the *depth of field.*

In a zoom lens selected elements are moved within the lens system to change the overall focal length, and hence the lens coverage (field of view; camera angle).

To adjust the focused distance a *fixed-optics* lens system is moved to and from the camera-tube. In a *zoom* lens, elements are repositioned.

The regular methods of attaching the lens system to the camera head are the screw-type *C-mount* and the quick-release *bayonet lock mount,* where the barrel fits into a slotted keyway in the camera head.

Camera microphone A microphone with omni, wide-angle, narrow-angle, or vari-angle (zoom) pickup pattern may be attached to the camera for program sound. It avoids the need for a separate operator, personal microphone or pre-positioned microphone (i.e. stand microphone, table microphone). However, this method of sound pickup has its limitations: The camera microphone too easily 'overhears' the sound of its own zoom and auto-focus motors operating, camera handling noises, etc. It is often too far away or wrongly angled to the subject for appropriate level or sound quality. The camera's AGC circuits controlling sound levels can lead to varying levels and overprominent background noises. Although the sound is continuously monitored (earphone or ear insert), there is little one can do about problems that arise. On balance, a separate properly positioned microphone is preferable wherever possible.

Camera-tube systems have ranged through many designs: from the early *Iconoscopes, Orthicons* and *Image Orthicons* used in black-and-white television to later *Vidicon, Plumbicon* and *Saticon* camera tubes for color systems. Although each had its limitations, modern camera tubes are capable of producing television pictures of the highest quality. However, with the arrival of cheaper, more compact and rugged solid-state *CCD* image sensors the camera tube's popularity declined.

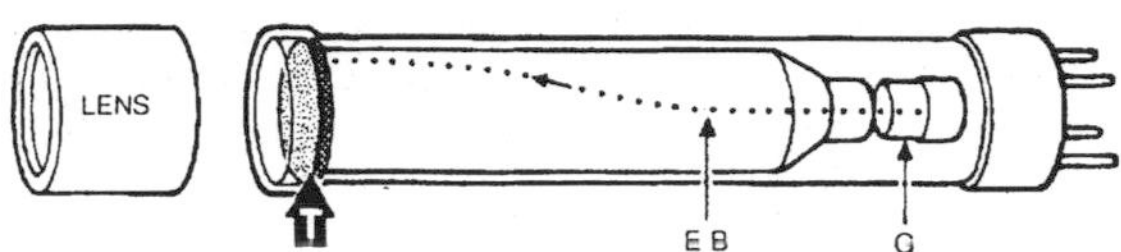

In photoconductive types of camera tube such as the *Plumbicon* the inside of its front glass face-plate is covered with a fine metallic coating (*signal plate*) on which a layer of photoconductive material is deposited. The lens' image is focused onto this target layer (T), and the electrical resistance of each point on its surface varies with the amount of light falling there to build up a charge pattern corresponding to light and shade in the lens image. A constant electron beam (E-B) produced by an electron gun (G) at the rear of the camera tube scans across the target in a series of close parallel lines, neutralizing each point (element) of the target in turn. The resultant recharging currents constitute the camera's video signal.

CCD – Generating the picture Although there are variations in the ways different *CCD* (*charge-coupled diode*) systems work, their underlying principles are similar. The lens' image falls onto a flat rectangular pattern or *matrix* of separate light-sensitive cells (*photodiodes*) which are located in the *image area* of a silicon chip. These cells are arranged in a series of horizontal rows, corresponding to the television scanning lines. While a typical consumer camera may have around 225 000 picture elements, a CCD for high definition TV can have some two million. Each of these minute elements or *pixels* produces an electrical charge (voltage) in the special silicon layer beneath its surface, which corresponds to the amount of light falling on that point.

By applying a suitable 'clock' voltage pulse to these matrix elements in turn the charges in the 'well' beneath each pixel can be progressively transferred (a line at a time) to a series of corresponding storage points in a light-proof *shift register* area on the chip. Here they are held briefly and read out by clocking pulses into a lower *output register,* and so conveyed to the output as the *video signal.*

All CCDs are essentially monochromatic; i.e they respond only to light and shade in the lens image. (An infrared filter may be fitted to suppress the CCD's sensitivity to infrared light.) To allow it to discriminate between colors, each CCD unit must be fitted with a color filter. In a *single chip* camera that may be in the form of a striped RGB filter or a mosaic pattern with complementary colors (yellow, blue, magenta). Although compact and economical, this reduces the overall resolution to one third of the total pixels.

For optimum color quality and resolution, three CCDs are needed. A block of prisms splits the lens' image into three separate paths. Crystalline surface coatings on the prisms produce *dichroic filters*. Unlike ordinary color filter media, which *absorbs* part of the light spectrum, and allows a reduced proportion of the rest through, a dichroic filter *reflects* light above and below a specific part of the color spectrum and passes the remainder with negligible light loss; a much more efficient process. The first prism in the block reflects blue light, and allows red and green light to pass. The second prism reflects red light, allowing green to pass. So the original color image is analyzed into the component R G B primaries. (See *Beam splitter*.)

CCD – Types of image sensor Currently, five types of image sensor are used in television cameras: *FT; IT; FIT; HAD; HyperHAD*. These differ in the position of their storage areas and in the way charges are transferred within the sensor.

FT (*Frame transfer type*) – Here the charge pattern corresponding to the lens image is built up by each field and rapidly transferred to a duplicate set of sensors for storage during the vertical blanking period. A *mechanical shutter* obscures the lens image during transfer to prevent the continuous lens image from contaminating the charge pattern while it is being moved into storage and degrading the next picture. Without the shutter, charges would continuously build-up and leak, causing a vertical smear on moving images.

The charges in the storage section are clocked out in the following field period and fed into the camera processing circuits. The design is claimed to provide a totally smear-free picture (particularly at high shutter speeds – e.g. 1/2000th second), absence of lag, and reduced aliasing effects. However, because the same pixels are used for both odd and even fields it is contended that the resolution is not as good as **IT** and **FIT** types.

IT (*Interline transfer type*) – This is the easiest and cheapest to make. As only about half of its pickup surface is light-sensitive, its overall sensitivity is reduced. Developed to eliminate the need for a mechanical shutter, the system has the disadvantage of *vertical smearing on strong highlights*, producing a vertical pink or red line on the picture. Improved design has reduced intrinsic deficiencies to a minimum, but these limit its applications. Smear is generally low, and fixed pattern noise (background) reduced. Fitted with an electronic shutter, performance improved: higher sensitivity; lower smear (white, not red). The IT is not used in broadcast cameras.

FIT (*Frame interline transfer type*) – A considerably improved storage method which is akin to the *IT* method, and virtually eliminates *vertical smear* due to highlight overloads. *Aliasing*, which causes a low beating moire patterning, is suppressed by offsetting the green CCD's position (by half a pixel) relative to the blue and red CCDs.

Both *IT* and *FIT* sensor designs can include tiny *micro lenses* fitted over each of the CCD's pixels. This results in doubled sensitivity, negligible picture noise and aliasing, and improved color quality. Both the FIT and FT cameras are high performance systems, and the latter has higher sensitivity. Although micro lenses collect more light from the lens image and improve sensitivity, their effect is much reduced when the lens is wide open (*non-linear sensitivity*). Micro-lenses may produce spurious halos and flares. (Considerably reduced by design developments; special anti-flare glass and shielding.)

HAD (*Hole accumulation diode/Hole accumulated diode*) – The sensor is coated with a thin conductive layer which significantly reduces electronic noise produced by surface irregularities in the CCD. Greatly improved sensitivity to blue. Lower lag.

Closed circuit Production being recorded, reviewed, etc. *locally*; as opposed to programs being *broadcast* for public viewing (off-air, or cable). Closed-circuit television (CCTV) is the general term for non-broadcast TV.

Coding Electronic process of encoding RGB video signals into NTSC, PAL, SECAM, color systems. (*Decoder*: circuitry for transforming the encoded signal into its RGB components.)

Color bars Video test signal presenting a series of vertical bars of fully saturated color: white, yellow, cyan, green, magenta, red, blue, black. Color bars are produced by inter-switching and combining varying proportions of the red, green, and blue channel signal voltages. The color system transmits the color primaries in different proportions to produce natural monochromatic (panchromatic) tones, so color bars reproduce in black-and-white as a progressive tonal step wedge. (See *Color definition*.)

Color definition The eye cannot readily detect fine color detail. Therefore, to save bandwidth in color TV systems, full detail is transmitted in *luminance* only – 4.2 MHz; i.e. 320 lines horizontal resolution – NTSC 525/60 (5.5 MHz. PAL. 625/50). Color information is deliberately restricted: I bandwidth (orange to cyan) 1.6 MHz; Q (green to magenta) bandwidth 0.8 MHz. The effect is of lower definition color 'overprinted' with tonal detail. Colors are transmitted in the proportions 30 per cent red, 59 per cent green, 11 per cent blue, to produce a suitable monochrome tonal balance.

Color synthesis Any color can be simulated in a TV system by supplying appropriately proportioned voltages to the red, green, and blue video channels. The color produced by the *color synthesizer/colorizer/color-field generator* may be switch-selected or controlled by a roller-ball or joy-stick control ('paintpot'). Its central position produces white, but the controller can be moved anywhere within a red, green, blue triangle. The synthesized color can be used as a source for electronic insertion: titling, title backgrounds, decorative effects, substituting picture colors or tones.

Color temperature Although all 'white' light includes colors of the entire visible spectrum (red, orange, yellow, green, blue, indigo, violet), the actual *proportions* of the spectral colors vary. We are unable to detect such variations because the brain compensates. But pictures from video and photographic systems reveal a color cast if they are used with lighting that does not color-match their particular color balance.

Because 'white' light is a very arbitrary term, a system is used, based on the Kelvin scale, to classify and compare the 'whiteness' of light sources. This system is based on the following concepts. If a hypothetical 'black body' is heated (actually tungsten filament or carbon) it will emit light. The color quality of the light changes throughout the temperature scale. (0 K = −273°C, i.e. the temperature at which molecular movement, causing heat, ceases.) At lower temperatures it will be predominantly red. But as the temperature is increased, the radiated light covers more and more of the spectrum, and includes an increasing proportion of blue.

Because the color quality of the light changes along the Kelvin temperature scale we can use these readings purely as *labels*; each figure corresponds to a particular light quality. Let us suppose that we measure the light from a candle with a pocket spectroscope, and check the proportion of each spectral color (its 'spectral distribution'). If we find that it has a color quality similar to that of 1930 K on the Kelvin scale, we say that it has a *color temperature* of 1930 K. That does not imply that this is the *actual* temperature of the candle! It is just a convenient method of classifying its overall color rating. Some light sources, such as fluorescent lamps, do not correspond very accurately to the Kelvin spectral coverage, but their quoted 'color temperatures' are a useful enough guide.

Knowing the color temperature of the light source, and that of our system, we can adjust either the light or the system, so that they match, and avoid a color cast in the picture.

Color temperature meters compare the proportions of red and blue light coming from any source, and this is transformed into a corresponding Kelvin reading.

Color film is designed to be used with a particular type of light (daylight 5500+ K; tungsten light 3200–3400 K). Under other conditions, a compensatory filter must be fitted.

Television systems are immediately adjustable to accept prevailing conditions ranging from a *clear sky* (10 000–20 000 K) to tungsten lighting (3000 K). Although studio lighting has a color temperature of about 3200 K, the lamps are usually slightly dimmed (under-run) as this improves lamp life. Cameras are lined up to this lower color temperature – around 2850–3000 K. Dimmer variations of 200 K are not generally noticeable as color changes in the picture. But where several lamps are lighting a light-toned surface, even 50–100 K differences may be detectable as bluish or orange-yellow variations.

Many video cameras contain switched compensation to adjust them to 'daylight' (5600 K) or 'tungsten light' (3200 K). Although these are arbitrary settings, they suit most conditions.

Color terms:

Achromatic values (*gray scale*). Progressive scale of brightnesses (luminance), from black through grays to white. Usually expressed as steps in a reflectance scale (Figure 3.8).

Brightness. Our *impression* of the amount of light received from a surface. The term is often used to indicate *luminosity* (US).

Chroma. See *Saturation*. (Term used in the Munsell system.)

Complementary colors. In *light*: two colors which, when added together, produce white light; e.g. blue and yellow; cyan and red; magenta and green. In *pigment or dye*: complementary colors produce black.

Hue. The predominant sensation of color; i.e. red, yellow, orange, etc. (Term used in the Munsell system.) A color's hue may be specified in several ways: by its *wavelength* in nanometers (nm); its *frequency* (e.g. 10^{12} Hz); as proportions of standard red, green, blue primaries. Hue may also be indicated graphically on a *color triangle* or located on a *color wheel*.

Lightness. Our impression of the brightness of surface colors.

Luminance. The *true* measured brightness of a surface. Snow has high luminance (reflecting 93–97 per cent of the light falling on it). Black velvet has a low luminance (reflecting 1.0–0.3 per cent of the light falling on it).

Luminosity. Brightness. Our impression of the amount of light received from a light source, or reflected from a surface.

Minus colors. If the visible spectrum is filtered, to hold back one primary color (e.g. red), the result is a 'minus red' mixture. 'Minus red' = blue + green – i.e. cyan. Similarly, minus green is magenta (red + blue); minus blue is yellow (red + green).

Monochrome. Generally refers to 'black-and-white' (achromatic) reproduction. Strictly means varying brightnesses of *any* hue.

Primary colors. Three colors (usually red, green, and blue) which, when mixed in correct proportions, can produce any other color of the spectrum.

Saturation (*chroma, intensity, purity*). The extent to which a color has been diluted with white (paled out). If a hue is pure and undiluted, it has 100 per cent saturation. As it becomes diluted, its saturation falls; e.g. 100 per cent red desaturates to pink (e.g. 15 per cent).

Secondary colors. In light, the hues resulting from the additive mixture of a pair of primary colors. (In printing, the orange-red, green, and purple-blue colours produced when pairs of *subtractive primary* colored inks are superimposed).

Shade. A hue mixed with black.

Spectral colors. The series of color bands seen when white light is diffracted by a lens, prism, or diffraction grating. Merging continuously from red (longest wavelength; lowest frequency) through orange, yellow, green, blue, indigo, violet (shortest wavelength; highest frequency).

Tint. A hue diluted with white; i.e. a desaturated color.

Value. Subjective brightness (Term used in the Munsell system.)

Color-under Several different techniques are used to record color information on videotape:

1 Recording a *composite* signal (which includes a chrominance-modulated subcarrier).
2 *Color-under recording*.
3 *Component recording*, in which luminance and chrominance (actually, *color difference signals*) are recorded separately.

The detailed information in a fully encoded color TV signal (i.e. NTSC, PAL, etc.) cannot be recorded accurately at the slower videotape speeds of small-gauge VTR systems (U-Matic, VHS, etc.). Instead, an ingenious *color-under* system is used. In principle this involves recording brightness (luminance) and color (chrominance) information simultaneously on two adjacent carriers (FM, AM), using filters on replay to distinguish between them. However, there are problems in differentiation, and various visible defects arise: detail loss (above about 2 MHz), chroma noise, moiré patterns, edge sparkle, color displacement, ringing (edge repeats), 'cartooning' (plain areas lack texture). Such interference may be reduced, and definition increased, by raising the carrier frequency of the luminance signal (as in S-VHS).

Compact disk formats – Principles and typical systems In this highly competitive field there is an ever-increasing selection of high-storage formats. Although *tape systems* are cheap, have considerable storage capacity, and can be used in both analogue and digital (DAT) modes, searching and recovering video or audio data from tape is a slow process. The storage capacity of disk systems capacities has now extended from a few hundred kilobytes to the several gigabytes needed to accommodate high-quality long-duration color recordings. (*Note*: The conventional spelling of **DISC** for *read-only media* and **DISK** for *read/write media* – e.g. floppies and hard drives – is not consistently observed.)

The following incompatible formats, have been explored in diverse fields:– **CD:** Audio (*M*). **DAD** (*M,U*). **Video CD** (*F,P*). **CD-I** (*E,G,H,T*) (Philips/Sony). **PhotoCD** (*C,I*) (Kodak). **CD-ROM** (*S,B*). **CD-R** (*A,D*). **CD+/Enhanced CD** (*M*). **VideoCD Plus** (*F,H,M*) (Omnimedia). **Digital Video Disc**; **DVD-ROM** (*E,F*). **MCD7** (*S*) (Phillips/Sony). **SD** (*F,U,V*) (Toshiba, Time/Warner).

The main applications of these formats are: (A) archiving; (B) publishing; (C) consumer; (D) production; (E) entertainment, (F) films; (G) education; (H) corporate communications; (I) professional imaging; (M) Music; (P) promos; (S) software; (T) training; (U) data; (V) video.

CD (Compact disc) – This universal music format uses a 120 mm (4.7 in.) single-sided disc of 79.8 min maximum duration. The digital audio signal is recorded as a pattern of shallow depressions (*pits*) of varying lengths along a fine-groove spiral track. (Typically 0.6–0.12 mm wide; minimum pit length 0.83 μm; track spacing 1.6 μm; over 16 000 tracks per inch.) During processing, this recorded track is stamped into a disc of clear polycarbonate plastic. On replay, the light from a small intense laser passes through the disc as it reads the track and is reflected by a thin aluminum sheet attached to the top surface. A photo detector senses interruptions in the reflected light; registering '*zero*' on the flat 'land' surface and '*one*' at each pit. A clear lacquer protective coating on the other face of the disc gives it an overall thickness of 1.2 mm.

The disc is scanned from inside to out. Rotating at 510 rev/min at its center, it first reads coded data on the playing time and the number of tracks (sections). The disc speed progressively decreases to 210 rev/min, as it scans outwards; so producing a constant reading speed of 1.25 m/s. The audio quality is exceptionally high, with a wide frequency range, virtually without rumble, flutter, wow, background noise, a high dynamic range (>90 dB); low distortion (<0.05 per cent peak). There is no actual wear as the disc is played; although bad surface damage can defeat compensatory circuitry and produce repeats, jumped sections, etc.

CD-R (Compact disc – recordable) – Basically similar to the CD, the reflective aluminum sheet is replaced with a thin layer of organic dye coated with a microscopic film of gold. During *recording* the digital audio signal controls a laser which burns a succession of scorch marks in the organic dye. On replay, these 'pits' modulate the replay laser's reflected light to reconstitute the original audio. This system provides a range of storage applications for PC use (e.g. text, audio, still images, video clips, HTMl). Unfortunately, the recording cannot be erased. In another system – the **CD-RW (CD-Re-Writable)** – the laser alters the refraction of a special surface, to simulate data pits for replay. After quick 'reformatting' the restored 'blank' surface can be re-used many times.

DAD (Digital audio disk) – A 5-in. high-density compact disk carrying 4.7 Gb of data. (In a double-sided format – 9.4 Gb.) This is achieved by using a very tightly focused laser, creating fine pits on the disk surface. The player is able to run standard CDs and video-CDs.

CD-ROM (Compact disc read-only memory) – A read-only 5 in. optical compact disc on which data is stored as a series of minute pits in digitized (binary) form. The component video is digitally recorded in compressed form (MPEG-1) 4:2:2. This popular format is widely used for *interactive video, data storage*, and *video games*. Some 800 million bytes of data can be stored.

Rewritable video disc – A 12 in. disc carried within a protective cassette case, allowing component analogue video and audio (2 analogue tracks; 1 PCM) to be recorded/replayed, and rewritten. Typical duration 12 min. Broadcast applications include recording/replaying brief sequencies (spot inserts). A **WORM** disc (*write-once-read-many*) allows the user to record information once on a blank disc; after which it can be reproduced many times.

CDi (CD-interactive) – Designed to be used with a television receiver, for interactive programming. (Used for most digital movies until 1994, when the VideoCD standard became available.)

DVD-ROM (digital versatile disk/digital video disk) – A single-sided single-density version can store nearly 5 Gigabytes of data (over seven 650 Mb CD-ROMS; while a single *double-sided double-layered* DVD-ROM can contain 17 Gb of data (i.e. 26 CDs or around 12 000 floppy discs). With MPEG-2A/V compression, offers over two hours of top quality video and stereo sound.

Examples of further developments – Currently these include **DVD-Ram** (a recordable disk format); joining the **DVD Video**, **DVD Rom**, and **DVD Audio** replacing the laser disc, computer and audio CD systems respectively, providing enhanced storage capacity and quality. A further **PC-RW** (*phase change read write*) system is also progressing. The **Multimedia CD (MMCD)**, a high-density compact disk in single and dual-layer formats. **Super Disc (SD)** and **SD-RAM** (rewritable/erasable optical disk).

Compositing This method of creating *digital video effects* involves a computer controlling a dedicated image processor. Software enables images of objects to be built up systematically by creating a simple '*wire-frame*' structure in which sections are formed and joined together. A suitable textural effect is chosen for each segment (*texture mapped*), surface contours selected (*bump mapping*), and a suitable material chosen for the object (e.g. simulating wood, metal, marble). This image is then integrated with the background picture and the effect of lighting is introduced (*light sourcing*) for both the object and its surroundings. Light and shade on its surface and reflections are created by *ray-tracing (environmental mapping)*. To animate the picture, a succession of *key frames* are created in which changes in the positions of this object and the 'camera viewpoint' are established. Then software calculates the *in-between* frames between the key frames (rather like *morphing* transformations). The total sequence is then stored on a computer hard disk; usually to be transferred to videotape.

Using a *layering* process one can draw a series of separate planes and place one over the other in any chosen order. This allows each contributory layer to be independently changed or manipulated when they have been combined to create a composite.

Many of the regular graphical tools found in *computer-graphic programs* are used to build up video images: *cropping* (cutting off areas), *pasting* (moving areas to new positions; duplicating features), *rotation in x-y-z modes* (i.e. left/right; up/down; to/fro), *perspective* effects, *borders, color fill, shading, blending, scaling, spray, textures, patterns, transparency, filters, color selection, color correction or adjustment*, etc. In addition, various forms of image manipulation can be introduced, such as: *flexing, stretching, shaping, twisting, bending, solarization, strobing, motion blur, glints, star filters*, etc.

From the *compositor unit* itself the artist may turn to *stand-alone boxes* which house a library of shapes (e.g. to transform an image into a heart shape or sphere), internal wipe patterns, positionable light source direction, as well as a range of effects such as quad splits, multi-tiles, spheres, page turns, cylinders, ripples, trails . . .

Compression (Compressed data storage) Even a brief picture sequence can produce a great deal of data. So when copying a program tape onto hard disk for editing or storage it can soon exceed the storage capacity available. (That is less of a problem with a lower resolution system such as VHS which involves less data than when using a high-grade system, such as a D-2 videotape.) To overcome this dilemma, the trick is to *compress* the material; reducing the effective amount of data that needs to be stored by putting the digital video and sound signals through a mathematical sampling process.

Restricted resolution – If a highly compressed version of the the picture is stored on the disk the copy's quality is noticeably degraded; depending on the system used. But it does allow long sequences of moving images to be stored on hard disks of quite modest capacity.

These versions are not suitable for transferring onto the final master videotape, but they do provide the videotape editor with instant access when overviewing the program material during editing; allowing preliminary editing decisions to be made before the actual editing/compilation session. After selecting and arranging the shots in this way the corresponding sections of the original tapes are automatically copied from the edit master onto a master tape. This approach is necessarily an off-line editing process.

Full resolution storage – Where high-density multi-disks are able, long periods of *high grade* images can be stored. This alters matters considerably, for where the original recorded data is copied and stored *without compression* the high-quality picture and sound (to D-1 system standards) can be duplicated directly during on-line editing – straight from the edit master hard disk to the final master (transmission) videotape – thus cutting out the need to go back and auto-assemble from the original videotape.

While compression has many advantages when storing or transferring data, it does impose limitations. For example, in order to work on picture or sound material during editing or compositing, data must be *de*compressed. Depending on the system used, compressing and decompressing digital data files may take some time, particularly when compiling from different sources, for many factors are involved.

Several systems are in use for compressing data: text, sound, still and moving pictures. For example, the *JPEG* compression techniques which are optimized for *still* pictures do not need to cope with motion compensation or audio, so are able to use different algorithmic refinements and considerable reduction ratios (up to 50:1). The international *Moving Picture Experts Group* (*MPEG working group*) developed common standards for compressing digital signals. Basically, the digital picture is subdivided into manageable blocks of data, which are interpreted by a mathematical encoding technique called *Intra-frame compression*. Where changes are detected in the picture content between frames, further selective reduction is introduced (*Inter-frame compression*). There are several sub-groups of the MPEG standards to suit various applications. MPEG 422 is used by broadcasters for studio operations, image processing and editing. Another is used for transmission purposes.

While compression has unquestionable advantages when storing data, or working with systems having limited capacity, there can be drawbacks. Ideally, the compression process should be a *lossless* or *transparent*, so that no adverse effects or distortions are visible when the image is restored. But objectionable *compression artifacts* which introduce spurious effects can develop in some compression systems. Where one compression process follows another (*cascading*), problems arise. Compressed signals may need to be transcoded from one format to another to allow certain operations such as chroma-keying or compositing, special effects or multi-generation processes. In the process, the image can become noticeably degraded.

Crossed gray scale (chipchart) A standard test graphic comprising two opposed horizontal nine-step tonal gray scales (from 3 per cent to 60 per cent reflectance).

Cut-back During editing, returning to the main scene after a series of interpolating close shots.

Decibel (dB) A logarithmic unit indicating ratios of powers, voltages, or currents and used to express transmission levels, gains, and losses. The human ear (like the eye) does not respond proportionally to changes, but follows a 'power law'. A decibel represents the smallest perceptible change in audio level.

Degaussing Demagnetizing. Tape recording heads must be periodically degaussed to prevent magnetic build-up from increasing tape hiss. Videotape is usually bulk erased before re-use.

Depth of field The *depth of field* available in a shot depends on the lens distance setting, angle of view (focal length) and the lens aperture (*f*/stop). You can use the following formulae to calculate how the depth of field changes with your particular lens:

$$\text{Nearest limit} = \frac{H \times D}{H + D} \qquad \text{Farthest limit} = \frac{H \times D}{H - D}$$

where H is the hyperfocal distance (see *Hyperfocal distance*) and D is the distance from lens to the focused plane.

Desktop video '*Desktop video*' has brought a new dimension to television, video and sound production. As the speed and storage capacity of personal computer systems (PCs) grew, desktop video systems developed, able to do jobs that would otherwise require costly dedicated equipment. Desktop video now ranges in complexity from regular PCs using special software to specifically designed multi-task *workstations*. Video, audio, graphics and text can now be integrated into a single seamless system, with quality and price to suit various program makers – from the needs of the hobbyist at the low end of the multimedia market, the high-grade requirements of corporate and institutional video production markets, up to the exacting demands of full broadcast standards.

The on-screen presentations of typical desktop video formats include:

- *Small viewing screens* – showing moving or still video pictures (the main channel and multi-source previews); with the associated strip soundtrack(s) laid against a time scale.
- A simulated *control* panel – with symbolic switches, faders, pushbuttons, rotating knobs, etc.
- *Indicators* – Showing the controls in use and their settings.
- *Information boxes* – Displaying menus, dialogue boxes, lists, messages, instructions, etc.
- *Selection icons (tools)* – Small 'press-button' symbols, used to call up different processes and procedures.

Digital desktop video systems have certain advantages over analogue processes. Like regular computers, they store picture and sound data on a hard disk or solid-state devices. Immediate access overcomes the time and problems of shuttling tape. Editing is therefore rapid and non-destructive. It allows you to quickly cut-and-paste material, to rearrange alternative treatments.

These ingenious systems do have their drawbacks. The limited screen size and crowded layout of some monitor displays can make the selection and one-handed operation of these controls awkward (using mouse, roll-ball/track-ball, or touch-screen selection). Correcting or revising a step can be time consuming; and more complex operations (e.g. increasing one fader setting while decreasing another) may be impracticable. On a multi-task station it may not be possible to leave one operation partly developed and move to another task (e.g. from 'graphics' to 'video effect' modes).

How important such limitations are in practice compared with dedicated equipment largely depends on design and on your particular application. Insufficient available memory may preclude full-screen high quality real-time video displays. (A minute of regular NTSC 4 by 3 aspect ratio picture can take up to 10 Mb of hard disk space.) PC-based systems are likely to have low resolution pictures of restricted duration, drop frames, show action at reduced speed. Nevertheless, for many checking purposes, high quality is not essential. Lower performance is quite adequate in multi-frame displays for storyboarding or for identification frames when editing. Similarly, where color reproduction is restricted (e.g. 8-bit; 256 colors) results may be quite acceptable for some purposes. However, for broadcast use, top-grade standards are essential (24 or 32-bits/pixel; over 16.7 million colors).

There are fundamental variations between brands or models of PCs. (Most use *sequential/progressive scanning* instead of broadcast-type *interlacing*.) Few personal computers output a broadcast format television signal (i.e. NTSC, PAL, SECAM), so cannot be used directly with video equipment. *Analogue/digital (A/D) encoders* or *digitizers* are needed to translate one form of signals to another: to interface the different systems, and convert digital data into standard TV signal form. The system must provide NTSC (756 × 486 pixels) or PAL (768 × 576 pixels) compatible interlaced video. Some units have separate **Y** (luminance) and **C** (chroma/chrominance) outputs, which provide higher picture quality. *Genlock* is also necessary to interlock and synchronize sources, particularly when titling or graphics are to be integrated into standard TV pictures (live or recorded).

To accommodate the particular requirements of broadcast-quality video production, special-purpose hardware and software may be needed. PC-based systems can also have various quality limitations: flicker on fine horizontal detail (between odd and even field scans); oversaturated color (too pure); jagged lines ('staircase', 'jaggies') on circles or diagonals – reduced by '*anti-aliasing*'. The aspect ratio of the computer's picture may be different from the broadcast standard. Detail which is visible on a computer monitor may be lost on the TV screen. There may be 'glitches' (visual disturbances), jumps, or bumps that are unacceptable for broadcast use.

Typical *desktop video* applications include: video and sound editing (real-time non-linear editing, edit controller); frame grabber; graphics; paint; animation; compositing; rotoscoping; character generator; video production switcher; audio mixer; 3-D digital video effects; storyboarding; chroma and luminance keying; matte generator; virtual sets; still stores; transitions generator; genlock; time base corrector. One popular facility is the *Video toaster*, which provides in a single unit a very extensive range of production facilities, including: production switcher, video effects, graphics, animation, keying (luminance, chrominance), character generator, tapeless editor, etc. Desktop video systems may be used to provide a range of technical test facilities, such as waveform monitors, vectorscopes, timebase correction, video control.

Dichroics A dichroic mirror reflects one color band while letting others pass through it. When a series of extremely thin semi-transparent layers of material are deposited on a glass surface, light waves are interreflected there, creating interference effects. (Similar to colors reflected when oil floats on water.) The exact effect varies with the wavelength (hue) of the light. Treatment can be selective, to allow only e.g. the blue-green part of the spectrum to pass, while e.g. the red region is reflected. Carefully controlled color light filters can be made using this process.

In *beam splitters* this principle is used to convert the lens image into three identical color images (R, G, B) of the scene. (See *Beam splitter.*)

In lighting, *dichroic filters* are placed over tungsten-halogen lamps to change their color temperature from the warmer 3200 K to the bluer color of daylight (5600 K).

Diffuser A sheet of wire mesh, spun glass, or opaque polyester placed over a light fitting: either to diffuse (soften) the illumination or to reduce the light output, without affecting the color temperature. If the fitting is insufficiently ventilated, overheating can result, reducing the life of the lamp.

Digital basics

The principles An *analogue* system handles a direct electrical replica of the original sound or picture. Each vibration of a violin's string produces a corresponding fluctuation in the strength of the audio electrical signal. Similarly, as the television camera scans the scene, the variations in light and shade it detects are matched by similar changes in the strength of the video signal.

As we saw earlier in Figure 12.3, even the purest sounds combine to produce complicated waveshapes in the audio signal. Imagine the intricate variations of a microphone's output voltage as it brings us the sound of a Wagnerian opera! It is not surprising that analogue signals easily become distorted as they travel through the system. Reproduced quality deteriorates, becoming less and less like the original. Spurious noises are picked up *en route* (hum, hiss, crosstalk, induction), to become intermingled as unwelcome background noise. We may accept or overlook these shortcomings, but they are there. In a color television system complications increase enormously.

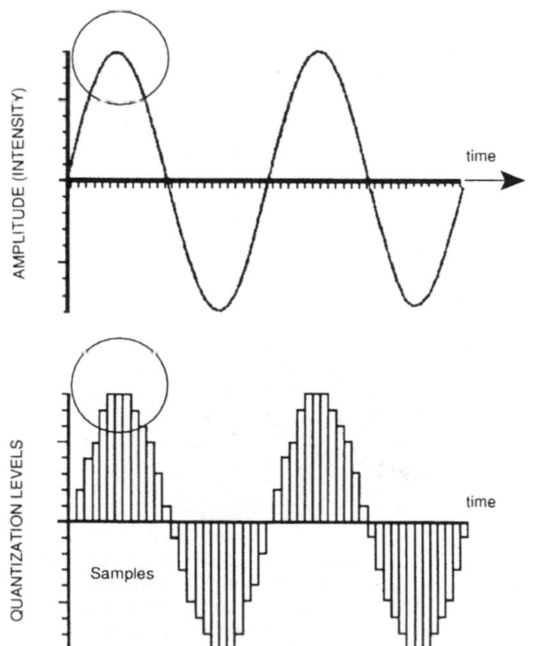

To overcome the various limitations of analogue systems, *digital* techniques were developed. These convert the audio or video signal into a different, less vulnerable form. As the original analogue audio or video signal passes through an *A/D (analogue/digital) converter* its strength is measured at rapid regular intervals (the *sampling rate*). The instantaneous value of each sampling (*quantization level*) is read off and this number (*digit*) is coded as a stream of eight *on-and-off* electrical pulses (*binary code*). If, for instance, the momentary signal strength is **1**, a binary code pattern **00000001** is sent through the system. If it is **2**, the sequence is **00000010** (**0** = **00000000**).

So now, instead of the subtle irregular fluctuations of the original signal, we have just straightforward on–off switching of a single voltage. To restore this data to its original analogue form it is fed into a *digital/analogue* (*D/A*) converter at its destination.

The advantages Although at first sight this technique might seem very cumbersome, like the dot–dash system of Morse code, it has proved to be a very 'robust', accurate method of sending and storing information (*data*). In practice, digital techniques have many advantages. Even if the *digitized* signal becomes badly distorted or accompanied by noise, the basic binary on–off pattern can still be read out, and it becomes possible to recapture the original signal.

Digital data is readily stored on tape, magnetic or optical disk, or in solid-state memory devices (ROM, RAM). It can be modified or manipulated in many ways with considerable precision. Whether the data represents text, graphics, music, speech or a series of pictures (graphics or video), you can rapidly access selected sections or sequences. We can even compensate for limitations in the original picture or sound, and immeasurably improve its quality. Digitized treatments of early acoustical phonograph recordings have produced minor miracles.

- *Sound* – You can take an entire sequence or a brief fragment of digitally recorded sounds and remove or add features, change their order, extend or shorten their duration, repeat, reverse, delay or advance, invert. Even the *character* of the sound can be varied. It is possible at the touch of a button in a *MIDI* system to transcribe a recording of music played on a piano to the sound of an entirely different instrument; an organ, guitar, flute, harpsichord, steel drums . . . The pitch and intonation of digitized speech can be modified; varied from soprano to deep bass; its speed changed; its delivery altered, from flat to emphasized.
- *Pictures* – The tones, colors, textures of a graphic or a photograph can be modified or replaced. Subjects or entire areas can be moved or multiplied, reversed, inverted, size and perspective changed. Selected material can be exported or imported to and from another picture. Opportunities are endless!

The technicalities The fidelity of this digitizing process depends on both the *sampling rate* and the subtlety of *quantization level* measurement. If these are insufficient, reproduction will suffer badly. On the other hand, high-speed sampling with high resolution is costly, with increased technical problems.

- *Sampling rate* – The *rate* at which the waveform is sampled needs to be at least twice the signal's maximum frequency (*Nyquist sampling theorem*). If it is too low, the reproduced version will have a characteristically 'crunchy' quality. The number of *bits* determines the resolution of the digital signal. The minimum analysis acceptable for broadcast television requires 8-bit sampling, giving a resolution of 1 in 256. Typical *audio* sampling rates are: *Compact disc* – 44.1 kHz; *digital audio tape* – 32, 44.1, or 48 kHz; *digital VTRs* (*D1, D2, D3*) – 48 kHz. For audio utilities where intelligibility is the only standard, sampling rates as low as 10 kHz may be sufficient.
- *Quantization levels* – Where differences in the signal's *strength* are measured in too few steps the system's *resolution* deteriorates. It cannot follow slight changes in the original signal, but crudely 'rounds them up' or 'rounds down' to the nearest level step, so introducing distortion when this digital signal is restored to analogue form. When errors arise due to differences between the actual analogue signal and the nearest sampling step size, *quantizing noise* develops. For many purposes, 8-bit sampling which identifies 256 loudness levels is sufficient.

Units The smallest amount of digital information is the *bit* (**BI**nary digi**T**). Whether we are considering audio, video, computer programs, or any other digital process, data is coded in the form of groups of ***on (1)*** and ***off (0)*** pulses measuring signal strength variations.

Decimal	Binary	Decimal	Binary	Decimal	Binary
1	00000001	6	00000110	11	00001011
2	00000010	7	00000111	12	00001100
3	00000011	8	00001000	13	00001101
4	00000100	9	00001001	14	00001110
5	00000101	10	00001010	15	00001111

When discussing digital *pictures*, one *bit* of picture information is usually termed a *pixel* (**pic**ture **ce**ll). A succession of 8 *bits* of information is a unit called a *byte*. And that is sufficient to define 256 shades of gray between black and white. For digital *audio*, 16 to 20 bits is a common rate. With the 16-bit resolution used for CD quality (65 536 levels are detectable) and quantizing errors are inaudible.

1 kilobyte (KB)	= 1024 bytes
1 megabyte (MB)	= 1024 × 1024 bytes = 1 048 576 bytes
1 gigabyte (GB)	= 1024 × 1024 × 1024 bytes = 1 073 741 824 bytes
1 terabyte (TB)	= 1024 × 1024 × 1024 × 1024 bytes = 1 099 511 627 776 bytes

Specific terms tend to vary with the application. The *bit* is the smallest element in a drawing, a line, or parts of letters; on a monitor, the smallest picture element is a *pixel*; while in a printout we speak of *dpi* (dots per inch).

Digital television systems

NTSC system In this 525-line 60-field system each picture frame (which is built up from two fields) involves 486 active lines, each of 640 pixels (i.e. bits). So 307 200 samples are involved in conveying the picture's light and shade variations (luminance). A color system entails three separate images (red, green, and blue), making a total of 921 600 bytes per frame. So in one second 30 picture frames (actually 29.97) of picture information totals some 27 648 Mbytes!

PAL system In this 625-line 50-field system each picture frame (two fields) involves 720 pixels to convey the variations in luminance. As each of the color difference signals involves a further 360 pixels, this amounts to 1440 pixels per line. There are 576 active lines in a picture, totalling 830 kBytes per picture. So for the 25 frames each second, a total of 21 MBytes of information is involved; or 1.26 Gbytes each minute.

A considerable amount of memory is needed to store or record full picture information. In an HDTV system these quantities increase by some four or five times. To reduce this data density, and to make handling easier, various methods of *compression* are used. (See *Compression*.)

Diopter A *diopter lens* is a simple supplementary lens placed over the main camera lens to alter its effective focal length. Mainly used for close-ups of small objects.

The *diopter* is the measurement of the power of a single lens; 100 divided by its focal length in centimeters. So a lens of power +15 diopters has a focal length of 100/15 = 6.66 cm (66.6 mm).

+ indicates that the lens is convering; – that it is diverging.

Disk, magnetic Two types of magnetic disk systems are used to store audio, video or computer data in digitized form – the *floppy disk* and the *hard disk*.

A *floppy disk* (typically 3.5 in. diam; capacity 1.44 megabytes) consists of a rotating flexible Mylar disk with a magnetic coating (e.g. iron oxide), centered within a slim rigid protective plastic case. A metal cover slides to one side when in the disk drive to allow the magnetic surface to be scanned by a moving pickup head. The 'floppy' is removable and readily stored.

Before use, the floppy disk is first *formatted* by recording on it a number of concentric-ring *tracks*, which are subdivided into *sectors*. When digitized data is stored on the disk as magnetized spots, its location is given by the track and sector numbers involved. Formatting details vary

with the computer system (platform) being used. A particular advantage of a disk system is that the moving head travels across the disk, allowing virtually instantaneous random access to any selected sector(s) – unlike magnetic tape systems, which must be spooled through to reach a selected point.

A *hard disk drive* (*HDD*) format consists of a double-sided 3.5 in. magnetically coated aluminum or glass disk, sealed within a shock-resistant case. (Available in permanently installed or removable forms; in single- or multi-disk arrangements.) Data is recorded and read from the rapidly spinning disk by a head on a pivoted arm on either face of the disk. Each head can be repositioned with precision anywhere on the tracks. As it arcs to and fro across the disk's surface a cushion of air prevents the head making direct contact with it – which would result in a '*head crash*' and data loss. Maximum storage capacity per disk currently exceeds 5 Gbs, and a disk pack of up to 20 independently read disks stacked one on top of another may be mounted on a common spindle to provide a centralized data bank (*server*) storing photo-stills, video-clips, statistical information, etc. Stacked tracks are known as *cylinders* and the location of any data is identified by selecting the appropriate read/write head and the sector and cylinder in which it is stored.

Drop-out Magnetic tape surface defect or damage causing momentary disturbance of reproduced video, resulting in small localized information gaps in a line (black flash, color loss). To disguise this brief loss of FM signal pick-up from the tape, a *drop-out compensator* can insert stored picture information from a corresponding part of the previous line. (This term is also used for the information loss, *noise* band at end of line/frame scanning in helical recording.)

Ducker/voice-over ducker An audio-fader circuit that automatically reduces the volume of e.g. music ('back-grounds' it) to enable an announcement to be heard; its level being restored as the speech stops.

Dupe neg A duplicate negative prepared from a positive print – when the original negative is not available, or to protect the original negative, or for special-effects work. By using *color reversal intermediate film*, duplicate negatives of the original color negative can be prepared, so eliminating one printing stage (reduced grain, improved color reproduction and sharpness).

Electronic cinematography (EC) Video cameras designed to produce typical 'film look' picture quality. Used for shooting 'motion pictures' that will subsequently be transferred to film for screening. These cameras are intended to handle and perform like 35 mm cine cameras. They have the merits of both media, i.e. the advantages of videotape over film stock, continuous monitoring, with interchangeable lens systems (prime and zoom), T-stops, the familiar angles of film camera lenses, and facilities for a separate focus-pulling operator.

Other design features include extended dynamic range, soft clip (i.e. a *knee* in the exposure curve, instead of the hard/sharp cut-off of high-lights in the normal TV white clipper/white limiter).

Electronic still store (ESS) Photographic slides are costly, vulnerable, bulky, need manual sorting and loading, etc. So magnetic video disc stores of various designs are increasingly used that provide a library of still video pictures. These pictures can be 'grabbed' from any video source (cameras, slide scanners, videotape, film, computer graphics) from artwork to photo-stills or titles.

Storage capacity may range from a few hundred to several thousand frames. Sometimes a number of work stations can load from one central library store or *server*. Individual stills are coded and may be selected at random, or arranged to play through in a programmable sequence.

As stills selection from store can be almost instantaneous, several can be shown in rapid succession to create animated effects. An index of descriptions/titles can be displayed on a monitor screen, and may enable a simultaneous multi-segment picture (e.g. 64 'slides') to be displayed (*browse mode*).

Exposure curve (transfer characteristic) Only where a picture system's output is directly proportional to the light input (unity gamma) will tonal reproduction be strictly accurate. Most systems have a linear (straight line) portion to their characteristics, but are less responsive to changes at exposure extremes. Lightest tones are therefore progressively compressed at the upper end of the exposure curve (knee, shoulder), while shadow detail merges at the lower end (toe).

Fiber optics A cable of fine glass filaments conveys intensity-modulated light from light-emitting laser diodes in a miniature transmitter to light detectors, which transform these light pulses into corresponding electrical signals (video and audio).

The advantages of optical fibers include: lightweight, small-diameter cable, no electromagnetic interference, no crosstalk between fibers, low losses, no radiation, no picture degradation, no equalization needed, wide bandwidth, independent of line-of-sight and weather conditions (unlike external radio links), rapidly routed, very robust (withstands vehicles, trampling, wet, mud, sand, snow, etc.).

Filter wheel Most cameras have an internal multi-position filter wheel fitted between the lens and the beam splitter. A control at the side of the camera rotates the wheel to select from the available filters. Usually, one of its openings is left clear. Another is blanked off, to allow the lens to be 'capped up', preventing any light from falling on the camera-tube or CCD. The rest of the wheel is used for three kinds of filters: neutral density, color correction, and effects.

Neutral density filters are an alternative to having to stop the lens down to avoid overexposure; particularly when you do not want to increase the depth of field. These gray-toned filters reduce all colors equally.

Color-correction filters compensate for the color quality of the prevailing light. Instead of readjusting the camera's *white balance* circuits on moving to light of a different *color temperature* (e.g. from artificial light to daylight), a color-correction filter can change it to suit the existing color balance.

Effects filters of several types may be fitted. The commonest are four- or six-point star filters (starburst) and diffusion discs.

Flash cutting A sequence structured from a series of very brief shots, each lasting only a few frames.

Flat display screens Flat display screens are gradually replacing regular cathode ray tubes in many applications. Currently there are several systems. *LCD (liquid crystal display) screens* are regularly used in smaller displays (hand-held TV receivers, etc.). In *plasma displays* two substrate sheets enclose an inert neon–xenon gas. The back sheet has many thousands of tiny cells coated with phosphors. When a voltage is applied to lines of electrodes on the front sheet opposite the cells the ultraviolet gas discharge causes the appropriate red, green, blue cell phosphor to glow. In *SED* displays (*surface-conduction electron-emitter display*) coated electrodes on a glass substrate are located on a multi-phosphor screen. An applied voltage generates a stream of electrons which strike the phosphors, causing them to glow.

Flying erase head In a standard helical scan VCR a fixed erase head wipes the entire tape width. Thus it erases parts of *several* video tracks simultaneously. It cannot erase one complete video track at a time. This precludes precision picture editing. To overcome this problem, recorders designed for *insert editing* have an auxiliary *flying erase head* fitted just before the record head, on the head drum. In some recorders there is also a *flying reproduce head* (*confidence head*) which immediately follows the record head; so allowing simultaneous off-tape monitoring during recording.

Forced processing When a film is developed at a higher temperature or for a longer period than normal its effective *speed* (sensitivity) is increased; although contrast, graininess, and fog are emphasized. Reversal films 'push' more successfully than negative film material. This technique is resorted to when light levels are too low for normal exposure.

Gamma *Gamma* is a logarithmic measurement that compares the tonal values in the scene with the way they are reproduced on the screen. If reproduced tones correspond with those of the subject (i.e. are directly proportional), the system is said to have *unity gamma* (*gamma = 1*). In fact, various parts of the television system may have gammas other than the ideal (e.g. a color picture tube with a gamma of around 2.2); but gamma-correction circuits can compensate for deviations.

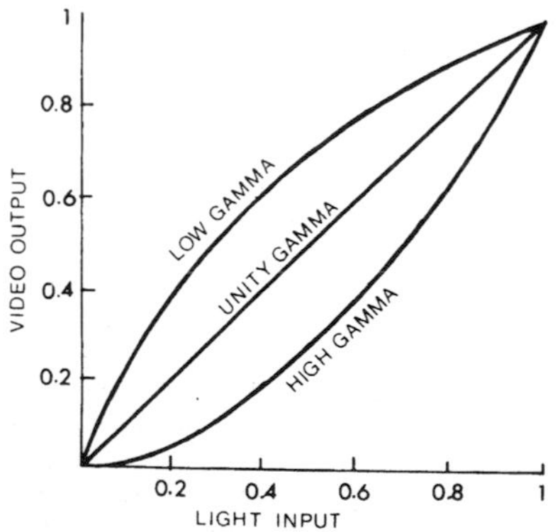

Gamma
The *gamma curve* reveals how a video system reproduces tonal gradation. Where a device is linear (gamma of 1) its output is proportional to the input. A *low gamma* device accepts a wide contast range, compressing it into the system's limits, resulting in reduced tonal contrast (thin). A *high gamma* device accepts only limited subject contrast, expanding it to fit the reproduction limits, giving exaggerated coarsened tonal values.

We can alter the subtlety or coarseness of tonal gradation in a picture by adjusting *gamma* controls. A *low gamma* results in thin, reduced tonal contrasts. A *high gamma* produces coarse, exaggerated tonal contrast. By readjusting the gamma, we can often provide greater clarity in shadows or lighter tones. However, there is the drawback that picture noise can become more pronounced with increased *gamma* correction. Occasionally one deliberately uses a higher gamma to emphasize tonal contrasts for dramatic effect.

High-definition television (HDTV) The original *NTSC* color system needed to be designed so that its transmissions could be viewed on existing 525 line black-and-white (monochrome) receivers. This necessitated many technical compromises. Various exploratory high-definition color television systems emerged, including the NHK/Sony system (1125 lines, 60-field scanning rate, having a picture aspect ratio of 5:3, interlaced 2:1, with the video bandwidth increased from the regular 4.5 MHz to 30 MHz).

When the US Grand Alliance Committee assessed standards for high-definition (*HDTV*) systems they approved 18 possible advanced TV formats, with differing resolution and scanning methods. All technical choices involve compromises, so while some organizations favor *interlaced scanning (i)*, others consider *progressive* or *sequential scanning (p)* preferable. The number of scanning lines for the three main DTV (*digital TV*) formats are 480 i, 720 p, 1080 i.

In 1997 the Technical committee of the World Broadcasting Union (WBU-TC) endorsed the unique HD-CIF standard of 1080 lines with 1920 samples per line, as a common standard for both 60 Hz and 50 Hz scanning rates, for high-definition program production and exchange.

Hyperfocal distance When the lens is focused at infinity (∞), focus remains sharp from infinity to a plane near the camera. When focused at this *hyperfocal distance (H)* the scene is sharp from about distance $\frac{1}{2}H$ to infinity:

$$H \text{ in meters} = \frac{(\text{focal length in cm})^2 \times 100}{\text{lens } f\text{-stop number} \times 0.05}$$

Image enhancement Electronic correction and improvement of video signals by a *video processor*. This includes corrections such as crispening edge sharpness (high-frequency synthesis), edge color-fringe removal, color-displacement correction (chroma/luma delay), reduced noise ('snow remover'), suppressing 'ringing' at edges, and improved small image detail, sync regeneration.

Image stabilizers Various forms of *image stabilizer* have been devised to compensate for unsteady pictures, random camera movement or vibration. The camera itself may be supported and stabilized by a *sprung counter-balanced system* attached to a body harness (*Steadicam/Panaglide*). A sophisticated *gyroscopically stabilized lens* which resists irregular camera movements is favored by film crews using heavier equipment. A different approach is to compensate for slight variations by deliberately displacing the picture image itself in the opposite direction. A *vari-angle liquid* *prism system* alters shape to relocate the image. A mechanical *mirror system* readjusts as the current image is electronically compared with that immediately preceding it. Totally *electronic systems* selectively sample and modify readout of the CCD's charge pattern.

Iris controls There are times when *manual* iris adjustments are essential. When an overall lighter or darker picture is dramatically more effective. When we are shooting against the light and want to avoid underexposing the shot. Some camera lens systems do not give *full* manual control of the iris. Instead, it can be opened and closed manually by a fixed amount without deactivating the *auto exposure (auto iris)* mechanism. This arrangement allows the operator to gradually increase or decrease the exposure, and once adjusted, that amount of over- or underexposure remains (relative to the auto setting) until the control is readjusted. In-camera fades by opening or closing the lens iris are not always possible because the iris does not close completely. (Anyway, it is usually preferable to leave fades until editing or postproduction, for the in-camera result may be unsatisfactory.)

LCD (liquid crystal display) LCD technology relies on complex molecular structures which flow like a liquid and bend (refract) light. The *active* or *TFT (thin film transistor)* display used for color screens consists of a thin layer of semiconductor or magnetic material deposited on a ceramic, metal, or semiconductor base. An 800 by 600 pixel VGA color screen display involves around 1 440 000 separate transistor elements. Each pixel in the picture requires three transistors (triads), each with its separate red, green, and blue filter. The resulting display is sharp, with good contrast and color, and flicker-free.

Lens angle The horizontal coverage (field of view) of the lens; from frame left to frame right. The vertical lens angle is 3/4 the horizontal coverage in a standard 4 by 3 picture format. The actual coverage of a particular lens will depend on its focal length, the size of the camera's CCD, and the distance at which you are focusing the lens.

- *What is the lens angle, when using a focal length of X mm* (2/3 in CCD)?
  Divide 4.4 by the focal length. Find the ATN (i.e. $\tan^{-1}$) of the result. Multiply by 2 for the angle. So for 17 mm lens on a 2/3 in. CCD: 4.4 ÷ 17 = 0.2588.
  ATN = 14.511. Multiply by 2 = 29° (For a camera with a 1/2 in. CCD, substitute 3.2 for 4.4 above.)
- *What focal length is needed to give a coverage of X degrees with a 2/3 in. CCD?* Divide the required angle by 2. Find its TAN. Multiply the result by 2. Divide 1 by the answer. Multiply the result by 8.8. This is the focal length. So to obtain 29° horizontal angle with a 2/3 in. CCD:

  29 ÷ 2 = 14.5° TAN = 0.2586. Times 2 = 0.5172
  Reciprocal = 1.9333 Times 8.8 = *17 mm focal length*

  (For a camera with a 1/2 in. CCD, substitute 6.4 for 8.8 above)
- *For details of shot coverage* (width, distance, lens coverage), etc., see Figure 18.7

Lens design The *lens system's* main function is to focus a sharp image of the subject onto the camera's image sensor (see *CCD*). Even a single convex (outward curved) lens can do this within limits. But to provide an image which is equally sharp overall and has negligible distortion requires a corrective combination of several different types of lens. Otherwise there would be geometrical distortions (barrel or pincushion effects), and various other optical *aberrations* (such as astigmatism, coma, spherical and chromatic aberration, field curvature). These would reduce image sharpness, and result in uneven image brightness, blurring, light flares, color distortions.

The lens elements are *coated* with a microscopic layer which reduces internal reflections, glare, haloing effects, and arranged inside a metal tube (the lens *barrel*). Some of these lens elements are fixed, while others move together to adjust the focal length and the focusing actions. As a ray of light passes through a lens it is deflected (*refraction*) in a direction depending on the lens shape and its material. But some of the light is absorbed (*transmission* depends on its thickness) and some is scattered. The more elements involved in its design, the greater the light losses.

Within the lens system, a variable *iris* or *lens* aperture is fitted, which adjusts both the effective *image brightness* and the *depth of field*. (Typical maximum aperture stop for a 1/2 in. CCD is *f*/1.4, and for a 2/3 in. CCD is *f*/1.7.)

The lens system is attached to the camera by its *lens mount*. There are several designs; including screw-types *C-mount* (6 turns to install; as on 16 mm cameras) and *bayonet-lock* quick-release types. The latter simply key into the camera head with a half-turn (so are less liable to wear and damage than screw types). Suitable *lens mount adapters* are available if the lens fitting does not match the camera's. Typically, the lens mount also incorporates multiple electrical contacts for iris control, zoom position, and often auto-focus circuits.

The image size and proportions produced by the lens should match the active area of the image sensor to avoid overscanning (*image overspill*) or underscanning (spurious black borders or corners). Certain optical defects such as vignetting (corner shading), color shading, or lens diffusion may be compensated electronically by microprocessors which monitor optical parameters (*dynamic lens correction*).

Light measurement
Lumen. A unit of light output (luminous flux).

Lux, foot candle. Units of incident light intensity falling on a surface (illumination).

Nit, foot lambert. Units of surface brightness; reflected light intensity (luminance).

Nanometers, micron, angstrom. All units specifying wavelength of light (e.g. identifying spectral colors) and other electromagnetic radiation.

Kelvin. A unit of color temperature. (See *Mired.*)

Linear matrix masking When the color camera analyzes the scene into red, green, and blue images their relative proportions must be accurate; otherwise color values in the final picture will be incorrect. Certain unavoidable errors that arise in the camera system (e.g. due to the pick-up tubes' color response, imperfections in filters and dichroics) may be compensated by special electronic circuitry; a process known as *linear matrix masking*.

Lock-up time The time taken from starting a VTR (or telecine) for it to reach a stable running speed. Some helical recorders use *stand-by idling* (for recording) and *timebase correctors* (on replay) to reduce start-up time and picture instability.

Low-frequency extender (line extender) Audio equipment permitting regular phone lines to be used for 'broadcast-quality' commentary speech by suitable frequency shifting, filtering, etc. to remove clicks, pops, hum, and compensating for limited audio bandwidth.

Mired (microreciprocal degrees) Unit derived to classify a color filter, or the color temperature of a light source. It enables easy calculation of the color shift required to modify a light source's color quality. Mired value equals one million divided by the Kelvin value, e.g. 2500 K = 400 mired.

Mixed-minus (clean feed) A commentator often needs to be able to monitor pictures and sound of the program to which he or she is contributing in order to suit the shots, and avoid speaking while others are on-air. If they listened to the complete program sound they would hear their own voice fed back into their earphones/earpiece as they speak. Instead, they can be supplied with a special source-selective feed of the program sound, termed *mixed-minus* or a *clean feed*. They hear all program sound *except* their own contribution. Video *clean feeds* are also used.

Multi-vision (multi-screen) A large presentation using an assembly of adjoining TV or projector screens to form an extensive composite single or multi-image display. Sometimes indicates several images appearing simultaneously in the same frame.

Munsell color frame System of notation defining color through a set of charts showing *hue* (five principal and five intermediate hues), *value* (brilliance) in a scale of 10 steps from black to white, and *chroma* (saturation).

Noise reduction (NR) (See Chapter 12.) The major audio background noise-reduction systems are incompatible. Audio recorded with a given system must generally be reproduced by the same method; although some can be played satisfactorily, through suitable equalization adjustments on any reproducer (Dolby B). Each system has its associated compromises (e.g. need for careful alignment, or performance limitations).

In the complex *Dolby A* system used for professional recording the audio-frequency spectrum is filtered into four sections (bands). Each is individually treated, boosting very quiet signals, while leaving louder ones virtually unaffected. When decoded on replay, the original relative audio levels are restored, and background noises correspondingly reduced.

The *Dolby B* system is widely used for audio-cassette recording. It is level-selective, but operates only on the high-frequency end of the audio spectrum. So tapes recorded with *Dolby B* noise reduction are subjectively compatible when played without correction.

Dolby C offers improved noise reduction. Widely used for audio-cassette recording, it uses pre-emphasis; the frequency at which the boosting begins depending on the volume at that moment. There is corresponding de-emphasis on replay.

During audio taping the strength of the fixed bias current applied to the recording head is normally a technical compromise. (Lower bias improves high notes but worsens bass distortion, modifying the system's overall response.) The *Dolby HX* (*headroom extension*) adjusts the tape bias automatically, according to the high-frequency energy content of the program, to produce lower distortion levels overall.

The relatively straightforward *dBx* system does not split the audio spectrum, but applies routine pre-emphasis/de-emphasis to the program. The Telefunken *Telecom* and *High-com* systems have features similar to Dolby A, but with a constant compression.

The *Dolby SR* (*Spectral Recording*) process combines aspects of the A, B, and C systems, the playback complementing the recording process. During recording, quiet sounds are selectively raised above tape noise. Loud sounds are reduced below distortion levels, according to their energy content at different frequencies, so as to suit the ear's characteristics. A further Dolby system *ADM* is used with high-quality *digital* stereo sound systems.

Further facilities for reducing unwanted background noise include *noise gates* which selectively suppress low-level signals; and *notch filters* which reduce a narrow selected part of the audio spectrum (e.g. hum reduction).

One and a half heads (1.5 heads) principle A separate head records the vertical interval information near the lower edge of the tape, thus retaining VIRS, VITS, teletext.

Optical printer A special film-printing machine in which a filmed image is projected onto the film stock rather than printed by contact with it. The projected image can be independently exposed to provide optical transitions, superimpositions, size changes, freeze frame, step printing, speed and direction changes, skip frame, multi-image, traveling matte, image-position changes, image distortions, etc.

Overlapping sound An introductory editing treatment used when flat cuts join two dissimilar scenes. The sounds of the next scene are heard before the vision switches.

Overscanning If a picture on a monitor is expanded so that its edges are lost beyond the surround mask it uses the full picture-tube screen, and appears subjectively to be larger. But in fact all the picture information around the edges is being lost – sometimes including subtitles. In any production areas, monitors should be *underscanned* to show the entire TV frame (*raster*) including corners; for this will reveal when any unwanted subjects are peeking into shot (mikes, another camera, distracting items); and also display certain technical defects more clearly (e.g. sync problems shown by ragged picture edges).

Padding (fill) Improvised action/dialogue introduced when a program is underrunning, or *stretching* available material to fill the allotted time.

Panning head (camera-mounting head) Several designs are widely used. The cheapest and simplest is the *friction head*. For lightweight cameras, it relies on surface friction (stiction) between parts to steady pan/tilt movements. But it is not easily controlled, due to excess friction at the start of movements, and vertical balance cannot be adjusted.

The *fluid head* is an excellent all-purpose mounting head for light- to medium-weight cameras. Layers of high-viscosity silicon fluid dampen head movement and produce very smooth action, unaffected by temperature changes. Pan and tilt friction can be adjusted. For very fast movements, damping can be switched off. A spring element compensates for imbalance during tilting. The head often incorporates a leveling indicator. *Serial drag* systems have closely controlled viscous drag which allows smooth camera movements at any speed, including whip pans, without readjustments.

The *cradle head* is often used for heavy cameras. Large and cumbersome, its balance is fairly good, as the camera's center of gravity is distributed, but its tilt range is limited. Friction settings (drag) tend to be unreliable, and change in use.

Cam heads overcome these problems. These incorporate cams or cylinders on either side of the head to control pan and tilt movements. Drag is adjustable, and the head can be locked in chosen positions. Particularly suitable for heavier cameras, control is extremely smooth.

Perspective distortion Perspective effects strongly influence interpretation of space. Where the camera's lens angle and your viewing angle to the screen are comparable you see 'natural perspective', showing proportions and spatial impressions similar to those of everyday life. When a *camera moves* towards a subject to obtain a larger image (i.e. a closer shot), perspective remains consistent, the proportions of subjects are compatible, their relative positions and spacing changing as you approach.

Zooming, on the other hand, simply alters the overall magnification of the lens image, so these natural effects do not result. Although by reducing the lens angle you can fill the screen with a distant subject – so suggesting that it is close – the resultant image is generally dissimilar from the impression you would actually get at a close viewpoint. Instead, subjects show characteristics you normally associate with *distance*: depth in the picture appears foreshortened, and there is often considerable overlapping. Sizes do not diminish naturally with distance. You interpret such incompatibilities as *spatial compression*. A *spatial exaggeration* effect arises when a very wide camera lens angle is used. (The illusion of natural perspective can be restored by changing your viewing distance proportionally to the lens angle used.)

Pick-up A loose term for any separate shots recorded after the main program to be inserted during VT editing. They may be *corrective* (e.g. to enable action, dialogue, technical errors to be removed) or *detail inserts* (e.g. showing close-ups, location action, reactions, etc.) that could not be shot during the original take. Another type of '*pick-up shot*' is used to create an impression of speech continuity between sequences recorded at different places or at different times. *The guide standing on a clifftop, points to the beach below: 'Yesterday's storm has badly weakened the sea defences . . .' Cut to a shot of her on the beach showing us the damage. She continues without a break: 'and here you see how the cliff has broken away . . .'* In reality, of course, it took quite a while for speaker and crew with all their equipment to scramble down to second location and set up the new shot. But a small audio-tape recorder replayed the earlier words, to cue-in the second sequence. When the shots are edited together, the dialogue appears to be continuous.

Picture defects Many picture defects are overlooked by the uncritical eye: picture noise, reduced texture, artificial edges to subjects (ringing, reflections), color distortions, spurious moiré-patterning effects, (chroma-luminance interference), displaced color, edge jitter, crushing of highlights and shadows, flattened-out tonal gradations (cartooning), poor resolution of detail, inaccurate focus . . .! These effects will be visible (or worsened) on the home TV picture, together with additional defects such as ghosting (multi-images), etc. For the program maker these shortcomings must be reduced to a minimum, as they worsen in the course of multi-generation copying, videotape editing, transmission.

Picture monitors One's opportunity to assess picture quality and video equipment performance largely depends on the standards and adjustment of the picture monitor. Where monitor performance drifts (loses focus, convergence alters, color balance changes) or reproduction varies with picture content, judgement is very arbitrary.

Various types of picture-tube are used (Figure 3.4). The color temperature of a white screen on a correctly aligned color monitor is CIE illuminant *D65* (formerly illuminant C). While delta-gun dot-mask (shadow mask) tubes provide generally superior pictures, their convergence drifts with time (so subjects seem to develop color fringes). PIL tubes have improved convergence stability, but coarser resolution.

In black matrix screens the phosphor dots are laid down on a low-reflectance black background, so that less light is reflected from the screen surface. The picture-tube's resolution depends on the closeness and size of the screen's dot: from typical broadcast tubes (pitch of 0.47–0.63 per inch), to high resolution (0.43), and ultra-high (0.31).

Typical picture-tube performance is around: white 25 fL (max.) to black ½ fL (minimum limited by flare and dispersion in glass). Maximum contrast of 50:1 is possible, but 15:1 in a lighted room is more typical.

Picture noise *Noise* is the general term for the unwanted background disturbances that are produced when generating a picture or sound signal; i.e. the 'grain' in a picture, tape noise, hum. In an ideal world, this noise is so slight as to be undetectable. Systems are designed to have as high a *signal-to-noise* (*S/N*) ratio as possible. This is measured in *decibels* (*dBs*) in which the ratio of voltages is indicated by 20 × log10 *signal voltage* divided by *noise voltage*. So where, for example, one is 10 times as large as the other (10:1), there will be a 20 dB difference between them.

Although these technical parameters are mainly of interest to the engineer, it is helpful if we appreciate that whenever we increase the *amplification* of the video signal (e.g. to compensate for failing light) the picture noise becomes correspondingly more prominent. Switch camera gain to + 18 dB and an original satisfactory overall S/N ratio of e.g. 48 dB falls to 30 dB, so that picture noise ('*grain*'; '*snow*') becomes prominent.

In *a* digital system, the S/N ratio improves as the number of sample bits is increased. Thus while an 8-bit system (which can detect 256 differences in signal level variations) provides an S/N ratio of about 48 dB, when the sampling rate is increased to 12 bits (4096 levels) there is an improvement to a 72 dB ratio.

Picture quality A subjective grading scale may be used to assess video or audio quality (CCIR/CCITT).

Quality	*Grade*	*Impairment*
Excellent	5	Imperceptible defects
Good	4	Perceptible, but not annoying
Fair	3	Slightly annoying
Poor	2	Annoying
Bad	1	Very annoying

Piezoelectric effect A property of certain crystals, which produce a corresponding voltage across their outer faces when bent or twisted; and conversely, move when a voltage is applied to them.

Pilot tone VTR development in which a special frequency is recorded (1.5 times the color subcarrier) to provide constant monitoring and correction of the system's chrominance, as well as checking scanning synchronizing errors for improved time-base correction.

Pixillation Jerky fast motion effect created by regularly omitting frames from film shot at normal speed. *Also* an animation effect obtained by conjoining a series of still frames.

PLUGE Electronically generated image used to adjust picture monitors to a uniform standard. Picture comprises a vertical white bar, an area of reference black, and two reference tones slightly higher and lower than the reference by 2.5 IEEE/IRE units (Institute of Electrical and Electronic Engineers). The monitor is adjusted so that the darker patch merges with reference background, the brighter patch still remaining visible.

Post-syncing The process of recording sound (speech, sound effects) to synchronize with an existing picture – as when replacing original dialogue with a different language, closely following the original lip movements; or when fitting convincing new sound to a mute print.

Pressure zone microphone A form of high-quality electret microphone. Its flat baseplate contains a narrow slot through which sound reaches a diaphragm. Reflected and direct waves are in phase in the *pressure zone*, so that when the microphone is placed against a large reflecting surface it becomes non-directional.

Program interrupt (switched talkback) Many shows use a central performer to introduce and link items, interview, provide commentary, etc. This person can wear an earpiece through which to receive instructions/guidance from the director or program associates, unheard by the studio microphone (typically, suggesting interview questions, explaining last-minute changes or emergency situations). This intercom circuit remains silent until activated by a switch in the production control room. Or alternatively, the earpiece circuit may carry program sound, which is interrupted and replaced by intercom whenever the director needs to contact the performer; who can acknowledge silently with a gesture, or speak over a local microphone.

Quadruplex (quad, transverse) VTR Now obsolete, this high-quality system uses a 2 in. wide magnetic tape moving at 38 cm/s. A full-width erase head demagnetizes the tape, which passes a transverse headwheel with four recording/replay heads. Mounted 90° apart, these scan across the tape in turn recording a series of parallel transverse video tracks (effective writing speed 3800 cm/s or 1500 ips). Each track records 16 lines in 525 systems (20 lines, 625 systems). Interhead switching ensures continuous recording/replay. The audio, control, and cue tracks are located along the tape edges.

Ramping As you adjust a lens' *aperture* (*iris*), the intensity of its image varies so affecting the picture's exposure. These changes in the image brightness are calibrated in. '*f*/stops'. (Each *f*/stop is 1.414 times the lower one.) A stop's value is calculated from the *effective diameter of the aperture (iris), divided by the focal length.* From this it follows that any changes in the zoom lens' *focal length* – e.g. through zooming – would normally alter the image brightness or exposure too! Zoom lenses are therefore designed to compensate for such exposure variation by adjusting the iris as the focal length is changed. The aperture is reduced slightly at the wide-angle setting and increased as the angle narrows to keep exposure constant throughout. However, if you are shooting under low-light conditions, with a fully opened wide-angle lens . . . and then zoom in to a close-up, there is a chance that the picture will now be underexposed, because the lens aperture has already reached its maximum, and can go no further! This fall in image brightness is called *ramping* (*f*/drop). If it happens, you can only attempt to compensate by increasing the video gain.

Remote control (See *Robotic cameras*) There are two forms of remote control. In *partial control*, a *camera operator* handles the actual camera while a remote *vision control operator* adjusts the lens *f*/stop (exposure) and various electronic parameters (gamma, black level, etc.). In *total remote* or *fully robotic control* all cameras are connected to a central desk by cable, wireless, or infrared systems, and controlled by a single operator, who may handle up to eight remote cameras. All camera operations including pan, tilt, zoom, focus, lens settings, and perhaps camera height and position are controlled through a touch screen and a joystick control at the control desk – although controls can be overridden at the camera if necessary. The robotic system stores miniature stills of preset shots, which are displayed on a control panel. Touching the required picture moves and adjusts the camera to that rehearsed shot or move.

Resolution The maximum vertical detail that any TV/video system can display is determined initially by the standard being used (i.e. 525 lines, 625 lines). While most of these scanning lines provide picture information seen on the screen (*active lines*), some occur during the vertical retrace period (i.e. when the scanning spot is returning from the bottom right of the picture, to the top left, ready to begin scanning the next field). So they do not contribute to the picture display.

Horizontal resolution is measured by the maximum number of black and white vertical lines that can be discerned. (A resolution of 480 TV lines allows 240 black and 240 white lines to be discerned.) Most manufacturers' specifications indicate the *extinction point* at which detail can no longer be seen – although in fact, the clarity of detail progressively deteriorates over about 350 TV lines in the scene. In practice, the overall resolution of a system will depend on the specification and performance of each stage in the system; from the lens to the picture monitor or television receiver.

Robotic cameras (See *Remote control*) Robotic camera system may be remotely controlled or function automatically to a programmed schedule. Robotics are generally used in semi-static situations, such as newscasts, where the action follows limited or predictable routines. The system can store program shot details, dolly movements, pedestal elevation, etc. and free-roaming robotic pedestals can be arranged to exactly follow an easily laid adhesive floor marked track.

Rostrum camera Two basic forms are used. (1) A vertical TV camera shoots an animation table, where successive drawings (or cells) are displayed on a horizontal surface; top lit, or illuminated by a light-box underneath. The results are recorded on a VTR or magnetic video disc. (With *two-frame animation*, changes are made after every other exposed frame.) In sophisticated designs, camera movements, zoom, table position changes (N/S, E/W), exposure rate, etc. are computer-activated. (2) Another system projects a video recording of live action (a frame at a time) onto a glass screen, where it is traced on a cell to derive an animated cartoon.

Rotoscope In film this is a frame-by-frame process which allows a series of pictures to be modified or adjusted in some way; e.g. to compensate for matting errors (spurious breakthrough effects). Typically, the original film frame is projected onto a peg-registered drawing board, and corrective hand-drawn '*garbage mattes*' used to hide defective areas. The corrected image is then photographed a frame at a time on a rostrum camera (animation rostrum). An allied technique is used in the aftertreatment of video images.

Scan converters To convert the *digital* output of a PC, Mac, or workstation display to a standard *video* signal you need a *scan converter*. Designs range in complexity from those that will transform their outputs into a NTSC, PAL, or S-Video signal for a regular TV monitor to more sophisticated versions providing precise signals that can be recorded on VHS and S-VHS videotape recorders. Higher quality scan converters overcome such problems as *flicker* (by converting the computer's *sequential/progressive* scanning process into the *interlaced scanning* process of the *video system*), and *genlock* (correcting picture instability and color shifts). A scan converter may also include freeze frame and overscan features.

Sensitivity, Camera Statistics showing the minimum light levels required by various camera systems can be misleading. In practice, standards used by manufacturers differ (IRE level varies). When assessing different types of camera there are variations between EFP, ENG, and high-end illumination required to give 'usable' picture quality (an arbitrary value). Even with the lens aperture wide open, the AGC control (automatic gain) on, and video amplification maximum (e.g. +18/+20 dB; 8 or 10 times gain), and disregarding picture noise, these conditions may still not give a full video signal. Some refer to the lowest light level that will give a 'usable' signal output. Others quote the amount of light needed at a particular *f*/stop, to obtain a full 100 per cent video signal. The *sensitivity of a camera system is best defined as:* the lens *f*-stop required to produce a full 100 per cent video signal of 100 IRE units, when the scene *illumination* is 2000 lux; the *video gain* is zero (0 dB); the *scene reflectance* is 89.9 per cent the *color temperature* is 3200 K; the system's *gamma* adjustment is on (+0.45); *black compression* is off; and *auto knee* correction is off.

Servers A multi-platter hard disk store forming a multimedia library which serves as a central supply point for video and audio information. Several users at diverse *workstations* can random access the server sumultaneously; extracting, updating, copying the same data. Photostills ('slides'), video clips, graphics, artwork, titles, text, scripts, music, reference material (e.g. maps) can all be accessed immediately. Data may be compressed to increase storage capacity. The server's overall capacity may range from several minutes to hundreds of hours of data. Cross-indexing allows browsing and rapid tracing. More limited facilities referred to as *disk packs* or *disk farms* provide data stores on disk drives, but without a sophisticated operating system database or filing system.

Shutter speed In a photographic system how long the lens shutter remains open when making an exposure is adjustable (*shutter speed*). It is independent of the *f*/stop used. If the film is exposed for too long relative to the speed of the subject movement, the result will be a blurred or trailing image of the action. The picture rate in a TV system is fixed at 30 (25). So the 'effective shutter speed' can only be shortened by electronically reducing the CCD's exposure time. Shortened exposure time results in sharper, more distinct pictures of movement. Details of a moving subject will be clearly defined in a frozen shot. However, short exposure times result in jerky, stroboscopic, flickering effects, even on simple movements (e.g. a moving arm). And to compensate for such brief exposure, the lens aperture may need to be increased, so reducing the depth of field. A multi speed electronic shutter may cover a range of: 1/50; 1/60; 1/125; 1/250; 1/500; 1/1000; 1/4000 second.

Simultaneous contrast (spatial induction) A visual illusion in which the apparent tone, color, and size of an area is modified by its background. A light-toned area appears lighter and larger against a dark background; a dark area even darker against a light one. Similar interaction arises in color, where an area may look cool (bluish) against a dark background and warm (red/yellow) against light tones. A colored background may modify the appearance of the foreground subject, often biasing its color towards a complementary hue. Juxtapose red and blue, and the red will seem quite orange while the blue has a greenish tinge. A strongly colored subject may similarly influence a neutral background tone.

Single-sensor color camera Simpler color TV cameras reduce cost and weight by using only *one* image sensor instead of the three in high-grade designs. The natural-color lens image is split into the three component colors R, G, B by attaching a striped color filter to the front of the camera-tube target (external or internal). This filter may have red, green, blue stripes overall, or a combined pattern of cyan/clear stripes and diagonal yellow/clear stripes.

In the latter type the red component of the scene is recovered from the clear (luminance) stripes and the cyan (minus red) stripes. The blue component is recovered from the yellow and clear (blue is 'minus yellow'). The green signal is derived from the other components. The result is ingenious, but inevitably of lower color quality and definition than more complex optical systems.

Single-system sound Audio recorded directly onto film soundtrack (or integrated VTR), using a mike on top of the camera. Automatic gain circuits control audio levels. In *double systems* a separate camera and synchronized audio recorder are used; picture and sound being combined during editing, or reproduced in sync on separate equipment (*double headed*).

Slate (clapperboard, clapstick) An identification board used during filming. Shown before a shot; or inverted if taken at its end. The hinged top section is brought down quickly to produce a loud noise, which enables the separate picture and soundtrack (double system) to be synchronized during editing. Electronic *time code* systems of synchronizing are increasingly used.

An electronically generated '*slate*' with a time-remaining clock is widely used as a VTR 'slate'/leader.

Slides

Standard 35 mm slide format. Mount 50 × 50 mm (2 × 2 in); aperture 36 × 24 mm; aspect ratio 3:2.

Superslide format. Similar mount size; aperture 40 × 40 mm (1.6 × 1.6 in).

Slide scanner An optical projector or flying-spot scanner used to televise transparencies. Plastic-mounted slides are fitted into pairs of drums, discs, or trays (typical capacities of 36–40). Selection may be sequential (instantaneous) or random (delayed) from the production switcher position. Scanners do not usually permit size and position adjustments of the image. (See *Electronic still store.*)

Slow motion Occasionally we need to replay a recorded action sequence in slow motion (*slo-mo*) to demonstrate movements more clearly or create an artistic effect. The three main methods of achieving slow motion use video tape, magnetic disk or RAM stored data. Which is most effective depends on the situation. Do you simply want to play an action sequence more slowly than normal (e.g. a dreamy dance)? Or to recapture and linger over an unexpected moment during game play – which may involve stopping and running back the recording, which is quickly replayed on cue?

SuperMotion tape uses a special video camera shooting at 75 frames per second. When replayed at around 25 fps, slow motion results. It cannot replay its high-quality pictures while continuing to record, but the tape winds rapidly to selected cue points. *Disk-based systems (EVS)* allow instant random access to over 31 hours of compressed material, as well as providing limited video effects (split screen; digital zoom). *Solid-state RAM-based recording* gives instant access for up to 5 min replay of continuously recorded material; with slow-mo, vari-speed, forwards/reverse replay effects.

Slow motion replay of pictures from standard TV and film systems can be disappointing. Shot at regular 30 (25) pictures or frames a second, the exposure of each is normally too extended to capture sharp images of fast movement. Although the resulting blurring is not obvious at normal speeds, it can be unacceptable in frozen frames or when replayed slowly.

Fast *electronic shutters* on video cameras reduce the exposure time, allowing movement to be captured more effectively. (See *Shutter speed.*) This reduces exposure time; but movement can appear jerky and unrealistic. Stroboscopic effects can develop. To successfully capture very fast movement (e.g. a falling raindrop) special *film* cameras are needed, shooting at 64–100 frames each second or much more.

For *fast-motion time-lapse effects* in which flowers grow rapidly and clouds speed across skies, a videotape recorder is arranged to make a series of brief recordings at selected intervals (every 10 seconds, every minute, hourly, daily) triggered by a timing device (e.g. *intervalometer*).

Slow-motion controller This device provides instant slow-motion replay on a 25 mm (1 in) helical VTR. A cue-mark is added while recording. When cued, the system rapidly rewinds the tape, ready to replay at variable slow speeds, with freeze-frame options.

Sound in syncs A system in which audio is digitally encoded, and introduced into the composite video signal, during the line syncs period. Thus both video and audio can be transmitted on one carrier instead of requiring two separate transmission systems.

Staging The design and arrangement of scenic elements (scenery, furniture, props) to create a practical and artistically suitable working environment; permitting appropriate action, shots, sounds.

Staircase (step wedge) Video test signal generated to provide a series of distinct brightness steps from black to white.

Standards converters (Transcoder) Used primarily to convert composite picture signals originating from one TV system (e.g. NTSC) to another incompatible system (e.g. PAL).

Conversion problems include: motion judder/blur, color errors, horizontal edge-flicker. Various degrees of design sophistication exist, but six-field storage equipment provides more accurate movement rendition, is free from drift, and includes such operational features as freeze frame, noise reduction, technical corrections (blanking errors, head-switching, frame break-up).

Teletext (Oracle, Ceefax, Antiope, Telidon) Systems for the digital transmission of written information and diagrams during vertical interval period – for selective display of data on visual display units or home TV receiver.

Television systems All color TV pictures are distributed or transmitted in coded form (not as separate RGB signals).

NTSC (National Television System Committee). The three primary color video signals (RGB) are transformed by a coder into a *luminance* (brightness) signal conveying the tonal values and two special *chrominance* or color difference signals (I and Q). I and Q signals are used to simultaneously modulate the chrominance subcarrier; its strength (amplitude) varying with a color's saturation at that moment, and its phase changing with the hue (quadrature modulation). The resultant complex transmitted wave therefore contains both chrominance and luminance information. Color errors can arise in the path from transmitter to receiver (phase errors). Corrective receiver circuits increasingly use *VIR* signals to regulate these errors. Overall bandwidth 4.2 MHz. Color subcarrier 3.58 MHz.

PAL (*Phase alternating line*). Basically a similar system, but one of the color difference signals is reversed in phase on alternate line, so that slight color errors due to phase shift are averaged out. (Greater errors become visible as *Hanover bars*.) Overall bandwidth 5.5 MHz. Color subcarrier 4.43 MHz.

SECAM (*Sequential color and memory*). Similarly derived, but here the chrominance signals are transmitted one at a time sequentially, on alternate lines of each field to average out phase errors. (A delay line stores and reinserts color information.)

All three systems can exhibit 'herringbone' (moiré) or 'crawling dot' patterns.

Time-base correction Any disturbance of synchronizing pulses in a color system can cause such picture defects as jitter, frame roll (vertical), skew or hooking at the top of frame, scalloping at edges, hue and saturation errors. (Helical scan recorders are very susceptible to such irregularities.) Ingenious circuitry can reduce such scanning errors by using delay lines (as in analogue *time-base correctors*, TBC), or by digital storage of a full frame of video information (as in *frame synchronizers*). Sophisticated digital correctors have overcome certain problems in video switching and remote source synchronizing, and in satellite transmission.

Time code This is a specially generated digital code based on the 24-hour clock; recorded with a video or audio program, to provide continuous shot identification. The original standard time code (*longitudinal time code – LTC*) is widely used, in NTSC and EBU forms.

Where time code is recorded on an edge track (*longitudinal time code – LTC*) the tape must move past a replay head at over one-fifth normal speed to be read reliably. On stopping the tape motion (for a still frame), code readout ceases altogether, although the video replay heads continue to scan, reading out the *picture information*. But during VT editing, tape motion varies considerably: fast search, slow motion, jogging (frame by frame). To overcome this dilemma, another time-code format was introduced (*vertical interval time code – VITC*) in which the code is recorded in the vertical interval (retrace) period, and read out by the video heads, so is always available with the picture at all tape speeds.

Whereas the LTC format codes at *frame rate*, decoded at the end of the video frame, the VITC format is a *field-rate code*, decoded at the start of each video field, and odd/even fields are identified. Unlike the LTC format, where picture and its corresponding time-code pick-up points are displaced along the tape (offset), the VITC is read with its picture.

Because the NTSC system scans at 59.9 Hz, using a 60 Hz power supply, there would normally be a progressive difference between the time code reading and clock time (3.6 seconds' error per hour). To compensate for this, a couple of frames are dropped from the time-code count for 9 minutes out of every 10 (i.e. 108 frames per hour). This *drop frame* convention has been widely adopted. Where time code is used in *zero start mode* this error is unimportant, and correction may not be used. But it is essential that computer facilities are not presented with a mixture of 'drop-frame' and 'non drop-frame' tapes. For non-critical applications where frame-accurate edits are not involved, *drop-frame* precision is not necessary. This makes editing correspondingly easier.

Simpler editor systems often count control track pulses (deriving 'user bits') to aid frame identification during editing. However, this process has several disadvantages compared with time code, when editing is at all complex. Reading errors arise while shuttling tape to and fro, so that frame counts are only approximate. Unlike time code, this method cannot locate specific tape points. Nor can it be used for precise control of other equipment during editing, such as multi VTR playbacks, audiotape replay, switchers (for transitions between shots), digital video effects. To summarize, there are several forms of time code in use today, which can be used to identify individual frames or time-positions throughout a video or associated sound recording:

EBU time code (European Broadcasting Union) – Relates to 25 frames/second, 625/50 scanning system. Used by most UK operators.
SMPTE time code – Relates to 30 fps (actually 29.97 ps), 525/60 scanning system specified by ANSI (American National Standards Institute).
LTC (Longitudinal time code – Written on an edge track of the videotape. Readings are frame accurate during normal speed and fast shuttling; but not at slow speeds or freeze frame. On some VTRs, this occupies a longitudinal audio track.
VITC (Vertical interval time code) – Recorded on free scanning lines during the vertical interval (framing bar). Read by the rotating video head, it is frame accurate at all tape speeds and on stationary tape. Part of the video signal, the TC cannot be added afterwards.
TCIV (Time code in vision) or *BITC (Burnt-in time code*) – The numerical display panel set into the screen, for off-line editing, showing the tape's LTC or VITC data.
User bits; RCTC (Rewritable consumer time code) – Spare digital data capacity available for custom use (manufacturer or user). Carrying a four-character code word during the vertical interval; can be used for log information.
Control track pulse count – A facility for locating a tape position by counting the control pulses. Poor accuracy; particularly following tape stretch.
CTL-TC (Control track time code – A facility on *S-VHS videotape recorders (JVC*), in which the width of the control track pulses on the tape is varied to carry time code information. So frame-accurate locations are available, even when the tape has been spooled or reinserted. This technique frees the edge track that would otherwise be used for time code information for other use (e.g. logging). This code can be added during recording, or later by '*post-striping*'. (This is not a *pulse-counting* operation.)

Time compression Circuitry that strategically adjusts the length of pauses on replay of a taped program, by just a few milliseconds, enables the overall duration to be adjusted automatically by e.g. 3–6 minutes in a 30-minute show (10–30 per cent contraction). Tape-transport speed is guided by a digital controller, which speeds up the tape very slightly, without obviously changing the audio pitch or showing perceptible visual disruption. This facility allows precise program-duration adjustment to a fixed time slot without having to edit the tape unduly.

Translator Equipment used to extend the service area of a TV station by receiving the transmitted signal, boosting it, and retransmitting at increased power.

Transmission numbers (T) The *f*-stop number is based on physical aperture size, and disregards light-transmission losses and reflections between. *T-stops* are based on the actual amount of light passed by the lens system. In practice, these systems are comparable.

Traveling matte A film-printing process in which a matte or mask silhouette is derived from a subject image to block out a selected area of another picture. This permits the subject (or other material) to be introduced into that area.

Traveling shot Any shots from a moving camera (e.g. tracking shot).

UHF Ultra-high frequency. TV transmission band *above* Channel 13, 470–890 MHz, (UK bands IV, V.)

Vectorscope A *vectorscope* is used to check and match the color fidelity of signals from various TV sources. A standard *color bars* test signal is fed into the source being tested (e.g. camera channel, VTR, telecine) and the resulting trace on the vectorscope's screen compared with small engraved boxes which show the precise NTSC standards. Simple readjustments of the video equipment ensure consistent accurate results.

That is just as well, for color generation in the NTSC system is a complex process, involving very precise changes in the *phase* (moment of starting) of chrominance signals relative to a constant standard (*color burst*). This is measured in degrees. Different phase angles result in different final colors. If this phasing is incorrect, all colors throughout the spectrum will be wrongly reproduced. A 'blue' area, for instance, could appear as a 'reddish-blue' or a 'greenish-blue' on the screen. We do not need to understand the technicalities involved, thanks to the vectorscope.

As the test signals's *red, green, blue, cyan, magenta, yellow* bars are scanned, a spot of light on the screen moves around the vectorscope's screen, which has a circular scale calibrated in degrees. It traces a twisting pattern as it moves to correspondingly-labelled boxes. Where the trace-ends fall outside these boxes, controls need to be adjusted on that channel's control unit. The spot's position round the circular display relates to the hue being scanned at that instant; while its distance from screen centre corresponds to its intensity. Colored pictures appear as spread jumbled patterns on the screen. A black-and-white picture traces a confused splotch of light at the center of the display. A white line out left from center, results from the television system's *color burst* reference signal, which determines its color accuracy and stability.

The vectorscope makes these precision measurements by comparing the chrominance components of the system's television signal: Q along the display's vertical axis, I along its horizontal axis (NTSC) – V and U in PAL systems. (See Figure 3.3).

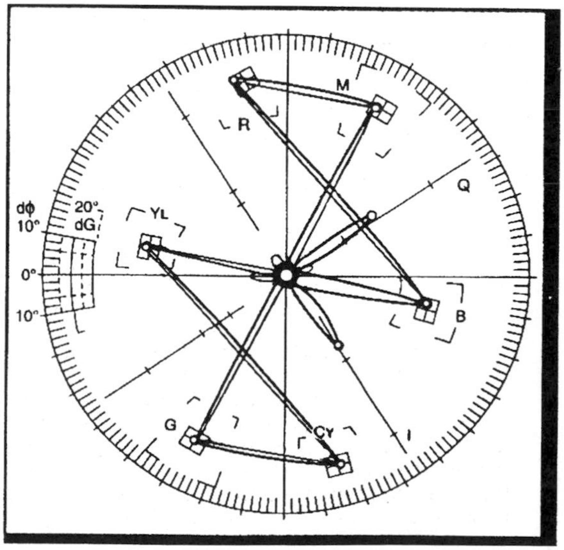

VHF Very high frequency. TV transmission band covering Channels 2–13, 54–216 MHz. (UK bands I, II.)

Video discs Following similar principles to the audio *compact disc*, the video disc format permanently stores picture and sound information digitally on a metalized disc surface in the form of a pattern of pits on a fine spiral. These are read optically by a reflected laser beam.

The video disc has unique storage merits, for it offers: continuous replay (e.g. an entire motion picture); *selective replay* (frame search, freeze frame, vari-speed); *still store* (thousands of individually selectable still frames); *interactive routing* (user-selected sequences from a menu); *disc/computer interfacing* (computer-selected stills, sequences, animation).

Although non-erasable, the video disc has the particular advantage over videotape systems that information is instantaneously selectable.

Video gain When a shot is underexposed due to insufficient light, or too small an *f*/stop, boosting the camera channel's *video gain (video amplification)* will brighten the image overall as the strength of the picture signal is increased. However, the brightness of the lens image falling on the CCD will still be below optimum, so any defects or noise arising from the image sensor itself will be greater than normal. Video gain may be increased in steps. A 6 dB increase will double the gain, and may provide very acceptable pictures with quite low light levels (around 150 lux (15 fc) at *f*/1·6. Increase the gain to a 12 dB boost, and only about 80 lux (8 fc) would be needed. Previously, high gains resulted in an unacceptable amount of picture noise ('snow', 'grain'), but now increases of some 24 dB to 36 dB offer considerably improved performance, thanks to advanced signal treatments (*integration techniques*).

Video signal The video signal is a voltage in analogue form of light and shade in the scanned image. During the

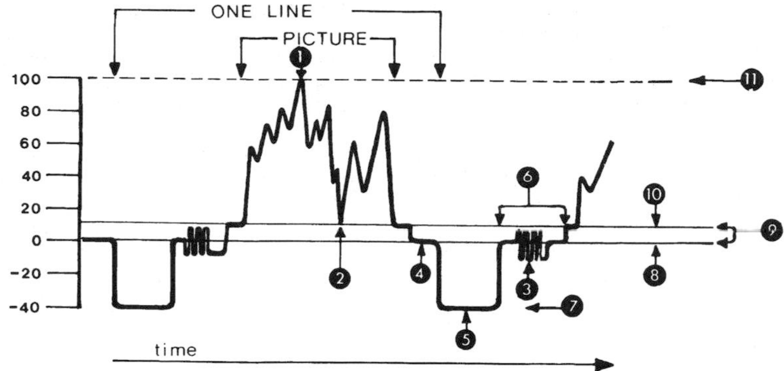

retrace periods after scanning a line any picture information is suppressed (*blanking*), and a horizontal (line) synchronizing pulse is inserted. This ensures that the entire TV system scans in step. In addition, a brief burst of subcarrier frequency provides a color reference signal to ensure color accuracy.

In a 525-line TV system the system scans the lens image in 262.5 lines in 1/60 second. When this *odd field* is complete, the system retraces to scan between the first set of scanning lines, to provide the *even field*. The odd and even fields are *interlaced* to form one complete *frame*. Thirty of these frames (i.e. 15 750 lines) are scanned each second. Of the 525 lines, 485 actually contribute to the picture information (are *active*). Others are scanning during the blanked-out vertical retrace period.

In a 625-line system the respective figures are: 312.5 lines per field, scanned in 1/50 second; 25 complete frames per second; 15 625 scanning lines per second.

At the end of each complete field a further synchronizing pulse is introduced for vertical stabilization (*vertical sync pulse*). Additional signals may also be included (*VIRS, Teletext*).

The illustration shows details of one complete scanning line, together with the names of its various features: 1 Peak white (peak modulation); 2 Peak black. 3 Color burst; 4 Front porch; 5 Horizontal (line) sync pulse; 6 Back porch; 7 Synchronizing level (sync level); 8 Blanking level; 9 Set-up (pedestal); 10 Reference black (black level); 11 Reference white (white level).

The video or picture signal from the camera may be transmitted through the television system in several different forms. So you will find a variety of input and output connections on video equipment from camera and videotape recorder to picture monitor.

- *Composite form*: Encoded as a single complex NTSC, PAL, or SECAM signal, complete with the synchronizing information (*sync pulses*). This has the advantage of being a simple one-wire system. Here the *luminance signal (Y)* provides brightness and detail, while color information (*chrominance (C)*) is integrated into two separate signals (IQ or UV) from the original red, green, blue ('*RGB*') color signals.

  This encoded color information is conveyed by a short burst of pulses within the sync period back porch (at 4.43 MHz). The composite signal is distributed in this form and decoded in picture monitors to recover the separate luminance and color components. Unfortunately, during the *decoding* process difficulties can arise in distinguishing between some luminance and color signals which results in visible interference patterns. These become more pronounced if the recording is copied, causing picture quality to deteriorate noticeably.

  In typical home videocassette recorders the *composite signal* is fed into a *modulator unit* (a miniature transmitter) where superimposed on an *RF (radio frequency) carrier*, it is routed to the antenna (aerial) socket of a TV receiver. Here it is subsequently *demodulated* (turned back into a composite signal) and then *decoded* to recover the R G B signals.
- *Component form*: The three video signals representing the red, green, and blue elements of the color picture are not equal. Because the human eye is more sensitive to the green/yellow part of the spectrum, the proportions of the primaries added together to produce the 'white' luminance signal Y differ; 59 per cent of the green signal, 30 per cent of the red, and 11 per cent of the blue, provide a panchromatic monochrome picture. In a *component-based* system, special *color difference* signals are derived which technically simplify handling of color information and compensate for this unbalance.

  Where a system works with video in *component* form, there is considerably less deterioration. Although the video signal needs to be translated back into *composite (NTSC, PAL, or SECAM)* form for transmission. There are *three* approaches to avoiding the decoding problems that are inherent in composite systems.

1 In '*Y, R-Y, B-Y component recording*' (or '*true*' component video) there are three signals: the luminance signal (Y) and two derived chrominance signals (R-Y and B-Y) which are kept entirely separate in the system. This format is used for *EFP (electronic fim production)* and *ENG (electronic news gathering)*, and is widely used for broadcast tape recording.

2 The '*Y/C*' (or '*color-under*') format is semi-professional. This method, which is used in VHS and S-VHS systems, involves two signals. It handles the luminance (brightness) signal (Y) as normal but the R-Y and B-Y elements are combined to form a single *chrominance signal (C)*. The luminance and chrominance (color) information is recorded on separate carrier frequencies, using filters on replay to distinguish between them.

Problems can arise in this differentiation, causing such visible effects as: detail loss (above about 2 MHz), chroma noise in color, moiré patterns, edge sparkle, color displacement, ringing (edge repeats), 'cartooning' (plain areas lack texture). However, these defects may be considerably reduced and definition increased, by raising the carrier frequency of the luminance signal, as in S-VHS systems.

3 In the *'digital'* approach, the analogue signals are digitized to provide virtually distortionless processing – although there can be visual inaccuracies as digital signals are translated into component or composite form within the system (*D to A, or A to D conversion*).

- *RGB form*: This is a three-signal method in which the red, green, and blue video signals are kept separate as they travel through the system from point of origin to display screen. This provides optimum color reproduction. Used in computer systems, it is not generally used for television videotape recording owing to technical complications.

Videotape formats This is a highly competitive field. Of the many systems that have reached the market, some are preferred in particular regions or by certain organizations. Some became established, while others lapsed. At the time of writing, Sony, Panasonic. JVC are offering broadcasters 13 different formats; and three new digital formats have become available – five including DV variants.

The equipment that records the video and its accompanying sound can take several forms, depending on its intended use: part of a permanent studio installation; a stand-alone field recorder, a dockable unit (which is attached to a portable camera), or integrated into a camcorder.

Some systems have features that make them particularly suitable for particular applications. For instance, Sony's *DVCAM* and Panasonic's *DVCPRO* formats lend themselves to news gathering. *DVCPRO* can transfer data at ×4 real-time speed to disk to facilitate quicker downloading preparation for editing. A *DVCAM* feature allows *key* frames to be stored on a chip, which will download instantly to its editor; so allowing an overview of shots for selection (*storyboard editing*) before the tape has even rewound.

The following survey outlines the basics of videotape formats in current use.

One-inch tape – Type-B format Widely used in countries with 625-line TV systems, this is a broadcast-standard open-reel video recorder making analogue composite recordings using a *segmented system*. Two video heads on a small split head-drum (190° *omega* wrap) scan the tape in turn, recording *total* picture information without loss or disturbance during the line-retrace/blanking period. Each records a succession of pictures (e.g. 52 lines) on their respective tape tracks. Their outputs are interswitched to provide continuous uninterrupted video output. (*'Banding'* can arise through inter-head switching.) The small head-drum mass results in greater speed stability, immunity to shock or gyroscopic effects during mobile recording. Simple tape threading (*lace-up*) reduces tape friction. High writing speed makes tape quality less critical. The short (80 mm) track length provides more accurate tracking and interchange compatibility. However, there is less room for confidence heads to check while recording. Along the tape edges are four independent longitudinal tracks; audio (two), time code; control track. There are differences between the *SMPTE/NTSC* and *EBU/PAL* formats. There are flexible recording and editing facilities, including slow motion, fast motion, and freeze frame (still frame). Tape speed 245 mm/s (9.65 in./s).

One-inch tape – Type-C format This broadcast-standard analogue composite video recorder is widely used in countries with 525-line TV systems. It uses a **non-***segmented* or *continuous system* of open-reel design in which the tape wraps round most of a split head-drum. A *single* video head mounted on the upper drum section (rotating at 60 or 50 rev/s field rate) records one *field* on each track. (Remember, it takes two interlaced fields, odd and even, to form one complete TV picture.) This method has certain technical advantages (simple freeze frame, vari-speed) but unfortunately, it omits 10 (or 12) picture lines from each field, and all the information during the vertical retrace interval as the rotating head loses tape-contact at the end of each scan. This lost information is either replaced from a *time-base corrector* store or recorded on a separate track by an additional *sync head* just in front of the *record head*. The 16 (or 19) lines the *sync head* records overlap the missing segment, so compensating for changes in tape tension, slow motion, and still-frame modes.

Where broadcast-quality slow motion or still frame is required, an extra video head is included, mounted on a piezoelectric element, which ensures optimum tracking accuracy (*dynamic tracking/autoscan*). Along the tape edges there are 3 (or 4) audio and one control track. All information in the TV vertical interval (blanking) period can be recorded where it contains control and logging data (e.g. for auto-opt-out or advertisement logging). In Europe an extra head can be fitted to record the vertical interval information or provide an extra high-quality fourth audio track. Audio tracks 1 and 2 are used for main program stereo sound (*SMPTE* record sum and difference signals; *EBU* record left and right hand channels) or provide an optional *PCM* digital stereo pair.

Because the rotating head-drum is large, gyroscopic errors may arise if the equipment is moved rapidly while recording which may not be within the range of a timebase corrector on replay. Scanner servos do help to reduce replay errors. Tape speed 244 mm/s (9.65 in./s)

Three-quarter-inch U-formats Initially designed for industrial/commercial/educational close-circuit use, the original *low-band (Standard U-format) ¾ – U-matic* was subsequently adapted to broadcast use, especially for ENG/EFP work. This obsolescent system is relatively bulky and sluggish in operation, and needs additional *timebase correction equipment (TBC)* or a *frame store synchronizer* to avoid picture jitter due to timebase irregularities, to achieve broadcast standards. *Tracking errors* develop when playback heads do not accurately follow the recorded track (tearing, flagging, picture breakup). Longitudinal tracks include two audio channels, control track, and time code address track (or lower quality audio), (Tape speed 95.3 mm/s)

- *¾-SP ('Superior performance')* – A development of the original analogue composite standard U-matic (but not compatible with it), specifically designed for broadcast use, and widely used in ENG/EFP production. The design includes slow- to high-speed search with picture; shuttling, jogging, freeze-frame facilities.

Half-inch formats Thanks to considerable developments in equipment design and tape performance videotape recorders have now become smaller and more efficient, with greatly enhanced picture and sound quality in both professional and consumer markets. Tape medium ranges from the regular magnetic oxide coating to cobalt-doped and metal-particle surfaces.

- *Betacam* – A widely used high-quality broadcast system derived from the earlier obsolete '*Beta*' (*Betamax*) system, run at high speed. Available as independent units or in dockable form to be fitted to camcorders. While the audio is recorded on longitudinal tracks, the video *luminance* and *color-difference* signals (R-Y; B-Y) are recorded in compressed form on separate alternate video tracks. (The original *Betamax* videotape recorder format is obsolete.) (Tape speed 118.58 mm/s)
- *Betacam-SP (Beta SP) – A 'superior performance'* development with greater video bandwidth, resulting in enhanced picture quality. Currently the main analogue component ½-in. MP cassette format used in broadcasting. Widely used for shooting and editing in news gathering, documentary, current affairs, corporate production. (Several design variants including *UVW* and *DVW*.) There are two longitudinal (linear) audio tracks. Two frequency-modulated audio tracks (AFM) may be recorded in addition to the compressed color-difference signals to provide very high quality analogue sound.
- *M-II* – A top-grade broadcast-quality ½-in MP cassette system, using an analogue component format, of similar quality to the *Betacam-SP* system. (Derived from '*VHS*'-type system running at high speed.) Two different audio recording modes: common audio mode, and PCM digital audio option. Available as independent units or in dockable form to be fitted to camcorders. A developed version (*M-II/LC*) has increased facilities and more flexible inputs (NTSC; RGB; Y/C). (Tape speed 67.69 mm/s)
- *VHS* – The ½ in. analogue composite '*Video Home System*' was originally marketed for home recording of of-air programs. Subsequently developed for broadcast and industrial use, it is extensively used for non-broadcast applications (industrial, corporate, educational, etc.). In broadcasting organizations, *VHS* recordings provide check copies of off-air programs, time-coded off-line editing copies, promotions, location reconnaissance, auditions, rehearsals, etc. The quality of the final picture and sound deteriorates noticeably if a copy is made of a copy of a *VHS* recording (third generation). (Tape speed 33.35 mm/s)
- *VHS-C (Compact)* – Similar system, using smaller cassette, used in small consumer cameras.
- *S-VHS* (Super VHS) – Development in which chrominance and luminance signals are more widely separated, providing superior performance very economically. *S-VHS* (like *Hi-8*) achieves a luminance resolution of +400 TV lines, compared with 240 lines of the *VHS* system. (A margin of 20 per cent over around 330 of today's television receivers.) Audio is recorded simultaneously on a CD-quality stereo multiplex *AFM* track with the video and on a mono edge (linear) track. The *audio dub* facility which allows existing audio track to be replaced on most VCRs is not practicable where the audio track has been multiplexed with the video as in *S-VHS* and *Hi-8*.

The quality of *a Super VHS*, like *Hi-8*, is sufficiently good to allow it to be broadcast effectively; either as a first generation picture or a version *dubbed-up* to a higher grade videotape format. So it may be used for newsgathering, particularly in hazardous or highly mobile situations, sports videography, etc. *S-VHS* is extensively used in small to midsize TV stations, cable and corporate TV, smaller production facilities of all kinds, including education, training, industrial use, as well as in the consumer field.

S-VHS recorders are available as independent units (portable or studio based) and as dockable units to be attached to an ENG/EFP camera. The recorder incorporates *time base correction (TBC)* to stabilize the picture during playback; an essential for accurate editing. While the *S-VHS* videotape recorder can effectively replay recordings made on a *VHS* machine, the reverse is not true. *S-VHS* (and *Hi-8*) systems use their own timecodes. (See *Time code*.) In an '*S-VHS supercam*' arrangement, program is recorded by an on-board *S-VHS* videotape recorder (which is subsequently used for off-line editing), while being *simultaneously recorded* at higher quality on a separate *Beta* VTR system for on-line use.

8 mm formats Developed to provide compact lightweight camcorders, this system has evolved from the original *8 mm* (*Video 8*) format to the superior *Hi-8* (*High 8; High-band 8 mm*) system which provides quality similar to *S-VHS*. Performance owes much to the high-grade tape used; metal particle (MP) or metal evaporated (ME) coatings. (Take care with ME tapes not to leave the VTR in '*record pause*' mode for any length of time as the tape coating can wear and stick to the head, subsequently producing dropout.)

- *Hi-8* – The *Hi-8* system is widely used as a *consumer format*. While professional, corporate, industrial program makers may use *Hi-8* for some ENG and EFP applications, they will invariably copy this tape onto a higher quality VTR system such as *Betacam* or *1-inch* (*dub-up, bump up*) before editing or duplication; because while pictures are initially superior, *Hi-8* picture quality deteriorates noticeably during multi-copying; and the audio progressively lags behind its video ('*generation lag*'). There is a tendency too for red areas to 'bleed' (a visual defect that digital versions overcome) and this becomes obvious in multi-generations.

  The recording process is rather more complex and less flexible than *S-VHS*. The information in each slanting track is laid down by rotating heads as a sequence of separate data segments: analogue component *video (Y/C), data area/time code*, followed by *audio*. Instead of a separate longitudinal *control track*, each helical track in the Hi-8 system recording includes *sync* information. A series of *flying erase heads* wipe tracks individually, so that the program can be edited (*insert or assemble*) without disrupting the picture. However, because the FM stereo sound is recorded as a series of brief segments, this not only results in '*generation lag*' but also means that this program audio cannot be substituted using regular *audio dub* methods. A separate edge track records analogue mono audio.

Digital formats Digital techniques offer considerable advantages in videotape recorder design; in data storage, image correction, stabilization. Several digital video recorder formats are used; more are being developed.

- *Digital Betacam* (BVW) *Sony* – A 'state-of-art' digital video recorder using ½ in. MP cassette tape. Component recording with bit-rate compression (2:1). Four digital audio tracks. One cue audio track (analogue). Duration: 6–124 min. Available in studio and portable (field recorder) configurations, for broadcast and facilities work.
- *Betacam SP* – Duration: 5–90 min.
- *Betacam SX* – A similar format, primarily intended for broadcast ENG and EFP work. Duration: 6–180 min.
- *Digital-S (JVC)* – Duration: 104 min.
- *DCT* – ¾-in. open-reel system. Digitally recorded component video, compressed 2:1. Two digital audio tracks. One analogue track. One cue track. Primarily used for postproduction work.
- *HDVS/HDD 1000* – An open-reel 1-in. high-density tape system for HDTV standards (1125/60). Component digital video. Three digital audio tracks. One cue audio track (8-bit). Duration up to 63 min. Mainly for HDTV film and TV production.

D-1 – This top-class *component* system records on ¾-in. (19 mm) metal particle tape and is mainly used for postproduction work. Its excellent resolution and low picture noise together with its separated color components make it particularly suitable for graphics applications, where pictures are combined – in compositing, layering, and multiple keying – and several generations of copying are involved. Because most regular video equipment (such as picture monitors, switcher, etc.) is designed for *composite* signals, compatibility problems can arise when introducing a videotape recorder with a *component* format into the video chain.

Data is recorded digitally on a special, fast-moving tape (287 mm/s) in the form of the usual parallel helical tracks, each containing six sectors: the video segment, and four *audio* segments (sampled at 48 kHz); two before, and two after the video. 250 consecutive lines from each picture field are recorded – as three segments of 85 lines each. A pair of opposite edge tracks record control pulses and time code respectively. A longitudinal track records audio *cue signals* (analogue) which are used for reference during editing.

D-2 – This top-grade system records *composite video* signals on a ¾ in. (19 mm) metal particle cassette tape. Because the format uses a composite (i.e. NTSC, PAL) configuration, the compatibility problems of the *D-1 format* do not arise. Where program making does not involve multigeneration copies and picture manipulation, but only straightforward editing, this system is particularly successful. Track arrangements are similar to D-1 format; six helical tracks are used to record each TV field. (Tape speed 131.7 mm/s)

D-3 – This compact portable high-quality digital format, records *composite video* in compressed form on ½-in. MP cassette tape. One video channel and four separate digital audio channels; each able to be edited independently. Horizontal edge tracks include (top edge) *cue track*, and *control* and *time code tracks* (lower edge). A full-width erase head is used for continuous recording and a flying erase head for insert editing. Track arrangements are similar to D-1 format; six helical tracks are use to record each TV field. (Tape speed 83.88 mm/s)

D-5 – Using a ½-in. MP cassette system, the digital video is *un*compressed (10-bit, 4:2:2). This format has the advantage that its sampling rate can be switched between 13.5 MHz and 18 MHz to accommodate both 4:3 and 16:9 screen formats. Each TV field is recorded on 12 tracks (525/60) or 16 tracks (625/50) by a ten-head central scanning drum. Each track includes a video sector followed by four digital audio channel sectors and a second video sector. The longitudinal tracks are for *cue, control*, and *time and control code*. (Tape speed 167.23 mm/s)

D-6 – A ¾-in./19 mm digital system, recording video and audio data of various image standards (up to e.g. 1 Gbit/s). Each slant track comprises a series of 270 *blocks* of data patterns (including sync information), distributed in three main sectors; audio – video – and audio. The total number of audio channels available (10/12) depends on the TV standard. Three longitudinal tracks carry *index, cue*, and *control information*.

D-7 – See *DVCPro* below.

Digital videotape systems Many digital tape formats are currently available, including:

High definition formats: *D-5* HD (P); HDCAM (S); Digital-S 100 (J); DVCPRO 100 (P)
Standard definition 1/2-in: *D-5* (P); Digital Betacam (S); Digital-S *(D-9)* (J); Betacam-SX (S)
DV-based 6.35 mm (1/4 in.) formats: DVCPRO 50 and DVCPRO (P); DVCAM (S); DV (various)
Consumer data format: D-VHS
Note: P = Panasonic; S = Sony; J = JVC.

Differences in the design of digital videotape recorders mean that while some are totally digital others also include edge tracks of analogue recorded information. The tape's slant tracks now include a variety of data rather than program video alone. Recorded by the same rotating heads, video data and sound data (generally using time compression) is stored in a series of sectors or blocks along the track. It is decoded on replay. Other data sectors may include timing signals, pilot signal, subcode, etc. Edge tracks may include control, cue, time code, and audio tracks, depending on design.

- *DV* – The lightweight DV digital tape system was primarily designed as a consumer standard, and may be replayed on DVCPro VTRs.
- *DVCPro* (*Panasonic*) – Standardized as the SMPTE *D-7* format, and intended for newsgathering (ENG), EFP, sport, cable, business and industrial applications. DVCPro (Professional) uses 1/4 in. (6.35 mm) tape. A double-speed professional version of the DVC consumer format, uses a 15 micron track pitch on metal evaporated tape. It includes two digital audio channels, and provides up to 2 hour of recording. The initial range includes camcorders, field videotape recorders and digital videodisk recorders. It records 4:1:1 component digital video, using 5:1 frame compression, to allow frame accurate editing, with LTC/VITC time codes. A × 4 normal speed player allows news

footage to be copied to disk rapidly for non-linear editing. Quality is comparable with the Betacam SP, D-1, D-5 formats. In a further development, a digital optical disk recorder provides up to 45 min of digitally compressed video and two audio channels. Duration: 6–123 min. Will replay *DVCam* tapes. 4:2:0 processing; eventually full 4:2:2 50 Mbit/s.

- *DVCam* (Sony) – Quarter-inch system. 4:2:0 processing. Primarily for business and industrial applications; and existing users of Hi-8, S-VHS, UVW Betacam. Uses a 15 micron track pitch and metal evaporated tape. Duration: 20/40; 60/180 min.
- Digital-S – A digital version of VHS. A quality format using half-inch metal particle tape, and designed as a lower-cost system for in-house corporate users, documentary, sports, and the industrial market. Using component processing (8-bit, 4:2:2) data is recorded on a 105 min tape at a rate of 50 megabits per second. It is DCT-compressed at 3.3:1. The two *pulse-code modulated* audio channels are sampled at 48 kHz (16 bits per sample). It can provide slow motion of plus/minus one third speed, and display color pictures up to ×32 speed.

D-VHS – A new digital tape format simultaneously recording up to 44 Gigabytes of data on a S-VHS formulation E-180 size videotape. Able to record up to six different digital TV channels simultaneously, and turn domestic video recorders into multi-media servers – for storing computer data, long-term video recording, etc. It records raw data, replaying it without alteration.

Disk-based camcorder Another approach to recording in the field is the *camcutter*, a *disk-based* camcorder recording system, mainly aimed at high-speed ENG operations. Its removable twin 2.5 in (2.4 Mbyte) magnetic hard disk drive, digitally records 20 min of program (M-JPEG compressed). This system includes a *loop-record* (*RetroLoop*) arrangement, which facilitates continuous recording while waiting for unpredictable action to begin. Pressing the record button dumps the last 3 min picture and sound from RAM to disk, to avoid a missed start or wasting footage. (Redundant material is recorded over.) The system includes a comprehensive time-code, auto clip numbering, coding, four DAT-quality audio tracks. Its particular advantages are that the program is recorded *digitally on a disk*, so can be rapidly transferred to the storage disk of a non-linear editing system; avoiding the usual slow tape copying process of analogue/digital conversion routines. Duration: 15–20/30 min.

Viewing conditions Preferred viewing conditions recommended by CCIR include – viewing distance four to six times picture height; peak screen luminance 60–80 cd/m^2; blank screen 0.02 of peak white.

VIRS (Vertical interval reference signals) As you know, the TV system scans each complete picture in two separate 'fields'. After scanning each field there is a brief *retrace* period when the system returns from the bottom-right corner of the screen to the top-left, ready to scan the next. During this brief *vertical interval/field blanking* period no picture information is transmitted. So the broadcaster takes the opportunity to introduce encoded data instead – (*VIRS, VITS*) and perhaps *teletext* information.

These inserted data are transmitted just before *picture* information begins, and are visible on the receiver screen as a dot pattern within the first few lines at the top edge of the frame. However, as most home receivers are overscanned (i.e. the picture is expanded to overlap the screen edges), the lines fall outside the normal viewed picture area.

VIRS can be used to provide identification of the program source, the point of origination, time and date of the original broadcast, etc. Technically, reference data can be included that automatically adjust the screen color balance to levels specified at the source, compensating for any signal distortions arising between the transmitter and the receiver. But this practice is not widespread.

Vertical interval test signals (*VITS*) are used for technical measurements, monitoring, and performance correction of transmission systems.

Volume indicators (*see Figure 12.24*) Our ears have a *logarithmic* response, i.e. they can detect slight changes in quiet sounds, but at higher volumes even quite large variations do not seem very different. So our subjective impressions of volume changes are not very accurate. They vary with the frequency (pitch) and the strength of the sound.

Audio equipment, on the other hand has a direct *linear* response to increases in sound level. The audio becomes distorted when it exceeds the system's limits; but our ears cannot accurately judge when it is about to reach that point. So we need some kind of volume indicator to show when to reduce the system's gain (amplification) in anticipation.

Several forms of volume indicator are used to guide our judgment and prevent accidental *overmodulation* (*overload distortion*) or *undermodulation* (as weak audio becomes intermixed with random background noise).

The widely used *VU meter* is a cheap, simple indicator of program *loudness*, i.e. how strong the sound appears to the *ear*. It has 'decibel' and 'modulation' scales (*volume units*) showing the audio system's limits. The continual rapid needle movement can be confusing and tiring to watch. The indicated readings for steady sounds (tone) are accurate but much less reliable for fluctuating audio, and very inaccurate for loud transient sounds (e.g. percussion), that can read low, so that the sound system overloads and distorts. Normal range used: –20 to 0 dB. Speech, –14 to 0 dB. True undistorted maximum modulation reading is around 50 per cent on the meter.

A *peak program meter* (*PPM*) responds to the audio signal's *peaks*, so gives a better indication of system overload. Readings are accurate for steady sounds, transients, and for complex audio, so reveal any possibilities of overload distortion. However, unlike the VU meter, the PPM's readings do not necessarily relate to the impression of loudness we actually hear. Normal range used: 2 to 6 (each scale step is 4 dB).

Various forms of *visual display* are becoming popular as peak-volume indicators including: bargraphs of LEDs (light-emitting diodes), gas-discharge devices, plasma displays, and light patterns on video monitors.

A problem encountered in all technical fields is the need for internationally agreed *standards*. Currently audio levels are measured using three different units: dBm, dBu and dBV. There are differences between the *standard operating reference levels* (SOLs) used. There are entrenched preferences for either VU meters or PPMs as methods of monitoring audio sound levels. And the respective calibration and display scales of audio level meters vary. (The *peak program meters* used in BBC, CBC, EBU, and German systems differ; as do the *VU* scales used by CBC and French systems.) As a result, today's manufacturers of audio equipment may offer systems with VU or PPM indicators having different rise/fall times.

Wall outlets (distribution boxes) At intervals around the studio walls various supplies are centered at combined outlet points. These can include:

AC outlets ('household current'/general service supplies) to power electrical equipment for demonstration apparatus, musical instruments, loud-speaker amplifiers, etc.

Camera cable outlets (to studio engineering area/apparatus room/master control). Outlets carry supplies to cameras, video from camera.

Audio outlets (tie lines from studio to sound control room): audio signals from each studio microphone (boom, personal, radio microphone).

Audio feeds (tie lines from sound control room to studio): to feed studio monitor loudspeaker(s) (e.g. sound effects; playback; foldback).

Sound-monitoring outlets (for earphone monitoring – studio sound output; selected sound sources; sound cues; incoming telephone calls; private line; 'mixed-minus'/'clean feeds').

Intercom outlets carrying production intercom/talkback. Also, switched intercom ('interrupted feedback' (IFB)/interrupted talkback). Only activated when keyed in production control room; for selective cuing (as opposed to general intercom/general talkback).

Video outlets (tie lines from engineering area) carrying studio video output to feed picture monitors; or providing a selected video source such as film channel, VTR output, video effects to picture monitors. Remote monitor switching (monitor display can be switched in production control room).

Cue-light circuits (push button cuing, from control room, of attached cue lights in studio).

Private wire outlets: tie lines for individual cuing/instruction of boom operators, floor workers, electricians, special-effects operators, etc.

Telephone to production control area (e.g. lighting).

Additional services such as water, compressed air, steam are provided elsewhere as wall outlets, away from distribution boxes.

Waveform monitor (WFM) A small oscilloscope tube displaying a fluctuating line which traces the variations of the video signal, sync pulses, and insertion pulses. Individual picture lines can be selected and examined (line strobe).

Workstation A desktop computer facility which allows access to central data or multi-media sources (e.g. a *server*) to contribute, organize, or draw upon stored material; as a news editor assessing, selecting, co-relating incoming stories.

Zoom microphone A specially designed camera-mounted microphone, containing electret capsules, which combine to provide adjustable coverage. This ranges from 'omni-directional' (equal sensitivity in all directions) to 'ultra-unidirectional' (narrow-angle). The apparent closeness of the sound can nominally be adjusted to match different zoom-lens settings: i.e. 'close' sound for close-ups, 'distant' sound for long shots. The arrangement is very arbitrary, but a useful compromise for a one-camera unit.

Further reading

If you want to explore further aspects of television/video production the following companion books by Gerald Millerson, published by Focal Press, are available.

Video Production Handbook (3rd edition)
This realistic practical guide to low-cost video program making explains how to achieve professional standards with limited facilities and a restricted budget.

Effective TV Production (3rd edition)
This is a 'succinct but thorough overview of the production process' (*American Cinematographer*) distilled for rapid study into a single volume.

Video Camera Techniques (2nd edition)
A quick, lucid guide to the essentials of handling video cameras.

The Technique of Lighting for Television and Film
An internationally established sourcebook, discussing in detail the principles and techniques of the art of lighting.

Lighting for Video (3rd edition)
A rapid guide to practical lighting techniques in television and video production.

TV Scenic Design (2nd edition)
A study in depth of the art, the mechanics, and techniques of scenic design for television and video production.

Index

M & E track, 333, 334